# ARGUMENT

ARGUMENT: THE ORAL ARGUMENT
BEFORE THE SUPREME COURT IN BROWN V.
BOARD OF EDUCATION OF TOPEKA, 1952-55.

# ARGUMENT

ARGUMENT: THE ORAL ARGUMENT
BEFORE THE SUPREME COURT IN BROWN V.
BOARD OF EDUCATION OF TOPEKA, 1952-55.

Editor
Leon Friedman

Introductions
Kenneth Clark and Yale Kamisar

1969
CHELSEA HOUSE PUBLISHERS
NEW YORK

# PREFACE

· Dean Louis H. Pollak of the Yale Law School has called the School Segregation cases *(Brown* v. *Board of Education)* "the most important American governmental act of any kind since the Emancipation Proclamation."[1] The Brown case not only affected millions of school children throughout the country but it acted as a catalyst for one of the most significant social movements in our history. Only the Dred Scott case, which was decided almost one hundred years before and led directly to the Civil War, had a more substantial effect on the political destiny of so large a part of the nation.

The Desegregation cases had their genesis in the 1930's when Charles Houston, then legal director of the NAACP, initiated the first attacks on segregated graduate schools in the south. It had been apparent at least since the Supreme Court's decision in *Buchanan* v. *Warley*[2] in 1917 that certain kinds of governmental classifications based on race would not stand up under the equal protection clause of the Fourteenth Amendment. Of course the "separate but equal" doctrine of *Plessy* v. *Ferguson* had provided a rationale for segregated schools. At first it was only the "equal" part of the doctrine that was attacked by the NAACP lawyers. Houston (a Harvard Law School graduate and later dean of Howard Law School) and his able lieutenants William Hastie (now a distinguished federal judge), James Nabrit (later dean of Howard Law School), Ralph Bunche, and Thurgood Marshall insisted that the southern authorities' practice of sending Negroes out of state for their graduate education did not provide them with "equal" facilities. Therefore, any refusal by a state-run graduate school to admit a qualified Negro applicant violated the Fourteenth Amendment. Beginning in 1938 with the decision in *Missouri* ex rel. *Gaines* v. *Canada,* the Supreme Court accepted that argument, and the first steps were taken toward the Brown decision. World War II interrupted the legal strategy begun in the Gaines case, but the NAACP Legal Defense and Educational Fund, Inc. (a separate organization designed to undertake legal attacks on segregation), under its director-counsel Thurgood Marshall, continued the effort to destroy the "separate but equal" doctrine. Yale Kamisar, of the University of Michigan Law School, outlines in his introductory essay to this volume the succession of cases by which Marshall and his staff gradually established the principle that any separate graduate school could not be truly equal because of the many intangible benefits that the white universities could give their students.

---

[1] 2 *The Constitution and the Supreme Court* 266 (Cleveland, 1966).

[2] 245 U.S. 60. The Court declared unconstitutional a city ordinance which denied to Negroes the right to occupy houses in blocks inhabited by a majority of whites.

In 1951, with that wedge in the door, the NAACP lawyers initiated in Clarendon County, South Carolina the first attack on segregated public schools per se. Suits were later brought in Prince Edward County, Virginia (largely because of the enthusiasm produced by a student strike in 1951 against the inadequacies of the Negro schools in that district), Kansas, Delaware, and the District of Columbia. The cases were heard in local federal district courts (except in Delaware, where the attack was made in the state courts) which found against the Negro plaintiffs on the basis of the continued validity of the "separate but equal" rule. (Those opinions appear in the appendix of this volume.) The Supreme Court decided to hear argument on the appeals from these cases, and the lawyers in all five of the cases appeared before the nine justices—first on December 9, 10 and 11, 1952, again on December 7, 8 and 9, 1953 and finally on April 11, 12, 13 and 14, 1955 to argue the question of relief.

The transcripts of the oral argument in the School Segregation cases, published here for the first time, are among the most revealing documents of contemporary history. On a strictly legal level, they show two of the greatest lawyers of our time displaying two diametrically opposite techniques in trying to persuade the Court of two totally different theories of law, government, and social ordering. John W. Davis, still a superb advocate in his seventy-ninth year, relied on the rhetoric of states' rights and warned of the danger of upsetting decades of precedents and the expectations of numerous state and local administrators and of violating the wishes of almost all the whites in the regions in question. Thurgood Marshall, on the other hand, pointed out the logic of the Court's new rulings in the Gaines case, *Sweatt* v. *Painter,* and the other graduate school cases decided since 1940. He focused on the beginnings of the breakdown of segregated patterns in the army and other phases on American life, and boldly challenged the Court to grant to the Negro the rights called for by federal law.

The arguments also show the problems that beset the Supreme Court in deciding a crucial question of Constitutional law that has wide social effect. Lawyers and legal scholars have long rejected the idea that precedent alone guides the Court's work. In fact, the Court usually has precedent to justify going almost any way it wants. Although the "separate but equal" doctrine had never been directly rejected before *Brown,* the Court had fashioned new legal principles in *Buchanan, Gaines,* and later cases which undermined the rationale of *Plessy* v. *Ferguson.* It was clear that the Court could decide either way and still find precedent to support its position.

The oral argument in the Brown case shows the Court functioning as both keeper of the nation's conscience (as the ultimate interpreter of "due process" and "equal protection") and as legislator on the broadest scale as it implements its decrees in specific cases. Even during the first argument on the merits the Justices were concerned with the ultimate reach of their orders, whom they would affect, and what immediate changes would be required. They saw that any decision they made would have a profound influence on the future of American life and thus sought to explore all the contours of any resultant change. They anticipated many of the problems which did in fact arise, such as the difficulty of dealing with subterfuge and evasion of their orders and the need for bold and prompt assertion of federal power. In hindsight, the deliberate speed formula which was suggested by the Solicitor General in his oral argument (see p. 256)[3] and appeared to offer the best hope for orderly change seems a strategic mistake, as Justice Black suggested recently. The Prince Edward County case, begun in 1951, was not resolved until 1964, after two further appeals to the Supreme Court and twenty-two reported decisions in other federal courts. In the process the entire school system in the county was shut down, and use of the full counterweight of the federal government was necessary to obtain relief for Negro school children.[4]

The Justices' purpose in the oral argument is to force the lawyers to think out the political, social, and Constitutional implications of their arguments. Oftentimes their inquiries are deliberately embarrassing and sometimes seem to express a point of view opposite to the anticipated position of the questioner. As Justice Frankfurter explained (at p. 20): "I want to ask you—and, may I say, particularly in a case of this sort, a question does not imply an answer; a question merely implies an eager desire for information . . ."

The Justices constantly seek to relate the immediate problem to analogous situations—Justice Jackson brought up the implications of the Court's decision to Indian school children—and try to cut through the rhetoric of the lawyers to see the concrete result of any argument advanced. Certain Justices excel in that type of scrutiny. Justice Frankfurter, a law professor for twenty-five years, treated even the great leaders of the bar as sloppy students and his probing, often testy questions of John W. Davis and the other lawyers helped elucidate many of the cloudy areas under review.

The transcript also suggests the importance of Chief Justice Earl Warren in the Brown decision. The first argument took place in December, 1952, when Fred Vinson presided over the Court. The Vinson Court had handed down a number of the graduate school cases, and he himself had written the Court's opinion in *Shelley* v. *Kraemer* and the *Sweatt* case. But even allowing for the possibility that Vinson's statements were merely to elicit information, his few questions indicated a lack of sympathy with the plaintiffs' position. (See p. 18-19, 78, 110-111.) The fact that the Court ordered reargument on the case in 1953 showed that unanimity had not been achieved. Earl Warren took over as Chief Justice in late 1953 and finally wrote the Court's unanimous opinion himself, sweeping away the "separate but equal" rule in a single sentence.

Another question about the Brown case is also answered by the oral argument. The sociological sources cited in the famous footnote 11 of the decision appeared to play a less important part in the Court's thinking than critics had claimed. The plaintiffs' lawyers cited the social science evidence only briefly in their argument. While the testimony of Dr. Kenneth Clark in the lower court and the "Social Science Statement" he prepared as an appendix to the plaintiffs' briefs

---

[3] Edward J. Bander has suggested that Oliver Wendell Holmes was the source for the phrase. The Justice wrote in Virginia v. West Virginia, 222 U.S. 17, 19-20 (1911), ". . . a state cannot be expected to move with the celerity of a private business man; it is enough if it proceeds, in the language of the English Chancery, with all deliberate speed." Justice Frankfurter, a friend of the old Justice and a careful student of his opinions, would doubtless have been familiar with the phrase. See Edward Bander, *Justice Holmes: Ex Cathedra* 539-40 (Charlottesville, 1966).

[4] For a study of the Prince Edward County case see Bob Smith, *They Closed Their Schools* (Chapel Hill, 1965).

undoubtedly had an important effect on the outcome, the court did not linger very long on the matter in the oral argument. In fact the southern lawyers made more of the sociological evidence introduced in opposition. (See p. 90-92.) Basically, it was justice that most concerned the Court.

The oral argument also had numerous dramatic moments—Thurgood Marshall's plea for justice for the Negro (p. 239), the explicit racist remarks of some southern lawyers (p. 428, 435), the rejoinder to that nonsense (p. 437), and the defiant remarks of some of the southern attorneys general who participated in the argument on relief (p. 433, 460).

What is most ironic, perhaps, is the fact that the defense of separate schools by white southern lawyers sounds suspiciously like the arguments recently presented by black separatists for black control of their schools. Milton Korman presenting the case for the District of Columbia in 1952 said (at p. 133-134):

> I say to the Court, and I say to my distinguished adversary, . . . these acts were not passed, this dual school system was not set up to stamp these people with a badge of inferiority. There was not this racial feeling that he speaks of with such fervor behind these acts. There was behind these acts a kindly feeling; there was behind these acts an intention to help these people who had been in bondage. And there was and there still is an intention by the Congress to see that these children shall be educated in a healthful atmosphere, in a wholesome atmosphere, in a place where they are wanted, in a place where they will not be looked upon with hostility, in a place where there will be a receptive atmosphere for learning for both races without the hostility that undoubtedly Congress thought might creep into these situations.
>
> We cannot hide our faces and our minds from the fact that there is feeling between races in these United States. It is a deplorable situation. Would that it were not so. But we must face these facts.
>
> We know that there have been outbursts between races north of here where there are not separate schools for white and colored. We know that these things exist, and constitutionally, if there be a question as to which is better, to throw these people together into the schools and perhaps bring that hostile atmosphere, if it exists, into the schoolroom and harm the ability to learn of both the races, or to give them completely adequate, separate, full educational opportunities on both sides, where they will be instructed on the white side by white teachers, who are sympathetic to them, and on the colored side by colored teachers, who are sympathetic to them, and where they will receive from the lips of their own people education in colored folklore, which is important to a people—if that is to be decided, who else shall decide it but the legislature, who decides things for each jurisdiction?

Roy Innes of CORE has called for an entirely separate school district for Harlem,[5] and Kenneth W. Haskins, principal of the Morgan Community School in Washington, D.C. has recently written that "The black community . . . has decided that it has to make the decisions about what can and cannot be tolerated for its children because society as a whole has largely failed the black community in this respect."[6]

---

[5] See Peter Schrag "Why Our Schools Have Failed," *Commentary* 31, 35 (March 1968).
[6] "The Case for Local Control," *Saturday Review* 52 (January 11, 1969).

Of course there is a difference between the white community providing by law for separate schools as a mark of black inferiority and the black community choosing to run its own schools because of the failure of white society to establish adequate educational facilities for its children. The controversy over community control is thus directly linked to the legal problems raised by the Brown case. It is only fitting that Dr. Kenneth Clark, one of the key witnesses in the original Virginia case, should examine the relation between black community control and black separatism on the one hand, and the broad aims of the original Brown case on the other.

This volume, therefore, represents an attempt to gather together the many different strands of this most crucial social and legal problem.

LEON FRIEDMAN

New York
April, 1969

# CONTENTS

# THE SCHOOL DESEGREGATION CASES IN RETROSPECT
## Some Reflections on Causes and Effects

by Yale Kamisar

> Lord, we ain't what we oughta be,
> we ain't what we wanna be,
> we ain't what we gonna be but,
> thank God, we ain't what we was.
>
> —The Rev. Martin Luther King, Jr.
> quoting an old southern preacher.

Recently, when asked to give a lecture on appellate advocacy, Justice Thurgood Marshall reminded his audience what Judge Benjamin Cardozo had once said: "The great tides and currents which engulf the rest of men do not turn aside in their course and pass judges by."[1] An outstanding example, he might have added, is *Brown* v. *Board of Education.*

In a sense, the significant changes which have occurred in the Black man's status in the last two decades had their beginnings in the rise of numerically, and hence politically, important Black communities in the North. For the importance of civil rights for the Black—and his political power to enhance these rights at the national level—has increased as he has moved northward and cityward.[2]

The Great Depression and the New Deal, as historian Alfred Kelly has noted, "nationalized the Negro's political significance in the great cities of the North by incorporating the colored voter as an essential ingredient in the new political machine which Franklin Roosevelt put together after 1933," and "for the first time since Reconstruction, the Negro had a recognized position in a winning political combination of national scope." World War II accelerated the growth of Black power and influence by creating an enormous demand for Black labor in northern cities. And this increase in power and influence led to the revival of a Black dream—"first-class citizenship" in an integrated nation.[3]

World War II had other consequences for the Black man in America. The

---

[1] Thurgood Marshall, "The Federal Appeal," in Charpentier ed., *Counsel on Appeal* 141, 143 (New York, 1968), quoting from Benjamin Cardozo, *The Nature of the Judicial Process* 168 (New Haven, 1921).

[2] See Alfred H. Kelly, "The School Desegregation Case," in Garraty ed., *Quarrels that Have Shaped the Nation* 243, 246–47 (New York, 1966) (Harper Colophon ed.); C. V. Woodward, *The Strange Career of Jim Crow* 115–117 (New York, 1957) (Galaxy Book ed.).

[3] Kelly, *supra* note 2, at 247.

"equalitarian ideology" of war propaganda, depicting democratic America bat-
tling racist Nazi Germany, must have instilled in the minds and hearts of not a few
white Americans "a new and intense awareness of the shocking contrast between
the country's too comfortable image of itself and the cold realities of America's
racial segregation."[4] No sooner had the Axis powers been defeated than we found
ourselves contesting Russia for the friendship of the world's great colored
races—and feeling the sting of Communist propaganda about racial discrimination and injustice in "the land of democracy." The establishing of the United
Nations headquarters on our shores "suddenly threw open to the outside world a
large window on American race practices." What delegates from all nations and
races saw for themselves, and the publicity generated by U.N. committees of
investigation and public debates on racial inequality, "caused genuine and practical embarrassment to the State Department in the conduct of foreign affairs."[5]
The United States Attorney General, in a brief filed in December of 1952 in connection with the School Segregation cases, told the Supreme Court:

> It is in the context of the present world struggle between freedom and tyranny
> that the problem of racial discrimination must be viewed . . . . Racial discrimina-
> tion furnishes grist for the Communist propaganda mills, and it raises doubts even
> among friendly nations as to the intensity of our devotion to the democratic faith.

During and after World War II, it became increasingly apparent that racial
equality was becoming an objective of our national policy. The Roosevelt administration expanded federal employment of Blacks, wrote "no discrimination"
clauses into war contracts, and established a Fair Employment Practices Commission. President Truman's Commission on Higher Education condemned inequality of opportunity on account of race, and his Committee on Civil Rights urged
the elimination of racial segregation from American life. And in 1948, Truman
issued executive orders designed to eliminate discrimination in federal employment and to end segregation in the armed services.

By the time *Brown* and its companion cases had reached the Supreme Court,
the order to achieve "equality of treatment and opportunity for all persons in the
armed services" had been thoroughly carried out in Korea, Japan, Germany, and
in the camps and bases of the Deep South. "For the full impact of the results
one needs the picture supplied by Lee Nichols of a company barracks at Fort
Jackson, South Carolina, where, 'busily cleaning their rifles, Negroes from Mississippi and Arkansas sat on double-decker bunkers among whites from Georgia
and South Carolina with no apparent antipathy.' "[6] With hundreds of thousands
of young Americans entering and leaving the armed services every year, the
impact of unsegregated military life on civilian life since the early 1950's probably
was enormous.

On the judicial front, the "separate but equal" doctrine, for which the 1896
case of *Plessy* v. *Ferguson,* 163 U.S. 537 (1896) had come to stand, was being
weakened by a series of cases in the field of higher education.

[4]Id. at 248. See also *Report of the National Advisory Commission on Civil Disorders*
224 (Bantam Books ed. 1968); John Roche, *Courts and Rights* 88–89 (New York, 1961);
Woodward, *supra* note 2, at 119.

[5]Woodward, *supra* note 2, at 119–22.

[6]*Id.* at 139.

*Missouri* ex rel. *Gaines* v. *Canada,* 305 U.S. 337 (1938) held that a state could not satisfy the test of separate but equal by offering to pay the tuition of a Black applicant to its law school at an out-of-state school of equally high standing: "The white resident is afforded legal education within the State; the negro resident having the same qualifications is refused it there and must go outside the State to obtain it. That is a denial of the equality of legal right to the enjoyment of the privilege which the State has set up, and the provision for the payment of tuition fees in another State does not remove the discrimination."[7] Although the State argued in *Sipuel* v. *University of Oklahoma,* 332 U.S. 631 (1948) that the State Regents was required by local law to provide a separate law school for Blacks upon demand or notice, and that petitioner had failed to seek relief from or against state officials who had to provide it, the Court, undoubtedly aware of the inevitable delay that establishing a new law school would involve, was unmoved: "The petitioner is entitled to secure legal education afforded by a state institution. To this time, it has been denied her although during the same period many white applicants have been afforded legal education by the State. The State must provide it for her in conformity with the equal protection clause of the Fourteenth Amendment and provide it as soon as it does for applicants of any other group."[8]

Oklahoma was back in the Supreme Court two years later. A Black student had been admitted to graduate instruction in a state university, but, pursuant to new state law, on a "segregated basis." Thus, for some time the section of the classroom in which he sat was surrounded by a rail on which there was a sign stating: "Reserved for Colored." He was also not allowed to use the desks in the library reading room, but forced to sit at a designated desk. Nor was he permitted to eat in the school cafeteria at the same time as other students. Oklahoma maintained that these separations were "merely nominal"; they did not detract from the fact that appellant used the same facilities as students of other races. The Court was not impressed. Indeed, in the course of striking down these restrictions in *McLaurin* v. *Oklahoma State Regents,* 339 U.S. 637 (1950), the Court seemed to shake the very foundations of the "separate but equal" doctrine:

> [These restrictions] signify that the State, in administering the facilities it affords for professional and graduate study, sets McLaurin apart from the other students. The result is that appellant is handicapped in his pursuit of effective graduate instruction. Such restrictions impair and inhibit his ability to study, to engage in discussions and exchange views with other students, and, in general, to learn his profession. . . .
>
> It may be argued that appellant will be in no better position when these restrictions are removed, for he may still be set apart by his fellow students. This we think irrelevant. There is a vast difference—a Constitutional difference—between restrictions imposed by the state which prohibit the intellectual commingling of students, and the refusal of individuals to commingle where the state presents no such bar. . . . The removal of the state restrictions will not necessarily abate individual and group predilections, prejudices and choices. But at the very least, the state will not be depriving appellant of the opportunity to secure acceptance by his fellow students on his own merits.[9]

[7] 305 U.S. at 349.
[8] 332 U.S. at 632–33.
[9] 339 U.S. at 641.

The "separate but equal" doctrine was further battered by another case handed down the same day, *Sweatt* v. *Painter,* 339 U.S. 629 (1950), which held that a new law school set up by Texas for Blacks did not—could not, really—provide equal protection of the laws. By taking into account human relationships, social experiences and other intangible but significant differences between the new state law school for Blacks and the existing one for whites, the Court all but said that no "separate" school for Blacks *could possibly be* "equal":

> What is more important, the University of Texas Law School possesses to a far greater degree those qualities which are incapable of objective measurement but which make for greatness in a law school. Such qualities, to name but a few, include reputation of the faculty, experience of the administration, position and influence of the alumni, standing in the community, traditions and prestige. . . .
>
> Moreover, although the law is a highly learned profession, we are well aware that it is an intensely practical one. The law school, the proving ground for legal learning and practice, cannot be effective in isolation from the individuals and institutions with which the law interacts. Few students and no one who has practiced law would choose to study in an academic vacuum, removed from the interplay of ideas and the exchange of views with which the law is concerned. The law school to which Texas is willing to admit petitioner excludes from its student body members of the racial groups which number 85% of the population of the State and include most of the lawyers, witnesses, jurors, judges and other officials with whom petitioner will inevitably be dealing when he becomes a member of the Texas Bar. With such a substantial and significant segment of society excluded, we cannot conclude that the education offered petitioner is substantially equal to that which he would receive if admitted to the University of Texas Law School.[10]

As the late Edmond Cahn has pointed out, "If you wish a judge to overturn a settled and established rule of law, you must convince both his mind and his emotions, which together in indissociable blend constitute his sense of injustice."[11] The *Sweatt* and *McLaurin* cases, he argues persuasively, supplied the intellectual and emotive conditions for the School Desegregation cases of 1954.

Texas' contentions might have seemed plausible to the Court, wrote Cahn, "if the school involved had not happened to be a school of *law.* Law was the only discipline that the judges understood thoroughly, the only one in which each considered himself wiser than any pedagogic expert." And if *Sweatt* suggested to the Justices' minds that "separate but equal" should be transformed into "separate therefore unequal," *McLaurin* "provided the propulsive power of empathy and indignation." Cahn continued:

---

[10]*Id.* at 634. As former Justice Tom Clark recently observed, after *Sweatt* and *McLaurin* were on the books, calling *Plessy* still "established doctrine" in public education "is but dealing with shadows rather than substance. * * * [Passages in these higher education cases] were a premonition of what was to come in public grade and high school segregation! Indeed, they were specifically used by the Chief Justice in *Brown* [347 U.S. at 494] when he said of the doctrine of *Sweatt* and *McLaurin* that their findings 'apply with added force to children in grade and high schools.' " Clark, Book Review, 36 *University of Chicago Law Review* 239, 241 (1968).

[11]*The Predicament of Democratic Man* 129 (New York, 1962) (Delta Book ed.).

What Oklahoma did . . . was to furnish the Court with a living tableau, an animated epitome of segregation that even the most insensitive could easily comprehend. For unlike other members of his race, McLaurin had not remained conveniently out of sight in his own schoolyard; he had entered the precincts of the white people and had asked to qualify for the highest academic degree in Education. And once within the university, in the name of "Education" and under the orders of the state and its chief educational officers, how was he treated?[12]

In the wake of *Sweatt* and *McLaurin,* "all over the South, white boards of education . . . began crash programs of Negro school building, calculated, as Governor Byrnes of South Carolina frankly confessed, 'to remedy a hundred years of neglect' of Negro education, lest the Supreme Court 'take matters out of the state's hands.' "[13] Although southern lawyers were to allude to these frenzied spending programs repeatedly in the School Desegregation oral arguments, "they came too late to deter either Negroes in their quest for equality or the Supreme Court in its role as the major organ for the enforcement of equality before the law. Accordingly, at the very time that the first serious measures were being taken to convert the fiction of separate but equal into physical reality, suits were pending which were to seal its doom."[14]

As the transcript of the oral arguments in the *Brown* case amply illustrates, many able lawyers participated in the five School Segregation cases. But the principal antagonists were John W. Davis and Thurgood Marshall. Davis, the Democrats' nominee for President in 1924, was a magnificent legal advocate.[15] If he lost the School Segregation case, it was only because in 1954 no lawyer could have won it. And although he lost, he left no doubt why he was reputed to be *the* leading advocate of his time. This is a sample:

> [I]t has been accepted that where there is a pronounced dissent from previous opinions in constitutional matters, mere difficulty in amendment leaves the Court to bow to that change of opinion more than it would of matters of purely private rights.
>
> But be that doctrine what it may, somewhere, sometime to every principle comes a moment of repose when it has been so often announced, so confidently relied upon, so long continued, that it passes the limits of judicial discretion and disturbance.
>
> That is the opinion which we held when we filed our former brief in this case. We relied on the fact that this Court had not once but seven times, I think it is, pronounced in favor of the "separate but equal" doctrine.
>
> We relied on the fact that the courts of last appeal of some sixteen or eighteen States have passed upon the validity of the "separate but equal" doctrine vis-a-vis the Fourteenth Amendment.
>
> We relied on the fact that Congress has continuously since 1862 segregated its schools in the District of Columbia.

[12] *Id.* at 130–32.

[13] Kelly, *supra* note 2, at 256.

[14] Robert Harris, *The Quest for Equality* 139–40 (New York, 1960).

[15] In a recent discussion of appellate advocacy, Judge Rifkind remembered "at least one judge who said to me that whenever he heard John W. Davis argue a case, he positively closed his mind to his argument for at least a week. He wanted the magic of Davis' voice to subside before he put his mind to the case." Charpentier ed., *Counsel on Appeal* 211 (New York, 1968).

We relied on the fact that twenty-three of the ratifying States—I think my figures are right, I am not sure—had by legislative action evinced their conviction that the Fourteenth Amendment was not offended by segregation, and we said in effect that that argument—and I am bold enough to repeat it here now—that in the language of Judge Parker in his opinion below, after that had been consistent history for over three-quarters of a century, it was late indeed in the day to disturb it on any theoretical or sociological basis. We stand on that proposition.[15a]

Davis' argument was carefully organized, and his urbaneness and splendid rhetoric is shown again, and again in the record. When one adds what all observers call the magic of his voice, the total effect was almost —almost—irresistible. Davis said in his peroration:

Let me say this for the State of South Carolina. It does not come here, as Thad Stevens would have wished, in sack cloth and ashes. It believes that its legislation is not offensive to the Constitution of the United States.

It is confident of its good faith and intention to produce equality for all of its children of whatever race or color. It is convinced that the happiness, the progress and the welfare of these children is best promoted in segregated schools, and it thinks it a thousand pities that by this controversy there should be urged the return to an experiment which gives no more promise of success today than when it was written into their Constitution during what I call the tragic era.

I am reminded—and I hope it won't be treated as a reflection on anybody—of Aesop's fable of the dog and the meat: The dog, with a fine piece of meat in his mouth, crossed a bridge and saw the shadow in the stream and plunged for it and lost both substance and shadow.

Here is equal education, not promised, not prophesied, but present. Shall it be thrown away on some fancied question of racial prestige?

It is not my part to offer advice to the appellants and their supporters or sympathisers, and certainly not to the learned counsel. No doubt they think what they propose is best, and I do not challenge their sincerity in any particular period but I entreat them to remember the age-old motto that the best is often the enemy of the good.[16]

As Justice John Harlan has said, "Each lawyer must proceed according to his own lights."[17] Although his organization was not nearly as tight as Davis' nor his presentation nearly as polished, Marshall was a powerful advocate in his own way. This was especially so on rebuttal where, perhaps stimulated by the sting of his opponents' argument, he really seemed to warm to his task. The following is an example of his earthy, homey touch:

Those same kids in Virginia and South Carolina—and I have seen them do it—they play in the streets together, they play on their farms together, they go down the road together, they separate to go to school, they come out of school and play ball together. They have to be separated in school.

There is some magic to it. You can have them voting together, you can have them not restricted because of law in the houses they live in. You can have them

[15] See p. 215 *infra*.

[16] See p. 216–17 *infra*.

[17] John M. Harlan, "The Role of Oral Argument" in Westin ed., *The Supreme Court: Views from Inside* 57, 58 (New York, 1961).

going to the same state university and the same college, but if they go to elementary and high school, the world will fall apart.[18]

Marshall was no less aware than Davis that, particularly in a great case, the advocate must "always go for the jugular vein."[19] If Davis the master craftsman told the Court *how* to write an opinion reaffirming *Plessy,* Marshall, spokesman for an oppressed race, never let the Justices forget *why* they had to overrule it. Nor was he about to let the Justices forget that the Court and the Constitution, as well as his own cause, were on trial:

> They can't take race out of this case. From the day this case was filed until this moment, nobody has in any form or fashion, despite the fact I made it clear in the opening argument that I was relying on it, done anything to distinguish this statute from the Black Codes, which they must admit—because nobody can dispute, say anything anybody wants to say, one way or the other—the Fourteenth Amendment was intended to deprive the States of power to enforce Black Codes or anything else like it.
>
> We charge that [the challenged state laws] are Black Codes. They obviously are Black Codes if you read them. They haven't denied that they're Black Codes, so if the Court wants to very narrowly decide this case, they can decide it on that point.
>
> So whichever way it is done, the only way that this Court can decide this case in opposition to our position, is that there must be some reason which gives the State the right to make a classification that they can make in regard to nobody else [but] Negroes, and we submit the only way to arrive at this decision is to find that for some reason Negroes are inferior to all other human beings.
>
> Nobody will stand in the Court and urge that, and in order to arrive at the decision that they want us to arrive at, there would have to be some recognition of a reason why of all of the multitudinous groups of people in this country you have to single out Negroes and give them this separate treatment.
>
> It can't be because of slavery in the past, because there are very few groups in this country that haven't had slavery some place back in the history of their groups. It can't be color because there are Negroes as white as the drifted snow, with blue eyes, and they are just as segregated as the colored man.
>
> The only thing it can be is an inherent determination that the people who were formerly in slavery, regardless of anything else, shall be kept as near that stage as is

---

[18] See p. 239 *infra.* Marshall's reference to the state university and college must have been quite deliberate. Years earlier Charles Houston and other NAACP lawyers had decided upon the strategem of an "indirect attack" on school segregation by law suits forcing the admission of Blacks to Southern graduate and professional schools, in part because Southern states did not even pretend to offer "equality" at this educational level and in part because providing genuinely equal facilities at this level would be enormously expensive, but also because they were persuaded that the South somehow regarded integration in higher education far less invidious than in primary and secondary schools. Years later, Marshall is reported to have commented: "These racial supremacy boys somehow think that little kids of six or seven are going to get funny ideas about sex and marriage just from going to school together, but for some equally funny reason youngsters in law school aren't supposed to feel that way. We didn't get it but we decided that if that was what the South believed, then the best thing for the moment was to go along." Kelly, *supra* note 2, at 253–54.

[19] J. W. Davis, "The Argument of an Appeal," 26 *American Bar Association Journal* 895, 897 (1940).

possible, and now is the time, we submit, that this Court should make it clear that
that is not what our Constitution stands for.[20]

## THE COURT AND THE CONGRESS

If one who was still in law school when the School Segregation cases were
being argued may second-guess a master of his profession, I venture to say that
John W. Davis made at least one mistake. On the eve of *Brown* the odds were
high that *Plessy* would be overruled, but, if not, it was very unlikely that the old
case would be reaffirmed. Rather, the Court would probably have taken a third
course—avoided a head-on confrontation with the equities of Marshall's position
by treating the issue as a "political question" to be resolved by Congress under
Section 5 of the Fourteenth Amendment, which provides: "The Congress shall
have power to enforce, by appropriate legislation, the provisions of this article."
Such an "evasive solution would itself have created new law, since hitherto, for
seventy-five years, Congress had left it to the Court to develop the content of the
equal-protection guarantee." But the South's best chance, however small, was
that the Court, inhibited by the magnitude of the issue and the difficulties of
enforcement, might pass the buck to Congress, which "would have been something of an Alphonse-Gaston game, with no one going through the door."[21]

Despite the apparent interest of both Justices Frankfurter and Jackson in
such a line of reasoning, neither Davis on the reargument nor his colleague Justin
Moore on the original argument wanted to argue that although the equal protection clause, of its own force, did not prohibit school segregation[21a], Congress
could invalidate such segregation, and, in effect, expand the substantive scope of
the clause, by enacting appropriate legislation under Section 5 of the Fourteenth
Amendment:

> MR. DAVIS: . . . Section 5 is not a Trojan Horse which opened to Congress
> a wide field in which Congress might expand the boundaries of the article itself.
> JUSTICE JACKSON: Mr. Davis, would not the "necessary and proper"
> clause apply to the [Fourteenth] Amendment as well as to the enumerated powers of
> the instrument itself? In other words, if Congress should say that in order to accom-
> plish the purposes of equality in the other fields the abolition of segregation was
> necessary, as a "necessary and proper" measure, would this not come under it, or
> might it not come under the "necessary and proper" clause?
> MR. DAVIS: Well, if you can imagine a necessary and proper clause which
> would enforce the provisions of this article by dealing with matter which is not within
> the scope of the article itself, which I think is a contradiction in terms, that is a para-
> dox. Congress could do what the Amendment did not warrant under the guise of
> enforcing the Amendment.
> JUSTICE FRANKFURTER: But you can look for the "necessary and prop-
> er" clause to determine whether it is something appropriate within the Amendment.

[20] See p. 239–40 *infra.*

[21] Paul Freund, "Storm Over the American Supreme Court," 21 *Modern Law Review*
345, 351 (1958). See also Charles Black, *The People and the Court* 139–42 (New York,
1960) (Spectrum Book ed.); Herbert Wechsler, "Toward Neutral Principles of Constitutional Law," 73 *Harvard Law Review* 1, 32 (1959).

[21a] See p. 93–94 *infra.*

MR. DAVIS: . . . [To] interpret the Amendment as including something that it does not include is not to interpret the Amendment but is to amend the Amendment, which is beyond the power of the Court.[22]

The questions raised by Justice Frankfurter and Jackson above, and in the original oral arguments, foreshadow *Katzenbach* v. *Morgan*, 384 U.S. 641 (1966), applying Section 5 of the Fourteenth Amendment to uphold §4(e) of the Voting Rights Act of 1965, prohibiting the application of an English literacy requirement to any prospective voter who has completed six grades in an American-flag school in which the language of instruction was other than English, whether or not, *apart from* the federal act, such a state requirement would violate equal protection. A 7–2 majority, speaking through Justice Brennan, took the position that "by including Section 5 the draftsmen sought to grant to Congress, by a specific provision applicable to the Fourteenth Amendment, the same broad powers expressed in the Necessary and Proper Clause."[23]

### SYMBOL AND CATALYST FOR A REVOLUTION

If I may make another criticism of a master, let me suggest that one line of Davis' argument would have been better left unsaid: "shall ['equal,' albeit separate, education] be thrown away on some fancied question of racial prestige?"[24] Many a white must have regarded this question quite appropriate. Disrupt long-established customs and life patterns for what? Just to accomodate some status-seeking Blacks? (No, to afford them the minimal dignity and respect to which every American is entitled.) Whites, certainly northern whites, are much less conscious of their color than are Blacks of theirs—and the stigma it connotes. The many whites who more or less take their whiteness and treatment as full human beings for granted—who have never felt, if they have even thought about, what it means always to be confined to the back of the bus—may well have wondered: Why do Blacks get so worked up about mere social amenities? Why do they rave so about their rights? Why are they so sensitive? Marshall's rebuttal was:

> I understand the South's lawyers to say that it is just a little feeling on the part of Negroes—they don't like segregation. As Mr. Davis said yesterday, the only thing the Negroes are trying to get is prestige.
> Exactly correct. Ever since the Emancipation Proclamation, the Negro has been trying to get what was recognized in *Strauder* v. *West Virginia* [1880], which is the same status as anybody else regardless of race.[25]

Of course, racial prestige was not the only thing at stake in *Brown*—but it was a great deal. As sociologist Joseph Gusfield has pointed out in his illuminating study of Prohibition and Temperance, the instrumental effects of governmental action may be slight compared to the response which it entails as a symbol. So long as men's regard for status, respect, honor and prestige are real and important, symbolic action will be real and important. And, though he treated this

---

[22] See p. 214 *infra*.
[23] 384 U.S. at 650.
[24] See p. 216 *infra*.
[25] See p. 236 *infra*.

aspect flippantly, Davis knew it every bit as well as Marshall. It is because political symbolism may affect the status order—may contribute to a glorification or
degradation of one group in opposition to others within the society—that "the
struggle to control the symbolic actions of government is often as bitter and as
fateful as the struggle to control its tangible effects."[26]

White southerners and Black men, as do *all* men, live by symbols. And in
large measure the School Desegregation cases were so fiercely contested and then
so bitterly resisted because school segregation is a special symbol. Indeed, to the
southern Black this racist institution must have seemed the epitome of American
hypocrisy. Had not Horace Mann called education "the great equalizer of the
conditions of men?" Had not Justice Frankfurter called the public school "the
symbol of our democracy and the most pervasive means for promoting our
common destiny?"[27] Were Blacks supposed to be less aware than other Americans
that "education is a fetish of our country; we have believed it somehow to be a
magic cure-all."[28]

The Blacks understood, no less than did white southerners, that for the
latter—or more accurately, for whites *everywhere*—to treat them as though they
were outside the community of man it was essential to nourish and preserve the
stereotype of Blacks, the stereotype that—

> depicts Negroes as relatively unteachable, and therefore ignorant; as insensitive
> to the demands of abstract ideals, and therefore less troubled by discrimination than
> the white man; as motivated solely by appetite for the creature comforts, and there-
> fore appeasable with access to fried fish, liquor and women; as devoid of moral fibre,
> and therefore predisposed to crime . . . [and] that segregation's significant function
> is not to deliver an insult but to preserve the group stereotype by minimizing contact
> between the races in situations where they would necessarily see and deal with each
> other as individuals, and by putting the official imprimatur on the proposition that
> Negroes and whites differ in a legally material way.[29]

Similarly, Anthony Lewis has observed:

> That racial separation should carry more emotional weight in schools than
> elsewhere was understandable: Attendance was compulsory, and in school children

---

[26] Joseph Gusfield, *Symbolic Crusade: Status Politics and the American Temperance
Movement* 167 (New York, 1963) See also *id.* at 22, 173.

[27] Frankfurter, J., joined by Jackson, Rutledge and Burton, JJ., concurring in
*McCullom* v. *Board of Education,* 333 U.S. 203, 231 (1948). Compare W. E. B. DuBois,
"My Evolving Program for Negro Freedom," in R. Logan ed., *What the Negro Wants* 68
(New York, 1944): "The underlying philosophy of our public school system is that the
education of all children together at public expense is the best and surest path to
democracy."

[28] Roy Wilkins, "The Negro Wants Full Equality," in *What the Negro Wants* 123.

[29] Louis Lusky, "The Stereotype: Hard Core of Racism," 13 *Buffalo Law Review* 450,
451–52 (1964). See also Gunnar Myrdal, *An American Dilemma* 657 (20th ann. ed. New
York, 1962): "Although the Southerner will not admit it, he is beset by guilt-feelings,
knowing as he does that his attitude toward the Negroes is un-American and un-Christian.
Hence he needs to dress his systematic ignorance in stereotypes. * * * [The Southern
whites] need the ceremonial distance to prevent the Negroes' injuries and sufferings from
coming to their attention."

of an impressionable age were exposed to a culture. Intermingling of the races could not help but affect their outlook. Putting it another way, any breakdown in school segregation necessarily endangered the perpetuation of the southern myth that the Negro is by nature culturally distinct and inferior. And there was the fear—surely felt deeply by many in the South, however others regarded it—that school integration was a step toward intermarriage.

It was these reasons that led Hodding Carter, one of the most enlightened voices in Mississippi, to write a year before the School decision that a Supreme Court ruling against segregation would be "revolutionary" in character.[30]

"Revolutionary in character?" Has it really turned out that way?

Up through the 1962–63 school year, less than 1 per cent of Black students attended school with whites in the eleven states of the old Confederacy. In the 1965–66 school year—in no small measure as a result of the Civil Rights Act of 1964 and guidelines promulgated by the United States Department of Health, Education and Welfare—the percentage increased to 6 per cent.[31] Local resistance has occasionally taken the form of spectacular open defiance, but far more effective have been the less flamboyant "guerilla activities" of public officials.[32]

The pace of desegregation, of course, has been most uneven. During the 1966–67 school year, although more than 90 per cent of Black pupils still attended all-Black schools in the Deep South states of Alabama, Georgia, Louisiana, Mississippi, and South Carolina, more than 80 per cent attended schools which were less than 95 per cent Black in the border States of Delaware, Kentucky, and West Virginia. Indeed, in Kentucky a majority of Black children attend schools which are less than 20 per cent Black. Although the rate of desegregation has accelerated almost everywhere in the South in recent years (the pace has been heartening in some states), the grim facts are that more Black students still attend all-Black schools in southern and border states than they did at the time of the first *Brown* decision—and this amounts to more than 75 per cent of all Black students in such states. Is this the stuff of "revolution?"

Even in the North, because of housing segregation, most Blacks, although legally eligible to attend white schools, are still in segregated ones. Indeed, in too many northern communities, because whites are moving away or sending their children to private or parochial schools, we are experiencing "resegregation." And most of the relatively few Black students who are no longer "separate" are not yet "equal" or meaningfully "integrated."[33]

The statistical story is disappointing, but it is only a small part of the whole story. The consequences of *Brown* cannot begin to be measured by cold statistics. Nor, although the Supreme Court quickly applied (or extended) the principle of

[30] Anthony Lewis, *Portrait of a Decade: The Second American Revolution* 5 (New York, 1964).

[31] See U.S. Commission on Civil Rights, *Southern School Desegregation* 5-9 (1967). See also Robert Carter, "The Warren Court and Desegregation," 67 *Michigan Law Review* 237, 245 (1968).

[32] See generally Louis Lusky, "Racial Discrimination and the Federal Law: A Problem in Nullification," 63, *Columbia Law Review* 1163 (1963).

[33] See generally Kenneth Clark, *Dark Ghetto* 111-153 (New York, 1965); Charles Silberman, *Crisis in Black and White* 249-307 (New York, 1964) (Vintage ed.).

its 1954 ruling to other public facilities—such as public transportation, parks, and beaches,[34] can its consequences be measured by the number of times it has been cited in other judicial opinions. Regardless of its practical, tangible, direct effects, and its judicial progeny, the symbolic quality of the decision was immeasurable; "the psychological dimensions of America's race relations problems were completely recast"; the "indirect consequences" "awesome."[35] It stimulated men everywhere—corporate executives, union officials, clergymen, hospital administrators, university executive officers and faculty members—to rethink and, sometimes at least, to reshape their policies. "Its educative and moral impact in areas other than public education and, in fact, its whole thrust toward equality and opportunity for all men has been of enormous importance."[36] This impact and thrust, for example, contributed mightily to the enactment of the Civil Rights Acts of 1957, 1960, 1964, 1968, and the Voting Rights Act of 1965— demonstrating once again that constructive political action "flows in no small part from an awareness of basic principles concretely illustrated in court decisions and constantly explained in opinions circulating among a wide audience."[37] And it greatly accelerated, perhaps even precipitated, the "revolution" in constitutional-criminal procedure. For "it is hard to conceive of a Court that would accept the challenge of guaranteeing the rights of Negroes and other disadvantaged groups to equality before the law and at the same time do nothing to ameliorate the invidious discrimination between rich and poor which existed in the criminal process."[38]

White America was never to be the same after *Brown*. Nor was Black America. As author Louis Lomax put it:

> It would be impossible for a white person to understand what happened within black breasts on that Monday. An ardent segregationist has called it "Black Monday." He was so right, but for reasons other than the ones he advances: That was the day we won; the day we took the white man's laws and won our case before an all-white Supreme Court with a Negro lawyer, Thurgood Marshall, as our chief counsel. And we were proud.[39]

That the case generated a feeling of hope and momentum is evidenced by such Black responses to a national poll, years later, as: "It started the ball rolling"; "the Supreme Court gave us heart to fight."[40]

---

[34] For a collection of Supreme Court and lower court cases, since *Brown*, holding racial segregation invalid in numerous areas, see W. Lockhart, Y. Kamisar & J. Choper, *Constitutional Law: Cases, Comments & Questions* 1228 (2d ed. 1967).

[35] Carter, *supra* note 31, at 247.

[36] John Kaplan, "Comment on School Desegregation," 64 *Columbia Law Review* 223, 228 (1964).

[37] Charles Wynzanski, "Constitutionalism: Limitation and Affirmation," in Sutherland ed., *Government Under Law* 473, 486 (New York, 1956).

[38] A. K. Pye, "The Warren Court and Criminal Procedure," 67 *Michigan Law Review* 249, 256 (1968).

[39] *The Negro Revolt* 84 (New York, 1963) (Signet ed.)

[40] These were typical responses to a 1963 *Newsweek* national poll which found two-thirds of all Blacks crediting the Supreme Court for their biggest breakthroughs. See Thomas Pettigrew, *A Profile of the Negro American* 10 (New York, 1964).

Last year, looking back at the School Desegregation cases, in which he played a major role, Robert Carter, former NAACP General Counsel, sadly observed that *"Brown* has promised more than it could give." Yet few commentators have better articulated how much it did give:

> Blacks were no longer supplicants seeking, pleading, begging to be treated as full-fledged members of the human race; no longer were they appealing to morality, to conscience, to white America's better instincts. They were entitled to equal treatment as a right under the law; when such treatment was denied, they were being deprived—in fact robbed—of what was legally theirs. As a result, the Negro was propelled into a stance of insistent militancy. Now he was demanding—fighting to secure and possess what was rightfully his. The appeal to morality and to conscience still was valid, of course, but in a nation that was wont to describe itself as a society ruled by law, blacks had now perhaps the country's most formidable claim to fulfillment of their age-old dream of equal status—fulfillment of their desire to become full and equal participants in the mainstream of American life.[41]

Southern conservatives understood perhaps better than northern liberals that revolution feeds on itself and that the time to stop one is at the beginning, not the end. But they couldn't. That is why *Brown* is a momentous decision.

Southern conservatives knew, too, that one Black success would lead to other Black demands. "They were undoubtedly wrong in thinking that they could hold the line by opposing all Negro demands, but the northern liberals were probably equally wrong in thinking that they could contain the Negro revolution by legal concessions."[42]

I realize that revolutions do not begin at a particular point in time; that they are not made, but come, out of the past. Nor am I unaware that many factors were working for change in American race relations on the eve of *Brown*. "But revolutions require a spark, a catalyst. For the revolution in American race relations, this was the School Segregation case." Anthony Lewis said further:

> The struggle to carry out the Supreme Court's decision created a climate that encouraged the Negro to protest against segregation on buses, to demand coffee at a lunch counter, to stand in long, patient lines waiting to take a biased test for the right to vote. It was easy to say, as many observers did during the [1954–64] decade, that it would be more logical for Negroes in the South to concentrate on obtaining the ballot because political power would open the way to all other rights. But that was only true in the abstract. In the real world the right to vote was too remote an idea to arouse the Negro of the South from apathy and fear. It took the drama of school desegregation, and then of the protest movements, to make the possibility of freedom come alive; then Negroes began demanding *en masse* the ballot to which the law had said they were entitled.

* * * * *

> However discouraged one may be at the continuing reality of discrimination, he should remember that this country is at least on the right course—and that the law put it there.[43]

[41]Carter, *supra* note 31, at 247.

[42]James Reston, "The Shame of the Cities" (1966), in *Sketches in the Sand* 370 (New York, 1967).

[43]Lewis, *supra* note 30, at 5, 8–9.

## DUBOIS AND SEPARATE SCHOOLS

In the course of his spirited defense of the "separate but equal" doctrine, John W. Davis turned for support to Dr. W. E. B. DuBois.—

Perhaps the most constant and vocal opponent of Negro oppression of any of his race in the country.

Says he:

"It is difficult to think of anything more important for the development of a people than proper training for their children; and yet I have repeatedly seen wise and loving colored parents take infinite pains to force their little children into schools where the white children, white teachers, and white parents despised and resented the dark chile, made mock of it, neglected or bullied it, and literally rendered its life a living hell. Such parents want their children to "fight" this thing out,—but, dear God, at what a cost!"

He goes on:

"We shall get a finer, better balance of spirit; an infinitely more capable and rounded personality by putting children in schools where they are wanted, and where they are happy and inspired, than in thrusting them into hells where they are ridiculed and hated."[44]

The irony of it! For the South to cite one who had been called "the most vital and compelling figure in the Negro world"[45]—one who, a full half-century earlier, had warned Booker T. Washington and other Black leaders that "the way for a people to gain their reasonable rights is not by voluntarily throwing them away and insisting that they do not want them"[46]—for the proposition that Black people did not want desegregation.

If Davis was implying, as he seemed to be, that if the militant DuBois were opposed to school desegregation, then surely so were virtually all other members of the Black race, he was plainly wrong. From the white South's viewpoint, the best that could be said was that Blacks were divided on this issue. Indeed, DuBois himself had pointed out, "In this matter of segregation I was touching an old and bleeding sore in Negro thought. From the eighteenth century down the Negro intelligentsia has regarded segregation as the visible badge of their servitude and as the object of their unceasing attack."[47]

Why are Blacks more fungible than Jews or Irishmen—or white Protestants? There are some prominent members of nonconforming minority religious groups, no doubt, who do not (or pretend not) to mind religious instruction in public school classrooms or the invocation of "official prayers" there, but how can they bind those who do object? How can any Black, however eminent, speak for *the* Black?[48] How can any Black, however renowned, prevent other Blacks from

[44]See p. 61 *infra* quoting from DuBois, "Does the Negro Need Separate Schools?," 4 *Journal Negro Education* 328, 330–31 (1935).

[45]See Preface to E. M. Rudwick, *W. E. B. DuBois: Propagandist of the Negro Protest* (New York, 1968).

[46]"Of Mr. Booker T. Washington and Others," in *The Souls of Black Folk* 51 (New York, 1903) (Crest Reprint).

[47]DuBois, *Dusk of Dawn* 305 (New York, 1940) (Schoken ed.).

[48]See S. A. Brown, "Count Us In," in *What the Negro Wants* 336–37.

asserting *their* constitutional rights? Did not the Court have to tear down the wall, regardless of the number of Blacks determined to climb over the rubble? It seemed sufficient, therefore, to remind Davis, as Marshall did, that "If all of the people in the State of South Carolina and most of the Negroes still wanted segregated schools . . . any individual Negro has a right, if it is a constitutional right, to assert it."[49]

Inasmuch as many Black activists view DuBois as a "symbol of dedicated, uncompromising militance,"[50] it may be profitable to dwell for a moment on what his views really were on school segregation—and why.

To begin with, his apparent preference for segregated schools was essentially a product of despair, not choice. In the long run DuBois, too, wanted all color bars down, but that day would only come when "the majority of Americans were persuaded of the rightness of our cause."[51] And he eventually became convinced that the white world was so resolutely opposed to racial equality that that day was far away—"many years, perhaps many generations."[52] The long run was too long. In the long run DuBois and his contemporaries would be dead and their children graduates of segregated schools.

In the meantime, his people had to come to terms with the brutal facts of racism. They had to fight for a fair share of public funds for Black schools and transform them, if possible, from "simply separate schools, forced on us by grim necessity" to "centers of a new and beautiful effort at human education"[53]—and otherwise develop their own facilities and resources as best they could. In the meantime, they had to do more than dream the impossible dream. DuBois lived long enough to see the School Desegregation case of 1954 and to exclaim, "I have seen the impossible happen."[54]

Once "the present attitude of white America toward black America" is recognized, insisted DuBois in 1935, "there is no room for argument as to whether the Negro needs separate schools or not. The plain fact faces us, that either he will have separate schools or he will not be educated."[55]

The NAACP, he maintained, "was not, never had been, and never could be an organization that took an absolute stand against race segregation of any sort under all circumstances. This would be a stupid stand in the face of clear and incontrovertible facts. . . . What we did say was

> Whenever we found that an increase in segregation was in the interest of the Negro race, naturally we had to advocate it. We had to advocate better teachers for Negro schools and larger appropriation of funds. We had to advocate a segregated

[49] See p. 65 *infra.*

[50] Rudwick, *supra* note 45, at 295.

[51] *Dusk of Dawn* 304.

[52] *Ibid.* See also *id* at 309: "I am certain that for many generations American Negroes in the United States have got to accept separate medical institutions. They may dislike it; they may and ought to protest against it; nevertheless it will remain for a long time their only path to health, to education, to economic survival."

[53] DuBois, *supra* note 44, at 332, 334–35.

[54] DuBois, "We Rejoice and Tell the World . . . but We Must Go Further," *National Guardian,* May 31, 1954, p. 5.

[55] DuBois, *supra* note 44, at 328–29.

camp for the training of Negro officers in the [First] World War. We had to advocate group action of Negro voters in elections. We had to advocate all sorts of organized movement among Negroes to fight oppression and in the long run end segregation.
. . .

So long as we were fighting a color line, we must strive by color organization. We have no choice.[56]

In the very article that John W. Davis quoted, DuBois made plain that he would "welcome" a time when "racial animosities and class lines will be so obliterated that separate schools will be anachronisms."[57]—Twenty years later he was to "rejoice" at the overruling of the "separate but equal" doctrine[58] for he was well aware that

Other things being equal, the mixed school is the broader, more natural basis for the education of all youth. It gives wider contacts; it inspires greater selfconfidence; and suppresses the inferiority complex. But other things seldom are equal, and in that case, Sympathy, Knowledge, and the Truth, outweigh all that the mixed school can offer.[59]

Lest we too hastily congratulate ourselves on the great distance we have traveled since 1935, the year DuBois made these grim observations, consider the sobering remarks of *New York Times* columnist James Reston, some thirty years later and ten years after the School Desegregation cases:

It will not do to wait for total racial integration to make substantial improvement in the schools still predominantly Negro. . . . [A] vast and expensive new effort will probably have to be made to make the predominantly Negro schools "equal" even if they are still largely "separate." This is opposed by some Negro leaders in the belief that making the predominantly separate Negro schools "equal" will weaken the fight against keeping them "separate."

Yet it is fairly clear from the history of the last ten years that the fight for legal equality is insufficient. Educational equality must go with it, or at the end of another

---

[56] *Dusk of Dawn* 309–11.

[57] DuBois, *supra* note 44, at 328.

[58] See note 53 *supra*. See also DuBois, "The Negro Since 1900: A Progress Report," *N.Y. Times Magazine,* Nov. 21, 1948, pp. 24, 59: "[The Negro] proposes to reach complete equality as an American citizen. And by equality he means abolition of separate schools, the disappearance of 'Jim Crow' travel; no segregation in public accommodations * * * [W]hether it takes thirty years or a thousand, equality is his goal and he will never stop until he reaches it."

[59] DuBois, *supra* note 44 at 335. Although DuBois dwelt on "chiefly negative arguments for separate Negro institutions of learning based on the fact that in the majority of cases Negroes are not welcomed in public schools and universities nor treated as human beings," he also advanced "certain positive reasons due to the fact that American Negroes have, because of their history, group experiences and memories, a distinct entity, whose spirit and reactions demand a certain type of education for its development." *Id.* at 333. But this rested largely on the premises that certain studies, *e.g.,* the history of the Negro race in America, would seldom be found in white institutions and that a white bias pervaded white study of anthropology, psychology and other social sciences. *Ibid.* In any event, a desire for the availability of desegregated public schools is not on a collision course with the view that "in history and the social sciences the Negro school and college has an unusual opportunity and role," *id.* at 334.

ten years we shall have a Negro generation with equal rights to jobs but few jobs, free access to restaurants and housing but no means to enjoy them, equal opportunity to vote but little understanding of the purpose of voting.[60]

Although DuBois never realized how near at hand was the 1954 Supreme Court decision, his estimate of the "living hell" many a Black child would experience on entering a previously all-white school was closer to the mark. But for the South this brutal factor was to backfire badly. Not only did it fail to stay the Court's hand in 1954, it was to strengthen its hand in the grim, tense years which followed. If there was irony—when the principle had not yet been announced—in the South drawing on DuBois' writings for support, there was more irony—when the viability of the principle was still in doubt[61]—in the Black cause thriving on the visibility of the racism which DuBois had foreseen.

For southern Black families, two Black psychiatrists have recently told us, "School . . . was seen in a very special way. Beset on all sides by a cruel enemy, school was often primarily a refuge—a place of safety for those who were to be protected—and in a sense it was a case of women and children first."[62] But after *Brown* little Black boys and girls left their refuge to face the cruel enemy.

The courage of these little pioneers of school desegregation inspired Blacks everywhere. And at a time when not a few northerners must have been growing a bit tired of it all—here as elsewhere people may go to great lengths to gratify reformers "in principle" only to find it rather tedious of them to insist on carrying principle to the point where it really bites—the ridicule, harrassment and hatred of the white adults who confronted these Black children mobilized northern opinion in support of the Court's decision.

Few northerners would be misled any longer by "the entirely sincere protestations of many southerners that segregation is 'better' for the Negroes, is not intended to hurt them"; many would now understand "that what is meant is that it is better for the Negroes to accept a position of inferiority, at least for the indefinite future."[63] On seeing the fury of the mobs and hearing "the ugly, spitting curse

---

[60] "Education and Integration" in *Sketches in the Sand* 165–66 (New York, 1967).

[61] As Professor Alexander Bickel has observed, "the Supreme Court's law, the southern leaders realized, could not in our system prevail—not merely in the very long run, but within the decade— * * * if it was opposed by a determined and substantial minority and received with indifference by the rest of the country." *The Least Dangerous Branch* 258 (Indianapolis, 1962). Inasmuch as this was more or less the situation in 1956–7, at this point at least the outcome was still in doubt. Although Professor Bickel underscores the March 11, 1956 Southern Congressional Manifesto's heavy contribution to this sorry state of affairs, *id.* at 256–58; Bickel, "The Decade of School Desegregation: Progress and Prospects," 64 *Columbia Law Review* 193, 202 (1964); and no doubt the manifesto made defiance of the Court and the Constitution "socially acceptable in the South," Anthony Lewis, *Portrait of a Decade: The Second American Revolution* 45 (New York, 1964); I share Professor John Kaplan's view that the indifference of President Eisenhower in particular and the national political institutions in general probably did more to inhibit Southern moderates and to slow down the pace of desegregation than did the Manifesto. See Kaplan, "Comment on School Desegregation," 64 *Columbia Law Review* 223, 224–26 (1964).

[62] William H. Grier & Price M. Cobbs, *Black Rage* 124 (New York, 1968) (Bantam Book ed.)

[63] Charles Black, "The Lawfulness of the Segregation Decisions," 69 *Yale Law Journal* 421, (1960).

'Nigger!' ", the abstraction of racism was "concretized" on millions of television screens and the "moral bankruptcy" and "shame" of the thing finally grasped.[64] The North was roused. And an aroused North meant an aroused Federal Government.

Many campaigns of the Black Revolution remain to be won—for example, de facto segregation and massive educational and economical issues. But on the fifteenth anniversary of *Brown,* in large part thanks to those who did not spare us the gory details of "the southern way of life," the outcome of the campaign against legal, formal segregation of schools and other public facilities is no longer in doubt.

There remain, to be sure, pockets of resistance, some discouragingly large, many bitterly defended. Flushing them all out will take not a few years and in the process, no doubt, more hate will be spewed and more blood spilled. But now *this* campaign is only a mopping-up operation.

University of Michigan Law School
March, 1969

---

[64] See generally Bickel, *supra* note 61, at 266–67; Lewis, *supra,* at 7–12.

# THE SOCIAL SCIENTISTS, THE BROWN DECISION, AND CONTEMPORARY CONFUSION

## by Dr. Kenneth B. Clark

### THE LEGAL STRATEGY OF BROWN v. BOARD OF EDUCATION AND SUBSEQUENT CASES

The Dred Scott decision of 1857 can probably be viewed as one of the earliest attempts to use the federal courts as a vehicle for attaining racial justice for the Negro in America. This decision, however, reinforced the inferior status of the Negro through the judicial doctrine that the Negro had no rights which the white man was bound to respect. One could interpret the Dred Scott decision as an indication that judicial decisions tend to reflect moral, social, and political realities of the society at a particular point in time.

The *Plessy* v. *Ferguson* decision of 1896 reflected some progress beyond *Dred Scott* but left essentially unchanged the social and judicial perception of the Negro as different from other American citizens. The doctrine of "separate but equal" which was enunciated in the Plessy decision, must have been predicated on the assumption that, in spite of the Emancipation Proclamation, in spite of rather strong civil rights legislation passed by Congress, and in spite of the Thirteenth, Fourteenth, and Fifteenth Amendments, the Negro was still viewed as a social and political inferior. Judicial sanction is still given to his second-class citizenship.

The legalization of the inferior status of the Negro implicit in the Plessy decision cannot be considered to have been inadvertent in view of the rather strong dissent of Justice Harlan to *Plessy*. Harlan spelled out quite clearly that the doctrine of "separate but equal" could only be accepted on racial terms, and that the Court, in propounding this doctrine was, in fact, providing a more palatable form of the Dred Scott decision itself. The history of civil rights litigation in state and federal courts up to the Brown decision of 1954 can be understood in terms of this basic struggle to determine how the Negro is to be perceived and treated in relation to the treatment of other human beings within the framework of American democracy.

The underlying problem was that the Negro was regarded as semi-human or in some subtle way as sub-human; and not only as different, but as different and inferior. The common denominator of *Dred Scott, Plessy* v. *Ferguson,* and almost all court decisions up to *Brown* was that the Negro in some way was special and inherently unworthy of the rights which white American citizens would be expected to have without question and without litigation. Indeed, the fact that the Negro was required to persist in seeking judicial determination of his rights was, in itself, indicative of the basic racist realities of the society of which he was a part.

Given this analysis, the Brown decision represents an attempt to use the judicial system and the method of litigation to remove, once and for all, the special and inferior category to which the Negro had been relegated—or, at least, to ensure that governmental power, and particularly the power of the judiciary, ceased to function as agents in reinforcement of the Negro's second-class status.

In this regard, it is significant that cases such as *Sweatt* v. *Painter* (1950) and *McLaurin* v. *Oklahoma State Regents* (1938) sought to attack the constitutionality of segregation per se. The lawyers for the NAACP, in presenting their arguments, attempted to outflank the implicit racial rationale of *Plessy* v. *Ferguson.* However, the Court's decisions in these cases were, nonetheless, still based on the *Plessy* v. *Ferguson* precedent of "separate but equal." One should add, however, that the standards of equality set by the Court in these cases were so high as to make it difficult, if not impossible, to maintain separate state-supported graduate and professional educational levels. But these decisions, in spite of their retention of the racially determined *Plessy* v. *Ferguson* formula, were so narrowly drawn in their specific restriction to graduate and professional education that they did not meet directly the general issue of the constitutionality of racial segregation in general, or even of segregation at other levels of education.

Given this fact, it was imperative that the legislative strategists of the NAACP decided to face head-on the issue of the inherent inferiority of racial segregation without regard to the equality of segregated facilities. It must have been assumed by those who planned the cases that, in view of the increasing erosion of the biracial system of education on a graduate and professional school level, an attack on segregation per se would be more likely to be successful if it were initially directed at segregation in state-supported elementary and secondary schools. It must have been further assumed that such a legal attack risked a court decision sustaining segregated schools, a decision which would tend to perpetuate laws requiring or permitting social segregation in other aspects of American life as well.

*Briggs* v. *Elliott,* the first of the cases which led to the Brown decision, was argued by the NAACP in Charleston, S.C., in May, 1951. On the three-judge court was the late Justice J. Waties Waring, who in an earlier hearing on the case had strongly urged the NAACP lawyers to redirect the case from reliance on relief for the plaintiffs within the Plessy precedent to a challenge to the constitutionality of segregation itself without regard to the quality of facilities. In a case which was finally brought before the district court on behalf of Negro plaintiffs from Clarendon County, South Carolina, the NAACP lawyers did attack segregation itself, and the lawyers for the state conceded the inequality of facilities, urging the court to provide them with time to make the Negro school in Clarendon County equal to the schools provided for whites in that county.

This defense strategy of conceding inequality and arguing for time to obey *Plessy* v. *Ferguson's* doctrine of "separate but equal" was also used in varying degrees by Kansas, Delaware, and Virginia in cases brought by the NAACP. It led to appeals to the Supreme Court and hence to the Brown decision.

However, the May 31, 1955 implementing decision of the Court in *Brown,* which enunciated a policy of guidance to the states for carrying out the Brown mandate to desegregate public schools "with all deliberate speed," was a conconscious effort to make fundamental social change less disruptive. The Court, in seeking to facilitate a rational and orderly transition from a system of segregation to one of nonsegregated schools asked that such criteria as "local conditions," "variety of local problems," "practical flexibility," "the need to reconcile public and private needs," and "the taking into account of public interest," be considered. It was clear that in this decision the Court was stepping outside the limited role of determining the constitutionality of segregation and was assuming the more complex role of establishing guidelines for administrative and social change. Some of the words in this decision clearly indicate this: "Courts of equity may properly take into account the public interest in the elimination of such obstacles in a systematic and effective manner. . . . Once such a start has been made, the courts may find that additional time is necessary to carry out the ruling in an effective manner."

Some observers interpreted this decision—with some justification—as the Court accepting the gradualist approach as means for effective desegregation. In retrospect the "deliberate speed" formula seems a serious error to many, including Supreme Court Justice Hugo Black who criticized the Court in a 1968 statement. In practice it seems to have led to more rather than to less disruption. Here, Court reliance on social science evidence would have been useful, for students of social change have observed that prompt, decisive action on the part of recognized authorities usually results in less anxiety and less resistance in cases where the public is opposed to the action than does a more hesitant and gradual procedure. It is similar to the effect of quickly pulling off adhesive tape—the pain is sharper but briefer and hence more tolerable.

Recent cases that have logically followed *Brown* into the lower courts and that will lead to significant new law as they reach the Supreme Court deal directly with the problem of de facto segregation—segregation of public schools resulting from gerrymandering, racially determined building and bussing patterns, discriminatory teacher and pupil assignment to schools, and the like. The earlier assumption that these patterns are an inevitable consequence of housing patterns and, hence, that school officials have no responsibility for changing them, is giving way in the light of accumulating evidence of deliberate intent to segregate on the part of educational officials and in the light of an expanding theory of social responsibility.

The 1967 decision by Judge J. Skelly Wright in *Hobson* v. *Hansen*[1] in the United States District Court of Washington, D.C. has been the most significant of such opinions. The decision insisted that the city of Washington must devise a plan to eliminate inequality of education and segregation from the public school system. In view of that system's almost total Negro population, this decision sets the stage for defining educational responsibility in terms of larger geographic units (for example, metropolitan areas), in order to counteract segregation resulting from a combination of the confinement of Negroes to the central city ghettos and

---

[1] 269 F. Supp. 401 (D.D.C. 1967).

the flight of whites to exclusive white suburbs.

A next step will be to test the legal possibilities of another aspect of *Plessy* v. *Ferguson* and of subsequent Court decisions—that is, the responsibility of the states to provide equal education to the children of all its citizens in terms of teachers' expectations and quality, administration, counselling; and the total pattern of schooling. It is possible that future decisions will contrast the equality of taxation paid by Negroes with the inequality of services furnished to them.

As long as segregated education is the reality in the central cities, as well as elsewhere, children who are denied the opportunity to benefit from the decision of *Brown* must not be abandoned to an essentially discriminatory and inferior education. Further generations of children cannot be lost while metropolitan planning and other such approaches are prepared and implemented.

Some questions which we must now dare to ask and seek to answer as the basis for a new strategy in the assault against the inhumanity of the American system of racial segregation are: (1) Is the present pattern of massive educational inferiority and inefficiency found in predominantly Negro schools inherent and inevitable in racially segregated schools?; and (2) Is there anything which can be done within the Negro schools to raise them to a tolerable level of educational efficiency, or even perhaps to raise them to a level of educational excellence? If the answer to the first question is *yes* and to the second question is *no,* then the strategy of continued and intensified assault on the system of segregated schools is justified and should continue unabated since there is no hope of raising the quality of education for Negro children as long as they are condemned to segregated schools. If, on the other hand, the answers to the above questions are reversed it would suggest that a shift in strategy and tactics, without giving up the ultimate goals of eliminating the dehumanizing force of racial segregation from American life would be indicated. This would suggest that given the present strong and persistent resistance to any serious and effective desegregation of our public schools, the bulk of the available organizational, human, and financial resources and specialized skills should be mobilized and directed toward obtaining the highest quality of education for Negro students without regard to the racial composition of the schools which they attend. This would demand a massive, system-wide educational enrichment program designed to obtain educational achievement through accountability.

It is from such a premise that many supporters of integrated education have also given support to demands of ghetto community groups for a central role in determining the quality of education their children receive.

School boards and public school officials seem as resistant to developing or implementing programs designed to improve the quality and efficiency of education provided for Negro children in segregated schools as they are deaf to all requests for effective desegregation plans and programs. The interests and desires of white middle-class parents, groups, and organizations and the interests of the increasingly powerful teachers federations and professional supervisory associations are invariably given priority over the desire of Negro parents for nonsegretated quality education for their children. The interests of the white parents, teachers, and supervisors are often perceived by them as inimical to the desires of the Negro parents. Furthermore, the capture and control of the public schools by white middle-class parents and teachers provided the climate within which the system of racially segregated and inferior schools could be developed, expanded, and reinforced; and within which the public schools became instruments for blocking rather than facilitating the upward mobility of Negroes and other lower status groups. One, therefore, could not expect these individuals and groups to be sympathetic and responsive to the pleas of Negro parents for higher quality education for their children. Negro parents and organizations must accept and plan their strategy in terms of the fact that adversaries in the battle for higher quality education for Negro children will be as numerous and as formidable as the adversaries in the battle for nonsegregated schools. Indeed, they will be the same individuals, officials, and groups in different disguises and with different excuses for inaction, but with the same powerful weapons of evasion, equivocation, inaction, or tokenism.

An effective strategy for the present and the future requires rigorous and honest appraisal of all of the realities, a tough-minded diagnosis of the strengths and weaknesses of the enemy, and an equally rigorous analysis of the strengths and weaknesses of the Negro and his allies. We cannot now permit ourselves to be deluded by wishful thinking, sentimental optimism, or rigid and oversimplified ideological postures. We must be tough-mindedly pragmatic and flexible as we seek to free our children from the cruel and dehumanizing inferior and segregated education inflicted upon them by the insensitive, indifferent, and affably and at times callously rigid custodians of American public education.

In developing a presently appropriate strategy and the related flexible tactics, it must be clearly understood that the objective of increasing the quality of education provided for Negro children is not a substitute for, or a retreat from, the fundamental goal of removing the anachronism of racially segregated schools from American life. The objective of excellent education for Negro and other lower status children is inextricably linked with the continuing struggle to desegregate public education. All of the public school, college, and professional school civil rights litigation instituted by the legal staff of the NAACP arose from recognition of the obvious fact that the segregated schools which Negroes were forced by law to attend were inferior and therefore damaging and violative of the equal protection clause of the Fourteenth Amendment.

The suggested shift in emphasis from desegregation to quality of education is not a retreat into the blind alley of accepting racial separation as advocated by the Negro nationalist groups; nor is it the acceptance of defeat in the battle for desegration. It is, rather, a regrouping of forces, a shift in battle plans, and an attempt to determine the most vulnerable flanks of the opposition as the basis for major attack. The resisting educational bureaucracies, their professional staffs, and that segment of the white public which has not yet been infected fatally by the American racist disease are most vulnerable to attack on the issue of the inferior quality of education found in Negro schools. The economic, political, military, social stability, international, democratic, humane, and self-interests arguments in favor of an immediate, massive program for educational excellence in predominantly Negro schools are so persuasive as to be irrefutable. The expected resistance should be overcome with intelligently planned and sustained efforts.

This first phase of an all-out attack on the inferior education now found in racially segregated schools should be coordinated with a strategy and program for massive and realistic desegregation of entire school systems. This more complicated phase of the overall struggle will continue to meet the resistances of the past with increased intensity. It will be necessary, therefore, to break this task down into its significant components and determine the time and phasing of the attack on each or on combinations of the components. For example:

(1) The evidence and arguments demonstrating the detrimental effects of segregated schools on the personality and effectiveness of white children should be gathered, evaluated, and widely disseminated in ways understandable to the masses of whites.

(2) The need to reorganize large public school systems away from the presently inefficient and uneconomic neighborhood schools to more modern and viable systems of organization such as educational parks, campuses, and clusters must be sold to the general public in terms of hard dollars and cents and educational efficiency benefiting all children rather than in terms of public school desegregation.

(3) The need to consolidate small, uneconomic, and relatively ineffective school districts into larger educational and fiscal systems in order to obtain more efficient education for suburban and exurban children must also be sold in direct practical terms rather than in terms of desegregation of schools.

(4) The need to involve large metropolitan regional planning in the mobilization, utilization, and distribution of limited educational resources on a more efficient level must also be explored and discussed publicly.

(5) The movement toward decentralization of large urban school systems must be carefully monitored in order to see that decentralization does not reinforce or concretize urban public school segregation, and to assure that decentralization is consistent with the more economically determined trend toward consolidation and regional planning allocation of resources and cooperation.

## THE ROLE OF SOCIAL SCIENCE IN THE BROWN DECISION, AND SUBSEQUENT CRITICISM

The role of social science in the Brown decision was crucial, in the Court's opinion, in supplying persuasive evidence that segregation itself means inequality. Social psychologists had testified in the courts as expert witnesses (most extensively in the Virginia case) on the effects of segregation on personality development, on the effects of school segregation in lowering motivation to learn, on the consequences of desegregation, and on other questions. The author examined the Negro children involved in several of the cases to determine whether evidence of personality distortion related to racial discrimination and segregation could be ascertained. At the request of the NAACP, psychologists also prepared an appendix to the NAACP appellants brief ("The Effects of Segregation and the Consequences of Desegregation: A Social Science Statement") endorsed by thirty-two social scientists, psychologists, and psychiatrists, with the author serving as liaison between the lawyers and the social psychologists. The introduction of social science testimony in these cases proved to be a significant extension of legal frontiers.

The essential questions faced by the Supreme Court were not questions of legal precedent, historical in nature, but questions relating to the social consequences of legally imposed segregation. Without such evidence, the Court could only speculate about the probable damage caused by the violation of constitutional rights implicit in segregated education. The social scientists testified concerning the damage inherent in the total pattern of segregation on the human personality. On the basis of their testimony, the Court held that separate educational facilities are inherently unequal by virtue of being separate. By providing such evidence, the social scientists made it possible to avoid the need to obtain proof of individual damage and to avoid assessment of the equality of facilities in each individual school situation. The assumption of inequality could now be made wherever segregation existed.

In this regard it must now be stated that in doing so the Court, which appeared to rely on the findings of social scientists in the 1954 decision, rejected the findings in handing down the 1955 implementation decision. An empirical study of various forms and techniques of desegregation suggested that the gradual approach to desegregation did not increase its chances of success or effectiveness. The findings further suggested that forthright, direct desegregation within the minimum time required for the necessary administrative changes tended to facilitate the process. Gradualism or any form of ambiguity and equivocation on the part of those with the power of decision is interpreted by the segregationists as indecision and provides them with the basis for increasing resistance, as well as giving them time to organize, intensify, and prolong their opposition. In this regard, it is relevant to note that the pattern of massive resistance and sporadic, violent opposition to desegregation occurred after the 1955 decision. There is no evidence that a more direct, specific, and concrete implementation decree would have resulted in any more tension, procrastination, or evasion than the seemingly rational, statesmanlike deliberate speed decision of the Court. It does not seem likely that the pace of public school desegregation could have been slower.

After footnote 11 of the Brown decision acknowledged the contribution of social science to the Court's findings, a significant debate ensued in legal and social science circles on the appropriateness of reliance on such testimony and on the accuracy of the evidence itself.

Interestingly enough, such controversy had not arisen earlier about the role of social science in industry, in government, or in the military. The fact that social science was now participating in social change in ways that raised questions about the fundamental injustice of American society and the power arrangements that supported it was probably not irrelevant to the anxiety such participation now aroused.

One of the most serious and consistent criticisms came from distinguished professor of jurisprudence Edmond Cahn of New York University Law School.[2]

2 See Chapter on Jurisprudence, Annual Survey of American Law, 30 *New York University Law Review* 150 (1955).

Cahn questioned the contribution of the social scientists' testimony to the decision and implied that their primary motive was not "strict fidelity to objective truth." The fact, however, was that the social scientists were careful to reject findings that could not be substantiated. Professor Cahn seemed to suggest that legal facts and scientific facts were two kinds of reality. This also we could not accept. For us there was but one order of reality, and science and law were part of it.

The most serious criticism, however, began to come from social scientists. Dr. Bruno Bettelheim of the University of Chicago stated publicly that there is no scientific evidence that racial segregation damages the human personality.[3] In view of the effect of Nazi concentration camps on their inmates—a primary subject of Dr. Bettelheim's own research—it is hard to understand the rationale for this statement. But it was Dr. Ernest van den Haag of the New School of Social Research who presented the most intense and specific criticism from social scientists questioning the validity of the evidence.[4] He assumed that science could not assess personality damage associated with social stigma, a curious position for a contemporary social scientist to hold.

On the whole, none of the criticism to date have offered solid evidence to refute the psychologists' appendix to the legal brief in *Brown*. The testimony offered then still stands.

Those who attempt to use the methods of social science in dealing with problems which threaten the status quo must expect opposition and even retaliation. They must be prepared to accept the risks their role entails. But to assume that such involvement is by definition unscientific is to betray the ideal goal of science itself, which is a total concern for truth wherever it may lead, whatever it may threaten. The valid goals of law and science are identical—to secure for man personal fulfilment in a just, stable, and viable society.

## The Aftermath of Brown in the South and in the North

The aftermath of the Brown decision must be seen in both positive and negative terms. In positive terms, the high sense of morale enkindled among Negro and civil rights leadership led directly to support for various direct action, essentially nonviolent strategies of confrontation—the Montgomery Bus Boycott of 1956 led by Dr. Martin Luther King, the student sit-in movement at restaurant counters, the Freedom Rides begun by white and Negro ministers at bus terminals and railroad stations, the campaigns to desegregate recreation facilities, and the struggle to achieve the right to vote and the right to legal justice in the Deep South.

The Court decision, therefore, had shock waves in the South that reached far beyond the public school system. Indeed, one could say that changes in the

[3] "Discrimination and Science," Review of *Prejudice and Your Child*, Commentary Magazine 384 (April 1956).

[4] Ernest van der Haag and Ralph Ross, *The Fabric of Society* (New York, 1957), Appendix to chapter 14, "Prejudice about Prejudice."

pervasive southern pattern of racial discrimination were far more easily and rapidly won in public accommodations than in the school system itself. The changes
came first in those areas of life that were most visible, while the basic elements
of life in education, housing, and employment were more resistant. But the relatively superficial changes—whether one could take any seat in a bus or enter an
amusement park—stimulated the Negro to fight for more fundamental change and
encouraged him in the faith that such change would naturally follow. The civil
rights legislation of 1957 and the 1960's reinforced that hope on a national scale,
commiting the federal executive branch and the Congress, as it seemed to do, to
redress of longstanding grievances. Voting rights were increasingly protected and
Negro voter registration in the South gained dramatically. The March on Washington in 1963 seemed an eloquent and fitting testimonial to the biracial triumph
of the civil rights movement and to the strength of the integrationist view.

On the negative side during the post-Brown period, numerous civil rights
leaders were beaten, imprisoned, and murdered in the South. Each gain was
won at great cost, frustrating the promises of massive and prompt desegregation.
Negro children in the South were spat upon and jeered and assaulted as they tried
to enter desegregated public schools. The murderers of three girls in a Birming-
ham Sunday School went free and the deaths seemed quickly forgotten. Two
things were clear—that desegregation of schools, supposedly ensured by the
Brown decision, was token at best in both North and South, and that residential
segregation in the North remained as rigid and strong as ever. Economic disparities between the average white and Negro remained and increased.

It also became apparent that the persistent problems of the Negro in northern
cities were not soluble by abstract civil rights victories. The positive consequences
of *Brown* had little if any effect on the deprivation under which Negroes were
required to live in the urban ghettos. Rather, the ugliness of the ghetto had intensified. The housing had deteriorated even further. The public school systems
in the largest cities became even more rigidly segregated and declined into a
profound state of decay. Whites, particularly middle-class whites, were escaping
in increasing numbers into white suburbs. The riots from 1964 on, coming as they
did on the heels of civil rights legislation and the March on Washington, must
be seen, in part, as an inchoate and self-destructive response of northern ghetto
residents to the realization that the promises of the Brown decision—and all the
other promises that followed—were not being kept and had no concrete meaning
for them.

In fact, in the North social changes since *Brown* have been more negative
than positive, with the possible exception of a gain in Negro political power as
Negro population figures in the central cities moved rapidly upward in consequence
of the white exodus and the earlier Negro migration from the South that had
reached its peak during World War II.

In the South where, admittedly, American racism was most violent and
primitive and deeply rooted, progress could be substantial and still leave a racist
society fundamentally untouched. After *Brown,* a number of southern states developed and tested strategies of resistance to the Court decision. Massive resistance of interposition was resorted to in defiance of the Court, and the degree
of integration in elementary and secondary schools has been minimal. Neverthe-

less, the South has accepted or initiated more overt changes than the North. There has been tremendous progress in integration in higher education and in professional and graduate education. The percentage of Negroes in undergraduate colleges has risen sharply. In the fifteen years since 1954, relative change has been unquestionably greater in the South than in the North. In fact, the South can look at the North with a certain ironic condescension in terms of the acceptance of rapid change toward a non-racist society.

The North, for its part, did not think the Brown decision applied to them. The North had joined earlier in the Negro reaction against southern resistance to change. Now it became clear that racism was also virulent in the North, all the more insidious for its long nonrecognition. Even Negroes had not consciously acknowledged the depth of racism inherent in northern society. And when the North discovered its racism, it tended to provide justification for it and to react defensively—white backlash—rather than to engage in a struggle for social transformation.

One cannot now escape the conclusion that all hope for effective and orderly transition from a system of segregated public schools to a more efficient and economical system of nonsegregated schools was wishful thinking. The belief that the Brown decision would be enforced in good faith, in ways consistent with sound administrative and educational practices, and with due regard to constitutional safeguards and the respect for law essential to a stable democratic government, has not been supported by the evidence and events of the intervening years. Rather, public school desegregation has been aborted, evaded, subjected to the mockery of tokenism, equivocation, and seemingly endless litigation, while generations of Negro children in these segregated schools continue to be damaged irrevocably.

The nation, generally, and those social scientists who fought for the Brown decision had tended to underplay the extent to which racism had been internalized in American society, not only institutionally but also in the degree of intensity that contaminated almost all human beings socialized in America. Initially, the attempt was to use the Brown decision as a form of therapy, to free American whites and Negroes from the depths of the disease. It became apparent, however, that the extent of the metastasis had been underestimated and misunderstood, that the pattern of resistance, evasion, and tokenism that followed Brown could only be explained by a racism that had rotted the roots of American life North and South.

Acknowledgement of the intensity and extent of the disease may, however, be positive in its effects. The North has, at the least, become more honest in its racism; it no longer hides behind the posture of nonracism. That may be an important first step toward genuine social change.

## WHITE RACISM AND INTELLECTUAL LEADERSHIP

The effort of the challenging NAACP brief in *Brown* to point also to the destructive influences of racism upon the dominant white culture was virtually ignored by the Court as well as by social scientists and the public.

With reference to the impact of segregation and its concomitants on children of the majority group, the report indicates that the effects are somewhat more obscure. Those children who learn the prejudices of our society are also being taught to gain personal status in an unrealistic and non-adaptive way. When comparing themselves to members of the minority group, they are not required to evaluate themselves in terms of the more basic standards of actual personal ability and achievement. The culture permits and at times, encourages them to direct their feelings of hostility and aggression against whole groups of people the members of which are perceived as weaker than themselves. They often develop patterns of guilt feelings, rationalizations and other mechanisms which they must use in an attempt to protect themselves from recognizing the essential injustice of their unrealistic fears and hatreds of minority groups.

The report indicates further that confusion, conflict, moral cynicism, and disrespect for authority may arise in majority group children as a consequence of being taught the moral, religious and democratic principles of the brotherhood of man and the importance of justice and fair play by the same persons and institutions who, in their support of racial segregation and related practices, seem to be acting in a prejudiced and discriminatory manner. Some individuals may attempt to resolve this conflict by intensifying their hostility toward the minority group. Still others react by developing an unwholesome, rigid, and uncritical idealization of all authority figures—their parents, strong political and economic leaders. As described in *The Authoritarian Personality*, they despise the weak, while they obsequiously and unquestioningly conform to the demands of the strong whom they also, paradoxically, subconsciously hate.[5]

Racism at that time was acknowledged primarily in terms of its damage to the victims of oppression; the moral and psychological erosion of the oppressor himself had not been faced. The implications of the Myrdal report, *An American Dilemma*, published in 1944 had not yet been carried out in social science or the law.

Racism emerges in both blatant and in more difficult to answer, subtle, manifestations. In the academic community, it began to be clear in the 1960's that apparently sophisticated and compassionate theories used to explain slow Negro student performance might themselves be tainted with racist condescension. Some of the theories of "cultural deprivation," "the disadvantaged," and the like, until recently popular in educational circles and in high governmental spheres, and still prevalent in fact, were backed for the most part by inclusive and fragmentary research and much speculation. The eagerness with which such theories were greeted was itself a subtly racist symptom. The theories obscured this orientation, but when challenged, some of their advocates posed more overt racist formulations.

The earliest explanations of the academic inferiority of Negro children had been given in terms of their inherent, racially determined intellectual inferiority. This approach not only dominated the thinking of laymen but was accepted and reinforced by the theories of educators and social scientists until the fourth decade of the twentieth century. It was not until the publication of the significant

---

[5] "The Effects of Segregation and the Consequences of Desegregation: A Social Science Statement," Appendix to Appellants' Briefs, Brown v. Board of Education, as quoted in Kenneth B. Clark, *Prejudice and Your Child* 168 (Boston, 1956).

research and interpretations of Boaz and Klineberg in the 1930's that such subtle or flagrant theories of inherent racial inferiority ceased to be fashionable among social scientists.

With the increasing acceptance of the Boaz and Klineberg findings, social and environmental explanations of the academic retardation of Negro children replaced racial and biological explanations in the literature of the social sciences, reflecting the general rise of liberal thought that characterized the decade.

The most recent specific explanation of the academic retardation of Negro children is the "cultural deprivation" theory, the contemporary form of environmental interpretations. It rejects explanations of inherent racial or biological inferiority and asserts that the total pattern of racial prejudice, discrimination, and segregation found in a racist society blocks the capacity of school personnel to teach minority group children with the same observable efficiency as that given other children. These children may, therefore, be expected to remain academically retarded no matter how well they are taught. Among the specific barriers emphasized by different writers in varying degrees are: environmentally determined sensory deficiencies; withdrawn or hyperactive behavior; low attention span; peculiar or bizarre language patterns; lack of verbal stimulation; absence of father or stable male figure in the home; and lack of books in the home.

In spite of the fact that these factors have dominated the literature and have been frequently repeated and generally accepted as explanations of the academic retardation of lower status children, they have not been verified as causal factors through any precise and systematic research reported in the published literature. The evidence, or indeed lack of evidence, suggests, therefore, that this concept has gained acceptance through intuition, general impressions, and repetition.

There is probability that the provocative work of Pasamanick might be an exception to this general observation.[6] These students of the problem have sought to define the general problem of cultural deprivation in terms of the effects of poverty on the nutritional deficiencies and inadequate diet of pregnant females, low income pregnant females, which in turn affects the neurological development of the prenatal and postnatal child. This approach, if verified by further more systematic and controlled research, will provide a most sophisticated combination of biological, physiological, neurological, and social environmental variables in the explanation of the academic retardation of low income and low status children.

Many students of this problem have asserted that motivation is the pivotal factor in the relationship between low socioeconomic status—"cultural deprivation"—and academic retardation. They maintain that low status children are not motivated towards academic success and therefore do not perform up to the level of more privileged children. An analysis of the literature containing this motivation explanation of the problem leaves many important questions unanswered.

Is the low motivation of low status children a primary factor directly re-

[6] Benjamin Pasamanick and Hilda Knoblack, "The Contribution of Some Organic Factors to School Retardation in Negro Children" 27 *Journal of Negro Education* 4 (1958).

flecting their low socioeconomic or racial status? Is the low motivation of these children peculiar to them—and specific to low academic performance? Is low academic motivation a consequence of low academic performance which in turn is caused by other factors?

It is important to obtain these answers because imperative changes in educational policy and practices which will affect the lives of human beings will be determined by them. Cultural deprivation theorists have not only provided the public school educational establishment with a respectable rationalization for maintaining the status quo of educational inefficiency for low status children, but the related technology of this theory—compensatory or educational enrichment programs—appears to provide the basis for inherent contradictions in its premises and assumptions.

An uncritical acceptance of this theory and explanation seems to be contradicted by:

(1) the concretely demonstrated psychological fact of the normal curve in the distribution of human intellectual potential, personality characteristics, motivation, and other personal characteristics believed to be related to academic performance;

(2) the modifiableness of human beings;

(3) the fact that normal human beings who are taught, motivated to learn, expected to learn, and provided with conditions conducive to learning, will learn up to or near the limits of their capacity.

Furthermore, the cultural deprivation theories are clear violations of the law of parsimony, since they seek more complex explanations without determining that more simple explanations are not adequate. Cultural deprivation theories appear to bypass more direct and specific educational variables such as quality of teaching and supervision, acceptance or rejection of the students by teachers, and educational methods and facilities.

Given the history of educational rejection of Negro children, it would seem obvious to one trained in the methods of science that much more direct variables would have to be held constant and checked out with more precision and more sensitive instruments than the widely quoted Coleman report[7] does before one could resort to the more elaborate, ambiguous, and seemingly uncontrollable catchall variable of cultural deprivation. In this regard it is significant that the literature, while eloquent and repetitive in its expansion of the cultural deprivation hypothesis, is almost totally silent on discussions or research which seek to determine the relationship between subtle or flagrant rejection of a child by his teachers because of race, color, economic status, and family income, and the level of his academic performance. These social, psychological, and educational variables seem worthy of a serious attention and research which they have not as yet received. The cultural deprivation explanation did not emerge in its present form until the 1950's and did not receive wide currency and general uncritical acceptance until after the Brown decision. It has since become an integral part of the controversy concerning the quality of education provided for Negro children in de jure and de facto segregated schools.

[7] Office of Education, U. S. Department of Health, Education, and Welfare, *Equality of Educational Opportunity* (Washington, 1966).

Such theories are often regarded as liberal because they posit environmental inadequacy rather than genetic inferiority and because they are often used to support demands for integration. The problem, exemplified by the Coleman report, which takes this approach, is that it concludes that it is the environmentally caused characteristics of white children which are the positive component of integrated schools, and that Negro children gain educationally primarily from association with white children. Further research is necessary to determine whether correlation and causal factors have been confused in this important study, but perhaps most important, it is necessary to study the majority white school as a total unit as compared to the majority Negro school, to determine what happens in the school itself *because* white children are present. Sensitive instruments must be sought to measure teacher and administrative expectations, counseling attitudes, quality of curriculum, and the like, but beyond the assessment of these individual factors, it is necessary to evaluate the total pattern of advantage of deprivation. On the basis of years of observation and research of ghetto education, I would advance the proposition that one would find a significantly high correlation between a pattern of deprivation and ghetto schools, and a pattern of advantage and white urban and suburban schools. It is not the white child *per se* whose presence leads to higher achievement for the Negro child who associates with him in class, but the quality of the education provided because the white child is there that makes the difference, or so I believe the empirical evidence indicates. To argue, without irrefutable proof, that this is not the case is to lend support to a racially defined environmental theory of academic achievement that is no less callous in its consequences than a genetic theory of racial inferiority would be.

In the fields of sociology, history, and anthropology racial insensitivity took various other forms. One is the "bootstrap" argument ("We did it, why can't you?"), which assumes class more significant than race in determining status in America. Its proponents urge Negroes to climb the ladder of success in imitation of the experience of upward mobility of the other ethnic groups; the implication is that failure to succeed can be laid at the door of the group that fails. Another is the pluralistic argument, which assumes that voluntary separatism is the genius of American democracy, and that the Negro's demand for integration is a threat to the pluralistic tradition and aspirations of various ethnic groups.

The problem here is that both theories obscure or deliberately evade the fact that the Negro's inferior status, unlike that of other American citizens, was historically fixed by law and reinforced by the cult of racism. The Negro was highly visible as the white immigrant was not. The Negro, unlike the white immigrant, had to overcome centuries of slavery, the reinforcement of inferior status in the post-Reconstruction conspiracy led by powerful political, financial, and real estate interests, and the continuing pattern of institutionalized racial oppression in the twentieth century. The Negro could not become indistinguishable from other Americans merely by changing his name, his speech, his style. Color was his continuing badge of inferiority.

The Negro has not been permitted pluralistic interaction. He has been restricted from integrated or equal status.

It is only recently that Negroes have been permitted to function in colleges and universities in even limited numbers. Du Bois, as great an intellect as America has produced, was never invited to teach at Harvard, his Alma Mater. Only recently have Negroes—in limited numbers—been admitted to high governmental positions. Negroes are still not admitted to the highest financial circles. Pluralism, if indeed it is desirable, must follow not precede integration, for it is meaningful only in a context of limited voluntary separation under conditions where all share in the necessarily integrated economic and educational system. Therefore, to argue for pluralism—when the status of the Negro is unequal—is to obscure injustice. Pluralism without equality would best be described by the caste model. The untouchables in stratified India lived in a pluralistic society of a kind. Calls for pluralism just at the time when the Negro is demanding full freedom of entrance into previously restricted neighborhoods, into previously insular colleges, into previously white-monopolized governmental employment, must be viewed with a suspicion that equal interaction is not the intent of white society.

The new theories of the genetic inferiority of Negroes, like those posed by Arthur Jensen,[8] are almost identical to the old, their statistical apparatus notwithstanding. And like the old, they are not verifiable:

(1) because the concept of race itself is so elusive that except for certain distinct physical characteristics—which themselves vary widely within and between groups—genetic differences identifiable by race have so far proved impossible to determine;

(2) because even if pure racist differences were ascertainable, the Negro is not a biological or "racial" entity. The American Negro is an historical intermixture—of white and Indian and African;

(3) because the American Negro as a socially defined group with common characteristics generated by social and institutional exclusiveness has existed for too brief a time to develop any meaningful genetic character by inbreeding;

(4) because the definition of inferiority resorted to is itself restricted in terms of the characteristics of human beings, that is, the instruments and tests used are assumed to measure genetically determined characteristics in groups that can be compared to other groups without significant overlap. The evidence is clearly against that. Also, the assumption is that if one consistently and positively modifies the experience of deprived groups, this modification will not be reflected in significant improvement. There is no evidence to prove this closed-end theory of environmental influences.

The fact is that the limits of environmental effect on intelligence have not been ascertained. Even under the most controlled conditions, tests of human beings in a racist society cannot eliminate the flagrant and subtle influences which permeate every aspect of American life. Even the prebirth environment would need to be controlled, for the damage to urban infants whose mothers are deprived of adequate health care and nutrition, of psychological security, and of self-respect, cannot itself be fully ascertained. Until the conditions of life of American Negroes are in all respects equal to those available to others, no valid test of genetic capacity can be devised. Such conditions of equality must be achieved as speedily as possible.

[8] "How Much Can We Boost I.Q. and Scholastic Achievement" 39 *Harvard Educational Review* (Winter, 1969).

The ambiguity of the concept of race was first raised by Franz Boas and Ruth Benedict in the 1930's. The ambiguity of the American Negro as a racial entity was raised by Otto Klineberg in the late 1930's. The ambiguity of the phenomena to be measured and the limits of the instruments and the definition of the group must be as rigorously questioned today.

There is today a growing and persistent counterattack against this neo-racist intellectual backlash among biologists, psychologists and social scientists. Further, more vigorous attention to the social responsibilities of social science is leading a number of scholars, particularly among the young, into an overt role in the struggle for positive social change. Objectivity and pure science are now perceived by a growing number to be consistent with, and not antithetical to, social responsibility. They are perceived to be appropriate though limited in themselves, but monstrous when taken to mean that conditions of injustice must not touch the spirit or motivate a man to act.

The involvement of social scientists in the Brown decision set social science and the law on a common path. There can be no turning from it.

### The Future Relevancy of Integration, and the Challenge of Black Separatism

In 1954 when the Brown decision was handed down, desegregation and integration were the priority of the civil rights movement and Negroes generally. Fifteen years later, many militants have proclaimed the death of the civil rights movement and have denied the value of integration itself, and specifically have questioned the significance of the Brown decision and the truth of the social science findings on which it rested. One must thus look at the decision and its social science foundation from a new perspective, and inquire whether these charges are justified.

During the period since 1954, black nationalism has experienced a sharp rise in support from young Negro militants and from many whites. This represents in some forms the continuation of the nationalism of the Garvey movement of the 1920's, identifiable in degree by the black nationalism of Malcolm X. In other, and more serious, manifestations it has gained support among Negro students and youth. The seeming common denomination of both is the repudiation of integration and the apparent repudiation of the struggle for desegregation, the rejection of the Brown decision, and the implicit rejection of the whole rationale and psychological approach to the meaning of racism. This would logically include a denial of the social science explanation of the inevitability of inferiority in segregated systems on which the Brown decision depended.

Under the guise of assuming a positive identity, black nationalism has adopted an imitation of white racism with its deification of race, its attempt to make a virtue out of color, its racist mystique. This rationale argues that the detrimental consequences of a biracial society are neutralized or transformed into positive consequences by virtue of the fact that Negroes themselves are now asserting the value of racism. This argument would give primary weight to voluntarism, that is, that racism would lead to affirmative not negative results if it is voluntarily accepted or sought by the previous victims, as it was voluntarily maintained by the oppressors. The character of racism would depend on the attitude one had toward it; it would have no objective reality of its own. Consistent with certain contemporary philosophical positions, the nature of reality and of ethical judgment about separatism would be governed not by objectively determined evidence or by consequences but by the subjective view.

Fifteen years ago, on the contrary, it would have been the consensus in the Negro and white liberal communities that white racism would have gained its greatest triumph had it been able to persuade its Negro victims that segregation was not only acceptable but desirable in itself, and that the justification for this separatism was color alone.

The paranoia of racism, whether imposed or sought, must rest on insecurity. It is the verification of the psychological interpretation of the negative consequences of segregation. Racism does produce doubts and insecurities in the victims as well as in the perpetrators. It increases hostility and aggression and self-hatred. Actually, the present separatist movement, the present intensity of the cult—though one must still question whether it reflects the position of the majority of Negroes—is certainly fashionable in terms of treatment given by the press, television, and publishing. The semantics has been effectively changed in an abrupt few years. Many, even most, Negroes and most white liberals in positions requiring public articulateness, as well as many moderate newspapers, have substituted the word "black" for "Negro", however awkward it may sound to them—some from the conviction that the one represents liberation and the other submission; but many out of dread of the unfashionable and of the perjorative judgment of black militants, who have mounted a campaign of verbal condemnation and threat against those whites and blacks who desist.

It could be argued persuasively and with reason, if reason too is not now to be repudiated or considered too middle class, that the term "black" adds to the confusion of America's racial dilemma. Certainly it is not an African term. Like Negro, it too is a "white man's" term. It is Anglo-Saxon, while Negro is Latin and, more recently, Spanish in origin. Not long ago it was considered militant to insist that newspapers capitalize the term "Negro."

The chief functions of the use of the term "black" now is to demonstrate that one is identified with the new militant thrust. (The new elite may include a highly select group of converted or contributing whites.) It is regarded as offering a basis for differentiating between the truly anointed among Negroes who will reserve for themselves the designation *blacks,* a test of racial loyalty consigning all middle-class Uncle Toms to the damnable category of "Negro."

The most serious new dimension to the new form of black nationalism is not the threat of violence which it poses for white society—a threat which is for the most part verbal and after the fact—but the very real threat which it presents to the middle class and middle-class aspiring Negroes. Some of the most incoherently articulate spokesmen seem more intensely and fervently against the middle-class educated Negro than they are anti-white.

While some advocates or interpreters of the Black Power movement are middle-class themselves—professors, college students, white and Negro clergymen—many of its advocates are dominated by deep feelings of racial self-hatred.

Part of the pattern of pretense and posturing includes a suicidal eagerness to ascribe all middle-class patterns of speech, grammar, dress, manners, and style of life to whites, while reserving for the exclusive use of Negroes the uncouth and the vulgar. This is garden variety racism at its most obscene—and no less so because it is now being sold by Negroes rather than by whites. Some racial "militants" have accepted the white man's negative stereotype of the Negro. It was not acceptable when fostered by white oppression; it can not be acceptable in the guise of flamboyant black militancy.

This Lorelei quest for identity is based on superstition. Despite the verbal transformation from self-contempt to apparent pride, the conditions of injustice remain. We are asked to obscure them by the rhetorical posturing of pride. In a strikingly similar analogy, it is psychologically obvious that any man who proclaims how irresistible and potent and virile he is must have deep doubts about it. He would clearly be regarded as preoccupied with sexual anxiety. Such self-pretense conceals—or attempts to conceal—deep, poignant, and tragic insecurity. Given the fact that the realities of racism in America have not changed, that the Negro is still condemned to segregated schools, to segregated and deteriorated residential areas, and to an economic role that is not competitive with the white society, the cult of blackness must be recognized as what it is—a ritualized denial of anguished despair and resentment of the failure of society to meet its promises.

Separatism is an attempt to create verbal realities as substitutes for social, political, and economic realities. It is another and intense symptom of the psychological damage which a racist society inflicts on its victims.

A specific indication of the damage of separatism is that the victims internalize racism. Some forms of black separatism involve genuine and deep self-destructive, suicidal dynamics. They reflect the most cruel, barbaric, tragic, dehumanizing consequences of white oppression—the wish of the oppressed to die—and in dying to destroy others in a similar predicament. The white racists who so damage their fellow human beings must be prepared to face the same judgment which the Nazis who sent millions to death camps must face.

Whatever the motivation for individuals associated with the black nationalist movement, I consider the movement as a whole to be sick, regressive, and tyrannical. It is anti-intellectual. Its main source of energy is emotionalism rather than thought.

Responding to a button reading "Being Black Is Not Enough", several Negroes said, "Well, being white has always been enough." But if one looks at the moral decay, the instability, and the unresolved problems of white society, one perceives that being white is not enough, that it is effective only in terms of self-aggrandizement and at the expense of exploitation of those who are not white. Its success depends on victimization, for racism is not only subjective, it also demands an object. Positive racism has the necessary obverse of rejection of those who do not meet the chosen racial criteria.

So, rather than refuting the social science assumptions that led to the Brown decision, the present cult of black separatism verifies it intensely. Black separatism can be seen as a "sour-grapes-and-sweet-lemon" reaction against the failure of the society to implement and enforce the findings of *Brown*.

The vocal, well-publicized, well-endowed cult has to be understood for what it is, for otherwise it can be cynically manipulated and used by white racists who are now the often silent allies of the separatists. The rationale of the sophisticated white intellectual who endorses black separatism in his university, his church, his political party, his academic or professional society, while continuing to live in a restricted suburb and continuing to support the institutional relegation of Negroes to inferior status, must be seen by Negroes for what it is, an attempt to handle racial antiviolence, to deal with guilt.

The basic standard for such understanding is that which functioned in the Brown decision, namely that racism and segregation are a reflection of superstition, institutionalized untruth, cruelty, and injustice, and that race is irrelevant as a criterion for preference or rejection. The poignant tragedy is that the society is using the victimized groups as the agent for the perpetuation of irreconcilable injustice and racial irrelevance. Any white or black intellectual who denies this must be more comfortable with superstition and rationalization. One cannot deal with the reorganization of society on a nonracial basis by intensifying racist symptoms.

Separatists tend to substitute rhetorical satisfactions of reiterated pride of race for confrontation of racist injustice. They rarely address themselves to immediate specific programs designed to reorganize society, but rather comfort themselves with grandiose ideology, "black awareness" campaigns, and long-range plans such as demands for separatist states or back-to-Africa movements. They seldom invest their energies in attempts to abolish deteriorated housing or deteriorated education. Black nationalism is the easier way.

Nether do poor white racists address themselves to specific problems, such as inadequate nutrition and the life chances of their children. Rather, they are caught up in the semantics of white superiority. Neither poor whites nor blacks can ever change the conditions of their lives as long as they remain so narcotized. Racists, white and black, are essentially hopeless people who have given up on the possibilities of justice and on their own capacity to further justice.

It is fashionable also among whites to defend black separatism to other whites not on its merits, as they may do in the company of Negroes, but as a necessary step toward eventual integration as a "phase" restless Negroes must go through. Indeed, some black separatists offer the same self-defeating rationale.

Yet, at the end of the nineteenth century in the post-Reconstruction period, institutionalized segregation was also explained as a "phase" by whites and blacks who argued that it was a necessary first stage to prepare Negroes for inclusion into society. Instead, such racism became institutionalized and rigid, and then was explained and defended for its own sake as a desirable way of life. In American society, segregation and separatism, which is the same thing semantically disguised and camouflaged by self-acceptance, tends to be self-perpetuating rather than self-neutralizing.

Nor can one build a solid pride on the quicksands of emotion, anger, rage, hatred—no matter how justifiable. Genuine pride—the pride that makes life worth the struggle with some hope of serenity—must come from solid personal achievement, from sensitivity and concern and respect for one's fellow man, from compassion and the willingness to struggle to give some substance to one's own life by trying to help others live with confidence in the possibility of positives. Pride, like humility, is destroyed by one's insistence that he possesses it.

Racism in any form is dangerous, but particularly, as is now true among many whites and Negroes, when it is intellectually supported. Such supporters often fail to follow the implication of their rhetoric to its logical conclusion—that if segregation and separatism are desirable and good as a phase, and as a means, they are even more to be desired as ends in themselves.

All the implications of the Brown decision and all the social science arguments in its support point to the inherent dangers of racism. The latest surge toward self-imposed separatism is the greatest verification of all. I read into the separatist movement among Negroes a more severe symptom than those described in *Brown*. It convinces me even more persuasively that we must redouble our efforts to obliterate racism whatever its manifestations, wherever it appears.

New York
April, 1969

ARGUMENT

# JUSTICES PRESENT AT ARGUMENT

Chief Justice Fred Vinson
(participated only in 1952 argument)

(1890–1953) Member, House of Representatives (1924–1929; 1931–1938); United States Circuit Judge, District of Columbia Court of Appeals, 1938–1943; Secretary of the Treasury, 1945–1946; Chief Justice of the United States, 1946–1953.

Earl Warren
(participated in 1953 and 1955 arguments)

(1891–    ) Attorney General, State of California, 1939–1943; Governor of California, 1943–1953; Republican candidate for Vice President of United States, 1948; Chief Justice of the United States, 1953–1969.

Hugo L. Black

(1886–    ) United States Senator from Alabama, 1927–1937; Associate Justice, United States Supreme Court, 1937–

Stanley F. Reed

(1884–    ) Solicitor General of United States, 1935–1938; Associate Justice, United States Supreme Court, 1938–1957.

Felix Frankfurter

(1882–1965) Professor, Harvard Law School, 1914–1939; Associate Justice, United States Supreme Court, 1939–1962.

William O. Douglas

(1898–    ) Commissioner, Securities and Exchange Commission, 1934–1936, Chairman, 1936–1939; Associate Justice, United States Supreme Court, 1939–

Robert H. Jackson
(participated in 1952 and 1953 arguments)

(1892–1954) General Counsel, Bureau of Internal Revenue; Assistant Attorney General of United States, 1936–1938; Solicitor General of United States, 1938–1939; Attorney General, Jan. 1940–June 1941; Associate Justice, United States Supreme Court, 1941–1954; Chief Counsel to prosecute war criminals before International Military Tribunal at Nuremburg, 1946–1947.

Harold H. Burton

(1888–1964) Mayor of Cleveland, Ohio, 1935–1940; United States Senator from Ohio, 1941–1945; Associate Justice, United States Supreme Court, 1945–1958.

Tom C. Clark

(1899–      ) Assistant Attorney General of United States, 1943–1945; Attorney General, 1945–1949; Associate Justice, United States Supreme Court, 1949–1967.

Sherman Minton

(1890–1965) United States Senator from Indiana, 1935–1941. United States Circuit Judge, Seventh Circuit Court of Appeals, 1941–1949; Associate Justice, United States Supreme Court, 1949–1956.

John Marshall Harlan
  (participated only in 1955 argument)

(1899–      ) United States Circuit Judge, Second Circuit Court of Appeals, 1954–1955; Associate Justice, United States Supreme Court, 1955–.

## ATTORNEYS FOR PLAINTIFFS

| | |
|---|---|
| Robert L. Carter | Assistant Counsel, NAACP Legal Defense and Educational Fund, Inc. at the time of the argument in Brown v. Board of Education; subsequently General Counsel for NAACP. |
| Thurgood Marshall | Director-Counsel of the NAACP Legal Defense and Educational Fund, Inc., 1940–1961; United States Circuit Judge for the Second Circuit Court of Appeals, 1961–1965; Solicitor General of United States, 1965–1967; Associate Justice, United States Supreme Court, 1967– |
| Spottswood Robinson, III | Southeast Regional Counsel NAACP Legal Defense and Educational Fund, Inc., 1951–1960; Dean, Howard University Law School, 1960–1964; Member United States Commission on Civil Rights, 1961–1966; United States Circuit Judge for the District of Columbia Court of Appeals, 1966– |
| George E. C. Hayes | Private practice Washington D.C.; Member of Board of Directors of NAACP Legal Defense and Educational Fund, Inc. |
| James Nabrit | Professor, Howard University Law School, 1936–1956; Dean 1958–1960; President, Howard University, 1960–1967; United States Deputy Representative to United Nations, 1966–1967. |
| Louis L. Redding | Private Practice, Wilmington, Del. |
| Jack Greenberg | Assistant Counsel, NAACP Legal Defense and Educational Fund, Inc., 1949–1961; Director-Counsel, 1961– |

## ATTORNEYS FOR DEFENDANTS

Paul E. Wilson            Assistant Attorney General, State of Kansas.

Harold R. Fatzer          Attorney General, State of Kansas, 1949–1956; Justice, Supreme Court of Kansas, 1956–

John W. Davis             Member, House of Representatives, 1911–1915; Solicitor General of United States, 1913–1918; Ambassador to Great Britian, 1918–1921; Member of law firm of Davis, Polk, Wardwell, Sunderland & Kiendl, 1921–1955; Democratic candidate for President, 1924; President of American Bar Association, 1922; declined nomination to United States Supreme Court, 1922.

Robert McC. Figg, Jr.     Counsel for Board of Trustees of Clarendon County, South Carolina School District.

S. E. Rogers              Counsel for Board of Trustees of Clarendon County, South Carolina School District.

T. Justin Moore           Counsel for Prince Edward County Virginia School System; Member of firm of Hunton, Williams, Gay, Powell & Gibson of Richmond, Va.

Archibald G. Robertson    Counsel for Prince Edward County Virginia School System; Member of firm of Hunton, Williams, Gay, Powell & Gibson of Richmond, Va.

J. Lindsay Almond         Member, House of Representatives, 1946–1948; Attorney General, State of Virginia, 1948–1957; Governor, State of Virginia, 1958–1962; Judge, United States Court of Customs and Patent Appeals, 1962–

Milton Korman             Assistant Corporation Counsel, District of Columbia.

H. Albert Young           Attorney General, State of Delaware.

Joseph D. Craven          Attorney General, State of Delaware.

## COUNSEL FOR *AMICI*

J. Lee Rankin

Assistant Attorney General, Department of Justice, 1953–1956; Solicitor General of United States, 1956–1961; Chief Counsel, Warren Commission, 1963–1964; Corporation Counsel, City of New York, 1966–

Simon E. Sobeloff

Chief Judge, Maryland Court of Appeals, 1952–1954; Solicitor General of United States, 1954–1956; United States Circuit Judge for the Fourth Circuit Court of Appeals, 1956–     , Chief Judge since 1958.

Richard Ervin

Attorney General, State of Florida; Justice, Florida Supreme Court, 1964.

Ralph E. Odum

Assistant Attorney General, State of Florida.

I. Beverly Lake

Assistant Attorney General, State of North Carolina.

Thomas J. Gentry

Attorney General, State of Arkansas.

Mac Q. Williamson

Attorney General, State of Oklahoma.

C. Ferdinand Sybert

Attorney General, State of Maryland, 1954–1961; Judge, Court of Appeals, Maryland, 1961.

John Ben Shepperd

Attorney General, State of Texas.

Burnell Waldrep

Assistant Attorney General, State of Texas.

1952  ARGUMENT

IN THE SUPREME COURT OF THE UNITED STATES

October Term, 1952

OLIVER BROWN, MRS. RICHARD LAWTON, MRS. SADIE EMMANUEL, ET AL
Appellants

vs.

BOARD OF EDUCATION OF TOPEKA, SHAWNEE COUNTY, KANSAS, ET AL
Appellees.

Case No. 8

Washington, D.C.
Tuesday, December 9, 1952.

The above-entitled cause came on for oral argument at 1:35 p.m.

PRESENT:

The Chief Justice, Honorable Fred M. Vinson, and Associate Justices Black, Reed,
Frankfurter, Douglas, Jackson, Burton, Clark, and Minton.

APPEARANCES:

On behalf of the Appellants:
ROBERT L. CARTER, ESQ.

On behalf of the Appellees:
PAUL E. WILSON, ESQ.

THE CHIEF JUSTICE: Case No. 8, Oliver Brown and others versus the
Board of Education of Topeka, Shawnee County, Kansas.

THE CLERK: Counsel are present.

THE CHIEF JUSTICE: Mr. Carter.

ARGUMENT ON BEHALF OF THE APPELLANTS

by MR. CARTER

MR. CARTER: This case is here on direct appeal pursuant to Title 28, section 1253, 2101(b), from the final judgment of a statutory three-judge court, District Court, for the District of Kansas, denying appellants' motion, application for
a permanent injunction to restrain the enforcement of Chapter 72–1724 of the
General Statutes of Kansas, on the grounds of that statute's fatal conflict with the
requirements and guarantees of the Fourteenth Amendment.

The statute in question empowers boards of education in cities of the first
class in Kansas to maintain and operate public elementary schools on a segregated
basis, with the exception of Kansas City, Kansas, which is empowered to maintain
segregated public high schools also.

The law of Kansas is clear, as construed by the highest court of that state,
that except for this statutory authority, the appellees in this instance would have
no power to make any distinction whatsoever in public schools among children on

the basis of race and color; or, to put it another way, the law of Kansas is this: that it is a violation of state law for any state officer to use race as a factor in affording educational opportunities unless that authority is specifically, clearly, and expressly granted by the legislature.

The state cases, which are set forth and would set this out, are cited at page 2 of our brief.[1]

Now, it is to be noted that this statute prohibits any type of color discrimination in high schools, with the exception of Kansas City, Kansas.

The Topeka school system is operated on a six-three-three plan: elementary schools going through the sixth grade, thereafter junior high schools through the ninth grade, and thereafter senior high schools.

So that in this instance, appellants are required to attend segregated elementary schools through the sixth grade, but thereafter they go to high schools without any determination being made as to which school they will attend on the basis of race.

If appellants are of Negro origin, they are minors who are not eligible at the present time to attend the public elementary schools in Topeka.

The appellees are empowered by state law to maintain the public school system in Topeka, Kansas. The City of Topeka has been divided into eighteen territorial divisions for public school purposes. In each of these divisions appellees maintain one school for white residents; in addition, they maintain four segregated schools for Negroes.

It is the gravamen of our complaint—it was the gravamen of our complaint below, and it is the gravamen of our appeal here—that the appellees have deprived—we have been deprived of the equal protection of the laws where the statute requires appellants to attend public elementary schools on a segregated basis, because the act of separation and the act of segregation in and of itself denies them equal educational opportunities which the Fourteenth Amendment secures.

In the answer below, the appellees, the school board, defended this action on the ground that they were acting pursuant to the statute; that appellants were not entitled to attend the elementary schools in Kansas, the eighteen elementary schools, which they maintained for white children, solely because of race and color, and that they wouldn't be admitted into those schools because they were Negroes.

The State of Kansas in the court below, and in its brief filed here, defends the constitutionality of the statute in question, and affirmatively asserts that the state has the power to authorize the imposition of racial distinction for public school purposes.

The only state or federal constitutional limitation which the State of Kansas concedes on that power is that when these distinctions are imposed the school physical facilities for Negro children must be equal.

With that limitation, they say that there can be no constitutional limitation on their power to impose racial distinctions.

[1]The briefs and records of all cases argued before the Supreme Court are deposited in approximately twenty law libraries throughout the country, including Harvard, Columbia, Yale, the New York Bar Association library as well as at the Supreme Court library.

A three-judge court was convened in the court below, pursuant to title 28 of the United States Code, section 2281 and 2284, and there a trial on the merits took place.

At the trial, appellants introduced evidence designed to conclusively demonstrate that the act of segregation in and of itself made the educational opportunities which were provided in the four schools maintained for Negroes inferior to those in the eighteen schools which were maintained for white children, because of racial segregation imposed which severely handicapped Negro children in their pursuit of knowledge, and made it impossible for them to secure equal education.

In the course of the development of this uncontroverted testimony, appellants showed that they and other Negro children similarly situated were placed at a serious disadvantage with respect to their opportunity to develop citizenship skills, and that they were denied the opportunity to learn to adjust personally and socially in a setting comprising a cross section of the dominant population of the city.

It was testified that racial segregation, as practiced in the City of Topeka, tended to relegate appellants and their group to an inferior caste; that it lowered their level of aspiration; that it instilled feelings of insecurity and inferiority with them, and that it retarded their mental and educational development, and for these reasons, the testimony said, it was impossible for the Negro children who were set off in these four schools to secure, in fact or in law, an education which was equal to that available to white children in the eighteen elementary schools maintained for them.

On August 3, the District Court filed its opinion, its findings of fact and its conclusions of law, and a final decree, all of which are set out at page 238 of the record.[2]

We accept and adopt as our own all of the findings of fact of the court below, and I wish specifically to call to the Court's attention the findings which are findings 4, 5, and 6, which are set out at page 245, in which the court found that there was no material difference between the four schools maintained for Negroes, and the eighteen schools maintained for white children with respect to physical facilities, the educational qualifications of teachers, and the courses of study prescribed.

Here we abondon any claim, in pressing our attack on the unconstitutionality of this statute—we abandon any claim— of any constitutional inequality which comes from anything other than the act of segregation itself.

In short, the sole basis for our appeal here on the constitutionality of the statute of Kansas is that it empowers the maintenance and operation of racially segregated schools, and under that basis we say, on the basis of the fact that the schools are segregated, that Negro children are denied equal protection of the laws, and they cannot secure equality in educational opportunity.

This the court found as a fact, and I will go into that finding, which is also set out on page 25 of the brief, later in the development of my argument.

But suffice it to say for this purpose, that although the court found that racial segregation created educational inequality in fact, it concluded, as a matter of law,

[2]The District Court decision is reported at 98 F. Supp. 797 and appears at p. 539 of this volume.

that the only type of educational inequality which was cognizable under the Constitution was an educational inequality which stems from material and physical factors; and absent any inequality of that level, the court said:

> We are bound by *Plessy* v. *Ferguson,* and *Gong Lum* v. *Rice* to hold in appellees' favor and uphold the constitutionality of that statute.[3]

We have one fundamental contention which we will seek to develop in the course of this argument, and that contention is that no state has any authority under the equal protection clause of the Fourteenth Amendment to use race as a factor in affording educational opportunities among its citizens.

We say that for two reasons: First, we say that a division of citizens by the states for public school purposes on the basis of race and color effect an unlawful and an unconstitutional classification within the meaning of the equal-protection clause; and, secondly, we say that where public school attendance is determined on the basis of race and color, that it is impossible for Negro children to secure equal educational opportunities within the meaning of the equal protection of the laws.

With regard to the first basis of our attack on the statute, Kansas has authorized, under certain conditions, certain boards of education to divide its schools at the elementary school level for the purpose of giving them education opportunities.

It is our position that any legislative or governmental classification must fall with an even hand on all persons similarly situated.

This Court has long held that this is the law with respect to a lawful classification, and in order to assure that this evenhandedness of the law in terms of classification exists, this Court has set standards which say that where the legislature of a state seeks to make a classification or distinction among persons, that that classification and those distinctions must rest upon some differentiation fairly related to the object which the state seeks to regulate.

Now, in this case the Negro children are—and other Negro children similarly situated are—put in one category for public school purposes, solely on the basis of race and color, and white children are put in another category for the purpose of determining what schools they will attend.

JUSTICE MINTON: Mr. Carter, I do not know whether I have followed you or all the facts on this. Was there a finding that the only basis of classification was race or color?

MR. CARTER: It was admitted—the appellees admitted in their answer—that the only reason that they would not permit Negro children to attend the eighteen white schools was because they were Negroes.

[3]Plessy v. Ferguson, 163 U.S. 537 (1896), held that a Lousiana state law providing for separate but equal accomodations on railroads for Negroes and whites did not violate the Constitution. It was thereafter cited as the source of the "separate but equal" doctrine. In Gong Lum v. Rice, 275 U.S. 78 (1927), a young Chinese girl sought admittance to a white public school in Mississippi. The authorities refused to admit her, saying she was classified as part of the colored race for the purpose of school attendance. The Supreme Court refused to intervene.

JUSTICE MINTON: Then we accept on this record that the only showing is that the classification here was solely on race and color?

MR. CARTER: Yes, sir. I think the state itself concedes this is so in its brief.

Now, we say that the only basis for this division is race, and that under the decisions of this Court that no state can use race, and race alone, as a basis upon which to ground any legislative, any lawful constitutional authority and, particularly this Court has indicated in a number of opinions that this is so because it is not felt that race is a reasonable basis upon which to ground acts; it is not a real differentiation, and it is not relevant and, in fact, this Court has indicated that race is arbitrary and an irrational standard, so that I would also like to point out, if I may, going to and quoting the statute, that the statute itself shows that this is so.

I am reading from the quote of the statute from page 3 of our brief. The statute says:

> [The Board of Education may] organize and maintain separate schools for the education of white and colored children, including the high schools in Kansas City, Kansas; no discrimination on account of color shall be made in high schools except as provided herein.

We say that on the face of the statute this is explicit recognition of the fact that the authorization which the state gave to cities of the first class, and so forth, to make this segregation on the basis of race, carried with it the necessary fact that they were permitted to discriminate on the basis of race and color, and that the statute recognizes that these two things are interchangeable and cannot be separated.

Now, without further belaboring our classification argument, our theory is that if the normal rules of classification, the equal protection doctrine of classification, apply to this case—and we say they should be applied—that this statute is fatally defective, and that on this ground, and this ground alone, the statute should be struck down.

We also contend, as I indicated, a second ground for the unconstitutionality of the statute, a second part of the main contention, is that this type of segregation makes it impossible for Negro children and appellants in this case to receive equal educational opportunities, and that in this case, the court below found this to be so as a fact; and I would turn again to quote on page 245 of the record, finding No. 8, where the court in its finding said, and I quote:

> Segregation of white and colored children in public schools has a detrimental effect upon the colored children. The impact is greater when it has the sanction of the law; for the policy of separating the races is usually interpreted as denoting the inferiority of the Negro group. A sense of inferiority affects the motivation of a child to learn. Segregation with the sanction of law, therefore, has a tendency to [restrain] the edutional and mental development of Negro children and to deprive them of some of the benefits they would receive in a racial integrated school system.

Now, as we had indicated before, this finding is amply supported by the uncontroverted testimony, and we feel that what the court did in this case in approaching this finding was that it made the same approach on a factual basis that this Court made in the McLaurin and Sweatt cases.[4]

It is our contention, our view, that when this Court was confronted with the question of whether McLaurin and Sweatt were afforded equal educational opportunities that it looked at the restrictions imposed to find out whether or not they in any way impaired the quality of education which was offered and, upon finding that the quality of education that had been offered under the segregated conditions, that this Court held in both instances that those racial restrictions could not stand.

The court below, based on this finding, starts its examination in this same way. It finds that the restrictions which the appellants complained of place them and other Negro children in the class at a disadvantage with respect to the quality of education which they would receive, and that as a result of these restrictions, Negro children are—the development of their minds, and the learning process is impaired and damaged.

We take the position that where there exists educational inequality, in fact, that is necessarily follows that educational inequality in the law is also present.

But the court below felt, as I indicated before, that the only concern of the Constitution with the question of educational equality, was that the physical facilities afforded had to be equal; and absent any inequality with regard to physical facilities, they say, "We are bound by *Plessy* v. *Ferguson* and *Gong Lum* v. *Rice*."

It is also clear from the court's opinion that it was in a great deal of confusion and doubt and, perhaps, even in torture in reaching these results.

I would again like to quote from the record the court's opinion, on page 243, and the court says:

> If segregation within a school as in the McLaurin case is a denial of due process, it is difficult to see why segregation in separate schools would not result in the same denial. Or if the denial of the right to commingle with the majority group in higher institutions of learning as in the Sweatt case and gain the educational advantages resulting therefrom, is lack of due process, it is difficult to see why such denial would not result in the same lack of due process if practiced in the lower grades.

We say that but for the constraint which the court feels was imposed upon it by the McLaurin case—

THE CHIEF JUSTICE: We will recess for lunch.

(A short recess was taken.)

THE CHIEF JUSTICE: Mr. Carter?

MR. CARTER: Just before the recess, I was attempting to show that in the opinion of the court below that it was clear from the opinion that the court felt

[4]In McLaurin v. Oklahoma State Regents, 339 U.S. 637 (1950), the Court ordered a Negro graduate student at the University of Oklahoma to be treated exactly as the white students and required the special seats and tables to which he was assigned in the classroom, library, and cafeteria removed. In Sweatt v. Painter, 339 U.S. 629 (1950), the Court found a new Negro law school opened by the State of Texas to be inferior to the University of Texas Law School and therefore required the University to admit a qualified Negro applicant.

that the rule of law applicable in the McLaurin and Sweatt cases should apply here, but felt that it was constrained and prevented from doing that by virtue of *Plessy* v. *Ferguson* and *Gong Lum* v. *Rice*.

We believe that the court below was wrong in this conclusion. We think that the rules of law applicable to McLaurin and Sweatt do apply, and that there are no decisions of this Court which require a contrary result.

JUSTICE REED: Was there any evidence in the record to show the inability, the lesser ability, of the child in the segregated schools?

MR. CARTER: Yes, sir, there was a great deal of testimony on the impact of racial distinctions and segregation, on the emotional and mental development of a child.

Now, this is, in summary, Finding 8 of the court, a summarization of the evidence that we introduced on that.

JUSTICE REED: And the findings go to the ability to learn or merely on the emotional reaction?

MR. CARTER: The finding says that—

JUSTICE REED: I know about the finding, but the evidence?

MR. CARTER: The evidence, yes, sir. The evidence went to the fact that in the segregated school, because of these emotional impacts that segregation has, that it does impair the ability to learn, that you are not able to learn as well as you do if you were in a mixed school, and that further than that, you are barred from contact with members of the dominant group and, therefore, your total educational content is somewhat lower than it would be ordinarily.

JUSTICE REED: Would those citations be in your brief on page 9?

MR. CARTER: Yes, sir. In fact, what we attempted to do was to pick up in summary and refer the Court to the record of the various disabilities to which our witnesses testified, and we covered the question of the content of education. They are all set out on page 9 of our brief as citations.

JUSTICE BURTON: It is your position that there is a great deal more to the educational process even in the elementary school than what you read in the books?

MR. CARTER: Yes, sir, that is precisely the point.

JUSTICE BURTON: And it is on that basis which makes a real difference whether it is segregated or not?

MR. CARTER: Yes, sir. We say that the question of your physical facilities is not enough. The Constitution does not, in terms of protecting, giving equal protection of the laws with regard to equal educational opportunities, does not stop with the fact that you have equal physical facilities, but it covers the whole educational process.

THE CHIEF JUSTICE: The findings in this case did not stop with equal physical facilities, did they?

MR. CARTER: No, sir, the findings did not stop, but went beyond that. But, as I indicated, the Court did not feel that it could go in the law beyond physical facilities.

Of the two cases which the court below indicates have kept it from ruling as a matter of law in this case that educational, equal educational, opportunities were not afforded, the first is the *Plessy* v. *Ferguson* case.

It is our position that *Plessy* v. *Ferguson* is not in point here; that it had nothing to do with educational opportunities whatsoever.

We further take the position that whatever the court below may have felt about the reach of the Plessy case, that this Court in the Sweatt case made it absolutely clear that *Plessy* v. *Ferguson* had nothing to do with the question of education.

The Court, in its opinion, after discussing the Sipuel case, the Fisher case, and the Gaines case[5], in the Sweatt opinion said that these are the only cases in this Court which control the issue of racial distinction in state-supported graduate and professional education.

We think this was a pointed and deliberate omission in *Plessy,* and that the Court is saying the *Plessy* v. *Ferguson* certainly has nothing to do with the validity of racial distinctions in graduate and professional schools.

By the same logic, we say that since *Plessy* had nothing to do with the higher level of education, it certainly has nothing to do with equal educational opportunities in the elementary grades.

For that reason we think that *Plessy* need not be considered; that it has nothing to do with this case, and it is out of the case entirely.

THE CHIEF JUSTICE: Well, in regard to the findings, it was found that the physical facilities, curricula, courses of study, qualifications and quality of teachers, as well as other educational facilities in the two sets of schools are comparable?

MR. CARTER: Yes, sir.

THE CHIEF JUSTICE: And the only item of discrimination, an item of discrimination, was transportation by bus for the colored students without that facility for the white students.

MR. CARTER: That is true. But the court—these are the physical factors that the court found, and then the court went on to show how segregation made the educational opportunities inferior, and this, we think, is the heart of our case.

[5]In Sipuel v. Board of Regents, 332 U.S. 631 (1948), the Court ordered the state authorities to admit a Negro to the University of Oklahoma Law School. In Fisher v. Hurst, 333 U.S. 147 (1948) a further order of the district court in the Sipuel case was affirmed. Missouri ex rel. Gaines v. Canada, 305 U.S. 337 (1938), was the first decision requiring a state (Missouri) to admit qualified Negro students to a graduate school (in that case a law school) where equal facilities were not available elsewhere in the state. The state could not discharge its duty under the equal protection clause by paying the student's tuition to go to another school in another state.

THE CHIEF JUSTICE: That is all that you really have here to base your segregation issue upon.

MR. CARTER: That is right.

THE CHIEF JUSTICE: I mean, of course, you could have the issue as to equal facilities on the other, but so far as all the other physical facilities, curricula, teachers, and transportation and all that, and so forth, there is a finding that they are equal?

MR. CARTER: Yes, sir, and we do not controvert that finding.

The other case that the court below cited was the *Gong Lum* v. *Rice* case. We do not think that that case is controlling here either.

In that case it is true that what was involved was racial distinction in the elementary grades.

JUSTICE DOUGLAS: Was that a Chinese student?

MR. CARTER: That was the Chinese student. But we think that case is so different from our case that it cannot control the decision in this case, because there the issue which was raised by petitioner of Chinese origin was that she did not at all contest the state's power to enforce a racial classification.

She conceded that the state had such power. What petitioner was objecting to was the fact that, as a Chinese, a child of Chinese origin, that she was required to have contact with Negroes for school purposes which, under the segregation laws of Mississippi, white children were protected against.

She said that if—her contention was, that if there were some benefits or harms that would flow to white children from being forced to have contacts with Negroes, that she had an equal right to benefit or to be free of that harm from such contact, and that to require her to be classified among Negroes for school purposes was a denial to her of the equal protection of the laws.

Our contention is that in that instance that case cannot control a decision when here we are contesting the power of the state to make any classification whatsoever, and we think that what the court did below, this Court, in defining what was the issue in this case, said that the question was whether an American citizen of Chinese origin is denied equal protection and classed among the colored races for public school purposes, and furnished equal educational opportunities.

It said that were this a new question:

> We would think it would need our full consideration, and it would be necessary for full argument, but it is not a new question. It is the same question that we have many times decided to be within the purview of the States, without the intervention of the Federal Constitution.

Now, we do not believe that *Gong Lum* can be considered as a precedent contrary to the position we take here. Certainly it cannot be conceded as such a precedent until this Court, when the issue is squarely presented to it, on the question of the power of the state, examines the question and makes a determination in the state's favor; and only in that instance do we feel that *Gong Lum* can be any authority on this question.

JUSTICE FRANKFURTER: Mr. Carter, while what you say may be so, nevertheless, in its opinion, the Court, in *Gong Lum,* did rest on the fact that this issue had been settled by a large body of adjudications going back to what was or might fairly have been called an abolitionist state, the Commonwealth of Massachusetts.

Going back to the Roberts case[6]—

MR. CARTER: Yes, sir.

JUSTICE FRANKFURTER: —I want to ask you—and, may I say, particularly in a case of this sort, a question does not imply an answer; a question merely implies an eager desire for information—I want to ask you whether in the light of that fact, this was a unanimous opinion of the Court which, at the time, had on its membership Justice Holmes, Justice Brandeis, Justice Stone—and I am picking those out not invidiously, but as judges who gave great evidence of being very sensitive and alert to questions of so-called civil liberties—and I should like to ask you whether you think that decision rested on the concession by the petitioner in that case, and the problem of segregation was not involved and, in fact, that underlay the whole decision, the whole adjudication—whether you think a man like Justice Brandeis would have been foreclosed by the concession of the parties?

MR. CARTER: Well, Your Honor, in all honesty, I would say that only partially would I consider that to be true. I think that what the Court did in *Gong Lum,* the Court was presented with the issue or the question, and it assumed that facilities were equal; and the Court at that time, with regard to this issue which was raised, although they conceded the power and did not have to make any full examination, it felt after reviewing those other decisions that the only question that they would have to consider or settle was the question of equal facilities.

JUSTICE FRANKFURTER: Yes. But the Court took as settled by a long course of decisions that this question was many times decided that this power was within the constitutional power of the state legislatures, this power of segregation.

MR. CARTER: Yes, sir.

JUSTICE FRANKFURTER: The more specific question I would like to put to you is this: Do we not have to face the fact that what you are challenging is something that was written into the public law and adjudications of courts, including this Court, by a large body of decisions and, therefore, the question arises whether, and under what circumstances, this Court should now upset so long a course of decisions?

Don't we have to face that, instead of chipping away and saying, "This was dictum," and "This was a mild dictum," and "This was a strong dictum," and is anything to be gained by concealing that central fact, that central issue?

[6]Roberts v. City of Boston, 59 Mass. 198 (1850). School segregation in Boston was upheld despite a Massachusetts constitutional provision that all persons were equal before the law. In 1855 segregation was eliminated in Boston's public schools.

MR. CARTER: Well, I do not think, Your Honor, that you have to face that issue.

My view is that with regard to this particular question this Court decided with *Sweatt* v. *Painter*—

In *Sweatt* v. *Painter* in this Court, the only decision here which was decided on the question of "separate but equal" was a dictum coming out from *Plessy* v. *Ferguson,* and this Court in the Sweatt case, it seems to me very carefully to have decided that it did not have to face the question because *Plessy* v. *Ferguson* was not involved.

I think in this particular case the only decision of this Court which can be said to have decided a question of the validity of racial distinction in elementary schools is this case that I am discussing.

Now, I think that in view of the concession, in view of the fact that the Court felt this was not a case of first impression, although I think it was and is a case of first impression in this Court at the time it came here, that this Court did not give the arguments at all a full consideration which we think that they require.

JUSTICE FRANKFURTER: You are quite right in suggesting that this question explicitly as to segregation in the primary grades has not been adjudicated by this Court.

This question is in that frame, in that explicitness, unembarrassed by physical inequalities, and so on before the Court for the first time. But a long course of legislation by the states, and a long course of utterances by this Court and other courts in dealing with the subject, from the point of view of relevance as to whether a thing is or is not within the prohibition of the Fourteenth Amendment, is from my point of view almost as impressive as a single decision, which does not mean that I would be controlled in a constitutional case by a direct adjudication; but I do think we have to face in this case the fact that we are dealing with a long-established historical practice by the states, and the assumption of the exercise of power which not only was written on the statute books, but has been confirmed and adjudicated by state courts, as well as by the expressions of this Court.

MR. CARTER: Well, Mr. Justice Frankfurter, I would say on that that I was attempting here to take the narrow position with regard to this case, and to approach it in a way that I thought the Court approached the decision in *Sweatt* and *McLaurin.*

I have no hesitancy in saying to the Court that if they do not agree that the decision can be handed down in our favor on this basis of this approach, that I have no hesitancy in saying that the issue of "separate but equal" should be faced and ought to be faced, and that in our view the "separate but equal" doctrine should be overruled.

But as I said before, as the Court apparently approached *Sweatt* and *McLaurin,* it did not feel it had to meet that issue, and we do not feel it has to meet it here, but if the Court has reached a contrary conclusion in regard to it, then we, of course, take the position that the "separate but equal" doctrine should squarely be overruled.

JUSTICE FRANKFURTER: May I trouble you to clarify that? Do I understand from what you have just said that you think this Kansas law is bad on the record, is bad in the Kansas case, on the "separate but equal" doctrine, and that even by that test this law must fall?

MR. CARTER: No, sir, I think—

JUSTICE FRANKFURTER: Then why do we not have to face the "separate but equal" doctrine?

MR. CARTER: Because in so far as this Court is concerned, as I have indicated before, this Court, with the exception of *Gong Lum,* has not at the elementary level adopted the "separate but equal" doctrine.

There is no decision in this Court, unless the Court feels that *Gong Lum* v. *Rice* is that decision.

As I attempted to indicate before, that was a case of first impression, although the Court did not seem to think it was, and that here actually we are now being presented—the Court is now being presented—with a case of first impression, when it has a full record, which you can give full consideration to, and that *Gong Lum,* which did not squarely raise the issue, ought not to be controlling.

All I am saying is that you do not have to overrule "separate but equal" at the elementary school level in deciding the Kansas case because you have never decided the "separate but equal" applied at the elementary school level.

JUSTICE FRANKFURTER: Are you saying that we can say that "separate but equal" is not a doctrine that is relevant at the primary school level? Is that what you are saying?

JUSTICE DOUGLAS: I think you are saying that segregation may be all right in street cars and railroad cars and restaurants, but that is all that we have decided.

MR. CARTER: That is the only place that you have decided that it is all right.

JUSTICE DOUGLAS: And that education is different, education is different from that.

MR. CARTER: Yes, sir.

JUSTICE DOUGLAS: That is your argument, is it not? Isn't that your argument in this case?

MR. CARTER: Yes.

JUSTICE FRANKFURTER: But how can that be your argument when the whole basis of dealing with education thus far has been to find out whether it, the "separate but equal" doctrine is satisfied?

JUSTICE DOUGLAS: You are talking about the gist of the cases in this Court?

JUSTICE FRANKFURTER: I am talking about the cases in this Court.

MR. CARTER: As I interpret the cases in this Court, Your Honor, as I interpret the Sweatt case and the McLaurin case, the question of "separate and equal," as to whether the separate and equal doctrine was satisfied, I do not believe that that test was applied there. In *McLaurin* there was no separation.

JUSTICE FRANKFURTER: But take the Gaines case, take the beginning of the "separate but equal," and unless I completely misconceive the cases I have read before I came here and those in which I have participated, the test in each one of these cases was whether "separate and equal" is relevant or whether it was satisfied, and we have held in some of the cases that it was not satisfied, and that in a constitutional case we do not have to go beyond the immediate necessities of the record, and we have said as to others that for purposes of training in the law you have a mixed situation; you cannot draw that line.

MR. CARTER: Well, take the Gaines case, Your Honor; the only thing that I would say on the Gaines case is that what the Court decided in the Gaines case was that since there were no facilities available to Negroes, that the petitioner Gaines had to be admitted to the white school.

Now, it is true that there is certain language in the Gaines case which would appear to give support to *Plessy* v. *Ferguson,* but the language in terms of the decision—you have to take the language in regard to what the decision stated in the Sipuel case—I think it is the same thing, and when we get over to *Sweatt* and *McLaurin,* we have a situation in which this Court went beyond certain physical facilities and said, "These are not as important as these other things that we cannot name," and it decided then to set standards so high that it certainly would seem to me to be impossible for a state to validly maintain segregation in law schools.

In the McLaurin case, without any question of separation, what the Court did was that you have the same teachers, and so forth, so there could have been no question of his being set apart, except in the classroom, and so forth—there could be no question of the quality of instruction not being the same.

This Court held that those restrictions were sufficient in and of themselves to impair McLaurin's ability to study and, therefore, to deprive him of the equal protection of the law.

So, in my view, although the Gaines case is a case where you have the language, the decisions really do not hinge on that.

JUSTICE REED: In the Gaines case it offered what they called equal facilities, did it not?

MR. CARTER: They offered facilities out of state, out-of-state facilities.

JUSTICE REED: But which they said were equal.

MR. CARTER: Yes.

JUSTICE REED: The Court said that they were not equal.

MR. CARTER: Yes, sir; this Court said not only were they not equal, but that the state had the obligation of furnishing whatever facilities it was going to offer within the state.

JUSTICE REED; Well, we did have before us in the Gaines case the problem of "separate and equal." We determined that they were not equal because they were out of the state.

MR. CARTER: Well, Your Honor, I do not conceive of "separate and equal" as being the type of offering that the State of Missouri offered when they attempted to give out-of-state aid.

JUSTICE REED: Neither did this Court; but Missouri claimed that they were equal.

MR. CARTER: I am sorry, I do not think you have understood my answer. I do not conceive of the out-of-state aid which Missouri offered to petitioner Gaines to go to some institution outside of the state as being within the purview of a "separate but equal" doctrine.

I think that in terms of the "separate but equal" doctrine, that there must be the segregation. The "separate but equal" doctrine, I think, concerns itself with segregation within the state and the setting up of two institutions, one for Negroes and one for whites.

All the state was doing, I think there, was that it knew that it had the obligation of furnishing some facilities to Negroes, and so it offered them this out-of-state aid. But I do not believe that actually it can be—I mean, my understanding is that this cannot be classified as a part of the "separate but equal" doctrine.

JUSTICE REED: No. This Court did not classify it that way. They said it is not separate and equal to give education in another state and, therefore, "You must admit him to the University of Missouri."

MR. CARTER: The University of Missouri, yes.

JUSTICE REED: Yes.

JUSTICE FRANKFURTER: But there is another aspect of my question, namely, that we are dealing here with a challenge to the constitutionality of legislation which is not just one legislative responsibility, not just an episodic piece of legislation in one state.

But we are dealing with a body of enactments by numerous states, whatever they are—eighteen or twenty—not only the South but border states and northern states, and legislation which has a long history.

Now, unless you say that this legislation merely represents man's inhumanity to man, what is the root of this legislation? What is it based on? Why was there such legislation, and was there any consideration that the states were warranted in dealing with—maybe not this way—but was there anything in life to which this legislation responds?

MR. CARTER: Well, Your Honor, I think that this legislation is clear—certain of this legislation in Kansas—that the sole basis for it is race.

JUSTICE FRANKFURTER: Is race?

MR. CARTER: Is race.

JUSTICE FRANKFURTER: Yes, I understand that. I understand all this legislation. But I want to know why this legislation, the sole basis of which is race—is there just some wilfulness of man in the states or some, as I say, of man's inhumanity to man, some ruthless disregard of the facts of life?

MR. CARTER: As I understand the state's position in Kansas, the State of Kansas said that the reason for this legislation to be applicable in urban centers, is that although Negroes compose 4 per cent of the population in Kansas, 90 per cent of them are concentrated in the urban areas, in the cities of the first class, and that Kansas has people from the North and the South with conflicting views about the question of the treatment of Negroes and about the separation and segregation, and that, therefore, what they did was that they authorized, with the power that they had, they authorized these large cities where Negroes appeared in large numbers to have segregated public elementary schools.

THE CHIEF JUSTICE: When did that first appear in the Kansas law?

MR. CARTER: I am not sure, but I believe in 1862.

THE CHIEF JUSTICE: In 1862, and the next amendment was 1868?

MR. CARTER: 1862, Mr. Wilson tells me. The legislation on which this statute arose was first enacted in 1862.

THE CHIEF JUSTICE: That was amended in 1868.

MR. CARTER: That is right. But our feeling on the reach of equal protection, the equal protection clause, is that as these appellants, as members of a minority group, whatever the majority may feel that they can do with their rights for whatever purpose, that the equal protection clause was intended to protect them against the whims, as they come and go.

JUSTICE FRANKFURTER: How would you establish the fact that it was intended to protect them against them? How would I find out if I liked to follow your scent; that is, what the amendment is intended to accomplish, how would I go about finding that out?

MR. CARTER: I think that this Court in, certainly since, *Plessy* v. *Ferguson*—this Court, and in *Shelley* v. *Kraemer,*[7] has repeatedly said this was the basis for the amendment. The amendment was intended to protect Negroes in civil and political equality with whites.

JUSTICE FRANKFURTER: Impliedly it prohibited the doctrine of classification, I take it?

MR. CARTER: I would think, Your Honor, that without regard to the question of its effect on Negroes, that this business of classification, this Court has dealt with it time and time again.

[7]334 U.S. 1 (1948). Attempts to enforce restrictive covenants excluding Negroes from owning or occupying real property were declared unconstitutional since judicial enforcement of the agreements amounted to state action within the meaning of the Fourteenth Amendment.

For example, in regard to a question of equal treatment between a foreign corporation admitted to the state, and a domestic corporation, where the only basis for the inequality is the question of the residence of the foreign corporation, this Court has held under its classification doctrine that there is a denial of equal protection.[8]

JUSTICE FRANKFURTER: Meaning by that that there was no rational basis for the classification?

MR. CARTER: Well, I think that our position is that there is no rational basis for classification based on that.

JUSTICE FRANKFURTER: But do you think that you can argue that or do you think that we can justify this case by some abstract declaration?

MR. CARTER: Well, I have attempted before lunch, Your Honor, to address myself to that point, and that was one of the bases for our attack; that this was a classification, an instance of a classification, based upon race which, under these decisions of this Court do not form a valid basis for the legislation.

JUSTICE REED: Mr. Carter, you speak of equal protection. Do you make a distinction between equal protection and classification, on the one side, and due process on the other? Is that your contention, that this violates due process?

MR. CARTER: We do not contend it in our complaint. We think that it could, but we thought that equal protection was sufficient to protect us.

JUSTICE REED: And do you find a distinction between equal protection and due process in this case?

MR. CARTER: I do not. I think that the Court would, in terms of equal protection and due process, decide that under the equal protection clause and, therefore, do not consider due process. But so far as my understanding of the law, I would see that there would be no real distinction between the two.

I would like to reserve the next few minutes for rebuttal.

THE CHIEF JUSTICE: General Wilson.

### ARGUMENT ON BEHALF OF THE APPELLEES

#### by MR. WILSON

MR. WILSON: May it please the Court, I represent the State of Kansas, who was an intervening defendant in this proceeding.

The issue raised by the pleadings filed by the state in the court below was restricted solely to the matter of the constitutionality of this statute, and I want to limit my remarks to that particular phase of the subject.

---

[8]See Hanover Ins. Co. v. Harding, 272 U.S. 494 (1926); Southern Railway Co. v. Greene, 216 U.S. 400 (1910); Wheeling Steel Corp. v. Glander, 337 U.S. 562 (1948); Terral v. Burke Construction Co., 257 U.S. 529 (1922).

This Court heretofore noted an apparent reluctance on the part of the State of Kansas to appear in this case and participate actively in these proceedings. Because of that fact I would like to digress for a moment and explain to you the position that the state takes with regard to this litigation.

As my adversary pointed out, the effect of the Kansas statute is local only; it is not statewide.

Furthermore, the statute permits, and does not require, boards of education in designated cities to maintain segregated school systems.

Pursuant to that statute, the Board of Education of the City of Topeka set up and does operate a segregated school system affecting students in the elementary grades.

Now, this lawsuit in the court below was directed at the Topeka Board of Education.

The school system set up and maintained by that board was under attack. The Attorney General, therefore, took the position that this action was local in nature and not of statewide concern. We did not participate actively in the trial of the case.

However, after the trial in the court below there was a change in personnel and a change in attitude on the part of the Board of Education. The Board of Education determined then that it would not resist this appeal.

The Attorney General thereupon determined that he should be governed, his attitude should be governed, by the attitude taken on the local level. Consequently we did not appear.

I mention this to emphasize the fact that we have never at any time entertained any doubt about the constitutionality of our statute.

THE CHIEF JUSTICE: General Wilson, may I state to you that we were informed that the Board of Education would not be represented here in argument, and would not file a brief, and it being a very important question, and this case having facets that other cases did not, we wanted to hear from the State of Kansas.

MR. WILSON: We are very glad to comply with the Court's request. I was simply attempting to emphasize that we did not intentionally disregard our duty to this Court.

THE CHIEF JUSTICE: I understand it.

As I understand it, you had turned it over to the Board of Education and expected them to appear here, is that right?

MR. WILSON: That is correct, sir.

THE CHIEF JUSTICE: And when we found out that they were not going to, we did not want the State of Kansas and its viewpoint to be silent.

MR. WILSON: Now, the views of the State of Kansas can be stated very simply and very briefly: We believe that our statute is constitutional. We did not believe it violates the Fourteenth Amendment.

We believe so because our Supreme Court, the Supreme Court of Kansas, has specifically said so. We believe that the decisions of the Supreme Court of

Kansas follow and are supported by the decisions of this Court, and the decisions of many, many appellate courts in other jurisdictions.

In order to complete the perspective of the Court with respect to the Kansas school system, I should like to allude briefly to the general statutes of Kansas which provide for elementary school education.

There are three types of municipal corporations in Kansas authorized to maintain public elementary schools. There is the city of the first class, cities consisting of 15,000 or more persons, of which there are twelve in the state; then, there are cities of the second class, and cities of the third class, which are included within the common school districts.

Now, this statute, I want to emphasize, applies only to cities of the first class, to those cities which have populations of more than 15,000.

It does authorize separate schools to be maintained for the Negro and white races in the elementary grades in those cities, with the exception of Kansas City, where a separate junior high school and high school is authorized.

My adversary has conceded, and the court below has found, that there was no substantial inequality in the educational facilities afforded by the City of Topeka to these appellants. The physical facilities were found to be the same, or substantially alike.

Not only was that finding made with regard to physical facilities, but the course of study was found to be that subscribed by state law and followed in both systems of schools.

The instructional facilities were determined to be substantially equal. There was the item of distinction wherein transportation was supplied to the Negro students and not to the white students. That certainly was not an item which constituted one of discrimination against the Negro students.

Therefore, it is our theory that this case resolves itself simply to this: whether the "separate but equal" doctrine is still the law, and whether it is to be followed in this case by this Court.

My adversary has mentioned—again I want to emphasize that the Negro population in Kansas is slight. Less than 4 per cent of the total population belong to the Negro race.

JUSTICE FRANKFURTER: What is that number?

MR. WILSON: Sir?

JUSTICE FRANKFURTER: What is that number?

MR. WILSON: The population of the State, the total population, is approximately 2\million. The total Negro population is approximately 73,000.

JUSTICE FRANKFURTER: And of those, how many are in the cities of 15,000, about nine-tenths, would you say?

MR. WILSON: Our brief says that nine-tenths of the Negro population lived in cities classified as urban.

The urban classification includes those of 2,500 or more. I should say that two-thirds of the Negro population lived in cities of the first class.

JUSTICE FRANKFURTER: And this, according to your brief, as I remember—the present situation in Kansas is that this segregated class of primary schools are in only nine of those cities?

MR. WILSON: In only nine of our cities.

As I recall, there are eighteen separate elementary schools maintained in the State under and by virtue of the statute. There is one separate junior high school and one separate high school.

In other communities we do have voluntary segregation, but that does not exist with the sanction or the force of law.

JUSTICE BLACK: Do you have any Indians in Kansas?

MR. WILSON: We have a few, Your Honor.

JUSTICE BLACK: Where do they go to school?

MR. WILSON: I know of no instances where Indians live in cities of the first class. Most of our Indians live on the reservation. The Indians who do live in cities of the first class would attend the schools maintained for the white race.

JUSTICE BLACK: Those who live on the reservations go to Indian schools?

MR. WILSON: Yes, sir; attend schools maintained by the Government.

JUSTICE BLACK: Do any people go to them besides the Indians?

MR. WILSON: I do not believe so, sir.

JUSTICE FRANKFURTER: May I trouble you before you conclude your argument, to deal with this aspect of the case, in the light of the incident of the problems in Kansas, namely, what would be the consequences, as you see them, for this Court to reverse this decree relating to the Kansas law, or to put it another way, suppose this Court reversed the case, and the case went back to the District Court for the entry of a proper decree. What would Kansas be urging should be the nature of that decree in order to carry out the direction of this Court?

MR. WILSON: As I understand your question, you are asking me what practical difficulties would be encountered in the administration of the school system?

JUSTICE FRANKFURTER: Suppose there would be some difficulties? I want to know what the consequences of the reversal of the decree would be, and what Kansas would be urging us the most for dealing with those consequences of the decree?

MR. WILSON: In perfect candor, I must say to the Court that the consequences would probably not be serious.

As I pointed out, our Negro population is small. We do have in our Negro schools Negro teachers, Negro administrators, that would necessarily be assimilated in the school system at large. That might produce some administrative difficulties. I can imagine no serious difficulty beyond that.

Now, the question of the segregation of the Negro race in our schools has frequently been before the Supreme Court of Kansas, and at the outset I should say that our Court has consistently held that segregation can be practiced only where authorized by the statutes.

The rationale of all those cases is simply this: The municipal corporation maintaining the school district is a creature of statute. It can do only what the statute authorizes. Therefore, unless there is a specific power conferred, the municipal corporation maintaining the school district\cannot classify students on the basis of color.

JUSTICE REED: Have there been efforts made to remove the act permitting segregation or authorizing segregation in Kansas?

MR. WILSON: I recall, I think I mentioned in my brief, in 1876 in a general codification of the school laws, the provision authorizing the maintenance of separate schools was apparently, through inadvertence, omitted by the legislature. It was nevertheless deemed to be repealed by implication.

But thereafter, in 1879, substantially the same statute was again enacted. Since that time, to my knowledge, there have been no considered efforts made in the legislature to repeal that statute.

JUSTICE JACKSON: Mr. Attorney General, you emphasized the 4 per cent, and the smallness of the population. Would that affect your problem if there were heavier concentrations?

MR. WILSON: It is most difficult for me to answer that question. It might. I am not acquainted with the situation where there is a heavier concentration, in other words.

JUSTICE JACKSON: I mean, your statute adapts itself to different localities. What are the variables that the statute was designed to take care of, if any, if you know, at this late date?

MR. WILSON: My theory of the justification of the statute is this: The state of Kansas was born out of the struggle between the North and the South prior to the war between the states, and our state was populated by squatters from the North and from the South.

Those squatters settled in communities. The proslavery elements settled in Leavenworth, in Atchison, and Lecompton. The Free Soil elements settled in Topeka, in Lawrence, and in Wyandotte. The Negroes who came to the state during and immediately subsequent to the war also settled in communities.

Consequently, our early legislatures were faced with this situation: In some communities the attitudes of the people were such that it was deemed best that the Negro race live apart. In other communitites a different attitude was reflected. Also in some communities there was a substantial Negro population. In other communities there were few Negroes.

Therefore, the legislature sought by this type of legislation to provide a means whereby the community could adjust its plan to suit local conditions, and we believe they succeeded.

JUSTICE JACKSON: You mentioned Topeka as one of the three state settlements, and that seems to be the subject that is involved here with the segregation ordinances. Is there any explanation for that?

MR. WILSON: As I explained these matters—I am speculating—we have in Kansas—

JUSTICE JACKSON: Your speculation ought to be worth more than mine.

MR. WILSON: We have in Kansas history a period of migration of the Negro race to Kansas which we call the exodus, the black exodus, as spoken of in the history books.

At that time, which was in the '80s, large numbers of Negro people came from the South and settled in Kansas communities. A large number of those people settled in Topeka and, for the first time, I presume, and again I am speculating, there was created there the problem of the racial adjustment within the community.

The record in this case infers that segregation was established in Topeka about fifty years ago.

I am assuming that in my speculation for the Court that segregation began to be practiced in Topeka after the exodus had given Topeka a substantial colored population.

JUSTICE REED: You spoke of the density of the Negro population, of about 4 per cent covering the State as a whole. Have you in mind what city has the largest concentration of residents by percentage?

MR. WILSON: The city with the largest concentration of Negro population is Kansas City, Kansas.

JUSTICE REED: That is by percentage?

MR. WILSON: By percentage, as well as in absolute numbers.

JUSTICE REED: How high is it there?

MR. WILSON: The Negro population, I should say—perhaps Mr. Scott can help me with this—I should say not more than 10 per cent, is that correct?

MR. SCOTT: That is about right, yes.

MR. WILSON: This statute has been squarely challenged in our Kansas Supreme Court and has been upheld, and I cite in my case the leading case of *Reynolds* v. *The School Board*[9] where in 1903 the Court held flatly that the Kansas statute does not violate the Fourteenth Amendment to the Constitituion of the United States.

That opinion is an exhaustive one wherein the Court drew on the Roberts case in Massachusetts, and numerous other cases cited in the appellate courts of the state, and the Court followed specifically the rule laid down in the Plessy case.

[9]Reynolds v. Board of Education, 66 Kans. 672, 72 Pac. 274 (1903).

It is our position that the principle announced in the Plessy case and the specific rule announced in the Gong Lum case are absolutely controlling here.

We think it is sheer sophistry to attempt to distinguish those cases from the case that is here presented, and we think the question before this Court is simply this: Is the Plessy case and the Gong Lum case and the "separate but equal" doctrine still the law of this land?

We think if you decide in favor of these appellants, the Court will necessarily overrule the doctrines expressed in those cases and, at the same time, will say that the legislatures of the seventeen or twenty-one states, that the Congress of the United States, that dozens of appellate courts have been wrong for a period of more than seventy-five years, when they have believed and have manifested a belief that facilities equal though separate were within the meaning of the Fourteenth Amendment.

JUSTICE FRANKFURTER: There is a third one—

JUSTICE BURTON: Don't you recognize it as possible that within seventy-five years the social and economic conditions and the personal relations of the nation may have changed so that what may have been a valid interpretation of them seventy-five years ago would not be a valid interpretation of them constitutionally today?

MR. WILSON: We recognize that as a possibility. We do not believe that this record discloses any such change.

JUSTICE BURTON: But that might be a difference between saying that these courts of appeals and state supreme courts have been wrong for seventy-five years.

MR. WILSON: Yes, sir.

We concede that this Court can overrule the Gong Lum doctrine, the Plessy doctrine, but nevertheless until those cases are overruled they are the best guide we have.

JUSTICE FRANKFURTER: As I understood my brother Burton's question or as I got the implication of his question, it was not that the Court would have to overrule those cases; the Court would simply have to recognize that laws are kinetic, and some new things have happened, not deeming those decisions wrong, but bringing into play new situations toward a new decision. I do not know whether he would disown me, but that is what I got out of it.

MR. WILSON: We agree with that proposition. But I repeat, we do not think that there is anything in the record here that would justify such a conclusion.

Now, something has been said about Finding of Fact No. 8 in the District Court, and I would like to comment briefly upon that finding of fact.

The Court will recall that that is the finding of fact wherein the lower court determined generally that segregation of white and colored children in the public schools has a detrimental effect upon the colored children.

It may be significant that this finding of fact was based upon the uncontroverted testimony of witnesses produced by the appellants in this case.

I should also like to point out that that finding of fact was based upon the uncontested evidence presented by the case.

We think it is obvious, however, that the District Court regarded Finding of Fact No. 8 as being legally insignificant because having made a finding of fact, Finding of Fact No. 8, wherein the general statement is made that Negro children might be benefited by attendance at an integrated school system, the District Court concluded in its conclusion of law simply this: The court has heretofore filed its finding of fact and conclusions of law, together with an opinion, and has held that, as a matter of law, the plaintiffs have failed to prove that they were entitled to the relief demanded.

In other words, Finding of Fact No. 8 is immaterial, we believe, so far as the issues of this case are concerned.

The court did find, and we have mentioned the finding specifically, that physical facilities were equal; the court found that instructional facilities were equal, the court found that courses of study were equal. Those are the items that the state and the school districts have within their power to confer.

This additional item, the psychological reaction, is something which is something apart from the objective components of the school system, and something that the state does not have within its power to confer upon the pupils therein.

Therefore, the District Court, and we believe rightly, regarded it as something that is inconsequential, immaterial, not governing in this case.

We make one further point in our brief that may be significant, and that is that Finding of Fact No. 8 is a general finding. It does not relate to these specific appellants.

As we understand the law, in order to obtain an injunction, obtain injunctive relief, which is prayed for here, it is necessary that these appellants show in the court below, first, that they have actually suffered personal harm from attending segregated schools in Topeka, Kansas; they must show that either they have been deprived of some benefit that is conferred on the rest of the population or they must show that they are being subjected to some detriment that the rest of the population does not suffer.

Now, we submit that there is nothing in the Finding of Fact No. 8 which indicates that these appellants specifically have suffered any harm by reason of being compelled to attend an integrated school system in the City of Topeka.

I think it is significant that all of the other findings of fact relate specifically to the Topeka school system. They use the definite article when describing "the" system, until Finding of Fact No. 8, and there the general statement is made indicating that the court believes that Negro children generally would be better off if they were attending an integrated school system.

Now, we submit on the basis of that finding of fact the plaintiffs below and the appellants here have not shown their right to injunctive relief because they have not shown the injury that the decisions of this Court seem to require.

The position of the State of Kansas, to emphasize again, is simply this: Our statute is constitutional; it does not violate the Fourteenth Amendment, and that position is supported by all of the decisions of the Kansas courts. That position, we think, is supported by the decisions of this Court.

Thank you.

## REBUTTAL ARGUMENT ON BEHALF OF APPELLANTS

### by MR. CARTER

MR. CARTER: We think that finding of fact of the court below makes necessary a reversal of its judgment.

Without regard to any other consideration, the court below found that inequality flowed from segregation, and our position, as stated previously, is if there are facilities, educational opportunities, in fact, that educational opportunities can not be equal in law.

JUSTICE BLACK: Why do you think that would apply?

MR. CARTER: Because of the fact, sir—

JUSTICE BLACK: Suppose it had been found differently?

MR. CARTER: If it had been found or I should say if the Court agrees that the findings are correct—

JUSTICE BLACK: Suppose another court finds strictly to the contrary with reference to the general principle, what would you say?

MR. CARTER: Well, this Court, of course, in a question like that reexamines the findings or the basis for the findings and can reach its own conclusion in that regard.

JUSTICE BLACK: Do you think the Court can make a finding independent of the basis of fact?

MR. CARTER: No, sir, they do not. What I meant to say was that this Court, if they agreed with the findings on an examination of this record, agreed with the findings of fact of the court below, and came to the conclusion that the court below had correctly found the facts on its own independent examination, that this/Court would—it would necessitate a reversal of that court's judgment. I do not mean that the findings of the court below come here and that you have to accept them. Of course, I do not agree with that.

JUSTICE BLACK: Do you think that there should be a different holding here with reference to the question involved, according to the place where the segregation might occur, and if not, why do you say it depends—why do you say that it depends on the findings of fact at all?

MR. CARTER: I say about the findings of fact because what I think the court below did was in approaching this question it followed the example of this Court in *McLaurin* and *Sweatt* and, I think, it approached the question correctly; so that it found that inequality in educational opportunity existed as a result of the racial restrictions.

JUSTICE BLACK: Is that a general finding or do you state that for the State of Kansas, City of Topeka?

MR. CARTER: I think I agree with the fact that the finding refers to the State of Kansas and to these appellants and to Topeka, Kansas. I think that the findings were made in this specific case referring to this specific case.

JUSTICE BLACK: In other words, if you are going to go on the findings, then you would have different rulings with respect to the places to which this applies, is that true?

MR. CARTER: Well, the only thing that I think the findings do when this Court reached the question and held this finding, it seems to me that the only thing that the findings would do is that—without regard to the question, the court below, examining the facilities found that they were unequal.

Now, of course, under our theory, you do not have to reach the finding of fact or a fact at all in reaching the decision because of the fact that we maintain that this is an unconstitutional classification being based upon race and, therefore, it is arbitrary.

But all I was attempting to address myself to was to the specific examination by the court below on the impact of segregation on the equality of educational opportunities afforded.

JUSTICE BLACK: Are you planning to attach relevance to anything except the question of whether they are separate but equal?

MR. CARTER: I think that they are relevant to the question of whether there are equal educational opportunities that are being afforded. I think whether, in fact, you have equal education in the opinion of the court below, that the findings are relevant, and I think that the court below found that the educational facilities were unequal as a result of segregation, but it felt that it could not reach the legal conclusion that they were unequal because of two decisions we have discussed.

Now, to conclude, our feeling is that this case could be decided on the question of the illegality of the classification itself.

This case also could be decided on the question of equal educational opportunities as they are examined by the approach of *McLaurin* and *Sweatt*.

We think that the court below did the same thing. The court below did what this Court did in *McLaurin* and in *Sweatt,* and we think that in the examination of the equality of education offered, that what it did was it found that these restrictions imposed disabilitities on Negro children and prevented them from having educational opportunities equal to white, and for these reasons we think that the judgment of the court below should be reversed and the Kansas statute should be struck down.

(Whereupon, at 3:15 p.m., the argument was concluded.)

HARRY BRIGGS, JR., et al.,
Appellants,

vs.

R. W. ELLIOTT, CHAIRMAN, J. D. CARSON, et al.,
MEMBERS OF BOARD OF TRUSTEES OF SCHOOL DISTRICT NO. 22,
CLARENDON COUNTY, S.C., et al.
Appellees.

Case No. 101

Tuesday, December 9, 1952.

The above-entitled cause came on for oral argument at 3:15 p.m.

APPEARANCES:
On behalf of the Appellants:
THURGOOD MARSHALL, ESQ.

On behalf of Appellees:
JOHN W. DAVIS, ESQ.

THE CHIEF JUSTICE: Case No. 101, Harry Briggs, Jr., et al., against Roger W. Elliott, Chairman, J. D. Carson, et al., Members of Board of Trustees of School District No. 22, Clarendon County, South Carolina, et al.

THE CLERK: Counsel are present.

ARGUMENT ON BEHALF OF APPELLANTS

by MR. MARSHALL

MR. MARSHALL: May it please the Court, this case is here on direct appeal from the United States District Court for the Eastern District of South Carolina. The issue raised in this case was clearly raised in the pleadings, and was clearly raised throughout the first hearing. After the first hearing, on appeal to this Court, it was raised prior to the second hearing. It was raised on motion for judgment, and there can be no question that from the beginning of this case, the filing of the initial complaint, up until the present time, the appellants have raised and have preserved their attack on the validity of the provision of the South Carolina Constitution and the South Carolina statute.

The specific provision of the South Carolina Code is set forth in our brief at page 10, and it appears in appellees' brief at page 14, and reads as follows:

It shall be unlawful for pupils of one race to attend the schools provided by boards of trustees for persons of another race.

That is the Code provision.

The constitutional provision is, again, on page 10 of our brief, and is:

Separate schools shall be provided for children of the white races—

This is the significant language—

and no child of either race shall ever be permitted to attend a school provided for children of the other race.

Those are the two provisions of the law of the State of South Carolina under attack in this particular case.

At the first hearing, before the trial got under way, counsel for the appellees, in open court, read a statement in which he admitted that although prior to that time they had decided that the physical facilities of the separate schools were equal, they had concluded finally that they were not equal, and they admitted in open court that they did not have equality, and at the suggestion of senior Judge Parker,[10] this was made as an amendment to the answer, and the question as to physical facilities from that stage on was not in dispute.

At that time, counsel for the appellants, however, made the position clear that the attack was not being made on the "separate but equal" basis as to physical facilities, but the position we were taking was that these statutes were unconstitutional in their enforcement because they not only produced these inevitable inequalities in physical facilities, but that evidence would be produced by expert witnesses to show that the governmentally imposed racial segregation in and of itself was also a denial of equality.

I want to point out that our position is not that we are denied equality in these cases. I think there has been a considerable misunderstanding on that point. We are saying that there is a denial of equal protection of the laws, the legal phraseology of the clause in the Fourteenth Amendment, and not just this point as to equality, and I say that because I think most of the cases in the past have gone off on the point of whether or not you have substantial equality. It is a type of provision that, we think, tends to get us into trouble.

So pursuing that line, we produced expert witnesses, who had surveyed the school situation to show the full extent of the physical inequalities, and then we produced expert witnesses. Appellees, in their brief comment, say that they do not think too much of them. I do not think that the District Court thought too much of them. But they stand in the record as unchallenged as experts in their field, and I think we have arrived at the stage where the courts do give credence to the testimony of people who are experts in their fields.

On the question that was raised a minute ago in the other case about whether or not there is any relevancy to this classification on a racial basis or not, in the case of the testimony of Dr. Robert Redfield[11]—I am sure the Court will remember his testimony in the Sweatt case—the District Court was unwilling to carry the case over an extra day. Dr. Redfield was stuck with the usual air travel from one

---

[10]Judge John J. Parker (1885–1958) was appointed to the Fourth Circuit Court of Appeals by President Coolidge in 1925 and became Chief Judge in 1931. He was nominated as a Justice of the Supreme Court by President Hoover in 1930 but not confirmed by the Senate because of allegedly anti-labor decisions and anti-Negro remarks. He also acted as alternate member of the International Military Tribunal at Nuremburg after World War II.

[11]Dr. Robert Redfield (1897–1960), noted anthropologist, taught at the University of Chicago and Cornell University. Among his many books are *The Folk Culture of Yucatan* (1941) and *The Primitive World and its Transformations* (1953).

city to another. And by agreement of counsel and with approval of the court, we placed into the record Dr. Redfield's testimony.

If you will remember, Dr. Redfield's testimony was to this effect, that there were no recognizable differences from a racial standpoint between children, and that if there could be such a difference that would be recognizable and connected with education, it would be so insignificant as to be unworthy of anybody's consideration.

In substance, he said, on page 161 of the record—I think it is page 161—that given a similar learning situation, a Negro child and a white child would tend to do about the same thing. I think I have it here. It is on page 161:

> Question: As a result of your studies that you have made, the training that you have had in your specialized field over some twenty years, given a similar learning situation, what, if any differences, is there between the accomplishment of a white and a Negro student, given a similar learning situation?
> Answer: I understand, if I may say so, a similar learning situation to include a similar degree of preparation?
> Question: Yes.
> Answer: Then I would say that my conclusion is that the one does as well as the other on the average.

He has considerable testimony along the lines. But we produced testimony to show what we considered to be the normal attack on a classification statute, that this Court has laid down the rule in many cases set out in our brief, that in the case of the object or persons being classified, it must be shown, (1) that there is a difference in the two, (2) that the state must show that the difference has a significance with the subject matter being legislated, and the state has made no effort up to this date to show any basis for that classification other than that it would be unwise to do otherwise.

Witnesses testified that segregation deterred the development of the personalities of these children. Two witnesses testified that it deprives them of equal status in the school community, that it destroys their self-respect. Two other witnesses testified that it denies them full opportunity for democratic social development. Another witness said that it stamps him with a badge of inferiority.

The summation of that testimony is that the Negro children have road blocks put up in their minds as a result of this segregation, so that the amount of education that they take in is much less than other students take in.

The other significant point in this case is that one witness, Dr. Kenneth Clark,[12] examined the appellants in this very case and found that they were injured as a result of this segregation. The court completely disregarded that.

I do not know what clearer testimony we could produce in an attack on a specific statute as applied to a specific group of appellants.

The only evidence produced by the appellees in this case was one witness who testified as to, in general, the running of the school system and the difference between rural schools and consolidated schools, which had no basis whatsoever on the constitutional question.

---

[12]Dr. Kenneth Clark, distinguished educator and psychologist, is the author of *Desegregation: An Appraisal of the Evidence* (1953), *Prejudice and Your Child* (1955), and *Dark Ghetto* (1965).

Another witness, E. R. Crow, was produced to testify as to the new bond issue that was to go into effect after the hearing this case, at which time they would build more schools as a result of that money. That testimony was admitted into the record over objection of the appellants. The appellants took the position that anything that was to be talked about in the future was irrelevant to a constitutional issue where a personal and present right was asserted. However, the court overruled the objection. Mr. Crow testified.

Then he was asked as to whether or not it would not be "unwise" to break down segregation in South Carolina. Then Mr. Crow proceeded to testify as an expert. He had six years of experience, I think, as superintendent of schools, and prior to that time he was principal of a high school in Columbia. He testified that it would be unwise. He also testified that he did not know but what the legislature would not appropriate the money.

On cross-examination he was asked as to whether or not he meant by the first statement that if relief was granted as prayed, the appellees might not conform to the relief, and Judge Parker made a very significant statement which appears in the record, that if we issue an order in this case, it will be obeyed, and I do not think there is any question about it.

On this second question on examination, when he was asked, who did he use as the basis for his information that this thing would not work in the South, he said he talked to gangs of people, white and colored, and he was giving the sum total of their testimony, or rather their statements to him. And again on cross-examination he was asked to name at least one of the Negroes he talked to, and he could not recall the name of a single Negro he had ever talked to. I think the basis of his testimony on that point should be weighed by that statement on cross-examination.

He also said that there was a difference between what happened in northern states, because they had a larger number of Negroes in the South, and they had a larger problem because the percentage of Negroes was so high. And again on cross-examination, he was asked the specific question: "Well, assuming that in South Carolina the population was 95 per cent white and 5 per cent colored, would your answer be any different?" And he said, no, he would make the same answer regardless.

That is the only evidence in the record for the appellees here. They wanted to put on the speech of Professor Odom,[13] and they were refused the right to put the speech in, because, after all, Professor Odom was right across, in North Carolina, and could have been called as a witness.

So here we have a record that has made no effort whatsoever—no effort whatsoever—to support the legislative determinations of the State of South Carolina. And this Court is being asked to uphold those statutes, the statute and the constitutional provision because of two reasons. One is that these matters are legislative matters, as to whether or not we are going to have segregation. For example, the majority of the court in the first hearing said, speaking of equality under the Fourteenth Amendment, "How this shall be done is a matter for the school

[13]Prof. Howard Odom of the University of North Carolina delivered a speech in Atlanta entitled "The Mid-Century South Looking Both Ways" which the defendants sought unsuccessfully to introduce into evidence.

authorities and not for the court, so long as it is done in good faith and equality of facilities is offered."

Again the court said, in Chief Judge Parker's opinion:

> We think, however, that segregation of the races in the public schools, so long as equality of rights is preserved, is a matter of legislative policy for the several states, with which the Federal courts are powerless to interfere.

So here we have the unique situation of an asserted federal right which has been declared several times by this Court to be personal and present, being set aside on the theory that it is a matter for the state legislature to decide, and it is not for this Court. And that is directly contrary to every opinion of this Court.

In each instance where these matters come up in what, if I say "sensitive" field, or whatever I am talking about, civil rights, freedom of speech, et cetera—at all times they have this position. The majority of the people wanted the statute; that is how it was passed.

There are always respectable people who can be quoted as in support of a statute. But in each case, this Court has made its own independent determination as to whether that statute is valid. Yet in this case, the Court is urged to give blanket approval that this field of segregation, and if I may say, this field of racial segregation, is purely to be left to the states, the direct opposite of what the Fourteenth Amendment was passed for, the direct opposite of the intent of the Fourteenth Amendment and the framers of it.

On this question of the sensitiveness of this field, and to leave it to the legislature, I know lawyers at times have a hard time finding a case in point. But in the reply brief, I think that we have a case in point that is persuasive to this Court. It is the case of *Elkison* v. *Deliesseline,*[14] a decision by Mr. Justice William Johnson, appointed to this Court, if I remember, from South Carolina. The decision was rendered in 1823. And in 1823, Mr. Justice Johnson, in a case involving the State of South Carolina, which provided that where free Negroes came in on a ship into Charleston, they had to put them in jail as long as the ship was there and then put them back on the ship—and it was argued by people arguing for the statute that this was necessary, it was necessary to protect the people of South Carolina, and the majority must have wanted it and it was adopted— Mr. Justice Johnson made an answer to that argument in 1823, which I think is pretty good law as of today. Mr. Justice Johnson said:

> But to all this the plea of necessity is urged; and of the existence of that necessity we are told the state alone is to judge. Where is this to land us? Is it not asserting the right in each state to throw off the federal constitution at its will and pleasure? If it can be done as to any particular article it may be done as to all; and, like the old confederation, the Union becomes a mere rope of sand.

There is a lot of other language and other opinions, but I think that this is very significant.

---

[14]8 Fed. Cases 493 (No. 4,366) (C.C.D.S.C. 1823). Justice Johnson sitting on circuit held unconstitutional the South Carolina Negro Seaman Act (requiring all Negro sailors from foreign ships to be housed in jail while their ships were in port). Johnson served on the Supreme Court from 1804 to 1834.

THE CHIEF JUSTICE: Mr. Marshall, what emphasis do you give to the words, "So long as equality of rights is preserved"?

MR. MARSHALL: In Judge Parker's opinion—

THE CHIEF JUSTICE: Yes.

MR. MARSHALL:—of physical facilities, because he ends up in this statement, and makes it, I think, very clear. On the second hearing, on three or four occasions, he made it clear that segregation was not involved in the case any longer.

JUSTICE REED: Segregation or equality of rights?

MR. MARSHALL: He said that segregation was out of the case, and that we had disposed of it. And page 279—I think I marked it—yes, sir, the question was asked of me about building the schools overnight, and down near the end of the page he mentions the fact of segregation:

Well, I understand you do not admit that any conditions exist that require segregation. I understand that.

MR. MARSHALL: Yes, sir, that is right.

JUDGE PARKER: But that has been ruled on by the Court. What we are considering now is the question: Whether the physical facilities, curricula—"

THE CHIEF JUSTICE: (Interposing)—"and the other things that can be made equal, without the segregation issue, are being made equal?"

MR. MARSHALL: He is talking about physical facilities.

THE CHIEF JUSTICE: He is also talking about the curricula, "and the other things that can be made equal."

MR. MARSHALL: I am sorry I mentioned that, sir. I considered curricula in the physical facilities.

THE CHIEF JUSTICE: That is a shorthanded question.

MR. MARSHALL: Yes, sir. But again on page 281, they asked the question of whether something can be done, and I said that they could break down segregation. Judge Dobie[15] said, "Let that alone."
Judge Parker said, "That is the same question."
So I think for all intents and purposes, the District Court ruled out the question of all of this argument that segregation had the effect on these children to deny the children their rights under the Constitution, and they passed upon curricula, transportation, faculty, and schools. At the second hearing, the report

[15]Judge Armistead M. Dobie (1881–1956), one of the three judges on the Fourth Circuit panel which upheld the South Carolina segregation laws, was a former dean of the University of Virginia Law School (1932–1939) and served on the Fourth Circuit from 1940 to 1956.

showed that they were making progress. The schools still were not equal. But the question was that if they proceeded the way they were as of March of last year, they would be equal as of the September just past.

But in this case in the trial we conceived ourselves as conforming to the rule set out in the McLaurin and the Sweatt cases, where this Court held that the only question to be decided was the question as to whether or not the action of the state in maintaining its segregation was denying to the students the equal protection of the laws.

Of course, those decisions were limited to the graduate and professional schools. But we took the position that the rationale, if you please, or the principle, to be stronger, set out in those cases would apply just as well down the line provided evidence could be introduced which would show the same type of injury.

That is the type of evidence we produced, and we believed that on the basis of that testimony, the District Court should properly have held that in the area of elementary and high schools, the same type of injury was present as would be present in the McLaurin or the Sweatt case.

However, the District Court held just to the contrary, and said that there was a significant difference between the two. That is, in the Sweatt case it was a matter of inequality, and in the McLaurin case, McLaurin was subject to such humiliation, et cetera, that nobody should put up with it, whereas in this case, we have positive testimony from Dr. Clark that the humiliation that these children have been going through is the type of injury to the minds that will be permanent as long as they are in segregated schools, not theoretical injury, but actual injury.

We believe that on the basis of that, on that narrow point of Sweatt and McLaurin—on that I say, sir, that we do not have to get to *Plessy* v. *Ferguson;* we do not have to get to any other case, if we lean right on these two cases—we believe that there is a broader issue involved in these two cases, and despite the body of the law, *Plessy* v. *Ferguson, Gong Lum* v. *Rice,* the statement of Chief Justice Hughes in the Gaines case, some of the language in the Cumming case,[16] even though not applicable as to here—we also believe that there is another body of law, and that is the body of law on the Fifth Amendment cases, on the Japanese exclusion cases, and the Fourth Amendment cases, language that was in *Nixon* v. *Herndon,*[17] where Mr. Justice Holmes said that the states can do a lot of classifying that nobody can see any reason for, but certainly it cannot go contrary to the Fourteenth Amendment; then the language in the Skinner[18] case, the language of Mr. Justice Jackson in his concurring opinion in the Edwards[19] case.

[16]Cumming v. County Board of Education, 175 U.S. 528 (1899). The Court decided that a Georgia school board could legally close down a Negro high school when it had sufficient funds only for the white schools and a Negro primary school. The Court refused to divest funds from the white schools or order them closed until money was made available, as requested by the plaintiffs.

[17]The Japanese exclusion cases are Hirabayashi v. United States, 320 U.S. 81 (1943) and Korematsu v. United States, 323 U.S. 214 (1944), described in n. 56 and n. 58 *infra.,* In Nixon v. Herndon, 273 U.S. 536 (1927), Justice Holmes held for a unanimous court that a Texas law barring Negroes from participating in a state primary election violated the Fourteenth Amendment.

[18]Skinner v. Oklahoma, 316 U.S. 535 (1942). A law providing for sterilization of habitual criminals was found to violate the equal protection clause.

So on both the Fourteenth Amendment and the Fifteenth Amendment, this Court has repeatedly said that these distinctions on a racial basis or on a basis of ancestry are odious and invidious, and those decisions, I think, are entitled to just as much weight as *Plessy* v. *Ferguson* or *Gong Lum* v. *Rice*.

THE CHIEF JUSTICE: Mr. Marshall, in *Plessy* v. *Ferguson,* in the Harlan[20] dissent—

MR. MARSHALL: Yes, sir.

THE CHIEF JUSTICE: Do you attach any significance when he is dealing with illustrations of the absence of education?

MR. MARSHALL: Yes, sir. I do not know, sir. I tried to study his opinions all along. But I think that he was trying to take the position of the narrow issue involved in this case, and not touch on schools, because of the fact that at that time—and this is pure speculation—at that time the public school system was in such bad shape, when people were fighting compulsory attendance laws, they were fighting the money to be put in schools, and it was in a state of flux, but on the other hand, in the majority opinion, the significant thing, the case that they relied on, was the Roberts case, which was decided before the Fourteenth Amendment was even passed.

JUSTICE FRANKFURTER: But that does not do away with a consideration of the Roberts case, does it?

MR. MARSHALL: No, sir, it does not.

JUSTICE FRANKFURTER: The significance of the Roberts case is that that should be considered by the Supreme Court at a time when that issue was rampant in the United States.

MR. MARSHALL: Well, sir, I do not know about those days. But I can not conceive of the Roberts case being good for anything except that the legislatures of the states at those times were trying to work out their problems as they best could understand. And it could be that up in Massachusetts at that time they thought that Negroes—some of them were escaping from slavery, and all—but I still say that the considerations for the passage of any legislation before the Civil War and up to 1900, certainly, could not apply at the present time. I think that every race has made progress, but I do not believe that those considerations have any bearing at this time. The question today is—

---

[19]Edwards v. California, 314 U.S. 160, 181 (1941). The majority opinion held that a California law making it a crime to assist in bringing into the state an indigent person was an unconstitutional burden on interstate commerce. Justice Jackson would have invalidated the law as a violation of the privileges and immunities clause.

[20]Justice John M. Harlan, (1833–1911), the only dissenter in Plessy, served on the Supreme Court from 1877 to 1911. He was the only voice for Negro rights in that period, dissenting in many anti-civil rights decisions, such as the Civil Rights Cases, 109 U.S. 3 (1883) and Berea College v. Kentucky, 211 U.S. 45 (1908).

JUSTICE FRANKFURTER: They do not study these cases. But may I call your attention to what Mr. Justice Holmes said about the Fourteenth Amendment?

The Fourteenth Amendment itself as an historical product did not destroy history for the state and substitute mechanical departments of law . . .[20a]

MR. MARSHALL: I agree, sir.

JUSTICE FRANKFURTER: Then you have to face the fact that this is not a question to be decided by an abstract starting point of natural law, that you cannot have segregation. If we start with that, of course, we will end with that.

MR. MARSHALL: I do not know of any other proposition, sir, that we could consider that would say that because a person who is as white as snow with blue eyes and blond hair has to be set aside.

JUSTICE FRANKFURTER: Do you think that is the case?

MR. MARSHALL: Yes, sir. The law of South Carolina applies that way.

JUSTICE FRANKFURTER: Do you think that this law was passed for the same reason that a law would be passed prohibiting blue-eyed children from attending public schools? You would permit all blue-eyed children to go to separate schools? You think that this is the case?

MR. MARSHALL: No, sir, because the blue-eyed people in the United States never had the badge of slavery which was perpetuated in the statutes.

JUSTICE FRANKFURTER: If it is perpetuated as slavery, then the Thirteenth Amendment would apply.

MR. MARSHALL: But at the time—

JUSTICE FRANKFURTER: Do you really think it helps us not to recognize that behind this are certain facts of life, and the question is whether a legislature can address itself to those facts of life in despite of or within the Fourteenth Amendment, or whether, whatever the facts of life might be, where there is a vast congregation of Negro population as against the states where there is not, whether that is an irrelevant consideration? Can you escape facing those sociological facts, Mr. Marshall?

MR. MARSHALL: No, I cannot escape it. But if I did fail to escape it, I would have to throw completely aside the personal and present rights of those individuals.

JUSTICE FRANKFURTER: No, you would not. It does not follow because you cannot make certain classifications, you cannot make some classifications.

[20a]Jackman v. Rosenbaum Co., 260 U.S. 22, 31 (1922).

MR. MARSHALL: But the personal and present right that I have to consider like any other citizen of Clarendon County, South Carolina, is a right that has been recognized by this Court over and over again. And so far as the appellants in this case are concerned, I cannot consider it sufficient to be relegated to the legislature of South Carolina where the record in this Court shows their consideration of Negroes, and I speak specifically of the primary cases.

JUSTICE FRANKFURTER: If you would refer to the record of the case, there they said that the doctrine of classification is not excluded by the Fourteenth Amendment, but its employment by state legislatures has no justifiable foundation.

MR. MARSHALL: I think that when an attack is made on a statute on the ground that it is an unreasonable classification, and competent, recognized testimony is produced, I think then the least that the state has to do is to produce something to defend their statutes.

JUSTICE FRANKFURTER: I follow you when you talk that way.

MR. MARSHALL: That is part of the argument, sir.

JUSTICE FRANKFURTER: But when you start, as I say, with the conclusion that you cannot have segregation, then there is no problem. If you start with the conclusion of a problem, there is no problem.

MR. MARSHALL: But Mr. Justice Frankfurter, I was trying to make three different points. I said that the first one was peculiarly narrow, under the McLaurin and the Sweatt decisions.

The second point was that on a classification basis, these statutes were bad.
The third point was the broader point, that racial distinctions in and of themselves are invidious. I consider it as a three-pronged attack. Any one of the three would be sufficient for reversal.

JUSTICE FRANKFURTER: You may recall that this Court not so many years ago decided that the legislature of Louisiana could restrict the calling of pilots on the Mississippi to the question of who your father was.[21]

MR. MARSHALL: Yes, sir.

JUSTICE FRANKFURTER: And there were those of us who sustained that legislation, not because we thought it was admirable or because we thought it comported with human notions or because we believed in primogeniture, but for different reasons, that it was so imbedded in the conflict of the history of that problem in Louisiana that we thought on the whole that was an allowable justification.

MR. MARSHALL: I say, sir, that I do not think—

[21]Kotch v. Pilot Commissioners, 330 U.S. 552 (1947).

JUSTICE FRANKFURTER: I am not taking that beside this case. I am not meaning to intimate any of that, as you well know, on this subject. I am just saying how the subjects are to be dealt with.

MR. MARSHALL: But Mr. Justice Frankfurter, I do not think that segregation in public schools is any more ingrained in the South than segregation in transportation, and this Court upset it in the Morgan case.[22] I do not think it is any more ingrained.

JUSTICE FRANKFURTER: It upset it in the Morgan case on the ground that it was none of the business of the state; it was an interstate problem.

MR. MARSHALL: That is a different problem. But a minute ago the very question was raised that we have to deal with realities, and it did upset that. Take the primary case. There is no more ingrained rule than there were in the cases of McLaurin and Sweatt, the graduate school cases.

JUSTICE FRANKFURTER: I am willing to suggest that this problem is more complicated than the simple recognition of an absolute *non possumus*.

MR. MARSHALL: I agree that it is not only complicated. I agree that it is a tough problem. But I think that it is a problem that has to be faced.

JUSTICE FRANKFURTER: That is why we are here.

MR. MARSHALL: That is what I appreciate, Your Honor. But I say, sir, that most of my time is spent down in the South, and despite all these predictions as to what might happen, I do not think that anything is going to happen any more except on the graduate and professional level. And this Court can take notice of the reports that have been in papers such as the New York *Times*. But it seems to me on that question, this Court should go back to the case of *Buchanan* v. *Warley*,[23] where on the question as to whether or not there was this great problem, this Court in *Buchanan* v. *Warley* said:

> That there exists a serious and difficult problem arising from a feeling of race hostility which the law is powerless to control, and to which it must give a measure of consideration, may be freely admitted. But its solution cannot be promoted by depriving citizens of their constitutional rights and privileges.

In this case, granting that there is a feeling of race hostility in South Carolina, if there be such a thing, or granting that there is that problem, we cannot have the individual rights subjected to this consideration of what the groups might do; for example, it was even argued that it will be better for both the Negro and the so-called white group. This record is not quite clear as to who is in the white group, because the superintendent of schools said that he did not know; all he knew was that Negroes were excluded. So I imagine that the other schools take in everybody.

[22]Morgan v. Virginia, 328 U.S. 373 (1946). A Virginia law requiring segregation on buses was declared unconstitutional as an improper burden on interstate commerce.

[23]245 U.S. 60, 80 (1917). A Louisiana ordinance forbidding Negroes from occupying residences on a block inhabited by a majority of whites was declared invalid.

So it seems to me that insofar as this case is concerned, whereas in the Kansas case there was a finding of fact that was favorable to the appellants—in this case the opinion of the court mentions the fact that the findings are embodied in the opinion, and the court in that case decided that the only issue would be these facilities, the curriculum, transportation, et cetera.

In the brief for the appellees in this case and the argument in the lower court, I have yet to hear any one say that they denied that these children are harmed by reason of this segregation. Nobody denies that, at least up to now. So there is a grant, I should assume, that segregation in and of itself harms these children.

Now, the argument is made that because we are drawn into a broader problem down in South Carolina, because of a situation down there, that this statute should be upheld.

So there we have a direct cleavage from one side to the other side. I do not think any of that is significant. As a matter of fact, I think all of that argument is made without foundation. I do not believe that in the case of the sworn testimony of the witnesses, statements and briefs and quotations from magazine articles will counteract what is actually in the brief.

So what do we have in the record? We have testimony of physical inequality. It is admitted. We have the testimony of experts as to the exact harm which is inherent in segregation wherever it occurs. That I would assume is too broad for the immediate decision, because after all, the only point before this Court is the statute as it was applied in Clarendon County. But if this Court would reverse and the case would be sent back, we are not asking for affirmative relief. That will not put anybody in any school. The only thing that we ask for is that the state-imposed racial segregation be taken off, and to leave the county school board, the county people, the district people, to work out their own solution of the problem to assign children on any reasonable basis they want to assign them on.

JUSTICE FRANKFURTER: You mean, if we reverse, it will not entitle every mother to have her child go to a nonsegregated school in Clarendon County?

MR. MARSHALL: No, sir.

JUSTICE FRANKFURTER: What will it do? Would you mind spelling this out? What would happen?

MR. MARSHALL: Yes, sir. The school board, I assume, would find some other method of distributing the children, a recognizable method, by drawing district lines.

JUSTICE FRANKFURTER: What would that mean?

MR. MARSHALL: The usual procedure—

JUSTICE FRANKFURTER: You mean that geographically the colored people all live in one district?

MR. MARSHALL: No, sir, they do not. They are mixed up somewhat.

JUSTICE FRANKFURTER: Then why would not the children be mixed.

MR. MARSHALL: If they are in the district, they would be. But there might possibly be areas—

JUSTICE FRANKFURTER: You mean we would have gerrymandering of school districts?

MR. MARSHALL: Not gerrymandering, sir. The lines could be equal.

JUSTICE FRANKFURTER: I think that nothing would be worse than for this Court—I am expressing my own opinion—nothing would be worse, from my point of view, than for this Court to make an abstract declaration that segregation is bad and then have it evaded by tricks.

MR. MARSHALL: No, sir. As a matter of fact, sir, we have had cases where we have taken care of that. But the point is that it is my assumption that where this is done, it will work out, if I might leave the record, by statute in some states.

JUSTICE FRANKFURTER: It would be more important information in my mind, to have you spell out in concrete what would happen if this Court reverses and the case goes back to the district court for the entry of a decree.

MR. MARSHALL: I think, sir, that the decree would be entered which would enjoin the school officials from, one, enforcing the statute; two, from segregating on the basis of race or color. Then I think whatever district lines they draw, if it can be shown that those lines are drawn on the basis of race or color, then I think they would violate the injunction. If the lines are drawn on a natural basis, without regard to race or color, then I think that nobody would have any complaint.

For example, the colored child that is over here in this school would not be able to go to that school. But the only thing that would come down would be the decision that whatever rule you set in, if you set in, it shall not be on race, either actually or by any other way. It would violate the injunction, in my opinion.

JUSTICE FRANKFURTER: There is a thing that I do not understand. Why would not that inevitably involve—unless you have Negro ghettoes, or if you find that language offensive, unless you have concentrations of Negroes, so that only Negro children would go there, and there would be no white children mixed with them, or vice versa—why would it not involve Negro children saying, "I want to go to this school instead of that school"?

MR. MARSHALL: That is the interesting thing in this procedure. They could move over into that district, if necessary. Even if you get stuck in one district, there is always an out, as long as this statute is gone.

There are several ways that can be done. But we have instances, if I might, sir, where they have been able to draw a line and to enclose—this is in the North—to enclose the Negroes, and in New York those lines have on every occasion been declared unreasonably drawn, because it is obvious that they were drawn for that purpose.

JUSTICE FRANKFURTER: Gerrymandering?

MR. MARSHALL: Yes, sir. As a matter of fact, they used the word "gerrymander."

So in South Carolina, if the decree was entered as we have requested, then the school district would have to decide a means other than race, and if it ended up that the Negroes were all in one school, because of race, they would be violating the injunction just as bad as they are by violating what we consider to be the Fourteenth Amendment now.

JUSTICE FRANKFURTER: Now, I think it is important to know, before one starts, where he is going. As to available schools, how would that cut across this problem? If everything was done that you wanted done, would there be physical facilities within such drawing of lines as you would regard as not evasive of the decree?

MR. MARSHALL: Most of the school buildings are now assigned to Negroes, so that the Negro buildings are scattered around in that county. Now, as to whether or not lines could be properly drawn, I say quite frankly, sir, I do not know. But I do know that in most of the southern areas—it might be news to the Court—there are very few areas that are predominately one race or the other.

JUSTICE FRANKFURTER: Are you going to argue the District of Columbia case?

MR. MARSHALL: No, sir.
If you have any questions, I would try, but I cannot bind the other side.

JUSTICE FRANKFURTER: I just wondered, in regard to this question that we are discussing, how what you are indicating or contemplating would work out in the District if tomorrow there were the requirement that there must be mixed groups.

MR. MARSHALL: Most of the schools in the District of Columbia would be integrated. There might possibly be some in the concentrated areas up in the northwest section. There might be. But I doubt it. But I think the question as to what would happen if such decree was entered—I again point out that it is actually a matter that is for the school authorities to decide, and it is not a matter for us, it seems to me, as lawyers, to recommend except where there is racial discrimination or discrimination on one side or the other.

But my emphasis is that all we are asking for is to take off this state-imposed segregation. It is the state-imposed part of it that affects the individual children. And the testimony in many instances is along that line.

So in South Carolina, if the District Court issued a decree—and I hasten to add that in the second hearing when we were prevented from arguing segregation, the argument was made that on the basis of the fact that the schools were still unequal, we should get relief on the basis of the Sipuel decision—the court said in that case, no, that the only relief we could get would be this relief as of September, and in that case the court took the position that it would be impossible to break into the middle of the year. If I might anticipate a question on that, the point would come up as to, if a decree in this case should happen to be issued by the District Court, or in a case similar to this, as to whether or not there would be a time given for the actual enrollment of the children, et cetera, and changing of children from school to school. It would be my position in a case like that, which is very much in answer to the brief filed by the United States in this case—it would be my position that the important thing is to get the principle established, and if a decree were entered saying that facilities are declared to be unequal and that the appellants are entitled to an injunction, and then the District Court issues the injunction, it would seem to me that it would go without saying that the local school board had the time to do it. But obviously it could not do it over night, and it might take six months to do it one place and two months to do it another place.

Again, I say it is not a matter for judicial determination. That would be a matter for legislative determination.

I would like to save my fifteen minutes for rebuttal.

JUSTICE JACKSON: Coming back to the question that Justice Black asked you, could I ask you what, if any, effect does your argument have on the Indian policy, the segregation of the Indians. How do you deal with that?

MR. MARSHALL: I think that again that we are in a position of having grown up. Indians are no longer wards of the Government. I do not think that they stand in any special category. And in all of the southern states that I know of, the Indians are in a preferred position so far as Negroes are concerned, and I do not know of any place where they are excluded.

JUSTICE JACKSON: In some respects, in taxes, at least, I wish I could claim to have a little Indian blood.

MR. MARSHALL: But the only time it ever came up was in the—

JUSTICE JACKSON: But on the historical argument, the philosophy of the Fourteenth Amendment which you contended for does not seem to have been applied by the people who adopted the Fourteenth Amendment, at least in the Indian case.

MR. MARSHALL: I think, sir, that if we go back even as far as *Slaughter-House* and come up through *Strauder*,[24] where the Fourteenth Amendment was passed for the specific purpose of raising the newly freed slaves up, et cetera, I do not know.

JUSTICE JACKSON: Do you think that might not apply to the Indians?

MR. MARSHALL: I think it would. But I think that the biggest trouble with the Indians is that they just have not had the judgment or the wherewithal to bring lawsuits.

[24]In the Slaughter-House Cases, 16 Wall. 36 (1873), the Court refused to strike down a Lousiana law granting a monopoly to certain white butchers in New Orleans. The decision gave a narrow reading to the privileges and immunities clause of the recently passed Fourteenth Amendment. Strauder v. West Virginia, 100 U.S. 303 (1880), held a West Virginia law forbidding Negroes from serving on juries unconstitutional.

JUSTICE JACKSON: Maybe you should bring some up.

MR. MARSHALL: I have a full load now, Mr. Justice.

THE CHIEF JUSTICE: Mr. Davis.

### ARGUMENT ON BEHALF OF THE APPELLEES

#### by MR. DAVIS

MR. DAVIS: May it please the Court, I think if the appellants' construction of the Fourteenth Amendment should prevail here, there is no doubt in my mind that it would catch the Indian within its grasp just as much as the Negro. If it should prevail, I am unable to see why a state would have any further right to segregate its pupils on the ground of sex or on the ground of age or on the ground of mental capacity. If it may classify it for one purpose on the basis of admitted facts, it may, according to my contention, classify it for other.

Now, I want to address myself during the course of this argument to three propositions, and I will utilize the remaining minutes of the afternoon to state them.

The first thing which I want to contend for before the Court is that the mandate of the court below, which I quote, "Required the defendants to proceed at once to furnish plaintiffs and other Negro pupils of said district educational facilities, equipment, curricula, and opportunities equal to those furnished white pupils."

That mandate has been fully complied with. We have been found to have obeyed the court's injunction. The question is no longer in the case, and the complaint which is made by the appellants in their brief that the school doors should have been immediately thrown open instead of taking the time necessary to readjust the physical facilities, is a moot question at this stage of the case.

The second question to which I wish to address myself is that Article XIV, section 7, of the Constitution of South Carolina, and section 5377 of the Code, both making the separation of schools between white and colored mandatory, do not offend the Fourteenth Amendment of the Constitution of the United States or deny equal protection.

The right of a state to classify the pupils in its public schools on the basis of sex or age or mental capacity, or race, is not impaired or affected by that amendment.

Third, I want to say something about the evidence offered by the plaintiffs upon which counsel so confidently relied.

I see that the evidence offered by the plaintiffs, be its merit what it may, deals entirely with legislative policy, and does not tread on constitutional right. Whether it does or not, it would be difficult for me to conceal my opinion that that evidence in and of itself is of slight weight and in conflict with the opinion of other and better informed sources.

I hope I have not laid out too much territory for the time that is allotted to me. Let me attack it seriatim.

I want to put this case in its proper frame, by reciting what has transpired up to this time, so that Your Honors may be sure that my assertion of full performance is not an idle boast.

When the first hearing was at an end, the court entered its decree, demanding us to proceed forthwith to furnish, not merely physical facilities, as my friend would have it, but educational facilities, equipment, curricula, and opportunities equal on the part of the state for the Negro as for the white pupil.

Now, the court could have stopped there, and for the enforcement of its decree it could have awaited the moment when some complainant would have come in and invoked process of contempt against the delinquent defendants. That would have satisfied the duty of the chancellor. He would have retained in its own hand the powers of enforcement which the rules of equity give him, and perhaps his conscience might have been at rest with the feeling that he had done all that judicially he was called upon to do.

But the court below went further. In order to ensure the obedience to its decree, it required the defendants within the period of six months, not later than six months, to report what progress they were making in the execution of the court's order. The court might have said, "You must do this tomorrow"; I gather from counsel that not even counsel for the appellants here contends so much.

Insofar as the equality, equalization required the building of buildings and, of course, the court knew, as every sensible man knew, that you do not get buildings by rubbing an Aladdin's lamp, and you cannot create them by court decree. To say that the day following this decree, all this should have been done would have been *brutus fulmen,* and no credit to the court or anybody else.

In December, within the allotted time, the defendants made report of progress. At that time, the case was on Your Honor's docket. Because of the fact that an appeal had been taken from so much of the decree below, they refused to strike down the constitution and the statute.

Thereupon, the District Court sent that report to you, and you, not desiring to pass upon it, remanded the case to the District Court, and called upon them to pass upon their report which had been made to them, and to free their hands entirely for such action as they might see fit. You vacated the order entered below.

The District Court thereupon resumed control of the case. It set it down for a hearing in March of 1952, at which time the defendants filed a supplemental report showing the progress up to that precise day and minute. Thereupon, the court declared that the defendants had made every possible effort to comply with the decree of the court, that they had done all that was humanly possible, and that by the month of September, 1952, equality between the races in this area would have been achieved.

So the record reads.

Now, I should just like briefly to summarize what the situation was that those reports exposed. They showed that in the State of South Carolina, under the leadership of its present Governor,[25] there was a surge for educational reform and improvement, which I suspect has not been exceeded in any state in this Union. It began with the legislature which adopted the act providing for the issuance of a maximum of $75,000,000 in bonds for school purposes, not an ultimate of $75,

---

[25]James F. Byrnes (1879–     ) was Governor of South Carolina from 1951 to 1955. He also served as United States Senator (1931–1941), Associate Justice of the Supreme Court (1941–42), and Secretary of State of the United States (1945–1947).

000,000, but a maximum at any one time of $75,000,000, and that to be supported and serviced by a 3 per cent sales tax. Speaking from some slight personal experience, I can assert that it escapes very few transactions in that state.

That being done, the legislature set up an educational finance commission, with power to survey the educational system of the state, to consolidate districts for better finance, to allot funds to the districts all over the state in such manner as this commission might find to be appropriate. Thereupon, the commission goes to Clarendon County, which is the seat of the present drama. It finds that in Clarendon County there are thirty-four educational districts, so-called, each with its separate body of officers and administrators, and all of them bogged down, I take it, by similar poverty.

It directed that that county be readjusted, redistricted, into three districts, one, District No. 1 to contain the contentious District No. 22, with which the litigation began, and six others. I gather that counsel wants to reverse that process. Having brought these districts into unity and strength, he has some plan, the mathematics of which I do not entirely grasp, by which the districts will be redistricted again with resulting benefit to all concerned.

District No. 1 was created. Its officers entered this litigation, and agreed to be bound by the decree, and are here present.

The first thing that the district did was to provide for the building of a new Negro high school at Scott's Branch, and for the repair of the secondary school at Scott's Branch, for which it expended the sum of $261,000 on a contract that they should be completed and put into use by September of 1952.

I speak outside the record, but that has been accomplished.

It was also provided that it should purchase the site for some two Negro secondary schools, which should be serviced by this fund.

$21,000 was appropriated immediately for additional equipment, and those secondary schools are now on the verge of completion.

But what could be done immediately—and with this I shall close for the afternoon—what could be done immediately by this school board was done. Salaries of teachers were equalized. Curricula were made uniform, and the State of South Carolina appropriated money to furnish school buses for black and white. Of course, in these days, the schoolboy no longer walks. The figure of the schoolboy trudging four miles in the morning and back four in the afternoon swinging his books as he went is as much a figure of myth as the presidential candidate born in a log cabin. Both of these characters have disappeared.

THE CHIEF JUSTICE: The Court will adjourn.
(Whereupon, at 4:30 p.m., the Court arose.)
(Oral argument was resumed at 12:10 p.m., December 10, 1952.)

THE CHIEF JUSTICE: Case No. 101, Harry Briggs, Jr., et al against R. W. Elliott, Chairman, et al.

THE CLERK: Counsel are present.

THE CHIEF JUSTICE: Proceed.

### ARGUMENT ON BEHALF OF APPELLEES—Resumed

#### by MR. DAVIS

MR. DAVIS: If the Court please, when the Court arose on yesterday, I was reciting the progress that had been made in the public school system in South Carolina, and with particular reference to the improvement of the facilities, equipment curricular, and opportunities accorded to the colored students.

I might go further on that subject, but I am content to read two sentences from the opinion of the court below. This is the opinion of Judge Parker:

> The reports of December 21 and March 3 filed by defendants, which are admitted by plaintiffs to be true and correct and which are so found by the Court, show beyond question that defendants have proceeded promptly and in good faith to comply with the Court's decree.

They add:

> There can be no doubt that as a result of the program in which defendants are engaged the educational facilities and opportunities afforded Negroes within the district will, by the beginning of the next school year beginning in September, 1952, be made equal to those afforded white persons.

The only additional fact which I want to mention, aside from leaving the remainder to my brief of the opinion of the court below is a fact of which I think Mr. Marshall should take cognizance when he proceeds to his redistricting program, and that is the fact that in District No. 1, the district here in controversy, there are now, speaking of the report of last March, 2,799 registered Negro students and 295 registered white students. In other words, the proportion between the Negroes and the whites is about in the ratio of ten to one. And whether discrimination is to be abolished by introducing 2,800 Negro students in the schools now occupied by the whites, or conversely introducing 295 whites into the schools now occupied by 2,800 Negroes, the result in either event is one which one cannot contemplate with entire equanimity.

I come, then, to what is really the crux of the case. That is the meaning and interpretation of the Fourteenth Amendment to the Constitution of the United States. We devote to that important subject but five pages of our brief. We trust the Court will not treat that summary disposition of it as due to any lack of earnestness on our part.

We have endeavored to compress the outline of the argument for two reasons. The first is that the opinion of Judge Parker rendered below is so cogent and complete that it seems impossible to add anything to his reasoning. The second is, perhaps more compelling at the moment, that Your Honors have so often and so recently dealt with this subject that it would be a work of supererogation to remind you of the cases in which you have dealt with it or to argue with you, the authors, the meaning and scope of the opinions you have emitted.

But if, as lawyers or judges, we have ascertained the scope and bearing of the equal protection clause of the Fourteenth Amendment, our duty is done. The rest must be left to those who dictate public policy, and not to courts.

How should we approach it? I use the language of the Court: An amendment to the Constitution should be read, you have said,

"in a sense most obvious to the common understanding at the time of its adoption." For it was for public adoption that it was proposed.[25a]

Still earlier you have said it is the duty of the interpreters,

to place ourselves as nearly as possible in the condition of the men who framed the instrument.[25b]

What was the condition of those who framed the instrument? The resolution proposing the Fourteenth Amendment was proffered by Congress in June, 1866. In the succeeding month of July, the same Congress proceeded to establish, or to continue separate schools in the District of Columbia, and from that good day to this, Congress has not waivered in that policy. It has confronted the attack upon it repeatedly. During the life of Charles Sumner,[26] over and over again, he undertook to amend the law of the District so as to provide for mixed and not for separate schools, and again and again he was defeated.

JUSTICE BURTON: What is your answer, Mr. Davis, to the suggestion mentioned yesterday that at that time the conditions and relations between the two races were such that what might have been unconstitutional then would not be unconstitutional now?

MR. DAVIS: My answer to that is that changed conditions may affect policy, but changed conditions cannot broaden the terminology of the Constitution, the thought is an administrative or a political question, and not a judicial one.

JUSTICE BURTON: But the Constitution is a living document that must be interpreted in relation to the facts of the time in which it is interpreted. Did we not go through with that in connection with child labor cases, and so forth?

MR. DAVIS: Oh, well, of course, changed conditions may bring things within the scope of the Constitution which were not originally contemplated, and of that perhaps the aptest illustration is the interstate commerce clause. Many things have been found to be interstate commerce which at the time of the writing of the Constitution were not contemplated at all. Many of them did not even exist. But when they come within the field of interstate commerce, then they become subject to congressional power, which is defined in the terms of the Constitution itself. So circumstances may bring new facts within the purview of the constitutional provision, but they do not alter, expand, or change the language that the framers of the Constitution have employed.

[25a] Eisner v. Macomber, 252 U.S. 189, 220 (1920) (Holmes, J., dissenting).

[25b] Ex parte Bain, 121 U.S. 1, 12 (1887).

[26] Charles Sumner (1811–1874) was a leading anti-slavery Senator from Massachusetts from 1851 to 1874. He was assaulted in the Senate by Representative Preston Brooks of South Carolina for his anti-slavery remarks, sustaining severe injuries. He continued his fight for Negro rights after the Civil War.

JUSTICE FRANKFURTER: Mr. Davis, do you think that "equal" is a less fluid term than "commerce between the states"?

MR. DAVIS: Less fluid?

JUSTICE FRANKFURTER: Yes.

MR. DAVIS: I have not compared the two on the point of fluidity.

JUSTICE FRANKFURTER: Suppose you do it now.

MR. DAVIS: I am not sure that I can approach it in just that sense.

JUSTICE FRANKFURTER: The problem behind my question is whatever the phrasing of it would be.

MR. DAVIS: That what is unequal today may be equal tomorrow, or vice versa?

JUSTICE FRANKFURTER: That is it.

MR. DAVIS: That might be. I should not philosophize about it. But the effort in which I am now engaged is to show how those who submitted this amendment and those who adopted it conceded it to be, and what their conduct by way of interpretation has been since its ratification in 1868.

JUSTICE FRANKFURTER: What you are saying is, that as a matter of history, history puts a gloss upon "equal" which does not permit elimination or admixture of white and colored in this aspect to be introduced?

MR. DAVIS: Yes, I am saying that.

JUSTICE FRANKFURTER: That is what you are saying?

MR. DAVIS: Yes, I am saying that. I am saying that equal protection in the minds of the Congress of the United States did not contemplate mixed schools as a necessity. I am saying that, and I rest on it, though I shall not go further into the congressional history on this subject, because my brother Korman speaking for the District of Columbia will enter that phase of it.

It is true that in the Constitution of the United States there is no equal protection clause. It is true that the Fourteenth Amendment was addressed primarily to the states. But it is inconceivable that the Congress which submitted it would have forbidden the states to employ an educational scheme which Congress itself was persistent in employing in the District of Columbia.

I therefore urge that the action of Congress is a legislative interpretation of the meaning and scope of this amendment, and a legislative interpretation of a legislative act, no court, I respectfully submit is justified in ignoring.

What did the states think about this at the time of the ratification? At the time the amendment was submitted, there were 37 states in the Union. Thirty of them had ratified the amendment at the time it was proclaimed in 1868. Of those 30 ratifying states, 23 either then had, or immediately installed separate schools for white and colored children under their public school systems. Were they violating the amendment which they had solemnly accepted? Were they conceiving of it in any other sense than that it did not touch their power over their public schools?

How do they stand today? Seventeen states in the Union today provide for separate schools for white and colored children, and 4 others make it permissive with their school board. Those 4 are Wyoming, Kansas, of which we heard yesterday, New Mexico, and Arizona, so that you have 21 states today which conceive it their power and right to maintain separate schools if it suits their policy.

When we turn to the judicial branch, it has spoken on this question, perhaps with more repetition and in more cases than any other single separate constitutional question that now occurs to me. We have not larded our brief with quotations from the courts of last resort of the several states. It would be easy to do so, but we have assembled in our appendix a list of cases which the highest courts in the states have decided on this question. I am not sure that that list is exhaustive. In fact, I am inclined to think that it is not exhaustive. But certainly it is impressive, and they speak with a single voice that their separate school system is not a violation of the Constitution of the United States.

What does this Court say? I repeat, I shall not undertake to interpret for Your Honors the scope and weight of your own opinions. In *Plessy* v. *Ferguson, Cumming* v. *Richmond County Board of Education, Gong Lum* v. *Rice, Berea College* v. *Kentucky,*[27] *Sipuel* v. *Board of Regents, Gaines* v. *Canada, Sweatt* v. *Painter,* and *McLaurin* v. *Oklahoma,* and there may be others for all I know, certainly this Court has spoken in the most clear and unmistakable terms to the effect that this segregation is not unlawful. I am speaking for those with whom I am associated.

We find nothing in the latest cases that modified that doctrine of "separate but equal" in the least. *Sweatt* v. *Painter* and similar cases were decided solely on the basis of inequality, as we think, and as we believe the Court intended.

It is a little late, said the court below, after this question has been presumed to be settled for ninety years—it is a little late to argue that the question is still at large.

I want to read just one of Judge Parker's sentences on that. Said he:
It is hardly reasonable to suppose that legislative bodies over so wide a territory, including the Congress of the United States, and great judges of high courts have knowingly defied the Constitution for so long a period or that they have acted in ignorance of the meaning of its provisions. The constitutional principle is the same now that it has been throughout this period, and if conditions have changed so that segregation is no longer wise, this is a matter for the legislatures and not for the courts. The members of the judiciary [it goes on to say] have no more right to read their ideas of sociology into the Constitution than their ideas of economics.

It would be an interesting, though perhaps entirely useless, undertaking to enumerate the numbers of men charged with official duty in the legislative and the judicial branches of the Government who have declared that segregation is not per se unlawful. The members of Congress, year after year, and session after session, the members of state constitutional conventions, the members of state legislatures, year after year and session after session, the members of the higher courts of the states, the members of the inferior federal judiciary, and the members of this

[27]211 U.S. 45 (1908). A Kentucky law forbidding colleges to enroll both white and Negro students was upheld. Justice John M. Harlan dissented.

tribunal—what their number may be, I do not know, but I think it reasonably certain that it must mount well into the thousands, and to this I stress for Your Honors that every one of that vast group was bound by oath to support the Constitution of the United States and any of its amendments—is it conceivable that all that body of concurrent opinion was recreant to its duty or misunderstood the constitutional mandate, or was ignorant of the history which gave to the mandate its scope and meaning? I submit not.

Now, what are we told here that has made all that body of activity and learning of no consequence? Says counsel for the plaintiffs, or appellants, we have the uncontradicted testimony of expert witnesses that segregation is hurtful, and in their opinion hurtful to the children of both races, both colored and white. These witnesses severally described themselves as professors, associate professors, assistant professors, and one describes herself as a lecturer and adviser on curricular. I am not sure exactly what that means.

I did not impugn the sincerity of these learned gentlemen and lady. I am quite sure that they believe that they are expressing valid opinions on their subject. But there are two things notable about them. Not a one of them is under any official duty in the premises whatever; not a one of them has had to consider the welfare of the people for whom they are legislating or whose rights they were called on to adjudicate. And only one of them professes to have the slightest knowledge of conditions in the states where separate schools are now being maintained. Only one of them professes any knowledge of the condition within the seventeen segregating states.

I want to refer just a moment to that particular witness, Dr. Clark. Dr. Clark professed to speak as an expert and an informed investigator on this subject. His investigation consisted of visits to the Scott's Branch primary and secondary school, at Scott's Branch, which he undertook at the request of counsel for the plaintiffs. He called for the presentation to him of some sixteen pupils between the ages of six and nine years, and he applied to them what he devised and what he was pleased to call an objective test. That consisted of offering to them sixteen white and colored dolls, and inviting them to select the doll they would prefer, the doll they thought was nice, the doll that looked bad, or the doll that looked most like themselves. He ascertained that ten out of his battery of sixteen preferred the white doll. Nine thought the white doll was nice, and seven thought it looked most like themselves. Eleven said that the colored doll was bad, and one that the white doll was bad. And out of that intensive investigation and that application of that thoroughly scientific test, he deduced the sound conclusion that segregation there had produced confusion in the individuals—I use his language—"and their concepts about themselves conflicting in their personalities, that they have been definitely harmed in the development of their personalities."

That is a sad result, and we are invited to accept it as a scientific conclusion. But I am reminded of the scriptural saying, "Oh, that mine adversary had written a book." And Professor Clark, with the assistance of his wife, has written on this subject and has described a similar test which he submitted to colored pupils in the northern and nonsegregated schools.[28] He found that 62 per cent of the colored

[28]The article referred to was "Racial Identifications and Preferences in Negro Children" appearing in *Readings in Social Psychology* (Newcomb & Hartley, ed. New York, 1947).

children in the South chose a white doll; 72 per cent in the North chose the white doll; 52 per cent of the children in the South thought the white doll was nice; 68 per cent of the children in the North thought the white doll was nice; 49 per cent of the children in the South thought the colored doll was bad; 71 per cent of the children in the North thought the colored doll was bad.

Now, these latter scientific tests were conducted in nonsegregating states, and with those results compared, what becomes of the blasting influence of segregation to which Dr. Clark so eloquently testifies?

The witness Trager,[29] who is the lecturer and consultant on curricular, had never been in the South except when she visited her husband who was stationed at an Army post in Charleston during the war. And I gather that the visit was of somewhat brief character. She also was in search of scientific wisdom, and she submitted that same scientific test to a collection of children in the schools of Philadelphia, where segregation has been absent for many years. She made as a result of that what seems to have been surprising to her, the fact that in children from five to eight years of age, they were already aware, both white and colored, of racial differences between them.

Now, that may be a scientific conclusion. It would be rather surprising, if the children were possessed of their normal senses, if they were ignorant of some racial differences between them, even at that early age.

I am tempted to digress, because I am discussing the weight and pith of this testimony, which is the reliance of the plaintiffs here to turn back this enormous weight of legislative and judicial precedent on this subject. I may have been unfortunate, or I may have been careless, but it seems to me that much of that which is handed around under the name of social science is an effort on the part of the scientist to rationalize his own preconceptions. They find usually, in my limited observation, what they go out to find.

One of these witnesses, Dr. Krech,[30] speaks of a colored school, gives, as he says, "what we call in our lingo environmental support for the belief that Negroes are in some way different from and inferior to white people, and that in turn, of course, supports and strengthens beliefs of racial differences, of racial inferiority."

I ran across a sentence the other day which somebody said who was equally as expert as Dr. Krech in the "lingo" of the craft. He described much of the social science as "fragmentary expertise based on an examined presupposition," which is about as scientific language as you can use, I suppose, but seems to be entirely descriptive.

Now, South Carolina is unique among the states in one particular. You have often heard it said that an ounce of experience is worth a pound of theory. South Carolina does not come to this policy as a stranger. She had mixed schools for twelve years, from 1865 to 1877. She had them as a result of the Constitutional Convention of 1865, which was led by a preacher of the Negro race, against whom

---

[29]Mrs. Helen Trager taught at Vassar and acted as educational consultant to city schools in New York, Philadelphia, Denver, San Diego, and Detroit.

[30]Dr. David Krech taught social psychology at Harvard and the University of California.

I know nothing, who bore the somewhat distinguished name of Cardozo, and he forced through that convention the provision for mixed schools.[31]

The then Góvernor of South Carolina, whose term was expiring, was the war governor, Governor Orr, who denounced the provision. He was succeeded by—I hope the term has lost its invidiousness—a carpetbagger from Maine, named Scott, and Scott denounced the provision. And Dr. Knight, the Professor of Education at the University of North Carolina, who has written on the subject, declares that it was the most unwise action of the period, and that that is a certainty.[32]

When South Carolina moved from mixed to segregated schools, it did so in the light of experience, and in the light of the further fact, these authorities state, that it had been destructive to the public school system of South Carolina for fifty years after it was abolished.

Now, these learned witnesses do not have the whole field to themselves. They do not speak without contradiction from other sources. We quote in our brief—I suppose it is not testimony, but it is quotable material, and we are content to adopt it—Dr. Odum, of North Carolina, who is perhaps the foremost investigator of educational questions in the entire South; Dr. Frank Graham, former president of the University of North Carolina; ex-Governor Darden, president of the University of Virginia; Hodding Carter, whose recent works on Southern conditions have become classic; Gunnar Myrdal, Swedish scientist employed to investigate the race question for the Rockefeller Foundation; W.E.B. DuBois; Ambrose Caliver; and the witness Crow, who testified in this case, all of them opposing the item that there should be an immediate abolition of segregated schools.[33]

Let me read a sentence or two from Dr. DuBois. I may be wrong about this,

[31]F. L. Cardozo was the son of a Charleston economist, J. N. Cardozo, and a half-Negro, half-Indian mother. He was Secretary of State of South Carolina (1868–1872) and Treasurer of the State (1872–1876).

[32]James L. Orr (1822–1873) served as a member of the House of Representatives (1849–1859), Speaker (1857–1859), Republican Governor of South Carolina (1866–1868). He was succeeded by Robert K. Scott of Ohio (not Maine) who served as Republican Governor from 1868 to 1872. The book referred to is Edgar W. Knight, *Public Education in the South* (Chapel Hill, 1922).

[33]Frank Graham served as United States Senator (1949–1950), President of the University of North Carolina (1930–1949), member of the Civil Rights Commission (1946–1949), and special envoy to Pakistan for the United Nations. Hodding Carter is editor and publisher of the Delta *Democrat-Times,* Greenville, Miss., winner of a Pulitzer Prize in 1946, author of many books including *Southern Legacy* (1950) and *Robert E. Lee and the Road of Honor* (1954). Gunnar Myrdal, the distinguished Swedish economist, is the author of *An American Dilemma* (1941), one of the most thorough examinations of the Negro problem in America. W. E. B. DuBois (1868–1963) was the noted Negro educator and author. A founder of the NAACP in 1909, leader of the Niagara Movement (1906), an early attempt by Negro leaders to end discrimination, and teacher at Atlanta University. He was the author of *The Philadelphia Negro* (1899), *The Souls of Black Folks* (1903), *Black Reconstruction* (1935). He moved to Ghana in 1961 where he became director of the Encyclopedia Africana. Ambrose Caliver was senior specialist on Negro Education in the United States Office of Education from 1930 to 1945.

but I should think that he has been perhaps the most constant and vocal opponent of Negro oppression of any of his race in the country. Says he:

> It is difficult to think of anything more important for the development of a people than proper training for their children; and yet I have repeatedly seen wise and loving colored parents take infinite pains to force their little children into schools where the white children, white teachers, and white parents despised and resented the dark child, make mock of it, neglected or bullied it, and literally rendered its life a living hell. Such parents want their children to "fight" this thing out—but, dear God, at what a cost!

He goes on:

> We shall get a finer, better balance of spirit; an infinitely more capable and rounded personality by putting children in schools where they are wanted, and where they are happy and inspired, than in thrusting them into hells where they are ridiculed and hated.

If this question is a judicial question, if it is to be decided on the varying opinions of scholars, students, writers, authorities, and what you will, certainly it cannot be said that the testimony will be all one way. Certainly it cannot be said that a legislature conducting its public schools in accordance with the wishes of its people—it cannot be said that they are acting merely by caprice or by racial prejudice.

Says Judge Parker again:

> The questions thus presented are not questions of constitutional right but of legislative policy, which must be formulated, not in vacuo or with doctrinaire disregard of existing conditions, but in realistic approach to the situations to which it is to be applied.

Once more, Your Honors, I might say, What underlied this whole question? What is the great national and federal policy on this matter? Is it not a fact that the very strength and fiber of our federal system is local self-government in those matters for which local action is competent? Is it not of all the activities of government the one which most nearly approaches the hearts and minds of people, the question of the education of their young?

Is it not the height of wisdom that the manner in which that shall be conducted should be left to those most immediately affected by it, and that the wishes of the parents, both white and colored, should be ascertained before their children are forced into what may be an unwelcome contact?

I respectfully submit to the Court, there is no reason assigned here why this Court or any other should reverse the findings of ninety years.

THE CHIEF JUSTICE: Mr. Marshall.

### REBUTTAL ARGUMENT ON BEHALF OF APPELLANTS

#### by MR. MARSHALL

MR. MARSHALL: May it please the Court, so far as the appellants are concerned in this case, at this point it seems to me that the significant factor running through all these arguments up to this point is that for some reason, which is still unexplained, Negroes are taken out of the main stream of American life in these states.

There is nothing involved in this case other than race and color, and I do not need to go to the background of the statutes or anything else. I just read the statutes, and they say, "White and colored."

While we are talking about the feeling of the people in South Carolina, I think we must once again emphasize that under our form of government, these individual rights of minority people are not to be left to even the most mature judgment of the majority of the people, and that the only testing ground as to whether or not individual rights are concerned is in this Court.

If I might digress just for a moment, on this question of the will of the people of South Carolina, if Ralph Bunche were assigned to South Carolina, his children would have to go to a Jim Crow school. No matter how great anyone becomes, if he happens to have been born a Negro, regardless of his color, he is relegated to that school.

Now, when we talk of the reasonableness of this legislation, the reasonableness, the reasonableness of the Constitution of South Carolina, and when we talk about the large body of judicial opinion in this case, I respectfully remind the Court that the exact same argument was made in the Sweatt case, and the brief in the Sweatt case contained, not only the same form, but the exact same type of appendix showing all the ramifications of the several decisions which had repeatedly upheld segregated education.

I also respectfully remind the Court that in the Sweatt case, as the public policy of the State of Texas, they also filed a public opinion poll of Texas showing that by far the majority of the people of Texas at this late date wanted segregation.

I do not believe that that body of law has any more place in this case than it had in the Sweatt case.

I think we should also point out in this regard that when we talk about reasonableness, what I think the appellees mean is reasonable insofar as the Legislature of South Carolina decided it to be reasonable, and reasonable [to the] people of South Carolina. But what we are arguing in this case is as to whether or not it is reasonableness within the decided cases of this Court on the Fourteenth Amendment. As to this particular law involved in South Carolina, the constitutional provision and the statute—the Constitution, I think, was in 1895—I do not know what this Court would have done if that statute had been brought before it at that time, but I am sure that this Court, regardless of its ultimate decision, would have tested the reasonableness of that classification, not by what the State of South Carolina wanted, but as to what the Fourteenth Amendment meant.

In the year 1952, when a statute is tested, it is not tested as to what is reasonable insofar as South Carolina is concerned; it must be tested as to what is reasonable as to this Court.

That is why we consider the case that Mr. Justice Johnson decided, cited in our reply brief, that even if this case had been tested back in those days, this Court would have felt a responsibility to weigh it against the applicable decisions of the Fourteenth Amendment, not on the question as to what is good for South Carolina.

Insofar as the argument about the states having a right to classify students on the basis of sex, learning ability, et cetera, I do not know whether they do or not, but I do believe that if it could be shown that they were unreasonable, they would feel, too, that any of the actions of the state administrative officials that affect any classification must be tested by the regular rules set up by this Court.

So we in truth and in fact have what I consider to be the main issue in this case. They claim that our expert witnesses and all that we have produced are a legislative argument at best; that the witnesses were not too accurate, and were the run-of-the-mill scientific witnesses.

But I think if it is true that there is a large body of scientific evidence on the other side, the place to have produced that was in the District Court, and I do not believe that the State of South Carolina is unable to produce such witnesses for financial or other reasons.

JUSTICE FRANKFURTER: Can we not take judicial notice of writings by people who competently deal with these problems? Can I not take judicial notice of Myrdal's book without having him called as a witness?

MR. MARSHALL: Yes, sir. But I think when you take judicial notice of Gunnar Myrdal's book, we have to read the matter, and not take portions out of context. Gunnar Myrdal's whole book is against the argument.

JUSTICE FRANKFURTER: That is a different point. I am merely going to the point that in these matters this Court takes judicial notice of accredited writings, and it does not have to call the writers as witnesses. How to inform the judicial mind, as you know, is one of the most complicated problems. It is better to have witnesses, but I did not know that we could not read the works of competent writers.

MR. MARSHALL: Mr. Justice Frankfurter, I did not say that it was bad. I said that it would have been better if they had produced the witnesses so that we would have had an opportunity to cross-examine and test their conclusions.

For example, the authority of Hodding Carter, the particular article quoted, was a magazine article of a newspaperman answering another newspaperman, and I know of nothing further removed from scientific work than one newspaperman answering another.

I am not trying—

JUSTICE FRANKFURTER: I am not going to take issue with you on that.

MR. MARSHALL: No, sir. But it seems to me that in a case like this that the only way that South Carolina, under the test set forth in this case, can sustain that statute is to show that Negroes as Negroes—all Negroes—are different from everybody else.

JUSTICE FRANKFURTER: Do you think it would make any difference to our problem if this record also contained the testimony of six professors from other institutions who gave contrary or qualifying testimony? Do you think we would be a different situation?

MR. MARSHALL: You would, sir, but I do not believe that there are any experts in the country who would so testify. And the body of law is that—even the witnesses, for example, who testified in the next case coming up, the Virginia case, all of them, admitted that segregation in and of itself was harmful. They said that the relief would not be to break down segregation. But I know of no scientist that has made any study, whether he be anthropologist or sociologist, who does not admit that segregation harms the child.

JUSTICE FRANKFURTER: Yes. But what the consequences of the proposed remedy are, is relevant to the problem.

MR. MARSHALL: I think, sir, that the consequences of the removal of the remedy are a legislative and not a judicial argument, sir. I rely on *Buchanan* v. *Warley,* where this Court said that insofar as this is a tough problem, it was tough, but the solution was not to deprive people of their constitutional rights.

JUSTICE FRANKFURTER: Then the testimony is irrelevant to the question.

MR. MARSHALL: I think the testimony is relevant as to whether or not it is a valid classification. That is on the classification point.

JUSTICE FRANKFURTER: But the consequences of how you remedy a conceded wrong bear on the question of whether it is a fair classification.

MR. MARSHALL: I do not know. But it seems to me that the only way that we as lawyers could argue before this Court, and the only way that this Court could take judicial notice of what would happen, would be that the Attorney General or some responsible individual officer of the State of South Carolina would come to this Court and say that they could not control their own state.

JUSTICE FRANKFURTER: No, that is not what I have in mind. I want to know from you whether I am entitled to take into account, in finally striking this judgment, whether I am entitled to take into account the reservation that Dr. Graham and two others, I believe, made in their report to the President.[34] May I take that into account?

MR. MARSHALL Yes, sir.

JUSTICE FRANKFURTER: May I weigh that?

MR. MARSHALL: Yes, sir.

JUSTICE FRANKFURTER: Then you have competent consideration without any testimony.

MR. MARSHALL: Yes, sir. But it is a policy matter. And that type of information, I do not believe, is more than persuasive when we consider constitutionally protected rights.

[34]Frank Graham (see n. 33, *supra*) was a member of the President's Committee on Civil Rights which in 1947 issued a comprehensive report on minority rights, entitled *To Secure These Rights.* Graham dissented from certain of the proposals recommended by the full committee.

JUSTICE FRANKFURTER: Of course, if it is written into the Constitution, then I do not care about the evidence. If it is in the Constitution, then all the testimony that you introduced is beside the point, in general.

MR. MARSHALL: I think, sir, that so far as the decisions of this Court, this Court has repeatedly said that you cannot use race as a basis of classification.

JUSTICE FRANKFURTER: Very well. If that is a settled constitutional doctrine, then I do not care what any associate or full professor in sociology tells me. If it is in the Constitution, I do not care about what they say. But the question is, is it in the Constitution?

MR. MARSHALL: This Court has said just that on other occasions. They said it in the Fifth Amendment cases, and they also said it in some of the Fourteenth Amendment cases, going back to Mr. Justice Holmes in the first primary case in *Nixon* v. *Herndon*. And I also think—I have no doubt in my mind—that this Court has said that these rights are present, and if all of the people in the State of South Carolina and most of the Negroes still wanted segregated schools, I understand the decision of this Court to be that any individual Negro has a right, if it is a constitutional right, to assert it, and he has a right to relief at the time he asserts that right.

JUSTICE FRANKFURTER: Certainly. Any single individual, just one, if his constitutional rights are interfered with, can come to the bar of this Court and claim it.

MR. MARSHALL: Yes, sir.

JUSTICE FRANKFURTER: But what we are considering and what you are considering is a question that is here for the very first time.

MR. MARSHALL: I agree, sir. And I think that the only issue is to consider as to whether or not that individual or small group, as we have here, of appellants, that their constitutionally protected rights have to be weighed over against what is considered to be the public policy of the State of South Carolina, and if what is considered to be the public policy of the State of South Carolina runs contrary to the rights of that individual, then the public policy of South Carolina, this Court, reluctantly or otherwise is obliged to say that this policy has run up against the Fourteenth Amendment, and for that reason his rights have to be affirmed.

But I for one think—and the record shows, and there is some material cited in some of the amicus briefs in the Kansas case—that all of these predictions of things that were going to happen, they have never happened. And I for one do not believe that the people in South Carolina or those southern states are lawless people.

Every single time that this Court has ruled, they have obeyed it, and I for one believe that rank and file people in the South will support whatever decision in this case is handed down.

JUSTICE FRANKFURTER: I have not heard that the bar of this case has suggested that South Carolina or Kansas will not obey whatever decree this Court hands down.

MR. MARSHALL: There was only one witness, and he was corrected by Judge Parker. That was in this particular case. So it seems to me, and I in closing would like to emphasize to the Court, if I may, that this question, the ultimate question of segregation at the elementary and high school levels, has come to this Court through the logical procedure of case after case, going all the way back to the Gaines case, and coming up to the present time.

We had hoped that we had put in the evidence into the record, the type of evidence which we considered this Court to have considered in the Sweatt and McLaurin cases, to demonstrate that at the elementary and high school levels, the same resulting evil which was struck down in the Sweatt and McLaurin cases exists, for the same reason, at the elementary and high school levels, and I say at this moment that none of that has been disputed.

The only thing put up against it is a legislative argument which would ultimately relegate the Negro appellants in this case to pleas with the Legislature of South Carolina to do what they have never done in the past, to recognize their pleas.

We therefore respectfully urge that the judgment of the United States District Court be reversed.

JUSTICE REED: Is there anything in the record which shows the purpose of the passage of the legislation of South Carolina?

MR. MARSHALL: No, sir. We did considerable research, and we had help on it. There is so much confusion and there are so many blank spots in between that we did not believe that it was in shape to give to anyone.

As a matter of fact, at that time there was a terrific objection to public education, one; and, two, an objection to the compulsory attendance laws.

So the three things got wound up together, the segregation and those two points.

JUSTICE REED: Is it fair to assume that the legislation involving South Carolina, as these cases do, was passed for the purpose of avoiding racial friction?

MR. MARSHALL: I think that the people who wrote on it would say that. You bear in mind in South Carolina—I hate to mention it—but that was right in the middle of the Klan period, and I cannot ignore that point. Considerable research in other states has shown that there were varying statements made in the debates, some of which could be interpreted as just plain race prejudice. But I think that the arguments back and forth in South Carolina, at least, you could draw no conclusion from them.

But we do know, and the authorities cited in the Government's brief in the Henderson case,[35] and, if you will remember, in the law professor's brief in the

---

[35]Henderson v. United States, 339 U.S. 816 (1950). The practice of a southern railroad permitting only one dining car table to be used by Negroes was held to violate the Interstate Commerce Act.

Sweatt case—the authorities were collected to show that the effect of this has been to place upon the Negroes this badge of inferiority.

JUSTICE REED: In the legislatures, I suppose there is a group of people, at least in the South, who would say that segregation in the schools was to avoid racial friction.

MR. MARSHALL: Yes, sir. Until today, there is a good-sized body of public opinion that would say that, and I would say respectable public opinion.

JUSTICE REED: Even in that situation, assuming, then, that there is a disadvantage ot the segregated group, the Negro group, does the legislature have to weigh as between the disadvantage of the segregated group and the advantage of the maintenance of law and order?

MR. MARSHALL: I think that the legislature should, sir. But I think, considering the legislatures, that we have to bear in mind that I know of no Negro legislator in any of these states, and I do not know whether they consider the Negro's side or not. It is just a fact. But I assume that there are people who will say that it was and is necessary, and my answer to that is, even if the concession is made that it was necessary in 1895, it is not necessary now because people have grown up and understand each other.

They are fighting together and living together. For example, today they are working together in other places. As a result of the ruling of this Court, they are going together on the higher level. Just how far it goes—I think when we predict what might happen, I know in the South where I spent most of my time, you will see white and colored kids going down the road together to school. They separate and go to different schools, and they come out and they play together. I do not see why there would necessarily be any trouble if they went to school together.

JUSTICE REED: I am not thinking of trouble. I am thinking of whether it is a problem of legislation or of the judiciary.

MR. MARSHALL: I think, sir, that the ultimate authority for the asserted right by an individual in a minority group is in a body set aside to interpret our Constitution, which is our Court.

JUSTICE REED: Undoubtedly that passes on the litigation.

MR. MARSHALL: Yes, sir.

JUSTICE REED: But where there are disadvantages and advantages, to be weighed, I take it that it is a legislative problem.

MR. MARSHALL: In so far as the state is concerned, in so far as the majority of the people are concerned. But in so far as the minority—

JUSTICE REED: The states have the right to weigh the advantages and the disadvantages or segregation, and to require equality of employment, for instance?

MR. MARSHALL: Yes, sir.

JUSTICE REED: I think that each state has been given that authority by decisions of this Court.

MR. MARSHALL: And some states have, and others have not. I think that is the main point in this case, as to what is best for the majority of the people in the states. I have no doubt—I think I am correct—that that is a legislative policy for the state legislature.

But the rights of the minorities, as has been our whole form of government, have been protected by our Constitution, and the ultimate authority for determining that is this Court. I think that is the real difference.

As to whether or not I, as an individual, am being deprived of my right is not legislative, but judicial.

THE CHIEF JUSTICE: Thank you.

MR. MARSHALL: Thank you, sir.

DOROTHY E. DAVIS, BERTHA M. DAVIS AND INEZ D. DAVIS, ETC., ET. AL.,
Appellants,

vs.

COUNTY SCHOOL BOARD OF PRINCE EDWARD COUNTY, VIRGINIA, ET AL.,
Appellees.

Case No. 191

Washington, D.C.,
Wednesday, December 10, 1952

The above-entitled cause came on for oral argument at 1:15 p.m.

APPEARANCES:

On behalf of the Appellants:
SPOTTSWOOD W. ROBINSON, III, ESQ.

On behalf of the Appellees:
T. JUSTIN MOORE, ESQ.

THE CHIEF JUSTICE: Case No. 191, Davis, et al, against County School Board of Prince Edward County, Virginia, et al.

THE CLERK: Counsel are present.

ARGUMENT ON BEHALF OF APPELLANTS

by MR. ROBINSON

MR. ROBINSON: May it please the Court, this case comes before this Court upon appeal from the final decree of the United States District Court for the Eastern District of Virginia, denying an injunction against the enforcement of section 140 of the Constitution of Virginia, and section 22-221 of the Code of Virginia, each requiring that white and colored children be taught in separate schools.

The appellants, who were the plaintiffs below, are infant high school students residing in Prince Edward County, Virginia, and their respective parents and guardians. The appellees are the County School Board of Prince Edward County and the Division Superintendent of Schools of the County, who were the original defendants below, and who as officers of the State of Virginia enforce its segregation laws, and the Commonwealth of Virginia, which intervenes as a party defendant after the filing of the action.

The complaint in this case alleged that the original defendants maintain separate schools for white and Negro high school students residing in the county, but the public high schools maintained for Negroes was unequal to the public high schools maintained for white students in plant, equipment, curricula, and other opportunities, advantages, and facilities, and that it was impossible for the infant appellants to secure public high school opportunities, advantages, and facilities equal to those afforded white children so long as the segregation laws are in force.

The complaint therefore sought a judgment declaratory of the invalidity of the laws as a denial of appellant's rights secured by the due process and equal protection clauses of the Fourteenth Amendment, and an injunction restraining the appellees from enforcing these laws or from making any distinction based upon race of color among the children attending the high schools of Prince Edward County.

In their answer, the original defendants admitted that they were enforcing the segregation laws of the State, admitted that the Negro high school was inferior in plant and equipment to the two white high schools, but denied that it was otherwise unequal and denied that segregation in the public schools contravened any provision of the federal Constitution.

After intervention by the commonwealth in its answer it made the same admissions and asserted the same defenses as did the original defendants.

There are three high schools in Prince Edward County, which are the Farmville High School and the Worsham High School, which are maintained for white students, and the Moton High School, which is maintained for Negro students.

Attendance of white children at the Farmville High School or the Worsham High School is largely determined according to the area in which the child lives. But the segregation laws of the state, so it was testified to in this record by the Division Superintendent of Schools, determine whether the child attends the Moton School, on the one side, or one of the other two schools on the other.

A three-judge District Court was convened pursuant to sections 2281 and 2284 of Title 28 of the United State Code, and at the trial both the appellants and the appellees introduced evidence, including expert testimony, first as to the extent of the existing inequalities in the Negro high school as compared with the two white high schools with respect to physical facilities and curricula, and secondly, on the issue as to whether equality of educational opportunities and benefits can ever be afforded Negro children in a racially segregated public school system.

The evidence on the second score will be summarized in a later portion of this argument.

At the conclusion of the trial, the District Court found that the Moton High School for Negroes was inferior to the white schools, not only in plant and equipment, but also in curricula and means of transportation. It ordered the appellees to forthwith provide the appellants with curricula and transportation facilities substantially equal to those afforded to white students, and to proceed with all reasonable diligence and dispatch to remove the existing inequalities by building, furnishing, and providing a high school building and facilities for Negro students in accordance with the program which the evidence for the appellees indicated would result in the availability for Negro students of a new Negro high school in September, 1953.

At the same time, the District Court refused to enjoin the enforcement of the segregation laws or to restrain the appellees from assigning school space in the county on the basis of race or color, and in its opinion it asserted the following grounds:

First, it said that on the issue of the effects of segregation in education, it accepted the decision in *Briggs* v. *Elliott*, the District Court's decision, and the decision of the Court of Appeals for the District of Columbia in *Carr* v. *Corning,*[36] cases which, as the court said, had upheld segregation and had refused to decree that it should be abolished.

Additionally, the court said that on the issue of the effects of segregation, of the effects upon the pupil resulting from the fact of segregation itself, the court could not see that the plaintiffs' evidence overbalances the defendants!

It further felt that nullification of the segregation laws was unwarranted in view of the evidence of the appellees that the segregation laws declare what the court called one of the two ways of life in Virginia, having an existence of more than eighty years, evidence that segregation had begotten greater opportunities for the Negro, including employment in Virginia alone of more Negro public-school teachers than in all thirty-one nonsegregating states, in view of evidence which was offered by the appellees that in 63 of Virginia's 127 cities and counties, the high school facilities are equal to those for whites, and in 30 of these 63 cities and counties, they are or soon will be better than those for whites, in view of the evidence, or testimony submitted by the appellees' witnesses that the involuntary elimination of segregation would lessen public interest in and support of the public schools, and would injure both races, which the court felt was, in the language of the court, "a weighted practical factor to be considered in determining whether a reasonable basis had been shown to exist for the continuation of the school segregation."

The court further felt that having found no hurt or harm to either race, that ended its inquiry, stating that it was not for the court to adjudicate the policy as right or wrong, but that the Commonwealth of Virginia must determine for itself.

An appeal was duly taken to this Court from this decision under the provisions of sections 1253 and 2101(b) of Title 28 of the United States Code.

Probable jurisdiction was noted by this Court on October 8, 1952, and presented for decision in this case are the following questions:

First, whether the segregation laws of Virginia are invalid because violative of rights secured by the due process and equal protection clauses of the Fourteenth Amendment;

Secondly, whether after finding that the buildings, facilities, curricula, and means of transportation afforded appellants were equal to those afforded whites, the court should have issued a decree forthwith restraining the appellees from excluding the infant appellants from the superior secondary school facilities of the county on the basis of race or color, and whether or not under the due process and equal protection clauses, the appellants are entitled to equality in all aspects of the public secondary educational process, including all educationally significant factors affecting the development of skills, mind, and character, in addition to equality merely in physical facilities and curricula, and whether the District Court should have so found on the evidence presented.

At the outset, I would like to place the Virginia case in what I consider to be its proper setting. Unlike *Gebhart* v. *Belton,* the Delaware case, this case does not

[36]Carr v. Corning, 182 F.2d 14 (D.C. Cir. 1950). The Court of Appeals for the District of Columbia upheld the validity of the District's segregated school system over the dissent of Judge Henry Edgerton.

present the situation of a finding of inequality of physical facilities and curricula coupled with an injunction against the continuance of segregation in these circumstances.

In this case, the District Court made a finding of inequality of physical facilities and curricula and still refused to enjoin the segregation practice in the school system in question.

Unlike *Brown* v. *Board of Education,* the Kansas case, this case does not present the situation of equal physical facilities and curricula coupled with a finding of injury resulting from the fact of segregation itself.

In this case, the facilities and curricula were found to be unequal, and the District Court erroneously, in our view, made a finding that no harm resulted to the student from the fact of segregation.

Unlike *Bolling* v. *Sharpe,* the District of Columbia case, the appellants in this case did not concede an equality of physical facilities and curricula. But like in *Bolling* v. *Sharpe* and unlike the other state cases, we urge that state-imposed educational segregation is a denial of due process, as well as a denial of the equal protection of the laws.

I submit that it is important to distinguish between two dissimilar approaches to the basic problem in this case. It has been urged that the segregation laws derive validity as a consequence of a long duration supported and made possible by a long line of judicial decisions, including expressions in some of the decisions of this Court.

At the same time, it is urged that these laws are valid as a matter of constitutionally permissible social experimentation by the states. On the matter of stare decisis, I submit that the duration of the challenged practice, while it is persuasive, is not controlling.

This Court has not hesitated to change the course of its decision, although of long standing, when error has been demonstrated, and courts are even less reluctant to examine their decisions when it is plain that the conditions of the present are substantially different from those of the past.

No court has ever considered itself irrevocably bound into the future by its prior determinations. As a matter of social experimentation, the laws in question must satisfy the requirements of the Constitution. While this Court has permitted the states to legislate or otherwise officially act experimentally in the social and economic fields, it has always recognized and held that this power is subject to the limitations of the Constitution, and that the tests of the Constitution must be met.

Upon examination in the past, it has found such experimentation to be constitutionally wanting when predicated solely on the facts of race.

JUSTICE FRANKFURTER: Mr. Robinson, if I heard you right—and I was looking at your brief to clarify my impression—if you are right, this injunction is reversible because it violates the Gaines doctrine?

MR. ROBINSON: I would submit, Mr. Justice Frankfurter, for the additional reason—that is correct, sir.

JUSTICE FRANKFURTER: Not for the additional reason. I should say it is for the prior reason. This Court ought not to pass on constitutional issues bigger than the record calls for.

MR. ROBINSON: Let me answer Your Honor's question this way. I believe, and I intend to argue, that by reason of the physical inequalities and the inequalities in curricula which the District Court found and which were supported largely by uncontradicted testimony, that alone should have justified the issuance of an injunction which would have admitted these appellants to share the high school facilities of the county without regard to race, in other words, would have unsegregated the schools at that point.

JUSTICE FRANKFURTER: We have specific appellants here, specific plaintiffs, and particular children, boys and girls, I take it—

MR. ROBINSON: That is correct, sir.

JUSTICE FRANKFURTER: —who want to get to a high school.

MR. ROBINSON: That is correct, sir.

JUSTICE FRANKFURTER: And you say that they ought to be allowed because they do not have adequate high schools with equal facilities?

MR. ROBINSON: I would answer the question this way. I do not know where they will go, sir. I do not mean to imply that all of them can get in a white high school, because I know that they cannot.

JUSTICE FRANKFURTER: I am talking about your clients.

MR. ROBINSON: That is correct, sir.

JUSTICE FRANKFURTER: And if you are right, then, any decree should have been issued according to *Gaines* v. *Canada*?

MR. ROBINSON: That is one of our decisions here. But we feel that the other question is also necessarily involved for additional reasons.

If we got that decree, I take it that it would unsegregate the schools and keep them in that fashion only so long as there would be a showing, or we would be able to maintain a showing, of physical inequality.

Now, the appellants in this case say that they will have a new Negro high school available in September of 1953.

But be that as it may, if their right to enjoy the superior facilities of public education depends upon the existence or the nonexistence of inequality, then it seems very fair to me that there is no permanency in the administration of the schools, and there is no permanency in the status of these appellants. Any way we look at the situation, it means that if the facilities are unequal, you cannot segregate. If the scope of the decision is limited to that, if the facilities are equal, you can segregate; consequently, as the facilities change in that regard, as equilibrium is disturbed by the variety of facts and circumstances present in any educational system, then under those circumstances we could have segregated or we have nonsegregated education.

JUSTICE FRANKFURTER: But this Court, constituted as it is at this moment, has faced that problem in several cases, and has decided that with inequality, the order will be issued on that basis, and we shall not borrow trouble in 1953 or 1954 or whenever it is.

MR. ROBINSON: I agree with Your Honor entirely. My understanding of the past cases has been that the basis of the decision under those circumstances has been one upon which it was pretty nearly impossible to resume segregation at some future time.

Looking at the Gaines case, for example, the factors which this Court enumerated in its opinion, in order to make out the showing of inequality, not merely inequality of physical facilities and curricula—they were there—but this Court considered, and it based its opinion upon what it termed the more important considerations which were involved in a situation of that sort. And I certainly take it that after the decision in the Sweatt case, it is no longer possible for any state to have hope of establishing a separate segregated law school for Negro students.

JUSTICE FRANKFURTER: But if Mr. Marshall is right, and your clients are going to go to present white schools, things might turn out to be so happy and so congenial and so desirable that you do not know what the result may be.

MR. ROBINSON: I am fully aware of that, if Your Honor please. But it seems to me that there should be more in the way of stability, in the disposition of a situation of this sort.

We have the matter of the administration of the schools, and also, I submit, we have the matter of the right of the pupils who are involved. And I just do not see how, if we simply rest the decision upon a narrow ground which will not afford any reasonable expectation, or let me put it this way, any sound assurance that whatever changes will occur in the system at the present time, as a consequence of those inequalities, will continue, but we might revert back to the situation where we are once the facilities are made physically equal and the same courses of instruction are put in, under those circumstances it seems to me that the normal disinclination to base a decision upon a broader ground—

JUSTICE FRANKFURTER: It is not disinclination. It is not a restriction of that order. It is not just a personal preference.

MR. ROBINSON: I understand that in the historical context, of course, considering the whole history of this nation, it is a fact that the legislation of a state should not be disturbed unless it is fatally in collision with the Constitution.

I should like to urge upon Your Honors in this connection that what we sought in this case was a permanent injunction. It seems to me that we do not get it. If we are simply limited to that particular phase of the matter, it means, as I have tried to emphasize here, that we are in a situation where we cannot depend on anything.

The schools may be unequal, if Your Honor please, tomorrow, and consequently we are shunted right on out.

JUSTICE REED: Assuming that you would be admitted by decree to the high schools that you seek to enter, would it not be necessary to admit them on a segregated basis as the law stands now?

MR. ROBINSON: Yes, I suppose so.

JUSTICE REED: As the law stands now, you will be admitted on a segregated basis?

MR. ROBINSON: That is correct, sir.

JUSTICE REED: Because you have not had a decision that below the grade of colleges you are required to have an association of students.

MR. ROBINSON: Then, of course, if Your Honor please, we might have the other situation where they will take the white students and put them into bad schools. So consequently, I think any way we look at it, I agree with Your Honor's suggestion in that regard.

I submit that at least we get to the point, it seems to me, where the basis of decision must be something more than a basis which would permit of a shuttling of pupils back and forth into segregated schools and into an unsegregated system, something which would have no assurance, and something which I cannot conduce will be helpful, either to the school authorities or to the pupils involved.

JUSTICE REED: This is not a class suit, is it?

MR. ROBINSON: Yes, it is; yes, Your Honor. We brought it as a class suit on behalf of all Negroes similarly involved.

I might say for the benefit of the Court that I do not intend to unduly consume the Court's time on behalf of the question of constitutionality per se. But in view of the fact that I do feel that the question is in the Virginia case, I would like to be indulged for just a moment to make reference to a few things that I think are particularly important.

I have just said that on examination this Court had in the past found that legislation or other types of state activity, official activity, which were predicated solely on the fact of race were unconstitutional. I was going to make reference to the decisions of this Court in the area of the ownership and occupancy of real property, the Buchanan and Shelley cases, specially.

The Takahashi case[37] opened the field of employment or occupation. Restrictions on the right to vote were *Nixon* v. *Herndon,* based solely on the question of race, and in the Court's decision, having no relationship whatsoever to the end which the legislation sought to attain; and in the area of professional and graduate education, *McLaurin* v. *the Oklahoma State Regents,* which, incidentally, was a case in which there was no inequality present at all, but quite on the grounds of other factors which the Court found to exist in the situation in which it was concluded that there was a violation of the Fourteenth Amendment.

[37]Takahashi v. Fish and Game Commission, 334 U.S. 410 (1948), held unconstitutional a California law prohibiting the issuance of fishing licenses to persons ineligible to citizenship.

JUSTICE REED: What do you conceive to be the purpose of the Virginia enactment of the statute?

MR. ROBINSON: If Your Honor please, I am in very much the same situation that counsel in the South Carolina case are. The only thing which appears in the record which might be helpful to the Court in that regard is the testimony of Doctor Colgate W. Darden, the present president of the University of Virginia, and a former Governor of the State.

That testimony commences in the record at page 451. Doctor Darden went into an examination—he gave rather an outline of the historical development of public education in Virginia, and he said, according to his testimony—and it is a fact as a check of the statutes will show—that segregation came into Virginia in pretty much the same way as it did in South Carolina, at the time when the public school system of Virginia was just getting under way.

Virginia embarked upon a broad program of public education about 1870, and the first provision with respect to the segregation of white and colored pupils appeared on the statute books of Virginia in that particular year. It did not appear in the Consitution of Virginia until about 1900.

On page 462 of the record, Doctor Darden characterized the problem before the court as a by-product, and a fearful by-product, of human slavery, and he went on to say that we are the inheritors of that system.

I think from the historical viewpoint, there is much to sustain the position that the original notion behind the school segregation laws was to impose upon Negroes disabilities which prior to the time of the adoption of the Thirteenth, Fourteenth, and Fifteenth Amendments they labored under. That is the only thing that I can offer to this Court in the way of a justification.

JUSTICE REED: You say, to impose disabilities?

MR. ROBINSON: I beg your pardon. I meant, the Thirteenth, Fourteenth, and Fifteenth Amendments were passed to eliminate disabilities which were upon the Negro prior to the time of the adoption of the Thirteenth, Fourteenth, and Fifteenth Amendments, which had as their purpose the elimination of those disabilities.

In so far as the statute is concerned, Doctor Darden speaks of it here, in his very words, as a by-product, and a fearful by-product, of human slavery.

Before moving to the next point I would like to urge upon the Court that the reasonableness or the unreasonableness of educational segregation per se at the elementary and high school levels has never been tested.

Its validity in the previous decisions of this Court has been assumed to follow from its duration and acceptance over a long period of time.

As Mr. Marshall made reference, the duration of the particular practice has not been considered by this Court in the past to prevent reexamination of the problem. We had the same thing, for example, to come before the Court in the cases dealing with this problem at the graduate and professional levels, where it came here with a history of long duration; yet the mere fact that the practice had existed for many years, the mere fact that it had become a part of the community life, did not, in the judgment of the Court, establish its validity.

The same thing is true with respect to the restrictive covenant area, the area of exclusion of Negroes from jury service, segregation of passengers in interstate commerce, all instances where there were practices of long duration, yet they were found to be constitutionally fatal, and this Court so held.

So it is our position in Virginia, on this particular score, that it should now be determined by the application of the normal constitutional standards, whether the legislation here involved meets the challenge of the Fourteenth Amendment, and we respectfully submit that upon such examination, they will be found to be lacking.

On the second point, as I have already said, the District Court found that there was physical inequality and inequality of curricula.

In these circumstances, we submit that the action which the District Court should have taken at that particular time was to have enjoined the enforcement of segregation under those circumstances.

I should also like to point out that in addition to the finding of the District Court, which is found on page 622 of the record, in which the court goes into some small amount of discussion of the extent of the inequality, our record is pretty well loaded with evidence, most of which was uncontradicted, showing physical inequalities in the various areas.

As a matter of fact, the appellees did not even bother to cross-examine the chief witness that we put on the stand, whose testimony established these inequalities.

I should like to request the attention of the Court to the fact that the Farmville High School, one of the two white high schools, is a school which is accredited by the Southern Association of Colleges and Secondary Schools, while the Moton School for Negroes is not.

As a consequence of this accreditation, the white graduate of Farmville will generally be admitted to institutions of higher learning outside the state on his record alone, while Negro graduates of Moton will generally be required to take examinations to get in, or, if admitted without examination, will be accorded only a probationary status.

Farmville also offers to its students the opportunity of membership in the National Honor Society, which creates educational motivation and affords preferences in college acceptance and employment.

Our evidence in this case shows not only these inequalities, but clearly demonstrated that these inequalities in themselves handicap Negro students in their educational endeavors and make it impossible for Negro students to obtain educational opportunities and advantages equal to those afforded white students.

While the District Court did forthwith enjoin the continuation of discrimination in curricula offerings, I think it is important to note—and this is uncontradicted on this record—that lack of, inferiority of proper facilities for teaching many of the courses prevents advantageous instruction in some of these courses, and in some instances prevents those courses from being taught at all.

Going back for just a moment, the Court will recall that the District Court here did enter an injunction requiring forthwith the elimination of discrimination with respect to transportation means and curricula, but while that is true, we are faced with the situation where, absent the particular facilities essential for teaching the course, or, if not that, the inferiority of the facilities for teaching the course, it simply is not possible, even though we have a decree which purports to forthwith equalize curricular offerings—

THE CHIEF JUSTICE: What is your solution to that problem?

MR. ROBINSON: The solution, we submit, was not the solution taken by the District Court—

THE CHIEF JUSTICE: I say, what is your solution?

MR. ROBINSON: That, under the circumstances, the Court should have immediately entered an injunction which would have prevented the school authorities from assigning school space in the county on the basis of race, would have removed—

THE CHIEF JUSTICE: If you did not have the facilities, and if you did not have the teachers, how would you take care of them, regardless of what kind of curricula you had?

MR. ROBINSON: There are a sufficient number of teachers in the county, Mr. Chief Justice, to take care of all of the students. There is a sufficient amount of school space in the county to take care of all the students.
The differences here are —

THE CHIEF JUSTICE: You mean, to take them out of this particular locality and transport them over to some other part of the county?

MR. ROBINSON: No. At the present time, if Your Honor please, we have the situation where the white children are getting these courses; Negro children are getting, not all of them, but they are getting some of these courses, anyway. But the trouble is that over in the Negro school you have these inferiorities.
Now, we submit that you cannot continue to discriminate against Negroes, or these Negro students; under the circumstances, what you do is, you simply make all the facilities in the county available to all the pupils, without restriction or assignment to particular schools on the basis of race.

THE CHIEF JUSTICE: What was the order of the District Court?

MR. ROBINSON: The District Court did not order—

THE CHIEF JUSTICE: I did not ask you what they did not do; what did they do?

MR. ROBINSON: The District Court on the matter of courses forthwith enjoined discrimination in the curricular offerings. That was the order of the District Court. I was trying to make the distinction, if the Chief Justice please, between the so-called equalization decree and what I would call an antisegregation decree.
In this regard—and I think that I have already pretty well indicated our position—we feel that in view of the fact that in this particular area we are dealing

with an exercise of state power which has been shown to affect rights which are secured by the Fourteenth Amendment, an area in which the authority of the state is subordinate to the mandate of the Amendment, that whatever the fate of educational segregation may be under other circumstances, it is perfectly plain that it cannot obtain in the face of these inequalities.

As this Court has on several occasions said, the rights which are involved are personal and present, and the Constitution does not countenance any moratorium upon the satisfaction of these particular rights.

So under the line of decisions of this Court, commencing with *Gaines* and going right straight through with *Sweatt,* we feel that the relief which I have suggested in arguing here today should have been granted by the District Court.

I should also like to point out that we feel that there are additional reasons why this equalization decree should not have been entered, and I think I can be brief in this regard, because Mr. Marshall in his argument touched upon this yesterday.

We feel that any undertaking by a court to establish or maintain constitutional equality by judicial decree simply means that the court is in the business of supervising the school system and is in there indefinitely.

We are not dealing with a physical thing. We are not dealing with a static thing. We are dealing with an educational system that has a number of variables and a number of dissimilarities. We have schools that are different in size, location, and environment, and we have teachers who differ in ability, personality, and effectiveness, and consequently their teachings vary in value.

So consequently, all up and down the educational system we are going to find points of difference. Additionally, education is an ever-growing and progressing field, and facilities and methods are constantly changing.

They get better as experience and need demonstrate the way. As a matter of fact, several of the witnesses for the appellees testified that notwithstanding an effort to provide equal buildings and facilities and equally well prepared teachers, identity of educational opportunity could not be afforded under any circumstances, and at the very best the facilities could only be made comparable or approximately equal.

Consequently, we submit that this is a task for which the Court's machinery is not entirely suited, and consequently the regulation or maintenance of constitutional equality by an equalization decree embracing, as it does, the necessity that pupils and school authorities almost constantly stay in court, should be avoided, if possible.

We have also set forth in our brief something of the history of the equalization decree in Virginia. There have been four cases in which permanent injunctions against discrimination upon a finding that there was inequality of curricula or inequality of physical facilities, have been forthcoming.

Nevertheless, in each instance it was necessary, after the decree, to have further proceedings in the court with respect to efforts to obtain that sort of educational equality.

On the final point, I should like to say this. As I indicated earlier in the argument, the evidence in Virginia was conflicting—I should put in this way. There was evidence on both sides, evidence offered by both sides on the question of harm or the effect resulting from segregation itself. The witness for the appellees—

THE CHIEF JUSTICE: What did the court say about that?

MR. ROBINSON: The court concluded that, first, it found no hurt or harm resulting from segregation to the pupils of either race.

Secondly, the court said that on the fact issue as to whether Negroes could obtain in a separate school an equal education, the court could not say that the evidence for the plaintiffs overbalanced the evidence for the defendants.

Our testimony went quite fully into the matter, and I will not bother at the present time—we set it forth in pretty good summary, I think, in our brief—to summarize it here.

But I should like to make these comments addressed to the disposition which was made of this evidence by the District Court.

Notwithstanding the fact that the District Court concluded that there was no harm or hurt to any student, upon the examination of the evidence submitted by the appellees, the situation actually is that all of their experts who testified except one admitted that there was either harm, or that there was a possibility of harm.

Additionally, on the question as to whether separate education can ever afford equal educational opportunity, the witnesses who expressed the opinion for the appellees that it was possible that there might be equality in a separate school based their conclusion upon the conditions existent in Virginia at the present time.

They were influenced by what the situation would be in the event race should be removed as a factor in the educational system, and consequently predicated the opinions under those circumstances.

We submit that under these conditions, a reexamination of this evidence will demonstrate that the conclusion of the District Court in this particular regard is without foundation and consequently it should not be held binding upon this Court.

I would like to reserve the remainder of my time for rebuttal.

JUSTICE REED: You spoke of the fact that you depended, not only on equal protection, but due process.

MR. ROBINSON: Yes, sir.

JUSTICE REED: Did I hear you make a distinction between the two?

MR. ROBINSON: I would be glad to do so at the present time.

JUSTICE REED: Is there a distinction, in your mind?

Mr. ROBINSON: I think that I can say this: Anything that due process will catch, I think equal protection will catch, in this area. But certainly a legislative enactment which makes a distinction based solely on race in the enjoyment of the educational program offered by the state, I think would be that type of arbitrary and unreasonable legislation which would be in violation of the due process clause.

JUSTICE REED: You could have a valid classification under equal protection; you could have a classification under due process?

MR. ROBINSON: That is correct, sir.

JUSTICE REED: You do not make any point on that?

MR. ROBINSON: It is also conceivable to me that you might have the other situation, though, by reason of the fact that I feel in this particular instance certainly the legislation is caught by the one or by the other.

THE CHIEF JUSTICE: Mr. Moore.

## ARGUMENT ON BEHALF OF APPELLEES

### by MR. MOORE

MR. MOORE: May it please the Court, we believe it to be particularly fortunate that the Court concluded to assume for argument all five of these cases together because while in theory each case stands on its own record, there is, of course, one main stream which runs through all of the cases, and it is obvious from the arguments already made by counsel for the appellants that that is the real question with which they are concerned, namely, to test finally, if possible, the issue as to whether the mere fact of segregation by law is a denial of equal protection.

Now, the Virginia case is one which is equally helpful, I believe not only in respect of its own setting, but in its bearing on these other cases.

I am going to undertake in the discussion of this case to deal with it in that sort of way, not merely from the standpoint of our case, but also in its bearing on the other.

There are several distinctive features of this Virginia case that I want to call to Your Honors' attention at the outset. The first is the nature of the record that you find here. You were impressed, I am sure, with the fact that you have a much larger record. We believe that was not unnecessarily made large. When we were requested to represent this little county of Prince Edward and also to be associated with the Attorney General in the representation of the commonwealth, we found that there had been these four or five cases in the federal court where the question of inequality of facilities had been the issue, and that was the only issue. Where the courts had found that to exist, they promptly made decrees requiring equalization.

We also found that the state had undertaken an amazing program of expenditures of money and expansion of the public school system, particularly over the last twenty years, with the view to making the facilities equal for Negroes and whites, so that perhaps with the exception of the State of North Carolina, Virginia stands probably at the top among all these southern states in that program, which I am going to refer to more fully a little later.

But we also found in comparing and getting the benefit of the Kansas and the South Carolina case, which has just been heard, that these appellants had laid all this great stress on what they call the psychological issue. But we also found that there was quite a conflict of opinion among the experts on that matter.

So we undertook to prepare a full record, and Your Honors would find, when you browse through this record that you have, instead of, as in the Kansas case where all of these teachers and educators and psychologists testified on one side, and in the South Carolina case on the appellant's side—you find a great array of very distinguished persons who testified in the Virginia case in direct conflict on this crucial question of fact.

So the first distinctive feature is the fuller record.

The second distinctive feature is the difference in the findings of the court.

The court, in contrast to the Kansas case, based upon the historical background in Virginia and upon all this evidence, found on the crucial questions which these gentlemen had stressed so much that they failed to prove their case, even on that point.

That is one of the main distinctive features in this case.

There also will be presented the difference as compared to, with the Kansas case, as to the great impact that would result in Virginia from a sudden elimination of segregation.

Now, those are among the issues. There is this other distinctive feature, which I should mention at the outset. This case on this point is similar to the South Carolina case, in large degree, because when the case of South Carolina was tried, the facilities were not yet completed on the first trial, and were not completed on the second hearing. But when the case reaches this Court, they have been completed.

Now, Virginia is just a little bit behind South Carolina in that respect. But there is no doubt about it, no question from this record, that the funds are in hand, the buildings are going up, and the facilities will be equal by next September.

Those are the four principal distinctive features.

Now, may it please the Court, in undertaking to make a very brief statement of the case, as to how the issues come here, there are several facts that I believe should be brought to your attention at the outset. This case arises in a comparatively small county of the 100 counties of Virginia, Prince Edward County. It has only about 15,000 population. It has one town of any size, much, in it the town of Farmville, where the old Hampden-Sydney College is located.

The population is divided about 52 per cent Negro and 48 per cent white in the county. The school population is higher among the Negroes than that figure. There is about 60 per cent of the school population that is Negro and 40 per cent white.

So, roughly, you may regard the situation as being one where the ratio is about three to one, whites three to one. Now, these appellants are high school students. This case relates entirely to high school students. The South Carolina case was elementary and high school. These cases vary. But this is strictly a high school.

JUSTICE BLACK: What did you say about the three to one?

MR. MOORE: I said that the ratio is about three whites to one Negro.

JUSTICE BLACK: Where?

MR. MOORE: Throughout the state. I am sorry, I did not clear that up.

JUSTICE BLACK: I thought you were referring to the county. That is quite different.

MR. MOORE: That is right. I am sorry.

Now, in the county, I should mention that this is a rather poor county financially, in the state. It has an assessed value of only about $9,500,000. The total assessed property, on the ratio of assessment of about 50 per cent—the total real and personal property value is about $18,500,000.

Now, there are three high schools in the county, two for white and one for Negro. As might be expected, they are not identical. In the three high schools in 1951, there were 400 white children and 460 Negro children.

In standing, the Farmville High School was shown to be the best high school. That is, the white high school in Farmville. The next is the Moton School, the Negro school at Farmville, and the worst is the Worsham, which is a white school, a small combination high school and elementary school.

Now, one of the principal reasons why the Moton School, which, as Your Honors will realize, is named for the distinguished colored educator,[38] who, by the way, was educated largely in Virginia, where there was segregation—one of the main reasons why Farmville is ranked first is because of the unequal growth in school population in the last ten years, particularly among the Negroes. The record shows that the Negro pupils increased in the last ten years 225 per cent, but unfortunately whites have declined about 25 per cent.

The school authorities, in view of that increase in Negro attendance, particularly in view of that, made a survey in 1947 as to school requirements, approval, and so on. And they finally have approved a program which the record shows will cost about $2,500,000 in all to carry out, with about $2 million of that being allocated for Negro schools, and about $500,000 for white schools.

Now, among other things, one of the main things in the financing program was a new Negro high school in place of the existing Moton School. They were trying to arrange a bond issue for that, but unfortunately, in April and May, there was a two week strike called in the Negro school, which the Negro principal claimed that he could not control. The record indicates—and the matter was argued in the District Court—that the strike was really inspired by outsiders.

However that may be, the strike came at a very unfortunate time. It lasted two weeks. But that absolutely put an end to any bond issue.

The school authorities then undertook to raise the money for the new school from the state, and the state, which does have ample funds in Virginia, I am glad to say, through two sources, provided all the funds required. We have what is called a Battle Fund in Virginia, which is named after our present Governor, Governor Battle, and I am going to refer to that a little later after lunch. But it is a great source of money for these purposes, and about $250,000 out of the $900,000 required for the new Negro school was granted from that fund, and the remaining $600,000 was made in the way of a loan from the Literary Fund at two per cent.

Now, this suit was filed in May of last year, shortly after the strike, and as I said, it broke up the bond issue, but the state provided the funds, so that we are in the fortunate position of having the cash, the building is right under way, there is no question about the fact from the record and from the decree of the court that it is going to be completed.

[38]Robert R. Moton (1867–1940), educator and teacher, succeeded Booker T. Washington as head of the Tuskegee Institute.

THE CHIEF JUSTICE: Has that money been obtained, and firm commitments made?

MR. MOORE: Yes, sir, all that has gone in the record.

THE CHIEF JUSTICE: When?

MR. MOORE: The money was obtained finally in June of 1951. You see, they were on the program of the bond issue when the strike created such a public sentiment that it was felt that they could not carry that through.

THE CHIEF JUSTICE: What is the present situation in regard to the building program?

MR. MOORE: The building is under way.

THE CHIEF JUSTICE: What do you mean by "under way," Mr. Moore?

MR. MOORE: It is about 25 to 30 per cent complete. A firm contract is made. The funds are available to be drawn on from the state, just as the funds are needed, and the record shows that there is no reason why the school should not be in operation, a better school than any school in the county or that whole area, by next September.

Now, the challenge which was presented in this trial, which required five days—the case was very fully heard—was on two grounds:

First, it was said that on the basis of the federal precedent the segregation in the schools at the high school level violated constitutional standards. On that issue, the court held, "We cannot say that Virginia's separation of white and colored children in the public schools is without substance in fact or reason. We have found no hurt or harm to either race."

I was astonished at the statement that my friend—I will defer that until we come back.

(Whereupon, at 2:00 o'clock p.m., the Court recessed to reconvene at 2:30 o'clock p.m.)

MR. MOORE: May it please the Court, when the Court rose for its luncheon recess, I had just mentioned the first of two very important findings that we feel the trial court made here.

The first was that on the basis of the record made, they found that the separation scheme that had been in effect in Virginia through these eighty years—we cannot say that it was without foundation in fact or reason, and there was no hurt or harm to either race.

Now, there is another finding. These are set out at great length there in the record at pages 19 through 21, and the facts proved in our case presently demonstrate or potently demonstrate, why nullification of the cited sections is not warranted.

In those pages of the opinion Judge Bryan, sitting with Judge Dobie and Judge Hutcheson,[39] had given a very much more adequate answer, may it please

---

[39]Judge Albert V. Bryan (1899–     ) served on the Eastern District Court of Virginia from 1947 to 1961 when he was appointed to the Fourth Circuit Court of Appeals. Judge C. Sterling Hutcheson (1894–     ) sat in the Virginia District Court from 1944.

Your Honor, Justice Reed, than our friends on the other side did to your question as to what was the real basis and, therefore, I was about to comment when we adjourned for lunch that I was very astonished at the comment that had just been made that there was such a scanty record.

Judge Bryan, in the opinion, went back and traced the history of this scheme to the acts of 1869 and 1870 in Virginia, with the various changes in those laws that were passed right during the reconstruction period when, as everyone knows, there was this zeal involved in protecting the Negroes' rights, but stemming right from the first Act of 1869–1870, the law has been substantially the way it is today.

Instead of President Darden of the University leaving the matter, as our friend on the other side suggested, if Your Honors would look at page 456 of the record, you will see a very much more illuminating comment, where he goes on to show quite a bit about this history.

Of course, this system did spring out of the system which was in effect in the South before the war, but because it sprang out of that system it does not follow that there was any intent to continue a form of slavery or form of servitude such as here argued.

He goes ahead and points out there that actually in the consideration of the Underwood constitution,[40] there were twenty-two Negroes in the convention, and they were split eleven to eleven—eleven voting against the proposal to include a prohibition against segregation. That was obviously because of the friction that was involved arising out of that period.

Now, there is another set of facts here that I believe to be very pertinent. We observe that during the argument of our opponents, there was distributed among the Justices of the Court, two very interesting sheets, which we were not able to obtain until a few days ago, from the Census, and you will see from those sheets that the problem, as exists in these seventeen states that have segregation, and the District of Columbia, is a very different problem from many of the other states.

You will observe on that first sheet entitled, "Relationship of White and Negro Population," that there is a factor of 10 per cent of the total population of the country today that is Negro, about 15 million, it is very interesting to see how that is distributed.

In the seventeen states and in theDistrict of Columbia, the total population in those states that is Negro is 20.5 per cent; in all these other states it is 4.6 per cent. But there is a concentration of the Negro population in those seventeen states and the District to the extent of approximately 70 per cent.

In the second sheet you will observe that there is a variation all the way from about one tenth of one percent in Vermont to 45 per cent in Mississippi, with about 22 per cent in Virginia, Justice Black—that is where I was confused just a moment ago, as you will see right there.

It is perfectly clear that that situation is a very pertinent thing in the consideration of this matter.

---

[40]John C. Underwood (1809–1873) was a judge for the federal Circuit Court for Virginia in the Reconstruction years (1864–1873). He presided over the constitutional convention of 1868 which drafted a new Virginia constitution ratified in modified form in 1869.

JUSTICE REED: Have you carried it out into the counties?

MR. MOORE: We do not have it in the counties. As a matter of fact, we had much difficulty getting it from the Census people to this extent. We have got it for the county that is in question here. I gave that just before we adjourned for lunch.

Sixty per cent of the school population is Negro in this county to 40 per cent white, and the total population is 52 per cent Negro and 48 per cent white.

May I just undertake in my remaining time to address myself very briefly to four questions which we believe are the controlling questions in this case: First, while we know that Your Honors are so familiar with the precedents that are here talked about so much, we do not feel we could do justice to this case without referring to them, at least briefly, and I then want to refer briefly to what we call the Virginia situation as shown on these facts and, third, I want to mention briefly the expert evidence that became so important in this case and, fourthly, I wish to talk briefly about the point that Justice Frankfurter mentioned a moment ago as to what is the kind of decree or remedy that should be granted in a situation like this where, as distinguished from South Carolina, we have not quite got our facilities in shape, although they have been able to do that in South Carolina. I am going to take up those four matters in that order just as briefly as I can.

Mr. Davis stressed in his argument so far as background for the issue, the main issue in all these cases, the question as to whether separation by law is per se a violation of equal protection. He stressed the legislative history primarily.

There is an equally important area, we believe, involving the legal precedents.

Of course, all these cases come down finally to the question as to whether this type of case falls over into the category of *Gong Lum* —really that is the closest case; *Plessy* v. *Ferguson* is, of course, its forerunner, but do they fall under the doctrine of *Gong Lum* or do they fall under the *Sweatt* v. *Painter,* and *McLaurin;* that is the real crucial question.

I am not going to labor the point. Judge Parker has worked it out better than any of these other courts have. He has done that better, more fully, but you have got not only these statutes that have been passed, but this large body of decisions which certainly over a period of eighty years has recognized that the thing that is existing here in the South, particularly, as you saw from those sheets, is a thing that has become a part of a way of life, as our court said in our case, in the South.

It is plainly based on real reason, and if that is so, then there is no reason why the equal facilities, equal but separate facilities, doctrine should not apply.

What the court held in *Sweatt* v. *Painter,* and in *McLaurin,* was that on the facts, that at that level equality could not be provided.

Now, we took the trouble here to obtain—there are three very distinguished experts that testified in our case, right on that point, that there are great differences at the high school level on this question as to whether equality of not only facilities and curricula and all can be afforded as compared with the graduate and professional schools.

We did not have to rely simply upon what the Court might take notice of, but Your Honors will find the testimony of Dr. Lindley Stiles, who is the head of the Department of Education of the University of Virginia, a man with wide experience all over the country, teaching and supervising segregated schools and⁻

nonsegregated schools, who stressed that there was a difference in that level at adolescent age; you find Dr. Henry E. Garrett, head of the Department of Psychology of Columbia University, who testified at great length on this subject; and then Dr. Dabney L. Lancaster, the president of Longwood College in Virginia, stresses that situation.

Now, there the gist of their testimony was that equality of opportunity really could be provided and, possibly better provided, at the high school level with separate schools provided you had equal facilities, just as good teachers, just as good curricula, and all the facilities that go along with it.

On that basis there is no occasion to approach this matter from the standpoint of *Sweatt v. Painter,* and *McLaurin.*

It is shown right here definitely—and that is what Judge Bryan's opinion rests on—it is shown by evidence that at this level you have not got the problem that exists at the graduate and professional school level.

These gentlemen on the other side at great length, cite a long line of cases in this Court which they say are pertinent, and which we contend are not pertinent, and I just list them and state our position.

They mention cases like these: The Jury Duty case,[41] the Right to Vote case,[42] the Right to the Fishing License,[43] the Florida Shepherd case,[44] the Right to Participate in Primary Elections,[45] the Right to Own Property,[46] *Shelley* v. *Kraemer,* and then they rely upon these commerce cases, *Morgan* v. *Virginia,* and the recent Chance case.[47]

Those cases are not comparable here. There you had a complete denial of a right. The question of separation but with equal facilities and equal opportunities really did not exist in those cases; there was a denial, a complete denial.

What really happened, as we see it, in the appellants' theory is that we believe they are quite confused. They come here and they first make their attack in this way: They say that the doctrine, the separate but equal doctrine, just per se amounts to an offense to the Constitution, the Fourteenth Amendment.

Now that, of course, as was pointed out in the first case, the Kansas case

---

[41]Strauder v. West Virginia, 100 U.S. 308 (1880), see n. 24, *supra.* See also Cassell v. Texas, 339 U.S. 282 (1950). A murder conviction was reversed when it appeared Negroes had been systematically excluded from a grand jury panel that had returned the indictment.

[42]Nixon v. Condon, 286 U.S. 73 (1932). The Court invalidated a resolution of the Executive Committee of the Democratic Party in Texas allowing only whites to participate in a primary election.

[43]Takahashi v. Fish and Game Commission, 334 U.S. 410 (1948), see n. 37, *supra.*

[44]Shepherd v. Florida, 341 U.S. 50 (1951). A conviction for rape was reversed on the authority of Cassell v. Texas, 339 U.S. 282 (1950), since Negroes had been systematically excluded from the grand jury that indicted the Negro defendants.

[45]Nixon v. Herndon, 273 U.S. 536 (1927), Smith v. Allwright, 321 U.S. 649 (1944), and Terry v. Adams, 345 U.S. 461 (1953).

[46]Buchanan v. Warley, 245 U.S. 60 (1917), see n. 23, *supra.* See also Oyama v. California, 332 U.S. 633 (1948).

[47]Chance v. Lambeth, 186 F.2d 879 (4th Cir. 1951). The Court of Appeals for the Fourth Circuit declared invalid a private railroad regulation attempting to segregate passengers in its trains.

yesterday, is just a direct attack on *Plessy* v. *Ferguson,* and the *Gong Lum* doctrine.

But then they come along and make a second contention. They say that as long as there is separation then, as a matter of fact, there cannot be equality, and the only basis they have for urging that is to draw on this so-called expert testimony of the psychologists, and they say that because of that line of testimony you can never attain equality as a fact.

Now, in the Virginia case, we meet head-on on that issue. It may be, as some of the questions from Your Honors have indicated, that, perhaps, all of that testimony may be irrelevant. If we are right in our first proposition that *Gong Lum* is still the law then, perhaps, all that testimony may be irrelevant. But we did not want to take any chances in the Virginia case. We knew that there was this great body of expert opinion which was in conflict with that which had been presented without conflict in Kansas and in South Carolina, and we presented it. So that if, as a fact, that issue becomes important, we have met it head-on, and we have a finding of the court in our favor.

May I just refer very briefly to what, for short, I may call the Virginia scene in which this whole problem arises?

Of course, it is obvious that it is not just Prince Edward County that is involved or Clarendon County, South Carolina, it is a state-wide question, and this record abounds with information that shows that over the last twenty years there has been a tremendous movement springing largely with the position that Dr. Lancaster, now the head of Longwood College, at Farmville, Virginia, right where this controversy arose, while he was the head of the Department of Education, he saw ahead that this problem was going to arise in the way in which it has, and the state, under his sponsorship, and his successors, put on this tremendous program which, perhaps, except for North Carolina, is the greatest program in the South, of expending these huge sums for building up these facilities.

You have a situation today where the State of Virginia has every reason to be proud of what has been accomplished, although complete perfection has not yet been attained in every one of the counties and cities of the state.

Let me give you just a few figures. As Dr. Darden pointed out, public education somewhat dragged in Virginia until about 1920. At that time there were only 31,000 high school students in the state. Today there are 155,000.

During these last ten years the state, according to this record, has reached the point where the Negro salaries have been equalized with the whites throughout; there are actually more four-year college graduates among the Negro teachers in Virginia than there are white teachers.

The Negro expenditures in this state have increased 161 per cent as compared with 123 per cent.

According to a survey that was put in evidence in our case, it appeared that approximately one-half of the counties and cities in the state are now or within a very short time will be carrying out programs now in effect—will be on the basis of as good as or better than the whites.

As a matter of fact, in the city of Richmond, the finest high school in the city is a Negro high school, and at Charlottesville there has just been completed the finest high school for Negroes that there is in all that area.

Now, as an indication of what has been accomplished—I sound as if we are trying to brag in comparison with South Carolina, and we do not mean it that way, but we believe these figures are very pertinent, Your Honors. We are telling that to you because we have no other way of getting these facts to you except by telling them to you.

In Virginia we have put on this program that I referred to as the Battle Fund. It is $60 million as compared with the $75 million in South Carolina.

Of that amount, $10 million have already been allocated for the Negroes, and $18 million for the whites. They are getting much more than their share.

We have this tremendous Literary Fund, as it is called in Virginia. We are more fortunate in Virginia financially than many of the states, and through that fund, loans are being made to these schools, with the Negroes greatly benefiting in proportion.

Of the $48 million that have been loaned out of—comparing the $48 million loaned for whites, are $16.5 million loaned for the Negroes at 2 per cent interest, at a 2 per cent interest rate.

THE CHIEF JUSTICE: Are those loans made to the boards of education?

MR. MOORE: That is right, sir, at 2 per cent and that was the $600,000 in this $900,000 program for this very high school. So you see the funds are really right there in hand. There is no trouble about going out with a sales tax like our friends have to do in South Carolina.

We have got the money, and we have got a contract, and we have got a court decree which tells us that we have got to go ahead as quickly as possible.

Now, there is just one more fact in this connection, and I am through with this point. It is very striking that in the four-year plan that the board of education has adopted there are 168 projects for whites, with 73 projects for Negroes, involving for whites $189 million, may it please Your Honors.

Just think of what that means in taxation and in burdens to the people of Virginia in carrying out this program, with $74.5 million for Negroes. In other words, they are sharing in all this huge program in a ratio of about two to one, although their ratio in the state is only about 22 per cent.

In view of all that, the court could not find that this program, so important to the welfare of the people of Virginia, rested on prejudice, but it represented a way of life, and it represented a firm determination on the part of the people of Virginia, because they were able to bear the burden better than many of the Southern states, but they were fully committed in good faith to provide for the Negro child just as good education as a white child could get, and they were doing it and, therefore, the court found that they could not find that that program rested on prejudice.

Now, isn't that of some importance in this matter when this matter reaches the stage of this Court? The trial court said that they found that the program rested neither upon prejudice nor caprice nor upon any nebulous foundation but rather the proof is that it declares one of the ways of life in Virginia.

May I just very briefly refer to this expert testimony because, perhaps that, together with the difference in findings of the court, is the most distinctive thing about this case.

We are glad to get the benefit among our brethren involved in the other cases, if that be appropriate, with their testimony.

We were able to profit by the trials in these other cases. They could have gotten the experts if they had deemed it essential or relevant to do it. They, proceeding in their own way, considered in the light of the decisions of this Court and the numerous decisions of the state courts that all that line of expert testimony presumably was irrelevant.

Now, the statement is made here that time after time there is consensus of opinion among social scientists that segregation is bad.

I was interested in the appendix which is signed by some thirty-two alleged social scientists who say that appendix is out on the frontiers of scientific knowledge; that is the way they describe it.

When you examine that appendix you find that five of the persons who signed that appendix were cross-examined in our case, and the appendix is really just an effort—I say this without any lack of respect—but it is just an effort to try to rehabilitate those gentlemen and add to it with some other persons.

Now, it is our view that when you consider the expert evidence on the two sides in this case, it is perfectly clear that the trial court was justified in finding as they did.

Let me just briefly give you a description as to the kind of expert testimony that was presented in the Virginia case. Some of these witnesses apparently travel around over the country quite a bit testifying in these cases.

There were four principal experts for the plaintiffs in our case: A man named Dr. John J. Brooks, who runs an experimental school in New York where about three hundred students attend, and he tries to get a cross section of the population, a certain number of whites, a certain number of Negroes, and a certain number of others.

He has had practically—he had no experience in Virginia. He had a little experience in Georgia. He testified, in effect, that he felt that segregation was bad.

The next was Dr. Brewster Smith, who was a professor of psychology at Vassar. His chief contribution was that he considered that as a matter of principle segregation in the abstract was an official insult. That is about what his testimony finally boiled down to.

One of the most interesting witnesses was Dr. Isidor Chein. He has written a great deal on this subject, and he testified as to a questionnaire that he had sent out to some 850 social scientists, he said, asking them two main questions: First, as to whether or not in their view segregation was harmful to those segregated; secondly, was it harmful to those who did not segregate, and he said that the replies he got were some 500, and that some 90 per cent of the people who answered said that it was bad on both groups.[48]

We showed on cross-examination and otherwise that there were some six or eight thousand persons who were eligible to have that questionnaire sent to them;

[48]Dr. Isidor Chein was Director of Research of the Commission on Community Relations of the American Jewish Congress. The article referred to is Deutscher and Chein, "The Psychological Effect of Enforced Segregation: A Survey of Social Science Opinion," 26 Journal of Psychology 259 (1948).

we showed that only thirty-two came from south of the Mason and Dixon line, and he was unable to show a single one from Virginia, and what you wind up with is that you get a statement in the air as sort of a moral principle—it is kind of a religious statement that you get—that, in principle or in theory, in the abstract that segregation is a bad thing to have.

JUSTICE FRANKFURTER: Mr. Moore, of what would the six or eight thousand people be specialists in or of?

MR. MOORE: Well, there is a great line—

JUSTICE FRANKFURTER: Who are these specialists in that field?

MR. MOORE: Well, they described them as sociologists, anthropologists, psychologists, and variations of those groups, principally, Your Honor.

JUSTICE FRANKFURTER: Everybody in the sociological field is an expert in his domain?

MR. MOORE: That is right, Your Honor.

We say it does not mean a thing except as a matter of starting something in the abstract. You might as well be talking about the Sermon on the Mount or something like that, that it would be better—

JUSTICE FRANKFURTER: It is supposed to be a good document.

MR. MOORE: Well, I say you might as well be asking people whether it is desirable for everybody to try to live according to the Sermon on the Mount as to ask them the kind of questions that they had put to them.

Now, let us look for a moment at the experts we called. We had eight people who testified, who were especially familiar with conditions in Virginia and in the South.

We started at the lower level with the superintendent of education, Mr. J. I. McIlwaine, who had been the superintendent for over thirty years in that very area.

We then moved up to the next level. We took the present superintendent of education of the state, Dr. Dowell J. Howard: we took the ex-superintendent, Dr. Lancaster.

Then we moved up to the university level. We took Dr. Stiles, who has had this broad knowledge and experience all over the country, as the head of the Department of Education, and then took Dr. Darden, and took them, and then we followed through with three other kinds of experts. We called a leading child psychiatrist, Dr. William H. Kelly, a leading man in all our area, who testified and who had wide experience all over the country; as a matter of fact, in the war among the soldiers and what not, he had such experience.

We then called a clinical psychologist, Mr. John N. Buck, who had had wide experience, and then—our friends like to chide us with the fact that our star witness was Dr. Garrett—they would have given their right eye to have gotten Dr. Garrett. He happened to be the teacher in Columbia of two of their experts, this very Dr. Clark who made these doll tests, and who studied under Dr. Garrett.

Dr. Garrett, it so happened, was born and raised very near this very place where this controversy arose in Virginia. He was educated in the Richmond public schools and at the University of Richmond, and then he went on to Columbia, and finished his graduate work, and for years has been a leading professor of psychology, years the head of the department of psychology, with some twenty-five professors and assistant professors under him, with wide experience as an adviser to the War Department in connection with the psychological tests among soldiers during the war.

I have not time—my time is going by so fast, I see it is almost gone—and I must read you one or two things about what Dr. Garrett said about this thing.

He said this. He said:

> What I have said was that in the State of Virginia, in the year 1952, given equal facilities, that I thought, at the high school level, the Negro child and the white child—who seem to be forgotten most of the time—could get better education at the high school level in separate schools, given those two qualifications; equal facilities and the state of mind in Virginia at the present time.
>
> If a Negro child goes to a school as well equipped as that of his white neighbor, if he had teachers of his own race and friends of his own race, it seems to me he is much less likely to develop tensions, animosities, and hostilities, than if you put him into a mixed school where, in Virginia, inevitably he will be a minority group.

Then he says again:

> It seems to me that in the State of Virginia today, taking into account the temper of its people, its mores, and its customs and background, that the Negro student at the high school level will get a better education in a separate school than he will in mixed schools.

It is a better education he is talking about because of this friction that would arise and these eighty years of history in Virginia.

Is all that to be ignored? Is that not, Your Honor, Justice Frankfurter, a basis for classification with eighty years in this background, just as in the pilot case you mentioned yesterday—I was not familiar with it yesterday until you mentioned it, but I read it this morning, but it is very important, the historical background in the light of this testimony.

JUSTICE REED: What am I to draw from this argument that you are making now?

MR. MOORE: I think you are to draw—evidently I have not been successful, as successful as I had hoped.

JUSTICE REED: Perhaps I should express my question a little more fully.

MR. MOORE: Yes.

JUSTICE REED: What if they had decided to the contrary?

MR. MOORE: You mean the trial court?

JUSTICE REED: The trial court; and your experts had not been so persuasive as they were, and there were other experts, and the trial court had accepted their conclusion that this was detrimental and was injurious to the ability of the Negro child to learn or of the white child to learn, and created great difficulties, what difference does it make which way they decided this particular question?

MR. MOORE: I think you can argue the matter two ways, Your Honor. I think, in the first place, you can argue that the difference, for instance, in the Kansas finding and the Virginia finding point up how important is the legislative policy that is involved, that Mr. Davis talked about so much this morning. It just illustrates how it really is a policy question.

JUSTICE REED: I can understand that. But is it your argument that there are two sides to it?

MR. MOORE: It illustrates there are two sides to it, and it points up that the real crux of the whole matter is that there is involved fundamentally a policy question for legislative bodies to pass on, and not for courts.

Now, in the second place, it emphasizes, I hope, that the historical background that exists, certainly in this Virginia situation, with all the strife and the history that we have shown in this record, shows a basis, a real basis, for the classification that has been made.

JUSTICE REED: There has been a legislative determination in Virginia?

MR. MOORE: That is right, sir.

JUSTICE REED: That the greatest good for the greatest number is found in segregation?

MR. MOORE: That is right; with these lawmakers continuously since 1870 doing their job to do their best in the general welfare.

It is significant that the Virginia statutes since 1870 have contained straight through a requirement that there should not only be a separation, but there should be treatment with equality and with efficiency all the way through; that is the policy.

My time is almost up.

JUSTICE JACKSON: Suppose Congress should enact a statute, pursuant to the enabling clause of the Fourteenth Amendment, which nobody seems to attach any importance to here, as far as I have heard, that segregation was contrary to national policy, to the national welfare, and so on, what would happen?

MR. MOORE: Your Honor, we thought of that in here, and that is a big question, as you realize.

JUSTICE JACKSON: That is why I asked it.

MR. MOORE: Our view of the matter is that it should not be held valid in this Court; that the only effective way to accomplish that is to be done through an act of Congress, which would be by amending the Constitution.

JUSTICE JACKSON: You think that the Fourteenth Amendment would not be adequate to do that?

MR. MOORE: We do not believe so, and I have not the time and I have no desire to engage in this very interesting discussion that Justice Burton and Justice Frankfurter engaged in, as to whether there is any difference through the passage of time and through progress which has been made between the commerce clause and the Fourteenth Amendment.

But I would suggest in that connection that it certainly is much more easy to find facts that demonstrate that as progress has gone on, such as in *Morgan* v. *Virginia,* where the separation of race on the interstate buses is involved, it is much easier to find facts which will show, as time has gone on, that there should be a different application than there is where a question of equal protection is involved.

We believe, as Mr. Davis pointed out this morning, I think touching this same point, although very slightly, that the Fourteenth Amendment here should be viewed in the light of what was really intended, and what was understood by Congress and by the legislatures at that time.

JUSTICE FRANKFURTER: But Justice Jackson's question brings into play different questions and different considerations, Mr. Moore, because the enabling act of the Fourteenth Amendment is itself a provision of the Fourteenth Amendment; patently Congress looked forward to implementing legislation; implementing legislation patently looked forward to the future, and if Congress passed a statute doing that which is asked of us to be done through judicial decree, the case would come here with a pronouncement by Congress in its legislative capacity that in its view of its powers, this was within the Fourteenth Amendment and, therefore, it would come with all the heavy authority, with the momentum and validity that a congressional enactment has.

Mr. MOORE: That may be so, your Honor, but that is another case.

JUSTICE FRANKFURTER: That is a good answer.

MR. MOORE: Yes, it is another case.

JUSTICE JACKSON: I wonder if it is. I should suppose that your argument that this was a legislative question might have been addressed to the proposition that the enforcement of the Fourteenth Amendment, if this were deemed conflicting, might be for the Congress rather than for this Court. I would rather expect and I had rather expected to hear that question discussed. But you apparently are in the position that no federal agency can supersede the state's authority in this matter which, I say, you have good precedents for arguing.

MR. MOORE: Your Honor will appreciate that you have asked a question that to try to answer adequately requires a lot more time than I have got.

JUSTICE FRANKFURTER: I understood you to say that that is a different case—

MR. MOORE: That is right.

JUSTICE FRANKFURTER: (Continuing)—meaning that you do not have an act of Congress.

MR. MOORE: That is right, sir. Now, of course, in the District—

JUSTICE JACKSON: What I am trying to get at is, do you attach any importance to the fact that there is not any act of Congress? Apparently you do not, because there could not be one.

MR. MOORE: I am very glad there is not; yes, sir, I am very pleased with that anyway.

May I just take one more minute or two? I wanted to take a couple of minutes on this last question that Justice Frankfurter asked, because it is a very important point in our case, and I would like to take a moment.

The question is posed as to whether or not we are in a different position in Virginia rather than that in the South Carolina case because our building is not yet finished.

I do not think so. In line with the doctrine that Your Honor, Justice Frankfurter, saw this Court declare in *Eccles* v. *Peoples Bank*,[49] there certainly must be some leeway here in a court of equity and in a declaratory judgment proceeding.

Our friend on the other side, Mr. Marshall, said yesterday he realized there must be a transition period. We are operating under a court decree which says, "Do that thing right now."

THE CHIEF JUSTICE: He was talking then, was he not, about segregation, and if it should be held that segregation per se was invalid, then he would be willing to let some time pass.

But as I have understood him here, he says it is of the present, and it should be here admitted presently.

Mr. MOORE: Well, the short answer here really is that as a practical matter in the situation we are in with the building under construction, under the court decree, with our knowing it is going to be ready in September, all we could really do practically would be to close the schools down until June, and then come along with equality.

Now, we do not believe that is in the interest of anybody.

I am sorry, I have encroached a little bit on Judge Almond's time. Judge Almond, the Attorney General, desires the remainder of the time.

### ARGUMENT ON BEHALF OF THE APPELLEES

#### by MR. ALMOND

MR. ALMOND: May it please the Court, just a few minutes are available to our side in which I would like to discuss with the Court what we conceive to be the historical background of this question in Virginia.

The question posed yesterday, or the remark made by Mr. Justice Frankfurter, is whether or not in the minds of some it may represent man's inhumanity to man or whether or not Virginia and the other Southern states made these provi-

---

[49]333 U.S. 426 (1948). The Court dismissed an action under the Declaratory Judgment Act by a bank against the Board of Governors of the Federal Reserve Board on the ground that the bank's grievance was too remote and speculative.

sions in its law, its statute, and its constitution, for the separation of the races in the field of education because she had the power to do it or, as answered by our worthy opponent, Mr. Robinson, this morning, that it was placed there to place disabilities upon the Negro.

Prior to 1865 there were no public free schools in Virginia supported by any government, state or local.

In 1865 kind missionaries from New England came into Virginia and established schools on a separate basis for the Negro children of former slaves.

The people were impoverished, and the poor white people—and nearly all of them were poor because the land was ravaged as a result of that unfortunate conflict, and they had no place to send their children to school except to do the very best they could through private tutorship.

So that arrangement lasted until 1870, when the public free school system of Virginia came into being virtue of the enactment of the Legislature of Virginia found here in substantially the same language that it was put into the Constitution of Virginia in 1902.

THE CHIEF JUSTICE: In 1865, General, you say there were missionaries who came down from the North?

MR. ALMOND: Yes, sir.

THE CHIEF JUSTICE: What funds did they have?

MR. ALMOND: They were private funds.

THE CHIEF JUSTICE: Private funds; and private schools, I take it?

MR. ALMOND: They were private schools.

THE CHIEF JUSTICE: For the Negro?

MR. ALMOND: For the Negro children.

But when the state took over or decided after a terrific conflict as to whether or not it should go into the field of public education, because it was the custom and tradition of our people prior to that time that every family should educate its own children—they were opposed to the expending of public funds for the education of the children of our people.

But a distinguished Virginian, a Dr. William H. Ruffing, became the first superintendent of schools in Virginia, and he wrote that statute which we have before us today, providing that white and colored children shall not be taught in the same schools, but under the same general regulations as to usefulness and efficiency.

As has been pointed out here, in the Underwood Convention of 1870, when the Underwood Constitution was adopted that Convention was presided over by an individual distinctly hostile to the great majority of the white people in Virginia, and the question came before that Convention as to whether or not a provision would be written into the Constitution requiring that the schools be mixed and operated by the state and the localities jointly on a mixed basis.

An amendment was offered by an eminent Negro doctor from the city of

Norfolk to bring that about and, to use an expression that is frequently used in my state today, I may say to the Court that the fur flew; but, as Mr. Moore has pointed out, there were twenty-two Negro members of the Convention, and on the vote, eleven of them voted not to have mixed schools in Virginia.

The debates in that Convention reflect what have been said here today relative to the mixed school which prevailed in the State of South Carolina for a period of twelve years, and that was discussed.

That was adopted in the light of the fact that they knew then that in 1862 the Congress of the United States provided for separate schools in the District of Columbia. That was adopted because they knew then, and discussed that when the Fourteenth Amendment was submitted to the people or proposed on June 16, 1867, and in the great debate raging in Congress relative to the adoption of the enabling Civil Rights Act, that Congress itself had established the policy of separation of schools, because of the feeling that had grown as an aftermath of that great struggle between the States, and because of the bitterness that ensued, unfortunately—it was determined in Virginia, not as a badge of inferiority, not to place the Negro man or the Negro child in the position where he could never rise to take his place in a free society, but the only way that we could have a free public school system was on a separate basis.

And then during the readjuster period, when impoverished as our public treasury and our peoples were, it became necessary to use tax funds for other purposes, and the public treasury and provisions for school purposes were raided to this extent, or diverted; and Dr. Ruffing made a big fight on that. But throughout the readjuster period, and not until 1920 did the people of Virginia awaken to the necessity of improvement of their public schools.

Sad to relate, I am ashamed to say, that during many of those years of the past we have been grossly neglectful of our responsibility in bringing about equal facilities for the Negro race in Virginia.

In 1920 there were only 31,000 children of high school age in Virginia going to school, and today there are something like 155,000 of them.

With that undertaking, our people have come to believe and to know and to feel as a moral proposition, if Your Honors please, that the only position we can take, the one that is morally defensible is that they are entitled to equal facilities, and there has been launched this great program in Virginia, appropriating millions of dollars and, Mr. Moore has pointed out, at this time we are spending more for facilities for Negro children than we are for whites, and we should do it because we were laggards in the years past in doing what we should have done.

THE CHIEF JUSTICE: General, I understood Mr. Moore to say that it was a legal responsibility for Virginia to have the equal facilities in the statute itself.

MR. ALMOND: In the statute itself there is a legal responsibility, and in the years past has not been discharged as it should have been discharged.

What I said about it is independently of his right that we should do it, it is our policy and it is our determination; we are irrevocably dedicated and our people are enthusiastically in support of equal facilities for Negroes at the secondary level in Virginia. That is our program today, and that is the program that we want to go forward with, and that we are going forward with.

The Legislature of 1950, on the recommendation of the Governor, almost without a dissenting voice, appropriated $50 million for school construction.

The Legislature of 1952 appropriated another $15 million, making a total of $60 million that have been appropriated in those two sessions of the Legislature of Virginia to be dedicated almost solely toward the improvement of facilities at the secondary level in Virginia.

THE CHIEF JUSTICE: Are those $60 million what you call the Battle Fund?

MR. ALMOND: That is right, Mr. Chief Justice.

THE CHIEF JUSTICE: What is the Literary Fund, for what purpose and in what amount? Is it temporary or permanent?

MR. ALMOND: No, sir. Written into the Constitution of Virginia are provisions for what we call a Literary Fund, and there goes into that Fund the collections of all fines that are paid in Virginia; they go permanently into that Fund, and that is a revolving fund from which the school boards of the various localities may make application for moneys for school purposes, principally for school construction, and meet certain minimum requirements laid down by the State Board of Education, and then they issue their bonds which are held at 2 per cent interest by the State Board of Education; and as the interest comes in and the funds are paid in, it revolves, and it self-perpetuates itself. Then it has been augmented from time to time by direct appropriations from the Legislature into that Literary Fund.

Today, as I cite from memory, and I think the record bears it out, there are loans either in actual operations or applications approved for in excess of $48 million from the Literary Fund, which have been applied to the construction of white schools, and something over $12 million which have been applied to the construction of the Negro schools.

If I may have just another moment—

THE CHIEF JUSTICE: All right, General, you may have five additional minutes, and you may have five minutes for rebuttal.

MR. ALMOND: Thank you, sir.
I just want to say a word—

THE CHIEF JUSTICE: I do not want to penalize you by my questions.

MR. ALMOND: I just want to say a word, if Your Honors please, relative to the impact of a decision that would strike down, contrary to the customs, the traditions and the mores of what we might claim to be a great people, established through generations, who themselves are fiercely and irrevocably dedicated to the preservation of the white and colored races.

We have had a struggle in Virginia, particularly from 1920 on, to educate our people, white and colored, to the necessity of promoting the cause of secondary education.

We think we have had great leaders to develop in that field. One, Dr. Dabney Lancaster, now president of Longwood College, I think, made himself very unpopular because he advocated and fought tooth and nail for the equalization of salaries between white and Negro teachers.

That has been accomplished. The curricula have been accomplished; facilities are rapidly being accomplished, and our people, deeply ingrained within them, feel that it is their custom, their use and their wont, and their traditions, if destroyed, as this record shows, will make it impossible to raise public funds through the process of taxation, either at the state or the local level, to support the public school system of Virginia, and it would destroy the public school system of Virginia as we know it today. That is not an idle threat.

Then, too, a thing that concerns us—

THE CHIEF JUSTICE: General, in what way will it destroy it?

MR. ALMOND: It would destroy it, Mr. Chief Justice, because we must have—it is a costly proposition—money with which to operate the public school system at both the state level and the local level, and the only source of income, of course, is the source of taxation at the state and local level, and bond issues at the local level, and the people would not vote bond issues through their resentment to it.

I say that not as a threat.

Then, another thing,we have 5,243 Negro teachers in the public school system of Virginia on an average of splendid qualification. That 5,243 exceed the Negro teachers in all of the thirty-one States of this Union, where there is not segregation by law.

They would not, as a hard fact of realism, and not in a spirit of recrimination do I say this, but simply as hard stark reality—those Negro teachers would not be employed to teach white children in a tax-supported system in Virginia.

Now, I know they tell us "Why didn't you raise that voice when the Negro was admitted to the University of Virginia?"

I did not raise it. I advised the University of Virginia that they had no defense, and I sat down with distinguished counsel in this case and agreed to the stipulations and helped prepare the decree that was entered by the court, and there was no evidence taken on it.

But here there is distinction, if Your Honor please, with 22.7 per cent of our population, the Negro population, with 59 per cent of the school population of Prince Edward County Negro population, to make such a transition, would undo what we have been doing, and which we propose to continue to do for the uplift and advancement of the education of both races. It would stop this march of progress, this onward sweep.

I thank you.

THE CHIEF JUSTICE: Mr. Robinson, you understand that you have five additional minutes.

### REBUTTAL ARGUMENT ON BEHALF OF APPELLANTS

#### by MR. ROBINSON

MR. ROBINSON: In addition to the time that was reserved to me, yes.

May it please the Court, in addition to the evidence in the record to which I have referred the Court to answer a question put to me by Mr. Justice Reed upon the opening argument, I should also like to request the attention of the Court directly to our statement as to jurisdiction, pages 9 to 11, where we did undertake to incorporate some historical evidence which we thought would be of value on the question of the basis, the original basis, of the segregation legislation, data which are not contained in the record in the case.

Examination of this material will indicate that prior to the time of the Civil War, as a consequence of the Dred Scott decision, the Negro did not enjoy citizenship rights equal to those enjoyed by a white person.

As a matter of fact, in that case the Court had decided that he possessed no rights which a white person was bound to respect at all.

And so it goes that after the Civil War, and even after the Negro was affirmatively ganted full and equal citizenship by the Thirteenth and Fourteenth Amendments, and even though his right to suffrage was given protection by the provisions of the Fifteenth Amendment, the white South was not content with this constitutional change. Consequently, we had the so-called period of the "Black Codes", which were a body of laws which were expressly intended and indeed did accomplish the disability of the Negro.

Examination of the records of the constitutional conventions of the Southern states during the period that legislative education of segregation had its beginning, gives, as I stated this morning, a reliable indication that the real basis of this legislation was not what it has been stated to this Court it is, but rather that the segregation laws themselves were intended to, and have, in fact, in Virginia accomplished, a matter which I shall get to in just a few minutes—were intended to limit the educational opportunities of the Negro, and place him in a position where he could not obtain in the state's educational system opportunities and benefits from the public educational program equal to those which flowed to white students.

We have incorporated in our statement as to jurisdiction as one piece of evidence specifically referable to Virginia, the report of the proceedings during the debates at the 1902 Constitutional Convention over one of the provisions which was then up for discussion, a resolution that state funds for schools must be used to maintain the primary schools for a certain period of time before these funds could be used for the establishment of high schools or indeed grades beyond the higher grades.

The question was then asked as to whether or not the effect of this provision would be to tend to prevent the establishment of schools in sections of the country where such schools ought to be prevented, and the eminent Mr. Carter Glass[50] answered the question by pointing out that this provision had been considered, that there was a discussion of this demand, stating as he did—and these are his words:

> Certainly, in my judgement, a very reasonable demand, that the white people of the black sections of Virginia should be permitted to tax themselves, and after a certain point has been passed which would safeguard the poorer classes in these communities, divert that fund to the exclusive use of the white children.

[50]Representative from Virginia (1902–1918), Secretary of the Treasury (1918–1922), Senator from Virginia (1920–1946).

It was at the same Constitutional Convention that Senator Glass made the statement that discrimination was one of the purposes for which the convention was called—I am speaking about discrimination over in the area of suffrage—and it was at this very same convention that he said that one of the purposes of the convention was to discriminate to the very extremity of permissible action under the limitations of the federal Constitution, with a view to the elimination of every Negro voter who can be gotten rid of legally without materially impairing the numerical strength of the white electorate. The so-called Virginia picture bears out this purpose.

I would like to ask the Court's attention—invite the Court's attention—to the data which we have incorporated in our reply brief commencing at page 11, the data pertaining to the present and the future educational system in Virginia.

Although Negroes constitute or they did constitute in 1950–51, 26 per cent of the total number of pupils enrolled in the schools of the commonwealth, they did not receive, when measured on a dollars and cents basis, anything like their fair share of the educational funds, anything like their fair share of the school property employed by the commonwealth in its educational program.

We have set forth there data to demonstrate that for each dollar invested in each category per Negro student, the investment for the 1950–51 school session per Negro student was 61 cents in sites and buildings, 50 cents in furniture and equipment, 67 cents in buses, and 61 cents in total school property. That is the situation in Virginia.

It was a situation in Virginia as we were able to present it up to the latest possible point at the time of the trial of this case.

JUSTICE JACKSON: I hope you will take time enough before you finish to tell me what your position is about the provision of the Fourteenth Amendment, that Congress pass appropriate legislation to enforce it, and what effect, if any, it has on these cases.

MR. ROBINSON: That are now before the Court, sir?

JUSTICE JACKSON: Yes, cases of this character.

MR. ROBINSON: I will be glad to do that, Mr. Justice Jackson, right now.

I disagree with counsel for the appellees that Congress does not have full power under section 5 of the Fourteenth Amendment to enact legislation that would outlaw segregation in state public schools.

But I do feel that insofar as the present cases are concerned that has relatively little merit.

We come before this Court presenting what we consider to be justiciable questions, questions that are not essentially different in character from those which have been presented in cases which in the past have been brought here.

In other words, I do not feel that the mere fact that under the authority of section 5 of the Fourteenth Amendment Congress could enact legislation which would settle this problem would in any way encroach upon the jurisdiction of this Court, if, as a matter of fact, a violation of the Constitution has been shown.

JUSTICE JACKSON: Of course, in the jury cases you have legislation by Congress; in the interstate commerce cases you have legislation by Congress.

MR. ROBINSON: That is correct, sir.

JUSTICE JACKSON: In a good many of our cases, but not all, you are quite right, that some do have them. But in a number of cases they rest on specific statutory implementation of this amendment.

MR. ROBINSON: Yes. I would like to make—

JUSTICE DOUGLAS: What statute of Congress regulates juries?

MR. ROBINSON: I think it is section 47 of Title 8 of the United States Code, I think it is; I have forgotten. [Now 42 U.S.C., section 1985 (2)]

JUSTICE JACKSON: I pointed it out in a dissenting opinion some time ago, but Justice Douglas apparently did not read my dissent.[51]

MR. ROBINSON: I do not remember the exact number, Mr. Justice Douglas, but it is up in Title 8, and, as I recall, it is somewhere in the forties; it is in the forties section.

I would like to make reference to this—

JUSTICE DOUGLAS: Has the Court ever held that the Fourteenth Amendment is not executed unless Congress acts?

MR. ROBINSON: No, I do not think so.

There is a large area of law which has been developed by this Court in which the decision has rested upon the provisions of the due process and equal protection clauses, and in a few instances of the privileges and immunities clause where there was not any implementing legislation by Congress.

As I understand the theory, particularly as it came as a consequence of the civil rights cases, that authority was there that Congress could exercise, if it desired to do so, but the position which we urge upon the Court is the mere fact that if Congress has not done it, it will not preclude this Court from deciding constitutional questions.

I can make reference, for example, to the situation which was recently presented to this Court in he so-called restrictive covenant cases,[52] and in those cases we had a piece of legislation involved that was section 42 of Title 8 of the United States Code. [Now 42 U.S.C., section 1981 *et seq.*]

This Court nevertheless held that a state court enforcement of those restrictions resulted in the denial of the equal protection of the laws, notwithstanding the fact in that situation we did have a case in which Congress, under its authority conferred by section 5 of the Fourteenth Amendment, might have outlawed the thing, to start off with, so that the question might never have gotten to this Court.

---

[51]Frazier v. United States, 335 U.S. 497, 514 (1948). The selection of federal juries is now governed by 28 U.S.C., section 1861 *et seq.* Interfering with jurors is made a crime by 42 U.S.C., section 1875 (2).

[52]Shelley v. Kraemer, 334 U.S. 1 (1948), see n. 7, *supra.*

JUSTICE REED: But if segregation is not a denial of equal protection or due process, legislation by Congress could do nothing more except to express congressional views, and wouldn't that be decisive?

MR. ROBINSON: Yes, I am inclined to—

JUSTICE REED: So you would be forced to decide whether or not segregation per se comes under that question.

MR. ROBINSON: Of course, that is our position here, sir.

JUSTICE FRANKFURTER: The Fourteenth Amendment is not unlike, in some aspect, the commerce clause. There are many things that the states cannot do merely because the commerce clause exists. There are many things that a state can do until Congress steps in.

MR. ROBINSON: That is right, sir. Under those circumstances—

JUSTICE REED: The state cannot violate the Fourteenth Amendment.

MR. ROBINSON: I beg pardon?

JUSTICE REED: The state cannot violate the Fourteenth Amendment.

MR. ROBINSON: That is right, and I was just about to observe that it cannot violate the commerce clause either.

JUSTICE FRANKFURTER: We would not be arguing for ten hours if it is clear that this is a violation of it. We do not argue for ten hours a question that is self-evident.

MR. ROBINSON: I understand, sir.

Now, going back to the so-called Virginia picture, reference was made and questions were asked concerning the Literary Fund allocations, the approximately $60 million allocated by the state Literary Fund for school construction in the state.

We have pointed out in our reply brief, and we have demonstrated statistically, that even with this large expenditure, when you add it to the present value of buildings and sites the ratio of investment in school property in Virginia will be increased from the present 61 cents to only 74 cents per Negro student.

I should like to also emphasize the fact that no time has been set for the completion of these projects and, consequently, we do not even know when the ratio is going to be realized; but even if all of the Negro projects which are proposed are completed, and even though no additional money whatsoever is invested in white schools, the amount of money invested in buildings and sites per Negro student over the entire state would only be $343.30 as compared with $366.73 that are already invested in school property per white student.

So, consequently, the Literary Fund program, the construction which is expected to develop out of the Literary Fund allocations would not seem to bring about this equality even of physical facilities within any point in the near future.

Reference was made in this case also to the so-called four-year program.

That is a program that has been developed, and that contemplates the expenditure of some $263 million for new construction and improvements, and it has been emphasized that 77.7 per cent of this money will be spent on white projects, and 23.3 per cent on Negro projects, and the emphasis is placed there by reason of the fact that the percentages of expenditures are slightly in excess of the percentages of school population.

The money for this program, as the record clearly shows, is not now available, and even if the money were available, and the entire program were completed by 1956, the amount invested in sites and buildings would only be 79 cents per Negro student for each dollar per white student, and thus, I urge the Court this is a very vast program.

Virginia does not have the money for it now. Even though Virginia could spend $263 million—an enormous sum by Virginia standards—all that we succeed in doing is moving from a present 61 cents to 79 cents per Negro student for each dollar that is invested in buildings and sites for white students.

THE CHIEF JUSTICE: Have you got any breakdown as to the number of school buildings that have been constructed in the last, say, five years? I heard about the high school of Richmond and Charlottesville. I am fearful that this percentage business does not make it very clear to me because it is a question of the number of schools, it is a question of how the students are grouped, as to whether they are getting the fair "divvy," I might say.

MR. ROBINSON: Yes, Mr. Chief Justice.

Now, maybe I can help. On the Literary Fund allocations that I was talking about just a few minutes ago, the evidence at the time of the trial showed that there had been projects—no, it does not give the number of schools. It simply shows the scope of the program, that is, the number of cities and counties over which the construction would extend.

If Your Honor will indulge me just a moment, I will look at the exhibit. If we have it in the record at all, might I make this suggestion: There are a large number of exhibits in this case, and all of this statistical information is contained in those exhibits.

Those exhibits are before the Court. If the information is available at all it will be found there.

We have in our reply brief a specific pointed and detailed reference in each case where we get to one of these particular things. I do not recall that the precise information concerning which Your Honor has asked me does appear in the record.

THE CHIEF JUSTICE: It would seem to me that if it did appear it would either show a stepped-up program or maybe retrogression in respect of the—if you had the breakdown it would show something.

MR. ROBINSON: Well, the appellees do insist that this is, in other words, a stepped-up program.

THE CHIEF JUSTICE: Do I understand that you take the same position that Mr. Marshall would take if we were to hold that segregation per se was unconstitutional in regard to the time element?

MR. ROBINSON: On the matter of necessity of the administrative problem in these segregated—oh, yes.

THE CHIEF JUSTICE: Then why, if you take that position there—and I assume you take it as a matter of necessity—why do you not take that position here under the equal facilities doctrine?

MR. ROBINSON: If Your Honor please, I think that there is a difference between a postponement of a right and a delay which is incidental to affording the remedies that we asked for.

I do not think that it would be possible without encroaching upon the previous decisions of this Court, to take the position that notwithstanding a present denial of the constitutional rights of the appellants, that notwithstanding that they must wait until the state gets around to fixing the schools.

THE CHIEF JUSTICE: Of course, I take it, that you recognize the distinction in the cases in regard to the number of students affected, and all that sort of thing, but if you agree that a reasonable period of time should be granted if we held segregation was unconstitutional, I just wonder why you take the position you do in regard to the equal facilities, unless you say that the stepped-up program is just not sufficient to meet the situation.

MR. ROBINSON: We do take the latter position, if Your Honor please, and we have set forth—and since my time is just about up—I can only now refer the Court to the data which we have set forth in our reply brief in that connection, in which we point out that this stepped-up program of this state is not going to produce even physical equality on a state-wide basis at any time in the near future, and we tried to calculate that time as best we could from the available information.

Now, with respect to the other portion of Your Honor's question, our position on it is simply this: I appreciate the fact that even though there has been a violation of legal right, in affording a remedy it may be necessary and it may be entirely necessary for there to be some delay incidental to the affording of that remedy.

A case that I can think of is if a court should decree specific performance of a contract to tear down a house, the man has got to have a reasonable opportunity to get the house down.

But I do not think in that particular case if the man is entitled to that decree—

THE CHIEF JUSTICE: A man might have to have a reasonable opportunity to get out of the house before it is torn down.

MR. ROBINSON: I agree with that, too.

In other words, we have the administrative practical problem arising from the affording of the remedy, and to that particular situation and to that particular extent, of course, we readily recognize some lapse of time. I am not in a position to suggest what it should be.

I think it is an administrative problem initially, at least, for the school authorities to work out. We appreciate that, but I do not see how we can, without encroaching upon the body of decisions of this Court which have established the rights involved in these cases, as present and personal, as to how we can say that notwithstanding that, we may delay the right; in other words, that a person must be compelled before he can get satisfaction of his rights—he may be postponed at some time into the future before he can get what the Constitution entitled him to, and what his white counterparts are getting already.

THE CHIEF JUSTICE: Now, take the South Carolina case. Would you say that, assuming the equal facilities rule will still continue, would you say that the lapse of time in their construction program was not fully justified by the lower court?

MR. ROBINSON: Well, I would have to answer that question, if Your Honor please, this way: I do not personally feel, and I could not urge upon the Court that suspension of the satisfaction of a constitutional right is ever justified.
In other words, I would—

THE CHIEF JUSTICE: But you realize you are in equity; you realize that you have got the rights of other people involved in regard to dislocation?

MR. ROBINSON: I appreciate that.

THE CHIEF JUSTICE: And in the South Carolina case there was some delay, but we are told here that when the new buildings were constructed and occupied in September—I recall there was some effort, special effort, made to get the material to build the gymnasium—at one time they thought they would not get it, but they worked around and got it for the gymnasium.

MR. ROBINSON: Yes. As I understand the "separate but equal" rule, even under that, at that particular time, at the time of the first hearing when the facilities were—

THE CHIEF JUSTICE: All right, go ahead.

MR. ROBINSON: —unequal, the court should, instead of entering an equalization decree, should have removed the segregation. That is what this Court said in the Gaines case is the consequence of trying to maintain segregation where you do not have equal physcial facilities.

THE CHIEF JUSTICE: Well, the Court did not—

MR. ROBINSON: The Court did not under those circumstances, and I say that at that particular point what the Court there was doing, the Court was not simply delaying the thing for purposes which would be incidental to giving to the plaintiffs the relief which, under that doctrine, they were then entitled to.
The Court was delaying it until conditions could be remedied in such a way that under the "separate but equal" doctrine, if limited to that particular point, they would not be entitled to any relief at all.

THE CHIEF JUSTICE: Well, now, what is your view in regard to the way it was handled by the lower court?

MR. ROBINSON: In the Virginia case?

THE CHIEF JUSTICE: No, in the South Carolina case, considering that they ruled segregation per se not unconstitutional? Do you have objection to that method of handling it?

MR. ROBINSON: Well, if the Court should rule—I want to make certain—

THE CHIEF JUSTICE: Well, they did rule. I say so far as they are concerned, they did so rule.

MR. ROBINSON: Yes. I am just trying to understand Your Honor's question.

THE CHIEF JUSTICE: Would you say that under the circumstances in the South Carolina case, having ruled on the segregation question as they did, that immediately, *eo instanti,* they should have said, "entry into white schools" or seeing the imminent construction that they should continue as they did?

MR. ROBINSON: Not the latter, if you please; the former, taking into consideration that immediately would not mean five minutes from now.

THE CHIEF JUSTICE: Well, now, how many minutes, how many days? That is the point.

MR. ROBINSON: I would not be able—I have tried to make plain that I consider that that is an administrative problem, and that gets into things that, frankly, I do not think that I am able to answer.

THE CHIEF JUSTICE: What about the courts?

MR. ROBINSON: I do not think that courts are, either. In other words, my position in that particular regard is that they are entitled to the relief immediately which should be afforded them just as soon as expeditious administrative arrangements can be made to unsegregate the schools, as I understand the Gaines and the subsequent cases, the doctrine of those cases, requires.

For these reasons, we respectfully submit that the decree of the District Court should be reversed.

(Thereupon, the argument in the above-entitled cause was concluded.)

SPOTTSWOOD THOMAS BOLLING, ET AL.,
Petitioners,

vs.

C. MELVIN SHARPE, ET AL.,
Respondents.

Case No. 413

Washington, D.C.
Wednesday, December 10, 1952.

The above-entitled cause came on for argument at 3:30 p.m.

APPEARANCES:

On behalf of the Petitioners:

GEORGE E. C. HAYES, ESQ., and JAMES M. NABRIT, JR., ESQ.

On behalf of the Respondents:

MILTON D. KORMAN, ESQ.

THE CHIEF JUSTICE: Number 413, Bolling, et al., versus C. Melvin
Sharpe, and others.

All right, Mr. Hayes.

### ARGUMENT ON BEHALF OF PETITIONERS

by MR. HAYES

MR. HAYES: May it please the Court, this case is here on a petition for a
writ of certiorari addressed to the United States Court of Appeals for the District of Columbia Circuit.

The jurisdiction of this Court to review by writ of certiorari is conferred by
Title 28, United States Code, section 1254 (1) and section 2101 (e).

This case was on appeal to the United States Court of Appeals for the District of Columbia, where no judgment had been rendered, and no order had been
entered, and the matter came up under the rule, as I have stated.

This case came before the court on a complaint and on a motion to dismiss,
and the facts are, therefore, not controverted.

The minor petitioners, Negroes, fully qualified to attend a junior high school
in the District of Columbia, accompanied by their parents, made application to
the Sousa Junior High School for admission, and they were denied admission to
the Sousa Junior High School solely on the ground of race or color.

Thereafter, through their attorneys, to each echelon in the administrative
setup of the schools of the District of Columbia, they made application for admission, and finally to the Board of Education, and in each of these areas they were
denied admission solely because of their race or color.

Thereafter, and having exhausted their administrative remedies, a suit was
filed asking for a declaratory judgment and for injunctive relief.

A motion was filed to dismiss. That motion was granted, and an appeal was
taken. Certiorari was granted in this case on November 10, 1952.

Your Honors have listened for a number of hours to discussions with respect to this matter of segregation.

In the case of the District of Columbia, in our opinion it presents an entirely novel question, one which this Court has not been called upon to pass upon, and in which we specifically and solely present the question as to whether segregation is unconstitutional per se.

There are no factual questions as to facilities; we raise no issue with respect to facilities.

Our proposition is baldly as to whether or not the respondents have the power, the statutory or constitutional power, to deny to these pupils admission to the Sousa Junior High School.

JUSTICE DOUGLAS: Where is the statute that is relied upon?

MR. HAYES: If Your Honor please, the statutes that are relied upon are in our brief beginning at page 23.

I want to call Your Honors' attention to the fact, at the very outset, that these statutes, contrary to the statutes to which Your Honors have listened for the last two days, nowhere, in and of themselves, require segregation. It, to our mind, is a matter solely of interpretation of these statutes as to whether or not segregation is required.

Our opponents take the position that these statutes do require it.

JUSTICE FRANKFURTER: Suppose we do not agree with your construction of the statute? Is that the end of the case?

MR. HAYES: No, Your Honor, that is not, because, if Your Honors were to determine that our construction of the statute was incorrect, and that by so much these statutes require segregation, we would then take the position that any such requirement is beyond the power of the Government to announce, and we would rely upon that for decisions of this Court as making that an impossibility.

JUSTICE FRANKFURTER: So your argument is that as a matter of construction this is not mandatory, but just exercising discretion by the educational authorities?

MR. HAYES: That is right, sir.

JUSTICE FRANKFURTER: And that in construing it, I suppose, that we should take into account that possibly a serious constitutional question is involved, even if on the face of it it does not yield to the construction that you argue; but you argue, in the third place, that if one cannot escape the constitutional question, then you assail it?

MR. HAYES: That is correct, sir; that is exactly our position, Mr. Justice Frankfurter.

JUSTICE DOUGLAS: Has this statute that you refer to consistently been interpreted by the Board of Education as requiring segregation?

MR. HAYES: Yes, sir; Mr. Justice Douglas, it has.

JUSTICE DOUGLAS: This is an old statute?

MR. HAYES: Yes, Mr. Justice Douglas; again, it has been in since 1864; originally there were the Acts of 1862, but the Acts here relied on go from 1864 forward.

JUSTICE REED: Why do you say an interpretation requiring segregation?

MR. HAYES: When I say interpreting as requiring, I mean by that, at any rate, they have required it.

JUSTICE REED: That may be permissive.

MR. HAYES: From our point of view, yes. They take the position, as I understand it, that they are required. From our point of view it could be purely permissive, and from our point of view, they are, if anything at all, simply permissive because they are in no sense—we take the position—mandatory.

JUSTICE DOUGLAS: Do you set forth the legislative history of this statute?

MR. HAYES: No, Your Honor, we do not set it forth in any—

JUSTICE DOUGLAS: Does it throw any light upon this?

MR. HAYES: I beg your pardon?

JUSTICE DOUGLAS: Does it throw any light upon this?

MR. HAYES: I am sorry.

JUSTICE DOUGLAS: Does it throw any light on this subject as to whether or not Congress intended there be segregation?

MR. HAYES: From our point of view it does not.

We say that because it is our belief that Congress, by the statutes, have indicated that it did not intend it because had they so intended, certainly the legislature would have been competent to have spelled it out in a manner so entirely different from the statute that we face because, as Your Honors well know, we have, for instance, the South Carolina statutes saying that these children shall never be educated together; we have the Virginia statute saying that they shall not be in the same schools.

There is no language in any of these which say any such thing, and so we say that Congress has never said that.

THE CHIEF JUSTICE: In seeking appropriations, the estimates that are put in, are they for the different schools in the city?

MR. HAYES: Yes, Your Honor.

THE CHIEF JUSTICE: Does that show that the schools are for Negroes and schools for whites?

MR. HAYES: It shows that, and we do not pretend that the legislature is not mindful of it.

THE CHIEF JUSTICE: And Congress throughout the period of years has been mindful of it?

MR. HAYES: Yes, Your Honor. We take the position that being mindful or being mandatory or being constitutional are entirely different propositions.

JUSTICE BLACK: What provisions of the Constitution do you assert this violates?

MR. HAYES: It violates, we will say, a number of them. I shall outline to you the manner in which we think they do violate it.

JUSTICE BLACK: Which?

MR. HAYES: It violates the due process clause of the Fifth Amendment; it violates, as we conceive it, the civil rights statutes; it is in violation of the public policy that this Government has just seen fit to announce in the Charter of the United Nations; all of them, we think, are violated by any attempts to deny to these people, the petitioners, admission into the Sousa Junior High School.

JUSTICE FRANKFURTER: Mr. Hayes, may I ask one other question?

MR. HAYES: Yes, Mr. Justice Frankfurter.

JUSTICE FRANKFURTER: Do I understand you to say that this legislation is not mandatory, but permissive?

MR. HAYES: If at all, it would be nothing but permissive.

JUSTICE FRANKFURTER: Wouldn't you, in your point of view, be attacking the constitutionality of legislation even if Congress authorizes it?

MR. HAYES: No, Your Honor, because from our point of view we take the position—if I stated it was permissive, then I am in error, we take the position—that this language is neither mandatory nor permissive.

JUSTICE FRANKFURTER: You say this does not even authorize it?

MR. HAYES: That is right, sir.

JUSTICE FRANKFURTER: And you say for how many years has the District been acting without authority?

MR. HAYES: We do not say without authority; we say that the fact that they acted with knowledge does not mean that the statute gives the authority.

JUSTICE FRANKFURTER: If the statute does not give the authority, then it was ultra vires for the District to have been doing what they have been doing; is that right?

MR. HAYES: No, if Your Honor please, because our position is that when the District recognizes that a situation exists, and when they appropriate for the sake of the statement, to an existing situation, that that does not mean that they themselves are given the authority nor does it mean that they are holding that it is mandatory, and this Court—

JUSTICE FRANKFURTER: Still somebody must have been doing something lawlessly for a good many years; is that it?

MR. HAYES: If Your Honor says lawlessly, perhaps, I cannot go along with the idea of lawlessness, but it has been done without constitutional authority, I do say that.

JUSTICE FRANKFURTER: Somebody has been asleep as to the illegality of what has been done?

MR. HAYES: No, I would not say asleep as to the illegality. I say rather—

JUSTICE FRANKFURTER: If I may say so, I am in deep sympathy with you in not trying to invalidate legislation if it can be dealt with otherwise. But I find a little difficulty in seeing how we can fail to reach the validity of this legislation unless you say that what has been done by the District authorities has been done, if not lawlessly, then without authority of law. How about that, would you accept that?

MR. HAYES: We would say, sir, if this Court were to determine that what has been done up to this time has been done validly, that then for the first time this Court has had the opportunity to say, "No, this is not the proper way."

We say that this is the opportunity for this Court to say that any such attempt as this, based solely on the question of race or color, is not within the Constitution.

JUSTICE FRANKFURTER: "Hereafter you have no lawful authority to do this, but we do not care about the past."

MR. HAYES: I would not want Your Honors' statement to indicate that we do not care about the past, but for the first time we have had the opportunity to pass upon it, and we frown upon it.

If Your Honor please, as I have indicated, these three propositions I have outlined are as follows:

We take the position, of course, that the court was wrong in having denied the relief sought, and in having granted the motion to dismiss.

This Government—and this is the point which seems to us so fundamental—that in these other situations where the question of these states has been involved, and where the question of equal facilities has been involved, that is one thing.

But in our case, this Government of ours is being asked to support a statute having as its basis nothing other than race or color, and we say that this Government cannot afford to do just that.

As I have said, the question of the right of this Government to legislate for the District of Columbia is without question because they expressly have been authorized to legislate for the District of Columbia. But this Court, with respect to that, acting for the District of Columbia, has said that they cannot do it and violate one's constitutional rights.

You have said so in *Capital Traction v. Hof,* and you said in *Callen v. Wilson*[53] that, as a matter of fact, the right to administer for the District of Columbia is restricted by the fact that you cannot violate the constitutional rights of persons in so doing.

This Court has seen fit to pass upon rights which come within the purview of the due process clause of the Fifth Amendment, and have explained and expressed what the word "liberty" means, and this Court has seen fit to indicate and incorporate in that word "liberty" things which we believe point out the way as to what should be done in this instance.

Governmental restrictions on the right to teach a foreign language, the right of a parent to send his child to a private school, the right for them to acquire knowledge, the right of parents and pupils to a reasonable choice with respect to teachers, curricula, and text books, the right of parents to secure for their children the type of education which they think best, and which is not harmful, have been held by this Court to be fundamental educational rights protected from arbitrary government action by the due process clause of the Fifth Amendment.

That language is found in *Meyer v. Nebraska, Bartels v. Iowa, Pierce v. Society of Sisters.*[54]

JUSTICE BLACK: Were those cases decided under the Fifth Amendment?

MR. HAYES: They were decided under the Fourteenth Amendment, if Your Honor please, but under the due process clause of the Fourteenth Amendment, and this Court, however, in the case of *Farrington v. Tokushige*[55] has seen fit to refer specifically to those three cases, indicating that the due process clause of the Fourteenth Amendment, as referred to in those cases, is incorporated and is taken over and assumed as being part of the Fifth Amendment.

As far as the Fifth Amendment cases are concerned, and so in the Takahashi case, this Court, it seems to us, has embraced these educational cases that might be referred to as coming within the Fourteenth Amendment, and has said that the Fifth Amendment applies in instances where due process of law is concerned and that, if Your Honor please, is the exact situation that we have here.

I would not pretend, because it would not be candid to pretend, that in those cases there was not something having to do with economic situations, with the question of ownership, that there was not a question of it being brought by owners

[53]Capital Traction Co. v. Hof, 174 U.S. 1 (1899); Callan v. Wilson, 127 U.S. 540 (1888). Both cases required the District of Columbia to follow the Constitutional requirements of trial by jury.

[54]Meyer v. Nebraska, 262 U.S. 390 (1923). A state law forbidding the teaching of a modern language other than English below the eighth grade was held invalid. Bartels v. Iowa, 262 U.S. 404 (1923) (same holding); Pierce v. Society of Sisters, 268 U.S. 510 (1925), upset an Oregon law requiring every parent to send his child to a public school.

[55]273 U.S. 284 (1927). Hawaii was not permitted to require a fee and a permit before a foreign language school could begin operation. The case discussed the relation between the Fourteenth and Fifth Amendments.

and teachers rather than by parents and children, so that for the sake of the statement someone might say it is dicta.

But I call the Court's attention to the fact that what you said in the Farrington case so entirely, as we conceive it, gave the concept of what this Court has in mind with respect to this question of liberty under this due process clause, and that there was no need to inquire whether or not it was in any sense any other than what this Court was embracing as being its doctrine.

JUSTICE REED: Do you take the same position that the Virginia counsel did, that this legislation was intended to be inimical to the interests of Negroes?

MR. HAYES: That this legislation was, if Your Honor means by inimical, the question of putting them in—simply segregating them?

JUSTICE REED: As I understood previous counsel, they urged that Virginia had passed these laws in order to deprive Negroes of educational opportunities.

MR. HAYES: I think, if Your Honor please, that unquestionably the answer must be that legislation of this character was pointed solely at the Negro, and that it was done purely and for no other reason than because of the fact that it pretended to keep for him this place of secondary citizenship.

I think it could have no other conceivable purpose. I have been concerned—

JUSTICE REED: You do not think that it had any relation to these prior considerations?

MR. HAYES: I do not think it had the slightest relationship to that, if Your Honor please; I do not think anyone can pretend in this jurisdiction that it has any such purpose because this question of the schools, if Your Honor please—this is the only governmentally constructed situation that has as its basis segregation in the District of Columbia, the only one, and to us it is entirely inconceivable and inconsistent that under those circumstances for any conceivable reason, that the argument can be had that it is necessary on account of any alleged difficulties that might arise.

This Court has seen fit to say that any legislation based on racism is immediately suspect. That is what this Court has said.

In the Hirabayashi[56] case this Court said that legislation of this character is suspect, and immediately that it is suspect we take the position that the burden then comes upon the Government to show as to why under those conditions any such thing should be allowed. We throw down that challenge to our friends on the other side, to indicate why this should be done if there be any purpose other than pure racism.

If there be any answer other than it is purely on account of color, then we ask them to indicate to us what that situation is.

THE CHIEF JUSTICE: Mr. Hayes, if it was solely due to racism, you mean that after the adoption of the amendments—of course, they would not affect

[56]Hirabayashi v. United States, 320 U.S. 81 (1943). The Court upheld wartime curfews restricting the movement of Japanese-Americans on the West Coast.

this particular area—that segregation continued solely for racism and, therefore, the Fourteenth Amendment should now declare that under such circumstances the resultant relationships were invalid as unconstitutional?

MR. HAYES: If Your Honor please, I say again—and this is said on something that I hope is not based on obsession because of the fact that I am a Negro—I said to you that I believe that any of the facts—the Fourteenth Amendment, which had in it the question of the equal protection clause—the equal protection clause, as I conceive it, was put into the Fourteenth Amendment not because of the fact that there was any attempt at segregation at that time, but it was the question of getting segregation for Negroes, not of administering it. It was a question of getting it, and I think that the Fourteenth Amendment, when it provided for citizenship, mindful of the situation, and saying that they should have full citizenship, I think that they could not consistently have had that in mind and passed that and, at the same time, had in mind the question of that we shall segregate in schools.

THE CHIEF JUSTICE: The point, to me, coming so close to the end of the war between the states, so far as the District of Columbia is concerned—

MR. HAYES: Yes, sir.

THE CHIEF JUSTICE: —were the people who were there in the Congress at the time the amendments were passed, and were there when ratified, and were there when this legislation was passed, and it is hard for me to understand that if it is racism, that it was not done deliberately, and the constitutional amendments were so interpreted, and I assume that you would not go that far, would you, in regard to the war amendments.

MR. HAYES: Mr. Chief Justice, I think that what was done was a matter of politics, was a matter of doing the thing which, at that time, was to them the opportune thing to do; it was the question of giving away this with the idea of pressing this which was the stronger thing.

It was the idea of putting through this act and giving up this, because of the fact that this was the expedient thing to do, and I think that that very situation was what occasioned them not writing into any of these acts anything specific with regard to it, because in the same vein in which Your Honor indicates that this was an allowable circumstance, if they had intended that it should be a matter of segregation they could have written into this this, that Your Honor has indicated.

THE CHIEF JUSTICE: I was just merely asking your view relative to the frame of mind in which the people who passed the amendments had in this situation in the District of Columbia to have separate schools at the time when the amendments—the Fourteenth Amendment was being ratified by the states, if they did this for the purpose of just punishing the Negro or was it their interpretation of what the Fourteenth Amendment meant?

MR. HAYES: I have attempted to indicate to Your Honor that in my opinion it was not given as punishment; it was given as an expedient. It was done as an expedient; it was done because, as a matter of fact, at that time it seemed for them, I presume, an expedient thing not to press for this particular thing, but rather to allow the amendment to go through and, as I say, I think it is for that reason expressly that they put nothing into it other than what they did.

May I make just this one additional suggestion, because my time has already gone, and my associate, Mr. Nabrit, is going to argue the other points, but I do want to say in these Japanese war cases, where the Court took the position, as I said, that any segregated thing based upon race alone was suspect, they took the position that the only justification for the denial of constitutional rights can be found where there is pressing public necessity such as the severity of war, and even there the Court must be satisfied in sustaining such restrictions that (1) the purpose of the restriction is within the competency of the Government to effect—we say that this is not within the competency of the Government to effect; (2) the restriction must be clearly authorized, and we call atention to the fact that this Government of the United States, with express powers and implied powers only to carry those express powers, has no such indication as to such clear authorization, and that they must, restrictions must have a reasonable relation to a proper purpose.

JUSTICE FRANKFURTER: Mr. Hayes, before you sit down I would like to put to you a question because of the candor with which I know you will answer. I do not suppose that anybody could deny that this legislation, all these enactments, concern drawing a line, drawing a color line. I suppose that is what this this is all about. As to motives, the devil himself, as some one wise man said some time ago, "Knoweth not the mind of man."

But I must want to ask you whether it is your position that the Fourteenth Amendment or the Fifth, for your purposes, automatically invalidates all legislation which draws a line determined because of race?

I do not want to have trouble tomorrow or the day after tomorrow, but one has to look ahead these days.

I wonder whether you would say, right off from your analysis of the Constitution, that marriage laws relating to race are ipso facto on the face of things, unconstitutional?

MR. HAYES: I would say to Your Honor, in answer to the first question as to whether or not in my opinion—

JUSTICE FRANKFURTER: Because I need hardly tell you there is a good deal of legislation in this country drawing the line in connection with it.[56a]

MR. HAYES: Oh, yes, I am aware of that, sir. But I think that the problem is an entirely different one. With respect to the first part of your query as to whether or not I think automatically it becomes—

JUSTICE FRANKFURTER: I mean that that denial to the states and to the Congress of the United States and to the District is written in by plain implication of the Fourteenth and the Fifth Amendment, that is what I want to know.

---

[56a]Miscegenation laws were finally declared unconstitutional in Loving v.Virginia, 388 U.S. 1 (1967).

MR. HAYES: I want to say my answer to that is this, if Your Honor please: I think that the very purpose of this Court is the very answer to that question. I think that this Court is called upon with that question now properly posed to make the answer.

JUSTICE FRANKFURTER: You mean as to schools?

MR. HAYES: Yes, sir; that is what your first question, I thought, was addressed to.

JUSTICE FRANKFURTER: Yes.

MR. HAYES: I answered that by saying as to schools this Court is called upon to say that this sort of thing cannot happen because it is a violation of the due process clause of the Fifth Amendment, and the due process clause of the Fifth Amendment does not lend itself to any substantial proposition. You can have substantial equality but you cannot have substantial liberty.

JUSTICE FRANKFURTER: Is that because no legislation which draws any line with reference to race is automatically outlawed by the Fifth and the Fourteenth Amendment? So that takes you over—I am violating my own rule against posing hypothetical cases and, particularly, one that is as full of implications as the laws relating to the marriage laws involved, but I think one has to test these things to see what is the principle which you are invoking before this Court.

Is it all-embracing, is it the all-embracing principle, that no legislation which is based on differentiation of race is valid?

MR. HAYES: I am invoking rather the principle which I think this Court involved in the Hirabayashi case when this Court said that legislation based upon race is immediately suspect; that is what I am invoking.

JUSTICE FRANKFURTER: Well, that is a very candid and logical answer. That simply means that it can be valid. It is not an absolute prohibition, that good cause must be shown or great cause must be shown for the rule.

MR. HAYES: That is right, sir; and it is for that reason that I move to the next position of public necessity that was pointed out in those cases, and of the fact that even with the public necessity you must meet the three requirements.

JUSTICE BLACK: Why do you have to equate the Fourteenth Amendment and the Fifth Amendment provisions on that score?

MR. HAYES: I am not attempting to equate them, if Your Honor please. I am attempting rather to say that as far as the Fifth Amendment is concerned there is no possibility of equating. You cannot make a quantum with respect to one's liberty.

JUSTICE BLACK: You have just referred to the fact that we said that under the Fifth Amendment such laws are suspect, which means that we look at them very carefully to see if they can discriminate on account of race or distinguish on account of race. Do you think the same rule applies with reference to the

Fourteenth Amendment which was passed under entirely different circumstances and for entirely different purposes?

MR. HAYES: Yes. I think the Fourteenth Amendment has within it inherent those possibilities. They have inherent within it the due process clause as well as the equal protection clause.

JUSTICE FRANKFURTER: But you have got to stand on the due process clause?

MR. HAYES: Yes. I am standing on due process.

JUSTICE FRANKFURTER: I take it that was what Justice Black had in mind, and which was behind Justice Black's question.

MR. HAYES: If that be the answer, that is what I was attempting to say. I was not attempting to equate them. We are relying on due process.

JUSTICE DOUGLAS: Your closest case in point so far as decisions go is Farrington?

MR. HAYES: Yes, Your Honor, and in fact, the Farrington case embraced the Meyer, Bartels, and the Pierce case. And that brings them into this.

## ARGUMENT ON BEHALF OF PETITIONERS

### by MR. NABRIT

MR. NABRIT: If the Court please, it would appear necessary that petitioners make clear the position which they take in the midst of these five cases.

It is our position, simply stated, that the respondents, the public school board officials, in the District of Columbia do not possess either the constitutional power or the statutory power to deny these minor petitioners admission to Sousa Junior High School solely because of race or color. Now, that, as we take it, is the sole question to be considered by this Court.

In considering that question, we would urge upon the Court that it consider whether these respondents possess that power under the due process clause, whether they possess it because these acts of Congress compel it or authorize it, either, whether they possess it in the face of sections 41 and 43 of Title 8 of the United States Code, known as the Civil Rights Act of 1866, or whether they possess it in light of the pledge which this Government has given towards the implementation of human freedoms and rights without any distinction on the basis of race or color; in other words, not as a requirement of the charge but as a policy which is enunciated by the charge.

Now, it would appear to petitioners that it is necessary also for this Court to consider the fact that we are not dealing with the State of South Carolina, we are not dealing with the State of Virginia, the State of Delaware, or the State of Kansas. We are not here concerned with those over-sensitive areas of state and federal relation. That is not involved in this case. We are not involved in this case with the question of the sensitiveness of states with the projection of federal power.

We are concerned here solely with the question of the relationship of the federal government to its citizens. It might be assumed as the basis for our approach to this problem that we go back and look at something of the history of our Constitution. We know that when the Constitution was adopted, there were provisions in there which made it possible for us to have an institution of slavery.

We also know that the juristic concepts were such, in *Dred Scott* v. *Sandford*,[57] that it was decided that a Negro could not be a citizen.

But along came the Thirteenth, Fourteenth and Fifteenth Amendments. The Thirteenth Amendment removed slavery as a condition, as a status. The Fourteenth, so far as the federal citizens are concerned, gave citizenship to those born or naturalized in the United States.

Now, those things together would appear to us to have removed from the federal government any power to impose racial distinctions in dealing with its citizens.

Now, we know that this is a government of limited powers, and we know that it has express powers, and one of these is to deal with the District of Columbia.

JUSTICE MINTON: Is it your thought that the adoption of the Fourteenth Amendment's due process clause changed the meaning of the Fifth Amendment's due process clause?

MR. NABRIT: No, Mr. Justice. I thought, with the abolition of slavery and the federal citizenship conferred in the first section of the Fourteenth Amendment, that those two things robbed any dubious power which the federal government may have had prior to that time to deal with people solely on the basis of race or color.

JUSTICE BLACK: Do you think that there is any doubt that they had complete power before that?

MR. NABRIT: No, not in the light of *Dred Scott* v. *Sandford*, I do not doubt it, because in the light of *Dred Scott* v. *Sandford*, they simply said that no matter whether you went to Missouri, or where you went, you are a Negro and you cannot be a citizen, and as soon as you cannot be a citizen, you cannot come within the purview of these things about which we are talking.

JUSTICE FRANKFURTER: We are talking about the District.

MR. NABRIT: That is right.

JUSTICE FRANKFURTER: We are talking about the District.

MR. NABRIT: Yes, I am saying the District, because if you could not be a federal citizen—and that is what *Dred Scott* held—it was for jurisdictional purposes, but everybody in the country took it as a finding of a lack of status as far as Negroes were concerned in 1856.

[57]19 How. 393 (1857). The famous Dred Scott case declared that even if a Negro slave settled in free territory he was still a slave and could never attain the rights of United States citizenship.

JUSTICE FRANKFURTER: You could not be a citizen merely by going to Missouri.

MR. NABRIT: Yes, I agree with you, Mr. Justice Frankfurter, if you say that the Court went further than it should have or had to. But I would say this, that after the citizenship that was conferred under the first clause of the Fourteenth Amendment, and after the abolition of slavery, that we would seriously question, as this Court questioned, the power of the federal government to deal with a federal citizen solely on the basis of his race. The only two cases that I can recall in the history of this Court where it is held that they could be done were in two cases where the Court said that there was an express power to wage war, that that was one of the all-embracing powers, and that as an implied power necessary to prevent sabotage and espionage, this Court said, under those circumstances, that a citizen of the United States might, one, be detained in his home overnight, and the other, be removed to a relocation center and there detained.[58]

So this Court itself, even when it recognized the all-inclusiveness of the war power, when the security of the nation was at stake—this Court has said, "We must test this detention, first, to see if it is authorized and see if the statute authorizes it." If it is a case like *Ex parte Endo*,[59] or it is not authorized, it is not good. Even if it is authorized, there must be a relationship between the purpose and the statute, and when we find that, as the Court said, we are not satisfied. There must also be some purpose which it is within the competency of this Government to effect.

JUSTICE REED: Who is to determine that?

MR. NABRIT: This Court.

JUSTICE REED: And Congress cannot determine it for itself?

MR. NABRIT: No, sir. Never in the history of this country have the individual liberties of the citizen been entrusted in the hands of the legislators. The very founders of the Government refused to agree to the Constitution itself until they could be satisfied, Jefferson and others, that they had a Bill of Rights, so as to protect individual liberties.

JUSTICE REED: That would mean that we would examine the basis, the foundation of Congressional enactments relating to race, such as the Japanese cases?

MR. NABRIT: It is my position—

JUSTICE REED: Who is going to make that determination as to whether it is necessary or proper or desirable? This Court?

[58]Hirabayashi v. United States, *supra*, n. 56 and Korematsu v. United States, 323 U.S. 214 (1944), where the Court upheld the exclusion of all Japanese from a West Coast military area during World War II.

[59]323 U.S. 283 (1944). The Court interpreted the law under which Japanese were relocated on the West Coast as not permitting indefinite detention of loyal Japanese-Americans.

MR. NABRIT: I would say this, that this Court, faced with a piece of legislation by Congress which did that, or an act under a piece of legislation which did that, would in my opinion test it by the same type of test that it used in *Korematsu* and in *Hirabayashi* and in *Endo*. This Court tested it by that same method and found that it had no such authority and released Mitsye Endo. In other words, we ask nothing different than that we be given the same type of protection in peace that these Japanese were given in time of war. We are not asking anything different.

We are simply saying that liberty to us is just as precious, and that the same way in which the Court measures out liberty to others, it measures to us, and Congress itself has nothing to do with it, except that in the exercise of a power which Congress has, if Congress determines that it has something that it must do as an implied necessity in order to carry out that power, and then we say it does not and we bring the question to this Court, this Court would decide it.

I cannot make the statement that there is no situation in which Congress might not use race. I do not know of one right now, except the war powers. But that certainly leaves it open for determination by this Court.

But at the same time, I assert that there is absolutely no basis that can be produced that would be accepted in our country in 1952 that would justify Congress making it such a racial basis for the exclusion of a student from a high school in the District of Columbia.

JUSTICE REED: Would that same test apply on it for Congress under the commerce clause?

MR. NABRIT: Under the commerce clause?

JUSTICE REED: I just happened to choose that.

MR. NABRIT: I was trying to think of one under the commerce clause.

JUSTICE REED: Or any of the other clauses?

MR. NABRIT: Or any of the other clauses, where the only purpose was the purpose of making a racial distinction, in affording it.

For instance, if they say that no Negro can ride the trains, the answer is yes; it would apply precisely.

JUSTICE REED: Could we examine the reasonableness of that decision?

MR. NABRIT: Because you have said already, Mr. Justice Reed, or this Court, that as soon as we see that, we suspect it. It is not to say that it is unconstitutional, but it is to say that it is suspect, and you have said in so many cases, race is invidious; race is irrelevant. So when we get over in the federal government where there is nobody to deal with, but just us, the federal government, we do not have to worry. We know it is irrelevant, invidious, odious and suspect. So this Court should examine it.

(Whereupon, at 4:30 p.m., the Court arose.)

(Oral argument was resumed at 12:10 p.m., December 11, 1952.)

THE CHIEF JUSTICE: Number 413, Bolling, et al., versus C. Melvin Sharpe, et al.

Mr. Nabrit.

### ARGUMENT ON BEHALF OF PETITIONERS—Resumed

#### by MR. NABRIT

MR. NABRIT: If it please the Court, at the close of the Court's session yesterday, we were attempting to outline the basic arguments of the petitioners. Unfortunately, we only have ten minutes left, and probably we can barely outline it.

We would like to address ourselves, however, to some of the questions which seem to be of concern to the Court in these cases.

JUSTICE FRANKFURTER: Before you sit down, I hope you will include in your answers the answer to this question, whether during the life of this statute there came before Congress periodically or at such periods as there did come, if any, the requirement to make appropriations for the enforcement of this statute, or, since you question whether they had the duty to enforce it the way they did, for the things that the District authorities did, and whether during that period there was any legislative effort to stop these appropriations or to prohibit the authorities from doing what I understand you and your colleagues said was not authorized by this legislation.

MR. NABRIT: I would be very happy to address myself to that at this moment, Mr. Justice Frankfurter.

In looking at these statutes enacted by Congress governing the schools in the District, I should like to preface my answer by saying that the first statute passed with respect to public education in the District of Columbia was passed in 1862.

Now, at the time petitioners drafted their briefs in support of our proposition, we had taken the position that the statutes did require it, and we did set out the history. However, if the Court is interested in the history, there is in the brief filed in this case amicus curiae for the eighteen organizations, on pages 20 and 21, some historical analysis of these statutes, which may be of help to the Court.

The Court may also take judicial notice of the Barnard Report, which is in the special report of the Commissioner of Education of the Public Schools of the District of Columbia in 1871, and in that volume at page 49 and page 267, they give the history of the public schools of the District of Columbia up to that time, and they also discuss the Act of 1864, to which I shall advert in just a moment.

JUSTICE FRANKFURTER: Is that report referred to in your brief or in the amici brief?

MR. NABRIT: No.

JUSTICE FRANKFURTER: What is the name of that report?

MR. NABRIT: The District of Columbia, the Barnard Special Report, Commissioner of Education on the Public Schools in the District of Columbia, 1871.

JUSTICE FRANKFURTER: Thank you.

MR. NABRIT: That is the Government Printing Office. It does not give any other name. It is the House of Representatives.

Now, if the Court please, in 1862, this was the situation in the District of Columbia. There were a number of private schools for whites and a number of private schools for Negroes in Georgetown, Washington, and the District of Columbia. As you recall, we had not yet combined all of those into what is now the District. But for purposes of this discussion I think that the Court may take those as one.

At that time, these private schools were supported by private philanthropy. In 1862, Congress, as discussions in Congress indicated—about that there is no dispute—being concerned about the support of the schools which existed in the District for the Negroes, enacted a measure which provided that these schools should be supported by tax funds derived from taxes levied upon free Negroes.

That did not appear either to produce revenue or to be satisfactory. So Congress then enacted a statute the latter part of that year in which Congress said that these schools should be supported by funds derived from the general revenue, that is, from the taxes of all of the inhabitants of the District.

Now, this, as you recall, was in 1862, before the Fourteenth Amendment and before the actual effect of the Emancipation Proclamation.

Now, at this time, the members of the legislature stated that they were concerned about what should be done for the Negroes who would be free. I think it is also fair to say to the Court that in the Barnard Report, to which I referred, the Congressmen, in presenting this to the House, and stating that there had been no printed report of the proceedings, stated that they were providing no separate schools for Negroes because they had no adequate financial support, and they were concerned about the educational situation.

In 1864, the basic acts out of which grow the present acts governing the schools in the District of Columbia were enacted. They provided in substance that suitable rooms and schools should be provided for the training of the colored pupils, and in addition to that they provided mandatory legislation to ensure that a proportionate share of the funds secured from revenue in the District should be allotted to these schools.

I might say to the Court that they did this because experience had shown that there was some diversion of funds that Congress had intended for these schools to the white schools.

Now, all of this is uncontroverted. There is no dispute about this.

Then, after the proposal of the Fourteenth Amendment in 1866, and after its adoption in 1868, there was, in 1874, a re-enactment of these statutes, in substance as they are found in our brief.

Now, it appears to petitioners that it is the contention of the respondents that that re-enactment after the adoption of the Fourteenth Amendment was a congressional construction of these acts that they permitted separate schools, and I think that it was the issue which underlies the question of Mr. Justice Frankfurter, as to re-enactment of these statutes and as to the appropriations in respect to these acts over all these years.

THE CHIEF JUSTICE: Do I understand that the schools were separate prior to the adoption of the Fourteenth Amendment?

MR. NABRIT: Yes, sir, they were.

THE CHIEF JUSTICE: And at one time they taxed property separately; they taxed colored property for the maintenance of colored schools and white property for the maintenance of white schools?

MR. NABRIT: No. They did not say anything about the white schools. I should say this—

THE CHIEF JUSTICE: The white schools were run out of general revenues?

MR. NABRIT: I presume so. I did not find that phrase. But I would answer your question by saying that they must have been supported out of the general revenue, since this special provision was made.

But I should say this, Mr. Chief Justice. At this time, public education—this is the first public education attempt in the District of Columbia—public education itself was suspect in the country, especially with these compulsory features that were attached to it, so that the least we can say is that at the beginning of public education, Congress indicated before the Fourteenth Amendment, by its support to these separate schools, that at that time separate schools existed, and could exist.

THE CHIEF JUSTICE: And in the District of Columbia, they did exist at the time of the passage and the adoption of the Fourteenth Amendment?

MR. NABRIT: That is correct.

Now, it is the petitioners' position at that stage in the history of these statutes that prior to the adoption of the Fourteenth Amendment, respondents can get no support from whatever Congress did with these schools; that they must gain their support by reason of the action of Congress thereafter. I think they joined in that position. It is therefore the position of petitioners that the action of Congress in 1874, in re-enacting these statutes, is not persuasive on this Court as to whether or not either (1) Congress intended compulsory or authorized segregation in the District, or (2) whether that is constitutional.

THE CHIEF JUSTICE: Mr. Nabrit, in view of the questions from the bench, you may have five minutes' more time, and the District may have similar time.

MR. NABRIT: Thank you.

As to the re-enactment of these statutes—

JUSTICE FRANKFURTER: I did not mean to divert you on any legal implication. I wanted to know what the facts were, whether from year to year appropriations had to be made, or whether the question was raised, and whether it got through without anybody's thinking about it.

MR. NABRIT: Yes, sir. I wanted to address myself to that, but I thought you were entitled to have some background for it.

Now, specifically addressing myself—

JUSTICE REED: Apparently there is no reference in the briefs to legislative history. Was there a discussion of the desirability or the undesirability of segregation in 1874?

MR. NABRIT: I do not know about 1874, but there was a discussion of it prior to 1874, in 1866 and 1864.

JUSTICE REED: Was it directed toward the adoption of segregation?

MR. NABRIT: That is right. And there was considerable difference of opinion among the Negroes in the District of Columbia on that question.

JUSTICE REED: I meant on the floor of the Congress.

MR. NABRIT: It was not printed, you see. So we just have to suppose that there was some discussion. I would say for the purpose of the Court, it might be assumed that there was discussions. But it was not printed.

THE CHIEF JUSTICE: But that was prior to the adoption of the Amendment?

MR. NABRIT: That is right. And we take the position that on this particular problem, it is not persuasive to the Court.

Now, as to your specific question, Mr. Justice Frankfurter, there have been acts in support of these schools, appropriation acts, directed to the support of this separate system in the District of Columbia each year, and also in 1906 a group of citizens went before Congress to urge in the appropriation bill the adoption of more powers for the then assistant Negro superintendent.

Also, subsequent to that, there was agitation for the creation of another first assistant superintendent for the white schools and for the Negro schools, and in each of those two instances, Congress provided the money and the position, and as to the first assistant, white and colored, they wrote that into the legislation, in addition to the appropriation.

Now, as to whether or not—

JUSTICE FRANKFURTER: You say they wrote into the legislation that there was to be an assistant, or deputy, superintendent for colored schools and for white schools?

MR. NABRIT: Precisely, in language as clear as that.

JUSTICE FRANKFURTER: That goes back to when, you say? 1906?

MR. NABRIT: Nineteen hundred six was when they enlarged the powers. This last act, I believe, was in 1947. I mean, this first assistant.

JUSTICE FRANKFURTER: But it was in 1906 that there was explicit legislative recognition that there is such a person as a superintendent for colored schools?

MR. NABRIT: This is correct.

There is no question so far as petitioners are concerned that that type of language has persisted in the District of Columbia. And as to the enforcement, there is no question about it, the Congress has done it.

It is petitioners' position (1) that there is nothing in this language that anybody can find that compels segregation. This is clear. There is language which may be said to permit it, or authorize it. About that, men may differ. Some may think that the differences are unreasonable, in view of the language. It is petitioners' position that it does not authorize it. But if it does authorize it, to the extent that it is implemented by these respondents, it is unconstitutional action on the part of respondents.

JUSTICE FRANKFURTER: You would say that providing whatever it is, X thousand dollars' salary, for an assistant superintendent for Negro schools is merely a provision that if there are to be Negro schools, and if there is to be the assistant superintendent, he is to get $6,000; is that it?

MR. NABRIT: I would go further than that. I would say, since there is in the District of Columbia a system of Negro schools—I mean, I would recognize the fact that they are.

JUSTICE FRANKFURTER: If you say that—

MR. NABRIT: I would.

JUSTICE FRANKFURTER: I wonder if you are not saying, since there is, and Congress appropriated for it, that it recognized the right, at least, under the statute, that there should be Negro schools?

MR. NABRIT: Now, the reason I do not say that, Mr. Justice Frankfurter, is that the language of this Court in *Ex parte Endo,* when they said that wherever there is implied legislation which restricts the individual, or curtails, to use the Court's language, the individual rights of citizens, that curtailment has to be explicitly stated in clear and unmistakable language.

JUSTICE FRANKFURTER: It does not touch on a constitutional point.

MR. NABRIT: Yes.

JUSTICE FRANKFURTER: I wonder if it does not carry permissiveness into a clear recognition by Congress here in the situation where they provide money, because the alternative is that Congress was providing money for something that they did not authorize.

MR. NABRIT: I would say yes, and I would say that that would not change petitioners' position. In other words, I agree to that.

Now, with this other principle, I want to say—

JUSTICE FRANKFURTER: In the course of these years, was there opposition to this legislation, or were there voices raised to the Congress, or objections to this? Did the issue ever come to discussion or to challenge?

MR. NABRIT: As to whether or not this system should be changed?

JUSTICE FRANKFURTER: Yes.

MR. NABRIT: In the early years—

JUSTICE FRANKFURTER: I am not meaning to draw any inference. I just want the facts.

MR. NABRIT: In the early years, there was such discussion. And I am also of the opinion that we may, on an exhaustive study of that question, find such language even later, and it is petitioners' position that, as this Court has said, Congress does not enact statutes, or does not deal with things in many instances for political or other reasons, so that petitioners would not consider that persuasive.

Now, I would like to say this final thing before my time runs out, that if the Court disagrees with us, which it may, and says that these statutes compelled and authorized, and therefore this action may be constitutional, we urge the Court not to do it, because, as this Court has said, where a possible interpretation might lead into the danger of declaring a statute unconstitutional, the Court will avoid that construction.

It is our opinion that if you do hold that these statutes compelled and authorized, they would then be unconstitutional under the due process clause of the Fifth Amendment, but more than that, we suggest to the Court that they would be in violation of Article I, section 9, clause 3, as bills of attainder, not under the classical concept of a bill of attainder, but under the concept of a bill of attainder as enunciated by this Court in *United States* v. *Lovett,*[60] and it would appear to us that denial of admission solely on the basis of race or color of petitioners to Sousa fits precisely the formula set forth by this Court in *United States* v. *Lovett.*

Now, if I have time, I will explain it. That is, in *United States* v. *Lovett,* this Court said that where Congress had named Lovett and two others in an appropriation bill and said that they should not receive funds from that until they had been recommended by the President and approved by Congress, that that was a permanent ban on employment. This Court went to the congressional discussion to find out whether they were trying to get them for disloyalty and subversive activities.

Now, we say that if this Court decides that these statutes prohibit Negroes from ever associating with whites or ever studying with whites in a white school, they have placed the same ban upon them, and they have done it without a trial, as in the other, merely because for some undisclosed crime, some status, some position, some matter of birth, appropriation, or something else in the past, these Negroes are unfit to associate with whites, and under the definition of a bill of attainder as laid down by this Court in *United States* v. *Lovett,* we suggest that there would be another danger that these acts would be unconstitutional.

Therefore, we urge upon this Court not to adopt that construction, and we

[60]328 U.S. 303 (1946). A law forbidding the payment of compensation to certain named government employees charged with subversive activities was held to be an unconstitutional bill of attainder.

say this to the Court: You would not reach the constitutionality, because if you find these statutes do not require it and do not authorize it, then the action of respondents is unlawful, and you may direct admission into Sousa Junior High School.

THE CHIEF JUSTICE: Mr. Korman.

### ARGUMENT ON BEHALF OF RESPONDENTS

#### by MR. KORMAN

MR. KORMAN: May it please the Court, questions have been asked by the Court concerning the history of this legislation, and my distinguished opponent, Mr. Hayes, has thrown the gauntlet down to us to show the real reason for this type of legislation setting up a dual school system in the District of Columbia.

I shall endeavor to point out to the Court the history of this legislation, and I accept the challenge of Mr. Hayes to show what the real reason for this legislation was.

In 1862, there was slavery in the District of Columbia. In April of 1862, by an Act of April 16, the Congress abolished slavery in the District. That was three and one-half years before the Thirteenth Amendment abolished it in the States.

There was a problem of doing something for these emancipated people. Up to that point, they had had no schools except some few private schools for the free Negroes.

So the first enactment of Congress on May 20, 1862, was to set up a system of schools in the County of Washington. At that time, the District of Columbia consisted of three parts: the City of Georgetown, the City of Washington, and the County of Washington. They were distinct entities.

The City of Georgetown had its own council, mayor, and board of aldermen; the City of Washington had the same setup; the county was governed by a levy court.

It appears that there were no schools of any kind, white or colored, in the county. There apparently were schools for white children, publicly supported, in the cities.

On May 20, 1862, the Congress passed an enactment which established a system of schools in the county, white and colored. It was a long act, with some thirty-six sections to it, and in section 35 they provided that the levy court in its discretion—apparently there were not many Negroes in the county at that time—but the levy court in its discretion might levy a tax of 1/8 of 1 per cent on property owned by persons of color for the purpose of initiating a system of education of colored children in said county.

But I remind you that in that same act, they set up for the first time a system of white schools in the county. Now, in that same paragraph 35, they said this:

> And said trustees are authorized to receive any donations or contributions that may be made for the benefit of said schools —

that is, the schools for colored children—

> by persons disposed to aid in the elevation of the colored population in the District of Columbia.

That was the purpose of these acts, to aid in the elevation of the colored population of the District of Columbia, and not to stamp them, as Mr. Hayes says,
with a badge of inferiority, this pure racism that he speaks of.

They were trying to elevate these people.

It goes on to say that:

Said trustees shall account for those funds.

Then the next day, May 21, the Congress passed another act for the Cities
of Washington and Georgetown, and with your permission I should like to read
that entire act, which is not lengthy, because to me it shows what the purpose of
this legislation was:

BE IT ENACTED, [and so forth]
That from and after the passage of this Act it shall be the duty of the municipal
authorities of the Cities of Washington and Georgetown in the District of Columbia
to set apart ten per-centum of the amount received from taxes levied on the real and
personal property in said Cities owned by persons of color, which sum received from
taxes as aforesaid shall be appropriated for the purpose of initiating a system of
primary schools for the education of colored children residing in said Cities.
BE IT FURTHER ENACTED that the board of trustees of the public schools in
said Cities shall have sole control of the fund arising from the tax aforesaid as well as
from contributions by persons disposed to aid in the education of the colored race, or
from any other source which shall be kept as a distinct fund from the general school
fund.

which I believe answers Mr. Justice Frankfurter's question.

It is made their duty to provide suitable rooms and teachers for the number of
schools as in their opinion will best accommodate the colored children in the various
portions of said Cities.

Section 3 deals with the setting up of boards of trustees, which says that they
shall have equal supervision over both the white and colored schools.

Section 4—this is the same Act, I remind Your Honors—

That all persons of color in the District of Columbia or in the corporate limits of the
Cities of Washington and Georgetown shall be subject and amenable to the same
laws and ordinances to which free white persons are or may be subject or amenable;
that they shall be tried for any offenses against the laws in the same manner as free
white persons are or may be tried for the same offenses, and that upon being legally
convicted of any crime or offense against any law or ordinance, such persons of color
shall be liable to the same penalty or punishment, and no other, as would be imposed
on or inflicted upon white persons for the same crime or offense and all acts or parts
of acts inconsistent with the provisions of this Act are hereby repealed.

Now, when we find those provisions in the same Act setting up schools for
colored children and saying that they may receive funds from those who may want
to help the colored race, and setting up these provisions for equal treatment of
both races before the law, there can be no question of what the intention of the
Congress was at that time.

On July 11, 1862, a few months later, Congress transferred to the board of
trustees of the schools for colored children—of the schools for colored

children—thereby created the powers with respect to such schools vested by the Act of May 21 in the board of trustees for public schools in the cities.

By an Act of June 25, 1864, Congress established the Board of Commissioners of Primary Schools of Washington County, District of Columbia, and in section 9 thereof authorized that Board to purchase sites, erect schools, regulate the number of children to be taught in each school, and the price of tuition, and so on, and said this:

> That any white resident might place his or her child in the schools provided for the education of white children in said county, and any colored resident should have the same rights with respect to the colored schools.

It seems to me that that definitely established an intent to set up separate schools.

Then in the Act of May 21, 1862, in section 18 of that Act, they authorized the municipal authorities of the Cities of Washington and Georgetown to set apart each year from the whole fund received from all sources applicable to public education such proportionate part thereof as the number of colored children between the ages of sixteen and seventeen in the respective cities bears to the total number of children to help support these colored schools.

Then in 1871, the Congress enacted the Legislative Assembly Act, which combined the Cities of Washington and Georgetown and the county into one unit, and they transferred all these schools to the combined board of education which governed all of the schools in the two cities and the county.

A question was asked by Mr. Justice Frankfurter, I believe, as to whether or not there were any specific attacks upon this system of separate schools, and it was intimated that while there were some before the adoption of the Fourteenth Amendment, there were none thereafter.

I specifically call the Court's attention to the fact, which is mentioned in our brief, that in the 41st, 42nd, and 43rd Congresses, between 1870 and 1874, there were three separate bills introduced by Senator Sumner of Massachusetts to strike down the dual school system in the District of Columbia, and they all failed of passage.

The Fourteenth Amendment was adopted in 1868, and all three of these things came after that.

Specifically, I call the Court's attention to the fact that the Civil Rights Act of 1875 was debated over a considerable period during the 42nd and 43rd Congresses, although that Act is not now constitutional, having been so declared on other grounds. But the bill which became the Civil Rights Act of 1875, as originally drawn, specifically provided for the abolition of separation in the schools of the United States, in and out of the District of Columbia, but as finally enacted, the word "schools" was stricken from that Act.

So it seems to me that as late as 1875, you have a specific declaration by Congress that there shall be a dual school system in the District of Columbia.

Now, what transpired thereafter? In 1900, Congress set up a new school board, a paid school board, of seven persons, and they provided at that time for a board of education, a superintendent, and two assistant superintendents, one of whom under the direction of the superintendent shall have charge of the schools for colored children.

That was the Act of June 6, 1900.

Then, in 1906, the Congress reorganized the whole school system here, and they established the present Board of Education as it exists today. The organic Act of 1906 was debated at some length, and there were lengthy hearings on that before a subcommittee of the Congress.

In our brief, I set forth some of the expressions of Negro leaders at that time, and I should ask the Court to please bear with me while I read some of them to you, because it seems to me that they go to the very heart of this question.

We find Professor William A. Joiner—

JUSTICE REED: What page is that?

MR. KORMAN: This is on page 25 of respondents' brief.

We find Professor William A. Joiner, of Howard University, addressing the committee, and I did not include the letter which he had presented to the committee, but I should like to read you one sentence from the letter, which he handed to the committee prior to making this statement. He says this, and this is found on page 199 of the hearings on that bill:

> Experience in the past dating back to the first organization of the schools for colored children in the District has tended to prove that the interests of these schools are most carefully guarded by those who are most deeply interested in the children who attend them.

Then he said this:

> I think, Mr. Chairman, that that embodies the main sentiment as expressed by that organization, an organization composed of those whose minds have led them into literary pursuits and those who have given attention to the best welfare and interest of their people. It may seem strange that this particular word 'colored' or the idea of colored schools thrusts itself into this argument. I would it were not so. Facts are stubborn things, and when we deal with facts we must deal with them as they exist and not as we would they were; and so, Mr. Chairman, it becomes our province and our duty to do what we can to see that in the administration of school affairs in that most precious birthright of equality of opportunity spoken to us by President Eliot (of Harvard) that there will not be the slightest divergence from the division, 'unto him who needs and most unto him who needs most.'

Then Professor Lewis B. Moore, of Howard University, said this at the same hearings, and I am reading from page 26 of our brief:

> Give us what is being asked for here by the colored citizens, give us that, and we shall conduct under the guidance of the Board of Education the colored schools of the District of Columbia in such a way as to produce just as good results as are produced anywhere else in this country.

As the result of those sorts of expressions, we find this in the report on the bill, which became the Act of 1906 setting up the school board: The bill does not change the number of assistant superintendents, merely enlarging the power of the colored superintendent so that he shall, besides having jurisdiction over the colored grade schools, also have entire jurisdiction over the colored normal, high, and manual-training schools. This was done at the earnest solicitation of the colored educators who appeared before the committee and was heartily endorsed by the superintendent of Howard University. The hearings developed that a great deal of friction had arisen between the director of high schools and the teachers in the colored high school, and to avoid this it was the unanimous opinion and desire of all who testified that not only should the colored superintendent have control, but that the colored schools in every instance should be designated as colored schools, so that no possible mistake could arise in that regard.

So in the Act of 1906, the Congress provided for a superintendent of schools and for two assistant superintendents of schools, one of whom, a colored man, should have charge of the colored schools.

That is not, however, the last expression by the Congress upon this point. As has been intimated, every year for practically ninety years there have been applications to the Congress for funds to operate these schools, and every year the justification for the appropriations has contained statements that so much is needed for colored schools, so much is needed for colored teachers, so much is needed for white schools, so much is needed for white teachers, so much is needed for new construction because the colored population has increased and we need another colored school, and so forth, and so forth.

In addition, in the Teachers' Salary Act of 1945, we find these expressions by the Congress:

> There shall be two first assistant superintendents of schools

—they are now first assistant superintendents—

> one white first assistant superintendent for the white schools, who under the direction of the superintendent of schools shall have general supervision over the white schools, and one colored first assistant superintendent for the colored schools who under the direction of the superintendent of schools shall have sole charge of all employees, classes, and schools in which colored children are taught

—not the colored schools, but the schools, classes, and employees under which colored children are taught.

The next section of that Act is:

> Boards of examiners for carrying out the provisions of the statutes with reference to the examination of teachers shall consist of the superintendent of schools and not less than four or more than six members of the supervisory or teaching staff of the white schools for the white schools, and of the superintendent of schools and not less than four nor more than six members of the supervisory or teaching staff of the colored schools for the colored schools.

Then in the next section:

> There shall be appointed a board of education on the recommendation of the superintendent of schools, a chief examiner for the board of examiners for white schools, and an associate superintendent in the colored schools shall be designated by the superintendent as chief examiner for the board of examiners for the colored schools.

and so on, almost identical language in the Teachers' Salary Act of 1947, two years later, and the latest expression by the Congress on that score was the Act of October 24, 1951, amending the Teachers' Salary Act, where we find in section 13—and this was one year ago, if the Court please:

There shall be appointed by the Board of Education on the recommendation of the superintendent of schools a chief examiner for the board of examiners for white schools and a chief examiner for the board of examiners for colored schools. All members of the respective boards of examiners shall serve without additional compensation.

It seems to me that that should dispose of this question of whether or not Congress intended that there should be separate schools for white and colored children.

In addition, however, twice in the history of these acts, the United States Court of Appeals for the District of Columbia Circuit has passed upon the question. In the case of *Wall* v. *Oyster,*[61] in 1910, the court specifically said that these acts of 1862 and 1864, and so on, that I read to the Court, and which were carried over into the revised statutes in 1874—the court said that they "manifest an intention by Congress that these schools shall be separate.

In the case of *Carr* v. *Corning,* and *Browne* v. *Magdeburger,* decided on a joint opinion in 1950,[62] the court came to exactly the same conclusion, the court saying:

These various enactments by the Congress cannot be read with any meaning except that the schools for white and colored children were then intended to be separate.

Now, in the light of those decisions by the highest court of the District of Columbia—and I remind the Court that this Court has said many times that it accepts the construction of purely locally applicable statutes as decided by the highest court of the jurisdiction—in the case of the states, the interpretation by the highest court of the state is, it has been said, completely binding on this Court, and in the case of the Court of Appeals of the District of Columbia, this Court has said several times that in most instances, and generally, you accept the interpretation of that court of locally applicable statutes.

I might read to you further from the expressions of leaders at the time the bill which became the Act of 1906 was being considered. There were expressions by Dr. Kelly Miller, one of the leaders of his people in this city, one of the foremost fighters for rights for the colored people. Indeed, one of the newest junior high schools for colored in the District is named after him, and he says essentially the same things that I have read to Your Honors in support of that Act of 1906.

What, then, is the situation? I say to the Court, and I say to my distinguished adversary, Mr. Hayes, these acts were not passed, this dual school system was not set up to stamp these people with a badge of inferiority. There was not this racial feeling that he speaks of with such fervor behind these acts. There was behind these acts a kindly feeling; there was behind these acts an intention to help these people who had been in bondage. And there was and there still is an intention by the Congress to see that these children shall be educated in a healthful atmosphere, in a wholesome atmosphere, in a place where they are wanted, in a place where they will not be looked upon with hostility, in a place where there will

[61]36 App. D.C. 60.
[62]See n. 36, *supra.*

be a receptive atmosphere for learning for both races without the hostility that undoubtedly Congress thought might creep into these situations.

We cannot hide our faces and our minds from the fact that there is feeling between races in these United States. It is a deplorable situation. Would that it were not so. But we must face these facts.

We know that there have been outbursts between races north of here where there are not separate schools for white and colored. We know that these things exist, and constitutionally, if there be a question as to which is better, to throw these people together into the schools and perhaps bring that hostile atmosphere, if it exists, into the schoolroom and harm the ability to learn of both the races, or to give them completely adequate, separate, full educational opportunities on both sides, where they will be instructed on the white side by white teachers, who are sympathetic to them, and on the colored side by colored teachers, who are sympathetic to them, and where they will receive from the lips of their own people education in colored folklore, which is important to a people—if that is to be decided, who else shall decide it but the legislature, who decides things for each jurisdiction?

And I say that the Constitution does not inveigh against such a determination by the legislature.

The Fifth Amendment contains a due process clause, as does the Fourteenth Amendment. It does not, however, contain an equal protection clause. It has been said by this Court that the Congress is not bound not to pass discriminatory laws. It can pass discriminatory laws, because there is no equal protection clause in the Fifth Amendment. This Court has likewise over a long period of time, some ninety years, said that under the Fourteenth Amendment separate schools for white and colored children may be retained.

If, therefore, this Court has said that such schools may be maintained under the Fourteenth Amendment where there is an equal protection clause, how can my friends here argue to the Court that there may not be a dual school system in the District of Columbia for such fine reasons as I have demonstrated to the Court, when there is no equal protection clause binding on the Congress of the United States?

And if there be questions concerning the long line of decisions leading up to this point where this Court has said that separation in schools is proper and constitutional, there can be no clearer statement than there was in the case of *Gaines* v. *Canada,* decided scarcely fourteen years ago, where this Court said, through Mr. Chief Justice Hughes:

> The state has sought to fulfill that obligation by furnishing equal facilities in separate schools, a method the validity of which has been sustained by our decisions.

That was the language, "a method the validity of which has been sustained by our decisions."

But then they went on to say that you cannot do it in this case because those equal facilities have to be within the borders of the state and not outside the state.

That is all that case said. But it established the principle that if there were separate but equal facilities within the state, then it was constitutional. And I say to the Court that it is conceded here by my distinguished opponents that there is no question of equality here.

You live here in the District of Columbia or in its environs. You know that we have a complete system of schools here. I invite your attention to the fact that it is so complete that we have two side-by-side complete systems of schools for white and colored, autonomous each in every respect, with one exception: one superintendent over them and a board of education laying down the policy for both systems. But from the janitor up to the first assistant superintendent, the colored schools are completely autonomous, and if we need an exhibit of what fine people they turn out, I will turn to my friend here, a product of the local schools.

What has changed the Constitution in fourteen years, since the Gaines case? What changes have occurred? What policy announcements have there been by the Congress?

Questions were directed to counsel all through these cases about changed conditions. Mr. Justice Burton asked counsel if it were not true that these other cases could be disposed of as being proper law at the time they were decided, but not now in the light of changed conditions.

I ask the rhetorical question, What changed conditions? What has happened in\fourteen years that we did not know in 1938 when the Gaines case was decided? What is there now?

I submit to the Court that the answer is, nothing is new. The Constitution is the same today as it was in 1938 at the time all these other decisions came from the lips of this Court.

It has been said here by our distinguished oppents—indeed, it has been said by the Attorney General of the United States that Washington, this District of Columbia in which we live, is the window through which the world looks upon us. It does not seem to me that is a constitutional argument, and I should like to read something to the Court, if I may, with the Court's indulgence. This comes from this Court. After I have read it, I will tell you the case it comes from:

> No one, we presume, supposes that any change in public opinion or feeling, in relation to this unfortunate race, in the civilized nations of Europe or in this country, should induce the court to give to the words of the Constitution a more liberal construction in their favor than they were intended to bear when the instrument was framed and adopted.

—or, if I may paraphrase by saying, that they were intended to bear at the time of each amendment of it—

> Such an argument would be altogether inadmissible in any tribunal called on to interpret it. If any of its provisions are deemed unjust, there is a mode prescribed in the instrument itself by which it may be amended; but while it remains unaltered, it must be construed now as it was understood at the time of its adoption.

—or, if I may paraphrase, at the time of its amendment—

> It is not only the same in words, but the same in meaning, and delegates the same powers to the Government and reserves and secures the same rights and privileges to the citizen; and as long as it continues to exist in its present form, it speaks not only in the same words but with the same meaning and intent with which it spoke when it came from the hands of its framers, and was voted on and adopted by the people of the United States. Any other rule of construction would abrogate the judicial character of this court and make it the mere reflex of the popular opinion or passion of the day.

This court was not created by the Constitution for such purposes. Higher and graver trusts have been confided to it, and it must not falter in the path of duty.

That, Your Honors, was from *Dred Scott* v. *Sandford,* oh, almost one hundred years ago.

But it is equally applicable today.

They speak there of the civilized nations and how we look to them, just as my friends say to us here today that we must be careful; as the Attorney General says, we must be careful because the Iron Curtain countries talk about us. But he admits that they tell some lies about us. Would the change in this system stop them from telling lies if they want to tell them?

As regards the question of the applicability of the Fifth Amendment, even the Attorney General concedes that it raises a grave constitutional question when we say, "Does the Fifth Amendment control the situation?"

To some extent, I am indebted to the Attorney General for some of the things he has said in his brief amicus curiae. He speaks of "vexing problems which may arise in eliminating segregation," and he suggests to the Court that if you should come to the point where you should strike down separate schools in the United States, then you should do it gradually over a period, which he suggests as much as fifteen years, class-by-class, starting in the kindergarten and going on up.

Why? Because I say to the Court, he recognizes that "vexing problems would arise in many places."

Before I leave the Fifth Amendment, there was a suggestion by Mr. Justice Jackson that there might be effect upon the Indians if this Court should hold that separate schools may not be maintained under the Fifth Amendment. And I suggest that there are whole chapters of the United States Code which are entitled "Protection of the Indians," and under which Congress has legislated especially for them, because it is recognized that there is a people that needs protection. You and I can go out and buy a bottle of liquor if we want. The Indian cannot, nowhere in the United States. And he is a citizen. Why? Because it is recognized that it is not good for him, and he needs protection.

That assumes, I know, that it is good for us.

JUSTICE JACKSON: I live very close to the Seneca Reservation, in New York, and I would just as soon deal with a drunken Indian as with a drunken white man, myself, under modern conditions. It may have been different in the days of scalping knives.

MR. KORMAN: Possibly so.

JUSTICE DOUGLAS: Referring to the educational system in the part of the country I come from, the Indians are not barred from the public schools, but the schools on the reservations are open only to Indians, and the white man would be barred from those schools.

MR. KORMAN: That is quite a different problem, Mr. Justice. In anticipation of that question, I talked to representative of the Indian Bureau, and I was told by them that there are some 230 schools on reservations which are restricted to Indians, and there are nineteen schools off reservations which are restricted to Indians.

JUSTICE DOUGLAS: That merely keeps the white man out. The public school systems of the West, at least, are open to Indians.

MR. KORMAN: That may be. But that is a state proposition, left up to the states in the individual case. If the states want to let them in and think that it will not cause a problem, that is up to the legislation of the states.

JUSTICE DOUGLAS: Some of these cases are state questions.

MR. KORMAN: Perhaps.

JUSTICE DOUGLAS: Not yours?

MR. KORMAN: Perhaps.

I call your attention to the fact that there is separation, I have learned, by sexes in many of the large cities of the country, not in all the schools, apparently, but in some, perhaps for some special reason. I find from the National Education Association that they have separate schools for the sexes in San Francisco, Louisville, New Orleans, Baltimore, Boston, Elizabeth, Buffalo, New York City, even, Cleveland, Portland, Philadelphia. Such cities as those separate by sexes. Those are the things which are left to the decision of the decision of the legislature, the competent authority in each case to decide what is best for that community.

Of course, this Court has said many times that it is not concerned with the wisdom of legislation or the policy except as it is expressed in acts of Congress.

Mention has been made that there is violation of the Civil Rights Act. The two sections of the Civil Rights Act that are set forth in the complaint and in the brief for the appellants are sections 41 and 43, and in the case which first had to deal with that, a case for Indiana, the Court reviewed the Civil Rights statute at some length, and said, after reading the language of the statute:

In this, nothing is left to inference. Every right intended is specified.[62a]

The Court of Appeals of the District of Columbia, in *Carr* v. *Corning,* came to exactly the same conclusion.

I should like to point out with reference to the Civil Rights Act that Mr. Justice Vinson in the case of *Hurd* v. *Hodge,*[63] pointed out the fact that the Civil Rights Act of 1866, as amended in 1870, was passed by the same Congress that submitted the Fourteenth Amendment to the States, and that that same Congress, as was pointed out in *Carr* v. *Corning,* as I pointed out to the Court earlier—that same Congress is the one which passed some of these laws setting up separate schools in the District of Columbia for the two races.

How, then, can it be said that the contemporaneous thought on this by the people who made these enactments had any idea that schools were to be included in the Civil Rights Act.

In *Hurd* v. *Hodge,* there was another section of the Civil Rights Act involved, section 42 of Title 8 of the United States Code, [now 42 U.S.C., section 1982] and

[62a] Cory v. Carter, 48 Ind. 327 (1874).

[63] 334 U.S. 24 (1948). Enforcement of restrictive covenants in the District of Columbia was forbidden under a provision of the Civil Rights Act of 1866.

that dealt only with the right to hold and own real property and to transfer it and lease it and contract for it, and so on. That has no bearing on the question of the right to integrate the schools in the District of Columbia.

My distinguished opponents have taken a different tack here than they have in their brief and than they took in their petition and in the argument in the District Court with regard to the provisions of the United Nations Charter. In their petition and in their brief they have said that these laws violate the provisions of the United Nations Charter. Apparently they recede from that position now, and they say only that the United Nations Charter expresses the policy of the United States. If it expresses the policy of the United States, it expresses the policy of the United States to enact legislation upon a particular subject, and that is all that it expresses.

It has been demonstrated rather clearly that the United Nations Charter is not a self-executing treaty. It is a non-self-executing treaty which must be implemented by Acts of Congress.

In Article 55 of the Charter it is said:

> With a view to the creation of conditions of stability and well-being which are necessary for peaceful and friendly relations among nations based on respect for the principle of equal rights and self-determination of peoples, the United Nations shall promote:
> A. higher standards of living, full employment, and conditions of economic and social progress and development;
> B. solutions of international economic, social, health, and related problems; and international cultural and educational cooperation; and
> C. universal respect for, and observance of, human rights and fundamental freedoms for all with distinction as to race, sex, language, or religion.

All that we say in there is that we pledge ourselves in future legislation to keep these things in mind. And as set forth in our brief, the framers of that Article 55 intended only that it was to give to the rest of the world those constitutional rights which we have here in America and which they are denied. That was the purpose of it. That was the purpose expressed to the Senate of the United States when they presented this charter to them for ratification. That was the purpose expressed to the President of the United States in the report on the charter as it came out of San Francisco.

What is the meaning of "human rights and fundamental freedoms"? It is not defined in the charter anywhere. "Fundamental freedom" is not defined. No one knows what it means. There has been set up a separate organization, an organization which I think is called the Council on Human Rights, which has attempted to define that term, but it has been stated specifically by Mrs. Roosevelt, who heads that, that that has no binding effect even on the General Assembly of the United Nations, much less on the signatory powers.

We bar people into this country on grounds of polygamy. Polygamy is a fundamental right and freedom in some nations. How can these things be justified together?

They cannot be.

My distinguished friend, Mr. Nabrit, has said that these laws constitute a bill of attainder. As I read the law of a bill of attainder, I shall give the definition as it comes from the leading case in the United States, *Cummings* against *Missouri,* 4 Wall. 277. At page 323 of that opinion, the court said:

> A bill of attainder is a legislative act, which inflicts punishment without a judicial trial. If the punishment be less than death, the act is termed a bill of pains and penalties. Within the meaning of the Constitution, bills of attainder include bills of pains and penalties. In these cases the legislative body, in addition to its legitimate functions, exercises the powers and office of judge; it assumes, in the language of the textbooks, judicial magistracy; it pronounces upon the guilt of the party, without any of the form or safeguards of trial; it determines the sufficiency of the proofs produced, whether conformable to the rules of evidence or otherwise; and it fixes the degree of punishment in accordance with its own notions of the enormity of the offense.

This Court has said that when it speaks of punishment, it may mean deprivation of rights, but it mean deprivation of rights, civil or political, previously enjoyed which may be punishment.

These people have never enjoyed anything which has been taken away from them. These laws which set up these schools for them were to give them something, and not to take something away from them. These laws which set up the dual school system in the District of Columbia are not to take anything from my friends and they are not to take anything from the white children. They are set up so that there will be schools which have an atmosphere wholesome to the reception of education by both races. That is the only thing that Congress has said is right for them in the District of Columbia.

They attempt to twist this word "punishment" in some way to say that they have punishment inflicted upon them by being required to go to schools to which white children are not admitted and by being denied the right to go to schools in which white children are taught.

I cannot really get their reasoning. Before that, they cite some of these sociologists, some of these psychologists that have been mentioned in earlier arguments. In this brief, I have set forth a list of publications, monographs, psychological treatises, and what-not that oppose the views of the psychologists that have been named by my friends and by those in other cases.

I do not say that either one or the other is right. I take no position on that. I do not know. I am not a sociologist. Frankly, I think the effect of that psychological testimony has been already demolished here in this Court by Mr. Davis and Mr. Moore.

I might say more upon it, but I do not think that the issue justifies further argument.

I leave with the Court the citations, however, if the Court thinks that they have any merit at all.

It seems to me, Your Honors, that I have answered specifically the points which have been raised by my adversaries, and I have answered, I believe, most of the questions which the Court has put to other counsel.

It seems to me, as I have listened to seven hours of argument that preceded my addressing the Court, this is the situation, that my friends say, "This is the time for a change."

JUSTICE BLACK: Does that have anything to do with the law in the case?

MR. KORMAN: I do not think so, sir.

JUSTICE BLACK: You do not.

JUSTICE JACKSON: There has been a promise of change.

MR. KORMAN: Sir, if there has been a promise of change and it comes through the proper channels, I certainly, and the respondents certainly, have no objection to it, if it comes in the proper way by the judgment of the Congress that should pass upon it. We do not object to it. But if they decide that there is no need further for separation of the children of white and colored people in the schools so that the two may benefit from being separated because of the receptive air, the wholesome atmosphere that pervades those schools, we do not object.

Perhaps this is the time. I do not know. But I say that this is not the forum for such arguments. I say that these arguments should be made in the halls of Congress, and not in this chamber.

Incidentally, while there has been talk about breaking down segregation in all fields, I note that it has not been completely broken down in the armed forces, where it could be done by executive order, where we do not have to go to the Court and we do not have to go to the Congress. There have been some moves in that direction, and incidentally, while we are talking about progress in that direction, I should like to call the attention of the Court—and I am indebted to my friends in the amici briefs for this, because they have pointed to those fields wherein there has been advancement, where there is no longer segregation, and I thank them for suggesting it to me, and I have looked into it myself and I find that here in the District of Columbia Negroes are admitted to all the legitimate theaters, that they are admitted to a number of downtown moving pictures, that they are admitted to a number of the fine restaurants, including the famous Harvey's Restaurant, that there is a gradual integration on the playgrounds, that they are admitted onto all the recreation areas, that they are accepted into many of our larger and better hotels, that they serve on the staffs of the hospitals—particularly I call your attention to the Gallinger Hospital, which is conducted by the District of Columbia—that they take part in entertainment and in athletic contests along with white people. I say to you that even in the school system there has been a movement toward the betterment, or a breaking down, let us say, a breaking down of any of the possible feeling of hostility, the possible thought that these races cannot get along together.

It has recently been ruled that mixed groups of entertainers may come into the schools and put on performances, which was denied them previously.

This is not generally known, but in the southwest section there have been joint meetings called of teachers, parents and pupils where they confer together for the betterment of their neighborhood. Those are steps which have been accomplished without the intervention of courts, without the intervention of legislative bodies, and if those things have been accomplished, pray God the day will come when all things will be merged and the white and colored men will meet together in every place, even in the school, and it will not require even arguments from my friends before the halls of Congress, because there will be a general acceptance of the proposition that these two races can live side by side without friction, without hostility, without any occurrences.

If that be so, then there will be a general movement without their taking any action to help it, without their seeking it, to bring those things about.

This legislation is now in the place where it can be handled by the Congress, and not where it will be cut off completely by this Court without power of change.

I should like to read to Your Honors what Judge Prettyman of the United States Court of Appeals said in 1950 in the Carr case:

> Since the beginning of human history, no circumstance has given rise to more difficult and delicate problems than has the coexistence of different races in the same area. Centuries of bitter experience in all parts of the world have proved that the problem is insoluble by force of any sort. The same history shows that it is soluble by the patient processes of community experience. Such problems lie naturally in the field of legislation, a method susceptible of experimentation, of development, of adjustment to the current necessities in a variety of community circumstances.

That is what I urge upon this Court, to leave this issue where constitutionally it belongs, in the body that can legislate one way or another as it finds the situation to be and as it finds the needs to be in each community. Particularly I speak for the District of Columbia. But I say it is true in all areas. And these allusions to the Japanese cases and the other cases that they have said to Your Honors control this situation, I say they do not. In those cases, there were complete denials. Hirabayshi, Korematsu, and Endo were kept in their homes as prisoners. They were taken from their homes and put in concentration camps. Takahashi was denied the right to fish, and in the Farrington case, which they say is the nearest approach to their problem, there was an attempt to legislate out of existence by regulation the foreign language schools of Hawaii.

In each of these cases, there was either denial or an attempt to completely deny. These people are denied nothing. They have a complete system of education, which they admit is equal in all respects. They do not raise that issue.

I say to the Court that this issue should be left to the Congress where it belongs. There is no constitutional issue here. It has been decided by this Court. It should be left where it now is.

## REBUTTAL ARGUMENT ON BEHALF OF APPELLANTS

### by MR. NABRIT

MR. NABRIT: If the Court please, I would like to adopt for the petitioners the complete argument of Mr. Korman with respect to changed conditions and to urge the Court that those changed conditions that he suggests are the very conditions that we have been saying to the Court should have a bearing upon the construction of these acts of respondents.

In the District of Columbia, contrary to the situation in the states, he has explained that the whole situation is one in which this action will create no problems, so that the question of "vexatious problems" which he mentioned does not exist in the District, and we adopt his answers to that.

Now, with respect to his statement that there is no constitutional issue, we think our brief deals with this whole argument. It appears that he does not believe that there is a constitutional issue, and refuses to meet it. Giving to his argument the full meaning of it, that is, that these statutes give the authority, he has failed to deal with the question as to whether or not, conceding that they are authorized by the statutes, that is a constitutional delegation of power, and he has not addressed himself to that.

Rather he has dwelt in the past upon the white man's burden, and he has seemed to feel that for some reason that exists today.

It would appear to me that in 1952, the Negro should not be viewed as anybody's burden. He is a citizen. He is performing his duties in peace and in war, and today, on the bloody hills of Korea, he is serving in an unsegregated war.

All we ask of this Court is that it say that under the Constitution he is entitled to live and send his children to school in the District of Columbia unsegregated, with the children of his war comrades. That is simple. The Constitution gives him that right.

The basic question here is one of liberty, and under liberty, under the due process clause, you cannot deal with it as you deal with equal protection of laws, because there you deal with it as a quantum of treatment, substantially equal.

You either have liberty or you do not. When liberty is interfered with by the state, it has to be justified, and you cannot justify it by saying that we only took a little liberty. You justify it by the reasonableness of the taking.

We submit that in this case, in the heart of the nation's capital, in the capital of democracy, in the capital of the free world, there is no place for a segregated school system. This country cannot afford it, and the Constitution does not permit it, and the statutes of Congress do not authorize it.

(Whereupon, at 1:27 p.m., the argument was concluded.)

FRANCIS B. GEBHART, ET AL.,

Petitioners,

vs.

ETHEL LOUISE BELTON, ET AL.,

Respondents.

Case No. 448

FRANCIS B. GEBHART, ET AL.,

Petitioners,

vs.

SHIRLEY BARBARA BULAH, ET. AL.,

Respondents.

Washington, D.C.,
December 11, 1952.

The above-entitled cause came on for oral argument at 1:27 p.m.

APPEARANCES:

On behalf of the Petitioners:

H. ALBERT YOUNG, ESQ.

On behalf of the Respondents:

LOUIS L. REDDING, ESQ., and JACK GREENBERG, ESQ.

THE CHIEF JUSTICE: Case No. 448, Francis B. Gebhart, and others, versus Ethel Louise Belton, and others.

THE CLERK: Counsel are present.

ARGUMENT ON BEHALF OF PETITIONERS

by MR. YOUNG

MR. YOUNG: May it please the Court, it seems that I have a Herculean task to perform in attempting to add to what has already been presented for some eight hours of argument before this Court. But there are some points which I will only touch upon briefly since it has been so ably presented by counsel in all of the other cases that preceded mine for argument.

In this case, involving the State of Delaware, a petition for writ of certiorari and supporting brief was filed on November 13 of this year.

The Delaware Supreme Court handed down its mandate on September 9, 1952, and certiorari was granted on November 24, 1952, the Court advising me that I would be permitted to file my brief not later than three weeks after argument, and I can assure the Court that the brief will be in before the three weeks are out.

Jurisdiction in this case is invoked under 28 United States Code, section 1257, paragraph 3.

The validity of the Delaware constitutional provisions and the statutes invoked was challenged by the respondents. The pertinent provisions of the Delaware constitution and statute are as follows, section 1, Article 10, of the Constitution of the State of Delaware being as follows:

> The General Assembly shall provide for the establishment and maintenance of a general and efficient system of free public schools, and may require by law that every child, not physically or mentally disabled, shall attend the public schools, unless educated by other means.
> Section 2. In addition to the income of the investments of the Public School Fund, the General Assembly shall make provision for the annual payment of not less than one hundred thousand dollars for the benefit of the free public schools which, with the income of the investments of the Public School Fund shall be equitably apportioned among the school districts of the State as the General Assembly shall provide; and the money so apportioned shall be used exclusively for the payment of teachers' salaries and for furnishing free textbooks; provided, however, that in such apportionment, no distinction shall be made on account of race or color, and separate schools for white and colored children shall be maintained.

The statutory counterpart provides:

> The State Board of Education is authorized, empowered, directed and required to maintain a uniform, equal and effective system of public schools throughout the State, and shall cause the provisions of this Chapter, the by-laws or rules and regulations and the policies of the State Board of Education to be carried into effect. The schools provided shall be of two kinds: those for white children and those for colored children.

The State contended that under our constitution and statutes, segregation in the public schools was lawful and not in violation of the equal protection clause of the Fourteenth Amendment, and that if inequalities were found to exist, any judgment in favor of the plaintiffs should be limited to an injunction directing the defendants to equalize the facilities within a reasonable time.

The Delaware Court of Chancery and the Delaware Supreme Court held that these provisions insofar as they require segregation in the public schools, based on race or color, do not offend against the provisions of the Fourteenth Amendment forbidding any state to deny any citizen the equal protection of the laws, so that the Delaware Supreme Court did sustain the State's position that segregation per se is valid in the State of Delaware.

The cases of *Plessy* v. *Ferguson,* and *Gong Lum* v. *Rice,* the Delaware Supreme Court said are decisive of the question.

It is important in the approach to the question in our case, which is a very narrow one with respect to the form of the decree, if Your Honors please, that I read from portions of the opinion in order to demonstrate to this Court how the Delaware Supreme Court arrived at its decision.

On page 43—and I am sorry that I cannot refer to a brief, but I can assure the Court that it will be fully covered—

JUSTICE BLACK: Page 43 of what?

MR. YOUNG: Page 43 of the opinion, which will be found in the supplementary appendix of appellees—it is the blue-covered book—at the bottom of page 43, the Supreme Court said:

A detailed review of these cases is unnecessary, since we are cited to no case holding to the contrary. They establish the principle that the constitutional guarantee of equal protection of the laws does not prevent the establishment by the state of separate schools for whites and Negroes, provided that the facilities afforded by the state to the one class are substantially equal to those afforded to the other (often referred to as the 'separate but equal' doctrine). The question of segregation in the schools, under these authorities, is one of policy, and it is for the people of our state, through their duly chosen representatives, to determine what that policy shall be. When so determined, it must be given effect by our courts, subject always to the rule enjoined both by the Constitution of the United States and our own statute, that substantially equal treatment must be accorded. . . .

The refusal of the Chancellor to enter the declaratory judgment prayed for was therefore, in our opinion, correct.

The Delaware Supreme Court, however, held that an injunction where an inequality is found to exist commanding the defendants to admit plaintiffs to the designated schools maintained for white children was required by the equal protection clause of the Fourteenth Amendment.

The asserted conflict, the court held, of our constitutional and statutory provision with the equal protection clause of the Fourteenth Amendment was the sole basis for the judgment of the Delaware court upholding the type of relief that was granted.

JUSTICE FRANKFURTER: Mr. Attorney General, may I ask you whether I am to assume that the finding of the Chancellor on page 193a of your blue appendix, Folio 579—

MR. YOUNG: What page is that?

JUSTICE FRANKFURTER: 193a, Folio 579.

MR. YOUNG: If Your Honor please, the reason for the confusion in these things—

JUSTICE FRANKFURTER: I will hand you mine.

Am I to assume that that is a finding which persisted through the decision of the Supreme Court of Delaware? I marked it.

MR. YOUNG: I see, Your Honor.

No, Your Honor, because the Supreme Court held that that was not—if it was a finding, it was an irrelevant finding, and that it had—as a matter of fact, the decision was that segregation per se is valid in the State of Delaware, and that had no relevancy to the finding or the conclusion.

JUSTICE FRANKFURTER: To the finding. But that paragraph is in terms of a finding on the evidence as to what factors, whether any legal inference is to be drawn from it or not. You will notice the terms in which your Chancellor stated that on the evidence—doesn't he say something about "on the evidence I find this is a fact"? Does that survive his modification of the decree by the Supreme Court?

MR. YOUNG: It does not.

JUSTICE FRANKFURTER: It does not?

MR. YOUNG: It does not, Your Honor, and I will come to that in the course of my argument.

The Delaware Supreme Court held that the right to equal opportunity is a personal right; that the rights under the equal protection clause are personal and present, and for its authority relied on the cases about which so much was said during the course of the arguments here, the Gaines case, the Sipuel case, and the Sweatt case.

Those cases, however, did not involve a constitutional provision of a state. Furthermore, there was no showing in those cases that equal facilities could be provided in a reasonable time.

There is quite a difference, I submit, between not being able to afford any facilities, and correcting certain disparities that exist, which would equalize the existing facilities and educational opportunities; and for that reason, I submit, that the Chancellor and the Supreme Court, which affirmed the decree of the Chancellor, were in error.

These cases, the Gaines case, the Sipuel case, and the Sweatt case, were not considered by the three-judge court in the Davis and Briggs cases as requiring any relief other than an injunction compelling the defendants to equalize the facilities, and giving them a reasonable time to do so.

Now, this case involved two school districts. One is known as the Claymont School District, and the other the Hockessin School District.

In the Claymont School District, there is one high school, the Claymont High School, for white children only. There is also a high school in the city of Wilmington, some nine miles away, the Howard High School for Negro children.

The plaintiff Belton, fifteen years of age, and of high school age, attending the tenth grade, and living in Claymont, was required to go to the Howard High School in the city of Wilmington.

There are about 404 pupils in the Claymont High School and there are 1274 pupils in the Howard High School.

I would like to point out that with the Howard High School there is an annex some nine blocks away known as the Carver School, which is devoted primarily to vocational study.

This particular plaintiff, who went to Howard High School, took up typing and shorthand, and two afternoons a week would be required to go from Howard High School to Carver in order to take up those studies.

The plaintiffs contended that there was inequality. The state took the position that there was no inequality; that the curricula were the same or substantially the same; that the physical facilities were the same, that the teacher preparation was the same, and many other factors to show that there was equality.

We also pointed out, if the Court please, that the Carver Annex, which was some nine blocks away from the Howard School, was to be abandoned, and that there were plans for its abandonment before the suit was even started, and that there was to be a consolidation at the Howard High School for Negro students with respect to its academic studies and vocational work.

The court found that there was disparity between the two schools, and they found that the disparity existed in some items, some factors, one being the gymnasium—not that the gymnasium at Howard High was not a good gymnasium—it was a fine gymnasium, but that it was overcrowded, and would be overcrowded because of the number of students attending.

They found that travel, not because of distance itself, made for inequality, but because the petitioner or the plaintiff had to go to Howard High, and then from Howard High had to walk the nine blocks to Carver which, we contended, would be abandoned, and the court also found that the physical education classes were larger than they should be in order to afford proper and adequate instruction.

They also found disparity with respect to the playground at Carver—Carver, the annex that we said was going to be abandoned, and that we had admitted was inadequate, but because Carver had no playground, although Howard High had the opportunity to permit its pupils to go to a park which adjoined Howard High consisting of some ten acres, the fact that Carver had no playground was considered as one of the factors making for inequality, and, of course, it was held that the Carver building itself was wholly inadequate.

We contested these questions but, nevertheless, we showed the court that the state had embarked upon a plan and program of improving the conditions in Howard High School, and we showed that Howard High School was going to be enlarged. We also showed that there was going to be a school built in the county, another school in Middletown for Negroes, which is not in the record, but I would like to say to the Court is about to be completed at a cost of $1,350,000, and we were going to show that the students at the Howard High School in the junior high grades were going to be transferred to another school known as the Bancroft School, which is presently occupied and attended by white children, and that will be a school primarily for Negroes, so that the tension of overcrowding will be relieved at the Howard High School.

The court, in finding these items of disparity with respect to the Carver building, which it was not going to ignore, the fact that this was a building that we said we were going to abandon, and the fact that the gym was overcrowded, and the fact that there was this travel required by the plaintiff from Howard High to Carver, found that as to the allocation of public funds, there was equality of treatment; that as to the buildings proper they were the same; that as to accreditation, they were equal; that as to equipment and instruction material, they were equal; that the libraries were the same, with the library of Howard being larger; that the physical and mental health and nursing services at Howard, the colored school, were superior; and the court went on to say that the other differences were too insubstantial to find—to support a finding of inequality.

The other case had to do with an elementary school in what is known as Hockessin, School 107, is the school for colored children, a two-room school, having forty-four pupils.

Number 29 is a four-room school having 111 pupils.

There are two teachers in 107; there are four teachers in 29.

In that case, travel, with respect to travel, no bus transportation was provided the plaintiff, although there was bus transportation provided for white children.

In that case it was held that 107 receives equal or greater support now, and it did receive equal and greater support at the time of the hearing, although there was evidence that prior thereto the colored school did not receive equal support, which, perhaps, made for the disparity in the maintenance and upkeep of that particular school.

Both buildings—both are brick buildings; both are substantially constructed, so that the court in the case involving the elementary schools which have classes from the first grade to the sixth grade, held there was disparity in value, in upkeep, in exterior painting and floors, in toilet facilities, fire hazard, auditorium and custodial services.

We contend that these items making for disparity, as was found in the Delaware case, are such as can be readily corrected, and that the state should have been given the time, or the Board of Education should have been given the time, where there was this recognition of the "separate but equal" doctrine, in order to correct the inequalities that exist.

The defendants show the court that there was under way in the City of Wilmington, as I stated before, a far-reaching program for the improvement of facilities in the Negro schools.

As I said, the Carver School was to be abandoned. The junior high school pupils at the Howard School, that is, the Negro high school, were to be transferred to the Bancroft School so as to relieve it from crowding, and the Howard School was to be enlarged.

There were to be new shops; the laboratories would be added, and the Bancroft School is to be a completely modern junior high school.

All of these things were to be equalized, and will be equalized, by September of 1953, and the Middletown High School, as I indicated before, will be completed at a cost of $1,350,000.

As to the form of the decree, the court enjoined the defendants from denying plaintiffs admittance to the two schools, retaining—

JUSTICE REED: Your objection here, Mr. Attorney General, is as to the fitness of the decree with respect to immediacy?

MR. YOUNG: Correct.

JUSTICE REED: Your contention is that it should wait until later?

MR. YOUNG: That is correct.

JUSTICE REED: Will you address yourself as to why we should overrule the findings of the Chancellor?

MR. YOUNG: Yes.

The contention is that based on the ground of the Chancellor and the Delaware Supreme Court, in affirming the Chancellor, did not interpret the cases upon which they relied, the Sipuel case and the Gaines case and the Sweatt case, in making a finding that unless they grant immediate relief it would be in violation of the equal protection clause of the Fourteenth Amendment.

May I refer to the portion of the opinion of the Supreme Court, on page 63:

In affirming the Chancellor's order we have not overlooked the fact that the defendants may at some future date apply for a modification of the order if, in their judgment, the inequalities as between the Howard and Claymont schools or as between School No.29 and School No. 107 have then been removed. As to Howard, the defendants, as above stated, assert that when the Howard-Carver changes are completed, equality will exist. The Chancellor apparently thought the contrary. We do not concur in his conclusion, since we think that that question, if it arises, is one which will have to be decided in the light of the facts then existing and applicable principles of the law.

The Chancellor properly reserved jurisdiction of the cause to grant such further and additional relief as might appear appropriate in the future, and we construe this reservation to be a general reservation to any party to the cause to make an application to modify the order in any respect if and when changed conditions are believed to warrant such action.

JUSTICE FRANKFURTER: Has this litigation had any effect upon other school districts in your state, Mr. Attorney General?

MR. YOUNG: Well, I must speak outside the record.

JUSTICE FRANKFURTER: Yes, that is my question.

MR. YOUNG: As a matter of fact, that is the reason I am here now, because of the terrific impact upon the rest of the state by this decision.

JUSTICE FRANKFURTER: Would not each district, whatever the units may be, call for a separate assessment of the conditions in that district, the way your court did here?

MR. YOUNG: What it would mean, Your Honor, is that each case might involve litigation.

JUSTICE FRANKFURTER: That is right.

MR. YOUNG: And it would also prevent, perhaps, the legislators from voting for particular allotments for particular school districts, not knowing whether they can maintain the "separate but equal" phase of it or not.

JUSTICE FRANKFURTER: I may be wrong, but I should assume that it is almost inevitable that the conditions in the various districts would not be identical, and therefore differentiation would be almost inevitable, and the claim that the two colored and white schools are not the same would almost inevitably be made, and it would have to be decided with proper reference to each set of circumstances.

MR. YOUNG: I absolutely agree with you, sir; I absolutely agree, but what I contend is this: that in a state which recognizes the "separate but equal" doctrine, where inequalities exist, and it can be shown that those inequalities can be corrected, let us say overnight or within a week, to make an order that the Negro children shall be admitted into the white school is indirectly saying—abolishing segregation.

JUSTICE FRANKFURTER: Am I to infer that you think that the thrust of the decision of the Supreme Court is that if inequality is shown, and this whole litigation is unlike the litigation in all the other records—that if inequality is shown, a decree must be issued at once, although it might be corrected overnight?

MR. YOUNG: That is correct. That seems to be my feeling about it and my understanding of that opinion—that as long as inequality—

JUSTICE FRANKFURTER: In other words, you are arguing on the assumption that that is what the opinion of your Supreme Court means?

MR. YOUNG: Exactly.

JUSTICE REED: How can you say that when you yourself, as I understood it, said that it would not be corrected until September 1, 1953?

MR. YOUNG: That, Your Honor, went as far as the Claymont School, the high school, was concerned, where we said a new building had to be constructed.
But in the Hockessin situation, a two-room school, where we could, perhaps, within ten days put on an additional room or improve the toilet facilities or those other things that Your Honor will note in the opinion, we feel that they can be corrected with dispatch.

JUSTICE REED: So it is a problem of weighing the time it would take to make the corrections?

MR. YOUNG: That is correct.

JUSTICE REED: Even in the one that is not to be ready until 1953?

MR. YOUNG: That is correct.

JUSTICE REED: You take the position that that is an adequate time?

MR. YOUNG: We think that is a reasonable time, as long as we have shown—

JUSTICE REED: As long as there are facilities and institutions afforded?

MR. YOUNG: Precisely; and as long as it is shown that we are willing and able to do it, and that there is every reason to believe that it will be done, the "separate but equal" doctrine being recognized by the court—there should be no immediacy for the entrance of those Negro pupils into the white schools.

JUSTICE REED: Has litigation of this type reached your Supreme Court in the last five or ten years?

MR. YOUNG: This is the first in the history of the state.

JUSTICE JACKSON: Do I understand that the inequality is largely a matter of overcrowding, relative overcrowding?

MR. YOUNG: I want to differentiate between the two cases.

JUSTICE JACKSON: Yes.

MR. YOUNG: In the Claymont High School, they claimed it was due to overcrowding, not in the school entirely, but only in physical education classes.

JUSTICE JACKSON: Has there been a shift or population? That is, have you had a migration which has occurred since the war, with war industries?

MR. YOUNG: Well, we have some, yes.

JUSTICE JACKSON: You have some.

MR. YOUNG: But I do not know whether we can attribute too much to that. But the fact is that the Howard High School had both the junior and the senior pupils there, and the fact that we are taking those pupils away from the Howard High School into this other school will certainly correct this situation.

But apparently the Delaware Supreme Court seemed to term this inequality only as to the overcrowding in a particular class, which did not make for proper instruction in physical education, but it seemed to hold that as to all other classes the difference in size between twenty-five pupils in white schools, and thirty or thirty-one or thirty-two in classes in the colored schools did not make for inequality so as to effect educational opportunity or instruction.

The State contends that where disparity exists under the equal protection clause of the Fourteenth Amendment, the rights of Negro children are protected by a decree compelling school administrators to equalize the facilities in the segregated schools involved where a state constitutional provision makes mandatory the maintenance of separate schools for white and colored children, and where school administrators have reasonably shown that the existing inequality can and probably will be corrected within a reasonable time.

So the Court of Chancery, of course, sat as a court of equity, and the form of the decree, we contend, violates the fundamental equitable principles as laid down in *Eccles* v. *Peoples Bank*.

In that case the court said:

> It is always the duty of a court of equity to strike a proper balance between the needs of the plaintiff and the consequences of giving the desired relief.

There was no showing that the state could not equalize or that it was unwilling to equalize, and the effect of the decree is demoralizing to the Negro pupils as well as to the white pupils, to the teachers, to the State Board of Education.

There is no permanency, there is no stability, as one of the counsel mentioned during the course of the argument in the Virginia case.

The decree in its present form, which says that the Negro children shall be permitted to go to the white school and that the Board of Education may come in next week, next month, and modify the decree would result in shunting those Negro children back and forth.

There would be no stability, there would be no permanency. I would rather if the court had said that segregation per se is bad; "Let the Negro children go the white schools."

(Whereupon, a luncheon recess was taken.)

MR. YOUNG: Mr. Justice Frankfurter, you asked me whether the Chancellor's finding on the evidence that segregation produces detrimental results so far as educational opportunities are concerned, if it is applied—and I call the Court's attention to the opinion of the Supreme Court of Delaware on page 44, beginning with the third paragraph:

> it is said that the uncontradicted evidence adduced by the plaintiffs shows that state-imposed segregation in the public schools and equality of educational opportunity are inherently incompatible, and that the Chancellor so held. The Chancellor indeed found on the evidence that segregation itself results in the Negro's receiving inferior educational opportunities, and expressed the opinion that the 'separate but equal' doctrine should be rejected. He nevertheless recognized that his finding was immaterial to the legal conclusion drawn from the authorities above cited. We agree that it is immaterial, and hence see no occasion to review it.

JUSTICE FRANKFURTER: Therefore, it is not before us.

MR. YOUNG: That is right.

JUSTICE BLACK: But does that necessarily follow? They did not set it aside, so that you have a finding of your Chancellor so far as segregation is concerned in Delaware that the result of it is the affording of an inferior opportunity of education and your Supreme Court says that nevertheless the Supreme Court of the United States, in effect, has held that that can never be a constitutional ground.

MR. YOUNG: So did the Chancellor, Your Honor.

JUSTICE BLACK: But you still have your finding that, so far as Delaware is concerned—and I presume he was not looking at evidence anywhere but Delaware, that the system of segregation there, even though the facilities, physical facilities, are equal, results in inferior education for them.

MR. YOUNG: He did so state.

JUSTICE BLACK: We have that finding without its being set aside.

MR. YOUNG: Well, I think we have it, in effect, set aside when the Supreme Court says that he considered it immaterial to the conclusion in his case and the decision in his case.

JUSTICE BLACK: That is right. He considered it immaterial, but nevertheless are we not faced with this situation: Do you conceive that segregation might be held on evidence in some places to supply equal opportunities for education, while in others it might be held that the situation was such that it gave an inferior opportunity for education?

MR. YOUNG: Depending on the facilities offered, and the educational opportunities.

JUSTICE BLACK: I mean, assuming that the facilities are the same—

MR. YOUNG: Yes.

JUSTICE BLACK: —do you conceive that it is impossible for segregation in one place to result in an equality of opportunity of education, while in another it might result in inequality of opportunity for education?

MR. YOUNG: No, I cannot conceive of that myself.
Now, it may be that—

JUSTICE BLACK: There might be many things involved, might there not?

MR. YOUNG: That is true, but I am not prepared to say whether, all factors being equal, mere segregation of and by itself will bring about inferiority so far as educational opportunities are concerned.

JUSTICE BLACK: Well, assuming that you had facts, and that your court found on the facts that in Delaware, where your two schools functioned, and with the general conditions of education in Delaware and the relationship between the races and all of that was such that even though the facilities were identical—physical facilities—nevertheless, in Delaware, the results of segregation were to give an unequal opportunity of education to the colored people.
Would you say that, assuming that finding on local facts, and it is accepted, that the separate but equal doctrine would not make it necessary to state that?

MR. YOUNG: I would not, if Your Honor please, under our Constitution and its statutory counterpart—we are required to maintain separate schools for white and colored as long as we afford them equal opportunities and equal facilities and I think that that would merely be an oblique way of striking down segregation, and desegregating schools.

JUSTICE BLACK: If you assume that the facts are correctly found. Suppose I asked you to assume that the court found those facts, and assume that he is right, and you had no way to overturn them. He would say that conditions in Delaware—given consideration on the facts—require him to see whether or not the colored people get an equal opportunity for education.
Now, I find that they do so far as the physical results are concerned, but I am led to the conclusion from the evidence and find from the evidence that they do not because the relationship that exists here, and by reason of the manner of going to school, and the mixture in other places, and so forth, I find that the effect on the children is that they get an inferior opportunity for education. Would you say that that would still not bring them within the "separate but equal" doctrine?

MR. YOUNG: I would, Your Honor. I would because I say that would be violative of the equal protection clause of the Fourteenth Amendment, and would also be violative of our own constitutional provisions, because we are assuming now facilities being equal, educational opportunities being equal; I would like to say I do not know what evidence Your Honor is referring to that the chancellor could rely on other than the sociologists and anthropologists and psychologists.

JUSTICE BLACK: I just read the findings, and I asked you the question at the beginning of these arguments, you may remember.

MR. YOUNG: I remember.

JUSTICE BLACK: About the difference in findings, and I wondered—both sides seem to be relying on the findings so much, and I wondered if the assumption we must make from that is that both sides believe that it could be found in one state and one locality by reason of a different situation that opportunities were unequal, even though the facilities were equal, while in another state that would not be the case.

MR. YOUNG: I do not subscribe to that, Your Honor.

JUSTICE FRANKFURTER: Mr. Attorney General, since I got you into this trouble, perhaps I might help straighten out the way the matter lies in my mind.

I had not read that sentence to which you called attention in the opinion of the Supreme Court. I think for myself this situation is very different from the Kansas situation.

In the Kansas situation we have a finding of fact similar to the finding made by your Chancellor, and the court said that finding does not bear on the legal question, namely, that the state has power to segregate, no matter what the psychological consequences may be, and that is what your Chancellor found.

As I understand it myself, when your Supreme Court came to review the decision of the Chancellor, it said that inasmuch as his finding of fact is irrelevant, it was not going to review it. Therefore, we have a finding of an inferior court specifically not reviewed by the highest court of the state.

The Chancellor found that on his appraisal of the evidence—insofar as I am concerned it may well be that your Supreme Court might not have reached that conclusion, and might not have weighed the evidence that the Chancellor did and, therefore, we have not got, for myself in this case, what we have in the Kansas case, a finding of fact which binds us, because for all I know your Supreme Court might have disagreed with your Chancellor, and then we would be in a position where the highest court said that the evidence does not yield to the conclusions that the Chancellor thought it yielded.

MR. YOUNG: That is precisely the point, Your Honor, and what is more, a review of the opinion would show that the Delaware Supreme Court did not agree with many things that the Chancellor said in his opinion in the lower court.

JUSTICE FRANKFURTER: Yes. The legal position that you take is on the assumption that was presented by the Kansas case. I think that your record presents a different set of facts.

MR. YOUNG: Exactly. There was no finding of fact that was considered at all. It was considered immaterial to the issue.

JUSTICE FRANKFURTER: A very powerful finding by the Chancellor.

MR. YOUNG: Oh, yes.

JUSTICE BLACK: I do not like to interrupt again, but taking that as true, if we assume and admit such a finding is relevant, you would be in a situation of having a finding by your Chancellor which is relevant, which might cause the case to turn one way or the other, which has not been reviewed by your highest court.

MR. YOUNG: That is right. But there is one thing I want to make plain: That notwithstanding that finding, and notwithstanding the fact that it was disregarded by the Supreme Court, I nevertheless address Your Honor's attention to the point that the shape of the decree, in any event, was not a proper decree under the circumstances, even if that were so.

Let us assume that were so, and it just desegregated the schools; nevertheless, the form of the decree being in conflict with the other jurisdiction, was not a proper decree, taking into account the needs and the relief to be granted, and the public interest involved.

This Court, as I contend, is not exercising—it was not a question of abuse of discretion, and it is not a matter of administration nor a matter of enforcing the injunction.

Both courts, my position is, said that under and only by reason of the Fourteenth Amendment was it justified to make the kind of decree it did.

The decree in the court below, while asserting that the plaintiffs were entitled to relief, made no attempt to assess the effect of its decree on the defendants, on the children and their parents, both white and colored, in the school districts affected.

No consideration was given to the ability of the defendants to equalize the facilities involved within a reasonable time; no consideration was given to the effect of a possible later decree based on changing circumstances; no consideration was given to the effect of the decree on the school administrators who would be faced with the problem of determining how and where to enroll children in the various school districts in the state.

No consideration was given to the effect of the decree on the public, generally, and on the legislature in planning for the future, in allocating funds for the maintenance and construction of school facilities.

The court below stated that the plaintiffs' rights were personal and present, and this does not necessarily mean that they are entitled immediately to admittance to the schools maintained for white children only.

The plaintiffs' rights are given full consideration when the court orders the defendants to proceed forthwith to make the facilities of the respective schools equal.

In this case, too, I am grateful to the Attorney General for his brief, and in his amicus curiae brief. On page 28 I would like the Court to take note of what he said:

> If, in any of the present cases, the Court should hold that to compel colored children to attend 'separate but equal' public schools is unconstitutional, the Government would suggest that in shaping the relief the Court should take into account the need, not only for prompt vindication of the constitutional rights violated, but also for orderly and reasonable solution of the vexing problems which may arise in eliminating such segregation. The public interest plainly would be served by avoidance of needless dislocation and confusion in the administration of the school systems affected. It must be recognized that racial segregation in public schools has been in effect in many states for a long time. Its roots go deep in the history and traditions of these states. The practical difficulties which may be met in making progressive adjustments to a nonsegregated system cannot be ignored or minimized.

JUSTICE REED: I asked a question similar to this before. Why do you contend that that is a problem here? Is it a violation of the federal law or a violation of the federal Constitution that the Delaware Supreme Court has acted somewhat precipitately, from your point of view?

MR. YOUNG It is because, Your Honor, we contend that the Supreme Court, affirming the Chancellor who acted in this matter, in shaping the form of the decree, said that he was compelled to make that kind of a decree under the equal protection clause of the Fourteenth Amendment. It was not a question of exercising discretion; in fact, it negated that proposition.

If, for example he would reach the same result by saying that he is exercising his discretion, perhaps we would have another matter. But he said he was compelled to issue that kind of a decree under the equal protection clause of the Fourteenth Amendment.

JUSTICE DOUGLAS: Is that because the right is personal?

MR. YOUNG: Because the right is personal, and depending upon the cases of Sweatt and the Gaines case and, of course, we differentiate between those cases, cases where there was no facility, there was no expectancy of any facility within a reasonable time, as compared with a case where there is the ability and the willingness to equalize.

JUSTICE REED: It is difficult for me to grasp what the state court of Delaware was saying when it said it was not acting within its discretion.

MR. YOUNG: Well, the Supreme Court pointed out in its opinion and stated that they were relying solely—

JUSTICE REED: It is on page 44.

MR. YOUNG: On page 57 the court cast aside—the Delaware Supreme Court—two preliminary matters upon which, perhaps, the injunction could have been or the decree could have been, handed down, but said:

> But we prefer to rest our decision upon another ground. With deference to the decisions in the Briggs and Davis cases, which we have carefully examined and considered, we cannot reconcile the denial of prompt relief with the pronouncements of the Supreme Court of the United States. If, as we have seen, the right to equal protection of the laws is a 'personal and present' one, how can these plaintiffs be denied such relief as is now available? The commendable effort of the state to remedy the situation serves to emphasize the importance of the present inequalities.

THE CHIEF JUSTICE: I think you will find some language in the Sipuel case, if I remember rightly, about "personal and present."

MR. YOUNG: Yes.

THE CHIEF JUSTICE: That was the admission into the school in Oklahoma. I think that language is in the Sipuel case.

MR. YOUNG: That is right.

THE CHIEF JUSTICE: I mean "personal and present."

MR. YOUNG: Well, there it was proper, I state, because there is quite a distinction between higher education and facilities that can or cannot be offered on a higher educational level as compared with the common school level; and the court—our contention is that the lower court, the inferior court, the Court of Chancery—was in error when it thought that it was compelled to issue the kind of decree it did without giving any regard to the public interest and to the parties involved.

JUSTICE REED: Your court says in the opinion:

To require the plaintiffs to wait another year—

I am reading at page 58—

MR. YOUNG: Yes.

JUSTICE REED: (Continuing)

—under present conditions would be in effect partially to deny them that to which we have held they are entitled. It is possible that a case might occur in which completion of equalization of facilities might be so imminent as to justify a different result, but we do not pass on that question because it is not presented.

Whether that is discretion—your position is that they are bound under the Sipuel case to give immediate relief; they thought they were bound to give immediate—

MR. YOUNG: Yes, they thought they were bound.

JUSTICE REED: To give immediate relief.

MR. YOUNG: Yes, that is correct.

In the light of what I have read from the amicus curiae brief, when it was urged that the Court should be slow in desegregating even where segregation per se was held to be invalid, our contention is that the fact that it is even more serious where the "separate but equal" doctrine is held to be valid, and where it is recognized that the state, upon a showing that any existing inequality relating to facilities and educational opportunities are capable of being corrected within a reasonable time, for a court to compel the immediate amalgamation of Negroes and whites in the same school, and then later upon a showing of equalization again separate the Negro children from the white school.

A decree requiring the defendants to equalize the facilities within a reasonable time would give the plaintiffs relief as quickly as practicable, consistent with an orderly administration of the school system and a specific adjustment of inequalities where such inequalities have been found to exist in the past.

The same situation occurred in the Virginia case and also in the South Carolina case, perhaps not with the finding that Your Honors find to exist in the opinion of the Chancellor in the lower court, but I believe that the language of—

THE CHIEF JUSTICE: The language can be found in the Virginia case, can it not?

MR. YOUNG: Not that particular finding that segregation of and by itself under the evidence is harmful. I think that they did—

THE CHIEF JUSTICE: They had findings there that it was not equal.

MR. YOUNG: That it was not equal, that is correct; and I believe there was some comment, as I recall, that whether it does harm or does not do harm is not for the Court to determine. But this is what Judge Parker had to say in disposing of the case, the South Carolina case:

> It is argued that, because the school facilities furnished Negroes in District No. 22 are inferior to those furnished white persons, we should enjoin segregation rather than direct the equalizing of conditions. Inasmuch as we think that the law requiring segregation is valid, however, and that the inequality suffered by plaintiffs results, not from the law, but from the way it has been administered, we think that our injunction should be directed to removing the inequalities resulting from administration within the framework of the law rather than to nullifying the law itself. As a court of equity, we should exercise our power to assure to plaintiffs the equality of treatment to which they are entitled with due regard to the legislative policy of the state. In directing that the school facilities afforded Negroes within the district be equalized promptly with those afforded white persons, we are giving plaintiffs all the relief that they can reasonably ask and the relief that is ordinarily granted in cases of this sort.

The Court, as it was said in the Briggs case, should not use its power to abolish segregation in a state where it is required by the constitution and laws of the state if the equality demanded by the Constitution can be attained otherwise.

This much, the court went on to say, is demanded by the spirit of comity which must prevail in the relationship between the agencies of the federal government and the state if our constitutional system is to endure.

What we ask in this case is that the Delaware Supreme Court's judgment be reversed and that the Delaware Supreme Court be instructed that affording reasonable time for the board of education to correct inequalities capable of being corrected, as we have shown, is not in violation of the Fourteenth Amendment.

JUSTICE FRANKFURTER: Mr. Attorney General, may I trouble you again? Has the Supreme Court, your Supreme Court, in terms, not as a necessary consequence of what it has decided, but has your Supreme Court in terms, taken the position that if the Chancellor finds inequality then the immediate opening of the doors of schools of whites who have no segregation in schools is a legal compulsion?

MR. YOUNG: That is, we contend, the position the Supreme Court took.

JUSTICE FRANKFURTER: Has it taken that in terms? Here is what troubles me. It is asking a great deal of this Court, for one-ninth of this Court, to overrule the judgment of the Chancellor, affirmed by the Supreme Court of the state, that the equity of the situation requires the decree that they entered.

If they base that on their interpretation of what the decisions of this Court require, then it was not the Chancellor's exercise of discretion, but it was a result caused by the requirement that they must follow the decisions of the Court.

As I read their opinions, they did not say that in terms, did they?

MR. YOUNG: No, but the general mandate, it would seem to me, the blanket mandate, in affirming the judgment of the Court of Chancery or the Chancellor—

JUSTICE FRANKFURTER: Did the Chancellor think that was the thing to do?

MR. YOUNG: He thought so, yes.

JUSTICE FRANKFURTER: That as soon as inequality is shown, then at once there must be—

MR. YOUNG: That is right.

JUSTICE FRANKFURTER: How could he? We did not do that in one of the cases.

MR. YOUNG: We tried to point out to the Chancellor that he was wrong, and we tried to point out to the Chancellor that that was not so.

JUSTICE FRANKFURTER: The question is whether he was wrong or what rule of law did he apply. If he said that in this situation, considering the circumstances in Delaware, your county or school district, or he may not have been explicit about it—that is one thing. If he says that the Supreme Court demands, "and I am an obedient judge," that is another thing.

MR. YOUNG: He said where there is an injury, as he found such to be here, then the injury should be redressed immediately.

JUSTICE FRANKFURTER: Well, that may be his view as an equity judge.

MR. YOUNG: But he based it on the equal protection clause of the Fourteenth Amendment.

JUSTICE FRANKFURTER: If I may say so, a chancellor who shows as much competence as this opinion shows, probably can read the opinions of this Court with understanding.

MR. YOUNG: There is no question about the Chancellor's competency, Your Honor.

JUSTICE FRANKFURTER: If I may say so, it was an unusual opinion, as opinions go.

MR. YOUNG: May I read from just the opinion of the Chancellor on page 203, at the bottom of the page:

Just what is the effect of such a finding of a violation of the Constitution, as has here been made. It is true that in such a situation some courts have merely directed the appropriate State officials to equalize facilities. I do not believe that such is the relief warranted by a finding that the United States Constitution has been violated. It seems to me that when a plaintiff shows to the satisfaction of a court that there is an existing and continuing violation of the 'separate but equal' doctrine, he is entitled to have made available to him the State facilities which have been shown to be superior. To do otherwise is to say to such a plaintiff: 'Yes, your Constitutional rights are being invaded, but be patient, we will see whether in time they are still being violated.'

Now, Judge Parker had that problem before him in the South Carolina case, and the same problem was there in the Virginia case. But is it a violation that is going to continue upon a showing that we, the state, are able and willing to correct the existing inequalities between the two races?

JUSTICE FRANKFURTER: Suppose your Supreme Court had said that "it is our view that when a violation of the Constitution is shown, that is such an overriding equity that we regard the inconvenience or the difficulties to the state as subordinate to that overriding equity." That would be a view of equity, the balancing of considerations by the local court, and not at all derived from the necessities of the Fourteenth Amendment?

MR. YOUNG: I agree with Your Honor.

JUSTICE FRANKFURTER: I was wondering whether that is not really implicit in these decisions?

MR. YOUNG: I do not believe so. I think that they were fully cognizant of the equal protection clause of the Fourteenth Amendment, and that they were aware of the South Carolina case at the time, the Virginia case, and that the leading cases, the Sweatt case and, of course, the Gaines case, and it was on that basis that they felt that they were compelled to make the kind of order—

JUSTICE FRANKFURTER: Automatically because there was a violation of the Fourteenth Amendment, and the Fourteenth Amendment requires automatic redress, that is your view of it?

MR. YOUNG: That is right, precisely. That is our view, and I think it is borne out by a reading of the two opinions in the Court of Chancery and in the Delaware Supreme Court.

JUSTICE REED: Mr. Attorney General, I call your attention to page 204 (a), as I understand it, of the Chancellor's opinion, and towards the bottom he says, "If it be a matter of discretion, I reach the same conclusion."

MR. YOUNG: Well, I think that is the language in the opinion, but it is clear that the decision rested—

JUSTICE REED: He thought to the contrary, too. He also said that if it is a matter of discretion "I reach the same conclusion."

MR. YOUNG: But he did reach the conclusion upon the basis and the interpretation of the equal protection clause of the Fourteenth Amendment, and that is the way the Delaware Supreme Court found that he ruled, and thought that it was proper because it was a matter of compulsion where there is such a finding.

I want to say, of course, there was much more that I would like to have brought to the Court's attention. I know it would be impossible for me to review the cases on the question of segregation per se that were so ably presented by my distinguished colleagues.

THE CHIEF JUSTICE: In addition to that, your time has expired.

MR. YOUNG: That is true. Is it at an end now?

THE CHIEF JUSTICE: Yes.

MR. YOUNG: Thank you.

### ARGUMENT ON BEHALF OF RESPONDENTS

#### by MR. REDDING

MR. REDDING: May it please the Court, in this fifth and last case before the Court on this subject, the fundamental question is still the same as in the four preceding cases, namely, what rights has the individual to protection against arbitrary action by government?

In four cases, including the Delaware case, the government involved is the state government; in the fifth case, the government involved is the federal government.

This case differs from the other cases in that the persons who were originally plaintiffs appear here not as appellants but as respondents.

Judgment in the trial court was rendered for the persons who were originally plaintiffs, and that judgment, as well as a finding of fact that there was substantial inequality in facilities, was affirmed by the state Supreme Court.

Now, that affirmance was not merely a formal affirmance. The state Supreme Court concluded that because a constitutional question was involved, that is, a question involving the constitution of the State of Delaware was involved, it had a right to completely disregard the findings of fact of the Chancellor and make its own independent findings of fact, and it did so, and it sustained the Chancellor's findings of fact that there was substantial inequality in physical facilities.

The Chancellor made a second finding of fact. He made a finding of fact which, in language, is something like this—and I think, perhaps, I had better refer to the exact language:

> I conclude from the testimony that in our Delaware society, State-imposed segregation in education itself results in the Negro children, as a class, receiving educational opportunities which are substantially inferior to those available to white children otherwise similarly situated.

Now, the respondents here say, first of all, just as has been said in the four preceding cases, that classification on the basis of race to determine what educational facilities may be enjoyed, is arbitrary and unreasonable, and because it is arbitrary and unreasonable, it is unconstitutional.

We say that such a classification has no relationship to the education of a state's citizens.

Now, there has been some discussion arising, I think in part, from questions from Your Honors as to the basis for the type of legislation that is here under attack.

I cannot answer what the basis for this type of legislation in other states was, but I should like to indicate what I think the basis was in Delaware.

Delaware has never, by the normal process of ratification, ratified the Fourteenth Amendment. The only ratification of the Fourteenth Amendment which has occurred in Delaware, is a ratification by implication from judicial action.

When the Fourteenth Amendment was being circulated among the states for ratification, the Delaware Legislature, in joint session, concurred in a joint resolution, the words of which I shall read:

> Whereas, this General Assembly believes the adoption of the said proposed amendment to the Constitution would have a tendency to destroy the rights of the states in their sovereign capacity as states, would be an attempt to establish an equality not sanctioned by the laws of nature or of God,

therefore they refused to ratify.

Now, this is not an isolated action. That action was taken in March of 1869, and it is found recorded in 13, Laws of Delaware 256.

This is not an isolated action.

The legislature took the same action with respect to the Fifteenth Amendment. In language which is as follows, it stated:

> It is resolved that the members of this General Assembly do hereby declare their unqualified disapproval of said amendment to the Constitution of the United States, and hereby refuse to adopt and ratify the same.

I say it is not isolated, and I refer to still another resolution, if Your Honors will indulge me. This resolution was unanimously adopted by a joint session of the Delaware Legislature, and I think its language will be self-explanatory:

> Resolved that the members of this General Assembly do hereby declare uncompromising opposition to a proposed act of Congress introduced by the Honorable Charles Sumner at the last session and now on file in the Senate of the United States known as the Supplemental Civil Rights bill, and all other measures intended or calculated to equalize the Negro race with the white race, politically or socially, and especially do they proclaim unceasing opposition to making Negroes eligible to public offices, to sit on juries and to their admission into public schools where white children attend, to their admission on terms of equality with white people in churches, public conveyances, places of amusement or hotels, and to any and every measure designed or having the effect to promote the equality of the Negro with the white man in any of the relationships of life.

We say, sirs, that that is the background of this legislation.

However, Delaware did not include in its State Constitution a requirement that there be separation of Negroes and whites in public schools until 1897, the year after this Court decided *Plessy* v. *Ferguson*.

Apparently, the Delaware Legislature, which passed the amendment of the Delaware Constitution—it was amended by two successive legislatures—apparently the Delaware Legislature felt that there was warrant in *Plessy v. Ferguson* for a so-called "separate but equal" doctrine.

Now, we think that these resolutions indicate that this separation of the Negro and white in public schools was not based on any rational consideration.

At the trial of the case evidence was introduced further to show that such legislation was not based on any rational or reasonable grounds.

I should like the indulgence of the Court to call attention to this testimony at page 122 of the appendix of the appellees, plaintiffs below.

Dr. Otto Klineberg, a professor of psychology at Columbia University was testifying. He was asked this question—

JUSTICE REED: What was the page, please?

MR. REDDING: I am sorry, sir, page 122 of the thick blue book.

Dr. Klineberg, are there differences in inborn intellectual capacity among individuals which are determined by whether an individual is Negro or white?
A. No. There are, of course, differences in intellectual capacity, but we have no scientific evidence that those differences are determined in any way by the racial origin of the individual.

We think that completely removes any possibility of a contention that this legislation today, with the advances in scientific knowledge about the measurement of mental capacities of human beings today, could have any rational basis.

Now, the Delaware statute provides for separate but equal education for Negroes and whites. The form of the statute itself predetermined the nature of the action, that is, these plaintiffs felt that they were required to show that there was not equality although there was separation, and they attempted to do it on two bases: They showed inequality of physical facilities, and they got a finding of fact from the Chancellor which was sustained by the Supreme Court on that, and then they attempted to show inequality flowing from the harm done by segregation on the individual student.

I might say that twelve expert witnesses testified with respect to this second aspect of inequality.

I should like to call the attention of the Court to just a small portion of that testimony. I should like to call the Court's attention to the testimony of a witness whom the Chancellor characterized in his opinion as one of America's foremost psychiatrists. This witness was not testifying merely from abstractions of scientific knowledge. This witness had examined, among other Delawareans, some of the respondents in this case and, as a result of his learning and as a result of this examination, this witness testified as follows, at page 76 of this same book, which is the transcript of the testimony. Dr. Fredric Wertham[64] testified:

Now, the fact of segregation in public and high school creates in the mind of the child an unsolvable conflict, an unsolvable emotional conflict, and I would say an inevitable conflict—it is inevitable that it cause such a conflict. This conflict is, in the child's mind, what a foreign body is in the child's body.

[64]Dr. Fredric Wertham is a noted psychiatrist and author. Among his works are *The Sign of Cain* (1967), *The Show of Violence* (1949), *Dark Legend* (1941), and *Seduction of the Innocent* (1954).

Further, Dr. Wertham testified that segregation, state-imposed segregation, created an important inequality in educational opportunities for the various reasons. He said:

> Now, of course, these facts that I have mentioned are not caused only by the school segregation, but the school segregation is important, of paramount importance, for a number of reasons.

JUSTICE BURTON: Where is that?

MR. REDDING: This, I am sorry, Your Honor, is at page 86 of this same transcript of testimony. He says:

> It is of paramount importance for a number of reasons.
> In the first place, it is absolutely clear cut.

Secondly, he says, the state does it; thirdly, it is not just the discrimination, it is discrimination of very long duration; it is continuous; and fourth, it is bound up with the whole educational process.

Now, sirs, I say that the Chancellor's finding of fact with respect to the harm done in Delaware society by state-imposed segregation on the minds of these children is based on that testimony.

Some discussion has been had as to what the Supreme Court of Delaware did with that finding of the Chancellor. It is our view that the Supreme Court did not reject that finding. It is our view that that finding survives, and because we have that view, and because the Supreme Court, in our view, did not give legal effectuation to a finding of fact made by the trial court, we ask that this Court give legal effectuation to such a finding.

JUSTICE FRANKFURTER: Aren't you really asking that the decree below be affirmed?

MR. REDDING: We ask, of course, that the decree below be affirmed, but we ask that it be affirmed not merely for the reason given by the Supreme Court of Delaware, but for other considerations which this Court has taken into account in, for example, the Sipuel case and the McLaurin case.

In those cases this Court did take into account factors like the isolation of the student from other students. The Delaware Supreme Court did not take that into account, and in affirming the opinion of the Delaware Supreme Court, we respectfully ask that this Court take those factors into account and grant a judgment of affirmance which will indicate that segregation in and of itself inflicts inequalities of educational opportunities on the respondents here. So that no matter what attempt to equalize facilities may be made by the Attorney General of the State of Delaware, there will still be inequality of educational opportunity which the state is not correcting.

We think that in the Sweatt case—

JUSTICE FRANKFURTER: If we just affirmed this decree below without an opinion, that would be an end of the matter, and the plaintiffs in this case would get all they asked, would they not?

MR. REDDING: No, sir.

JUSTICE FRANKFURTER: They would be admitted into the school into which they wanted to be admitted.

MR. REDDING: They ask for the equality of educational opportunity.

JUSTICE FRANKFURTER: That is what they would get if the decree was affirmed.

MR. REDDING: They would get it, sir, but they would get it under the shadow of the threat of the Attorney General that the moment he has shown to the court that facilities are equalized they would then be ejected from the schools.

THE CHIEF JUSTICE: Was it the threat of the Attorney General or was that the condition stated by the Court?

MR. REDDING: Well, the Attorney General now threatens that, sir.

THE CHIEF JUSTICE: I say though—

MR. REDDING: I say that is the explanation of his appearance here.

THE CHIEF JUSTICE: (Continuing)—isn't that what the court said?

MR. REDDING: Yes, the court said that.

THE CHIEF JUSTICE: And he held that it would be contingent, and motions might be made if conditions were changed.

MR. REDDING: We think that—

THE CHIEF JUSTICE: Isn't that what the court said?

MR. REDDING: That is correct, sir.

JUSTICE FRANKFURTER: Did the court say that they would exclude those children if new arrangements were made? Did the court say what they would do if in the future an application were made to deal with this decree? They simply let the decree open. Almost every decree in equity is left open.

MR. REDDING: That is correct, sir. But we have no reason to believe that the court at that time will not take the same position with respect to its limitation that it took originally.

JUSTICE FRANKFURTER: Mr. Redding, we have had cases where we had to dismiss a case as moot because the child had gone through the education, a case from New Jersey, and it was a case in a totally different field[64a]—so that by the time there may be a new threat, these boys and girls might be in various universities of the country.

MR. REDDING: We feel, sir, that the decree should be affirmed.

[64a] Doremus v. Board of Education, 342 U.S. 429 (1952). The Court held that a parent could not challenge public school bible-reading after his child had graduated from high school.

## ARGUMENT IN BEHALF OF RESPONDENTS

### by MR. GREENBERG

MR. GREENBERG: If it please the Court, we are seeking affirmance of the judgment below. In addition to the reasons submitted by Mr. Redding, which, we submit, will permanently settle respondents' right to the relief which they sought, and settle on the basis of the really important factors present in this case, we submit that the judgment rendered below should at least be affirmed for the reasons given by the court below.

The court below found that the state was offering education to respondents inferior to education offered white children similarly situated.

The petitioners, on page 4 of their petition for certiorari, expressly disclaim any challenge to this finding of inequality.

To give the Court an idea of the degree of the more measurable inequalities present in this case, I had merely intended to mention a few of them, but since the Attorney General had taken them up in detail, I should like to, for a moment, go through our brief where they are listed on pages 27 through 41, and outline them rapidly so that the Court will have an idea of the severe degree of the inequality.

There is travel, and the significance of travel, as testified to by a psychologist, who indicated that travel has important consequences for the learning process, that it induces fatigue and irritability and takes up valuable portions of the child's time when he could be engaged in self-initiated activity, that is very important to the learning process.

There were inequalities in sites and buildings and inequalities in teacher preparation and there was inequality in teacher load, which the Attorney General did not bring out.

We contended there were inequalities in curricula and extracurricular activities; there was no finding that these were equal, but we submit, and the Supreme Court of Delaware found that, perhaps, they were de minimus, and nothing to be taken into account in a case of this sort, and it is our contention, concerning inequalities of, perhaps, this small nature, that a child should not be submitted to them merely because of his race.

There were inequalities in the elementary school case in sites and buildings, which the Attorney General brought out, in instructional materials and accessories, which the Attorney General brought out; there were inequalities in relative expenditures for schools 29 and 107, which I do not believe were brought out; and, very important, there were inequalities in teaching in the cases.

The teachers in the Negro elementary school were not as well trained and were not as highly rated by the County Supervisor, who had rated them as B teachers, whereas he had rated the teachers in the white schools as A teachers.

So, we submit, that the palpable, perhaps the more measurable, inequalities in this case are of a very severe and extensive nature.

The Attorney General expressed willingness in both courts below, and he expresses it in this Court to accept the decree ordering the state to equalize the schools in questions.

But, as was pointed out in a portion of the Chancellor's opinion which was read here before, the Chancellor wrote:

This would be to say, 'Yes, your constitutional rights are being invaded, but be patient, we will see whether in time they are still being invaded.'

The Chancellor cited *Sweatt* against *Painter* for this proposition, and he ruled that respondents were entitled to relief immediately in the only way that relief was available, namely, by admission to the schools with the superior facilities, and he wrote:

To postpone relief would be to deny relief,

and the Supreme Court of Delaware affirmed on this express ground.

JUSTICE JACKSON: Is it your position that the court, finding a right being denied, has no power to take into consideration the time that it will take to correct it?

MR. GREENBERG: It is our position, Your Honor, that if constitutional rights are being denied our respondents, they are entitled to those rights as quickly as those rights can be made available; and in this case they could be made available most quickly by admission to the superior facilities—that is, without regard to the other factors that have been discussed in the other cases.

JUSTICE JACKSON: You do not agree with the Attorney General's suggestion, then?

MR. GREENBERG: No. It is our position, for example, that if the state guarantees a child ten years of education, and the child has spent approximately five of those years in inferior schools, and it is possible to give him the remaining five years on a parity with white students, that to deny him the sixth, seventh, and eighth year of equality is to inflict an irreparable injury on him.

Those three years cannot be completely recaptured, and we feel there is no reason in justice or under the Fourteenth Amendment why we should not demand it.

JUSTICE FRANKFURTER: When you say there is no reason in justice, of course—

MR. GREENBERG: And under the Fourteenth Amendment.

JUSTICE JACKSON: When you say that the Attorney General's plan for a gradual correction of this situation is impossible, it has to be done all at once?

MR. GREENBERG: That is our view.

First of all, it does not afford the right and, second of all, as I intend to come to in a moment, there is no showing on this record, no showing whatsoever, and both courts so found there is no evidence that equality would occur at any time in the future.

JUSTICE FRANKFURTER: What is there in the Constitution which prevents a chancellor from taking into consideration the consequences of a decree in cases involving constitutional rights or any other rights?

MR. GREENBERG: There is nothing in the Constitution one way or another on the question.

JUSTICE FRANKFURTER: He behaved the way a chancellor should behave, in the way of balancing the public interest on one side as against an immediate relief on the other?

MR. GREENBERG: But there is no showing of any public interest—

JUSTICE FRANKFURTER: That is a different story. A chancellor has no business not to enforce a right which he decrees in the ordinary property case—

MR. GREENBERG: I think that if a showing had been made on that point, something of that sort might be taken into consideration.

JUSTICE FRANKFURTER: I was referring to the broader question that Justice Jackson raised by referring to the considerations of the Attorney General's previous answers, the whole broad problem of relief in these cases on the assumption that rights are involved.

MR. GREENBERG: That is right, sir.
I would like to address myself to something close to that question, Your Honor. There have been questions apparently in this case and in other cases concerning the administrative problems that might be involved in the integration which was involved in these cases. As to this case, we can only say that the decree of the Supreme Court of Delaware came down, I believe, on August the 28, at which time both counsel for the respondents were on vacation, and before we could even return from vacation, the children who had read about the decree in the newspaper had applied to the schools and had been admitted, and there was no more administrative problem involved than admitting anybody else. I certainly heard of nothing unusual in this particular case that would indicate any serious administrative, or any administrative, difficulty.

JUSTICE FRANKFURTER: Are you suggesting that on the broader issue there is no problem at all in just eliminating segregated school systems throughout the country, no problem at all?

MR. GREENBERG: Of course, there may be a problem, but in this case, there was no problem, and in fact no problem whatsoever.

JUSTICE FRANKFURTER: Then there is no occasion for not doing what the Delaware court did?

MR. GREENBERG: As far as administrative problems are concerned, I see no problem.
The Attorney General's contention that the schools can be equalized within one year does not take several factors into account. The first one is, how the Wilmington School Board, which is not a party to this case, and which would have to equalize the Howard School in question, can be compelled to equalize the Howard School, since it is not a party to the case. The Court of Chancery and the Supreme Court of Delaware both know that they could not order the Wilmington

Board to do anything to which it was not a party. And the Attorney General in his petition for certiorari and also in his argument nowhere indicated how Delaware courts of equity could administer the type of decree which he said that they should have handed down, as both the Court of Chancery, which would have to administer such a decree, and the Supreme Court of Delaware have ruled that they cannot engage in the sort of business which he wants them to become involved in.

I read from page 57 of the thin blue book, at the end:

> . . . It is difficult to see how a court of equity could effectively supervise and direct the expenditure of state funds in a matter committed to the sound administrative discretion of the school authorities.

The Chancellor wrote similarly that he did not see how he could order the state to put into effect the equalization which the Attorney General suggests this Court should order the state to do.

A reference to the pages of the record to which the Attorney General referred for his assertion that equality will occur sometime in the future does not reveal that there is any likelihood of equality at all in the future. Both courts below found no likelihood of future equality.

The Court of Chancery wrote on page 352 of this thick white book:

> I do not see how the plans mentioned will remove all the objections to the present arrangement.

And on page 353:

> I conclude that the State's future plans do not operate to prevent the granting of relief to these plaintiffs . . .

And on page 356, he indicated that the same considerations applied to the elementary school cases. I was talking about the high school cases in the other two.

The Supreme Court of Delaware likewise noted that the Attorney General had proffered no evidence whatsoever of future equalization, and he noted that claims of equality would have to be judged when made in the future. That is on page 58 of the thin blue book.

So the Attorney General's request for a decree ordering equalization is based upon a factual premise that such equalization will occur at some ascertainable time in the future, and it is nowhere supported in the record in either of the opinions of the courts below.

THE CHIEF JUSTICE: You mean to say that the record does not show about the construction of the new high school, costing a million and a quarter dollars, that the Attorney General referred to?

MR. GREENBERG: Yes, Your Honor. It showed that a new high school is being constructed. That high school is thirty miles south of where respondents live, in the high school case, and it nowhere indicates what effect that high school will have upon the future education of respondents.

THE CHIEF JUSTICE: Does it consider the additions at Howard, and how they would be ready for use next September? Is that in the record, or is the Attorney General speaking out of the record?

MR. GREENBERG: There is a stipulation, Your Honor, which I will quote in full, and I think it will thoroughly answer your question. The stipulation is on page 36 of the clipped-in portion of the thin blue book, and Item 3 of that stipulation states:

> The present schedule of the Wilmington Board of Education calls for a transfer of grades seven, eight and nine of the Howard High School to the Bancroft School and the closing down of the Carver School at the beginning of the school year in September, 1953.

THE CHIEF JUSTICE: Is there anything about the additional facilities at Howard? We were told that there is quite a bit of it, and that that would be ready in September.

MR. GREENBERG: I think, in justice to the Attorney General, I can take the petition for certiorari and refer to every record reference that he gives. On page 5 of his petition for certiorari, speaking of future equalization, he refers first to pages R-36 and 57, which are in the clipped-in portion of this thin blue book. On page R-36 is Item 3, which we just read. On page 57, there is the statement that the court held:

> As to the Howard-Carver buildings, plans have been approved for the transfer of the junior high school pupils at Howard to another junior high school, for the enlargement of the Howard building, with additional equipment, and for the closing of Carver and the transfer of its pupils to Howard. It is said that all these changes are expected to be completed by September 1953, and that they will completely equalize the Howard facilities. It is also shown that plans are under way to build a modern high school for Negroes at Middletown, New Castle County.

That is our item. I might say that this nowhere takes into account contemplated future changes at the Claymont School, and the record indicates a very vast expansion program is under way there.

He then refers in that same paragraph to page 57, which I read, and then he refers to page A-312, which is page 312 of the thick white book. George Miller, who was State Superintendent of Education, stated:

> The construction program in New Castle County provides for a four-year high school in Middletown which is under way now, and we are just waiting for materials until that is completed.

But it nowhere indicates what effect that will have. This is thirty miles south of where respondents live. It in no way indicates what effect that will have on respondents' education.

He then in the elementary school case refers to pages R-59 to 62, where it is stated that until recently the white elementary school was favored in the receipt of public funds, and that that inequality has been eliminated, and on page 62, there is the statement that, speaking of the fact that the inequality of funds had been eliminated:

> the burden was clearly upon the defendants to show the extent to which the remedial legislation had improved conditions or would improve them in the near future. This the defendants failed to do. It is natural to suppose that with the equality of funds any

substantial disparities will shortly be eliminated, but we must take the record as it was made below.

And that only refers to the equalization of teachers in the two schools. It does not refer to any other disparities.

As Mr. Redding indicated, Your Honor, it is our contention in this case that from the Attorney General's position in this case and from the express provision in the opinion of the Supreme Court of Delaware, this litigation is open to re-segregate those plaintiffs at any time that the physical facilities, they believe, may become equalized.

Now, if the physical facilities were all that were involved in this case, it would be our contention that this merely might be another unfortunate burden that these respondents have to bear solely because of their race. But where the record proves that the injury from which the right flows will exist in segregated schools so long as segregated schools exist, we submit that this court should recognize these facts and assure the respondents' admission permanently.

JUSTICE BLACK: Do you say that the record shows that? What are you depending upon? The findings?

MR. GREENBERG: We are depending upon the findings and the evidence upon which the findings were made.

JUSTICE BLACK: Do you take the position that the findings affect the matter generally, or only in Delaware?

MR. GREENBERG: The findings expressly referred to Delaware, Your Honor, in our Delaware society. As to the other states, I have read the record in some of these other states, and there is similar evidence. But speaking of the Delaware case, the findings refer to Delaware specifically, and indeed, by our witnesses there was a very heavy emphasis upon the fact that these Delaware children were examined by one of America's most eminent psychiatrists, and by psychologists. An ex-head of the Delaware Psychological Association testified for us. The head of the Sociology Department of the University of Delaware testified for us. A professor of education at the University of Delaware testified for us. It was all to the effect that in Delaware society, this is the effect.

JUSTICE BLACK: Is that what you are limiting this part of your argument to, that on the basis of cases of this kind and the findings of fact based on oral testimony it may be expected, under the "separate but equal" doctrine to show that there is an inferiority in educational opportunity in one community where there might not be in another?

MR. GREENBERG: Yes, Your Honor, that is part of what you might call a three-prong attack. But that is only one part of it. We also contend, of course, that the classification is entirely unreasonable, but we are urging all the reasons we can for affirmance of the judgment below. And that is one of the reasons.

So as I said, in the doctrine announced in the case of *Helvering* v. *Lerner Stores*,[65] which is in our brief at page 11, we urge these additional reasons for affirmance of the judgment below.

[65]314 U.S. 463 (1941). The Court held that claims of unreasonable classification raise no question under the Fifth Amendment which contains no equal protection clause.

We urge again that this Court recognize the unreasonableness of the classification involved in this case, and also that this Court adopt as its own the factual finding of the Chancellor that state-imposed segregation in Delaware society injures the Negro child.

JUSTICE FRANKFURTER: How can we do that? The Supreme Court says that we are not going to review that. That means that we must take the testimony of Dr. Fredric Wertham, for whom I have a great respect, and say that his testimony, his appraisal and his judgment are like mathematical pronouncements, and there they are.

MR. GREENBERG: Well, Your Honor, there are several things involved. It is a very full and completely uncontradicted record. Secondly, there was a thorough review by the Chancellor.

JUSTICE FRANKFURTER: But the testimony of a witness is subject to intrinsic limitations and qualifications and illuminations. The mere fact that a man is not contradicted does not mean that what he says is so.

MR. GREENBERG: As far as that is concerned, the Chancellor—

JUSTICE FRANKFURTER: If a man says three yards, and I have measured it, and it is three yards, there it is. But if a man tells you the inside of your brain and mine, and how we function, that is not a measurement, and there you are.

MR. GREENBERG: That is true, Your Honor. But it is our contention that as far as the value to be placed upon the facts, the trial judge was able to see and hear the witness, and that is certainly in the record. The Chancellor saw him. Now, as far as the record is concerned, Your Honors are as free to review that record as the Supreme Court of Delaware. They cannot recapture the mood and the word of the witness, either, and this bears on a constitutional right.

JUSTICE FRANKFURTER: I do not know about that. They are dealing with Delaware conditions. They are dealing with situations that they know about. It makes a lot of difference, whether you have two so-called minority children in a group of twenty or two out of fifty or ten out of forty. Those are all local conditions, as to which the Supreme Court of Delaware has some knowledge, having lived there and thought about these things.

MR. GREENBERG: All we can say is that whatever consideration was given to the matter by the Delaware court, all added up to the fact that segregation injured these children. And as far as what I assume Your Honor is referring to, I assume Your Honor is referring to what other counsel has referred to, the untoward effects of the abolition of segregation.

JUSTICE FRANKFURTER: I am not referring to anything, except that we are here in a domain which I do not yet regard as science in the sense of mathematical certainty. This is all opinion evidence.

MR. GREENBERG: That is true, Your Honor.

JUSTICE FRANKFURTER: I do not mean that I disrespect it. I simply know its character. It can be a very different thing from, as I say, things that are weighed and measured and are fungible. We are dealing here with very subtle things, very subtle testimony.

MR. GREENBERG: Our only answer to that is that to the extent that it did receive a review below, and to the extent that the Chancellor was able to view these witnesses, and to the extent that the cross-examination affected their testimony, and to the extent that the Supreme Court of Delaware felt that the abolition of segregation would have any untoward effect, none of that weakens this testimony at all, because in fact segregation was abolished as far as these particular children were concerned, and they are now attending the schools.

JUSTICE FRANKFURTER: I do not mean to raise the question of testimony. All I am saying is that I do not have a record such as I would have if I merely had the Chancellor's findings or if the Supreme Court had said, "We agree with the Chancellor."

MR. GREENBERG: I agree that if more people had reviewed this—

JUSTICE FRANKFURTER: Not more; the very simple fact, the fact that the Supreme Court said, inasmuch as we deem this immaterial, we do not review it, and therefore we have merely a finding of an intermediate court, as to which I know not what the highest court of Delaware would have said if they had reviewed it.

JUSTICE BLACK: Did you say that the children are now attending these schools?

MR. GREENBERG: That is right, sir. They registered from the beginning of the semester. I thought I mentioned that the decree—

JUSTICE BLACK: I thought the argument was that they could not get in, that it would disrupt the schools.

MR. GREENBERG: The Attorney General of Delaware applied for a stay of execution, but it was not granted to him. One of the reasons was that he applied too late, and another reason was that to grant the stay would be inconsistent with the mandate.

And so for the reasons that Mr. Redding has submitted, and particularly for those reasons, because we feel that our respondents' rights can be more fully protected and more permanently protected in that way, we urge that this Court affirm the judgment below, and assure that the respondents' stay in the schools to which they have been admitted and which they are now attending will be one unharassed by future litigation, and attempts to segregate them once more.

(Whereupon, at 3:50 p.m., the argument was concluded.)

1953 ARGUMENT

No. 8. BROWN ET AL. v. BOARD OF EDUCATION OF TOPEKA ET AL.;

No. 101. BRIGGS ET AL. v. ELLIOTT ET AL., MEMBERS OF BOARD OF TRUSTEES OF SCHOOL DISTRICT #22, ET AL.;

No. 191. DAVIS ET AL. v. COUNTY SCHOOL BOARD OF PRINCE EDWARD COUNTY ET AL.;

No. 413. BOLLING ET AL. v. SHARPE ET AL.; and

No. 448. GEBHART ET AL. v. BELTON ET AL.

Each of these cases is ordered restored to the docket and is assigned for reargument on Monday, October 12, next. In their briefs and on oral argument counsel are requested to discuss particularly the following questions insofar as they are relevant to the respective cases:

1. What evidence is there that the Congress which submitted and the State legislatures and conventions which ratified the Fourteenth Amendment contemplated or did not contemplate, understood or did not understand, that it would abolish segregation in public schools?

2. If neither the Congress in submitting nor the States in ratifying the Fourteenth Amendment understood that compliance with it would require the immediate abolition of segregation in public schools, was it nevertheless the understanding of the framers of the Amendment

(a) that future Congresses might, in the exercise of their power under section 5 of the Amendment, abolish such segregation, or

(b) that it would be within the judicial power, in light of future conditions, to construe the Amendment as abolishing such segregation of its own force?

3. On the assumption that the answers to questions 2 (a) and (b) do not dispose of the issue, is it within the judicial power, in construing the Amendment, to abolish segregation in public schools?

4. Assuming it is decided that segregation in public schools violates the Fourteenth Amendment

(a) would a decree necessarily follow providing that, within the limits set by normal geographic school districting, Negro children should forthwith be admitted to schools of their choice, or

(b) may this Court, in the exercise of its equity powers, permit an effective gradual adjustment to be brought about from existing segregated systems to a system not based on color distinctions?

5. On the assumption on which questions 4 *(a)* and *(b)* are based, and assuming further that this Court will exercise its equity powers to the end described in question 4 *(b)*,

*(a)* should this Court formulate detailed decrees in these cases;

*(b)* if so, what specific issues should the decrees reach;

*(c)* should this Court appoint a special master to hear evidence with a view to recommending specific terms for such decrees;

*(d)* should this Court remand to the courts of first instance with directions to frame decrees in these cases, and if so what general directions should the decrees of this Court include and what procedures should the courts of first instance follow in arriving at the specific terms of more detailed decrees?

The Attorney General of the United States is invited to take part in the oral argument and to file an additional brief if he so desires.

IN THE SUPREME COURT OF THE UNITED STATES

October Term, 1953

HARRY BRIGGS, JR., et al.,
Appellants,

vs.

R. W. ELLIOTT, CHAIRMAN, J. D. CARSON, et al.,
MEMBERS OF BOARD OF TRUSTEES OF SCHOOL DISTRICT NO. 22,
CLARENDON COUNTY, S.C., et al
Appellees.

DOROTHY E. DAVIS, BERTHA M. DAVIS AND INEZ E. DAVIS, ETC., et al.,
Appellants,

vs.

COUNTY SCHOOL BOARD OF PRINCE EDWARD COUNTY, VIRGINIA, et al.,
Appellees

Case No. 4

Washington, D.C.
Monday, December 7, 1953.

The above-entitled causes came on for oral argument at 1:05 p.m.

PRESENT:

The Chief Justice, Honorable Earl Warren, and Associate Justices Black, Reed, Frankfurter, Douglas, Jackson, Burton, Clark, and Minton.

APPEARANCES:

On behalf of the Appellants, Dorothy E. Davis, et al.:
SPOTTSWOOD W. ROBINSON, III, ESQ.

On behalf of the Appellants, Harry Briggs, Jr. et al.:
THURGOOD MARSHALL, ESQ.

On behalf of the Appellees, R. W. Elliott, Chairman, J. R. Carson, et al.,
Members of Board of Trustees of School District No. 22, Clarendon County, S.C., et al.:
JOHN W. DAVIS, ESQ.

On behalf of the Appellees, County School Board of Prince Edward County, Virginia, et al.:
T. JUSTIN MOORE, ESQ., and J. LINDSAY ALMOND, ESQ.

On behalf of the United States:
J. LEE RANKIN, ESQ., Assistant Attorney General

THE CHIEF JUSTICE: No. 2, Harry Briggs, Jr., et al versus R. W. Elliott, et al.

THE CLERK: Counsel are present.

### ARGUMENT ON BEHALF OF THE APPELLANTS
### by MR. ROBINSON

MR. ROBINSON: May it please the Court. At the outset I should like to point out that the argument in No. 2 and the argument in No. 4 are being combined. Mr. Marshall and I are offering two separate appeals, as I have already outlined, the appeal in No. 2 and the appeal in No. 4, and for this reason at the outset I would like the indulgence of the Court, before stating the facts, to outline the argument and the part that he will present and the part that I will undertake to present.

After stating the facts and the procedural matters, I propose to address myself to questions one and two of the Court, and to discuss the historical evidence which we submit demonstrates that the Congress that submitted it and the legislatures and conventions that ratified the Fourteenth Amendment, contemplated and understood that it would abolish segregation in public schools; that future congresses might in the exercise of their power under section 5 of the Amendment abolish segregation, and also, that it would be within the jurisdictional power in the light of future conditions to construe the Amendment as abolishing segregation of its own force.

Mr. Marshall will then address himself to questions three, four, and five and will present our arguments demonstrating that it is within the jurisdictional power in construing the Amendment to abolish segregation in public schools and our position with respect to the disposition that this Court should make of these cases in the event that it is decided that segregation in public schools violates the Fourteenth Amendment.

Both of these cases are rearguments of appeals from final decrees of three-judge District Courts, in the instance of No. 2 from the Eastern District of South Carolina, in the instance of No. 4, from the Eastern District of Virginia.

In each of these cases Negro children and their respective parents and guardians sued competent county school authorities alleging that by requiring these and other Negro children to attend separate Negro schools as commanded by the Constitutions and the laws of South Carolina and Virginia respectively, they denied them rights secured by the Fourteenth Amendment.

In each of these cases the appellants sought decrees declaring the invalidity of the state school segregation provisions and injunctions restraining the appellees from enforcing these provisions and from restricting Negro children on a racial basis in their requiring attendance in the public schools.

In case No. 2, the majority of the District Court, with Judge Waring[1] dissent-

[1]Judge J. Waties Waring (1880–1968). United States District Judge for South Carolina, 1942–1952. He ruled in 1947 that the South Carolina Democratic primary must be open to Negroes, Elmore v. Rice, 72 F. Supp. 516 (E.D.S.C. 1947). Thereafter, Waring's life was threatened and his home was stoned. An unsuccessful effort was made to impeach him in the House of Representatives. After dissenting in the lower court decision in Briggs v. Elliott, he received more personal abuse for his pro-Negro ruling and soon afterward resigned from the bench. He moved to New York and became active in various civil rights organizations.

ing following the original hearing of that case in that court, filed an opinion and entered a final decree requiring the appellees to afford the appellants involved in that case equal facilities, but declaring that the contested constitutional and statutory provisions were valid, and refusing to grant the requested injunctive relief.

On appeal from this decree this Court, Mr. Justice Douglas and Mr. Justice Black dissenting, vacated the judgment, that is, the first decree of the District Court, and remanded the case for the purpose of obtaining the view of the District Court upon additional facts in the record presented by a report which was subsequently filed in the District Court by the appellees, and to give the District Court the opportunity to take such action as it might deem appropriate in the light of the facts disclosed by that report.

The District Court then proceeded to have a second hearing. Judge Waring, in the meanwhile, had retired from the bench.

Upon this occasion after the hearing the District Court filed another opinion and entered another final decree, this time unanimously, again declaring the school segregation provision valid, and refusing to grant injunctive relief.

In case No. 4, the District Court for the Eastern District of Virginia likewise found inequalities in physical facilities and curricula, and likewise, it ordered that these inequalities be eliminated. But as to the District Court, in No. 2, it refused to invalidate or to enjoin the enforcement of the school segregation provisions.

These cases were argued before this Court at the last term. On last June 8 the Court entered an order directing reargument in the case and requesting counsel to address themselves to five questions set forth in the order so far as those questions would be relevant to the issues involved in the respective cases. It is pursuant, of course, to that order that we are here today.

I think that it is highly significant at the outset to note that each of these cases was brought pursuant to the authority conferred by the Act of April 20, 1871, section 1 of that Act, which is now codified in large measure in Title 8 of the United States Code, section 43 [now 42 U.S.C. section 1983]. That Act was entitled:

> An Act to enforce the provisions of the Fourteenth Amendment to the Constitution of the United States and for other purposes.

As the Court is well aware, the Act provided, as does the present section, although the present section does not exactly conform to the original Act, though essentially the same provisions are there, that:

> Any person who, under color of any law of any State, subjects or causes to be subjected any person within the jurisdiction of the United States to the deprivation of any rights secured by the Constitution of the United States shall be liable to the party injured in any action at law, a suit in equity or other proper proceeding for redress.

Involved in these cases is a statute which in the viewpoint of the appellants is in violation of the provisions of section 1 of the Fourteenth Amendment. In section 43 of Title 8 we have a statute which, in the enforcement of the provisions of the Fourteenth Amendment, creates a cause of action and confers both the power and the duty upon the federal courts to enforce that cause of action.

We submit that the statute imposes a positive duty upon the courts to determine whether, under the Fourteenth Amendment, the action of a state in imposing racial segregation in public education is valid.

I would like now to proceed to an examination of the history of the formulation, the proposal and the ratification of the Fourteenth Amendment as an aid to the Court's determination of whether the laws involved in these cases can stand consistently with the prohibitions of the Fourteenth Amendment.

Our position is this: considering the overall evidence derived from the debates and proceedings on the Fourteenth Amendment, these conclusions are supported.

First: that the Amendment had as its purpose and effect the complete legal equality of all persons, irrespective of race, and the prohibition of all state imposed caste and class systems based upon race.

And secondly, that segregation in public schools, constituting as it does legislation of this type, is necessarily embraced within the prohibitions of the Amendment.

Going first to the debates on the Fourteenth Amendment itself, there is considerable evidence of the intention of the framers to broadly provide for the complete legal equality of all men, irrespective of race, and to broadly proscribe all caste and class legislation based upon race or color.

There is also some reference specifically to the impact which the proposed Amendment would have upon State imposed segregation in public schools. I propose to address myself to both categories of evidence.

When the 39th Congress, which formulated the Fourteenth Amendment, convened in December of 1865, it was cognizant of, and it was confronted with, the so-called Black Codes which had been enacted throughout the southern states.

In brief summary, these laws imposed and were designed to maintain essentially the same inferior position which Negroes had occupied prior to the abolition of slavery. As a matter of fact, they followed pretty much the legal pattern of the antebellum slave codes.

For example, they compelled Negroes to work for limited pay, they restricted their mobility, they prohibited their testimony in court against a white person, and contained innumerable provisions for segregation on carriers and in public places. In some of these codes there were expressed prohibitions upon the attendance by Negroes of the public schools provided for white children.

I would like to emphasize, as this Court has in its previous decisions recognized, that the existence of these laws was largely responsible for the Fourteenth Amendment and the contemporaneous civil rights legislation.

We find in the debates and proceedings on the Fourteenth Amendment abundant evidence demonstrating that the radical Republicans in the 39th Congress desired and intended that the Fourteenth Amendment would effect both the invalidation of the existing Black Codes and any and all future attempts to impose governmentally caste distinctions predicated upon race.

Among the items of evidence which demonstrate this broad overall purpose in effect of the Amendment, I would like to make reference to the following: When the resolution was introduced into the Senate which embraced the provision which is now section 1 of the Fourteenth Amendment, with simply the addition of the citizenship clause, in other words, House Resolution 127, Senate Howard[2] opened

[2]Senator Jacob M. Howard (1805–1871) of Michigan. Whig representative, 1841–1843; one of the founders of the Republican party in 1854; Republican senator, 1867–1871.

the debate in the Senate—as a matter of fact, he was speaking for the Joint Committee on Reconstruction, which had formulated the provision, mindful, as I said before, that it did not yet contain the citizenship clause, but did contain the privileges or immunities, the equal protection and due process clauses—speaking for the Joint Committee, because Senator Fessenden,[3] one of its co-chairmen, was ill, he made these significant statements.

He referred to the last two clauses of the first section. He said that these two clauses disabled a state from depriving not merely a citizen of the United States, but of any person, whoever he may be, of life, liberty or property without due process of law, and from denying him the equal protection of the laws.

This, Senator Howard says abolishes all class legislation in the states and does away with the injustice of subjecting one caste of persons to a code not applicable to another.

It prohibits the hanging of a black man for crime for which the white man is not hanged. It protects the black man in his fundamental rights as a citizen with the same shield which it throws around the white man.

Here we have an explicit declaration by one of the co-chairmen of the committee of Congress which formulated what is now essentially section 1 of the Fourteenth Amendment, and that is the scope that he ascribed to it.

As a matter of fact, during the course of the same speech introducing the bill into Congress, Senator Howard had this to say:

> I look upon the first section taken in connection with the fifth section as very important. It will, if adopted by the States, forever disable every one of them from passing laws infringing upon those fundamental rights and privileges which pertain to citizens of the United States and to all persons who may happen to be within their jurisdiction.
> It establishes equality before the law, it gives to the humblest, the poorest, the most despised of the race the same rights and the same protection before the law that it gives to the most powerful, the most wealthy and the most haughty.

Consequently, certainly in the opinion of Senator Howard, the due process and equal protection clauses would sweep away, in his language, all class legislation.

Similarly, during the Senate debates, Senator Poland[4] addressed himself to section 1, and he made a somewhat similar declaration. As a matter of fact, he pointed out the existence of the Black Codes. He made reference to them specifically:

> We know that State laws exist and some of them of very recent enactment, in direct violation of these principles.

Then he went on to give the Amendment the scope which he thought it was entitled to.

[3]Senator William P. Fessenden (1806–1869) of Maine. Whig representative, 1841–1843; Whig and Republican senator 1854–1864; Secretary of the Treasury, 1864–1865; Republican senator, 1865–1869. He was one of the seven Republican senators who voted to acquit President Andrew Johnson in his impeachment trial in May, 1868.

[4]Senator Luke P. Poland (1815–1887) of Vermont. Republican senator, 1865–1867; representative, 1867–1875 and 1883–1885.

The statements in this regard were by no means confined to the proponents of the Amendment. As a matter of fact, after the citizenship clause had been added to the Amendment, Senator Davis[5] of Kentucky had this to say:

> The real and only object of the first provision of this section [speaking of the citizenship clause which the Senate has added to it] is to make Negroes citizens, to prop the Civil Rights Bill and to give them a more plausible if not a valid claim to its provisions, to press forward to a full community of civil and political rights with the white race, for which its authors are struggling and mean to continue to struggle.

Over in the House when Representative Stevens[6] introduced Resolution 127, he made a similar declaration with respect to scope.

> I can hardly believe that any person can be found who will not admit that every one of these provisions [in the first section] is just.

As a matter of fact, Congressman Stevens says they are all asserted in some form or another in our Declaration or organic law. He pointed out, however, that the Constitution limits the action of Congress; that in this area it was not a limitation upon the States and said that the Amendment supplied that defect and allowed Congress to correct the unjust legislation of the states, and here again referring to the Black Codes, in so far as that law which operates upon one man shall operate equally upon all.

He later on made further reference to the fact that the Amendment was necessary by what he termed the oppressive codes which had become law in the southern states, pointing out that unless the Constitution should restrain these states, "those States will, I fear"—to use his language—"will all keep up this discrimination, and crush to death the hated Freedmen."

And just as in the Senate, we had others who took the floor in the discussion. I might make reference to the statement which was made by Congressman Randall[7] of Pennsylvania, the statement that was made by Congressman Rogers of New Jersey.[8] Now, they were men who opposed the Amendment.

Yet, their statements which we have set forth in our brief show that they also recognized as one of the clauses, as the great occasion for the Fourteenth Amendment, the existence of these racial laws in southern states, and recognized that if the Amendment were in fact adopted, it would have an impact upon such laws of the character which we describe.

I should also like to direct the Court's attention specifically to the statement of Mr. Bingham,[9] who has very appropriately been described as the Madison of

[5]Senator Garrett Davis (1801–1872) of Kentucky. Whig representative, 1839–1847; Whig and Democratic senator, 1861–1872.

[6]Representative Thaddeus Stevens (1792–1868) of Pennsylvania. Whig and Republican representative, 1849–1853 and 1859–1868; Leader of the radical Republicans after the Civil War and Chairman of the managers of the House conducting the impeachment proceedings against President Andrew Johnson.

[7]Representative Samuel J. Randall (1828–1890) of Pennsylvania. Democratic representative, 1863–1890.

[8]Representative Andrew J. Rogers (1828–1900) of New Jersey. Democratic representative, 1863–1867.

[9]Representative John A. Bingham (1815–1900) of Ohio. Republican representative, 1855–1863 and 1865–1873; one of the House managers in the impeachment proceedings against President Andrew Johnson.

the first section of the Fourteenth Amendment. Mr. Bingham made a very notable speech in the House during the debates on the Amendment.

He said that the need for the first section was, to use his language, "one of the lessons that had been taught by the history of the past four years of terrific conflict."

He pointed out that the Amendment did not take away rights which were properly reserved to the states, for in his opinion, and in his language, no state ever had the right under the forms of law, or otherwise, to deny to any Freedmen the equal protection of the law or to abridge the privileges or immunities of any citizen of the Republic, although many of them have assumed and exercised that power and that without remedy.

Going specifically to the evidence which was directed to the issue of public school segregation, I should like first to point out that on the Fourteenth Amendment debates proper, we find only one specific reference to school segregation, and that was the reference that was made in the House by Representative Rogers at the time that Resolution No. 63 was up for consideration. Resolution 63 was the predecessor of 127, and the relationship between the two of them I shall undertake to establish in just a moment.

But during this speech, Representative Rogers made a direct attack upon the proposed Amendment which at that time simply provided that Congress should have the power to make all laws which shall be necessary and proper to secure to the citizens of each state all privileges and immunities of citizens of the several states, and to all persons in the several states equal protection in the rights of life, liberty and property.

Perhaps I should undertake at this moment to demonstrate that connection which I mentioned. H.R. 63 was the bill which had been reported by the Joint Committee on Reconstruction, and it was a bill drafted by Mr. Bingham. H.R. 127, which eventually became, with two significant changes, the Fourteenth Amendment, was also drafted so far as the provisions of section 1 of the Amendment were concerned by Mr. Bingham.

Mr. Bingham introduced Resolution 63 in the House first, and it is notable at this point to say two things which I think are very significant.

In the first place, H.R. 63 was proposed simply to grant to Congress the power to enact laws of a certain character. Pursuant to this authority, assuming as I do that this would have been the construction given to H.R. 63 had it become a constitutional amendment, pursuant to this authority Congress might undertake to pass laws which would outlaw this or that embraced within the scope of the prohibition.

Later on—and the proceedings of the Joint Committee on Reconstruction indicate the various drafts, the various attempts, the various procedures which were gone through and finally deriving the present language of the trilogy of the first section—the form was changed, and it was changed and rewritten by Mr. Bingham to state as a direct prohibition upon the states the disabilities with respect to the things which were embraced within that section.

Now it was, as I said before, at the time that H.R. 63 came up for consideration in the House that Representative Rogers made reference to school segregation. As a matter of fact, he attacked this proposal. He termed it "more dangerous to the liberties of the people and the foundations of the Government than any proposal for amending the Constitution heretofore advanced". He said this amendment would destroy all state legislation distinguishing Negroes on the basis of race.

With respect to schools specifically he had this to say:

> In the State of Pennsylvania there are laws which make a distinction with regard to the schooling of white children and the schooling of black children. It is provided that certain schools shall be designated and set apart for white children, and certain other schools designated and set apart for black children.
>
> Under this amendment Congress would have the power to compel the state to provide for white children and black children to attend the same school upon the principle that all the people shall have equal protection and all the rights of life, liberty and property and all the privileges and immunities of citizens of the several States.

I think that it is also highly significant that during these debates no one denied that H.R. 63 had the scope that Mr. Rogers said that it did.

Throughout the debates there is practically no dispute as to the scope of H.R. 127, which eventually became the trilogy of the Fourteenth Amendment. As a matter of fact, Representative Bingham, who was contemporaneously amending the 1866 Civil Rights Act, to which I will make reference shortly, because of its broad anti-discrimination provisions, and claiming that it lacked constitutional foundation, naturally did not make any dispute of Representative Rogers' appraisal of the wide scope of H.R. 63.

On the contrary, Mr. Bingham in a colloquy with Mr. Hale,[10] two days later indicated his appraisal in just about the same terms. He was asked at that time a question in that regard, and at that time Mr. Bingham pointed to the equal protection clause of his constitutional proposal as justifying the scope which he attributed to the amendment.

In addition to the debates and proceedings on the Fourteenth Amendment proper, there is other evidence which in our opinion is helpful in promoting an understanding of the purposes and effects of the Fourteenth Amendment and of the correctness of our conclusions in this regard.

One of the most important of these items of evidence in my opinion is the Civil Rights Act of 1866. The 39th Congress had an occasion to contemporaneously consider, in addition to the Fourteenth Amendment, this piece of civil rights legislation.

I think that it is very important that at the outset I should point out that these two measures are related, this measure, rather, is related to the Fourteenth Amendment by something more than a mere coincidence in terms of time or subject matter.

The Fourteenth Amendment was actually proposed after members of the 39th Congress stated that the civil rights guaranteed by statute, particularly the Civil Rights Act of 1866, were vulnerable to future political attack or might be struck down as unconstitutional.

Consequently the legislative history of the Act of 1866 is a relevant and important part of the background of the Fourteenth Amendment. This is particu-

[10]Representative Robert S. Hale (1822–1881) of New York. Republican representative, 1866–1867 and 1873–1875.

larly true in our opinion since, as I will later undertake to show, the scope of the Fourteenth Amendment was broader than the scope of this Act.

Going through this as deeply as time will permit, the Civil Rights Act came about in the form of a bill introduced by Senator Trumbull[11] which intended to prohibit in the terms of the bill "any discrimination in civil rights or immunities among the people of the United States on account of race, color or previous condition of servitude," and also containing other provisions to the effect that all persons should have full and equal benefit of all laws for the security of their persons and property, and enumerating certain rights, the right to sue, the right to make contracts, to own and inherit property and that type of thing, which the latter provision would provide.

Senator Trumbull introduced the bill and, upon its introduction, he gave it a very broad scope. He said that in his opinion any statute which was based on race, which was not equal to all persons and which deprived any citizen of civil rights which are secured to other citizens, is in fact a badge of servitude which in his opinion was prohibited by the Constitution.

When the bill was introduced, there were two things that were considered by the houses of Congress with regard to this act. First was its constitutionality, and I don't think I need to needlessly consume the time of the Court on that issue, but simply point out that opponents of the bill took the position there was nothing in the Constitution at that time to justify the enactment of such a law.

There were others on the other side who asserted that the bill was constitutional.

And the second big issue that was involved in the proceedings in this regard was the scope of the bill. Time and again the Democrats and the more conservative Republicans in the Senate and in the other House of Congress had occasion to state that this bill, if Congress passed it, would have a very, very broad effect.

It would have an effect which would deprive the states of all power to make or impose racial distinctions or classifications, and some of these people made specific reference to the impact of the provisions of the first section of this bill, the "no discrimination" of this bill upon public school segregation.

JUSTICE FRANKFURTER: Mr. Robinson, what attitude do you think the Court is called upon to manage, what weight is to be given, or how is it to ever deal with individual utterances of this, that or other congressmen or senators?

MR. ROBINSON: I do not, Mr. Justice Frankfurter, take the position as this Court has on previous occasions stated that it would insist that the meaning of a constitutional provision or of a statute is to be determined by any isolated statement of any individual proponent or opponent of the legislation.

At the outset, however, I tried to point out what was the great occasion, in other words, what there was in the history of the times which presented the occasion for the constitutional amendment. Perhaps I should have earlier pointed out that the same thing, the racial laws in the southern states, constituted the basis,

---

[11]Senator Lyman Trumbull (1813–1896) of Illinois. Republican senator, 1855–1873; one of seven Republican senators to vote against the impeachment of President Andrew Johnson.

the occasion for the enactment, for the promulgation and eventual enactment in limited form, of the Civil Rights Act of 1866.

JUSTICE FRANKFURTER: Do you think we can get out of the debates anything more than Mr. Justice Miller[12] got out of them at the time of the *Slaughter-House Cases?*

MR. ROBINSON: Yes, I think so, Mr. Justice Frankfurter. As I recall Mr. Justice Miller's opinion in the *Slaughter-House Cases,* he recognized also that the great purpose of the Fourteenth Amendment, the occasion for the enactment of it, for the adoption of the Fourteenth Amendment—and I think that what additionally we got out of the debate is not simply a statement here or a statement there with respect to the broad overall purpose and effect, the fundamental thing that a constitutional amendment is supposed to accomplish, but what we get is a general understanding by people who are in the body promulgating that provision as to what scope it was intended to have.

JUSTICE FRANKFURTER: And the understanding you get or you think we ought to get goes beyond the terms which Justice Miller put it in the *Slaughter-House Cases.*

MR. ROBINSON: Well, I do not in any wise, of course, intend in any way to cut down on anything that Mr. Justice Miller stated in that connection. We offer the evidence in the congressional debates on the Amendment and other debates—

JUSTICE FRANKFURTER: I grant you we solicited and elicited that. But I just wondered now that we have got it, what are we to get out of it? The fact that a man in your position says, "This is a terrible measure and if you pass it we will do this and that," does that tell me that this measure does do this and that?

MR. ROBINSON: To this extent, sir. So far as the statement standing alone is concerned, I would attribute no value to it. But when a man makes that statement and he is joined in it by others, he is not disputed by anyone, we have a condition of general understanding that is demonstrated by the overall statements pro and con in that particular connection. I think we get assistance.

JUSTICE FRANKFURTER: You think if an opponent gives an extreme interpretation of a proposed statute or constitutional amendment in order to frighten people on the other side, and the proponents do not get up and say "Yes, that is the thing we want to accomplish," that means they believe it, do you?

MR. ROBINSON: Well, I will have to put it in these terms. I would not, of course, sir, know the motive of the person making that statement.

---

[12]Justice Samuel Miller (1816–1896) of Iowa. A doctor until he was thirty, he then studied law and became a leading lawyer in his state before being appointed to the Supreme Court by President Lincoln in 1862. One of the outstanding Justices of his time, he sat on the Court until 1890. He wrote the Court's opinion in the Slaughter-House Cases, 16 Wall. 36 (1873).

JUSTICE FRANKFURTER: I know, but what does silence mean?

MR. ROBINSON: I think when you have statement after statement with respect to broad overall purpose—

JUSTICE FRANKFURTER: By individual members?

MR. ROBINSON: By individual members.

JUSTICE FRANKFURTER: That the proposal has—

MR. ROBINSON: On other sides, if you please, on both sides, coupled with the fact of almost an entire absence of evidence to the contrary showing that anyone there had a different understanding or a different opinion as to what scope it would have.

JUSTICE FRANKFURTER: Namely, they wanted this proposal to put an end to treating white and colored differently before the law in all its manifestations?

MR. ROBINSON: That is correct, sir.

JUSTICE FRANKFURTER: That is all you get out of it?

MR. ROBINSON: In all of its manifestations.

JUSTICE FRANKFURTER: Then the question is whether this is one of its manifestations.

MR. ROBINSON: I beg your pardon, sir.

JUSTICE FRANKFURTER: Then the question is whether this is one of its manifestations.

MR. ROBINSON: Our position in this regard, Mr. Justice Frankfurter, is that when you consider overall what these people said, what from the facts of history it appears, what Mr. Justice Miller, if you please, said was the purpose and the intended scope of the Amendment, we come up with a broad, general purpose that necessarily embraces a prohibition against the type of state activity which we have presented to the Court in these cases.

I do not mean in any respect to divorce from the other factors which this Court normally utilizes to determine the scope of a constitutional amendment, the debates and proceedings, but simply to relate them in the fashion in which I have undertaken to do.

I will simply make brief reference to the remaining congressional legislation, out of the consideration of time. As I have pointed out, Senator Cowan,[13] of Pennsylvania, in the Senate made a specific reference to the scope of the Civil Rights Act in its original form, stating that it would outlaw school segregation.

[13]Senator Edgar Cowan (1815–1885) of Pennyslvania. Republican senator 1861–1867; opposed Reconstruction policy of radical Republicans and was not reelected.

Senator Howard made a statement with respect to its outlawing all state laws discriminating on the basis of civil rights. As a matter of fact, as we have set forth in our brief, there was speech after speech in each House devoted not only to the broad general intention of the Act, but also with respect to segregation in public schools.

Over in the House the same Representative Rogers, who said that the Fourteenth Amendment would abolish school segregation, said that the original form of the Civil Rights Act would also have that effect.

Now the importance of all that comes to this. After all of this discussion, particularly the raising of objections as to the constitutionality of the Act, Representative Bingham took the floor, stated that he was thoroughly in favor of the provisions of the things which the proponents of the Act were attempting to accomplish. He had an objection not to the scope of the bill, but he did have one to its constitutionality.

He then stated that in his opinion while the objectives that were objectives properly to be attained, they were to be attained by a constitutional amendment, and not by a statute which, in his opinion, was not justified by the provisions of the Constitution as it then existed. He made it very plain, however, that his objection in this particular regard was not the scope. His objection was to constitutionality.

Now, as a matter of history, Mr. Bingham had just introduced in the House a few days before H.R. 63 which was, as I have said, the forerunner of the Fourteenth Amendment, so consequently, he already had before the Congress a proposal which, if adopted, would, in his opinion, constitute or provide a constitutional basis for the type of legislation which was involved in the Civil Rights Act.

Now, at this point the discussions and the debates make it perfectly plain that the action of the Congress in eliminating the broad no-discrimination clause in the first part of the Civil Rights Act of 1866, and enacting the rest, the balance of the Act in a more limited form, did so for the reasons that were suggested by Mr. Bingham.

As a matter of fact, in this regard we haven't been able to find anything in history that discloses, as our opponents contend, that the rights which are embraced in, and the prohibitions imposed by, the Fourteenth Amendment are no larger than those which are embraced in or imposed by the Civil Rights Act of 1866.

I think this contention ignores the evolution of the Fourteenth Amendment in so far as its relation to the Civil Rights Act of 1866 is concerned. It will be recalled, as I have previously said, that some members of Congress stated that the bill in its original form would outlaw school segregation.

It is another fact that Mr. Wilson[14] in the House claimed that the Act as originally proposed would not effect school segregation, and it was at that point that Mr. Bingham disputed his construction of the Act and asserted that the bill was as broad as the conservatives charged and that while he favored such sweeping objections, he felt that they could not be legally justified except by a new constitutional amendment.

[14]Representative James J. Wilson (1828–1895) of Iowa. Republican representative, 1861–1869; Republican senator, 1883–1895; one of the House managers in the impeachment trial of President Andrew Johnson.

Consequently, when the 39th Congress eliminated the no-discrimination clause and restricted the scope of the Act, they did so both on the basis of Mr. Bingham's construction of the breadth of the Act and his assertion that there would be forthcoming a constitutional amendment of broad scope.

It is very evident that House Resolution 127, which finally became section 1 of the Fourteenth Amendment, with the addition of the citizenship clause, was even broader than H.R. 63 which was before Congress at that time.

Now, I should like to point out that during the debates on the proposed Amendment, it was charged that the radical Republicans were simply undertaking to provide a constitutional basis for the Civil Rights Act which had already been enacted. At this point the proponents of the Amendment made their purpose clear.

They pointed out that they intended not to adopt a constitutional amendment of restrictive scope, but first they wanted to place the rights to be secured by the constitutional amendment beyond the power of repeal by future congresses. A congressional act would not do this, but a constitutional amendment would.

They also made it plain that what they wanted to assure was the constitutionality in the future of any subsequent legislation which would have as broad a scope as did the '66 Act at the time it was originally introduced. And they also made it plain that they intended to enable the judiciary to give full and complete protection to the rights secured.

We don't find in the debates, nor do we find elsewhere, any such limiting scope attributable to the Fourteenth Amendment as is claimed. As I have had occasion to say, Senator Howard in the Senate, and Mr. Stevens in the House, introducing the bill for the Joint Committee on Reconstruction—I am speaking about 127 now, the Fourteenth Amendment—gave it a scope which far exceeded the Civil Rights Act of 1866.

I should also like to make this final point. That in adopting the Civil Rights Act of 1866, Congress enumerated in its final form as it was enacted, enumerated the rights protected.

I have already explained the reasons why that was done. But unrestricted by this consideration in drafting a constitutional provision, Congress used broad, comprehensive language to describe the standards necessary to guarantee complete Federal protection.

In one of the very early cases, construing the Fourteenth Amendment, *Strauder* v. *West Virginia,* this Court had occasion to point that out. It said:

> The Fourteenth Amendment makes no effort to enumerate the rights it designs to protect. It speaks in general terms, and those are as comprehensive as possible.

I will make brief reference to the legislation following the proposal of the Fourteenth Amendment by Congress and indeed, following its ratification by the states. We have set forth in our brief in considerable detail the proceedings in Congress relating specifically to school segregation. By reason of the division of time which we desire in undertaking to present the argument in these two cases, time simply will not permit me to get into it.

I would like to point out, however, that from beginning to end, all the way through, considering the evidence over all, there was an overwhelming mass of opinion that under the Fourteenth Amendment Congress could constitutionally legislate with respect to the elimination of segregation in public education.

JUSTICE REED: Do you think that legislation by Congress would add anything to the strength of your position?

MR. ROBINSON: In so far as this—

JUSTICE REED: In so far as segregation is concerned in the schools.

MR. ROBINSON: Oh, yes, I think if we had a congressional act, sir, that we probably would not have to be here now. However, I do not think that legislation by Congress in anywise detracts from the power of the judiciary to enforce the prohibitions of the Fourteenth Amendment.

JUSTICE REED: [The] provision granting new legislative power to Congress is useless?

MR. ROBINSON: Well, I would put it this way. As I understand section 5, section 5 was designed to give Congress the authority to legislate in this area if it so desired, within the scope of its legitimate sphere. I am speaking, of course, about the limitations of section 1. However, the separation of the provisions of section 1 and 5 we think is very, very significant.

JUSTICE REED: Was 5 intended only for punishment of violations?

MR. ROBINSON: For remedies, for remedies in so far as congressional action could afford them with respect to the prohibitions of section 1. But actually, as a matter of history, Mr. Justice Reed, the change was made from the original form of the Fourteenth Amendment as it was set up in H.R. 63 and H.R. 127 to make this a direct prohibition on the states not necessitating any congressional action, and as a matter of fact, of course, thereby empowering the courts to determine as a judicial matter acts of a state which were claimed to be in contravention thereof.

I should like to make brief reference to the evidence with respect to state ratification. We have again in our briefs set this forth in considerable detail.

I think the states will pretty largely fall in these general classifications. First we have the states which had seceded from the Union and which were seeking readmission. We have ten in this class who were not in the Union at the time the Fourteenth—well, the ten southern states which had seceded, except Tennessee. I think for all practical purposes Tennessee can be classified in about the same fashion.

Our position in that regard simply is that in view of the fact that these states were specifically required to adopt new constitutions in all respects in conformity with the provisions of the federal Constitution, in view of the highly significant fact that at the time these states came back into the Union they contained in their constitutions no reference to race, no reference to school legislation, I mean to racial segregation in schools, in view of the fact that these restrictions appear in the laws of those states only at a later time, that under those circumstances that fact is of great significance in so far as a determination as to what their understanding of the Fourteenth Amendment was to serve.

Additionally, the point which I urge in that connection was the fact that they were required to ratify the Fourteenth Amendment as a condition of readmission. Also, the newly admitted state, Nebraska, which came in at this time, the history which we set forth in our brief I think is sufficient to demonstrate that Nebraska's understanding with respect to the meaning of the Fourteenth Amendment was that it was not of a character which would permit of public school segregation.

Now, the rest of the cases fall in different categories. We have cases in which there were segregation laws at the time the Amendment was adopted. When the Amendment was adopted, those laws were eliminated, more or less at longer or shorter intervals after the adoption of this Amendment.

We think that the action of the states in this connection is of great significance. There were also states in which segregation in public schools was practiced administratively, some instances in which it was practiced without any statutory authority at all, and we have pointed out in our effort to respond to the Court's question in this particular regard the fact that in a good many instances those states changed their laws as well. Time will simply not permit me to go down the list with respect to the others, but I want to emphasize this point.

We do not claim that every state in the Union understood the Fourteenth Amendment as abolishing school segregation. But we do submit that considering the evidence overall, there was substantial understanding which is to be derived principally not from what the states said, because you can't get that, but from what the states did, that the Fourteenth Amendment would have the scope that we attribute to it, and that consequently, school segregation laws would be invalidated.

In conclusion, with respect to this historical evidence, I would like to say this. I think it is very clear that the framers intended to destroy the Black Codes. I think it is clear that they intended to deprive the states of all power to enact similar laws in the future.

I think the evidence overall is clear that it was contemplated and understood that the state would not be permitted to use its power to maintain a class or caste system based upon race or color, and that the Fourteenth Amendment would operate as a prohibition against the imposition of any racial classification in respect of civil rights.

I think secondly, it is very clear that the breadth of the Amendment is such that it necessarily encompasses school segregation, consequently is one of the activities which the Amendment was designed to protect. Necessarily, it would be invalidated by its provisions.

I further submit that the overall evidence establishes substantial understanding by the states ratifying the Fourteenth Amendment that it would prohibit such segregation. The historical evidence in our opinion, also demonstrates—well, there isn't any question about this—that under section 5 Congress could abolish such segregation and that the judiciary in the enforcement of the provisions of section 1, in the light of future conditions, could construe the Amendment as abolishing segregation of its own force.

(Short recess)

AFTER RECESS

THE CHIEF JUSTICE: Mr. Marshall.

### ARGUMENT ON BEHALF OF APPELLANTS

#### by MR. MARSHALL

MR. MARSHALL: May it please the Court, Mr. Robinson has addressed himself particularly to the congressional history and specifically to the first two questions asked by the Court. I would like for a moment to review particularly questions two and three.

As I understand it, the second question raised the question about Congress in submitting the Amendment as to whether future Congresses would have the power; and (b) was as to whether or not it was within the judicial power in the light of future conditions to construe the Amendment as abolishing such segregation of its own force; and then we get to question three, which is the one I would like to address myself to for the first part of this argument, namely, that, as I understand it, the Court is first requesting us to make the assumption that the answers to questions two (a) and two (b) do not dispose of the case, and on this assumption we are requested to direct our attention [to] the specific question as to whether or not the Court—this Court—has judicial power in construing the Fourteenth Amendment to abolish segregation in the public schools. And our answer to that question is a flat "yes."

But in answering the question, we want to develop from the legal precedents in this case the necessary answer, and to us these legal precedents divide themselves into three groups; and it would be normal and, perhaps, would be more logical to cover these groups of cases in chronological order.

But, however, with the permission of the Court and for the purpose of this argument, we would like to divide them as follows: in the first group to discuss the cases this Court has handed down in the recent years construing the Fourteenth Amendment and the Fifth Amendment, in both instances in regard to the power of the Government, federal or state, to use race, class or national origin for classification purposes.

Then, we would like to go to the second group, being the decisions of the Court construing the Fourteenth Amendment during the period immediately subsequent to the ratification of the Fourteenth Amendment.

We believe that a review of these two groups of cases will show that during these two periods, this Court uniformly gave to the Amendment the broad scope which the framers intended, as set forth by Mr. Robinson.

If there were no other cases on the point, the answer to question three would be simple. However, there is a third group of cases, including at least two decisions, and some others inferentially in that group, which are heavily relied upon by the appellees as compelling a contrary decision of this Court. These cases, obviously, are the ones alleged to support the "separate but equal" doctrine.

With that preliminary statement, I would like to get to this first group of cases.

JUSTICE JACKSON: May I suggest, I do not believe—

MR.MARSHALL: Yes, sir.

JUSTICE JACKSON: I do not believe the Court was troubled about its own cases. It has done a good deal of reading of those cases.

MR. MARSHALL: And the first group are all from this very Court; I was just trying to relate them.

JUSTICE JACKSON: Good.
Maybe the question was more nearly, instead of power—in the strong sense—I only speak for myself not for others—it is the question of the propriety of exercising judicial power to reach this result, if the result would be reached, in the absence of any legislation. I do not think it was a question of power in the sense that our cases have dealt with it. It is a question—

MR. MARSHALL: Well, so far—if I understand you correctly, Mr. Justice Jackson, you mean power that would come from the legislative history of the Fourteenth Amendment?

JUSTICE JACKSON: Whether the Amendment, with what light you can throw on it, makes it appropriate for judicial power, after all that has intervened, to exercise this power instead of—

MR. MARSHALL: Leaving it to the Congress.

JUSTICE JACKSON: That is right.
I do not like to see you waste your time on a misunderstanding, because I do not think we had any doubt about our cases. Things are so often read—

JUSTICE FRANKFURTER: And the books.

MR. MARSHALL: Believe it or not, I have read about it.
I think then that I should change and leave out the first group, for the time being, and go to the other group beginning with *Slaughter-House,* because the reason I would like to discuss those—because, for example, Mr. Justice Frankfurter raised the question about Mr. Justice Miller in the *Slaughter-House Cases,* and I wanted to add to that the fact that we cannot ignore the opinion of Justice Strong[15] in the *Strauder* v. *West Virginia* case, and at that stage of the argument I wanted to say that in these decisions at that period of time they recognized the exact same legislative historical argument that we have just completed; and the *Slaughter-House Cases,* as I read it, stands for the proposition, and at least it has been cited by this Court all the way up at least to the covenant cases of *Shelley,* that the Fourteenth Amendment and the intent that you get from the framers of it, is definitely on the broad purpose that we allege here.

[15]Justice William Strong (1808–1895) of Pennsylvania. Although originally a Democrat, he switched to the Republicans and strongly supported the Union cause, voting to uphold federal conscription and the Legal Tender Act while on the Pennsylvania Supreme Court (1857–1868). He was appointed to the Supreme Court by President Ulysses Grant in 1870 and wrote a number of opinions interpreting the Civil War amendments and the new civil rights statutes enacted under them.

As to whether or not Congress intended to leave this matter to Congress, I submit that one of the short answers is that Title 8, section 43, [now 42 U.S.C. section 1983] which is the statute that we base all of these cases on, says specifically in its enacting clause adopted in 1871, which we have in our brief, that "this bill is enacted for the purpose of enforcing the Fourteenth Amendment."

Congress has already acted and, in that act I am sure it will be remembered that it says that anyone acting under color of state statute, who denies anyone rights guaranteed by the Constitution or laws of the United States shall have a right of action in law or in equity. The original statute said "in the District Court or Circuit Courts," and in codifying it they, of course, have left out the Circuit Court point.

But if there is a need for congressional action, it is there, and in *Strauder* against *West Virginia* Mr. Justice Strong, in his opinion and we quote it in our brief on page 22 and 23 the language which we believe—either I have the wrong brief or—it is there, 33.

THE CHIEF JUSTICE: I would like to have you discuss the question of power because I believe that is the question the Court asked you to discuss.

MR. MARSHALL: The power.

THE CHIEF JUSTICE: Yes, the power.

MR. MARSHALL: Yes, sir. On the power, Mr. Chief Justice Warren, we take the position, and we have covered it in the brief—

THE CHIEF JUSTICE: Yes.

MR. MARSHALL: —and that was the part that Mr. Robinson was to deal with this morning, and it is our understanding that the Fourteenth Amendment, following the Civil Rights Law, but not limited to the Civil Rights Act of 1866, in the debates, it is obvious, especially in the later debates, that left with the courts of the land was this problem of deciding as to the interpretation, so that as to power, it is our position that the Court gets specific power in addition to the regular judiciary act, in this Act of 1871, Title 8, which is not Title 8, section 43 which, I submit, not only gives the federal courts power, but imposes upon the federal courts a specific duty which is different, and this is where we get our power point, and we thought that was sufficient.

THE CHIEF JUSTICE: Yes.

JUSTICE FRANKFURTER: Mr. Marshall—

MR. MARSHALL: Yes, Mr. Justice Frankfurter.

JUSTICE FRANKFURTER: —you trouble me about saying there has been legislation.

You are not resting your claim here on the Act of 1871 and are then discussing whether that Act is constitutional?

MR. MARSHALL: No, sir.

JUSTICE FRANKFURTER: You have to—you are resting, as I understand it, on the compulsions, the implications, derived from the Fourteenth Amendment, as such, in your cases?

MR. MARSHALL: Yes, sir.

JUSTICE FRANKFURTER: So I do not know why you constantly revert to the fact that Congress has already exercised the power. I do not understand what you mean by that.

MR. MARSHALL: Well, as I understand, running through the questions, especially those in number two, the second question—and, fortunately, in so far as this case is concerned, the appellees here claim that Congress has no power to legislate in this field at all and, as I understand their position, the courts and Congress and nobody else can touch it, it is a matter solely for the states.

JUSTICE FRANKFURTER: That we have not got here.

MR. MARSHALL: No, sir; but it is our position that the Fourteenth Amendment was intended to leave to the courts the normal construction of the statute—I mean of the Constitution—and this Act of 1871 is merely recognizing that.

JUSTICE FRANKFURTER: I do not know what that Act has to do with this, our problem. If your claim prevails, it must prevail by virtue of what flows out of the Fourteenth Amendment, as such?

MR. MARSHALL: And would be—

JUSTICE FRANKFURTER: And so far as I am concerned, 1871 need not be on the statute books.

MR. MARSHALL: And we would still have a valid—

JUSTICE FRANKFURTER: And does not help me any.

MR. MARSHALL: Yes, sir.

JUSTICE FRANKFURTER: All right, I understand.

MR. MARSHALL: As I understand it, Mr. Justice Frankfurter, if I may for a minute leave the congressional debates, because I think on the matter of time—and go to the *Strauder* and the *Slaughter-House Cases* which, I think, are the key to this situation, because they were decided at the time nearest to the Fourteenth Amendment—and the *Slaughter-House Cases,* Justice Miller's opinion has been, as I said, cited over and over again, and there is no question that that opinion makes it clear that the Fourteenth Amendment was adopted for the express purpose, and the purpose was, to correct the situation theretofore existing in regard to the treatment of Negroes, slave or free, in a different category from the way you treated the others.

Then, in that particular instance on page 81, which is cited on page 33 of our brief, it is stated that, "The existence of laws in the States where the newly emancipated Negroes resided, which discriminated with gross injustice and hardship against them as a class, was the evil to be remedied by this clause, and by it such laws are forbidden." That is the expression that is nearest to the time of the Amendment.

JUSTICE FRANKFURTER: Wouldn't you say, sir, we do not have to elaborate that because the whole point—not the whole point, but one of the difficulties or one of the assumptions that has to be remedied by later cases—was the intimation of Justice Miller that it was related exclusively to equalizing things?

MR. MARSHALL: Yes, sir.

JUSTICE FRANKFURTER: So one does not have to argue that the Fourteenth Amendment, the target of the Fourteenth Amendment, was to give Negroes certain rights.

MR. MARSHALL: I think so, sir.

JUSTICE FRANKFURTER: I do not see that that needs any argument.

MR. MARSHALL: The only thing that was preliminary to this, Mr. Justice Frankfurter, was that in the Strauder case—and I think that is the one that is really on the point for this particular issue, in *Strauder* v. *West Virginia*—it was made clear, one thing which I would have considered obvious all along—and that is the constitutional amendments are setting down rules—I mean broad principles and not rules—of conduct, as such, and they are put in broad language.

Well, *Strauder* mentions that.

But the important point is that in the Strauder case the decision in that Court makes it clear that they did not intend to enumerate these rights; and that, to my mind, is the crux of whether or not the Court has power to deal with segregation.

Certainly it did not mention it in the Amendment itself, and a lot of items it did not mention. But when you read the debates, as Mr. Robinson explained, you cannot escape this point: that the Amendment was adopted for the express purpose of depriving the states of authority to exercise and enforce the existing Black Codes; that by putting it in the Constitution it was obviously intended that the states would not have power in the future to set up additional Black Codes; and to use the language of this Court in one case, *Lane* v. *Wilson*,[16] whether it is sophisticated or simple-minded; and the part that is to my mind crucial in this case, is that until this time the appellees have shown nothing that can in any form or fashion say that the statutes involved in these cases are not the same type of statutes discussed in the debates and in the decision of the Court nearest to that, namely, the Black Codes, and I do not see how the inevitable result can be challenged, because they are of the exact same cloth, when you go to these Black Codes.

They do, however, on the question of power argue that the State of South Carolina and the State of Virginia have themselves worked out this problem, and for that reason they have found they have to have segregation.

[16]Lane v. Wilson, 307 U.S. 268 (1939). The Supreme Court upheld a suit for damages by a Negro against Arkansas officials who had unlawfully prevented him from voting.

The only way they can keep schools would be to keep segregation and for that reason, as I understand their argument, that reason takes them out of the general flow of invidious legislation under the Fourteenth Amendment; and then they say that there is no definite material in the debates that shows the intent of Congress to include segregation in public education. We submit that that is not the way to approach this problem.

Once we admit, either by reading the legislative debates or reading cases such as *Strauder,* the *Slaughter-House Cases* and the other cases, once we arrive at the conclusion that the Fourteenth Amendment was intended to strike down all types of class and caste legislation [that] on its face involves class, then it seems to me that the only way the appellees can destroy that very clear and logical approach is to show that it was intended not to include schools, not include segregation, and then we have the very interesting position—they immediately recognize that in their briefs, especially in the South Carolina brief, because they say that the McLaurin case involves "separate but equal" doctrine, and certainly if ever there was a case that did not involve "separate but equal," it was *McLaurin,* because as soon as the McLaurin case recognizes the broad intent of the Fourteenth Amendment to cover in progressive stages education, graduate education, I mean, excuse me, legal education, then graduate education; and, as I understand the task the appellees have by force addressed themselves to, it is that even admitting that education is within the purview of the Fourteenth Amendment, when you get to elementary and high schools this Court loses its power to decide as to whether or not segregation in elementary and high schools is illegal.

Now, as to the power argument, it seems to me that that is it in the simplest fashion, and despite the fact that we thought we were obliged to develop it, I think that is a shorthand statement of our position on it, and I think it has not been met, at least up to this point, in any of the briefs and cases.

JUSTICE FRANKFURTER: I should suggest that the question is not whether this Court loses its power, but whether the states lose their powers. I understand the answer you make to it—

MR. MARSHALL: It is my understanding, yes, sir, I think definitely, Mr. Justice Frankfurter, that a reading of the two briefs in this case demonstrates clearly that as of this time we have a test to see whether or not the public policy, customs and mores of the states of South Carolina and Virginia or the avowed intent of our Constitution—as to which one—will prevail.

For example, in their briefs they rely on the fact that, they mention the fact that there is such a thing as racial prejudice, and this is this and that is that, and I would like to, if I could, quote to you one case in our reply brief which, at least is I know, not news to the Court, but it was news to us. I am sure the Court is familiar with the case of *Tanner* v. *Little.*[17] I am not advocating the actual final decision in that case as of this time, but in the language in that case, which involved as you may remember, the green stamps by trading stores—the language is cited on

[17]Tanner v. Little, 240 U.S. 369, 382 (1916). The Court upheld a Washington state law requiring a tax of $6,000 on businesses that gave away trading stamps.

pages 8 and 9 of our brief, and I submit that it is in the middle of a paragraph, is that:

> Red things may be associated by reason of their redness, with disregard of all other resemblances or of distinctions. Such classification would be logically appropriate. Apply it further: make a rule of conduct depend upon it, and distinguish in legislation between red-haired men and black-haired men, and the classification would immediately be seen to be wrong; it would have only arbitrary relation to the purpose and province of legislation.

In these cases the only way—and if I will stay with the power point a short while longer, there would have to be a showing in order to sustain this legislation under the broad power of this Court to construe statutes under the reasonable classification doctrine.

They would have to show, and we have shown to the contrary—they would have to show, one, that there are differences in race; and, two, that differences in race have a recognizable relationship to the subject matter being legislated, namely, public education. That is a rule that has been uniformly applied by this Court in all other challenges that a classification is unreasonable. Those cases, of course, are also set out in our brief.

The other side in the South Carolina case says that the rule is a general rule, and the state has these powers; and they cite, of all cases to support that, *Yick Wo* v. *Hopkins*,[18] which this Court is thoroughly familiar with, the principle established in that case, which is directly to the contrary.

So, on the power point, it seems to me that there are only two relative groups of arguments: one, the congressional side, and the other, in addition to the recognized cases, the regular reasonable classification cases.

Now, with that, it seems to me that if I am correct in interpreting Mr. Justice Jackson's position, that that is what that point involves, it seems to me that is a sufficient answer to it, and if it is, I would conclude it by going back to the difference between the cases and the cases on the other side, because I feel obliged to touch the cases that the other side, of course, relies on and the lower courts relied on, beginning with the *Plessy* v. *Ferguson* case, and its doctrine.

In our brief we have pointed out the obvious ways that those cases could be distinguished. For the purpose of this argument and for the purpose of answering the specific question of this Court, we believe that it is proper for us to say here and now that the distinction, for example, in the *Plessy* v. *Ferguson* case, that it involved railroads instead of education, transportation against education, is a point of distinction, but for this point there is none, in fact, because it has been recognized as the originator of the "separate but equal" doctrine.

The next case that is near to the point is the *Gong Lum* v. *Rice* case, which was different; they did not raise the issue of the validity of the classification. All they were objecting to, and possibly it is understandable that the Chinese child was

---

[18]Yick Wo v. Hopkins, 118 U.S. 356 (1886). A San Francisco ordinance required all laundries to be made of brick or stone but permitted the board of supervisors at its discretion to give licences to wooden structures. The Supreme Court held that the law, although seemingly impartial and fair, was directed against Chinese laundries, generally built of wood, and thus violated the equal protection clause.

objecting to being classified as a Negro and put in an inferior school. Maybe that is—but so far as the law in the country today is concerned, that decision stands for the proposition that a state has a right to classify on the basis of class, race or ancestry, and our position on that is merely that the Gong Lum case, and the "separate but equal" doctrine of *Plessy* v. *Ferguson,* is just out of step with the earlier decisions in *Slaughter-House* and *Strauder* v. *West Virginia,* and the recent cases in this Court.

The other point which is made—

JUSTICE REED: But to reach that you have to take the Sweatt case based on the "separate but equal" doctrine.

MR. MARSHALL: No, sir; I only say the McLaurin case does not embrace the "separate but equal" doctrine.

I think in *Sweatt* v. *Painter,* the truth of the matter is that the decision was able to find that these intangibles produced inequality, and to that extent—

JUSTICE REED: But didn't the McLaurin case—

MR. MARSHALL: There was none of that.

JUSTICE REED: Granting the facts in the statement showed that they were equal—

MR. MARSHALL: Yes.

JUSTICE REED: But didn't the fact that they did not have the opportunity for association or discussion have any effect on it?

MR. MARSHALL: Yes, sir.

JUSTICE REED: And that, therefore, since they were graduate students, they did not have equal opportunities.

MR. MARSHALL: As I read it, sir—the best I could do is read it—as I understand it, the conclusion in there in two particular places, he says that in a situation of this type the state is deprived of the power to make distinctions, and the other point it says, to make any difference in treatment, but it was my idea that the thrust of the *McLaurin* opinion is that segregation in and of itself, at least as far as graduate training is concerned, is invalid, and that it was that conclusion was reached by first finding out—

JUSTICE REED: But they gave the reasons why, for undergraduate students, because they did not give equal opportunity.

MR. MARSHALL: But the only reason, I submit, Mr. Justice Reed, on the McLaurin case and these cases is age, age of students, and the fact that obviously graduate training is different from elementary training and high school training. But it has a difference, to use the language about another point in the McLaurin case, there is constitutional difference or rather it is insignificant as to the minor points, because if I understand, if we follow that to the logical conclusion, I do not have the slightest idea of where the line would be; whether the line would be at the college level, the junior college level, or the high school level, as to where this discussion with other pupils is of benefit.

JUSTICE FRANKFURTER: Am I wrong in thinking that you must reject the basis of the decision in McLaurin for purposes of this case?

MR. MARSHALL: You mean reject the basis of the fact that they were not allowed to associate?

JUSTICE FRANKFURTER: No. The basis was the criterion of those cases was whether each got the same thing. Your position in these cases is that that is not arguable, that you cannot differentiate, you cannot enter the domain of whether a black child or a white child gets the same educational advantages or facilities or opportunity. You must reject that, do you not?

MR. MARSHALL: We reach—

JUSTICE FRANKFURTER: Therefore, that is what I mean by saying you must reject the basis on which those cases went.

MR. MARSHALL: We reject it to this extent: I think I am—

JUSTICE FRANKFURTER: You reject the Delaware ground of decision, don't you?

MR. MARSHALL: Absolutely.

JUSTICE FRANKFURTER: Well, therefore, you reject the basis of the McLaurin case.

MR. MARSHALL: I think so far as our argument on the constitutional debates is concerned, and these two cases, that the state is deprived of any power to make any racial classification in any governmental field.

JUSTICE FRANKFURTER: So I understand.

MR. MARSHALL: But I do have to qualify it to this extent: I can conceive of some governmental action—to be perfectly frank, sir, we have discussed the point of census-taking—so they could take the census and name in the census, but so long as it affects not either group—but in any area where it touches the individuals concerned in any form or fashion, it is clear to me, to my mind, under the Fourteenth Amendment that you cannot separate people or denote that one shall go here and one shall go there if the facilities are absolutely equal; that is the issue in this case, because in the South Carolina case especially it is admitted on record that every other thing about the schools is equal, schools, curricula, everything else. It is only the question as to the power of the state to—

JUSTICE FRANKFURTER: Well, the Delaware case tests that. You are opposed to—you are in favor of the requested equality there, because I do not know whether you are—

MR. MARSHALL: Yes, sir.

JUSTICE FRANKFURTER: That is generally under your wing?

MR. MARSHALL: It is not only under our wing, sir; we are very proud of the fact that the children are going to school there, and they are demonstrating that it can be done.

JUSTICE FRANKFURTER: All I am saying is that with reference to the basis on which the Delaware decision went, you reject—

MR. MARSHALL: Yes sir.

JUSTICE FRANKFURTER: I follow that.

MR. MARSHALL: Well, it seems to me, sir, that there is considerable— there is an opening for argument that, after all, the Court is interpreting the phrase "equal protection" underlining the word "equal," and for that reason, that is the reason in our record in the case we felt obliged to show that these, what we considered as intangibles in the Sweatt case, were there in this case and, if necessary, the doctrine of *Sweatt* and *McLaurin* could automatically on all fours come there except for the question of difference of schools.

JUSTICE FRANKFURTER: But the point is important whether we are to decide that the facilities are equal or whether one says that is an irrelevant question, because you cannot apply that test between white and black.

MR. MARSHALL: In this case it is irrelevant—

JUSTICE FRANKFURTER: All right.

MR. MARSHALL: (continuing) —for two reasons: one, it is not in the case because we have agreed that equality is outside the case, and our argument is deliberately broad enough to encompass a situation regardless of facilities, and we make no issue about it.

JUSTICE FRANKFURTER: I understand that, but that will be a ground on which the series of cases in the McLaurin case—the point of my question is that I think we are dealing with two different legal propositions; *McLaurin* is one and what you are tendering to the Court is another.

MR. MARSHALL: The questions raised by this Court in June, as we understand it, requested us to find out as to whether or not class legislation and, specifically segregation, whether or not it, in and of itself, with nothing else, violated the Fourteenth Amendment.
We have addressed ourselves to that in this brief, and we are convinced that the answer is that any segregation, which is for the purpose of setting up either class or caste legislation, is in and of itself a violation of the Fourteenth Amendment, with the only proviso that normally, in normal judicial proceedings, there must be a showing of injury or what have you. That is our position and that is up—

JUSTICE REED: That is solely on the equal protection clause?

MR. MARSHALL: Solely on the equal protection clause except, sir, that is true in South Carolina, but we are arguing two cases together.

In Virginia we rely on equal protection and due process both, but the argument in our brief is limited to equal protection; not that we have discarded due process, but we did not have to get to it because of the wording of the questions of the Court.

But we think it is a denial of both. I urge particularly the equal protection clause because it seems to me, at least from the restrictive convenant case, the Shelley case on that. These rights are beginning to fall into the equal protection clause rather than the due process clause, but we do not abandon the due process clause at all.

JUSTICE FRANKFURTER: In the District of Columbia case—

MR. MARSHALL: Automatically—

JUSTICE FRANKFURTER: (continuing) —the opposite would happen.

MR. MARSHALL: In the District of Columbia—we are not the lawyers in that case—we are all working together on it—they, of course, are relying on the due process clause and they have the cases that support that; so I would say that in so far as there is a due process argument to be in the District of Columbia and Virginia, they would be related except for the difference that in the District of Columbia this Court has broad power—

JUSTICE FRANKFURTER: Your argument comes down to this: If in one of the states in which there is a large percentage of Negro voters, a preponderance, where we get a situation where X state has a preponderance of Negro voters who are actually going to the polls, and actually assert their preponderance and install a Negro governor to the extent that more money is spent for Negro education, better housing, better schools, more highly paid teachers, where teachers are more attracted, better maps, better schoolbooks, better everything than the white children enjoy—and I know I am making a fantastic, if you will, assumption—

MR. MARSHALL: Yes.

JUSTICE FRANKFURTER: (continuing) —and yet there is segregation, you would come here and say that they cannot do that?

MR. MARSHALL: If it is done by the state, the state has been deprived of—

JUSTICE FRANKFURTER: That is your position; that is the legal—

MR. MARSHALL: I think, sir, that is our flat legal position, that if it involves class or caste legislation—

JUSTICE FRANKFURTER: That is the antitheses of the McLaurin and the Gaines doctrine.

MR. MARSHALL: Well, of the Gaines case, certainly so, sir, because I, for one, do not believe that the language used by Chief Justice Hughes was—I mean, I just do not consider it as dictum when he said that they operated under a doctrine, the validity of which had been supported.

I think that *Gaines* was interpreted within the "separate but equal" doctrine.

I think *Sipuel* was, with the addition of "you have to do it now."

I think that *Sweatt* and *McLaurin,* if I could disagree for a moment, are moving between the two; that is the way I look at it.

JUSTICE FRANKFURTER: My only purpose is to try to see these things clearly without a simplifying darkness, and to try to see it clearly.

MR. MARSHALL: Yes, sir. But I do not believe—the point I wanted to make clear is that we do not have to—this Court does not have to—take my position to decide this case. Because of what I told you a minute ago, they could take up that material in those other records and find that the children were not getting an equal education, but it would not help in the situation.

JUSTICE FRANKFURTER: No, but if that line is taken, then the whole problem that you bring your weight to bear on is opened, and in each case we have to decide that.

MR. MARSHALL: I think so, sir.

JUSTICE FRANKFURTER: I did not suppose that you would say that we had to open this case, that they were not equal, whether psychologically, whether buildings, whether they spent X million dollars for white, or X minus Y for the black, that does not open any doctrine?

MR. MARSHALL: No, sir; and the Delaware case, if I can go to that without going outside of the record, demonstrates a situation more so than it does in South Carolina, because in Delaware so long as the schools are unequal, okay. And then the schools are made equal, and if I understand the procedure, you move the Negroes back to the colored school, and then next year you put ten more books in the white school, and the colored school is unequal, and I do not see how that point would ever be adequately decided, and in truth and in fact, there are no two equal schools, because there are no two equal faculties in the world in any schools.

They are good as individuals, and one is better than the other, but to just—that is the trouble with the doctrine of "separate but equal"; the doctrine of "separate but equal" assumes that two things can be equal.

JUSTICE REED: There is not absolute equality, but substantially equal, in accordance with the terms of our cases.

MR. MARSHALL: Yes, sir; starting with *Plessy* the word "substantial" and we say in our brief—I mean we are absolutely serious about it—that the use of the word "substantial" emphasizes that those cases in truth and in fact amend the Fourteenth Amendment by saying that equal protection can be obtained in a substantially equal fashion, and there is nothing in the debates that will hint in the slightest that they did not mean complete equality—they said so—to raise the

Negro up into the status of complete equality with the other people. That is the language they used.

"Substantial" is a word that was put into the Fourteenth Amendment by *Plessy* v. *Ferguson,* and I cannot find it, and it cannot be found in any place in the debates.

If it please the Court, we would like to, if possible, conserve the balance of the time for rebuttal. Mr. Robinson was a little over his time, and I cut mine down. Unless there are any questions on this particular point, because we still have some time left, I would like to leave that for rebuttal.

THE CHIEF JUSTICE: Thank you.
Mr. Davis?

### ARGUMENT ON BEHALF OF APPELLEES R. W. ELLIOTT, ET AL

#### by MR. DAVIS

MR. DAVIS: May it please the Court, I suppose there are few invitations less welcome in an advocate's life than to be asked to reargue a case on which he has once spent himself, and that is particularly unwelcome when the order for reargument gives him no indication whatever of the subjects in which the Court may be interested, and, therefore, I want to at the outset tender the Court my thanks and, I think, the thanks of my colleagues on both sides of the desk for the guidance they have given us by the series of questions which they asked us to devote our attention to, and in what I shall have to say, I hope to indicate the answers which, for our part, we give to each one of them.

At the previous hearing of this case I think all counsel on both sides of the controversy, and in every case, realizing that it was an act of mercy and, perhaps, even of piety, not to increase the reading matter that comes to this Court, briefed the case in rather concise fashion. An effort was apparent, and I am sure I shared it, to condense the controversy to the smallest compass it would bear.

Now, for a rough guess I should think the motion for reargument has contributed somewhere between 1500 and 2000 pages to the possible entertainment, if not the illumination, of the Court. But I trust the Court will not hold counsel responsible for that proliferation.

Most of us have supported our answers to the Court's questions by appendices addressed to the action of Congress, to the action of the ratifying states, and in our particular case, to the history of the controversy within the State of South Carolina.

In view of the fact that His Honor, the Chief Justice, was not on the bench at the time of the other argument, perhaps I should outline the present posture of the South Carolina case of Briggs and Elliott.

It was brought, as Mr. Robinson correctly stated, upon two grounds: A suit by infant Negro children in Clarendon County School District No. 22 which, by a subsequent reorganization, became a part of District No. 1, by their parents and next friends, asserting that they were denied the equal protection of the laws on two grounds: first, that section 7 of Article 11 of the Constitution of South Carolina forbade integrated schools; commanded that the white and colored races should be taught in separate schools, and that the statute, in pursuance of that

Constitution, section 5277 of their code, made a similar provision, and that both were in violation of the Fourteenth Amendment to the Constitution of the United States per se.

Second, that be that as it may, inequalities existed between the educational facilities furnished to the white and black children, to the detriment of the black.

The State of South Carolina came in and admitted that those inequalities existed, and declared its intention to remove them as promptly as possible.

Evidence was taken, the District Court decreed that the Constitution and statute of South Carolina did not violate the Amendment; found the existence of the admitted inequality, and enjoined its immediate removal, gave to the State of South Carolina the period of six months to report what steps had been taken to implement that decree.

At the end of that time a report came in which came to this Court, and was returned to the District Court, and upon a second hearing, a further report came in.

It was made to appear that the promise of the State of South Carolina to remove this inequality was no empty promise; that it had authorized, its legislature had authorized, a bond issue of $75 million to equalize the physical facilities of the schools, supported by a 3 per cent sales tax; that the curricula had been equalized, the pay of teachers had been equalized, transportation had been provided for children, white and black; and the accuracy of those reports being admitted—and I am merely summarizing it—the court below held that it was clear that by the first of September, 1952, that the inequalities had disappeared.

It then entered an order enjoining the further removal of such inequalities as might have existed, and declared the Constitution and the statute to be valid and non-violative of the Fourteenth Amendment.

We have then in South Carolina a case, as Mr. Marshall has so positively admitted, with no remaining question of inequality at all, and the naked question is whether a separation of the races in the primary and secondary schools, which are the subject of this particular case, is of itself per se a violation of the Fourteenth Amendment.

Now, turning to our answers, let me state what we say to each one of them. The first question was what evidence is there that the Congress which submitted to the state legislatures and conventions which ratified the Fourteenth Amendment contemplated or did not contemplate, understood or did not understand that would abolish segregation in public schools?

We answer, the overwhelming preponderance of the evidence demonstrates that the Congress which submitted, and the state legislatures which ratified, the Fourteenth Amendment did not contemplate and did not understand that it would abolish segregation in public schools, and in the time that is afforded, I hope to vindicate that categorical reply.

Our friends, the appellants, take an entirely contrary view, and they take it, in part, on the same historical testimony; certain fallacies underlie, I think, their course in reaching that conclusion. Some of them are apparent in their brief, and I have not found that they touched upon them in oral argument.

The first fallacy which appears in their brief, in their recounting of history, is the assumption, wholly unwarranted, as I think, that the antislavery pre-Civil

War crusade, the abolitionist crusade, was directed not only against slavery but against segregation in schools.

I do not think that thesis can be sustained, for the thrust and movement of the abolitionist crusade was directed toward one thing, and one thing only: the abolition of the institution of slavery, and from that nothing can be deduced which is helpful to the Court in its study of this section of history.

I think the next unjustified assumption which, again I am referring to my adversaries' brief and not to their oral presentation, was that the radical Republicans controlled the action of the 39th Congress. That again is an unwarranted assumption.

The 39th Congress never went as far as some of the radical Republicans wished it to go and, perhaps, there has never been a Congress in which the debates furnished less real pablum on which history might feed. It was what Claude Bowers calls in his book *The Tragic Era*, well-named—flames of partisan passion were still burning over the ashes of the Civil War.

In the Senate there were such men as Sumner, who made a lifelong crusade in favor of mixed racial schools from the time that he was counsel for the plaintiff in *Roberts* v. *Boston* in '49—he never missed an opportunity to bring the question forward, and never succeeded in having it enacted into law, except by the legislature of Massachusetts in 1855.

There were men who stood with Sumner, his colleague, Henry Wilson of Massachusetts,[19] and on the other side, equally critical, men like Cowan of Pennsylvania, and Garrett Davis of Kentucky,[20] and others, resented all of the Civil War Reconstruction legislation, and whenever they had an opportunity to attack it, painted it in the blackest colors that they could devise.

In the House, Thaddeus Stevens, called by historians perhaps the most unlovely character in American history, more concerned to humiliate the aristocrats of the South, as he called them, even than to preserve the rights of the Negro. His policy was confiscation of all estate over $10,000 and two hundred acres, of which $40 an acre should be given to every adult Negro, and remainder should be sold to pay the expenses of the war. He wanted the South to come to Washington as suppliants in sackcloth and ashes. He had his echoes.

On the other side there were resistors like Rogers of New Jersey, a Democrat from New Jersey, who never missed an opportunity to criticize every one of the bills that were presented on the ground that they would forbid segregated schools. That echo came from Rogers almost as regularly as the contrary view came from Sumner.

Now, if I gather my friends' position both in brief and argument, they hope from the debates of such a Congress to distill clear, specific evidence of congressional intent.

I do not think that is possible, but there is a source from which congressional intent can be gathered, far more reliable, far less hope for challenge by anyone.

What did the Congress do? And when we study the legislation enacted by

[19]Senator Henry Wilson (1812–1875) of Massachusetts. Free Soil and Republican senator, 1855–1873; Vice President of the United States under President Ulysses S. Grant, 1873–1875.

[20]See no. 5, *supra*.

Congress immediately before, immediately after, and during the period of the discussion of the Fourteenth Amendment, there can be no question left that Congress did not intend by the Fourteenth Amendment to deal with the question of mixed or segregated schools.

There is another fallacy in the presentation of the case by the appellants. They take for granted they can quote any senator, congressman, or other character in favor of racial equality, they can count him down in the column of those who were opposed to segregated schools, which is a clear non sequitur and a begging of the question.

We are not concerned here with the mandate of the Constitution that the Negro, as well as the white, shall enjoy the equal protection of the laws.

The question with which Your Honors are confronted is, is segregation in schools a denial of equality where the segregation runs against one race as well as against the other, and where, in the eye of law no difference between the educational facilities of the two classes can be discerned.

Now, I think those remarks sum up most of what I care to say by way of direct reply to the argument of the appellants.

There is a third point of view presented to Your Honors. We say the intent of Congress was clear not to enter this field. We say the intent of the ratifying states was equally clear, the majority of them, not to enter this field.

The Attorney General is present, acceding to the invitation of the Court, with a brief, and a very large appendix reciting the history of the legislation. He reaches the conclusion, or those who speak for him—I am not speaking in the personal sense but only of the office—he reaches the conclusion, as stated in his brief, historical facts, after some four hundred pages of recital, are too equivocal and inconclusive—I am having some trouble with my own chirography here—the historical facts are too equivocal and inconclusive to formulate a solid basis on which this Court can determine the application of the Amendment to the question of school segregation as it exists today.

After so prolonged a study, as has evidently been made, it does seem rather a lame and impotent conclusion, not calculated to be of a great deal of help to the Court, and I think the cause of that despair on the part of the learned Attorney General and his aides, is that they have fallen into the same fallacy into which the appellants have fallen. They endeavor by collating all that was said on either side whenever the question raged, and it was not a single instance—they hope out of that to distill some attar that will exhibit what can fairly be called the congressional intent.

It is no wonder, that having plunged into that Serbonian bog, they are in a state of more or less despair when they are able to emerge.

Now, Your Honors then are presented with this: We say there is no warrant for the assertion that the Fourteenth Amendment dealt with the school question. The appellants say that from the debates in Congress it is perfectly evident that the Congress wanted to deal with the school question, and the Attorney General, as a friend of the Court, says he does not know which is correct. So Your Honors are afforded the reasonable field for selection. (Laughter.)

Now, we say that whatever may have been said in debate, and there is not an angle of this case that would not find, if that were the decisive question, support in what some person might have said at some time, but Congress by its action demonstrated beyond a peradventure what scope it intended to employ.

I hoped at one time that it would be possible to take up each action of Congress upon which we rely and vindicate our interpretation of it. I see now that I underestimated the time that would be at my disposal, or overestimated my power of delivery.

I shall have to speak now more or less in word of catalog and leave to our brief and to our appendices confirmation of the relevancy of these incidents.

In the 39th Congress the first supplemental Freedmen's Bureau bill passed, giving the Freedmen's Bureau power to buy sites and buildings and schools for freedmen, refugees, and their children; and, of course, the freedmen and the refugees were of the colored race.

There was provision that if certain cataloged rights were denied, military protection should be given. What was that catalog? To make and enforce contracts, sue, be sued, be a party and give evidence, inherit, purchase or dispose of real or personal property; have full and equal benefit of all laws and proceedings for the security of person and estate, and be subject to like punishments, pains and penalties as with others, and none beside.

What did the Freedmen's Bureau do? It was the pet and child of Congress and, acting under its constant supervision, they installed separate schools throughout the South, so separate indeed that history records one complaint by the City of Charleston that they had seized, occupied, and taken over all the school buildings in the city, filled them with their Negro wards, and the white children no longer had any buildings to which to resort; the Civil Rights Act of 1866, where the rights to be protected by it were cataloged almost in the identical language of the Freedmen's Bureau Bill, the difference being that the Freedmen's Bureau Bill ran only in those states in which the process of the courts had been interrupted, which was a euphemism, being those states that had been occupied by the Confederate and Federal army, and the Civil Rights Act of 1866 was designed to be nation-wide.

It is not surprising that its language conformed to the language of the Freedmen's Bureau. They were both introduced at the same time by Senator Trumbull, the chairman of the Judiciary Committee of the Senate, and they made their way through Congress in much the same fashion.

After the Civil Rights Act of 1866 had passed the Senate, it went to the House for consideration. There it was introduced, sponsored, discussed by Congressman James Wilson[21] of Iowa, who was chairman of the Judiciary Committee, and when Brother Rogers, with his usual complaint that it would do away with the separate schools, and others joined him in taking that point of view, at that time Wilson said on the floor that the Act did not mean that their children should attend the same school, and, in effect, that it was absurd so to interpret it.

Now, the pertinency of that is due to the connection which counsel has stated between the Civil Rights Act and the Fourteenth Amendment. It was the constant claim of those who favored the Fourteenth Amendment, Stevens and Sumner, both speaking to it, that it was intended to make the Civil Rights Act not only constitutional and quiet Bingham's doubt and conscience, but to make it irrepeal-

[21]See no. 14, *supra.*

able so that, as Stevens said, whenever the Democrats and their Copperhead allies came back to Congress, they would not be able to repeal it.

I will pass over, for the moment, some other legislation, which I will come back to, that occurred in the 39th Congress.

We came to the reinstatement of the seceded states. Congress passed an Act, by virtue of which they might, in compliance, send their senators and congressmen back.

Now, in the 39th Congress, Sumner had put forward his prescription for their readmission. He had five headings for it, of which the fourth was this: that the seceding states, if they wished to return, should adopt constitutions, which among other things, would provide for the organization of an educational system for the equal benefit of all, without distinction of color or race.

The Reconstruction Act was adopted in the succeeding Congress and it called for a catalog of performances to be carried out by the states desiring readmission. Did they say anything about Sumner's educational plank? Not a word. Was any requirement made of the state as to educational provision? None whatever.

When they came to admit the State of Arkansas, Senator Drake[22] of Missouri offered an amendment in which he provided that the constitution of the petitioning state should provide no denial of the elective franchise or any other right. He offered that as an amendment to the bill admitting the State of Arkansas.

Controversy arose as to the meaning of "any other right." Then it was asserted that there would enter the question of schools. It was stricken out, and the Drake Amendment adopted without—and Senator Frelinghuysen,[23] who had been chairman of the Joint Committee on Reconstruction, said that neither the Drake Amendment or the Fourteenth Amendment touched the question of separate schools. That is once I think it is proper to quote from a debate.

There came then the amnesty bill amendments. Congress passed an amnesty bill. When it was before the Senate, Sumner offered his supplemental Civil Rights Act, which provided expressly for mixed schools.

The Judiciary Committee twice reported it adversely, and Sumner flanked them by offering it then as an amendment to the amnesty bill. In that form it was debated and, finally, a vote was taken which was 28 to 28, and the Vice President broke the tie in Sumner's factor. It was the high-water mark of his achievement.

The amnesty bill, so amended, went to the House.

It failed of passage in the Senate, where it needed a two-thirds vote under the terms of the Fourteenth Amendment. It failed of passage in the Senate and the Senate did nothing more with it.

Then it went to the House, and the House failed to pass it. The weight of the Sumner Amendment was too much for the bill to carry.

Bills to require mixed schools in the District of Columbia were defeated in the 41st and the 42nd Congress.

---

[22]Senator Charles D. Drake (1811–1892) of Missouri. Republican senator, 1867–1870; Chief Justice of Court of Claims, 1870–1885.

[23]Senator Frederick T. Frelinghuysen (1817–1885) of New Jersey. Republican senator, 1866–1869 and 1871–1877: Member of Hayes-Tilden Electoral Commission (1877); Secretary of State under President Chester A. Arthur, 1881–1885.

Then came the Civil Rights Act of 1875, which was passed only after the Kellogg Amendment[24] striking out the reference to schools, churches, cemeteries, and juries, and passed in that form.

Then, in 1862 Congress set up its first school for Negroes in the District on a segregated basis. In 1864 it dealt with that question again on a segregated basis.

In 1866, the 39th Congress, it passed a donation of certain lots to be given to schools for Negroes only. It passed a second Act in the same Congress dealing with the distribution of funds between the Negro and the white schools.

In 1868 it dealt with the question again on the segregated basis, and has so continued to this day.

I know that Your Honors are shortly going to hear a case which challenges the validity of those statutes; and be they valid or invalid, for the purposes of my present argument it is immaterial. They are enough to show what the sentiment of Congress was, what its determination was on this specific question, and it is no answer to say that Congress is not controlled by the Fourteenth Amendment. Of course, it is not; but is it conceivable to any man that Congress should submit to the states an amendment destroying their right to segregated schools and should contemporaneously and continuously institute a regime of segregated schools in the District of Columbia?

I should think that if a congressman, who was responsible for submitting to the state an amendment shearing them of power—he would have quite an explanation to make if he got home, if he said he had not done exactly the reverse in the District of Columbia.

Then it is suggested in the brief for the learned Attorney General—and I think similar comment, perhaps, by the appellants—that these two instances in the 39th Congress, these two legislative recognitions of separate schools in the District, which was taking place when the Fourteenth Amendment was taking form and substance—they say that those were mere routine performances, that they came very late in the congressional session, that they were not even honored by having any debate.

Apparently, to have a law which is really to be recognized as a congressional deliverance, it must come early in the session, it must be debated, and the mere fact that it is passed by unanimous consent and without objection more or less disparages its importance as an historical incident. I have never, that I can recall, heard a similar yardstick applied to congressional action.

There isn't time to go over the states. They are covered by our appendix and these other appendices. We classified them, too.

We say that there are nine states that never had segregated schools. There were those states in the northern territory, and there weren't enough Negroes to make it worthwhile. There were five states—I am speaking now of the ratifying states, not of the ratifying—of the thirty-seven states that were then in existence, there were about five states where there had been segregation, and they contem-

[24]The original version of the bill which became the Civil Rights Act of 1875 contained a clause requiring integrated schools. The House Judiciary Committee added a provision permitting separate but equal school facilities to be maintained. Representative Stephen W. Kellogg of Connecticut introduced a successful amendment striking all references to schools in the bill whether for or against separate schools.

poraneously discontinued. Those were Connecticut, Louisiana, Michigan, Florida and South Carolina. Three of those states returned to segregation as soon as the Reconstruction period was over. There were four states that had segregation. I am speaking of the period now from '66 when the Amendment was submitted to '68 when it was proclaimed.

There were four states with segregation who refused to ratify and continued segregation. They were California, Kentucky, Maryland and Delaware. Delaware didn't ratify it until 1901.

There were two border states that had segregation both before and after ratification, and have continued it to this day. They are Missouri and West Virginia.

There were nine northern states that either continued segregation they already had or established it immediately after the ratification of the Fourteenth Amendment: Illinois, Indiana, Kansas, Nevada, New Jersey, New York, Ohio, Oregon and Pennsylvania.

And then—and I can find no evidence that my friends appreciate the significance of this fact—of the reconstructed states who ratified in order to get their delegate, their congressmen and senators back to Washington, eight Reconstruction states in the same Reconstruction legislature, Republican controlled, the same legislature which ratified the Fourteenth Amendment passed statutes continuing or immediately establishing segregated schools. I regard that as a fact of great significance.

If there was any place where the Fourteenth Amendment and its sponsors would have blown the bugle for mixed schools and asserted that the Fourteenth Amendment had settled the question, surely it would have been those eight states under Reconstruction legislation, sympathetic to the party which was responsible for the submission of the Fourteenth Amendment.

Now the appellants say in their brief that three-fourths of the ratifying states gave evidence that they thought the Fourteenth Amendment had abolished segregated schools. I can find in the history as detailed by all of these appendices no warrant whatever for any such assertion, for any such proportion of nonconcurring states. That is before Your Honors in the appendices, and you must, between the three points of view that I have indicated, make your selection.

The second question: Neither the Congress, in submitting, or the states, in ratifying, the Fourteenth Amendment understood that compliance with it would require the immediate abolition of segregation in public schools.

It was nevertheless the understanding of the framers of the Amendment that future Congresses might, in the exercise of their power under section 5 of the Amendment, abolish segregation or, (b), that would be within the judicial power in light of future conditions to construe the Amendment as abolishing such segregation of its own force, and to that we answer it was not the understanding of the framers of the Amendment that future Congresses might, in the exercise of their power under section 5 of the Amendment, abolish segregation in public schools.

And, (c), it was not the understanding of the framers of the Amendment that it would be within the judicial power, in light of future conditions, to construe the Amendment as abolishing segregation in public schools of its own force.

It was not the understanding of the framers that Congress might, in the exercise of the power under section 5 of the Amendment, abolish segregation, and if we are right in the initial proposition that neither Congress nor the states thought the Amendment was dealing with the question of segregated schools, obviously section 5 of the Amendment could not give Congress more power than the Amendment itself had originally embraced.

But the power given to Congress we had noted in section 5 is the power that—I thought I had the exact language—to enforce the provision of this article. And section 5 is not a Trojan horse which opened to Congress a wide field in which Congress might expand the boundaries of the article itself.

JUSTICE JACKSON: Mr. Davis, would not the necessary and proper clause apply to the Amendment as well as to the enumerated powers of the instrument itself? In other words, if Congress should say that in order to accomplish the purposes of equality in the other fields, the abolition of segregation was necessary, as a necessary and proper measure, would that not come under it, or might it not come under the necessary and proper clause?

In other words, I mean is it limited to just what is given in the Amendment or does the necessary and proper clause follow into the amendments?

MR. DAVIS: Well, if you can imagine a necessary and proper clause which would enforce the provisions of this article by dealing with matter which is not within the scope of the article itself, which I think is a contradiction in terms, that is a paradox. Congress could do what the Amendment did not warrant under the guise of enforcing the Amendment.

JUSTICE FRANKFURTER: But you can look for the necessary and proper clause to determine whether it is something appropriate within the Amendment.

MR. DAVIS: Quite so. That is if you use, choose, a monetary clause, related to congressional wisdom and policy, and to the judicial power, in answer to that question, we say that you interpret the Amendment as including something that it does not include is not to interpret the Amendment but is to amend the Amendment, which is beyond the power of the Court.

The third question: On the assumption the answers to questions 2 (a) and (b) does not dispose of the issue, is it within the judicial power in construing the Amendment to abolish segregation in the public schools, and we answer it is not within the judicial power to construe the Fourteenth Amendment adversely to the understanding of its framers as abolishing segregation in the public schools.

Before we answer, we preface that with an expression of the extreme difficulty we have in making the initial assumption on which that question is based, where in our humble judgment the answers to questions 1 and 2 (a) and (b) do dispose of the issue in this case and dispose of it in the clearest and most emphatic manner.

We go on in our answer: Moreover, if in construing the Amendment the principle of *stare decisis* is applied, controlling precedents preclude a construction which would abolish segregation in the public schools.

Now we are cognizant of what this Court has said not once but several times, and what some of us have heard outside the Court as to the scope of *stare decisis* in constitutional matters, and it has been accepted that where there is a pronounced dissent from previous opinions in constitutional matters, mere difficulty in amendment leaves the Court to bow to that change of opinion more than it would of matters of purely private rights.

But be that doctrine what it may, somewhere, sometime to every principle comes a moment of repose when it has been so often announced, so confidently relied upon, so long continued, that it passes the limits of judicial discretion and disturbance.

That is the opinion which we held when we filed our former brief in this case. We relied on the fact that this Court had not once but seven times, I think it is, pronounced in favor of the "separate but equal" doctrine.

We relied on the fact that the courts of last appeal of some sixteen or eighteen states have passed upon the validity of the "separate but equal" doctrine vis-a-vis the Fourteenth Amendment.

We relied on the fact that Congress has continuously since 1862 segregated its schools in the District of Columbia.

We relied on the fact that twenty-three of the ratifying states—I think my figures are right, I am not sure—had by legislative action evinced their conviction that the Fourteenth Amendment was not offended by segregation, and we said in effect that that argument—and I am bold enough to repeat it here now—that in the language of Judge Parker in his opinion below, after that had been the consistent history for over three-quarters of a century, it was late indeed in the day to disturb it on any theoretical or sociological basis. We stand on that proposition.

Then we go on that even if the principle of *stare decisis* in controlling precedents be denied, the effect of the Amendment upon public school segregation examined de novo, that the doctrine of reasonable classification would protect this from the charge of any policy that is brought against us.

In Clarendon School District No. 1 in South Carolina, in which this case alone is concerned, there were in the last report that got into this record something over a year or year and a half ago, 2,799 Negroes, registered Negro children of school age. There were 295 whites, and the state has now provided those 2,800 Negro children with schools as good in every particular.

In fact, because of their being newer, they may even be better. There are good teachers, the same curriculum as in the schools for the 295 whites.

Who is going to disturb that situation? If they were to be reassorted or comingled, who knows how that could best be done?

If it is done on the mathematical basis, with 30 children as a maximum, which I believe is the accepted standard in pedagogy, you would have 27 Negro children and 3 whites in one school room. Would that make the children any happier? Would they learn any more quickly. Would their lives be more serene?

Children of that age are not the most considerate animals in the world, as we all know. Would the terrible psychological disaster being wrought, according to some of these witnesses, to the colored child be removed if he had three white children sitting somewhere in the same school room?

Would white children be prevented from getting a distorted idea of racial relations if they sat with 27 Negro children? I have posed that question because it is the very one that cannot be denied.

You say that is racism. Well, it is not racism. Recognize that for sixty centuries and more humanity has been discussing questions of race and race tension, not racism.

Say that we make special provisions for the aborginal Indian population of this country, it is not racism.

Say that the twenty-nine states have miscegenation statutes now in force which they believe are of beneficial protection to both races. Disraeli said, "No man," said he, "will treat with indifference the principle of race. It is the key of history."

And it is not necessary to enter into any comparison of faculties or possibilities. You recognize differences which racism plants in the human animal.

Now, I want to spend some time on the fourth and fifth questions. They give us a little disturbance, and I don't feel they will greatly disturb the Court.

As to the question of the right of the Court to postpone the remedy, we think that adheres in every court of equity, and there has been no questions about it as to power.

The fifth question, whether the Court should formulate a decree, we find nothing here on which this Court could formulate a decree, nor do we think the Court below has any power to formulate a decree, reciting in what manner these schools are to be alternative at all, and what course the State of South Carolina shall take concerning it.

Your Honors do not sit, and cannot sit as a glorified Board of Education for the State of South Carolina or any other state. Neither can the District Court.

Assuming, in the language of the old treaties about war, it is not to be expected and that God forbid, that the Court should find that the statutes of the State of South Carolina violated the Constitution, it can so declare.

If it should find that inequality is being practiced in the schools, it can enjoin its continuance. Neither this Court nor any other court, I respectfully submit, can sit in the chairs of the legislature of South Carolina and mold its educational system, and if it is found to be in its present for unacceptable, the State of South Carolina must devise the alternative. It establishes the schools, it pays the funds, and it has the sole power to educate its citizens.

What they would do under these circumstances, I don't know. I do know, if the testimony is to be believed, that the result would not be pleasing.

Let me say this for the State of South Carolina. It does not come here as Thad Stevens would have wished in sack cloth and ashes. It believes that its legislation is not offensive to the Constitution of the United States.

It is confident of its good faith and intention to produce equality for all of its children of whatever race or color. It is convinced that the happiness, the progress and the welfare of these children is best promoted in segregated schools, and it thinks it a thousand pities that by this controversy there should be urged the return to an experiment which gives no more promise of success today than when it was written into their Constitution during what I call the tragic era.

I am reminded—and I hope it won't be treated as a reflection on anybody—of Aesop's fable of the dog and the meat: The dog, with a fine piece of meat in his mouth, crossed a bridge and saw the shadow in the stream and plunged for it and lost both substance and shadow.

Here is equal education, not promised, not prophesied, but present. Shall it be thrown away on some fancied question of racial prestige?

It is not my part to offer advice to the appellants and their supporters or sympathisers, and certainly not to the learned counsel. No doubt they think what they propose is best, and I do not challenge their sincerity in any particular period but I entreat them to remember the age-old motto that the best is often the enemy of the good.

## ARGUMENT ON BEHALF OF APPELLEES, COUNTY SCHOOL BOARD OF PRINCE EDWARD COUNTY, VA., ET AL.

### by MR. MOORE

MR. MOORE: May it please the Court, in undertaking to present the Virginia case, and in view of the fact that the facts are now so similar to those in the South Carolina case, I am aware that there will necessarily be covering of much of the same ground that my distinguished friend and associate, Mr. Davis, has covered. But we feel that we should present our own point of view.

Starting first with a very interesting table, if Your Honors will look at page 211 and 212 of our brief, you will get a very quick and vivid conception of the impact that a decree such as is asked for against South Carolina and Virginia in these cases would produce.

As you will see from page 212, we have there shown you the population by race in every state in this Union, and according to the 1950 census, and as you will see from that table, the proportions vary from practically zero up to 45.3 per cent in Mississippi, with, near the bottom there, 22.1 per cent in Virginia.

Now, if you look at page 211, you will see another very striking set of figures which shows that in these seventeen states in which segregation is now required, plus the District of Columbia, there is, according to this census, ten and a half million Negroes, 40,400,000 white, and that approximately 70 per cent of the entire Negro population of the Nation is in these seventeen states and in the District of Columbia.

It is very striking that the total percentage of the Negroes to total population is approximately 10 per cent, as you will notice there, 10 per cent of the total.

In other words, there are 15,000,000 Negroes, according to the last census in the Nation as a whole, with ten and a half million of those Negroes, or approximately 70 per cent, in these seventeen states plus the District, so that when our opponents talk about the effect of segregation in some of these Northern and Western States, they are not talking about the practical condition with which we are here faced.

In other words, there is actually today one-third of the nation in these seventeen states which, by law, has required segregation, approximately one-third of the population which lives in that situation.

Now, that focuses attention, we believe, at the outset, upon the facts of each situation, so that you cannot talk about this problem just in a vacuum in the manner of a law school discussion.

Now, this particular case, I believe, should be very briefly referred to as to the facts just as was done in the South Carolina case, particularly in view of the fact that the present Chief Justice was not sitting at that a year ago.

This case comes from one of the smaller and poorer counties in Virginia, Prince Edward County. It is about 130 miles from this very spot.

There were three high schools in Prince Edward County at the time this litigation arose. The best of those was the Farmville High School for whites, the poorest was the Worsham High School for whites, and in the middle was the Moton School for Negroes.

Now the record shows that the school authorities during the ten-year period just before this suit was filed had had a very unexpected and difficult problem. In 1941 there were 540 white high school students in the county and only 208 Negro students. In ten years, by 1951, those relationships had changed tremendously.

The white school students numbered 405 while the Negroes had increased to 463. In other words, there had been a decline of 25 per cent in the white, but an increase of 120 odd per cent in the colored.

Now, of course, during that period, during much of the time, it was not practical to obtain the necessary materials for construction of facilities that would be absolutely equal. But we are glad to say that in quality that does not any longer exist. The new Moton Negro High School has now been completed, which was in process of construction when we were here a year ago. It has been completed at a cost of something more than $800,000.

The details of that are shown in Appendix at the end of our brief where there are certificates furnished there by the architects and Superintendent of Schools, showing that money being furnished either through loans or grants from the State of Virginia.

And it is a striking fact that this is just not an isolated case. This brand new high school which has now been completed and was occupied beginning the first of September, is only one of a large number of similar projects. The state has in effect a program over the next four years of more than 250 millions of dollars, with a view to equalizing the facilities. They are able to do it, they intend to do it, and according to the records in this case, about half of the job has been done.

Now, just as in the South Carolina case, this suit was brought with two purposes. The first was the charge that segregation per se was a violation of the Fourteenth Amendment, and to support that charge, the appellants here introduced expert testimony. I, of course, cannot go into that in detail here. We reviewed that a year ago. But it is sufficient to say that if expert testimony ever was discredited, the testimony in this case was.

Now, on the other hand, on our side of the case—and this is the most distinctive feature of this case—we called seven distinguished experts ourselves and attacked the theories, the factual theories that were relied on by the other side, four distinguished educators, a psychiatrist, a psychologist and a distinguished professor of Columbia University, the head of the Department of Psychology.

And through our testimony we show perfectly clearly that the factual contentions that were made by the other side as to detriment to the Negro child were not borne out, as a matter of fact. And the court found on the crucial point in its opinion to this effect. The court said:

> In this milieu we cannot say that vast separation of white and colored children in the public schools is without substance in fact or reason. We have found no hurt or harm to either race.

Now, it is striking that in three of these five cases there was no evidence presented countervailing the Negro's evidence. In the Kansas case, the District case and the Delaware case, expert evidence was presented which was not contradicted by opposing evidence.

In the South Carolina case there was some opposing evidence, not to any great degree such as was in the Virginia case, so that the Virginia case really stands out in opposition, for example, to the Kansas finding where the Virginia court has found on the evidence, after five days of hearings, that the Negroes have failed to prove their case as a matter of fact.

Now, there was an inequality of facilities which we admitted. We were required by the lower court to equalize. We have now done that, and so far as we know, we are precisely in the same situation as the South Carolina case. I don't think there is any dispute about that now from our friends on the other side.

Now, may I just, for a moment, touch questions four and five. Question four in substance is an inquiry as to our position on the question of gradual adjustment if the Court finds against us. We think it is perfectly clear, as Mr. Davis has pointed out, that in the event we are faced with the distressing situation of an adverse decree, that the Court as a court of equity plainly has the power and the duty, in situations like this, to permit a gradual adjustment, as a court of equity considering a balancing of equities. That is all briefed and I don't want to take up time in that discussion.

On the fifth question, the question is whether or not if there is an adverse decree, whether the case should be remanded to the lower court or should a master be appointed, or some other way that the matter should be handled.

We think it is perfectly clear that if there should be this unhappy, unfortunate decree, that the case should be remanded to the lower court where local conditions could be considered, where new evidence would be received. Considering what might be appropriate in Kansas, wouldn't necessarily be appropriate in South Carolina or Virginia.

JUSTICE FRANKFURTER: What kind of guidance, if any, should be given to the district court on this unhappy hypothesis of your argument?

MR. MOORE: It really distresses me to face that question. About all I can say, Your Honor, is we feel the courts should be given the broadest possible discretion to act along reasonable lines. It is a matter of a reasonable exercise of discretion. That is the best answer, I believe, I can give.

JUSTICE FRANKFURTER: I suppose, and Mr. Davis touched on it before when it was asked, it is one thing to ask a district court to lay out districts, school districts.

MR. MOORE: Yes.

JUSTICE FRANKFURTER: I suppose that is one thing. But to have the parties or the state which would be involved, whatever the political unit, say "This is what we are going to do" and have the district court pass on whether that conforms to this hypothetical decree, is another thing, isn't it?

MR. MOORE: Well, Your Honor, we think, to further answer the question—I did not intend to just drop it summarily.

JUSTICE FRANKFURTER: I beg your pardon, I am sorry. Please go your own way, Mr. Moore.

MR. MOORE: No, no, I want to answer Your Honor. We think that following the theory of, say, the antitrust cases, that the party certainly should be allowed to present a plan, rather than for the Court just to hand down a plan. Perhaps that is a more accurate and a better answer. I did not give quite as fluent an answer as I should have originally.

JUSTICE FRANKFURTER: In the Paramount Case in New York,[25] as you know—

MR. MOORE: Yes.

JUSTICE FRANKFURTER: —there was I don't know how long a proceeding before Judge Hand and his associates in which there was conformity by the parties going on as proposed by what this Court decided, which was made a matter of independent extensive litigation and consideration.

MR. MOORE: That's right.

JUSTICE FRANKFURTER: Is your suggestion that kind of solution?

MR. MOORE: That's right. I think undoubtedly that the decree should be a decree that would give broad discretion and permit the parties involved to present an appropriate plan that would be in conformity with the decision of this Court, but leaving a great deal of latitude for the parties to present their own kind of plan.

Now in view of the discussion of Mr. Davis, I am going to pass rather rapidly on the first question.

The remaining questions which Your Honors posed for us to investigate and discuss might be summarized very briefly in this way. The Court said to us to investigate what was the Congressional understanding and intent of the framers of the Fourteenth Amendment with respect to this matter of its impact on schools, both from the standpoint of that time and from the standpoint of what they contemplated future Congresses might do or what this Court might do.

Secondly, what was the understanding and intent of the 33 out of the 37 States that ratified, and the third question was what is the judicial power of this Court? To what extent is it properly within the judicial power of this Court to outlaw segregation just by force of the Amendment and the decision of this Court.

Now there are six major pieces of legislation that were involved in that first question. I will just enumerate them for convenience, and then touch only the more important ones.

The first one was the Freedmen's, the first supplemental Freedmen's Bureau Bill in this 39th Congress of 1866 which, as Mr. Davis pointed out, provided for certain relief, authorized certain relief for these freedmen, but nowhere is the effect on mixed schools really involved in that at all.

[25] United States v. Paramount Pictures, 334 U.S. 131 (1948). The practice of motion picture companies charging uniform license fees to exhibitors and requiring uniform booking arrangements was found to violate the Sherman Act. Extensive litigation on appropriate relief followed the original Supreme Court decision.

The second is the Civil Rights Act of 1866. The third is the Fourteenth Amendment Resolution. The fourth is the legislation with regard to district schools. The fifth are the amnesty bills and sixth is the Civil Rights of 1875.

Now it is a striking thing that that first supplemental Freedmen's Bill undertook to cover almost precisely the same rights, the same subject matter as the Civil Rights Act of 1866.

The supplemental Freedmen's Bill covered only the seceding states.

The Civil Rights Act of 1866 covered all the states. The Rights bill fell into five groups, and everywhere through the debates you will see these five groups of rights being dealt with.

The first was the right to contract. The second was the right to hold property, to inherit it, to transfer it, to lease it and what not.

The third was the right to sue and be sued and give evidence in court.

The fourth was the right to equal security, no improper seizures, no searches and so forth. Equal rights in respect of security.

And the fifth was a group of rights that assured equal punishment for the same offenses.

Now, it is very striking that when this Civil Rights Act of 1866 was submitted, it was submitted by Senator Trumbull, who, as we show repeatedly in our brief, very clearly and finally came out very definitely on the specific point—and he was the proponent—that the right to go to public school was not regarded as a civil right. That is what he said repeatedly in those days.

Now that was the five groups of rights that was covered. Notice what he said. I want to just leave in these few moments in your minds two quotations.

I agree entirely with the thought expressed this morning that you can't judge the intent of Congress by what one senator might have said here or what another congressman said there, but as this Court has repeatedly said, what the sponsors of the legislation say is entitled to particular weight.

That is the Duplex doctrine,[26] that is the doctrine in the Calvert case[27] which Mr. Justice Douglas repeatedly delivered the opinion on, and I want to leave in your minds what these two sponsors said.

Trumbull, as the sponsor of the Civil Rights Act, Wilson in the House, who was Chairman of the Judiciary Committee, and here is what Trumbull said:

> The first section of this bill defines what I understand to be civil rights, the right to make and enforce contracts, to sue, to be sued, to give evidence, to inherit, purchase,

[26]Duplex Printing Press Co. v. Deering, 254 U.S. 443 (1921). The Supreme Court upheld an action for damages under the antitrust law against a union despite a labor organization exemption granted by the Clayton Act. In commenting on the Congressional debates on the labor exemption, the Court noted: "it has come to be well established that the debates in Congress expressive of the views and motives of individual members are not a safe guide . . . in ascertaining the meaning and purpose of the law-making body." 254 U.S. at 474.

[27]Schwegmann v. Calvert Corp. 341 U.S. 384 (1950). The Supreme Court found that fair trade laws passed by Louisiana did not permit a manufacturer of liquor to stop non-signing merchants from selling below the fair trade price despite the Miller-Tydings Act generally sanctioning fair trade laws. In referring to the statutory history of the Act, Justice Douglas noted: "The fears and doubts of the opposition are no authoritative guide to the construction of legislation." 341 U.S. at 394.

sell, lease, hold, convey real and personal property. It is confined exclusively to their civil rights.

And you couple that with his own statement that the right to go to school is not a civil right. Here is what Wilson said over on the House side:

Nor do they mean that children shall attend the same schools. These are not civil rights.

Later on he said:

When he talks about setting aside the school laws of the States by the bill now under consideration, he steps beyond what he must know to be the rule of construction which must apply here.

And when you read these debates, as I hope to show you tomorrow, there were three types of rights which they all finally admitted were not civil rights.

The first one was the right to vote, which was never given until the Fifteenth Amendment. The second was the right to marry a white woman or the other way. The third was the right to go to mixed schools.

Now as I hope to show Your Honors tomorrow morning, those were certainly three vital rights in spite of all this talk about equality of men which was never intended to be given under that bill.

Now the Attorney General, as Mr. Davis points out, says that in view of this conflict, he sets one off against the other. He says he doesn't believe any interpretation is practical here.

He asserts that the proponents and opponents both express the view that the act would outlaw or would not outlaw separate but equal schools. Two of the people he refers to are Kerr and Delano,[28] I will have you bear in mind. They were speaking of cases where there were schools for whites and no schools for Negroes.

Senator Cowan, the only senator who insisted on the point of view that it might open up the schools, as we point out in our brief, later changed his mind in the light of further debate, and he said he became convinced that the rights are here, that the rights are those which I here enumerated.

And only Rogers of New Jersey, the most bitter opponent, stands out in the House in the final showdown, who was insistent that the right to go to school, the mixed schools, might be produced.

As we said in the Calvert case, may I just close this part of the discussion with this question. The Court said here: "The fears and doubts of the opposition are no authoritative guide to the construction of legislation. It is the sponsors that should be looked to when the meaning of the statutory words is in doubt." Now that brings me to the Fourteenth Amendment itself.

(Whereupon at 4:30 p.m., the Court arose.)

(Oral argument was resumed at 12:10 p.m., December 8, 1953.)

[28]Representative Michael C. Kerr (1827–1876) of Indiana. Democratic representative, 1865–1873 and 1875–1876. Representative Columbus Delano (1809–1896) of Ohio. Republican representative, 1865–1862 and 1868–1869; Secretary of the Interior under President Ulysses S. Grant, 1870–1875.

THE CHIEF JUSTICE: This is in the matter of a hearing before the United States Supreme Court in the segregation cases held on Tuesday, December 8, 1953.

### ARGUMENT ON BEHALF OF THE APPELLANTS—Resumed

#### by MR. MOORE—Resumed

MR. MOORE: May it please the Court, at the adjournment yesterday afternoon I had referred briefly in presenting our side of the Virginia case, to the fourth and fifth questions.

Perhaps I was very brief, but we felt in comparison with these other great questions, that we dealt with those very fully in our brief, and I hope my statement was sufficient as to our position as to gradual adjustment and as to the kind of decree in the event of an adverse decision.

I started in the discussion of the first great question, one, as to congressional intent and understanding. In view of Mr. Davis' very extensive discussion on that matter and also on the question of the states' understanding, I shall try to be quite brief on those two next questions, and will simply try to pinpoint what we regard as the high points as to both those matters, and give the greater part of my time to what we believe now, in view of questions from the Court as well as from the former hearing, what is perhaps the larger question as to judicial power.

Your Honors will recall that I had pointed out that there are six classes of legislation which throw a great deal of light on the intent of Congress. I had touched on the first two, the Freedmen's Bill which is significant here only in this respect: that that was the first bill in which Congress had undertaken to provide for the Negro for public schools at public expense, and the significant thing is they were separate schools.

I had then proceeded to discuss the 1866 Civil Rights Act and had undertaken to point out to you the great change that was made in that Act.

As the Act was originally introduced, it had broad language which provided that all discrimination in civil rights and immunities as to all inhabitants on account of race is prohibited. And because of constitutional questions that had been raised and arguments on policy, that language was changed around to the specific language that you now find in the bill as it was finally passed.

Now I had pointed out that there were these five groups of rights that were listed, and the sponsors of the bill made clear that those were the rights intended, and only those.

Now there is no difficulty about *Strauder* when you look at it in that light.

The fourth group of rights was their right to equal security, and all that *Strauder* held was the right to have a Negro possibly on the jury was a part of his right of equal security.

I also tried to point out that there were three classes of rights which, by debate, was clearly eliminated in that list of rights. The first was the right of suffrage which, as we all know, in spite of this argument about equal rights was never given the Negro until two years later in 1870 when the Fifteenth Amendment was passed, although the Thirteenth had freedom from slavery.

The second was the right of intermarriage which was clearly not intended to be included, in spite of the broad language, and this right of mixed schools. Now those were three that were clearly pointed out in all the debates and were not intended to be covered.

That brings us therefore to the third important piece of legislation which was the Fourteenth Amendment itself. As Your Honors recall, that Amendment really sprung out of the debates on the Civil Rights Act, because it was argued that the Civil Rights\Act, even in spite of the Thirteenth Amendment that freed the slaves, was still not constitutional. So the Amendment sprung from that.

It came from the Joint Committee on Reconstruction. That Committee was composed of nine representatives and six senators. The majority were radicals, although Senator Sumner was considered too radical for membership, we find, from a very interesting letter from Senator Fessenden's son. It is in our opinions. His friends wouldn't put him on there.

The chairman was Senator Fessenden of Maine and he was ill much of the time, and Senator Howard of Michigan took the lead in his place. The House leader was the famous co-chairman, that is, Stevens.

Now the Amendment here again is debated in two forms very much like the Civil Rights Act. In its first form it purported to confer on Congress the affirmative power to make all laws that were necessary to secure privileges and immunities and equal protection. That version though was considered too broad, just as was the broad language in the original Civil Rights Act.

And finally in May of that year the Amendment was reported in the form that is now found, and as Your Honors probably are thoroughly familiar with it, there are two sentences really in the first section.

The first was the sentence put in by Senator Howard which defined citizenship, that everyone born and naturalized in this country, regardless of race, was a citizen, and the second sentence which Mr. Bingham wrote, was the same section we are here concerned with, which switched around the approach to the matter from a grant of affirmative power to Congress to a denial of power to the states.

Now in both the House and the Senate the debates made one thing clear. The purpose of the first section of the Amendment was simply to write the Civil Rights Act into the Constitution. Stevens, the sponsor in the House, said that, Howard of Michigan said that, and numerous others, which I will not take time to enumerate.

The reasons were very interesting. The Democrats persistently charged the Republicans with trying to constitutionalize the Civil Rights Act. They said, "That is all you are trying to do is to legalize it."

On the other hand, the Republicans replied, "Yes, that is what we want to do, but we want to nail it down so it can't be repealed."

That is what Stevens said in perfectly clear language as the leader, and as I pointed out yesterday, we look primarily to Stevens and Howard, people like that, and Wilson in the House, to find out really what they are talking about, the proponents.

Now the appellants here assert two things. They first quote these broad statements about equal privileges and immunities that certain members of Congress and the Senate wanted to assure, and next they assert that the Amendment went beyond those civil rights that we have in the Civil Rights Act.

Neither statement in our judgment is a safeguard to this Court because it is perfectly plain from the extracts in our brief and appendix and in the South Carolina brief, that these radical people never were able to go as far as they wanted. Stevens admitted that frankly. So did Howard at the end.

So the Amendment was proposed in the form with these two sentences, Howard's definition of citizenship and Bingham's statement of denial of rights to the States to deny equal protection of the laws.

Now the debates give convincing evidence that it was not intended to abolish segregated schools, but confirmation comes from two other sources which were mentioned, one of them particularly yesterday. I will just touch it very briefly.

The next step is the District school legislation which our opponents, our colored friends, saw fit in their brief to completely ignore, and which the Attorney General comes in and dusts off with just a gesture, saying it was dealt with casually.

The most significant thing in that legislation, Your Honors, aside from the fact that just a month after slavery was abolished here in the District in 1862 and separate schools were set up for Negroes, is this fact: I am not going to review it all, but keep in mind this fact, that in 1866, in July, 1866, within one month after the Fourteenth Amendment was proposed in June, 1866, this Congress, the same 39th Congress passed these two bills in which they dealt with these separate schools.

In one case they provided for property to be transferred for the use solely of those schools. In the second bill they appropriated money in proportion to the number of Negroes to whites, and yet these gentlemen are bold enough to come up and say because that legislation passed without great debate, that it was not carefully considered.

Now passing on from the District school legislation, let's take the next important piece of legislation. I will mention it. It was the amnesty bills.

Those bills were debated with greatest heat in Congress with a view to granting amnesty to Southerners who participated in the war. And on two occasions Charles Sumner undertook to draft, to tack onto those bills his Civil Rights bill, which included a requirement that the Negroes should be given equal status as to schools, churches, cemeteries, theaters and what not. And in respect to each of those he lost out, and the bills were finally passed without them.

Now one more reference and I am through with this part of the case. We should not lose sight of the 1875 Civil Rights Act. This matter was not finally ended until the 1875 Act was dealt with, the famous right, the famous act, which was held unconstitutional in the *Civil Rights Cases.*

And therein in respect of that Act which was introduced by General Butler of Massachusetts,[29] the effort was being made as the last effort on this matter to write into the civil rights bill the fact that the Negroes should be given equal status in schools, churches, cemeteries, theaters and what not.

Finally, in order to get something passed because the Republicans lost out, there were a hundred people who lost their seats in Congress just about that time

[29]Representative Benjamin F. Butler (1818–1893) of Massachusetts. Major General of the Union Army, Republican representative, 1867–1875 and 1877–1879. He was one of the radical Republican leaders in Congress and one of the House managers in the impeachment proceedings against President Andrew Johnson. He also served as Governor of Massachusetts, 1882–1884.

on the Republican side, and to try to get something through, they struck out all reference to schools and the cemeteries and things of that sort and the Act was passed without it, and that was the last effort made to write into this legislation all of this business about equal rights as to schools.

So how our friends on the other side can get comfort out of that story when they can point only to Rogers of New Jersey and occasionally to a remark made by Senator Cowan is beyond us to understand.

Now let me turn just very briefly to the state end of this. There is a very interesting chart in our brief. I have called Your Honors' attention to one yesterday, which was the chart of the 1950 Census.

If you look at page 150, you will see the Census of 1870 where for the first time after the Amendment was adopted, we get a Census including the Negro, and that chart is very illuminating as to what was done with these states.

Mr. Davis discussed it yesterday, and I will not take much time on it. I will just comment on two or three points.

As you see from that chart, there are five states, including Maine, New Hampshire, and so forth, where the question of segregation never was even pertinent at all, never even came up, and in those states the Negro was not quite two-tenths of one per cent of the population.

There is another group of states, such as Massachusetts, Michigan, and so forth, where slavery had been abolished before the Amendment, or where it was abolished about that time, and it is less than one per cent of the Negroes in those States, so it was of no moment.

You then turn to the twenty-three states, the principal ones that are left. My friend, Judge Almond, who will follow me in a brief talk about the seceding states as to which there is an abominable conspiracy charged here by our opponents, is going to talk about the seceding states. But there what happened was that the same legislature that adopted the Fourteenth Amendment passed these laws that required segregation.

Well, how could that be clear evidence that they didn't understand that the Amendment prevented that? But I submit to you that the significant thing in this whole state story is the fact that there were seven of the great states—and I will name them, New York, New Jersey, California, Illinois, Missouri, Ohio and Pennsylvania—as to which our opponents are unable to lay any finger of scorn, and every one of those states had segregation before the Amendment was adopted, and they continued segregation for years thereafter; in California until 1880, in Illinois until 1874, in New Jersey until 1881, in Ohio until 1887, in Pennsylvania until 1881, and in New York until 1930.

And in addition to that, we have the Supreme Courts of those states—Ohio was the first in 1871—which passed directly on the matter and held that the equal facilities, equal doctrine, was not in violation of the Constitution. California filed suit with the decision of its Supreme Court, then Pennsylvania and New York. I will not take further time on it. The record is perfectly clear. And how these gentlemen try to explain away that record with respect to those states is beyond our understanding.

Now turning finally to the third question as to judicial power, as we understood that question, we understood that the Court had in mind in asking us whether the Court had judicial power of itself to abolish segregation, we understood that the Court had in mind perhaps three approaches to it, which I will deal with very briefly.

The first is whether or not this is a case where there should be a restraint of judicial power and the matter left to the legislative bodies.

The second is whether or not in the light of precedents this is a case lasting over these hundred years where it would be an abuse of power in the light of that history. It is what Mr. Davis called yesterday the time when there should be some time a period of repose when a matter is really settled. That is the second question.

And the third branch is whether or not there is some idea here of a living constitution and changing conditions that should make a difference. I am going to talk just very briefly about those three.

As we pointed out, segregation in education does exist in these seventeen states and the District where 55 million people live. In many of these states it is written into the constitution.

And we submit that the first point to bear in mind on this phase of the case is the principle that was mentioned in Justice Jackson's opinion here yesterday, and so well put by Justice Brandeis many years ago: that in a situation like this the statute of a particular constitution comes before Your Honor with a presumption of constitutionality.[30]

In the second place, we point out that this is not a case of some novel or modern experiment such as has been involved in so many cases before Your Honors where these old doctrines have been attempted to be applied to some modern situation. Here the statute is as old as the Constitution itself, and the novel principles are those that are brought in issue here by our opponents.

Finally, we must refer to the field of legislative action. Mr. Justice Holmes has very well expressed the thought when he said:

> Legislatures are ultimate guardians of the liberties and the welfare of the people in quite as great a degree as the courts.[31]

We submit that the Court must coordinate the field for its operations with that of the legislative branch in a case particularly of this kind. What we urge is that the size, the history of this problem before the Court here, makes it clear that the solution should be left with the legislatures.

This case presents a matter, we submit, for judicial restraint if there ever was a case presented. We don't mean judicial restraint here in the sense of these political cases such as have been referred to by the other side. What we do urge is that this question should be left to the duly elected representatives of the people.

Now in touching just the second question as to what is the true situation here in the light of history of the decisions of this Court and the many state courts, in view of questions between Mr. Justice Frankfurter and Mr. Marshall yesterday, I can touch that very briefly.

[30]United States v. Gambling Devices, 346 U.S. 441 (1953). On December 7, 1953, the Court in an opinion by Justice Jackson upheld the constitutionality of a federal law prohibiting the shipment of gambling machines in interstate commerce.

[31]Missouri, Kansas and Texas Ry. Co. v. May, 194 U.S. 267, 270 (1904).

I need only point out that his "separate but equal" doctrine is not a new doctrine. It is more than one hundred years old.

It was first presented to the nation in *Roberts* against *Boston* in 1849, and there was upheld under the Massachusetts Constitution in fundamentals like we have here.

From that time on it got written in the various state statutes, as I have just pointed out. It was continued, it was debated back and forth in the halls of Congress here between 1862 and 1875. In states like Virginia and Georgia it was written into fundamental law in 1870.

These state court cases came along in 1871, 1873 and 1874. In *Hall* v. *DeCuir* in 1877 Mr. Justice Clifford there in the Steamboat case, where the State of Louisiana in a legislature dominated by Negroes and carpetbaggers had passed a law requiring the mixing of people on these boats, that was held unconstitutional under the commerce clause, and he had recognized the doctrine in his concurring opinion there.[32]

So the Court came in 1896 to *Plessy* v. *Ferguson.* There was nothing new to present, and I am glad to find that our gentlemen on the other side here differ from their position here a year ago. They do not come here trying to distinguish *Plessy* v. *Ferguson* and *Gong Lum* from this case. They were here a year ago saying *Plessy* v. *Ferguson* was a railroad case, and the Gong Lum case was a Chinese case, and they could be distinguished, but I am very glad Mr. Marshall marched right up to the point.

He said, "Now, we are asking that this Court go further than it has ever gone before and overrule *Plessy* v. *Ferguson* and *Gong Lum*" because that is what has got to be done for the decree that he asks to be entered.

I am not going to review these more recent cases. As was pointed out, it was admitted here yesterday these gentlemen are not happy with these recent cases of *Sweatt* v. *Painter* nor *McLaurin,* for that matter. McLaurin there in the Department of Education in Oklahoma was set apart, true enough, but he was set apart in a way so it was just as if he had the sign, "Here is a leper, here is a leper, don't touch him." In very proper words said, "Well, you can't do that. That is not any proper application of the doctrine."

So we find the Court under the Chief Justice saying in *Sweatt* v. *Painter,* which they don't like on the other side, "Nor do we need to reach the petitioners' contention that *Plessy* v. *Ferguson* should be reexamined."

Now coming finally to the last phase of this matter that I just spoke of, and that is whether or not there are changed conditions that may warrant some different application of the doctrine.

The appellants urge that these precedents should be overruled. They don't urge merely changed conditions. Practically every argument these gentlemen present, Your Honors will find that Charles Sumner presented just as effectively and just as oratorically in 1870 and in that period as they presented it.

The real crux of their argument is the fact they contend that the mere act of

[32]Hall v. DeCuir, 95 U.S. 485 (1878). A Louisiana state law passed in 1869 by a Reconstruction legislature required integration of common carriers within the state. It was held unconstitutional as a burden on interstate commerce.

separation is a badge of inferiority, and that was his theme, that is what he dedicated his life to long before the Amendment and until his death in 1874.

Now if we are going to look at this matter from the standpoint of precedent, the rule is pretty simple. The rule is that the state may classify and the test of its classification is merely within the bounds of reason. Mr. Justice Hughes well said, quoting him:

> The inquiry must be whether considering the end in view, the statute passes the bounds of reason and assumes the character of a mere arbitrary fiat.[33]

Now how is "reasonable" to be decided here? It can't be decided in a vacuum. It has got to be decided in the light of all the surrounding facts.

Now what are the local conditions in Virginia where we are concerned? In our case the superintendent, State Superintendent of Public Construction testified that the people, Negroes and whites alike, believed that the best interests of both the whites and the Negroes are that the separate schools are best. A former Superintendent of Public Education testified that segregation caused no warped personalities, and that the general welfare would be definitely harmed by mixed schools in Virginia.

A distinguished child psychiatrist testified in this case that the amalgamation would result in increased anxieties which would be detrimental to both races.

The Chairman of Psychology in the Department of Columbia testified—and he is a Virginia boy educated in Virginia, went up to the big city where he has been a great teacher for these many years—he testified with full knowledge of Virginia conditions that the result of segregation in Virginia produced better education for both races.

Now what are we going to do with that testimony? Are we just going to disregard it? Can this Court now say that on the basis of this record, segregation is beyond the bounds of reason, that it is an arbitrary fiat? We don't believe so.

I would like to say this in conclusion, may it please Your Honors. We are trying to be fair as we know how about this matter. It is a matter on which there is great feeling in these seventeen states.

We recognize that there are a great many people of the highest character and position who disapprove of segregation as a matter of principle or as ethics. We think that most of them really do not know the conditions, particularly in the South, that brought about that situation.

That was true of all these witnesses, these experts that appeared in our Virginia case. They did not know a thing about Virginia, they all admitted, and they are not familiar with the way in which it is gradually being worked out. But those feelings that I refer to are not relevant here.

Mr. Justice Holmes had very well put the thought when he said:

> There is nothing that I deprecate more than the use of the Fourteenth Amendment beyond the absolute compulsion of its words to prevent the making of social experiments that an important part of the community desires, in the insulated chambers afforded by the several States, even though those experiments may seem futile or even noxious to me and to those whose judgment I most respect.[34]

[33]Purity Extract and Tonic Co. v. Lynch, 226 U.S. 192, 204 (1912).
[34]Truax v. Corrigan, 257 U.S. 312, 344 (1921).

Is that sound? We believe it is. And just look at the picture that faces the seventeen states as I leave this matter with you.

These states start at Maryland. They go all the way down to Texas, to the Gulf of Mexico. They go out as far west as Missouri and Oklahoma, with a third of the nation included in those states with ten and a half million Negroes in those states, 70 per cent of the Negroes in the whole nation in those states.

During this hundred-year period since *Roberts* and *Boston* has been the law, millions and millions of dollars have been spent in building up these systems. There are thousands of school houses, fine school houses, all over these seventeen states. As a matter of fact, these gentlemen here have one of the finest school buildings in the Nation just completed, which they moved into on September the first.

What are we to do with that situation? Are we to go and put in this county—there are about five and a half Negroes to every five white persons—shall we put one Negro along with every white child in high school when that is the best high school?

I say to you that there is looking down on you from every one of these high school sections, every elementary school in these seventeen states with anxiety as to what you shall do with this.

In our humble judgment there is not anything that could be more serious than an adverse decision. And I want to leave that matter just with this thought which our friend Judge Parker in the South Carolina case has expressed better than anywhere I know. Here is the way he summed it up, after referring to *Plessy* v. *Ferguson* and *Gong Lum* and the great judges that sat in those cases. He said:

> To this we may add that, when seventeen states and the Congress of the United States have for more than three-quarters of a century, required segregation of the races in the public schools, and when this has received the approval of the leading appellate courts of the country including the unanimous approval of the Supreme Court of the United States at a time when that Court included Chief Justice Taft, Justices Stone, Holmes and Brandeis, it is a late day to say that such segregation is violative of fundamental constitutional rights.
>
> It is hardly reasonable to suppose that the legislative bodies of so wide a territory, including the Congress of the United States, and the great judges of high courts, have knowingly defied the Constitution for so long a period or that they have acted in ignorance of the meaning of its provisions. The constitutional principle is the same now that it has been throughout this period; and if conditions have changed so that segregation is no longer wise, this is a matter for the legislatures and not for the courts. The members of the judiciary have no more right to read their ideas of sociology into the Constitution than their ideas of economics.

Thank you.

THE CHIEF JUSTICE: General Almond.

ORAL ARGUMENT ON BEHALF OF THE APPELLEES
COUNTY SCHOOL BOARD OF PRINCE EDWARD COUNTY, VIRGINIA, ET AL

by MR. ALMOND.

MR. ALMOND: May it please the Court, Mr. Moore assigned to me a rather Herculean task, and I have no time in which to address myself to that phase of the case which I would like to discuss.

As the only official of one of the seceding states privileged to actively participate in this case, I just want to, if Your Honors please, take a few moments, the
few moments which remain, to bring to your attention this phase: what are they
here asking for?

They are asking this Court, contrary to the intention of the Congress which
proposed the Fourteenth Amendment, as evidenced irrevocably by the records of
that historic session and during those years, they are asking you to make a decision contrary to the spirit, the intent and purpose of the Fourteenth Amendment.

They are asking you to amend the Constitution of the United States and to
go further than the Congress ever intended that this Court should go.

They are asking you to disturb and tear down the principle of *stare decisis*
enunciated so clearly in 1896 in *Plessy* v. *Ferguson,* reimplemented again in
1899 in *Cumming* v. *Board,* clearly enunciated again in 1927 in *Gong Lum* v.
*Rice,* and even though driven to the wall yesterday, the ingenious counsel of the
opposition in a fruitless effort to confess and avoid, finally admitted that the very
basis of the latest decisions of this Court on that subject beginning with *Gaines* v.
*Canada* in 1938, followed by *Sipuel* in 1948, by *Sweatt* v. *Painter* and *McLaurin* in
1950, that the very basis of those latter cases was predicated upon the doctrine
enunciated in *Plessy* v. *Ferguson:* separate but equal facilities do not offend any
provision of the Constitution of the United States.

They are asking you to overturn the principle of *stare decisis* laid down by
this Court and the courts of last resort of every state in this Union that a solemn
constitutional provision or legislative enactment carries with it the highest presumption known to law, that it is a valid exercise of the powers of the body which
enacted it.

They are asking you to disturb the unfolding evolutionary process of education where from the dark days of the depraved institution of slavery, with the help
and the sympathy and the love and respect of the white people of the South, the
colored man has risen under that educational process to a place of eminence and
respect throughout this nation. It has served him well.

In those days as now, the states were dealing with the question of policy.
Questions have been asked here or submitted by this Court as to what directions
there should be in any adverse decree handed down, adverse to the appellees in this
case. I like the language of Mr. Justice Holmes when he said—I believe it was Mr.
Justice Holmes—no, probably not, but in the case of International Salt in 332
U.S.:[35]

> It is not the province of the appellate court to write decrees. That is within the
> province and the equipment of the District Court.

I would say to this Court on that question, in the event of an adverse decision
to our side, that the case be remanded with direction to the lower court to conduct
a hearing taking into consideration the vast administrative difficulties which
would be occasioned as a result of such a decision.

[35]International Salt Co. v. United States, 332 U.S. 392 (1947). The International Salt
Co. leased its patented machines with a requirement that the lessee could purchase only
International Salt products for the machine. This was held to violate the Sherman Act. The
District Court was directed to frame an appropriate decree for relief.

We must determine from Virginia what we are going to do with our compulsory attendance law in the event of an adverse decision. We must determine whether we will have one system or three systems, if the dual system is destroyed.

It is a matter, sir, of great import to these states affected. What crime has Virginia committed? She has within the last fifteen years gone further in the promotion of education on an equal facilities basis than almost, I can say, any state in the South.

Within the last four years she has appropriated 75 millions of dollars which has been more than matched by the political subdivisions, to increase the facilities of our public school system, and most of that has been spent to equalize facilities which needed to be equalized.

JUSTICE FRANKFURTER: General Almond, let me ask you a question to see whether I understand your suggestion.

MR. ALMOND: Yes.

JUSTICE FRANKFURTER: Of these systems, the choice is of going to what is called an integrated school but in default of that, deciding of the choice than, it will be shepherded into one or the other, is that what you mean by the decree?

MR. ALMOND: I didn't mean, Mr. Justice Frankfurter, shepherding in that sense.

JUSTICE FRANKFURTER: That is a bad word. If they do not choose to go to unmixed schools, then they would have to go to a separate school, is that right, if they do not choose to go to a mixed school which is open to them, then they would have to go to one or the other, is that what you mean, General Almond?

MR. ALMOND: I said, sir, that that is the matter of policy which the states—

JUSTICE FRANKFURTER: Yes, I understand, but is that what you meant?

MR. ALMOND: Yes.

JUSTICE FRANKFURTER: Those are the three which you have in mind?

MR. ALMOND: That is right, sir, which the state would have to determine.

JUSTICE FRANKFURTER: Yes, I understand that. It is a very hypothetical answer on that, but I just wanted to understand you.

MR. ALMOND: That is a matter of legislative policy.

Now, if Your Honors please, I guess my time has just about expired. I would like to say one thing in behalf of the seceding states, if there was ever such a thing, why they have been indicted by the opposition of treachery, of fraud, of conniving to subvert the Fourteenth Amendment.

I ask our friends of the opposition to consider this: That when the constitutional conventions were created in the South, think of their composition. There were 101 delegates to the constitutional convention which framed the new constitution of the great State of Alabama. Of these there were 18 Negroes, 38 carpetbaggers and 45 scalawags.

Now I do not use those two latter terms in any sense of approbium. Mr. Webster defines a carpetbagger as a roving venturer meddling in the politics of a locality in which he has no interest. History defines a scalawag as a white southerner who associated with the machinations of the carpetbaggers.

Now Georgia's constitutional convention of 1867 and '68 consisted of 131 scalawags, 37 Negroes, 9 carpetbaggers and 12 conservative whites. The convention that prepared the new constitution for Virginia was composed of 24 Negroes, 26 carpetbaggers, 14 scalawags and 35 conservative whites.

I ask them when they indict these states for perpetrating a fraud by not placing certain provisions in their constitutions until after readmissions has been accomplished, and then turning around as they said and enacting mixed school law, if a fraud was perpetrated, who was the perpetrator.

We should remember also in this indictment against the southern states that governors were sent in as importations from as far away as Maine, Kansas and Pennsylvania, and those governors recommended to the very legislatures which ratified the Fourteenth Amendment that a school system should be established on a segregated basis. They did that because they understood the facts of life and knew that in no other way could that question then, as we maintain now, be solved to the benefit of both races.

### REBUTTAL ARGUMENT ON BEHALF OF APPELLANTS, HARRY BRIGGS, JR., ET AL.

#### by MR. MARSHALL

MR. MARSHALL: May it please the Court, there are several points I would like to clear up preliminarily, and then I would like to make sure that our position is correctly stated, and as it relates to statements made by counsel on the other side.

JUSTICE FRANKFURTER: Mr. Marshall, I do not want to interrupt your closing argument, but I hope before you sit down you will state to the Court whether you have anything more to say on the question of remedies.

MR. MARSHALL: Yes, sir.

JUSTICE FRANKFURTER: In case you should prevail, more than is contained in your brief.

MR. MARSHALL: Yes, sir, I would be glad to get to that first, Mr. Justice Frankfurter.

In our brief we found ourselves, after having given as much research as we could, in a position where we intelligently could not put forth a plan. We find that in the briefs of the other side they recognized there would be certain administrative problems involved, and anything else that they mentioned we, of course, well, not of course, we do not recognize as being valid for this Court to consider.

On the other hand, we spent as much time as we could during the time of filing and the present time on the United States Government's suggestion as to the decree, and so far as we are concerned, it appears to us that there are administrative problems, there would be administrative problems, and that the decree of this Court could very well instruct the lower court to take into consideration that factor, and if necessary give to the state involved a sufficient time to meet the administrative problems, with the understanding so far as we are concerned that I do not agree with the last part of the Government [brief], that if it isn't done within a school year, that they could get more time for this reason, sir.

I can conceive of nothing administrative-wise that would take longer than a year. If they don't have staff enough to do these administrative things, the sovereign states can hire more people to do it.

So for that reason I don't think it should take more than a year for them to adequately handle the administrative techniques, and I submit that a longer period of time would get the lower court into the legislative field as to whether or not to do it this way or that way.

Specifically, I am a firm believer that especially in so far as the federal courts are concerned, their duty and responsibility ends with telling the state, in this field at least, what you can't do.

And I don't think anybody is recommending to this Court that this Court take over the administrative job. Obviously, that is not recommended by anyone. So with that, I think that is our position.

We said in the opening brief that if any plans were put forth, we would be obliged to do it, we wanted to do it, and that is our position on the limited point.

It gets me, if it please the Court, to one of the points that runs throughout the argument in the brief on the other side, and that is that they deny that there is any race prejudice involved in these cases. They deny that there is any intention to discriminate.

But throughout the brief and throughout the argument they not only recognize that there is a race problem involved, but they emphasize that that is the whole problem. And for the life of me, you can't read the debates, even the sections they rely on, without an understanding that the Fourteenth Amendment took away from the states the power to use race.

As I understand their position, their only justification for this being a reasonable classification is, one, that they got together and decided that it is best for the races to be separated and, two, that it has existed for over a century.

Neither argument, to my mind, is any good. The answer to the first argument is in two places, if I may for a moment address myself to it. This one that Mr. Davis and Mr. Moore both relied on, these horrible census figures, the horrible number of Negroes in the South—and I thought at some stage it would be recognized by them that it shows that in truth and in fact in this country that high percentage of Negroes they talk about can be used to demonstrate to the world that in so far as this country is concerned, two-thirds of the Negroes are compelled to submit to segregation.

They say that is the reason for it. The best answer is in the record in the Clarendon County case, where the only witness the other side put on on this point—and a reading of it will show he was put on for the express purpose—he is a school administrator—of explaining how the school system would be operated under the new bill that was going to tax people, but they dragged this other point in and made him an expert in race relations and everything else.

He emphasized—well, the best way to do it is this way on page 119 of the record in the Briggs case:

> What I was saying is that the problem of the mixed groups and racial tensions is less in communities where the minority population is small. That has been true of the testimony I have heard.
>
> Then the question: "Well, Mr. Crow," incidentally, that was his name, Mr. Crow, assuming that in Clarendon County especially in School District No. 22 the population was 95 per cent white and 5 per cent Negro, would that change your opinion? Answer. No.
>
> Question. Then that is not really the basis of your opinion, is it?
>
> Answer. The question that you have asked me is in my opinion, will the elimination of segregation be fraught with undesirable results, and I have said that I thought it would. That may not be stating your question exactly, but that is still my answer.
>
> Question. As a matter of fact, Mr. Crow, isn't your opinion based on the fact that you have all of your life believed in segregation of the races? Isn't that the reason, the real reason, the basis of your opinion?
>
> Answer. That wouldn't be all.
>
> Question. But it is a part of it?
>
> Answer. I suppose it is.

And that answers all of those arguments about this large number of people involved. They are all American citizens who, by accident of birth, are a different color, and it makes no difference one way or another in so far as this Court is concerned.

Then, in that same vein, Attorney General Almond gets to the name-calling stage about these state conventions. Well, let's go up to the later convention in his State of Virginia. I don't believe that the man I am now going to quote can be characterized as anything but a respected former senator of the United States, and in debating the section in the latter Constitution of Virginia, not the one in this period, but the later one, Senator Carter Glass, who was a delegate to the convention, spoke thusly in the debates:

> Discrimination, that is precisely what we propose. That exactly is what this Convention was elected for, to discriminate to the very extremity of permissible action under the limitations of the federal Constitution.

That is quoted in the statement of jurisdiction in the Virginia case on page 11. And another answer I submit is quoted in our reply brief involving the University of North Carolina Law School case which was decided adversely to the Negro applicants in the district court, and on appeal to the Fourth Circuit Court of Appeals, the very Circuit that is involved here, in an opinion by Judge Soper of Maryland met this question of what we are doing is for the benefit of the white and Negro people alike, saying:

> The defense seeks in part to avoid the charge of inequality by the paternal suggestion that it would be beneficial to the colored race in North Carolina as a whole, and to the individual plaintiffs in particular, if they would cooperate in promoting the policy adopted by the State rather than seek the best legal education which the State provides. The duty of the federal courts, however, is clear. We must give first place

to the rights of the individual citizen, and when and where he seeks only equality of treatment before the law, his suit must prevail. It is for him to decide in which direction his advantage lies.[36]

As to this time of how long segregation has been in existence in the South, the same argument has been made in every case that has come up to this Court, the argument of *stare decisis,* that you should leave this because it has been long standing, the "separate but equal" doctrine, and that there are so many states involved, was made in even more detailed fashion in the Sweatt brief filed by Attorney General Price Daniel,[37] and as an aside, it is significant that in the Virginia brief on the last page they go out of their way to pay acknowledgement to that brief filed by the Attorney General, which was obviously discarded by this Court.

There is not one new item that has been produced in all of these cases. And we come to the question as to whether or not the wishes of these states shall prevail, as to whether or not our Constitution shall prevail.

And over against the public policy of the State of Virginia and the State of South Carolina is an Amendment that was put in the Constitution after one of the worst wars that was ever fought, and around that constitutional provision we say that the public policy of the United States does not look to the state policy, but looks to our government.

And in the brief we have filed in our reply brief, we quote from a document which just came out, at least we just got ahold of it a couple of weeks ago, monograph, which we cite in our brief from the selective service of our Government, and we have some quotes in our brief.

I don't emphasize or urge the quotes as such, but a reading of that monograph will convince anyone that the discriminatory segregation policies, education and otherwise in the South, almost caused us to lose one war, and I gather from the recommendations made in there that unless it is corrected, we will lose another.

Now that is the policy that I understand them to say that it is just a little feeling on the part of Negroes, they don't like segregation. As Mr. Davis said yesterday, the only thing the Negroes are trying to get is prestige.

Exactly correct. Ever since the Emancipation Proclamation, the Negro has been trying to get what was recognized in *Strauder* v. *West Virginia,* which is the same status as anybody else regardless of race.

I can't, for the life of me—it seems to me they recommend to us what we should do. It seems to me they should show some effort on their part to conform their states to the clear intent of past decisions.

For example, the argument was made in *McLaurin* and *Sweatt* of what would happen if these decisions were granted, and indeed the brief, joint brief filed by the Attorneys General of all the states, and if I remember correctly it was signed by General Almond, said that if this Court broke down exclusion and segregation in

[36]McKissick v. Carmichael, 187 F 2d 949, 953–54 (4th Cir. 1951). One of the plaintiffs in that action was Floyd McKissick, later chairman of CORE and a militant civil rights leader.

[37]Price Daniel (1910–    ) former Governor of Texas (1956–1963), U.S. Senator (1953–1956), and State Attorney General (1946–1953). He argued Sweatt v. Painter for the State of Texas.

the graduate and professional schools, or maybe it was the law schools—I know exactly what they said—the schools would have to close up and go out of business.

And the truth of the matter—and we cite in our record the figures that show that since that decision there are now 1500 Negroes in graduate and professional schools in heretofore all white universities, 1500 at least in twelve states, one of the states significantly out of the group being South Carolina.

It is also pointed out in our brief a very long list of private schools in the South, which as a result, with no legal binding upon them at all, do so.

It is also significant that in states like Arkansas—I could name four or five—without any lawsuit, segregation was broken down. The truth of the matter is that I for one have more confidence in the people of the South, white and colored, than the lawyers on the other side. I am convinced they are just as lawful as anybody else, and once the law is laid down, that is all there is to it.

In their argument on the congressional debate, they do a job too well. They say no education was intended to be covered by the Fourteenth Amendment.

Obviously, that is not correct, because even their pet case, *Plessy* v. *Ferguson,* recognized that education was under the Fourteenth Amendment.

Then Mr. Moore goes to great detail to point out that the Fourteenth Amendment could go no further than the Civil Rights Act, and he emphasized yesterday and he emphasized today that in addition to that, there were some rights that were deliberately excluded.

His language is "clearly eliminated," and then he says, "Suffrage was clearly not intended to be included."

And how anyone can stand in this Court, having read the opinion of Mr. Justice Holmes in the first Texas Primary case,[38] and take that position is beyond me, because that decision, in the language of Mr. Justice Holmes, said specifically that they urged the Fourteenth and Fifteenth Amendments, but we don't have to get to the Fifteenth Amendment because the Fourteenth Amendment said that the states can do a lot of classifying which we, speaking as a Court, can't seem to understand, but it is clear that race cannot be used in suffrage. So I don't see the purport of any of that argument.

JUSTICE FRANKFURTER: Do you think the Fifteenth Amendment was redundant, superfluous?

MR. MARSHALL: No, sir, definitely not.

JUSTICE FRANKFURTER: So if it had not been there, it would have been included in the Fourteenth?

MR. MARSHALL: I think definitely under the reasoning of Mr. Justice Holmes, it would have been.

JUSTICE FRANKFURTER: That is superfluous, then it is an extra.

[38]Nixon v. Herndon, 273 U.S. 536 (1927). The Texas statute barring Negroes from participating in Democratic party primary elections was held unconstitutional. Later attempts by Texas to keep Negroes from voting in the primary were voided in Nixon v. Condon, 286 U.S. 73 (1932), Smith v. Allwright, 321 U.S. 649 (1944) and Terry v. Adams, 345 U.S. 461 (1953).

MR. MARSHALL: It is an extra.

JUSTICE FRANKFURTER: An extra.

MR. MARSHALL: I just—maybe it is timidity, but I just can't say a constitutional amendment is superfluous, but if you are asking me if I think Mr. Justice Holmes was absolutely correct, definitely, yes, sir.

That brings me to the other point which I want to make clear. It involves the questions yesterday about our position as to the McLaurin case, and I am a little worried in thinking of what I said yesterday as to whether the position was absolutely clear. And it is suggested today that the position we take in this case is a negation of the McLaurin case, and as to whether or not the McLaurin case is a negation of the "separate but equal" doctrine, and it is argued that McLaurin had a constitutional grievance, because he was denied equality, but in the McLaurin case the answer is that the only inequality which he suffered is that which is inherent, emphasis on "inherent," if you please, in segregation itself.

He had the same schools, same everything else, but he had this segregation, so that is inherent. And if McLaurin won because he was denied equality, it is also true and much more important that he suffered constitutional inequality in the enjoyment of these identical offerings.

And it follows that with education, this Court has made segregation and inequality equivalent concepts. They have equal rating, equal footing, and if segregation thus necessarily imports inequality, it makes no great difference whether we say that the Negro is wronged because he is segregated, or that he is wronged because he received unequal treatment.

We believe that what we really ask this Court is to make it explicit what they think was inevitably implicit in the McLaurin case, that the two are together. But most certainly I do not agree, and I want to make it clear, that the McLaurin case is under the one-way, and I think that with this understanding, the Court has no difficulty in our position at least.

And finally I would like to say that each lawyer on the other side has made it clear as to what the position of the state was on this, and it would be all right possibly but for the fact that this is so crucial. There is no way you can repay lost school years.

These children in these cases are guaranteed by the states some twelve years of education in varying degrees, and this idea, if I understand it, to leave it to the states until they work it out—and I think that is a most ingenious argument—you leave it to the states, they say; and then they say that the states haven't done anything about it in a hundred years, so for that reason this Court doesn't touch it.

The argument of judicial restraint has no application in this case. There is a relationship between Federal and State, but there is no corollary or relationship as to the Fourteenth Amendment.

The duty of enforcing, the duty of following the Fourteenth Amendment is placed upon the states. The duty of enforcing the Fourteenth Amendment is placed upon this Court, and the argument that they make over and over again to my mind is the same type of argument they charge us with making, the same argument Charles Sumner made. Possibly so.

And we hereby charge them with making the same argument that was made before the Civil War, the same argument that was made during the period between the ratification of the Fourteenth Amendment and the *Plessy* v. *Ferguson* case.

And I think it makes no progress for us to find out who made what argument. It is our position that whether or not you base this case solely on the intent of Congress or whether you base it on the logical extension of the doctrine as set forth in the McLaurin case, on either basis the same conclusion is required, which is that this Court makes it clear to all of these states that in administering their governmental functions, at least those that are vital not to the life of the state alone, not to the country alone, but vital to the world in general, that little pet feelings of race, little pet feelings of custom—I got the feeling on hearing the discussion yesterday that when you put a white child in a school with a whole lot of colored children, the child would fall apart or something. Everybody knows that is not true.

Those same kids in Virginia and South Carolina—and I have seen them do it—they play in the streets together, they play on their farms together, they go down the road together, they separate to go to school, they come out of school and play ball together. They have to be separated in school.

There is some magic to it. You can have them voting together, you can have them not restricted because of law in the houses they live in. You can have them going to the same state university and the same college, but if they go to elementary and high school, the world will fall apart. And it is the exact same argument that has been made to this Court over and over again, and we submit that when they charge us with making a legislative argument, it is in truth they who are making the legislative argument.

They can't take race out of this case. From the day this case was filed until this moment, nobody has in any form or fashion, despite the fact I made it clear in the opening argument that I was relying on it, done anything to distinguish this statute from the Black Codes, which they must admit, because nobody can dispute, say anything anybody wants to say, one way or the other, the Fourteenth Amendment was intended to deprive the states of power to enforce Black Codes or anything else like it.

We charge that they are Black Codes. They obviously are Black Codes if you read them. They haven't denied that they are Black Codes, so if the Court wants to very narrowly decide this case, they can decide it on that point.

So whichever way it is done, the only way that this Court can decide this case in opposition to our position, is that there must be some reason which gives the state the right to make a classification that they can make in regard to nothing else in regard to Negroes, and we submit the only way to arrive at this decision is to find that for some reason Negroes are inferior to all other human beings.

Nobody will stand in the Court and urge that, and in order to arrive at the decision that they want us to arrive at, there would have to be some recognition of a reason why of all of the multitudinous groups of people in this country you have to single out Negroes and give them this separate treatment.

It can't be because of slavery in the past, because there are very few groups in this country that haven't had slavery some place back in the history of their groups. It can't be color because there are Negroes as white as the drifted snow, with blue eyes, and they are just as segregated as the colored man.

The only thing can be is an inherent determination that the people who were formerly in slavery, regardless of anything else, shall be kept as near that stage as is possible, and now is the time, we submit, that this Court should make it clear that that is not what our Constitution stands for.

Thank you, sir.

THE CHIEF JUSTICE: Mr. Rankin.

### ARGUMENT ON BEHALF OF THE UNITED STATES

#### by MR. RANKIN

MR. RANKIN: May it please the Court, as this Court well knows, the United States appears in this action as a friend of the Court, and the only excuse for us to be here is because of the assistance that we may be able to give the Court in regard to this problem before it.

When these questions were asked by the Court as a part of the request for reargument in this matter, we approached them with the idea of how much we might be able to help the Court in answering the questions, and we felt it incumbent upon us in the Department of Justice to try to arrive at the truth in the background and the history as the Court inquired for it. And we saw it as our duty to approach that history much as historians would, and try to draw from it the facts just as objectively as any party could on either side, for someone who had no personal interest in the case. That was the approach that we made to this case in trying to help the Court in the answer of these questions.

We have been chided because we did not come forth in our brief in answer to the questions with certain history. We did not conceive it as our duty to develop any history. We thought it our duty to present what the history showed, whether it hurt or helped either side.

We have no apology to Your Honors or to the country for the manner in which we have developed the history involved in this case and the Fourteenth Amendment, and on behalf of the Attorney General and myself personally, I want to express publicly my appreciation for the work that was done, as some of you well know, by others and myself on this, in order to present a factual history of the entire matter that the Court could rely on and not have to do independent work in regard to it.

But these questions were not in vain. There are great lessons that can be drawn from them, and they are important to this Court in helping them to decide this, one of the greatest cases that this Court has had before it.

Why do those questions seem important? Because they clean out some of the unimportant elements, some of the claims that cannot be sustained by history, and leave the Court with the naked problems of what this Amendment means to every American citizen who loves this country and this Constitution.

Many claims have been made in these cases about the acts of Congress, and the only way to determine the validity of those claims is to look at what Congress did, what was said about them, and we have rejected masses of material and tried to boil it down.

I apologize for the size of the work we left for the Court, but it is the best we could do, and we tried to eliminate all we could. However, in looking at what happened, we have tried to follow the standards this Court has laid down in many decisions, *Maxwell* v. *Dow*[39] is one of them, in which the Court would not pick out an isolated remark, part of debates, something of the opponents or the proponents, in connection with a certain piece of legislation, and even that rule did not apply in constitutional matters.

And we have rejected purposely those various statements, but pointed them out to the Court so the Court could consider them for what they are worth.

But we say when Congress considered the question of segregation in the schools in the debates that extended over a period of months in this matter, that you cannot rely on those statements as showing that Congress decided this particular question before the Court.

They are too sketchy under the rules laid down by this Court to rely on. There we get to the middle of the road. We are not satisfactory to either side. We turn up with conclusions that the evidence does not sustain the plaintiff's position nor the position of the states. But regardless of who it hurts, it is there and it cannot be overlooked.

Now to deal directly with a few of these problems, let us look at what happened in the District of Columbia, and on its face the fact that two enactments were passed by the same 39th Congress dealing with this question of schools and separate schools in the District might seem of grave importance as to the interpretation by Congress.

But we show you what happened. We show the consideration or lack of it that Congress gave to that particular problem.

The separate schools question was considered by Congress back in 1862. The 39th Congress considered only two things. One was whether to give three lots for the use of the colored schools in the District, and the other was to allocate certain funds. There were no committee reports, no participation by the members of the Reconstruction Committee. There was no debate, and we show you on page 71 in the supplement to our brief the detail of the material that Congress considered on the same day.

Now, gentlemen, with your experience I am sure that Your Honors know that in that particular instance the history is of great help to this Court, because it does not show that Congress determined at that time that segregation should be continued as the policy under the Fourteenth Amendment to the Constitution.

Congress just did not consider that matter, and they did not have time for it and it wasn't the way that those matters are determined by Congress as we well know, and the things that this Court considers in regard to it.

In addition to that, we must keep in mind, as the Court well knows in connection with the Thompson[40] case, that at that time Congress did not have the same

[39]176 U.S. 581 (1900). The Supreme Court held a state need not proceed in a criminal action by indictment, nor must it try a defendant before a twelve man jury under the Fourteenth Amendment. Thus, a conviction for robbery returned by an eight man Utah jury was upheld. The case has been overruled by the Supreme Court in Duncan v. Louisiana, 391 U.S. 145 (1968).

[40]District of Columbia v. John R. Thompson Co., 346 U.S. 100 (1953). A District of Columbia restaurant was prosecuted for refusing to serve Negroes under an 1873 law passed by a temporary legislative assembly of the District. The law was held to be still in force.

responsibility in the administration and conduct of the District of Columbia that it has today; that it had its own government, and it wasn't until 1871 that the change was made where Congress undertook the detailed supervision of the District.

So we are saying that that event in itself doesn't show the Congress understood that the Fourteenth Amendment was to permit segregation in the schools of this nation.

Then we turn to the action of the states.

JUSTICE FRANKFURTER: Before you do that, Mr. Attorney General, I suppose you would say that the action since 1871 is too ex post facto to be relevant.

MR. RANKIN: Very largely, Your Honor. It all is removed from the scene. Changes have occured in Congress over the years. The framers were not participants in most of that action, and the Fourteenth Amendment was not involved in those questions.

JUSTICE FRANKFURTER: But it could in any event be involved, but I think so far as any inference is to be drawn from what Congress did or did not do, the early legislation, you put to one side for the reason that you have given. That would be significant becamse Congress was then contemporaneous, it was the same Congress about the same time as those that submitted the Fourteenth Amendment.

But since 1871 Congress has continued to pass legislation year after year acknowledging or authorizing—which is it—acknowledging or authorizing segregation in the District, both. Whatever it is, there have been appropriations recognizing the fact of segregation, and such has been the policy of the District, is that correct?

MR. RANKIN: That is right.

JUSTICE FRANKFURTER: To this day.

MR. RANKIN: That is right.

JUSTICE FRANKFURTER: From 1871, when Congress had sole charge, you would say we can't attribute constitutional verification to Congress passing the appropriations act.

MR. RANKIN: That is correct. That is our position.

JUSTICE REED: I understood you to attribute it to after 1896. What about the period from 1866 until '96, where the question hadn't been raised, where they went ahead and appropriated for the District schools which had segregation. Does that give any indication to you of the attitude of the Congress or the meaning of the Fourteenth Amendment?

MR. RANKIN: We don't consider that there is anything to show that that was an interpretation with knowledge as required by the opinions of this Court in the past concerning the meaning of the Fourteenth Amendment with regard to segregation in the schools in the District or any place else.

When you go back into the—

JUSTICE REED: What about the 1875 Act?

MR. RANKIN: When you go into the history of the 1875 Act, as we have set out in detail, the consideration before Congress was whether or not the law would be passed with a provision for mixed schools or with an amendment that was offered for separate and equal. Both of them lost.

How you can possibly draw any inference from such action that one side won that contest rather than the other is what we cannot follow. We think that Congress by not enacting separate and equal, and failing to enact for mixed schools, left the question in abeyance as far as that particular action is concerned.

JUSTICE REED: Or left it to the states.

MR. RANKIN: No, I think it left it to the Fourteenth Amendment which had already been passed by the Congress and ratified by the states, and it was appreciated at that time that this Court would have the problem to protect those rights as they were declared in section 1.

JUSTICE REED: The Fourteenth Amendment, in the light of the history that had gone on from 1866 to 1875—

MR. RANKIN: Well, that history as we saw it—

JUSTICE REED: I mean the history of the states.

MR. RANKIN: Well, the history of the states, if the Court will look—

JUSTICE REED: You are coming to that next?

MR. RANKIN: Yes. We will look into that picture.

JUSTICE JACKSON: Before you go into that, isn't the one thing that is perfectly clear under the Fourteenth Amendment, that Congress is given the power and the duty to enforce the Fourteenth Amendment, by legislation. You don't disagree with that, do you? You believe that, don't you?

MR. RANKIN: No, there is no question but—

JUSTICE JACKSON: And the other thing that is clear is that they have never done, have never enacted an act that deals with this subject.

MR. RANKIN: There is no question but what Congress has the power under section 5 to enforce the Fourteenth Amendment.

JUSTICE JACKSON: And if the Amendment reaches segregation, they have the power to enforce it and set up machinery to make it effective. There is no doubt about that, is there, and it hasn't been done.

Now if our representative institutions have failed—is that the point?

MR. RANKIN: No, because this Court has in our understanding concurrent jurisdiction.

JUSTICE JACKSON: Have you taken it over?

MR. RANKIN: No. You both have a responsibility, and neither one can give that responsibility up to the other in our conception. There is a concurrent responsibility, and the Court has recognized it in numerous cases where it has interpreted and applied the Fourteenth Amendment.

It has not waited for Congress to act under section 5, but it has looked at section 1 and the other sections of the Amendment to see what they meant, and the force of that language that was used at that time in adopting the intention and purpose of the framers as expressed and tried to give a liberal interpretation to carry out the purposes that were pervading in the passing of the Amendment.

JUSTICE JACKSON: I suppose that realistically the reason this case is here was that action couldn't be obtained from Congress. Certainly it would be here much stronger from your point of view if Congress did act, wouldn't it?

MR. RANKIN: That is true, but there are many cases that the Court well recognized I know, upon any reflection, and has in its opinions, that if the Court would delegate back to Congress from time to time the question of deciding what should be done about the rights, the constitutional rights of a party appearing before this Court for relief, the parties would be deprived by that procedure from getting their constitutional rights because of the present membership or approach of Congress to that particular question.

And the whole concept of constitutional law is that those rights that are defined and set out in the Constitution are not to be subject to the political form which changes from time to time, but are to be preserved under the holdings of this Court over many, many years by the orders of this Court granting the relief prayed for.

JUSTICE FRANKFURTER: The thing to be said, or is it to be said fairly, that not only did Congress not exercise the power under section 5 with reference to the States, but in a realm which is its exclusive authority, it enacted legislation to the contrary.

Now I understand the argument that from 1871 to date you do not get that which has contemporaneous significance, but it does indicate, or does it indicate—I ask you that—any understanding on the part of successive Congresses that segregation was not ruled out by the Constitution, not the Fourteenth Amendment. I take that whatever you have to say about the District you will be saying during this hour?

MR. RANKIN: Yes.

JUSTICE FRANKFURTER: The Fourteenth Amendment apart, which does not bind the federal government of course, but whatever is to be drawn out of the Fifth Amendment through the action of Congress for what is now eighty years, has contradicted the assumption that the Fourteenth Amendment as reflected by the due process of the Fifth, bars such action.

MR. RANKIN: Well, we think that the action regarding the District back in 1862 when the Amendment was before the 39th Congress does not give any bearing upon the action in adopting the Fourteenth Amendment.

JUSTICE FRANKFURTER: I understand that. Because after all what precedes, as Justice [Bradley] said in the *Legal Tender Cases*[41] when we got that Amendment and the antecedent—but it does seem to be underlying some implicit belief on all the Congresses from 1871, that such legislation does not contravene the deepest presuppositions of our Constitution, or am I overstating what that means or are you saying that legislation does not mean anything but what it does? It just segregates, that is all.

MR. RANKIN: Well, not exactly. It seems that you have to find a conscious determination by Congress that segregation was permitted under the Fourteenth Amendment.

JUSTICE FRANKFURTER: You think legislation by Congress is like the British Empire, something that is acquired in a fit of absentmindedness? (Laughter)

MR. RANKIN: I couldn't make that charge before this Court, and I wouldn't want to be quoted in that manner. There might be times that that occurred, but I think Congress is well aware that when that does happen, the subject matter does not deserve greater consideration than it has at the moment, and that it is ordinarily pretty well taken care of under the processes.

With regard to the entire question, it seems that there should be another factor that the Court should consider in this matter.

JUSTICE REED: Are you going to discuss later the action of the states?

MR. RANKIN: Yes. I will proceed now to the question of the legislation of the states in regard to this matter.

JUSTICE REED: The issue of the states, the seceding states?

MR. RANKIN: Yes. In the ratification of the Amendment and the readmission of the seceding states, much is assumed in connection with that by the parties. We find that the evidence, the record of history, does not sustain that.

There were no references to the Fourteenth Amendment and its effect, and the history of the times shows why there were not. We must look back to that period and recognize the condition of the entire country, and particularly the South that had just been occupied, was in the process of occupation, the condition of the Negroes who were entirely illiterate but were freedmen, and the problem of what to do about their education, and the many things dealing with them in the situation where they had just been slaves.

We must remember the condition of education throughout the North. It was far different than the progress that had been made up to this day. And that in the South there were very few public schools.

---

[41]Legal Tender Cases, 12 Wall. 457 (1871). The Court upheld the issuance of greenbacks without specie backing during the Civil War and the requirement that they be accepted in repayment of all debts, public and private. A contrary decision in Hepburn v. Griswold, 8 Wall. 603 (1870) was overruled. Justice Joseph P. Bradley (1813–1892) in a concurring opinion examined the practice of states issuing paper bills of credit at the time the Constitution was adopted to show that such power existed in the colonial period.

The public schools were largely for the poor, and other people went to the private schools, and there was a prohibition against the Negro going to any school because it might make him rebellious.

Now when you take all of that into account and consider what happened at that time, it seems to us that it is very revealing, but you can't draw any conclusions from that legislation that there was any conscious understanding that the Fourteenth Amendment provided or permitted segregation in the public schools.

A perfect example is shown in the appendix to our brief on page 352 where we set out the history about South Carolina. There was a state where reconstructionists, scalawags, the radical Republicans, carpetbaggers, and all of the others that have been remarked about here, had control of the convention that ratified this Amendment. And you recall the circumstances. They had to do certain things, three things in order to get back into the Union.

Now arguments were made at great length about the terms of the Constitution for the State of South Carolina, and during those arguments much was said about the schools, and the facts were that the Negroes had taken over the public schools, such as they were, in the important cities at that time in South Carolina, and had them in their possession, to try to teach the Negroes something, because they had to start from scratch.

And during those debates when the question was presented about whether they should have mixed schools or separate schools, nothing was said about the effect of the Fourteenth Amendment, although it was provided in the Constitution that there could be no distinction in the schools based upon race or color.

Now that is in a convention that was under complete control of the Reconstruction forces, and we say from that you just cannot properly say that the history shows that anyone had any conscious understanding at the time those various acts were passed that the Fourteenth Amendment would permit segregation in public schools.

It just wasn't there, because in those debates, as shown in the appendix again, all they would have had to say was "look at the Fourteenth Amendment, it prohibits this very thing."

Instead of that, one of the parties who was in control of the schools actively trying to get education for the Negroes, said, "Maybe the Negroes will attend the same schools as the whites, or the whites will come into the schools of the Negroes now in our possession." Nobody saw fit to say anything about the effect of the Fourteenth Amendment.

Now if you will look back at the history of the schools in the North and also throughout the South, you will see that everybody was involved in the problem of "What are we going to do to educate the Negro? He is a free man, he is a part of our citizenry like any white man. He has no background for education. Many of them are of mature years, as well as the children."

And they were so involved in that problem that the effect of the Fourteenth Amendment and whether it permitted or would allow segregation in the public schools was just not discussed by anyone.

And I don't think you can draw from that any assumption that by those legislative acts when there was not discussion of the problem, that it was intended or understood by anyone that the Fourteenth Amendment would permit, in spite of its language, segregation of the Negro in the public schools.

JUSTICE JACKSON: Mr. Rankin, I would like to ask you this. You have studied this much more than I have had a chance to, and I almost hesitate to ask a question in a case of this kind because people jump to the assumption that if you want information, it is stating a judgment that I have.

How do you account for the decisions of the State of New York, for example, holding the Amendment did not reach this question,[42] when there was a state where there was no problem of numbers, there were few Negroes, the court that last decided this was predominantly a Republican court, predominantly from up-state New York, where the underground railway had plenty of stations, all kinds of things to fight the war, a popular war.

How do you account for judges like that not understanding what this Amendment meant? The very section that promulgated it—it was a northern product, there was no getting away from that.

You studied the history of this a great deal. How do you account for those interpretations?

JUSTICE REED: May I ask this question before you answer that, also the question of the legislatures of the northern states on the Amendment, the same legislatures in some instances passed legislation which recognized segregation, allowed segregation amendments.

MR. RANKIN: Well, first, if I might answer in regard to the courts, apparently there was no detailed study of the history and background of the Fourteenth Amendment in connection with some of the decisions of the cases.

JUSTICE JACKSON: You can't say that of the New York case. It is one of the—

MR. RANKIN: And the Court will find that in later periods there was reliance placed upon *Plessy* against *Ferguson* and some of the earlier cases where the history was not reviewed in such detail, that will explain fully the decisions that the court made without examining the question in detail.

JUSTICE JACKSON: These men had lived with the thing. They didn't have to go to books. They had been through it. They didn't have to go to books any more than we have to read books on what is going on today.

MR. RANKIN: Well, if the Court is looking—

JUSTICE JACKSON: And the Grand Army of the Republic was the strongest force in that community, don't make any mistake about that.

MR. RANKIN: If the Court is looking for someone who knew, who lived through the period, to give it aid in regard to this problem, I think it has to look no further than its own decisions, and going back to the *Slaughter-House Cases* and the Strauder case, Justice Miller comments upon the fact in the *Slaughter-House Cases* that it was within five years of the time when all of this occurred and that

[42]Dallas v. Fosdick, 40 How. Pr. 249 (1896); People ex rel. Dretz v. Easton, 13 Abb. Pr. (N.S.) 159 (1872); People ex rel. King v. Gallagher, 93 N.Y. 438 (1883); People ex rel. Cisco v. School Board, 161 N.Y. 598 (1900).

they had the matter fresh in their minds, and then he reviews the background, the history and the detail and the reasons for the Amendment and what they were trying to reach in the greatest of detail, and we recommended to the Court something superior to anything else that can be found with regard to a fresh appraisal of the basis for the Fourteenth Amendment and the history back of it.

In the Strauder cases we have a later period, but we do have a period not too far removed, and a thorough consideration of what the Fourteenth Amendment means in all of its various reaches.

JUSTICE JACKSON: Then the assumption is that they didn't understand what it was about.

MR. RANKIN: Well, in those days—

JUSTICE JACKSON: That is what it comes to, isn't it?

MR. RANKIN: It was considered that education as such was a state matter, and we had the question of whether schools would be provided as public schools. We also had a good portion of the problem handled by private schools. We had areas where there were mixed separate schools and also where there was no restriction on attendance, and the two races did mix, but there was no provision legally for such mixture.

JUSTICE REED: So the very men that sat on the Plessy-Ferguson case on this Court were thoroughly familiar with all the history in that case.

MR. RANKIN: Well, the Court in that case was not giving any consideration to this particular situation. It was considering the question of segregation in public utilities and railroads.

JUSTICE REED: That is the difference, isn't it?

MR. RANKIN: There is a very material difference in the question of whether or not segregation is to be permitted in public schools furnished by the state itself and the monies of the state, although this Court has recognized that that may be and is a privilege, but that the state has no power to restrict that privilege based upon race in regard to the schools. If it is going to provide education at all, it must provide it equally to the citizens.

It does not have to provide education, and to that extent it is a privilege, but if it provides it at all, it must do it equally to all citizens.

Apparently that was not fully understood, the difference between it being privileged and the later decisions of this Court in regard to the requirement that even such a privilege had to be granted to citizens alike, but we think that question is now decided by this Court that it cannot be contravened at this time.

Regarding the question of the power of the Court, we do not think this is a matter that involves the right to abolish segregation in the public schools. It is a question whether or not the Fourteenth Amendment permits the state to determine that it shall have segregation as an order of the state in the conduct of its public education, and that we think is within the peculiar competency of this Court to determine.

It is a civil right to have education on the same basis as every other citizen.

When Congress deals with these matters, it must deal with them generally, and the courts deal with them specifically.

The courts deal with whether or not a certain litigant before it is entitled to relief, has not been permitted to have the rights he was entitled to by the wording of the Constitution, and this Court has never seen fit to determine that a man has been denied his constitutional rights, and then referred him to Congress to see what type of relief he should be granted from it.

JUSTICE DOUGLAS: The Department of Justice goes no further than to say that first we can decide this case, these cases, and second, we can decide them under what, on the basis of history?

MR. RANKIN: No, Your Honor, no. Our position is that the history helps the Court in showing that some of the conclusions that have been asserted from history are not borne out. The history as related by the *Slaughter-House Cases* and the Strauder case is the history that the Department of Justice found to be correct in its review of the entire matter.

That by reason of that history, it is shown that the pervading purpose of the Fourteenth Amendment was to establish that all men are equal, that they are equal before the law, that they are entitled to equal protection of the law, that no distinction can ever be made upon the basis of race or color, and that therefore this Court, in applying the rules it has laid down in many cases looking to that pervading purpose, can find only one answer to this case, and that is when they stand before the bar of this Court and say that "the reason that we want to segregate black children from white children is because of racism, just because of their color," that the Fourteenth Amendment does not permit that to happen, because if there was anything the Fourteenth Amendment tried to do for this country, it was to make it clear that no discrimination could ever by made, based upon race or color, and that is the position of the Department of Justice in this matter.

JUSTICE FRANKFURTER: That is your third conclusion on page 186 of your brief, isn't it?

MR. RANKIN: Yes. We think that the history is of great help to the Court in regard to the basic question of the rights of the parties, and this Court has the problem of deciding two things: First, whether or not the constitutional rights have been abridged, and we think that is clear. The history shows the pervading purpose.

JUSTICE DOUGLAS: The provision that Justice Frankfurter referred to doesn't say that, in my opinion. I am just inquiring to find out what it says.

You start on page 185, the Government brief reads as follows:

—The Government respectfully suggests to the Court that, if it holds school segregation to be unconstitutional, the public interest would be served by entering decrees in the instant cases providing in substance as follows:
(1) That racial segregation in public schools be decreed by this Court to be a violation of rights secured by the Constitution.

I would think that would be obvious, that if the Court holds segregation would be unconstitutional, that we would—and it was within the judicial competence, it would be within our duty to enter an appropriate decree to that effect. But my question went further than that. It was what are the merits, whether the Department of Justice had taken a position?

MR. RANKIN: Yes. I think Your Honor is correct in that regard, and the way I answered the question was due to the formulation of the question, but in order to answer your question specifically, it is the position of the Department of Justice that segregation in public schools cannot be maintained under the Fourteenth Amendment, and we adhere to the views expressed in the original brief of the Department in that regard. We did limit our brief in our—

JUSTICE DOUGLAS: I just wanted to clear up that confusion in my mind.

MR. RANKIN: Yes.

JUSTICE FRANKFURTER: You say this is the kind of a question where you are responding to the inquiry of the Court as to what the form of the decree should be. The Department has already in its prior brief and in this brief, if I can interpret the entire brief, made its position perfectly clear that it thinks segregation is outlawed by the Fourteenth Amendment, and on pages 186 and 187 you indicate the kind of a decree that should follow such a declaration, is that correct?

MR. RANKIN: That is correct. The problem about the questions that the Court presented that gave us the greatest trouble was the question of relief. Because of the statements of the Court, there are a number of decisions that when a person has had his constitutional rights abridged, that he had a present and personal right to immediate relief.

JUSTICE REED: Are you leaving the third question?

MR. RANKIN: I thought I had dealt with it, but I will be glad to try to answer any further questions.

JUSTICE REED: I did not quite understand what you were saying in regard to that. The third question is on the assumption the answers to question 2 (a) and (b) do not dispose of the issue, is it within the judicial power of the Fourteenth Amendment to abolish segregation. Now that is saying that the argument over history is inconclusive, as I understand it.

MR. RANKIN: That's right.

JUSTICE REED: Assuming that that is inconclusive, then does this Court through its own power have the right—is that the belief of the Government—have the power to declare segregation unconstitutional?

MR. RANKIN: The position of the Government is that the Court does have the power and that it has the duty.

JUSTICE REED: Where do we get that power, and how?

MR. RANKIN: By reason of the power given to it under the Constitution and by act of Congress and the—

JUSTICE REED: So far as the Fourteenth Amendment is concerned by the very words of the Fourteenth Amendment?

MR. RANKIN: Yes, by reason of section 1 which says that these rights shall not be denied by any state, and in the interpretation of that language the Court, in applying it, has the right to find, and according to its decisions will find, that the parties are entitled to this.

JUSTICE REED: Regardless of the view of Congress, regardless of the history of it, which you say is inconclusive, that the wording covers segregation?

MR. RANKIN: I think the best answer to that would be the history in regard to—

JUSTICE REED: Is that what we are trying to determine now?

MR. RANKIN: Yes.

JUSTICE REED: It could very well be. That is what is striking to me, if you lay aside the history, lay aside what has happened, and the intention as expressed in Congress, then we have nothing left except the bare words.

MR. RANKIN: That is correct.

JUSTICE REED: And those you say require the invalidation of all the laws of segregation?

MR. RANKIN: Yes. And the Court has in other cases seen fit to examine the question and not finding any specific language about, for instance, jury trials, has found that the Fourteenth Amendment would not permit any abridgement of those rights by reason of race or color.

And this Court has said many times that it does not have to find that a particular matter or subject was examined by Congress.

JUSTICE JACKSON: We have a statute on juries. Congress passed a statute on juries.

MR. RANKIN: Yes.

JUSTICE JACKSON: So it is clear that Congress acted on that subject.

MR. RANKIN: We don't have any statute, as I recall, about [petitions] or freedom of speech, but this Court has not hesitated to protect the provisions of the Constitution and the litigants before this Court in regard to them, and the history also does show that the framers of this constitutional amendment desired to avoid having it submitted to Congress, and they recognized that they might lose control of the Congress in the future, and they wanted to frame their change deliberately, section 1, in order to make certain that it wouldn't be a question for Congress, because you will recall the history that we relate.

Originally it was to empower Congress, in section 1, to take certain action, and they feared and they expressed the fears that Congress by that might change it and they would lose control and they said maybe they can get a majority, but two-thirds they will never get, and so they provided the specific right in such a form that it was like the provisions of the Bill of Rights. It was a declaration of a right that every citizen could look to and say, "That is mine, equality before the law."

JUSTICE REED: Which clause of the Fourteenth Amendment of the first section is that applicable to, to any person within its jurisdiction providing equal protection of the law?

MR. RANKIN: We think that there are two clauses that are controlling. One is the equal protection of the laws and the other is the depriving of any person of life, liberty or property without due process, both of them. Congress deliberately put the words so that no state could deny them.

JUSTICE REED: And is this a denial of liberty or property, segregation?

MR. RANKIN: Well, I would think it would be a denial of part of liberty rather than property.

JUSTICE REED: It has to be one or the other, or both, doesn't it?

MR. RANKIN: Yes, it could be a combination.
(A recess was taken from 2:00 p.m. to 2:30 p.m. this same day.)

AFTER RECESS

ARGUMENT ON BEHALF OF THE UNITED STATES—Resumed

by MR. RANKIN

MR. RANKIN: May it please the Court, I would like to deal briefly with the question of relief, and try to give to the Court our points on that problem.

THE CHIEF JUSTICE: Which problem is that, you say?

MR. RANKIN: The question of relief.
After the Court determines whether or not rights have been violated in these cases then there is the question of the relief that should be granted.
We do not regard lightly the question of presenting to this Court a policy of delaying at all the relief that should be granted to citizens of this country when constitutional rights are found to have been violated, as we feel that they have been in this case.
However, upon careful study of the entire problem, we do think there are considerations that we can recommend to this Court should be taken into account in the decision of these cases. These cases do not deal only with the particular plaintiffs. The Court knows that they deal with certain classes, in addition to these plaintiffs.
But beyond that, we think it is fair to take into account the fact that the precedents established by the Court in the decision of these cases will necessarily bear upon the educational systems of some seventeen states and the District of Columbia.

There have to be adjustments to take care of the children attending these schools, and to provide them a program of mixed schools that will be adequate; and there will also have to be the problems of the administration and the various financial problems involved. It seems unrealistic not to take into account those factors, and that some time may be involved in providing for them.

We, therefore, suggest that it should be—the burden should be—upon the defendants to present and satisfy the lower court as to the extent of time that is necessary to make such an adjustment in the school system, and that plan should be presented to the Court, not for the purpose of determining at all the wisdom of the plan, but only to determine and satisfy that court that, according to criteria presented and set out by this Court, that the plan satisfies the constitutional requirements of our Constitution and its amendments.

We, therefore, recommend to the Court, although we do not think it is squarely in point, the history of the Court in regard to the American Tobacco case[43] and the possibility that this decree may lay out, at least in a measure, a plan for handling these cases in returning them to the lower courts for final disposition.

We suggest a year for the presentation and consideration of the plan, not because that is an exact standard, but with the idea that it might involve the principle of handling the matter with deliberate speed.

JUSTICE JACKSON: Mr. Rankin, may I ask you a question or two about this remedy you suggest. We have no state before us, have we? We have several school districts.

MR. RANKIN: Yes, that is correct.

JUSTICE JACKSON: I suppose that even if we said that the state statutes or state constitutional provisions authorizing segregation were unconstitutional, local custom would still perpetuate it in most districts of the states that really want it; I assume that would be the case, would it not?

MR. RANKIN: We do not assume that once this Court pronounces what the Constitution means in this area that our people are not going to try to abide by it and be in accord with it as rapidly as they can.

JUSTICE JACKSON: I do not think a court can enter a decree on that assumption, particularly in view of the fact that for seventy-five years the "separate but equal" doctrine has prevailed in the cases that came before us within the recent past, indicating it still had not been complied with in many cases.

The only people we can reach with the judicial decree are the people who are before us in the case.

MR. RANKIN: That is correct.

JUSTICE JACKSON: So that if it is not acquiesced in and embraced, we have to proceed school district by school district, is that right?

[43]United States v. American Tobacco Co. 221 U.S. 106 (1911). The American Tobacco Co. was held to violate the Sherman Act by its monopolization of the tobacco industry. The District Court was given wide power to fashion an appropriate decree.

MR. RANKIN: Well, this Court traditionally handles each case as it comes before it.

JUSTICE JACKSON: Yes. It means that private litigation will result in every school district in order to get effective enforcement, and that is why, I suppose, this "separate but equal" doctrine has never really been enforced, because many disadvantaged people cannot afford these lawsuits. But the judicial remedy means just that, does it not, lawsuit after lawsuit?

MR. RANKIN: Well, it is probably true in every Fourteenth Amendment case that comes before the Court, each litigant has to come and say, "My rights have been infringed, and I have to be provided a remedy."

JUSTICE JACKSON: That is right; that is the nature of judicial process; that is why in some cases it has been necessary to set up something like the SEC to enforce individual rights in security transactions, and the Interstate Commerce Commission.

But what I do not get in your statement here are any criteria that we are to lay down to the lower court in your view to determine what shall be taken into consideration.

Now, you mention the antitrust cases, but we have been fifty years in interpreting the antitrust cases in this Court, laying down the criteria, the standards.

Some districts may have to have bond issues, some may have to submit to a vote; commissioners may resign; no commissioners would take the job—I wouldn't want it, to be caught between these forces.

What criteria are we going to lay down? I am all for having the district courts frame decrees and do all the rest of the work that we can put on them, but what are we going to tell them: "This is something different from antitrust? This is something that hasn't been before?"

What are we going to do to avoid the situation where in some districts everybody is perhaps held in contempt almost immediately because that judge has that disposition, and in some other districts it is twelve years before they get to a hearing? What criteria do you propose?

MR. RANKIN: If I may try to answer some of the questions that Your Honor—

JUSTICE JACKSON: It is all one question: What are the standards?

MR. RANKIN: In the first place, I do not think the country would ever be satisfied with anybody but the Supreme Court saying what the Fourteenth Amendment means; and, secondly—

JUSTICE JACKSON: We would not be, anyway.

MR. RANKIN: No. (Laughter)
Secondly, I think that this Court does not have the duty or the function to try to determine what is a wise educational policy for each one of the various school districts in the country.

JUSTICE JACKSON: I am with you there.

MR. RANKIN: It has the duty and the obligation to say that when the Constitution says that men shall be equal before the law, and the states shall regard them as equal in all of the various things that it does for them, that it cannot take one group of people and say, "You shall be separated just because of your color and from another group," and that is not equality.

JUSTICE JACKSON: That leads you squarely to Mr. Marshall's position that they have the right; children are getting older, they get out of school before they get this right and, therefore, it should be done, and then you say there are some conditions that should postpone that.

Now, what is to be taken, financial conditions, unwillingness of the community to vote funds? What are the conditions that the lower court should consider?

MR. RANKIN: I think that that problem will have to be tried as these matters are constantly before the lower courts and the federal courts in the determination as to whether or not the equities of the particular situation are such that the defendant has established the burden that it is unreasonable under those conditions to require them to act more rapidly than they propose, and those standards are well-established as a part of our judicial process and experience, and in the statements of this Court.

JUSTICE JACKSON: I forsee a generation of litigation if we send it back with no standards, and each case has to come here to determine it standard by standard.

MR. RANKIN: Well, experience has demonstrated that the common law procedure of trying to decide each case as it comes before the court has been very wise in the experience of mankind, and many of the decisions, problems, are handled by the lower courts in the federal system, and never reach this Court for final decision.

JUSTICE FRANKFURTER: Isn't there a difference between the applicable standard—it is one thing to talk about a standard—and another thing, the means by which this standard can be satisfied?

This Court might decree that as between state and state, one state is maintaining a nuisance; but how a nuisance should be abated is a very different question.

It does not bring into play what standards you apply, but what, in fairness to the public interest which determines their decree, should dictate as to the time or the circumstances under which that standard of equality has been caused, assuming that the standard of equality here requires what the Government says it requires.

Certainly the fact that local people do not like the result is not any condition that should influence or in any wise influence the court; but whether you actually have a building in which children can go to school, and what distances there are, and things like that, like questions of abating a nuisance which the local fellow has to determine is or is not an evasion of the requirements, are one of those facts of life that not even a court can overcome.

MR. RANKIN: That is right.

JUSTICE FRANKFURTER: If there is no appropriation by a legislature to build a school, the court cannot raise the taxes, the court cannot raise taxes by a court decree; or if a state makes a redistribution, the court cannot say, "You are indulging in educational gerrymandering."

MR. RANKIN: That is right.

JUSTICE FRANKFURTER: I am not suggesting that I have exhausted the difficulties because we still have them, but I do suggest that the standard is inherent in the very contention made by the Government, namely, that the standard of equality is not satisfied, indeed is violated by a separation based merely on color. Assuming that is so, then I do not see how you can escape some of the things which worry my Brother Jackson, and I know raise some questions.

JUSTICE JACKSON: They do not worry me; they will be worrying our children.

MR. RANKIN: May it please the Court, it is the position of the Government in this case, these cases are peculiarly those that deserve the most wise judgment of the members of this bench in the interests of this country.

We are dealing with a problem of equality before the law for little children. We are busy in the educational process throughout the country in saying to these children that our Constitution means that all men, regardless of race, color or creed, are equal. None are better, none are worse, and to do—

JUSTICE REED: I do not want to disagree with you on that, Mr. Rankin. But the problem we have here is how is that to be implemented if the case should be decided that segregation was unconstitutional? These parties in these several cases have asked us for a decree of court that they be admitted to certain schools. Are they entitled to that in case of segregation?

MR. RANKIN: It is our position that unless it can be shown by the defendants that that cannot be accomplished at once in accordance with the precedents of this Court of granting them their present and personal rights when their constitutional rights are invaded, that they should have them.

JUSTICE REED: Isn't it necessary in every school district at the present time that they have certain facilities, necessary facilities?

MR. RANKIN: That is right.

JUSTICE REED: They will be admitted, I suppose, tomorrow, if they wanted to take them.

MR. RANKIN: We also take the position that it is reasonable for this Court to remand the matter to the lower court and to take into consideration, as equity courts have for generations, the problems that have to be dealt with in any inequities that can be presented, and that the lower court can properly then determine how rapidly a plan can be achieved to come within the criteria established by this Court and the requirements of the Fourteenth Amendment, and that upon consideration of that, with all diligent speed, the lower court can enter a decree accordingly, and we visualize problems, but our courts have many problems, and they deal with those problems, and they weigh the various problems against the rights involved to accomplish the result in the best manner and as rapidly as possible.

JUSTICE REED: Mention one problem, mention just one.

MR. RANKIN: Well, the question is whether or not children should attend tomorrow or the next school term; and I do not see any great problem in that for the federal district court.

JUSTICE JACKSON: What is the criteria though; what considerations would you say would justify postponing it until next term, if he has a present right to enter?

MR. RANKIN: Whether or not it was a deliberate attempt to evade the judgment of this Court of equality or whether or not there are sound reasons that the action should be delayed because of transportation problems, whether or not the building is adequate, all of those matters—

JUSTICE JACKSON: Suppose you have two schools; you have a school that has been used by white pupils, a pretty good school; you have a pretty poor one that has been used by colored children. What are you going to do? How are you going to decide—you either have got to build a new school or you have got to move some white people into the poor school, which would cause a rumpus, or you have got to center them all in the good school. What would the court take into consideration?

MR. RANKIN: Well, time after time the courts have said that they were not going to be bothered by the worries and difficulties of the litigants about meeting the requirements of the Constitution or other principles laid down by this Court; and I think those are the problems that have to be dealt with by the local school districts, and they would have the obligation to bring in a plan to accomplish this in accordance with the order of this Court, as rapidly as could be obtained, and the details of it would not be a problem of the Court unless it found that the plan was unreasonable, that it was a deliberate attempt to evade the order of the Court, or that it was not equitably proper. Those standards—

JUSTICE JACKSON: This is the most definite one, what appears on page 186, being the most definite thing that you have been able to devise?

MR. RANKIN: We explored the possibility of more definite decrees, but experience seems to dictate that the more definite courts are, appellate courts, in trying to describe the activities of lower courts, the more often they are apt to not give them the opportunity to solve the problem in the best manner possible.

We conceived that the position and the duty of this Court is to establish the broad general principles of what could be obtained, what the Fourteenth Amendment meant with regard to equality in the attendance of schools; that there could not be a distinction because of race.

JUSTICE FRANKFURTER: Am I right in assuming, if not in inferring—I do not think I have the right to infer—but in assuming that the Government in its suggestions as to the kind of a decree, is not dealing with these cases on the assumption that what is involved are just these individual children, but you have indicated a while ago that underlying your suggestions lies the assumption that these cases will settle a widespread problem, as indicated by both Mr. Davis and Mr. Moore, involving, whatever it is, the relationship of ten million Negroes in seventeen states, and that it is not a question of putting one child in a school, but how to make a readjustment of an existing system throughout the states where this present practice prevails; is that right?

MR. RANKIN: Yes. We thought—

JUSTICE FRANKFURTER: Rather than looking forward to having endless lawsuits of every individual child in the seventeen states for the indefinite future.

MR. RANKIN: We felt that your question, Your Honor, reached that far and, further, for the Department of Justice of the United States to close its eyes to the effect of the precedent established by this Court, if it should so decide, was not the help that this Court was entitled to receive, and that we should view the extent of the reach that the decision might properly obtain and try to give the help that we could in regard to it.

THE CHIEF JUSTICE: Thank you, Mr. Rankin.
(Oral argument was concluded at 2:50 p.m.)

OLIVER BROWN, MRS. RICHARD LAWTON, MRS. SADIE EMMANUEL, ET AL.,

Appellants

vs.

BOARD OF EDUCATION OF TOPEKA, SHAWNEE COUNTY, KANSAS, ET AL.,

Appellees.

Case No. 1

Washington, D.C.,
Tuesday, December 8, 1953.

The above-entitled cause came on for oral argument at 2:50 p.m.

APPEARANCES:

On behalf of the Appellants:

ROBERT L. CARTER, ESQ.

On behalf of the Appellees:

PAUL E. WILSON, ESQ.

THE CHIEF JUSTICE: No. 1, Oliver Brown, Mrs. Richard Lawton, Mrs. Sadie Emmanuel v. Board of Education of Topeka, et al.

THE CLERK: Counsel are present, sir.

THE CHIEF JUSTICE: Mr. Carter.

ARGUMENT ON BEHALF OF APPELLANTS

by MR. CARTER

MR. CARTER: Mr. Chief Justice, the facts in this case are similar to those involved in the cases preceding.

The appellants are of elementary school age, of Negro origin, and they are required to obtain their elementary school education in segregated elementary schools maintained pursuant to the laws of the State of Kansas, and pursuant to the rules and regulations of the Topeka School Board.

The statute in question, whose constitutionality we are here attacking, is chapter 172 of the Kansas statutes of 1949.

JUSTICE FRANKFURTER: Is your case moot, Mr. Carter?

MR. CARTER: I hoped that I would get a little further into the argument before that question was asked. (Laughter.)

We take the position, Your Honor, that the case is not moot. The Government, the state, that is, takes the same position. We take that position because of the fact that although the plan which I had hoped to get to when I discussed questions four and five—but if you want me to discuss it now, I will—the plan which is presently in operation, and the resolution of the School Board of Topeka under which they have decided that they will eliminate segregation in the elementary schools in Topeka—under this plan, two schools have been desegregated, and the Negro children have been admitted.

However, with respect to the remaining schools, Negro children are still segregated.

The brief which the Topeka Board filed with this Court gives no indication as to how long they feel the plan which they now have in operation will take before the other Negro children will be able to go to an integrated school system.

We feel further that the case is not moot because the statute is still involved, and if the Court were without these problems being settled, we still have—while we have only one appellant here who has been admitted to the school, unsegregated school, pursuant to this plan—our position is that the case is not a moot case, and we have to address ourselves to the questions which the Court asked.

JUSTICE FRANKFURTER: Is Topeka here apart from—I understand the state takes a different view. Is the immediate respondent-appellee here?

MR. CARTER: If Your Honor will remember, last year the Topeka School Board did not appear.

JUSTICE FRANFKFURTER: No.

MR. CARTER: This year they did not appear. So far as I know, they have no intention of appearing, if I am right in that, Mr. Wilson?

JUSTICE FRANKFURTER: They have every intention of giving you what you want, is that it?

MR. CARTER: I beg your pardon?

JUSTICE FRANKFURTER: They merely have the intention of giving you what you want, and not contesting your claim?

MR. CARTER: That is right.

JUSTICE FRANKFURTER: That is what I call a moot case. (Laughter.)

JUSTICE JACKSON: Do I understand that the parties you represent here are now admitted to unsegregated schools?

MR. CARTER: No, sir. One of the appellants has been admitted to a school in the district in which he lives; that school has been opened to Negroes. Just one of the appellants has been admitted.

JUSTICE JACKSON: What about the others?

MR. CARTER: The others are still attending the four segregated schools.

JUSTICE JACKSON: You have clients then who are still subject to the rule of segregation?

MR. CARTER: Yes.

JUSTICE FRANKFURTER: But by the authorized pronouncement of the appellee, they will be admitted just as soon as it is physically or administratively or whatever the adverbs are—Topeka is able to admit them, and they do not contest your position.

MR. CARTER: That is true.

JUSTICE FRANKFURTER: Kansas does contest?

MR. CARTER: That is right.

JUSTICE FRANKFURTER: That is a different story. But Kansas is not a party.

MR. CARTER: Well, Kansas appeared in the court below as a party. It intervened in the court below as a party, specifically for the purpose of defending the constitutionality of the statute.

JUSTICE FRANKFURTER: Yes. But abstractly to defend a statute does not give this Court jurisdiction to pass upon it.

MR. CARTER: Well, frankly, Your Honor, my only feeling on this is that with respect to the plan which is in operation, the appellees have certainly indicated an intention—

JUSTICE FRANKFURTER: And you do not question the good faith?

MR. CARTER: I certainly do not.

But the point that I think that we need to, that we have to have in mind, one, I think, in so far as the plan itself is concerned, I have serious questions about—with respect to the plan; as to whether this is the forum to raise that, I do not know.

Also, I think in so far as the other appellants are concerned, as I indicated, I do not know when they will be free from the imprint of the statutes, and it does not seem to me that at this point in the litigation I can say that the case is moot, when the State of Kansas—

JUSTICE FRANKFURTER: Perhaps I ought to change my inquiry. I do not mean to shut off your argument. Having heard you before, it gives me pleasure to hear you again. But as I understand it, then, the position is that the respondent, the appellee, meets your claim, and you do not question the purpose is to meet it, and the question is whether, as a matter of formality, in fact, the concession of your claim would be appropriately carried out.

So I suggest what you ought to say to us is that we ought to enter a decree sending the case back to the district court to enforce that which the respondent or the appellee concedes. Therefore, it is a question of the terms of the decree, is it not, in your case?

I am sure that you must feel it is a welcome thing if a board of education accedes to your wishes and of its own volition stops—it has a desire not to oppose desegregation, and I am sure that is a welcome thing to you. I am not talking about the general question; I am talking about the specific thing, that the board of education has taken the position, and you just want to be sure that they will carry it out; is that right?

MR. CARTER: That is right. If that is the general view of the Court, I would certainly—

JUSTICE REED: What about the state? As I recall it, the state was admitted as a party.

MR. CARTER: Yes, sir; the state was admitted as a party.

JUSTICE REED: Or merely as a friend of the court.

MR. CARTER: No, they intervened as a party in the court below, defending the constitutionality of the statute under which the segregation was practiced and permitted and was, in fact, practiced in Topeka.
In the original—

JUSTICE REED: And is there authority in the State of Kansas for the Attorney General as intervenor in the litigation in which part of the state is involved or a city in the state or the board of education?

MR. CARTER: No.

JUSTICE REED: Has that been pointed out as to the Attorney General's right to intervene in the case and take charge of the case?

MR. CARTER: Well, that wasn't what occurred.

JUSTICE REED: They did not approach it on that basis?

MR. CARTER: No, sir. I will explain briefly what happened. We went before a statutory court, and we attacked the constitutionality of the statute.
The clerk of the court advised the Attorney General that a state statute was under attack.
The Topeka Board appeared and defended their action and the statute, and the state appeared separately in order to defend the constitutionality of the statute. They are in that position here. They appeared in the original argument, and they reappeared—

JUSTICE FRANKFURTER: They did not appear; we had to bring them in. We had to ask them whether they would let the thing go by default. They did not appear; they were not so anxious. They did not claim that they had a great right, that they had a right to defend here.

MR. CARTER: Well, I think—

JUSTICE FRANKFURTER: Perhaps "cajoled" is a better word.

MR. CARTER: If you are expressing—if that is the view of the Court, Your Honor—

JUSTICE FRANKFURTER: Mr. Carter, nobody knows better than you that I can speak only for one poor lone voice.

MR. CARTER: I certainly have no real desire to proceed with an argument.

JUSTICE FRANKFURTER: But, Mr. Carter, if all the appellants had been admitted—suppose all of them were in the position of this one child—

MR. CARTER: I would have no question about it.

JUSTICE FRANKFURTER: Then the state would not say "We want to be heard," could they?

MR. CARTER: No, sir. I would have no question about it if all the appellants had been admitted; I think that the question of mootness would have been clear. But my problem with respect to it is that some are admitted and some are not.

JUSTICE FRANKFURTER: I understand it then, that it is a question of whether Topeka will carry this out as quickly with these other children as they have with Leah—

MR. CARTER: Leah Carter, and I also have no way of knowing whether this would be so, because the appellees do not appear before the Court, and the state cannot speak for the appellees with respect to this question.

But if it is permissible, I would yield my time to the state, and see what the state has to say about this, and I would answer it, if that is permissible so far as the Court is concerned.

JUSTICE JACKSON: You have the privilege of rebuttal under our rules, if he says anything that you wish to answer.

THE CHIEF JUSTICE: Mr. Wilson, will you please address yourself to the question of whether it is moot or not.

### ARGUMENT ON BEHALF OF THE STATE OF KANSAS

#### by MR. WILSON

MR. WILSON: If it please the Court, it is our position that the case is not moot from our standpoint for several reasons. In the first place, the appellant has pointed out that only one of the group of appellants that counsel represents has been admitted to the integrated public schools of Topeka.

JUSTICE REED: Why is that?

MR. WILSON: The Board of Education—may I preface this remark by pointing out that our statute is a permissive one. The local boards of education are authorized to make the determination on the local level as to whether separate or integrated schools shall be maintained in cities of the first class.

Now, as a matter of policy, and as a matter of policy only, and without reference to this case, the Topeka Board of Education has determined that segregation will be abandoned in the elementary schools of Topeka as soon as practicable. That is the language of their resolution.

Now, we think if they are simply exercising their prerogative under the statute, another city in the State of Kansas, the City of Atchison, has adopted a similar resolution that does not reflect at all on this case.

It was our view that the constitutionality of this statute is still under attack. We were permitted to defend the constitutionality of the statute in the district court.

We were asked to defend it in the Supreme Court a year ago, but we feel that we must, in order to maintain a position consistent with the expressed intent of this Court, answer the brief and the arguments that the appellants have supplied us.

JUSTICE FRANKFURTER: May I trouble you to tell me what are the cities of the first class in Kansas?

MR. WILSON Yes, sir. May I refer you to Appendix D in our brief, the very last page. There are set out in tabular form the nine cities of the first class where segregation is maintained on a complete or partial basis in the elementary schools.

Now, in addition to that, there are three cities, namely, Wichita, Hutchinson, and Pittsburgh, that do not maintain segregated elementary schools.

Two of those cities, as we point out in our brief, have completed a process of integration during the past two years. We feel that—

JUSTICE FRANKFURTER: Is there any litigation pending as to any of the other cities?

MR. WILSON: No, sir.

JUSTICE REED: Why did one of the parties, appellants, disappear from the case?

MR. WILSON: The plan adopted by the Topeka Board of Education was this: You will recall from the record last year and the arguments that the city then maintained within the entire district eighteen geographic areas. In each geographic area there was a school attended by the white students living within the limits of that area.

In addition to the eighteen white schools, there were four Negro schools spaced at wider intervals throughout the city. The first affirmative step taken by the Board of Education in carrying out its policy to abandon segregation as soon as practicable eliminated segregation in two of the geographic areas, namely, Randolph and Southwest.

There were nine Negro students living within the limits of those geographic areas. Consequently, they are admitted to the integrated schools, and one of these appellants is one of those children.

JUSTICE FRANKFURTER: As I understand it, the present situation is that the only litigation that is rife is the one now before the Court?

MR. WILSON: That is correct, if the Court please.

JUSTICE FRANKFURTER: As to which the educational authorities, with an authority not challenged by the state to stop segregated schools, in fact formally and officially announced that they are going to integrate their schools, and have begun the process of integration, is that correct?

MR. WILSON: I should point out that not only is the authority not challenged by the state, the authority is specifically granted by the statute that is here being attacked.

JUSTICE FRANKFURTER: So they are doing what they can do, no matter—

MR. WILSON: They are doing, as a matter of policy, as a matter of legislative policy, may I say, what they can do without reference to this case.

JUSTICE FRANKFURTER: But if they did what it wanted, the state cannot say "You are exceeding your authority," and no case could come here on that ground, could it?

MR. WILSON: Certainly not.

JUSTICE REED: If they were to reverse their position tomorrow, these children who seek admission would have no right to go unless it was unconstitutional?

MR. WILSON: That is right.

JUSTICE FRANKFURTER: Do you think it is an alarming assumption that in 1953 where a state has stopped segregation, and in the next year is going to begin segregation in Topeka, Kansas. Do you think we ought to do business on that assumption?

MR. WILSON: If the Court please, may I distinguish between the State of Kansas and the Board of Education of Topeka, Kansas, which is a separate municipal corporation.

The Board of Education of Topeka, Kansas, has announced its intention to abandon the policy of segregation. I think the Board is acting in complete good faith, and I have no notion that they will reverse that trend.

On the other hand, the State of Kansas is here to defend its statute, and I emphasize, and the Court emphasized, we came a year ago, at the express invitation of the Court, and there are other cities that are concerned, and, therefore, the State had hoped to be heard with respect to the questions that the Court submitted to it on June 8.

If the case is moot, obviously, after five or six hours, argument does reach a point of diminishing returns, and certainly we do not want to discuss a matter that is moot, if the Court deems that to be the case.

JUSTICE JACKSON: Is there anything that would distinguish your case and that would save your statute if the statutes in the other states went down?

MR. WILSON: I think not, Your Honor.

JUSTICE JACKSON: So that your case is governed by what—is there anything that you have to add that Mr. Davis or Judge Moore have not covered, in defense of your statute?

MR. WILSON: In preparing my argument, I examined the same authorities that both the other appellees and the appellants have examined. As a matter of fact, I cite both the same authorities that both the parties, as well as the Attorney General, have examined.

My conclusions, my interpretations, are substantially those that Mr. Davis and Judge Moore have presented to this Court.

MR. MOORE: That is Mr. Moore, I would just like to correct that.

MR. WILSON: I am not sure whether it is proper to apologize under the circumstances or not. (Laughter.)

THE CHIEF JUSTICE: You may proceed, Mr. Wilson.

MR. WILSON: In view of the comments by the Court, I shall proceed somewhat summarily. I shall not make an effort to review in detail the evidence that I base the conclusions that I shall present to the Court.

I think the facts—Mr. Carter started to state the facts in this case. Perhaps, in order to give proper perspective to my argument, some further statement would be proper.

We pointed out that the Board of Education in Topeka is a separate municipal corporation, is the party defendant in the court below; that the State of Kansas, with consent of the court below, intervened for the sole and only purpose of defending the statute that is under attack.

We further pointed out the permissive nature of our statute. It applies to cities of only—only cities of the first class, that is, cities of more than 15,000 population, of which there are twelve in the State of Kansas. It applies only on the elementary school level.

The school systems in the cities that are included in this group are divided generally into elementary, junior high, and senior high school levels. The elementary category includes only the kindergarten and the first six grades of instruction, and it is there only that the statute under attack applies, except in the single case of Kansas City where, under an exception in the law, the practice of segregation is authorized in the high school, in addition to the elementary grades.

Now, I emphasize that it is our position that the action of the Topeka Board of Education, which had been discussed here at some length, does not in any way alter the position or the status of the State of Kansas.

We are here as appellees; we are defending the constitutionality of the statute that is under attack.

The Board of Education of the City of Topeka, as a matter of policy and not—there is nothing in the record to indicate that it is a concession to the appellants in this case, but as a matter of policy—and exercising their power under the statute, the Board of Education has determined to abandon segregation as early as practicable.

JUSTICE BLACK: Do you think this is a case of a controversy between these people and the City of Topeka?

MR. WILSON: Sir?

JUSTICE BLACK: Do you think this is a case of a controversy between these people and the City of Topeka in the present situation? If so, what is it?

MR. WILSON: The appellants have denied the right of the Board of Education of the City of Topeka to maintain separate schools, pursuant to our statute. The City of Topeka has never agreed that it does not have such a right.

JUSTICE BLACK: It has been agreed to desegregate schools.

MR. WILSON: It has agreed as a matter of policy to put them in the schools. Now, there may be a controversy as to the means of accomplishing this stated intention.

The Board of Education has filed a separate brief here in which they point out numerous administrative difficulties that will be encountered, and in brief, they are asking for time, but they do not believe—

JUSTICE BLACK: You could not rest on that, could you?

MR. WILSON: I think we could not.

JUSTICE FRANKFURTER: To follow up Justice Black's question, is there any controversy between these appellants and the State of Kansas, any justiciable controversy?

MR. WILSON: These appellants allege and contend that a statute enacted by the legislature of Kansas is unconstitutional.

JUSTICE FRANKFURTER: Suppose I allege that a statute, an Act of Congress, is unconstitutional; and I have no secular damage of mine that is affected. I think such a profound Act of Congress, passed in this heedless way we have been told about, is unconstitutional. Can I go to court?

MR. WILSON: No, obviously not.

JUSTICE FRANKFURTER: Obviously not.

MR. WILSON: However, when you consider the peculiar circumstances under which the State of Kansas got into this case—

JUSTICE FRANKFURTER: Litigants sometimes get in, and then find themselves out. (Laughter)

MR. WILSON: Unless the Court desires, I do not wish to proceed with argument; that is, I have no intention to burden the already overburdened Court.

JUSTICE FRANKFURTER: That is not my question. There is no suggestion about your not arguing the appropriateness; it is just the question of whether it is one of those cases where you have to say there is no controversy in a judicial sense before the Court.

MR. WILSON: Well, to repeat my earlier statement, I think there still is a controversy because under the authority that the Board of Education presumes to exercise, it does maintain segregation in sixteen of its eighteen geographic areas, and it requires the children living in those areas to go to segregated schools.

THE CHIEF JUSTICE: I consider that a problem; I would like to hear some light on it anyway. I think when both parties to the action feel that there is a controversy, and invited the Attorney General to be here and answer these questions, I, for one, would like to hear the argument.

MR. WILSON: Thank you, sir.

At the outset I should point out—I have pointed out—that we are not here defending a policy, and the determination that has been made is one of policy.

We are here solely for the purpose of defending the right, the constitutional right, we contend, of the State of Kansas and of its own communities to make these determinations as to state and local policy on state and local levels.

We think that regardless of all that has been said, and regardless of the extreme difficulty of these cases, of the fact that they do involve great moral and ethical and humanitarian principles, there are still some very basic considerations, so basic in fact, that I am a little bit embarrassed to mention them to this Court after there has been so much argument.

But, nevertheless, they are so very important that I think I must suggest, in the first place, that this is a union of states that are sovereign, except for only those purposes where they have delegated their sovereignty to the national authority, and I think further to determine the scope of the national authority we must look at the intent and the purpose of the instrument by which the authority was delegated.

I think in these arguments we frequently lose sight of the historic doctrine of separation of powers. We fail to distinguish between the legitimate sphere of judicial activity and the legislative or policy-making function; and if I may presume, it may have been that the Court had these things in mind when it suggested to us last summer that we answer certain questions by way of reargument, for certainly my studies, and apparently the studies of other counsel, have reinforced these basic considerations that this is a federal union; the national Government only possesses power delegated to it, and that the legislative must always be distinguished from the judicial function.

Now, as to the specific intent of the framers of the Fourteenth Amendment, the evidence has been examined in detail and I should not wish to report that which has been said.

I can state generally, and I have stated generally, that we agree with the other appellees. We find the evidence to be persuasive that the Congress which submitted the Fourteenth Amendment did not contemplate that it would affect segregation in the public schools.

It may not be significant that all of the appellees in these cases—that is, all of the states, including the State of Delaware—have reached that conclusion working independently, but we do think it is significant that the Attorney General, in his brief, finds that the legislative history does not conclusively establish that Congress which proposed the Fourteenth Amendment specifically understood that it would abolish racial segregation in the public schools.

Now, we thought the question was rather specific. We thought the Court asked was it specifically understood. We contend it was not. The Attorney General agrees it was not. That should dispose of that question.

I think perhaps in the discussion here there has been too much emphasis on contemporary intent. I want to suggest very briefly that the concept of equality and equal protection was not something that originated with the 39th Congress.

For a long time prior to that the term "equal protection" had had a place in the understanding of the people and in the philosophy of government.

Equal protection, as we study the record, the aims and objectives of the abolitionist societies, equal protection was meant to include those very basic rights, rights for which governments are established, the right to life, to liberty and property, and we think that it is in that sense that the term "equal protection" is used in the Fourteenth Amendment.

We would point out that—we have pointed out in our brief—there is probably no occasion for pointing it out further—that there were specific denials in the Congress that civil rights and equal protection did comprehend the public schools and racial segregation therein.

Mr. Davis quite eloquently in his statement yesterday expressed to the Court the conviction that the thrust of the Fourteenth Amendment was toward the institution of slavery. We think that is the case, and nothing more.

The Fourteenth Amendment was intended to embody the rights that are cataloged in the Civil Rights Act, and they are cataloged rather specifically. They are set out in this language:

> That citizens will have the right in every State and Territory to make and enforce contracts, to sue, to be parties, to give evidence, to inherit, purchase, lease, sell, hold and convey real and personal property, and to the full and equal benefits of all laws and proceedings for the security of person and property as is enjoyed by white citizens.

Now, we think this is the fruition of the whole abolitionist movement and the most complete expression of the consensus of abolitionist aims.

We think that the only purpose of the Fourteenth Amendment was to give constitutional status and dignity to these aims and objectives expressed in the Civil Rights Act of 1866, and in them we find no place for the contention that racial segregation or the absence of racial segregation would be comprehended within their terms.

Turning to the states, we again find the same result, but our colleagues or at least the other appellees in these cases, have discovered—we were unable to find a single instance where it appeared to us that a state, by reason of deference to the Fourteenth Amendment had eliminated segregation from its public school system.

On the other hand, we found that some twenty-four of the states, either at the time of the adoption of the Amendment or within a few years thereafter, did legally sanction separate public schools.

We found that ten states, including my own State of Kansas, that by the same legislature in the same year and, I think perhaps in the same session, legislated with respect to segregated schools and ratified the Fourteenth Amendment.

Now, we think that is positive evidence that the states, of at least a majority of the states, did not contemplate, did not understand, did not comprehend that the Fourteenth Amendment would preclude segregation in the public schools.

Kansas is, perhaps, unique in this case because Kansas is a state with a pronounced abolitionist tradition. The other states, Virginia and South Carolina, were members of the Confederacy; Delaware, we are told by the Attorney General's brief, was sympathetic toward the Confederacy, although it remained in the Union.

On the other hand, Kansas was an abolitionist state. The settlement of Kansas was inspired and financed by the Immigrant Aid Society of Boston.

The first positive political influence in Kansas was the Free Soil Party, an offshoot of the abolitionists of the East.

Certainly, Kansas is not subject to the accusation that can be hurled, perhaps, at the other states that its tradition is rooted in the slave tradition.

But I mentioned a while ago the same legislature, and I might point out that this legislature was composed largely of Union veterans. Our historians tell us that Kansas contributed more troops to the Union armies in proportion to its population than any other state. Almost to a man, the legislature of 1867 was composed of those Union veterans, of men who had offered their lives for the cause of Negro freedom, and that legislature ratified routinely, as a matter of course, the Fourteenth Amendment.

We infer from the Governor's message that ratification was deemed desirable because it was a part of the national Republican program, and the Republicans were in the ascendancy in Kansas. That same legislature, within about six weeks, enacted a statute providing for separate education for children of white and Negro races in cities of the second class.

Prior thereto the statutes had provided for separate education, for optional separate education, in common school districts, that is, in the rural areas.

A little later, a statute had been enacted authorizing separate education in cities of the first class, which then was cities of more than 7,000.

Then you have the gap between the rural areas and the cities of more than 7,000, where segregation was not authorized.

By the action of the legislature of 1867, which ratified the Fourteenth Amendment, the picture was completed in Kansas. Segregation was then authorized on all levels.

Now, I point this out because it seems to me if we can infer any intention from our own legislative act, we must infer that the legislature recognized that within the State of Kansas there were areas where, by reason of lack of mutual understanding between the races, it would be impossible to provide equality of opportunity, assured by the Fourteenth Amendment in integrated schools.

Therefore, as a special benevolence, as a special device whereby equality to be assured in the Fourteenth Amendment could be complied with, the legislature of Kansas made it possible to establish separate schools in those areas.

Now, again that is only my inference. However, my adversaries infer also.

Now, to pass quickly to the other questions that are submitted, I think I have emphasized our position. We find that the Congress nor the state legislatures intended or comprehended or understood that segregation would be precluded by the Fourteenth Amendment.

The next question, of course, concerns the contemporary understanding of future intent, and again, we answer both questions in the negative.

We cannot understand, we cannot conceive, of how a Congress or how state legislatures, in ratifying an amendment, could contemplate that in the future the limitations that they imposed upon that amendment might be enlarged by any agency or any branch of the federal government.

The limitations were fixed by the intent that preceded and existed at the time of the adoption of the Amendment. We think those limitations were present in the minds of the Congress that submitted, and the states that ratified, the Amendment.

We do not believe that any member of Congress intended that the basic relationship between the states and the federal government should be altered by the Amendment. We do not think that they contemplated they were providing a means for amending the Constitution and giving it a meaning that it did not presently have.

We must admit that if we are impelled in this instance, and looking only at the intent, to choose between the judicial and the congressional power, the choice would necessarily be the congressional. My understanding is not, perhaps, mature on this phase of the question but, as I read these debates, there was throughout an emphasis on congressional power.

Undoubtedly the abolitionists had contemplated that Reconstruction might be affected by congressional action. The fact was that the Congress trusted neither the executive nor the judiciary to any extent, and so looking at the intent of the Congress and the intent of the legislatures, we must concede that should the issue before this Court be one within the Amendment, within the federal competence, that it was then the intent of the framers that the Congress and not the courts should supply the re-definition or the impetus by which the particular subject is comprehended within the terms of the Amendment.

With respect to the judicial power, our argument is limited pretty much by our conslusions with respect to the intended future effect of the Amendment. Certainly, in commenting upon the subject of judicial power, we are confronted with a considerable amount of difficulty.

Obviously, the judiciary has the power to determine the limitations of its power. Furthermore, any decision that this Court makes in this case will become the law of the case. In that sense, certainly the entire matter is within the judicial power.

However, when we consider the historic exercise of the judicial power, we are constrained to recognize a great deal of limitation and restraint upon that exercise.

There is a case in which Justice Holmes has commented on the judicial power and, particularly, on the judicial power to legislate, in these words. He says that:

I recognize, without hesitation, that judges do and must legislate, but they do so only interstitially. They are confined from molar to molecular motion.[44]

We think that, at least that is the key or that is the essence of our understanding of the judicial power, to move from molar, from mass, to molecular motions, to refine the broad and general concepts that are included in the statute and in the constitutional provisions that are presented to the Court.

[44]Southern Pacific Co. v. Jensen, 244 U.S. 205, 222 (1917).

Certainly, it is not moving from the molar to the molecular to move outside the original intention, and with a sweeping gesture to bring into the Constitution a meaning, a view that was not entertained by the framers and those that gave the Amendment its effect.

That disposes of our general arguments with respect to the first three questions.

The latter two questions of the Court deal with the remedy to be applied which, in this case, may be moot.

The State of Kansas, of course, is not concerned with the immediate problems that will confront the Board of Education in complying with whatever decree or order this Court may enter. We have taken the position that this Court need not concern itself in the Kansas case with a decree in detail, but should simply, in the event of reversal, remand the case to the district court with directions to form an appropriate decree.

There are a number of considerations which must be taken into the purview of that court, but they are not for consideration here.

We appreciate very much the opportunity to be heard somewhat summarily in the circumstances of a moot case, and we hope that in considering this matter, this matter of constitutional right, the Court will not be unmindful of the constitutional right of the State of Kansas to set up and maintain its own school system and to initiate and maintain there the policies that are most beneficial to all of its people.

Thank you.

THE CHIEF JUSTICE: Thank you, Mr. Wilson
Mr. Carter?

### REBUTTAL ARGUMENT ON BEHALF OF APPELLANTS

#### by MR. CARTER

MR. CARTER: I would like to say this, Your Honors, I do still have doubt with regard to the question of mootness in this case.

However, as Mr. Justice Frankfurter pointed out, I would think it would not be likely that, having made this step, that Topeka would reverse itself, not in 1953.

I am also confident that the State of Kansas, if this Court declares the statute unconstitutional with respect to South Carolina and Virginia, that the State of Kansas would abide by that decision.

I might add that, in so far as I am concerned with respect to the arguments that have been urged by the Attorney General, since I do not feel he has opened any new avenues, it seems to me that in order to conserve the Court's time, I will not speak.

THE CHIEF JUSTICE: Thank you
(Whereupon, at 3:40 p.m., the argument was concluded.)

SPOTTSWOOD THOMAS BOLLING, ET AL.,
Petitioners,

vs.

C. MELVIN SHARPE, ET AL.,
Respondents

Case No. 8

Washington, D.C.
Tuesday, December 8, 1953.

The above-entitled cause came on for oral argument at 3:40 o'clock p.m.

APPEARANCES:

On behalf of the Petitioners:
GEORGE E. C. HAYES, ESQ., and JAMES M. NABRIT, JR., ESQ.

On behalf of the Respondents:
MILTON D. KORMAN, ESQ.

THE CHIEF JUSTICE: Number 8, Spottswood Thomas Bolling, et al., vs. C. Melvin Sharpe, et al.

THE CLERK: Counsel are present.

THE CHIEF JUSTICE: Mr. Hayes.

ARGUMENT ON BEHALF OF PETITIONERS

by MR. HAYES

MR. HAYES: May it please the Court, the case of *Bolling* v. *Sharpe* comes before this Court by reason of certiorari granted to the United States Court of Appeals for the District of Columbia, and the problems that we face are problems which are different from those which the Court has been hearing for the past two days; different, because of the fact of our federal relationship; different because of the fact that there are no state-federal conflicts; different because of the fact that in our case there is no question of equality of facilities.

It is probably proper that I should begin by saying something by way of background in order to acquaint the Court again of the problems, as we see it, that we face in this jurisdiction.

The minor petitioners in this case presented themselves to the authorities at the Sousa Junior High School, seeking admittance as students.

They were denied admittance, and expressly denied it for no other reason than because of their race and color.

They followed that up by going through each of the echelons with respect to the administrative authorities in the District of Columbia, and at each of the levels they were denied admission for no reason other than the question of their race or color.

This suit was then filed asking by way of injunction that they be admitted to these schools and that the Board of Education should not use as a means of excluding them the race and the color of these petitioners.

I have heard comment within the last few days about the concern that the seventeen states may have as to what this decision of this Court might be so as to know what they should do.

I respectfully submit to this Court that not seventeen states but the world at large is waiting to see what this Court will do as far as the District of Columbia is concerned, to determine as to whether or not the Government of the United States will say to these petitioners if they are not entitled to the same liberties as other persons, that they are denied it simply because of their race and color.

When my colleague, Mr. Nabrit and I—I should, perhaps, interrupt myself to say to the Court that it is our purpose to open our argument, divide fifty minutes of time between us, and then allow ten minutes for the closing—so I shall address myself to the feature with respect to the history as far as the statutes are concerned, and Mr. Nabrit will address himself to the things which seem pertinent to us by way of the inquiries made by this Court.

Turning then to this question of the history of the statutes, there has been a great deal said in the last few days about the statutes here in the District of Columbia having to do with the Fourteenth Amendment.

I do not need to say to this Court that we are not concerned primarily with the Fourteenth Amendment. We rely rather upon the Fifth Amendment because of the fact that that applies to our jurisdiction.

But a great deal has been said, as I have indicated to you, and as you will realize, with respect to the question of statutes here in the District of Columbia.

We find ourselves in the company of the distinguished Attorney General of the United States and his associates when we take the position that, as far as the statutes are concerned, as we conceive it, they are permissive and voluntary; they are not compulsory; and we believe that this Court can find, by looking at these statutes, or must find, either one of two things: either that they are permissive and voluntary, and that by so much, if they find that the Board of Education has construed them as being compulsory and has used them as a means of segregating Negroes, that then by its mandate this Court will say that the Board of Education is wrong in any such interpretation; or, if on the other hand, it were to be determined that they are, as a matter of fact, compulsory, that then this Court must, of necessity, say that they are unconstitutional if, as a matter of fact, they use as their yardstick nothing other than race or color.

It may, therefore, become important for us to look and see what was the atmosphere under which the statutes came upon the books.

JUSTICE REED: Whether they are permissive or mandatory, would they not be unconstitutional in either case?

MR. HAYES: If they are permissive and voluntary, the answer would be that they would be unconstitutional; but that the constitutional question—and this is where we think the issue is as we presently see it—that until the issue is raised, that then, of course, the question of constitutionality has not been passed upon, and it is our position that we are presently at the place where that issue, as far as this Court is concerned and as far as the statutes are concerned, is for the first time being raised and, therefore, Your Honor, to specifically answer your question, Justice Reed, the answer is, yes, we think it is unconstitutional in both instances, unconstitutional whether permissive and voluntary, unconstitutional whether by actual compulsion, and we think it is the present time when this Court should so determine.

JUSTICE FRANKFURTER: Mr. Hayes, may I ask what you mean by permissive? I am not talking about any legal implications, but am I wrong in thinking that Congress year after year passed appropriations for the maintenance of a system of segregation?

MR. HAYES: Your Honor is entirely correct with respect to the fact that they have passed appropriations.

It is our position that the fact that Congress, having found a certain situation and having acted upon it, and having supplementarily issued or allowed appropriations, that that inaction on the part of Congress or that acceptance of a situation on the part of Congress does not still avoid the fact of the unconstitutionality which we ask Your Honors to determine.

With respect to the history of these statutes I say there may be, therefore, some appropriate comment.

Slavery was abolished in the District of Columbia in April of 1862. In May of 1862, within approximately one month after the time of the abolition of slavery, two of these statutes that are presently on the books and under which the Board of Education is acting, were promulgated. Those are referred to, and they use the expression of "initiating education."

That was not an actual fact, because they amounted to nothing other than appropriations, appropriations to an existing situation.

What had happened had been that public education, as such, even among the whites at that time, had taken on no actual status.

As I have heard the suggestion within the last couple of days, I think it was from the Attorney General's office, from the Assistant there, that, as a matter of fact, from their point of view, what they were at that time attempting to do was to reach a situation which they found. It was not a question of them actually appropriating, of them actually initiating. It was the fact of their appropriating.

They found a situation existing. Public education was for the poor people. The persons who had money sent their children to private schools, and public education had no such concept as is the present concept with respect to public education; and so, what happened was that Congress, finding that situation and desiring, as it unquestionably did desire, that something should be done for the Negro, just emancipated from slavery, attempted to do something in the way of appropriating moneys.

It is to be noticed that what they did or attempted first to do was to tax Negroes for their properties, with an idea of Negro education in the public sense.

As I say, at that time it was not with respect to any public education but rather in the nature of appropriations. There were no public schools so far as Negroes were concerned.

It was not until 1864 that there was anything that purported to be a public school, as far as Negroes were concerned, and that was then in a private church, showing again that public education did not have the connotations that it presently has.

What they did was to attempt to give this Negro some opportunity for an education, and so it became a part of what the background was, that there was this appropriation for Negro education, and the things that happened subsequently, significantly, too, were that in 1864 there was a requirement of compulsory education.

Now, that takes on, too, a different aspect because as far as we are concerned, we find ourselves in a question of compulsory segregation, either announced, created or sanctioned by the federal government.

In 1864, I say then, they required compulsory education, and also provided that there might be the right of selection of persons who were white persons to send their children to a white school of their choice, and for Negroes to send Negro children to colored schools of their choice, the language at each time, if Your Honors please, being permissive in its character.

At no place in any of these enactments do we find language which specifically says, as they do in instances when the legislature feels disposed to say, "that this shall be a compulsory proposition as far as Negroes and whites are concerned," and the language in these statutes does not lend itself to anything other than permission rather than compulsion.

The enactments that came from that time forward, if Your Honors please—the question has been referred to of three lots which were to be given for the use of Negroes; another act which required that the money should be turned over to the Board of Education for Negro students because of the fact that moneys had been allocated and had not been properly applied.

Further along, the question of legislation having to do with assistant superintendents of the schools—there was that legislation—or with respect to the question of Boards of Examiners, all simply addressing themselves to a situation begun back in 1862, and which had been, shall I say, winked at and carried forward from that time forward, but not legislated upon, not made compulsory.

With respect to that situation, there has been, perhaps, some addressing of itself to the question as far as our courts are concerned, and I say our courts now, meaning the courts of the District of Columbia.

But I would call Your Honors' attention to the fact, in the first instance, the case of *Wall* v. *Oyster* that there was no question there raised of a character which is being raised before this Court.

What happened then was that the person who was the petitioner desired not to be placed in a colored school. She had taken a position that she would rather be held a part of the white race and, therefore, was asking not to be put into a colored school.

As Your Honors will see, that begins with the premise that the segregation in and of itself was all right; that all that the person wanted to do was to be put into a school which they believed would not put them among the Negroes, and so we say to you in that case there was no issue of the character that is here being raised.

My attention is called to the fact that as far as an interpretation of the statute was concerned—and this has significance which I want to bring to Your Honors' attention—that back in 1869, and I am reverting now—that back in 1869 there was an issue that was raised as to whether a colored child who had been given a permit to go to a white school should be allowed to go to that school, and that question was posed to the Office of the Corporation Counsel of the District of Columbia, who appears for the respondents in this case, and the Corporation Counsel at that time, in 1869, took the position that there was nothing in the statute that avoided this child being admitted to the white school, and the record seems to indicate that the child was admitted to this school, continued to go there until they finished the colored school.

We call Your Honors' attention to that not that we think it in any sense changes the situation, but rather to show the indecision that was a part of the picture, rather to show that even there then at the time of the early promulgation of the statute, there was the interpretation by the substantial office of the Government that it permitted of going into the white school and that that being the allowed circumstance, it was accepted as such, and no issue was raised further with respect to that.

JUSTICE FRANKFURTER: Mr. Hayes, in those days roughly what was the proportion of the colored population to the total population, just as a rough guess? Don't bother if you—

MR. HAYES: I would not like to give Your Honor an inaccurate statement. We did have calculations, and I think that somewhere—

JUSTICE FRANKFURTER: Don't bother.

MR. HAYES: Mr. Nabrit suggests there were in the District some 11,000 Negroes at that time. I do not know the proportion that there were, I mean, that held to the total population, but there were some 11,000 Negroes, and at that time, as I have indicated to Your Honors, the education which they were getting was that of the benign gentlemen who were the philanthropists, and that type of thing rather than any question of public education.

There was also at that time, as a part of the population situation which Your Honor has just asked me, after the time that slavery was abolished in the District, there was a great influx of freedmen into this area because of that circumstance, naturally because of that circumstance—there was this great influx.

I was addressing myself to the question of litigation in some sense that had come up. This litigation came again in the case of *Carr* v. *Corning,* and in that case—well, there were two cases, *Carr* v. *Corning* and *Browne* v. *Magdeburger,* and the two cases were combined because of the fact that inherent in them was the same proposition.

The *Browne* v. *Magdeburger* case—this proposition the question as to whether or not there was a violation of the constitutional right of a student because of the fact of being required to go into a school where there was the alleged inequality; that they were required to go where there was a double shift of students, so far as they were concerned, and the same proposition was raised in *Carr* v. *Corning,* but there was the additional proposition in the *Carr* v. *Corning* case, which we have raised in this case, and that was as to whether or not segregation as such, whether or not segregation per se, was unconstitutional.

That is the position which we are taking with respect to these cases, that segregation per se is unconstitutional, and that without regard to physical facilities, without regard to the question of curriculum, and that if, as a matter of fact, there is a designation that one must go to a particular school for no other reason than because of race or color, that that is a violation of the constitutional right, and as this Court has said, wherever the issue is raised with respect to color, then it is upon the Government to show that the reason for it—that there is a reason that is a justifiable reason. I shall address myself to that in a moment or two, if I have the time.

But with respect to this *Carr* v. *Corning* case, we take the position that as far as the *Carr* v. *Corning* case was concerned, it simply was decided incorrectly; that our Court of Appeals was simply wrong in its decision.

We call attention to the fact that there was in that case a dissenting opinion by Mr. Judge [Henry W.] Edgerton,[45] which we commend to this Court as being more nearly what the law should be with respect to that case.

In that case, Judge Edgerton went on to say that it was an improper concept to be able to have education based solely upon race or color.

Judge Edgerton in that case says, "Appellees say that Congress requires them to maintain segregation"—reading from page 48—page 48, Mr. Korman, in our original brief—"the President's Committee concluded that congressional legislation 'assumes the fact of segregation but nowhere makes it mandatory.' I think the question irrelevant, since legislation cannot affect appellant's constitutional rights."

That is the position which we urge upon this Court, that it cannot be affected—that the constitutional rights of these people cannot be affected by legislation of any character, and Mr. Judge Edgerton in that case was saying the thing which we say to this Court, that in his opinion there was not any such showing as made the Board of Education take such a step, but that from his point of view it was irrelevant as to whether they did or not, because if it purported to affect the constitutional rights of these persons, that then there was no alternative but that the Court should declare it to be unconstitutional.

I have heard the question asked today as to under what heading it should come. This Court has told us under what heading it should come. It should come under the heading of liberty because this Court in *Meyer* v. *Nebraska* said it was a violation of the liberty of the person, which is the language of the Fifth Amendment upon which we stand, to deny to him their constitutional right, and that constitutional right was then an educational right, just as has been indicated to Your Honors before.

May I say this final word: that we believe that this Court has already determined this proposition in the *Farrington* v. *Tokushige* case where, with respect to the Hawaiian legislation, this Court struck down legislation saying that it was a violation of the person's constitutional right, talking about education, and referred to *Meyer* v. *Nebraska, Bartels* v. *Iowa, Pierce* v. *Sisters,* saying, "Yes, admittedly, they come under the Fourteenth Amendment, but, as far as the Fifth Amendment is concerned, the same thing is to be adopted," and so we say to this Court that under whatever angle the situation is looked at in the District of Col-

---

[45]Henry White Edgerton (1888–     ). United States Circuit Judge for the District of Columbia Court of Appeals, 1938–     ; Chief Judge, 1955–1958.

umbia, from whatever aspect we take it, that this Court, as we conceive it, cannot say to a waiting world that we sanction segregation in the District of Columbia for no other reason than because of the fact that the skin of the person is dark. That, this Court has said, is suspect; that, you have said, is void; that, you have said, should not be sanctioned; that, we believe, must be your decision.

THE CHIEF JUSTICE: Mr. Nabrit.

ARGUMENT ON BEHALF OF PETITIONERS

by MR. NABRIT

MR. NABRIT: If the Court please, we have for the past two days been engaged continuously in a concentrated and thorough attempt to recapture the spirit and mood of a significant period in the history of our country.

The danger in this, as I see it, is that in a worthy attempt to project ourselves into the remote scenes of the 1860's and '70's, that we shall lack either the normal apperceptions of men of that day which, though inarticulate, nevertheless were a part of their own concept of day-to-day events, or we shall miss the motivations of legislators, though known then by all, though not set forth in specificity by any, which agitated both men and events eighty-eight years ago.

At best, I fear that we shall recapture only the overtones of these historical settings, the outlines of the broad sweep of events, but I hope at least we shall have grasped the general delineation of the primary purpose and objectives.

Men do not always set forth explicitly the motives which cause them to act as they do nor do congressmen always explain in detail either the objectives which they seek in proposed legislation or the reasons why they support or fail to support a particular bill.

In this posture of these cases then it seems to us that we need to be reminded of two facts of great importance and significance, as we consider the District of Columbia case.

First, none of this exhaustive discussion of history, however illuminating it may be, can conceal the blunt fact that under a system of legalized segregation millions of American Negroes live in this land of opportunity, equality and democracy as second-class citizens, suffering all types of civil disabilities imposed upon them in every aspect of their daily lives solely because of their race and color.

Today we deal only with one significant aspect of it, segregation in public school education.

In the second place, in this posture of the cases, we should single out the District of Columbia for different treatment, not alone because the District of Columbia brings this case under the Fifth Amendment, but because this is the federal government dealing with federal citizens. Here is no question of the delicate relationship of state and federal government. Here we are dealing with the capital of the free world.

In this framework we submit to the Court that the question before the Court is not merely the technical question of the construction of school statutes or the propriety or the reasonableness of the action of the respondents complained of here, but it is also the basic inquiry as to whether under our Constitution the federal government is authorized to classify Negroes in the District of Columbia as untouchables for the purpose of educating them for living in a democracy.

We say to the Court that this is not in line either with the principles of the Constitution of the United States, our ideals of democracy, nor with the decisions of this Court, nor with the executive orders of the President of the United States, nor with the orders of the Commissioners of the District of Columbia; and that so far as we have been able to find, with the exception of these school statutes, the training school in the District of Columbia and one or two other instances of that ilk, that there is in the District of Columbia no authority, no official, no body of responsible persons who takes the position that racial distinction should be imposed upon Negroes because of color, except for the respondents complained of here, and we say that these respondents do this in defiance of the decisions of this Court, the executive orders of the President of the United States, the policy of the District of Columbia Commissioners, and in that framework they violate federal policy, and that inconsistent position should lead this Court to deny these respondents the power which they claim to possess.

JUSTICE FRANKFURTER: Have the Commissioners of the District expressed themselves on this subject?

MR. NABRIT: They have expressed themselves, Mr. Justice Frankfurter, as not having authority over the school board and, therefore, it is one of the phases of the life in the District of Columbia to which the thrust of their power does not reach.

JUSTICE FRANKFURTER: Is the legislation of Congress clear that the school board is autonomous as to this question?

MR. NABRIT: I would like to—I will answer that, but I would like to answer it, instead of a yes or no—

JUSTICE FRANKFURTER: You do whatever you want to; you give that before you get through.

MR. NABRIT: Yes.

I want to answer that right now, Justice Frankfurter, because it is a peculiar situation.

In the District of Columbia the school board is not appointed by the President of the United States, it is not appointed by the District Commissioners, it is not chosen by the voteless inhabitants of the District of Columbia. Rather it is appointed by the District Court of the District of Columbia, and, as we understand the situation in the District of Columbia, we do not know to whom they are responsible. (Laughter) That is the status of the school board in the District of Columbia.

JUSTICE FRANKFURTER: They are appointed for a term?

MR. NABRIT: Of three years, and then they are either not reappointed or they are reappointed by the District Court of the District of Columbia.

JUSTICE FRANKFURTER: By the District Court you mean the whole bench of judges of the District, the United States District Court?

MR. NABRIT: Yes, sir; the United States District Court, a very unusual situation. (Laughter).

JUSTICE FRANKFURTER: Does the District Court define their powers or does the Code of the District of Columbia define their powers?

MR. NABRIT: Their Code—you know, under our setup in that area we have some adminstrative functions in the courts.

JUSTICE FRANKFURTER: Does the Code say anything about this problem, the segregation of the grade schools?

MR. NABRIT: No, sir.

JUSTICE FRANKFURTER: This is just a pronouncement by the board?

MR. NABRIT: That is right .

JUSTICE FRANKFURTER: And the board has pronounced—

MR. NABRIT: The board has pronounced it, although I notice—and this is something that the Court may reprimand me for, but I noted—in the brief and in the papers that counsel for the respondent is not certain as to what the positions of all his respondents are on this matter.(Laughter).
They are sued individually, you know.

JUSTICE FRANKFURTER: All you have to do is to read his brief; I do not know for whom he speaks.

MR. NABRIT: I neither, Mr. Justice Frankfurter.

JUSTICE FRANKFURTER: I take it he will tell us before we get through. (Laughter.)

MR. NABRIT: Yes, I hope so.
So, in this posture of the cases, we would like to say to the Court—and I say this primarily, if this is proper, so that the Chief Justice might have this because I said it to the Court—but I want it understood that our position is that, number one, the statutes governing the schools in the District of Columbia, which were passed immediately prior to and during the Civil War, without any thought of whether segregation was good or bad, when schools in the United States, public schools themselves, were at issue as to whether people ought not to educate their children privately or not—they were only thirty years old at that time—in the District of Columbia they were only six years old—and here were these Negroes; there were these three systems of schools, public schools for whites, Negroes excluded, a private school for Negroes, and a private school for whites—system of schools, these are all systems—Congress looked at these schools for Negroes getting no support, and authorized support for them from taxes from the Negroes themselves; that is the first bill. Obviously that did not do much good.

They then authorized taxes from all of the persons in the District to be used for that purpose, and in this four-year period, ending in the middle of the Civil War, all of the basic statutes governing the schools in the District of Columbia were enacted.

Under that circumstance and in that case, it is inconceivable that Congress would do anything but make a provision for people who had no schooling, no question of separate or anything else. It was just providing for schools that were found there.

Now, our position is that the Court should construe those statutes as voluntary, meaning by that what the congressman said in talking about them, and I do not cite him for history, but I cite him for the point, for his saying the point that I want to say on this point, that he said Negroes could go to the schools. That is all I need.

That is voluntary. If that be true, until somebody complains in this Court about the exertion of the power of government to compel him to go to one of these schools, there is nothing unlawful about that situation.

Therefore, we do not have a history of lawless action by people in the District of Columbia.

Now if the Court takes that view, it can dispose of the District of Columbia case simply by saying the statutes do not authorize compulsory segregation of races in the District of Columbia in the public schools, and your action complained of here is unlawful and violates the due process clause.

We don't have to go into any constitutional question. We just find they don't have the authority.

Now I suggest that this Court has always done that when it was faced with the statute which it had not interpreted, and one interpretation would be to a constitutional result, and the other interpretation would lead to a non-consititutional result.

And since we suggest to you that if these statutes compel it, they would violate our federal policy, they would violate the due process clause of the Fifth Amendment, the liberty aspect of it, it would violate section 41 and 43 of Title 8 of the Civil Rights Act, that under these circumstances the Court should construe these as merely voluntary statutes, and that in the event the Court doesn't agree, it has still to deal with the question of whether they are not in the nature of bills of attainder. So we suggest as our line of argument that the Court say there is no authority for the actions complained of. It is out of line with the District of Columbia. Now the counsel for the respondents—

JUSTICE REED: On whose part was the complaint?

MR. NABRIT: On the part of the pupils and the parents. Here are two systems of education. Everybody has been going in there without any complaint for sixty or seventy years.

JUSTICE FRANKFURTER: Who has kept these children out of this?

MR. NABRIT: Before this?

JUSTICE FRANKFURTER: Now.

MR. NABRIT: Oh, these respondents, these people—we have got them named. We have them all pointed out.

JUSTICE FRANKFURTER: Do they make a justification for that?

MR. NABRIT: They do.

JUSTICE FRANKFURTER: What do they say?

MR. NABRIT: On the grounds of race and color and that "we are compelled by these statutes."

JUSTICE FRANKFURTER: Do they say the statutes compel them or the statutes authorize them?

MR. NABRIT: Oh, no. They say they are compelled to do it. They don't make any technical differential between authority and compel. They say they are compelled by these statutes to do it.

JUSTICE FRANKFURTER: Suppose we say the statutes do not compel them and then they say it is a matter of discretion, "We ourselves think it is a matter of discretion"?

MR. NABRIT: Well, all we would do—

JUSTICE FRANKFURTER: Start a new suit?

MR. NABRIT: I was just going to tell you, we would file suit that day. (Laughter.)

JUSTICE FRANKFURTER: I am merely suggesting it is multiplying litigation instead of subtracting it.

MR. NABRIT: Well, at least we are going along with the line that the Court follows of restraining itself from engaging in decisions of constitutional questions when it may resolve the problem by a step less than that.

One other thing the Court may do, and I like the Schneiderman[46] case because the Court did something there that I think we don't use enough.

JUSTICE FRANKFURTER: You are for opinions that you like, is that it?

MR. NABRIT: That's right. I like this Schneiderman opinion, Mr. Frankfurter, because in that case the Congress passed, you will recall, an attachment statute in 1906. An alien was naturalized in 1927. About 1919, I believe, Mr. Justice Holmes enunciated that clear and present danger doctrine.

In '42 when this Court passed on that statute for the first time, they read into that statute the intent which Mr. Holmes first discovered—I won't say discovered—announced, twenty years almost after the statute was passed.

Now why can't the Court in this case read into these statutes an intent on the part of Congress not to segregate Negroes by compulsion following the Schneiderman case?

[46]Schneiderman v. United States, 320 U.S. 118 (1943). The government sought unsuccessfully to denaturalize the defendant (represented in the Supreme Court by Wendell Willkie) for failing to disclose that he was a Communist in 1927 when he secured his citizenship papers. The Court found that the defendant could have believed in the Constitution in 1927 despite his Communist associations.

JUSTICE FRANKFURTER: That is easier than worrying about what they debated in '66.

MR. NABRIT: Precisely. That is precisely our position.

Now I would say, I want to say—I want to save ten minutes, but I want to say one thing on this matter of due process, because it seems to me the Court has had a remarkable record in dealing with the exertions of power by the federal government on its citizens where it was faced solely on race or color, and if I am correct, the only instances where the Court has permitted that to be done since Dred Scott has been in the case where war power was involved, and implied power essential to effectuate the war power. With great reservations the Court has permitted the federal government to make racial distinction.

Now I think that that establishes the fundamental principles upon which our case rests, and that it is in line with the policy of this Court, and we would there urge the Court under these considerations to hold that the respondents are without power in the District of Columbia to discriminate or segregate the Negro pupils solely on the basis of race and color.

THE CHIEF JUSTICE: Mr. Korman?

### ARGUMENT ON BEHALF OF RESPONDENTS

#### by MR. KORMAN

MR. KORMAN: Mr. Chief Justice, may it please the Court, at the outset I should like to state the position of the corporation counsel of the District of Columbia in this matter. I stand before the Court to defend acts of Congress which we believe to be lawful and constitutional. I stand before the Court to assert that this is not the forum wherein laws should be attacked because change is wanted. I stand before the Court, as we stood before the Court on May 1 of this year, to defend legislation which we think is valid legislation and constitutional legislation. I refer to the Thompson Restaurant case.[47]

At that time, we found statutes enacted in 1872 and 1873 which required service to all well-behaved persons in any restaurant, hotel, or other place of assembly in the District of Columbia, irrespective of race and color.

For seventy-five or eighty years no one had attempted to enforce those laws. They were believed to be dead. They were called to our attention; we looked into the history of them; we studied the statutes and acts of legislatures thereafter. We studied the Constitution of the United States and the decisions of this Court, and we came to the conclusion that those statutes were valid, even though lying dormant for all those years, and that they were constitutional, and we came here to defend them.

Now, we say to the Court that there are statutes enacted by the Congress of the United States which provide for separation of races in the schools; that they have not lain dormant for seventy-five or eighty years, but they have been repeatedly legislated upon by the Congress of the United States. It appears that they are still valid, that it is still the policy of the Congress to maintain separate schools for

[47]See note 40, *supra*.

the races in the District of Columbia, and we are here to defend the validity and the constitutionality of those laws.

JUSTICE FRANKFURTER: When you say "we," am I to infer that means the Board of Education of the District of Columbia?

MR. KORMAN: You are, sir. I speak for the Board of Education of the District of Columbia, although I admit very frankly in our brief that I have not talked to the individual members so far as their position on the sociological issue is concerned.

JUSTICE FRANKFURTER: I do not know what that means.

MR. KORMAN: It means this: (Laughter) From public statements that I have seen in the press, it appears that at least some members of the Board of Education are strongly convinced at this time that the time has come for a change in the system; that the time has come to integrate the schools of the District.

Indeed, I concede that there is a strong movement in the District of Columbia from a number of sources to strike down segregation in all fields. The President of the United States has made the pronouncement that he expects to use all the power of his office to accomplish that end. The Commissioners of the District of Columbia have made a pronouncement that they intend to try to implement the statement of the President, and they have, in fact, taken action in that direction.

I say that there are many people in the District of Columbia who feel that way.

By the same token, statements have come to me from a number of sources that there are others who think otherwise; indeed, I am constrained to believe that some members of the Board of Education believe otherwise.

But as we see it, that issue, which is the one I called the sociological issue, is not the one involved here.

JUSTICE FRANKFURTER: But my question is to elicit, not by anything other than what I read in your own brief, that this is a strictly legal position which you take as an officer of the Court. I supposed the corporation counsel must represent appellants or respondents before the Court.

MR. KORMAN: That is right.

JUSTICE FRANKFURTER: And it becomes relevant to know whether the Board of Education of the District maintains and has instructed the corporation counsel to maintain the position which you are putting and which you now plead before the Court.

MR. KORMAN: Yes, Your Honor.

JUSTICE FRANKFURTER: Then you do speak for the Board of Education?

MR. KORMAN: Yes, I do.

JUSTICE FRANKFURTER: All right.

MR. KORMAN:  I speak for the Board of Education in that the position we take here today is the same position that we took here one year ago, and slightly more than a year ago, when we filed the original brief, and we have not changed our position on that. We advised the Board of Education what the law is; they do not tell us what the law is.

JUSTICE FRANKFURTER:  No, but clients do not have to pursue their rights under the law. They may take a position in advance of the law, and lawyers do not maintain positions. They merely maintain their clients' positions.

MR. KORMAN:  May I say this to the Court: that the Board, while it is sued individually, is sued individually because it is not an entity, as a matter of law.

The petition in this case asserts, and it is a fact, that the Board of Education itself denied these petitioners entry into the school that they claim they have a right to enter into.

JUSTICE FRANKFURTER:  I do not want to take needless time. It is a simple question. You tell the Court that you are here, as other counsel are here, under instructions appropriately given by their clients, and, of course, I will accept your word for it.

MR. KORMAN:  At the time this case was first filed, the corporation counsel was asked by the Board of Education to defend it in the  district court. We were definitely apprised of the position of the Board of Education.

The case arose in 1950. Since that time there has been a decided change in the personnel of the Board of Education. There are some eight of the nine members who have been replaced. Only one, Mr. Sharpe, still remains of the original defendants in the district court.

There has been no notification to us that the new Board—the Board as now constituted, and which denied to these petitioners the entry into the school which they claimed the right to enter, has changed its position in that regard.

We have seen some statements in the press by some members of the Board which have been alluded to in the briefs.

JUSTICE FRANKFURTER:  I do not care about that, and the reason why I think it is important is—I hope this is not improper for stating my own individual responsibility—to the extent that problems of this sort are settled outside a court of law, to that extent, in my opinion, the public good is advanced; and if, by any chance, settlements are made in various jurisdictions through the power of those who have power to settle it, I call it all to the good, without the need of litigation and adjudication and controversy.

Therefore, I raised the question. If you will give me assurance that you are here by the same right by which the State of South Carolina is represented by its counsel, and the State of Virginia, and the Commonwealth of Virginia by its, of course, I repeat, I will accept your word.

MR. KORMAN:  We are here on that condition; yes, sir.

JUSTICE FRANKFURTER:  Very well.

JUSTICE BLACK: May I ask you, I do not quite understand you, because you stated—when was it, a year ago that you said the Board had changed? Will you let us know in the morning, when the case comes up, whether the Board wants you to defend this case. It has raised some question in my mind, and I think—

MR. KORMAN: I do not know whether I can or not, Your Honor.

The Board is composed of nine members; I do not know whether it is possible to get them together tonight or not.

JUSTICE JACKSON: Isn't the corporation counsel by law made the representative of the Board?

MR. KORMAN: That is right.

JUSTICE JACKSON: I think that settles it. You may have a row with your own clients, but that is not our business.

JUSTICE FRANKFURTER: The question is, your client at the moment—

MR. KORMAN: My client is the Board of Education.

JUSTICE FRANKFURTER: Yes, but they do not know it, apparently.

MR. KORMAN: There are a number of other respondents, who are the superintendents of schools, and some of the assistant superintendents of schools, and the principal of the Sousa Junior High School.

They are all respondents in this case, and we were directed to represent them by order of the Commissioners of the District of Columbia specifically because there were other respondents or defendants in the case, as originally filed than the actual members of the Board of Education, and in those instances we get an order from the Commissioners of the District of Columbia to represent the parties. We have such an order.

(Whereupon, at 4:30 p.m., the Court arose.)

(Oral argument was resumed at 12:07 p.m. December 9, 1953.)

THE CHIEF JUSTICE: No. 8, Spottswood Thomas Bolling, et al, v. C. Melvin Sharpe, et al.

THE CLERK: Counsel are present.

THe CHIEF JUSTICE: Mr. Korman.

### ARGUMENT ON BEHALF OF RESPONDENTS, resumed

#### by MR. KORMAN

MR. KORMAN: May it please the Court, when the Court rose on yesterday, we were having some discussion concerning the right of corporation counsel to appear here as counsel for the respondents. On yesterday I made certain statements to the Court. I should now like to document those statements to some extent.

Section 1301 of the Code of Law for the District of Columbia provides that the corporation counsel "shall be under the direction of the Commissioners and shall have charge of the conduct of all law business of said District among other things."

And it provides further that "he shall perform such other professional duties as may be required of him by the Commissioners."

I said to you on yesterday that the last action of the respondent members of the Board of Education as set forth in the complaint filed in this case below was to deny to the petitioners admission to the Sousa Junior High School which is set apart for the instruction of white students. You will find that statement on page 7 of the record.

I have in my hand a copy of a letter sent by Mrs. Elise Z. Watkins, the secretary of the Board of Education, to Mr. George E. C. Hayes, with copies to Mr. Merican and Mr. Nabrit under date of November 6, 1950. I shall not read the whole letter.

It acknowledges receipt of a letter from Mr. Hayes, Mr. Merican and Mr. Nabrit under date of October 31, 1950, requesting admission of the petitioners to the Sousa Junior High School. The letter continues:

> In reply to your letter, you are advised that the following motion was passed by the Board: 'That the Board feels it has fulfilled its obligation as far as it is capable and that the request to send children to the Sousa Junior High School be denied.'

On the bottom of that is this certification by Mrs. Watkins:

> I hereby certify that this letter embodies the action of the Board of Education taken at its meeting on November 1, 1950. I am familiar with all of the actions of the Board of Education since that time, and the Board of Education has taken no action to rescind or change in any manner its action on November 1, 1950, as reflected in this letter to Mr. George E. C. Hayes, dated Nobember 6, 1950.

I said to you on yesterday that the Board of Education—

THE CHIEF JUSTICE: What was the date of that certificate, sir?

MR. KORMAN: That certificate is dated—it is not dated, Your Honor. It was signed yesterday evening. It is a copy of a letter written November 6 with an up-to-date certification as of today.

THE CHIEF JUSTICE: Thank you.

MR. KORMAN: I said to you on yesterday that the Board of Education had requested the Commissioners to direct the corporation counsel to represent them in this action, and that the Commissioners had so directed us.

I have in my hand a copy of a letter prepared by Mrs. Watkins, the secretary of the Board of Education, and I have also in my hand a duplicate original of that letter dated November 13, 1950, which came to the office of the corporation counsel.

The letter is to the Board of Commissioners of the District of Columbia, and without burdening the Court to read the whole thing, it asks the Commissioners to direct the corporation counsel to represent all of the respondents in two civil actions, one of which is *Bolling* v. *Sharpe*. Mrs. Watkins has put this certification as of last evening on a copy of that letter:

> I hereby certify that the foregoing is a true and correct copy of the letter sent by me to the Board of Commissioners, D.C., under date of November 13, 1950, at the direction of the President of the Board of Education.
>
> This is the usual letter which is sent to the Board of Commissioners whenever the Board of Education or its members or its public school officers have been sued, and is in accordance with Chapter 1, Article 9, section 1 of the rules of the Board of Education which provide when legal advice or service as counsel is desired by the Board of Education upon matters relating to the administration of school affairs, application shall be made to the Commissioners, D. C., for the services of the corporation counsel of the District of Columbia.

Mrs. Watkins continues:

> I am familiar with all of the actions of the Board of Education since the date of the letter of which the foregoing is a copy, and certify that the Board of Education has taken no action to rescind the request of the president of the Board of Education that the board members, the superintendent of schools, and the public school officers be represented by the corporation counsel of the District of Columbia in regard to the civil actions enumerated in the foregoing letter.

In the case of *Denney* v. *Callahan* in 294 Federal 992, it was held that the rules of the Board of Education have the force and effect of law.

I have in my hand a certification by Mr. G. M. Thornett, secretary for the Board of Commissioners, D. C., prepared last evening certifying—I shall read it:

> I hereby certify that the following is a true and exact excerpt from the minutes of the meeting of the Board of Commissioners of the District of Columbia on November 14, 1950.

I shall not read the whole order, but I say to the Court that it contains a direction to represent the various members of the Board of Education and the various school officers named as respondents in this case denominated *Spottswood Thomas Bolling, et al* v. *C. Melvin Sharpe, et al*. There has been no withdrawal of any of that, and I should be very glad if the Court desires to file these copies with the clerk of this Court, with sufficient copies for each member of the Court, if required.

I may say to you further that on last evening Mr. West, the corporation counsel, Mr. Gray, the assistant corporation counsel, and I held what might be called a four-way telephone conversation with Mr. Sharpe, the president of the Board of Education, and we were assured by him that we have the right to stand before you and say that we represent the members of the Board of Education in this controversy.

This morning Mr. Sharpe telephoned me about ten thirty to say that of his own volition he had contacted all the members of the Board of Education and that he could say to me that, in his own words, 100 per cent they say that I have the right to stand before you to represent them in this controversy; that they want decided the question of the constitutionality and the validity of the acts of Congress under which the dual school system in the District of Columbia is being maintained.

JUSTICE BLACK: May I ask you then this question? The reason I asked you the question yesterday was not that I doubted your right as corporation counsel to defend them if they wanted the case defended. You say they want the constitutionality decided.

MR. KORMAN: And the validity of these acts.

JUSTICE BLACK: I understand that. The thing that disturbed me, more from what had been said, I gathered the impression there is the implication that perhaps the majority of the board were going to change the rules; and, if so, I did not think that the Court should be called upon to decide the constitutionality of the rules.

MR. KORMAN: May I say this, Mr. Justice Black. I do not understand that there is a majority of the board that has such a feeling. I am not sure. It may be that that is the case.

JUSTICE BLACK: That was the cause of my interest in the question I asked you. That was the point in my mind.

MR. KORMAN: But I may say to you further, sir, that our position as legal advisers to the board is that they have not the right to make any change in the system, because we believe firmly, and I hope to establish to you in argument today, that the acts of Congress require the maintenance of separate schools for white and colored children in the District of Columbia, and that those acts of Congress are constitutional.

I may say to you further that that has been passed on indirectly by this Court in the case of *Plessy* v. *Ferguson* in 1896, directly by the United States Court of Appeals for the District of Columbia in 1910 in the case of *Wall* v. *Oyster,* and directly and specifically in the cases of *Carr* v. *Corning* and *Browne* v. *Magdeburger* in 1950 by the United States Court of Appeals for the District of Columbia Circuit, holding in so many words that the acts of Congress required the maintenance of separate schools for white and colored children, and that those acts of Congress are constitutional.

It does not lie in my mouth to say to the members of the Board of Education that they have a right to fly in the face of such decisions and I say to you that they could not make any change as we understand the law, and I think as they understand the law, however much any of them might want the law to be otherwise.

JUSTICE BLACK: Of course, that would be a different lawsuit. I don't suppose that the corporation counsel would have a right to defend the board or require them to appear as defendants if a majority of them decided that they wanted to change the rule.

Now I can understand mandamus might be filed againt them or something of that kind.

MR. KORMAN: I would think that under those circumstances, sir—I don't know whether we would be called on to represent them or not, but if we were, I would feel constrained to go before the Court and confess error, because we believe the law is otherwise.

As I said to the Court on yesterday, we stand here to maintain the validity of these acts of Congress, just as we stood before this Court in May and asked this Court to sustain the validity of other legislative enactments in the Thompson Restaurant case. That in the one case segregation is inveighed against and that in the other it is required, is to us a legal immateriality.

We say that Congress has a right and that the legislature which enacted the other laws had the right to pass such laws, and they are in effect in the District of Columbia.

I should like to touch on the question of the kind of decree which might be entered by the Court in the event of unconstitutionality. I take this up at this point because I believe that the Court will not reach that point, but I think that in respect of the Court's wishes, I should say something about it, because the question was asked.

JUSTICE DOUGLAS: Are you going to reach the legal questions, whether the District of Columbia statutes—

MR. KORMAN: I expect to cover that further.

JUSTICE DOUGLAS: —are mandatory or are merely permissive?

MR. KORMAN: Yes, I expect to reach that. We have suggested in our brief on reargument that the Court should not enter any detailed decree.

On page 17 of our brief we merely make this suggestion:

> The soundest suggestion that counsel for respondents can make to the Court concerning the nature of the order, if unconstitutionality is to be decreed, is that the Court make recognition of the necessity for proper preparation and changes which appear essential to perfect integration in all jurisdictions and remand the cases to the respective District Courts with instructions for such courts to prepare decrees directing the immediate commencement of such preparation, with periodic investigation by the District Courts of the progress thereof, with direction that, in accordance with the principle of unconstitutionality of separation of races in schools, integration be commenced at the earliest possible date, and that complete integration be accomplished by a definite future date, not to exceed in any jurisdiction more than a maximum period of time.

And we do not suggest any maximum period of time.

JUSTICE JACKSON: If you can't, how are we going to? How are we going to be better informed on that than you?

MR. KORMAN: I don't know that you can be, Your Honor, and I don't know that I can help, and I don't know that any counsel here can help the Court, for the reason that it appears in the District of Columbia and in many of these States legislation may be necessary, as has been suggested by members of the Court.

Some officers may move slower than others, some may resign, not want to serve at all, and so forth. Those are contingencies which I frankly don't know how the Court can deal with.

Perhaps it might be better—and I know that my friends on the other side will disagree with this—that no positive future date be set, but that the matter be left to the District Courts, because I don't think that anyone can now determine what those lengths of time will be. Certainly I can't predict what time may be required to get Congress to act on something.

THE CHIEF JUSTICE: Mr. Korman, is there any legal question involved in remanding this to the District Court of the District of Columbia, in view of the fact that the District Court itself appoints the members of the Board of Education who are the appellees in this case?

MR. KORMAN: I don't think so, sir. I may say, sir, that there have been many cases that have come before that court involving the Board of Education since the organic act of 1906, when they got the authority to appoint members of the Board of Education, and the record will show that they have dealt quite firmly and severely with the members of the board when necessary.

I don't think there is any tie between the members of the bench and the members of the board so that it would be at all embarrassing in any way for them to take positive and firm action if necessary, even in opposition to wishes of some of the members of the board. I don't anticipate that that would ever come up.

Indeed, my thought is that the matter would be worked out quite amicably. I am inclined to believe that the Board of Education, if there should be a mandate from this Court that segregation is unconstitutional, would take immediate steps to try to plan and work out the desegregation of the schools of the District of Columbia as quickly as possible.

I have made some suggestions in the brief concerning things that I believe are necessary to be done before the actual reshuffling of children takes place. I don't believe that my opponents agree with me.

Indeed, I am not at all sure that all of the members of the Board of Education, from some public statements I have seen in the press, agree with some of the things that I have said, but I assure the Court that I did not pluck them out of the air.

I consulted with the chief executive of the Board of Education, the Superintendent of Schools at some length. I consulted with representatives of the United States Government, in the United States Department of Education. I consulted with others, and I have read on the subject, and I am firmly of the belief that some preparation and indoctrination of the teachers to handle integration is a prime prerequisite.

My friends on the other side take me to task for this, and they say that these things are not necessary, but yet there is a strange situation developed. In their reply brief on page 17 and on page 16, they have an indication that the American Friends Service Committee has conducted courses of instruction for some 120 enrollees in four classes or seminars extending from last March until November of this year.

It is not shown whether the 120 enrollees were thirty who enrolled four times in each of the four seminars. There are, however, 3,500 to 3,600 teachers in the public school system. I should like to call the Court's attention to the fact that in the appendix to the brief which we have filed on reargument, there is a letter from the Superintendent of Schools of the District of Columbia which shows that instructional courses have been provided for recreation workers, so that they will be properly indoctrinated in the handling of integration in recreation areas, and we find that those courses were put on on a voluntary basis, and at the expense of these organizations:

The National Conference of Christians and Jews, the Jewish Community Council of Greater Washington, the American Friends Service Committee, the Washington Interracial Workshop, the Washington Federation of Churches, the Catholic Interracial Council, the Washington Urban League, and the Unitarian Fellowship for Social Justice.

Now strangely enough in this yellow-backed brief which was filed as a friend of the Court last year, before this case was argued, we find these organizations among others that are advocating the striking down of segregation in the District Court:

The Catholic Interracial Council, the Commission on Community Life of the Washington Federation of Churches, the Friends Committee on National Legislation, the Jewish Community Council of Washington, the Unitarian Fellowship for Social Justice, the Washington Interracial Workshop, the Washington Urban League.

And so we see that the organizations that are urging this Court to strike down segregation are conducting courses to instruct teachers and workers in the proper way to handle integration, and if that is not an acknowledgment that it is necessary, then I don't know what is.

May I say one thing further. The complaint in this case asks for a declaratory judgment that the acts of Congress under which separate schools are conducted in the District of Columbia are unconstitutional. It would seem to me that a decree by this Court that segregation is unconstitutional would require the lower court to enter such declaratory judgment, and that would indeed cover the whole situation in the District of Columbia, and not just this handful of students who have brought this suit, and so I don't think we have the problem that was suggested by Mr. Justice Jackson, that the decree would only go to the immediate petitions.

JUSTICE JACKSON: You have all of your authorities here?

MR. KORMAN: Sir?

JUSTICE JACKSON: All of your authorities are in this litigation, aren't they?

MR. KORMAN: Yes.

JUSTICE BLACK: The petition asks that we enter a declaratory judgment, or the Court does, stating that the defendants are without right, construing the statutes having to do with public education, as requiring the board to do this. That is the first question that has to be decided, isn't it?

MR. KORMAN: I think so, sir.

JUSTICE BLACK: And I would assume that it should be construed in a way possible so that we don't reach a constitutional question.

MR. KORMAN: That has been the policy of this Court, but by the same token it has been the policy of this Court as expressed in the Butler[48] case, every presumption is to be indulged in favor of faithful compliance by Congress with the mandates of the fundamental law.

Courts are reluctant to judge any statute in contravention of them, but under the frame of our government, no other place is provided where the citizen may be heard to urge that law fails to conform to the limit set upon the use of a granted power.

When such a contention comes here, we naturally require a showing that by no reasonable possibility can the challenged legislation fall within the wide range of discretion permitted to the Congress.

Now I realize that that is not completely apposite, because it does not go to the constitutionality but to construction, which is a different thing, but I believe I can demonstrate to you that these acts of Congress do require the maintenance of separate schools.

JUSTICE BLACK: Has it been construed by the local District Court or the local Court of Appeals—

MR. KORMAN: Yes, sir.

JUSTICE BLACK: —in this respect?

MR. KORMAN: In this respect. They have been twice so construed, in the case of *Wall* v. *Oyster* in 1910, and in the combined cases which were consolidated for argument and consolidated opinion, *Carr* v. *Corning* and *Browne* v. *Magdeburger,* decided in 1950.

JUSTICE FRANKFURTER: Did Judge Prettyman[49] in the Carr case explicitly deal with this problem? He sustained the segregation and he sustained the constitutionality, but was it an issue in that case, whether the segregation was to be sustained, because that was the system which the board enforced, or that segregation was sustained because the statutes compelled the court to enforce them?

MR. KORMAN: The question was raised in that case, and Judge Prettyman—

JUSTICE FRANKFURTER: Did he discuss that problem, Mr. Korman? That is what I want to know.

MR. KORMAN: He reviewed all of the statutes, and then he said—

JUSTICE FRANKFURTER: And said segregation is constitutional?

---

[48]United States v. Butler, 297 U.S. 1 (1936). The Agricultural Adjustment Act, one of the more important New Deal enactments, was declared unconstitutional.

[49]Judge E. Barrett Prettyman (1891–     ). United States Circuit Judge for the District of Columbia Court of Appeals, 1945–     ; Chief Judge, 1958–1960.

MR. KORMAN: No. He said this. It is set forth more fully in the brief we filed last year. I have this quote in my notes. After citing the various statutes, he said:

> These various enactments by Congress cannot be read with any meaning except that the schools for white and colored children were then intended to be separate.

That was his conclusion, and I think I can demonstrate that to you by reviewing the statutes, which I should like to do.

JUSTICE FRANKFURTER: I am not questioning that, but as I remember his opinion and as I remember Judge Edgerton's dissent, they did not clinch, if I may use a vulgarism, on that question.

MR. KORMAN: I am quite in agreement with you that Judge Prettyman and Judge Edgerton did not clinch on that question.

JUSTICE FRANKFURTER: That is all I am trying to find out, the scope of the decision on that question.

MR. KORMAN: But Judge Clark[50] clinched pretty well on that.

JUSTICE FRANKFURTER: In that case?

MR. KORMAN: Yes.

JUSTICE FRANKFURTER: Was there an opinion by Judge Clark?

MR. KORMAN: No. He joined Judge Prettyman in the majority.

JUSTICE FRANKFURTER: How can a concurring judge go beyond what he concurs with, unless he says so? I don't understand that.

MR. KORMAN: Well, my understanding—

JUSTICE FRANKFURTER: He may have done so from the bench, but so far as my reading goes, which is all I have in these matters, I did not see that that issue was in contest between the judge who wrote the majority opinion and the judge who wrote the dissent.

MR. KORMAN: I don't think it was in contest between those two, no.

JUSTICE FRANKFURTER: All right, that is all there is in the books. I have no private edition of their opinion.

MR. KORMAN: Well, sir, Judge Clark joined with Judge Prettyman—

JUSTICE FRANKFURTER: But he could not join more than what Judge Prettyman wrote.

---

[50]Judge Bennett Champ Clark (1890–1954). United States Democratic senator from Missouri, 1933–1945; United States Circuit Judge for the District of Columbia Court of Appeals, 1945–1954.

MR. KORMAN: No, but he joined that much, and Judge Prettyman wrote—

JUSTICE FRANKFURTER: So I read Judge Prettyman's opinion—

MR. KORMAN: And I think it bears out my opinion.

JUSTICE FRANKFURTER: Very well.

MR. KORMAN: May I then proceed to a review of these enactments? I think it should be said to the Court that in 1862 Congress passed an Act on April 16 by which the slaves in the District of Columbia were freed, and slavery was abolished.

At that time there was in the District of Columbia two cities and a county, all of which were ruled by Congress. There was the City of Washington and the City of Georgetown, and the county which was ruled, governed, by a levy court, and the legislation for all of them was by Congress. About a month later, on May 20, Congress provided for schools for the county. Up to that time there had been no schools at all in the county.

There had been for some years public schools in the cities for white children, but not for colored children.

In the Act of May 20 setting up the colored schools, setting up the schools in the county, there was a law enacted, some thirty-six sections, and in one of those sections, section 35, as I recall, they provided schools, separate schools, equal schools, for the colored children. May I refer to the Act itself and read you some of the—

JUSTICE DOUGLAS: What act is this?

MR. KORMAN: This is the Act of May 20, 1862.

JUSTICE DOUGLAS: That was the first one?

MR. KORMAN: Yes, sir. That was the one which set up schools in the county for white and colored children.

JUSTICE DOUGLAS: Is this in your brief?

MR. KORMAN: No, this is in the petitioners' brief on page 23. It is set out in extenso, and we did not set it out again.

And be it further enacted, that the said levy court may in its discretion, and if it shall be deemed by said court best for the interest and welfare of the colored people residing in said county, levy an annual tax of one-eight of one per cent on all the taxable property in said county outside the limits of the cities of Washington and Georgetown, owned by persons of color, for the purpose of initiating a system of education of colored children in said county.

Discussions on this indicate that there were not many colored people in the county.

—levy an annual tax of one-eighth of one per cent on all the taxable property in said county outside the limits of the cities of Washington and Georgetown, owned by

persons of color, for the purpose of initiating a system of education of colored children in said county, which tax shall be collected in the same manner as the tax named
in section 13 of this Act. And it shall be the duty of the trustees elected under section
9 to provide suitable and convenient rooms for holding schools for colored children,
to employ teachers therefor, and to appropriate the proceeds of said tax to the payment of teachers' wages, rent of school rooms, fuel and other necessary expenses
pertaining to said schools, to exercise a general supervision over them, to establish
proper discipline, and to endeavor to promote a full, equal and useful instruction of
the colored children in said county.

I think I might skip down to the last sentence at the bottom of that page:

And said trustees are authorized to receive any donations or contributions that may
be made for the benefit of said schools by persons disposed to aid in the elevation of
the colored population in the District of Columbia.

And so you see that here is Congress setting up a system of schools in the
County of Washington for white children, and in one section of the same Act, setting up separate schools for colored children, and saying that they shall be equal in
all respects. It seems to me that that is the beginning of the "separate but equal"
doctrine.

Now, then, on the next day, May 21, 1862, the Congress set up schools for
colored children in the cities, the cities of Washington and Georgetown, and
therein they provided a tax of 10 per cent on the property of colored persons for
the maintenance of these colored schools.

Now unusually enough—and I have to burden the Court with reading—but
that is an Act of four sections.

My friends yesterday spoke about the striking down of the Black Codes, and
here we see in one Act the establishment by the Congress in the District of Columbia, of separate schools for Negro children and the striking down of the Black
Codes, all in one Act:

Be it enacted by the Senate and House of Representatives of the United States of
America in Congress assembled, that from and after the passage of this Act it shall
be the duty of the municipal authorities of the cities of Washington and Georgetown,
in the District of Columbia, to set apart 10 per centum of the amount received from
taxes levied on the real and personal property in said cities owned by persons of
color; which sum received for taxes, as aforesaid, shall be appropriated for the purpose of initiating a system of primary schools, for the education of colored children
residing in said cities.

This is section 2:

And be it further enacted, That the boards of trustees of public schools in said cities
shall have sole control of the fund arising from the tax aforesaid, as well as from
contributions by persons disposed to aid in the education of the colored race, or from
any other source, which shall be kept as a fund distinct from the general school fund;
and it is made their duty to provide suitable rooms and teachers for such a number of
schools as, in their opinion

—not classes but such number of schools as in their opinion—

will best accommodate the colored children in the various portions of said cities.
Section 3. And be it further enacted, that the board of trustees aforesaid shall pos-

sess all the powers, exercise the same functions, have the same supervision over
the schools provided for in this Act as are now exercised by them over the public
schools now existing in said cities by virtue of the laws and ordinances of the Corporation thereof.

Obviously they mean the setting up of separate schools for the Negroes.
Now, section 4, and this strikes down the Black Codes in the same Act:

And be it further enacted, That all persons of color in the District of Columbia, or
in the corporate limits of the cities of Washington and Georgetown, shall be subject
and amenable to the same laws and ordinances to which free white persons are or
may be subject or amenable; that they shall be tried for any offenses against the laws
in the same manner as free white persons are or may be tried for the same offenses;
and that upon being legally convicted of any crime or offense against any law or
ordinance, such persons of color shall be liable to the same penalty or punishment,
and no other, as would be imposed or inflicted upon free white persons for the same
crime or offense; and all acts or parts of acts inconsistent with the provisions of this
Act are hereby repealed.

So it seems to me that thereby is a positive demonstration that Congress
wanted to do something for these newly freed slaves, but at the same time while
giving them these rights of the white man, the right to be tried in the same courts,
the right to be subject only to the same punishments and so on, all of these things
in the same Act, and sets up for him separate schools.

JUSTICE REED: What act is that?

MR. KORMAN: That is the Act of May 21, 1862, 12 Stat. 394, page 407.

JUSTICE REED: Is that in here?

MR. KORMAN: The citation is in there but the full text is not in my brief.

JUSTICE DOUGLAS: It is 12 what?

MR. KORMAN: 12 Stat. 407.

Now, then, that was on May 21. On July 11, in the same year, Congress
established a board of trustees for colored schools. You see, these schools had
been set up under the existing board of trustees which handled the white schools,
and they established a separate board of trustees for the colored schools, and they
transferred the authority from the board of trustees of the schools as set forth in
the Act of May 21 to the new board of trustees for colored schools, and in that
connection may I read to the Court something that was said by Senator Grimes[51]
on the Senate Floor at the time that was being considered:

I am instructed by the Committee on the District of Columbia to whom was
referred the bill of House of Representatives No. 543, relating to schools for the
education of colored children in the cities of Washington and Georgetown in the
District of Columbia, to report it back and recommend its passage.

[51]Senator James W. Grimes (1816–1872) of Iowa. Governor of Iowa, 1854–1858;
Republican senator, 1859–1869.

And then, after something further which is not concerned here, he said this: "The motion was agreed to—" this is from the Congressional Globe—

The motion was agreed to and the bill was considered as in the Committee of the whole. It provides that the duties imposed on the board of trustees of the public schools of the cities of Washington and Georgetown in the District of Columbia, by virtue of an Act entitled 'An Act Providing for the Education of Colored Children in the Cities of Washington and Georgetown, District of Columbia, and for Other Purposes' approved May 21, 1862 be transferred to Daniel Breath, Zales J. Brown, and Zena C. Robbins and their successors in office who are now to be created a board of trustees of the schools for colored children in those cities who are to possess all of the powers and perform all the duties conferred upon and required of the trustees of public schools in Washington and Georgetown by the Act referred to.

These trustees—

And I am still quoting—

are to hold their offices for the respective terms of one, two, and three years to be determined by lot, and it is to be the duty of the Secretary of Interior on the first day of July, 1863 and annually on that date thereafter to appoint from among the residents of those cities a trustee in place of the one whose term has expired.

And so on. The bill became law.

The next enactment that we find with reference to the schools in on June 25, 1864, which established a board of commissioners of primary schools in the county, and that provided for the purchase of sites, for the erection of schools, for the regulation of the number of children, the fixing of tuition and so on. That contained in section 16 this provision:

That any white resident of said county shall be privileged to place his or her child or ward at any one of the schools provided for the education of white children in said county he or she may think proper to select, with the consent of the trustees of both districts and any colored resident shall have the same rights with respect to the colored schools.

But I can't see how possibly anyone could think that Congress intended otherwise than that those schools should be separate.

Section 18 provided funds to be set up or collected for the maintenance of those schools according to the census, the proportion of colored children to white children of school age. Now in that connection I would like to read to you something that was said by Representative Patterson[52] in the House when that bill was being considered. He said this:

In the twentieth section we have endeavored to give efficiency to the system by requiring attendance at school under a penal enactment. This is in accordance with the school laws in most of our northern cities, and would seem to be especially necessary here.

[52]Representative James W. Patterson (1823–1893) of New Hampshire. Republican representative, 1863–1867; Republican senator, 1867–1873.

And then further on he said this:

> But the most important feature of the amendment is to be found in the seventeenth
> and eighteenth sections, and in the proviso of the nineteenth section which provides
> for separate schools for the colored children of the District. To accomplish this, we
> have provided that such a portion of the entire school fund shall be set aside for this
> purpose as the number of colored children between the ages of six and seventeen bear
> to the whole number of children of the District.

Now let us follow the chronology of some of the things done by Congress, and
I should like to point out to you, which I think probably is rather well known to
the Court, that because of its plenary legislative power over the District of Columbia, the Congress, if I may use the expression, frequently uses the District for testing purposes. They put through bills here which they later enact into national policy, and I find in Bryan's *History of the National Capital,* page 133, this statement:

> Some years prior to the attempt to commit the Government to a national policy of
> internal improvements through a District measure, the District had been made the
> battleground upon which for nearly four decades the contest over slavery was waged.
> The field of action was chosen not because of concern in the District, but because
> there the Congress had the power of exclusive legislation and could at a stroke do
> away with the entire system.

And so we find that in 1862 they struck down slavery in the District, but it
was not until three years later that they proposed the Thirteenth Amendment
which accomplished it for the rest of the nation. And so it was with other things, as
I shall demonstrate to you.

And further on in this same book, at page 259, we find this statement. It is
only indicative of the thinking of the time:

> In Alexandria, the loss of the banks was especially felt and there was great anger
> and excitement. At a town meeting held in that place, resolutions were adopted
> declaring that if Congress looked upon the District as a 'field of legislative experi-
> ment' the people of the several states are called upon to relieve us of political
> bondage.

That was the attitude of the people in those times, and that was what Congress did. And so it seems to me that when you find the Congress making these
enactments for the District of Columbia, setting forth as they abolish slavery here,
later on for the whole country as I shall show you, giving the right of suffrage to
the Negroes in the District, later on for the whole country, the District of Columbia is the testing ground, and it seems to me it should lend weight to some of the
arguments that were made here earlier concerning the intention of Congress in
framing the Fourteenth Amendment, but I won't touch on that. I think that has
been fully covered.

On February 1, 1865, there was a resolution proposing the Thirteenth
Amendment abolishing slavery. I have already pointed out to you that that was
done for the District in '62.

In March of '65 there was the right of the Negro to ride on street cars. The
act of July 23, 1866, was—that was right at the time the same Congress was proposing the Fourteenth Amendment—passed an act enforcing the payment of the

proportionate share of the taxes for the colored schools, which had been provided for earlier, as I read you.

Apparently it wasn't being paid on time, and they put some teeth in it, and put a 10 per cent penalty in it if it wasn't paid on time.

And then on July 28, 1866, that same Congress which proposed the Fourteenth Amendment passed this act transferring certain lots, and this was the language.

For the sole use of the schools for colored children.

And further on in the act,

To be used for the colored schools.

And providing that if they were not so used, there should be reversion to the United States. Then, as I told you earlier, on January 8, 1867, the right to vote in elections in the District was given to the Negro. And in 1869 there was the bill to abolish the separate school boards and transfer all of this to one school board, and it passed, but it was vetoed because the President said the Negroes here did not want that, and it was not passed over the President's veto. It died.

And then my friends refer to a memorial by the City Council of Washington to the Congress. They refer to that on pages 44 and 45 of their brief, that the City Council of Washington memorialized Congress to strike down segregation in the schools, and that is true.

The City Council of Washington did memorialize Congress to strike down segregation in the schools, but it was a fruitless gesture. It was a vain effort. Nothing came of it. So that we see that the Congress, in spite of the memorialization by the Council of the city, refused to take such action and it seems to me that that definitely establishes the intent of Congress.

But my friends made one mistake in their brief when they cited the memorial by the City Council to the Congress to change the school system. They cited a page, and I thought I had better look at it, and so if you will refer to—and I shall not take the time to read it, because I see my time is running out—the Washington, D. C., Council, 67th Council, 1869–1870, at pages 828 and 829, and later on—

JUSTICE JACKSON: Are those set forth in your brief?

MR. KORMAN: No, Your Honor.

JUSTICE JACKSON: I wonder if you are going to rely on our memory?

MR. KORMAN: I shall be very glad to submit these references in writing, if the Court would permit. These are things which I found only recently.

JUSTICE JACKSON: It is pretty hard to—I would think you would file a supplemental brief setting forth this. It would be advisable if you think it is important, because it will all be out of mind.

MR. KORMAN: Well, let me say this: I shall briefly refer to what this says.

JUSTICE JACKSON: All right, I am not trying to stop the argument. I am simply suggesting—

MR. KORMAN: Yes, I understand that. The Council of the City of Washington took to task rather severely by a resolution a member of the school board who had issued a certificate to a colored girl to enter a white school. They quoted a report, and opinion by the corporation counsel. There was no corporation counsel at that time. There was an opinion by some lawyer for the District of Columbia Government then that once having got the ticket, they couldn't deny this girl the right to enter this school, and the Council takes that very much to task and says that the man ought to be fired for doing such a thing.

On February 21, 1871, the legislative assembly of the District was created combining the cities of Washington and Georgetown and the county into one, but there was no integration of the schools provided for. In the 41st Congress, there was the specific bill by Senator Sumner to integrate the schools, and there was a great deal of debate found in the Congressional Record, but the bill did not pass.

In the 42nd Congress, in 1872, there was a bitter debate on a similar bill to integrate the schools, but it failed of passage. And then the Legislative Assembly passed the acts which I mentioned earlier which gave to the Negro the right to enter all restaurants and places of public assembly, but they did not legislate on this subject of schools, because they knew they could not.

They gave the Negro all sorts of rights and powers in the District, but they did not legislate on schools because they couldn't, and that was at the time when Mr. Sumner, the Senator from Massachusetts, was a member of the District Committee in the Senate, and I have no doubt that they acted under his prodding, and yet they took no action because they knew that the schools were intended to be separate.

And then in 1900 a school board was provided for of seven paid members of the school board, a superintendent and two assistant superintendents, one of whom under the direction of the superintendent shall have charge of the schools for colored children and the organic act of 1906 came along when they reorganized the whole school system, and the reason, Mr. Nabrit, why they provided for the appointment for the Board of Education by the judges was because they felt that the judges were incorruptible and that the school board appointed by them would not be subject to the vagaries of politics and pressure groups. And you will find that in discussion on the subject.

Then I should like to call your attention to the Teachers' Salary Act of 1945, and of 1947, which says essentially the same thing. May I read some of those provisions to the Court:

> There shall be two first assistant superintendents of schools, one white first assistant superintendent for the white schools who, under the direction of the superintendent, shall have charge of general supervision over the white schools, and one colored first assistant superintendent for the colored schools who shall have direction of those schools.

And so on through enactments right up to the present day. Each year, as has been pointed out, Congress appropriates for this separate system of schools and provides so much money for the colored schools, so much money for the white schools, as is set up in the requests for appropriations.

I might call your attention further, in addition to the appendix which was filed and which is the order of the Commissioners of the District of Columbia striking down segregation in certain areas and which contains in it a recognition by them that there are certain areas in which they have no power to act because it has been taken care of and provided for by the Congress of the United States, and with that I shall leave it to the Court and ask the Court to take into account the arguments which were set forth in our brief filed in 1952.

JUSTICE REED: Mr. Korman.

MR. KORMAN: Mr. Justice?

JUSTICE REED: The matter referred to here as being acts of the Congress for the benefit of the District of Columbia Government, are they stated in your brief?

MR. KORMAN: The Act of the Congress relating to the District of Columbia?

JUSTICE REED: Yes.

MR. KORMAN: All of the Acts?

JUSTICE REED: That you referred to this morning. For instance, 12 Stat. 407.

MR. KORMAN: Yes, sir, they are referred to in my brief. They are not set out in extenso, but they are referred to and those citations of statutes are set forth in the brief.

JUSTICE REED: Which brief is that?

MR. KORMAN: That is the 1952 brief. The brief that was filed this time touched only upon the fourth and fifth questions asked by the Court. We took the position—

JUSTICE REED: There is a section called "The Acts of Congress providing for education of children in the District of Columbia," which is section 2 of your brief.

MR. KORMAN: The latest brief?

JUSTICE REED: No. This is the 1952 brief.

MR. KORMAN: Yes, sir. That contains those acts, the reference to them. You will find at the bottom of page 12 the list of these enactments.

JUSTICE REED: That you referred to this morning?

MR. KORMAN: That's right, sir.

THE CHIEF JUSTICE: Thank you. Mr. Nabrit.

## REBUTTAL ARGUMENT ON BEHALF OF THE PETITIONERS

### by MR. NABRIT

MR. NABRIT: If it please the Court, counsel for respondents in answer to the question of referring the decision as to action to be taken, if the Court would find that segregation in the District of Columbia is not authorized, to the district court as satisfying some inquiries upon the Court, he quoted from the act in which the authority for the judges to do this—in which it was stated that the purpose was to confer the power of appointment in a group of persons who were noncorruptible.

Under American jurisprudence, however, we would suggest to the Court that in considering due process, we have not let the incorruptibility or noncorruptibility of the persons involved permit us to entrust to them both the appointive and reappointive power of boards, and then the judicial power to distinguish between litigants who are contesting the rights of the board and the board on the basis that their incorruptibility satisfies the requirements of due process.

We don't suggest in any way or question the corruptibility or the impeccability or the character of the judges. All we suggest to the Court is that there appears to be an impropriety in the District of Columbia where the District judges appoint the members of the board, and if they don't like them, they don't reappoint them, and when I say "don't like them," I mean it in the high sense. They don't reappoint them. And yet when we sue the Board of Education, these same judges pass upon the actions of the board.

Now we merely suggest to the Court that there appears to be some impropriety in that. And again counsel for respondents take the position that the attitude of Congress with respect to racial distinction in the District of Columbia can be gathered by reading certain phrases in these statutes. Now, counsel neglects some very important things in doing that.

Number one, out of the eleven basic statutes governing the control of schools of the District of Columbia, nine of those statutes were passed between 1862 and 1866. Of those nine, seven of them were passed before 1864 by the end—between 1862 and 1864.

At that stage of history in this country two things ought to be borne in mind by the Court. One, we were on the verge of the Civil War in 1862. We were in the midst of the Civil War thereafter until 1864. I merely speak of that period because the war continued.

Number two, during that period public education itself was in an elementary stage of development. The public education for anybody in the District of Columbia, even the whites, was in such a fragmentary and rudimentary situation as not to be dignified by the name of public educational system.

Now, in that historical framework, where Congress provided funds, and Mr. Grimes said in both of these Acts to which Corporation Counsel referred your attention, that these were revenue acts to give to systems—I should not use the word "systems"—to Negro schools some financial support in a situation where there were three types of schools, a so-called public school system for whites, private schools for whites, and private schools for Negroes.

Now, without using the word "separate," without using any words of compulsion, when Congress provided that sort of system, to say that the intent of

Congress was to provide for racial distinctions in education, when at the same time in every other Act of Congress beginning with the Emancipation Act which he referred to, the elimination of the Black Codes which he referred to, the Civil Rights Act, the Acts giving the District of Columbia Negroes electoral rights, the Acts enacted immediately after the enactment of the Fourteenth Amendment, those dealing with restaurants, public places in the District of Columbia, those in the Civil Rights Act of 1875, every one of those Acts of Congress provided against any distinction on the basis of race or color with respect to Negroes.

It is inconceivable that in this type of fragmentary educational system the Congress there intended to manifest an intention to impose a racial distinction. There is no basis for such a supposition. So that we must read these statutes if we are going into history in the light of the historical background where we find it.

Now, we suggest to the Court, however, if it does not agree, that it is not necessary to do that. They can look in these statutes in vain for any language which provides any type of penalty or punishment or disability for the mixing of Negroes and whites in the public schools in the District of Columbia.

In *Ex parte Endo* this Court has said this: that when the Government, the federal Government, imposes restraints upon its citizens based upon race, or when it restrains its liberty, I think we can say the Court went that far, that the restraint must be justified by the language used in specificity. The justification for the restraint must be found in the words used, and we suggest to the Court that no such condition exists with respect to these statutes.

Now, in the third place we say with respect to these statutes that the Court does not agree with that, that the Court should give these statutes an intent which is in conformity with the decisions of this Court, the policy of the Government, both executive and legislative as we have indicated.

I think it also highly important to call this to the attention of the Court: that the President of the United States, President Truman, the Attorney General of the United States during Mr. Truman's Presidency, President Eisenhower, the Attorney General now under President Eisenhower, Attorney General Brownell, both of the executive officers of the highest position in this country of the major political parties, including the highest legal officers of the United States, have stated: 1. These statutes do not compel or authorize segregation. 2. That segregation is unlawful and unconstitutional in the District of Columbia.

Now I suggest that under those circumstances that is much more persuasive than the position taken because some statute authorizes the corporation counsel to represent the Board of Education. Those statutes do not authorize him to determine, contrary to all of the legal opinion, that these persons must compel segregation in the public schools. He says that is his opinion and he cites for that *Carr* v. *Corning.*

Now, in *Carr* v. *Corning,* the Court decided that these statutes in the framework with which we have been dealing with them, indicated that Congress did not intend to lift the question of segregation in education out of the hands of Congress, and under the facts in that case they found equality.

The Court did not reach the question which we ask the Court to decide here, whether or not the Government has the power to impose racial distinction in affording educational opportunity to citizens in the public schools in the District of Columbia solely on the basis of race or color, so that *Carr* v. *Corning* is no help;

and if *Carr* v. *Corning* had decided that there would be no doubt about our position, that would have no binding effect on this Court when, for the first time, this Court is called upon to decide as to the lawfulness of this type of action by the federal government.

Now, as far as *Wall* v. *Oyster* is concerned, that was the case in which a Negro girl was admitted to the white schools. Shortly after she was admitted it was found out that some far ancestor of hers in the past had a few drops of Negro blood, but it could not be discerned by looking at her.

They put her out, and she tried to get back, and the issue was on the basis of classification, and the court said that the District had the power to classify, and that their classification of you as a Negro could not be contested.

Now, the court said that, well, underlying that wasn't there an assumption that this was a proper separation of the races in the District? I would say yes, but that was not the issue.

Furthermore, *Wall* v. *Oyster* points out the basic thing that is wrong in this whole situation, and that is there is no justification for the separation of these races except on a basis of inferiority, because in *Wall* v. *Oyster* this girl was in the school, no question being raised about her, the same person. When they found out she had this drop of Negro blood in her, she became unfit to associate with the others in the classroom, and she was put out not because of anything that was wrong, other than that she possessed this Negro blood.

That, we say, is inconsistent with the Constitution of the United States, and nothing has been said by the corporation counsel in this Court in the last argument or this, which offers to this Court any suggestion of any reason or any justification for this separation of races by the exertion of governmental power, save and except there is something in the nature of the Negro which makes him unfit to associate with the whites in the public schools. And that, we say, is against the policy of the federal government and against the Fifth Amendment of the Constitution of the United States.

Now, I did want, if I have a minute or two, to say something to the Court about this matter of relief and about the question of—well, I did not mean to say anything about the power of the Court.

My answer to the question about the power of the Court is, of course, the Court has its power under its equitable power to give any type of relief which the Court thinks is desirable, and with that we have no quarrel.

We think, however, that the Court might raise a question itself as to whether it should exercise the power in these cases so as to give any type of gradual relief.

In the District of Columbia we go further, we say to the Court that the District of Columbia itself does not ask for any gradual relief. We assert no gradual relief is necessary.

Under those circumstances we would think that the Court, having no reason to give gradual relief of itself, would consider gradual relief not to be involved in the District. If that be sound, that would leave the question of what type of decree the Court should enter. In our judgment, the Court should not enter a detailed decree.

In our judgment, we have a time within which we think the Court should require the respondents to grant the relief requested, and that is that the Court enter a decree that these respondents be restrained from operating and managing these schools in the District of Columbia on the basis of racial distinctions alone, by the beginning of the next school term succeeding the issuance of the decree.

So that if the decree were issued—it is a supposition contrary to fact—if the decree were issued in January, the next term would be September; if it were issued in May, the next term would be September.

Now, if it were issued in June, the last day, it would still be September. In our judgment, there would then be sufficient time for whatever normal administrative problems arise in the adjustment of an integrated system to be resolved in the District.

We like to point that out to the Court: Number one, they talk about the reshuffling of students. There are 105,000 students. A normal administrative procedure would take the cards of all the students in the elementary grades, group them, group those cards of the students in junior high, group those in the senior high, so that you have your school populations in your cards; get maps for your areas in the District of Columbia divided for convenience; select either five or ten or whatever number of students you want represented by a pin, and put a pin in that map to show the number of students in each area.

You have the capacity of every school building in the area in each of the categories, and it is a simple proposition to distribute them; so simple is it that in the District of Columbia they do it every year, if not every other year, for the separate Negro system, and for this separate white system which they impose on us.

Now, in order to do it for both, all you do is to coalesce this mechanical action.

The second thing they say that is so difficult is that they have some teachers with different seniorities, and that when you get two lists together of these eligibles, you do not have any way to do that.

This Court has decided in any number of these labor cases that where we have collective bargaining agreements, and you have seniority and these lists, in the decision of the Court these lists are put together and there is no difficulty.

As a matter of fact, the superintendent of schools has announced that they are going to combine the lists for all teachers of physical education this year. It is just as simple to combine lists for all else; so there is no difficulty as to that.

The next thing they say it is difficult because you have got to indoctrinate the teachers. We know it is much better, the more the teachers have some training in intercultural relations, the better it is. We do not dispute that.

But in the District of Columbia 85 per cent of the teachers of the 3,500 teachers have served and are serving today on integrated committees, so they have not been isolated in a vacuum. All of the officers operate that way, largely groups of students operate that way. All of that is in our brief.

In addition to that, over two hundred of them will have been trained for intergroup living and activities and work before March, so that we have a nucleus if we only use those trained or if we only use those who belong to their amalgamated or integrated teachers union, to furnish a nucleus of teachers experienced enough to do this.

All of that calls for simply administrative judgment.

So that these evils and obstacles which the corporation counsel—although he takes the position that gradualism is not necessary, he postulates to this Court in a form to require the same time that gradualism requires—seems to have no substantial basis or merit and, therefore, we suggest to the Court that these respondents be required to conform to a mandate of this Court, assuming the Court decided that segregation is unconstitutional, that this or that that action is not lawful, that they do this at the beginning, by the beginning of the next succeeding school term; and, to be specific, since we hope the decision will come some time during this next year, that it be September, 1954, at the beginning of the school year.

I would like to say as one final sentence, if I may, that America is a great country in which we can come before the Court and express to the Court the great concern which we have, where our great government is dealing with us, and we are not in the position that the animals were in George Orwell's satirical novel *Animal Farm,* where after the revolution the dictatorship was set up and the sign set up there that all animals were equal, was changed to read "but some are more equal than others."

Our Constitution has no provision across it that all men are equal but that white men are more equal than others.

Under this statute and under this country, under this Constitution, and under the protection of this Court, we believe that we, too, are equal.

(Whereupon, at 1:20 p.m., the argument was concluded.)

FRANCIS B. GEBHART, et al.,
Petitioners,

vs.

ETHEL LOUISE BELTON, et al.,
Respondents.

Case No. 10

FRANCIS B. GEBHART, et al.,
Petitioners,

vs.

SHIRLEY BARBARA BULAH, et al.,
Respondents.

Washington, D.C.,
December 9, 1953

The above-entitled cause came on for oral argument at 1:20 p.m.

APPEARANCES:

On behalf of Petitioners:
H. ALBERT YOUNG, ESQ.

On behalf of Respondents:
JACK GREENBERG, ESQ., and THURGOOD MARSHALL, ESQ.

THE CHIEF JUSTICE: No. 10, Francis B. Gebhart, et al, v. Ethel Louise Belton, et al.

THE CLERK: Counsel are present.

THE CHIEF JUSTICE: Mr. Young.

ARGUMENT ON BEHALF OF PETITIONERS

by MR. YOUNG

MR. YOUNG: The petitioners in this case, Your Honors, seek review of final judgments of the Supreme Court of the State of Delaware affirming orders of the Court of Chancery.

The petitioners are members of the Board of Education of the State of Delaware, and the boards of the Claymont Special School District and the Hockessin School District.

The provision from which the petitioners seek relief is the same in both cases:

That the defendants, and each of them, are enjoined from denying to infant plaintiffs and other similarly situated, because of colored ancestry admittance to the public schools.

In the Court of Chancery the respondents urged the proposition that segregation in and of itself is contrary to the Fourteenth Amendment and prayed for a declaratory judgment to that effect.

The petitioners appealed from other rulings of the chancellor which enjoined the petitioners from refusing admittance to the plaintiffs to schools maintained for white children.

The basis of these rulings was that the physical and educational facilities of the schools maintained for Negro children were inferior.

Simultaneously the respondents appealed from the denial of a declaratory judgment, and the Delaware Supreme Court affirmed the decrees of the Chancellor.

The petitioners applied for certiorari to this Court on the narrow issue, namely, the type of relief which should have been granted, the form and shape of the decree, and asked for an opportunity to equalize the facilities.

The respondents did not file a cross petition nor did they seek any review of the decision that segregation in and of itself is not contrary to the Fourteenth Amendment.

The basic question then of segregation per se is, therefore, not before this Court in the Delaware case, but the respondents, however, take a different view, and because of this position taken by the respondents and the importance of the questions raised, and the wishes of this Court, and a sense of duty, we have attempted to answer the questions that are posed to counsel.

There is no evidence that Delaware refused to ratify the Fourteenth Amendment because of a belief that it would require the state to admit Negroes into its public schools on a mixed basis.

The respondents draw from the historical facts in Delaware the remarkable conclusion that the General Assembly, in a series of discriminatory statutes, demonstrated that it fully understood that equality before the law demanded non-segregation, and that school segregation in Delaware is based upon white superiority.

A few important facts, taken out of the pages of history from the State of Delaware, will throw some light on its position with respect to the Fourteenth Amendment and segregated schools.

Delaware did not secede from the Union nor did it join the Confederacy.

Its geographic position alone was sufficient to assure Delaware's loyalty to the Union. Its situation on the Wilmington-Philadelphia-Baltimore Railroad and the Delaware Railroad, along which troops could be moved south, and on the Delaware River, controlled by the Union fleet which lay off Hampton Roads in Virginia, would have made resistance hopeless. In addition, the material prosperity of the state had become increasingly dependent upon Northern markets.

Reinforcing the material ties was a long Delaware tradition of loyalty to the Constitution, and pride in having been the first state to ratify it.

Delaware's adherence, however, to the Union cause was a reluctant one. Attempts to obtain from the legislature a resolution of adherence to the Union failed. There were many manifestations of Southern sympathies throughout the state, throughout the war, and although slave-owning was clearly on the decline, particularly in Wilmington and other sections of New Castle County, one of the three counties of the State of Delaware, and although a vast majority of the Negroes were no longer slaves, it was pretty clear that slavery was a part of the social and economic life of the citizens of the remaining two counties, Kent and Sussex, as it was a part of the lives of the citizens of the Southern states.

Throughout the Civil War, the Democrats maintained firm control of the state government. It proclaimed itself the White Man's Party, and was in power until the late eighties or early nineties. It disapproved of suffrage or political or social equality for Negroes.

The dominant mood in Delaware, both during and after the Civil War, was opposed to abolitionism and equality for the Negroes, and in our own state legislature, in a joint resolution of the House and Senate opposing the Freedmen's Bureau Bill, the Civil Rights Bill, the Negro Suffrage, we witnessed the expression of the feeling that equality cannot be sanctioned under the laws of God or nature, and Senator Saulsbury[53] at that time stated that he was proud that his state was the last to abolish slavery.

The Thirteenth Amendment was unqualifiedly rejected by the legislature in 1865. The legislature expressed its unqualified disapproval of the Fourteenth and Fifteenth Amendments, and refused to adopt them in 1867 and 1869, respectively.

After the passage of the Fifteenth Amendment, poll tax laws in Delaware, designed particularly to disfranchise the Negroes, were adopted with great effect.

In the meantime, Negroes' education in Delaware had made small progress. In the Constitution of 1792 we provided for a public school system; in 1829 we provided for schools for white children by statute, and by the Constitution of 1831 we reaffirmed what we had said in our Constitution of 1792 and provided for a public school system. This was all before any consideration of the Fourteenth Amendment by the State of Delaware.

In 1875 there was a statute imposed upon Negro property-holders, and the funds that were obtained were used to supply and furnish education to the Negroes through a Delaware Society for the Advancement of Negro Education.

It was in 1881, for the first time, that Delaware did make some appropriation from its treasury for the education of Negroes, but the provision was rather meager and rather inadequate, but it is significant that it was the first step and the first stride forward in helping the Negro in his education in the State of Delaware.

In 1897 the Constitution that was rewritten and now under attack by our friends, and now in force in the State of Delaware, provided for segregated schools on an equal basis in the State of Delaware.

That section read as follows:

> In addition to the income of investments of the public school funds, the General Assembly shall make provision for the benefit of the free public schools which shall be equitably apportioned among the school districts of the state; provided, however, that in such apportionment no distinction shall be made on account of race or color, and separate schools for white and colored children shall be maintained.

In the late eighties or early nineties, a political revolution took place in the State of Delaware. The Republicans began to be a serious threat to the control of the Democrats, who proclaimed themselves as the White Party.

This was partly due to the activities and the financial contributions of a political adventurer, John Addicks by name, who was a wealthy stock manipulator from Pennsylvania, and reading of the contest for the United States senatorship

[53]Senator Willard Saulsbury (1820–1892) of Delaware. Democratic senator, 1859–1871.

in 1889, came to Delaware and stated he was available, and because of his contributions to the party at that time, the Republicans got in control, and he also accomplished the enfranchisement of a great many of the Negroes by paying their poll tax.

JUSTICE FRANKFURTER: To an outsider it does not appear as one of the great social reforms of this country, does it?

MR. YOUNG: That is correct, Your Honor.

And by 1898 the Republican Party, through his efforts, however, had upset the Democrat control so that the white supremacists in the State of Delaware had been overthrown. It was against this background that the Constitution of 1897, now in force, was adopted.

It is evident that the constitutional provision and its statutory counterpart in Delaware were in the cause of education of the Negroes, a long stride forward.

The attitude of the people of Delaware had undergone a change, for the slogan "White Man's Party" had finally lost its political potency, and the ineffaceable stamps of superiority were no longer present, and the doctrine of Negro inequality was no longer a guiding force in the framing of the statute.

The change may be said to have been formalized on February 12, 1901, when the Delaware legislature, without a dissenting vote, accepted and ratified the Thirteenth, Fourteenth, and Fifteenth Amendments.

In Delaware we ratified those three Civil War amendments thirty years after they had been submitted for ratification. Thus, the argument of the respondents to the effect that school segregation in Delaware is based on the doctrine of white superiority is refuted.

The resolutions about white superiority cited by the respondents in support of their argument belong to an era in Delaware history that had passed when the present school law and the present school system were enacted.

The constitutional provision for a separation of the races in the public schools in Delaware was not based upon any declaration of natural or God-made inequality or inferiority of the Negro. It was adopted in the light of the history and tradition of the people of the State of Delaware as the wisest and most workable and most acceptable method of educating the youth in that state, both white and colored.

Now, in answer to Question 1, I do not want to burden the Court—I know much argument has been presented—but it seems to me that in connection with Delaware's position, in order for the Court to obtain some idea of what the thinking was in the Congress at the time, I would like to touch upon some of the action and debates, although briefly, if I may, of Congress.

JUSTICE REED: May I ask a question whether there is any other case in the courts of Delaware? I should like to be informed.

MR. YOUNG: No, Your Honor.

JUSTICE REED: Just for my information.

MR. YOUNG: This is the only case.

JUSTICE REED: This is the only case?

MR. YOUNG: This is the only case, the first case of its kind.

JUSTICE REED: We know nothing then as to the federal performance?

MR. YOUNG: No, this is the only case.

In attempting to evaluate the understanding of Congress, of course, we have got to consider the debate in Congress and the actions of Congress, the action of Congress, for example, on the bill to enlarge the Freedmen's Bureau; the Civil Rights Act of 1866, the Fourteenth Amendment, and also the debates on the Civil Rights Act of 1875.

The debates in Congress on legislation of a similar character afford strong evidence that the Fourteenth Amendment was considered to have no effect on public school segregation.

A majority of the Senate and House came from the states which had segregated school systems. I have no doubt that Senator Sumner and Representative Stevens wanted to include in the Fourteenth Amendment mixed schools for white children and colored children.

I have no doubt that those who opposed the amendment attempted to stigmatize the bill, and made every effort they could to see to it that the Negroes received no rights, civil, political or social; but I do believe that between the proponents of those measures and the opponents of those measures there was that responsible majority that saw the distinction between civil and political rights and social rights.

The members of Congress, I respectfully submit, would not have remained silent if they thought it would invalidate segregation in the schools in the states which they represented and which held to segregation of public education.

The suggestions that it would do so came from the white supremacists who sought to stigmatize the bill; they sought to present a parade of horror to the existing state of public opinion, and their expressions should be taken cautiously.

Much has been said about the legislation in the District of Columbia at the time when they provided for a segregated school system and, at the same time, also abolished certain acts of discrimination, and did so both prior to any consideration of the Fourteenth Amendment, and also took up the question of the Negroes' rights during a consideration of the Fourteenth Amendment, and after a consideration of the Fourteenth Amendment. But at no time did they change the system in the District of Columbia with respect to segregated schools.

Mr. Grimes or Senator Grimes of Iowa, in reporting the bill, had this to say in offering an amendment, and if Your Honors would permit me I would like to read from it because it illustrates that Congress did not sit by nor was Congress asleep, apparently, or that this act of providing segregated schools in the District of Columbia was not just a perfunctory or routine matter about which no one knew anything.

Mr. Grimes. Before the bill is read, I wish to propose some amendments on which the question can be taken altogether. In line 7 of section 9, after the word 'the' and before the word 'taxable,' I move to insert the word 'white'; in line 19 of section 9 before the word 'inhabitants,' insert the word 'white'; in line 30–3 of section 9, after the word 'District,' insert the words 'owned by white persons.'

and so forth and so on; and then he concludes:

> The purpose is to make the bill conform to the view of the committee—the bill was not printed in consonance with their views—and to confine the levy of taxes to white persons in the District, and to open the schools to the admission of white children.

It does not seem likely that with this language, and with this introduction with respect to the provision for segregated schools in the District of Columbia, the window of the Republic at that time, that such equalitarians as Ben Wade of Ohio[54], and Senator Sumner and Senator Sprague[55], and Representative Stevens and all the other equalitarians would have sat by and said nothing.

The amendment was adopted and another amendment offered by Senator Grimes to provide separate schools for Negroes in the county, without any dissent, and it is interesting to know that these amendments were adopted without any opposition, even though twenty-three members of the 39th Congress that considered the Fourteenth Amendment, served in the Senate at that time, and not a single member of the House raised his voice against segregation in schools in the District of Columbia.

In the 40th Congress no suggestion was made to abolish segregation in schools in the District of Columbia when a bill to transfer the duties of the trustees of the colored schools for the cities of Washington and Georgetown came under consideration, and this bill was passed after the Fourteenth Amendment was declared and ratified; and again the 41st and 42nd Congresses, in those Congresses attempts were made to abolish segregation in the public schools, and in 1874 Congress reaffirmed its segregation policy in the District of Columbia.

It is hardly conceivable that the Congress which proposed the Fourteenth Amendment was attempting to prohibit the states a type of school which it had endorsed and failed or refused to change in the District of Columbia.

It is clear that the Fourteenth Amendment was not intended, as contended by the respondents, to write into the Constitution the principle of absolute and complete equality so as to include the prohibition by the states against school segregation.

Thaddeus Stevens realized that this notion of equality had not been achieved in the passage of the Amendment when, at the opening of the debate on the Fourteenth Amendment, he had this to say:

> This proposition is not all that the Commission desired. It falls far short of my wishes. But it fulfills the present state of public opinion. Not only Congress but the several states are to be consulted. Upon a careful survey of the whole ground we do not believe that nineteen of the loyal states could be induced to ratify any proposition more stringent than this.

[54]Senator Benjamin F. Wade (1800–1878) of Ohio. Whig and Republican senator 1851–1869. He was President pro tempore of the Senate, 1867–1869 and would have succeeded to the Presidency of the United States if Andrew Johnson had been found guilty of the impeachment charges against him. Wade refused to disqualify himself and voted against Johnson.

[55]Senator William Sprague (1830–1915) of Rhode Island. Republican senator, 1863–1875. He married Katherine Chase, daughter of Chief Justice Salmon P. Chase.

Then at the close of the debate on July 13, 1866, he said this:

We may perhaps congratulate the House and the country on the new approach to the completion of a proposition to be submitted to the people for the admission of an outlawed community into the privileges and advantages of a civilized and free government. When I say that we should rejoice at such a completion, I do not thereby intend so much to express joy at the superior excellence of the scheme as that there is to be a scheme, a scheme containing much of positive good as well, I am bound to admit, as the omission of many better things.

I am going to skip some of it, but he concluded:

Do you inquire why, holding these views and possessing some will of my own, I accept so imperfect a proposition?

He is talking about the Fourteenth Amendment.

I answer because I live among men, and not among angels; among men as intelligent, as determined and as interested as myself, who, not agreeing with me, do not choose to yield their opinions to mine. Mutual concession, therefore, is our only resort or mutual hostilities.

There is no doubt that one of the things which Stevens at that time found lacking was a provision to compel the elimination of school segregation, and that he thought then, as we urge now, that it is a matter of policy for the states, within their police power.

The debates and the absence of reference to school segregation in the House led to the conclusion that the House understood that the Fourteenth Amendment did not affect the right of the state to educate the Negro in segregated schools. Of the 183 or so congressmen, 129 came from states which either had mandatory segregation or no education for the Negroes, and at least six others from states which had segregated school systems.

It is unlikely that they would have ignored the consequences of such measures on the school systems of their own states if they believed that they were abolishing school segregation.

The respondents state that the debates which followed the bill to enlarge the power of the Freedmen's Bureau amounted to a forthright assault on the idea that there could be racial segregation in the public schools, and then they rely upon Representative Hubbard of Connecticut, who made no mention of racial segregation in public schools; they rely on Representative Rousseau of Kentucky, who opposed the bill because he said the Bureau would take over all the schools used by white children; and they rely upon Representative Dawson, a white supremacist who, every time the occasion arose, castigated the extreme radicals and suggested that the bill would permit white and Negro children to sit side by side.[56]

In the debates on the Civil Rights bill, Representative Rogers of New Jersey

---

[56]Representative Richard D. Hubbard (1818–1884) of Connecticut; Democratic representative, 1867–1869. Representative Lovell H. Rousseau (1818–1869) of Kentucky; Major General in the Union Army during the Civil War, Republican representative, 1865–1867. Representative John L. Dawson (1813–1870) of Pennsylvania; Democratic representative, 1851–1855 and 1863–1867.

and Kerr of Indiana stated that the bill would outlaw segregation in the common schools of the various states.

However, Representative Wilson of Iowa, chairman of the Judiciary Committee and floor leader of the bill in the House, stated that it did not mean that Negro children would attend the same schools as white children, these not being civil rights or immunities.

In the amendment to the Freedmen's Bureau bill proposed by Representative Donnelly of Minnesota[57] to require the Commissioner to provide common school education to all refugees and freedmen who shall apply therefor, was defeated—not a single reference or quotation by any proponent of the bill to support the statement that this was an assault on the idea that there could be racial segregation in the public schools.

In the debates in the Civil Rights bill in the Senate, only Senator Cowan of Pennsylvania suggested that the bill would abolish segregation in the school systems in his state. No such suggestion appears to have been made in the Senate with respect to the Freedmen's Bureau or the Fourteenth Amendment.

The silence in the Senate on the school question leads only to the conclusion that it was the understanding of the Senate that the measures would not affect segregated education. The senators and representatives were not oblivious to the effect of these measures on the school systems in their own states, nor would they have failed to discuss the consequences if they believed that segregation would be outlawed.

The respondents state on page 91 of their brief that none of the bill's supporters in the House, except Wilson, deny that the bill had any effect of ending all caste legislation, including segregated schools, and that this was the view of the Senate.

Well, the significant thing is not that no one contradicted the white supremacists, such as Rogers and Kerr and Cowan, but that no one contradicted Wilson, the man responsible for the bill, on the floor of the House, who specifically stated that the bill did not mean that Negro children would attend the same school as white children, holding that these were not civil rights or immunities.

Wilson's statement constituted an official interpretation, and neither Stevens nor Conkling[58] nor Bingham nor Donnelly nor any other radical Republican contradicted him; and the respondents have produced nothing to explain the silence of the proponents of the bill with respect to segregation in schools.

The actions of a majority of the state legislatures which ratified the Fourteenth Amendment, in re-enacting school segregation laws or allowing such laws to stand, demonstrate the understanding of those legislatures, that the Fourteenth Amendment did not abolish such segregation, and we agree with the appellants' statement on page 140 of their brief that if there was any authorization or requirement of segregation in state school laws, and after ratification, the legislature took

[57]Representative Ignatius Donnelly (1831–1901) of Minnesota. Republican representative, 1863–1869.

[58]Senator Roscoe Conkling (1829–1888) of New York. Republican representative, 1859–1863 and 1865–1867; senator, 1867–1881. A leading figure in the Grant and Hayes Administrations, he also declined nomination as Chief Justice of the United States in 1873 and as Associate Justice in 1882.

no action to end this disparity, undoubtedly it would appear that this state did not understand the Amendment to have the effect which appellants urge, and all the more reason, we state, that if the state legislature actually took action to continue or to compel school segregation, the legislature must have understood the Fourteenth Amendment not to abolish such segregation.

In some of the cases the legislatures which ratified the Fourteenth Amendment provided for segregation; others permitted segregation; others had no segregation.

In some instances the segregation in schools was declared invalid under state laws, but not under the Fourteenth Amendment.

In some cases, as in the case of New York, of ringing declarations that Negroes shall have full equality and the enjoyment of all civil and political rights, segregation was not regarded as a violation of such rights. Wherever segregation was abolished, whether by statute or by court decisions, there is no evidence that the Fourteenth Amendment entered into the question.

As to the action by future Congresses under section 5, we state that the enforcement clause, section 5, was inserted in order to give Congress the power to supplement any civil remedies or other protection which might be available or through the courts by providing penalties for violation of the Amendment.

The provisions of the Fourteenth Amendment do not permit Congress to broaden the Amendment, but merely provides for more effective remedies than those which might be obtained through the normal judicial process.

It cannot logically be argued that although the Amendment was properly understood to be broad enough to eliminate segregation in public schools at the time it was enacted, that it was, nevertheless, understood that Congress might in the future make segregation illegal.

In answer to question three, we take the position that the problem obviously is a legislative one and not a judicial one.

To construe the Amendment as requiring the abolition of segregation in the public schools would be to give the Amendment a meaning and an effect directly contrary to the understanding of the framers.

It was clearly understood by both Congress which submitted, and the states which ratified, the Amendment that it was to have no effect on the public school system of the state.

The Court, if it should abolish segregation, would not be interpreting the document to meet new conditions, but would be meeting a problem which existed at the time of the Fourteenth Amendment—the time the Fourteenth Amendment was adopted—in a manner directly contrary to the intent of those who proposed and adopted the Amendment.

The wisdom of abolishing segregation in public schools of the states was considered by Congress at and about the time the Fourteenth Amendment was adopted.

Congress consistently, whenever the matter arose, decided to leave this problem to the states.

This Court is not in a position to judge to what extent the prejudices and tensions which gave rise to the segregation laws and the Congressional decision to leave those matters to the states, have abated in any particular state or district, or to judge the wisdom of abolishing segregation in public schools of that state.

The matter should be left where Congress originally left it, in the state legislatures.

The problem before the Court is whether the people of those states, providing for a segregated school system, in the exercise of their judgment, based on first-hand knowledge of local conditions, decide that the state objective of free public education is best served by a system of separate but equal schools; and if I may borrow from—

THE CHIEF JUSTICE: General, may I ask you what is the situation in Delaware today as of this moment?

MR. YOUNG: In Delaware, in the high school district which is the Claymont School District—and I might say it is the northern part of the state, almost on the borderline of Pennsylvania—there are nineteen school children in that school out of twenty-two eligible Negro children. The total enrollment, you might be interested in knowing, is five hundred in the high school, but about eight hundred in the entire school; it is a combination elementary and high school.

Now, in the other district, which is the elementary school district, and which is referred to as the Hockessin School District, there are six out of forty-six that are attending that school, and that is also in New Castle County and on—near the Pennsylvania border, but more towards the west, the southwest; and I might add here that I heard the statement from—one of counsel, our adversaries, said that he was very happy to report that they were in those schools.

Well, I do not know to what extent he is happy, but I might say, if I am permitted to say it outside the record, that in a recent survey there was an indication that there was not too much happiness in the district, in the school, particularly where the six out of the forty-six are attending, and that situation is not solved in that particular district in New Castle County.

JUSTICE JACKSON: At any rate, Mr. Attorney General, we have no question in your case of shaping the remedy? I suppose the questions accidentally went to you as well as to the other counsel?

MR. YOUNG: That is right, yes.

JUSTICE JACKSON: But in your case we have no problem of a decree?

MR. YOUNG: If segregation per se is declared invalid, that is the end of it.

JUSTICE JACKSON: It goes to the state courts?

MR. YOUNG: That is right.

JUSTICE JACKSON: So we have nothing to do with that?

MR. YOUNG: That is right.

JUSTICE JACKSON: So that those questions should not really have been addressed to you, I think.

MR. YOUNG: It would have been very much appreciated if they had not been. (Laughter.)

JUSTICE FRANKFURTER: We have had the benefit of your observations.

MR. YOUNG: Thank you, Justice Frankfurter.

JUSTICE REED: In that county are there still existing segregated schools?

MR. YOUNG: Yes.

JUSTICE REED: All except in two districts?

MR. YOUNG: Just the two districts are affected.

JUSTICE REED: And they are maintaining segregated schools?

MR. YOUNG: They are maintaining segregated—

JUSTICE REED: There are Negro residents and it is—

MR. YOUNG: That is right.

If I may borrow from a statement made by the venerable Mr. John W. Davis, and quote from his brief this statement, he said:

> An emotional approach to this question is a poor substitute for a rational discussion of the problem at hand, which is to be judged by the application of well-settled principles governing the effect of the Fourteenth Amendment on the police power of the state.

The arguments, I respectfully submit, such as I have heard in this courtroom for three days by our adversaries, have great emotional appeal, but they belong in an entirely different forum and in a different setting.

Any change in state policy is for the legislature. The Fourteenth Amendment is a pact between the federal government and the individual states.

The intention of the parties was clear at the time it was adopted and ratified. In order to make that provision in the Constitution cover the question of public school segregation, it must be done within the framework of the Constitution, for as between providing for integrated or mixed schools in those states, where it is deemed best to maintain separate but equal schools, and preserving the meaning and intent of the provision of the Fourteenth Amendment, and the sanctity of the pact between the federal government and the states, it is more important that this problem, however worthy, be dealt with within the meaning of our Constitution.

As author Stanley Morrison, in conjunction with Charles Fairman, in a very scholarly article which appeared in the Stanford Law Review on "The Judicial Interpretation of the Fourteenth Amendment" aptly put it:

> No matter how desirable the results might be, it is of the essence of our system that the judges must stay within the bounds of their constitutional power. Nothing is more fundamental, even the Bill of Rights. To depart from this fundamental is, in Mr. Justice Black's own words, 'to frustrate the great design of a written Constitution.'

I would like to reserve the balance of my time for rebuttal.

THE CHIEF JUSTICE: Mr. Redding.

### ARGUMENT ON BEHALF OF RESPONDENTS

#### by MR. GREENBERG

MR. GREENBERG: Mr. Greenberg.

If it please the Court, Mr. Redding and I shall argue only briefly in support of our position.

In this case, as the Attorney General of Delaware has indicated, plaintiffs prevailed in the courts below. The plaintiffs and members of their class, are now in schools to which they sought admission, but the Attorney General is trying to get them out, and we appear here in an effort to keep them in the schools permanently.

As respondents here, we urge that the decision of the court below did not give respondents all that the Constitution guaranteed. Therefore, in this Court we urge that the decision below should be affirmed on grounds other than those given by the court below, and that segregation in elementary and high schools in the State of Delaware should be declared unconstitutional.

At the argument last term we submitted it was clear that the decision below could be affirmed on independent state grounds, and that this Court need not reach the constitutional question. But since this Court has seen fit to address two respondents in this case the same questions which it addressed to petitioners in Nos. 1, 2, and 4, we inferred that this Court believed that the constitutional question may be reached in this case.

JUSTICE FRANKFURTER: I do not quite understand the general invitation to counsel to submit arguments on a certain point changes the relevant issue within a controversy; I do not quite understand that.

MR. GREENBERG: I do not believe it changes the relevant issues, but we thought, perhaps, the Court was interested in the question of the constitutionality of segregation in the Delaware case.

JUSTICE FRANKFURTER: As with the Attorney General of Delaware, I am glad to get his observations; and I am glad to get yours, but I do not see that something which is not in issue before we asked specific questions in a group of cases, becomes the issue because we had asked them.

MR. GREENBERG: We submit that although the decision below may be supported on an independent state ground, that in reality, equal protection of the laws will not be given to the respondents unless the constitutional question is reached because, in truth and in fact, they are attending the schools in which they now are, so to speak, under a cloud. They are not like the rest of the students in the school, they are under—

JUSTICE FRANKFURTER: I think you should have cross-appealed.

JUSTICE JACKSON: You have not cross-appealed.

JUSTICE FRANKFURTER: I understand you can sustain a decision below on any ground, but I do not understand that you can object to a decision below on a ground that you have not appealed from.

MR. GREENBERG: Well, we did not cross-appeal, Mr. Justice Frankfurter, because we believed that we could urge other grounds for the affirmance of the judgment below.

JUSTICE FRANKFURTER: You can urge any ground you please that will justify the decree below; but you cannot go outside of the decree below.

MR. GREENBERG: Well, it is our understanding—

JUSTICE FRANKFURTER: I am glad to get your observations, but I might suggest I do not think the nature of the issues has been changed.

JUSTICE JACKSON: I think the question was addressed in this case along with all the others, so if there were any variations they could be called to your attention.

I do not think that we—speaking for myself—took into account the fact or expected in this case to deal with the problem of the decree and the relief or questions addressed to those things, because we cannot direct the state court as to what decree it shall enter. All we can say is, "You shall not go beyond a certain point," which we say is the constitutional limit. Here affirmance is as far as we can go. We could not order them to shape their decree.

MR. GREENBERG: It is our position, Mr. Justice Jackson, that the decree below does not give equal protection of the laws.

JUSTICE JACKSON: You did not appeal.

MR. GREENBERG: No, we did not.

JUSTICE JACKSON: So far as this case is concerned, the most that we can do would be to affirm the decree, but you probably will have the benefit of anything said in any other case that is helpful.

(Whereupon, at 2:00 p.m., a recess was had.)


AFTER RECESS


ARGUMENT ON BEHALF OF RESPONDENTS—resumed

by MR. MARSHALL

MR. MARSHALL: May it please the Court, during the luncheon recess counsel in this case conferred, and it was agreed among at least, so far as we are concerned, that instead of going into the main part of the argument, that we would merely make a brief statement on it.

And, in the first point we wanted to make it clear the reason that we did not file cross-petitions in the court, and we have set out in our brief on the argument, the small one, on page 2, three cases, *Helvering* v. *Lerner,* and *Langnes* v. *Green*[59], and we gathered from those cases that in the situation such as this where we were not opposed to the decision of the lower court and merely wanted to urge other grounds for the decision in the case, that we should proceed with the case and merely urge in argument the point, specifically the point as to the validity of the segregated school statutes.

We are afraid that in that particular posture of the case, if the Court should rule that we should have cross-applied, it could be interpreted that we have waived the other part of the case, and I merely wanted to briefly state our position on the main part, and that is that our primary responsibility here is to urge the Court not to reverse the judgment of the Supreme Court of Delaware, and not to take the position urged by the Attorney General to reverse and send the matter back.

In other words, so far as we are concerned, we are asking that the Court affirm the decision of the Supreme Court of Delaware.

The other point we wanted to urge upon the Court was even if the Court is of the opinion that they should not pass upon the validity one way or the other of the Delaware statutes, because we did not cross-appeal or for some other reason, it appears to us that these cases are all consolidated, the state cases in particular, and that if the Court, in the Virginia and the South Carolina cases in particular, should make it clear that the state was without power to enforce such statutes in the State of Virginia and the State of South Carolina, then merely affirm the decision of the Delaware case, I have no doubt at all that the Supreme Court of Delaware would follow the rationale of the decisions in the Virginia and South Carolina cases, so that if, as has been urged over and over again—and as I understand the position of the Attorney General of Delaware—that when these physical facilities become equal they will then either put the colored children out or take some proceedings to have them removed, that if the Court goes the way I have just suggested, I have no doubt that at that time the same Supreme Court of Delaware, having considered the decision in the Virginia and South Carolina cases, would hold that the Attorney General could not have the children removed because as of that time it would clearly be the decision of this Court that in such instances the State of Delaware as well as the State of Virginia and South Carolina are without power to enforce such statutes.

So it seems to me to narrow down to the position that in this case if the Court merely affirms the decision of the Supreme Court of Delaware, the first task that we have before this Court is to urge this Court to affirm that decision, at least go that far, because to us the decision in the Supreme Court of Delaware is the minimum that we could expect on our theory of what the Fourteenth Amendment

---

[59]Helvering v. Lerner Stores Corporation, 314 U.S. 463 (1941). A taxpayer unsuccessfully challenged the federal government's system for determining capital stock tax liability on the ground that it was an unlawful delegation of legislative authority since the taxpayer was free to choose any valuation he desired for the capital stock. The constitutional point was considered by the Court although no appeal on that issue had been taken. Langnes v. Green, 282 U.S. 531 (1931) was an action to limit liability of a shipowner following a collision at sea. He was allowed to raise a question decided adversely below although he did not appeal that issue.

requires. And with that I don't need the McLaurin or any of the other cases to urge that upon the Court.

I go all the way back to the Gaines case, where Chief Justice Hughes said that the laws segregating the races depend upon their validity on the equality that is offered under it. So I think in that case, and despite all Mr. Young said earlier about what was peculiar to Delaware and what have you, I do not find anything that says that this Court should reverse the decision which said merely that in the absence of equal physical facilities the colored children have to be admitted to the existing facilities.

So on that very narrow basis, it seems to me that the judgment of the Delaware court should be affirmed, at least on that narrow basis.

Our other ground that we urged, which was that in the decision and opinion of this Court, the expression be—or rather not, instruction—but that it should be made clear to the Delaware court that they are not required as they thought by the prior decisions of this Court to uphold the validity of the statutes so that at future times it can be applied to the same plaintiffs in this case.

Furthermore, I do not think that we should reply in detail to the Attorney General of Delaware's argument about the meaning of the Fourteenth Amendment, because our argument in the other cases has been full, and I do not know anything to add to our other argument, and I do not see anything that has been added by Mr. Young's argument, which would require us to meet it, except the peculiar situation in Delaware.

He thinks it is peculiar, we think it is peculiar. We have both dealt with it in great detail in our briefs, and I think that is as far as I would like to go on that.

I agree that the remedy point is most certainly not involved in this case. I think, as in the South Carolina and Virginia cases, the only points involved are the points as to the Congressional intent and the reliance that I understand from Mr. Young's argument runs the same as the others.

We have the segregation in the schools of the District of Columbia, that they did not intend to exclude—rather, they did intend to exclude—school segregation.

All of the lawyers have repeatedly argued that since the states had segregation statutes when they ratified the Fourteenth Amendment, we would gather something from that, when in truth and in fact, this Court in the case of *Neal* v. *Delaware*[ii] and specifically—of course, they were speaking of the jury situation—in that case the Court said specifically, this Court:

> The Fourteenth Amendment was intended to strike the word 'white' out of all those statutes.

So it seems to me when you pick up one point or another point it will do the Court no good.

The other point urged by the Attorney General is on the power argument and what this Court can do in the situation, and as I understand the power argument, it is, so far as we are concerned, that the authority of this Court is clear, and no one disputes that.

---

[ii]Neal v. Delaware, 103 U.S. 370 (1881). The Delaware Constitution permitting only white men to serve on juries was declared unconstitutional.

The real question involved is as to whether or not the states involved as of now, today, do or do not have power to use race and race alone for the basis of segregation, and that applies, our theory, that the states have been effectively deprived of that power hold as true—Mr. Young emphasized this—in Delaware, which is just beside Pennsylvania.

It applies as well there as it applies in South Carolina and Virginia, and therefore, unless there are questions, we submit this case and urge the Court to affirm the judgment of the Supreme Court of Delaware.

Thank you, sirs.

JUSTICE FRANKFURTER: Might I ask General Young whether the specific judgment we have before us is the final order that was entered by the Chancellor which was adopted by the court? Is that your understanding?

MR. YOUNG: That is right. There is nothing in rebuttal.

(Whereupon, at 2:40 p.m., the Court adjourned.)

FINAL DECISION ON THE MERITS

# BROWN ET AL. v. BOARD OF EDUCATION
# OF TOPEKA ET AL.

*NO. 1. APPEAL FROM THE UNITED STATES DISTRICT COURT
FOR THE DISTRICT OF KANSAS.\**

Argued December 9, 1952.—Reargued December 8, 1953.—
Decided May 17, 1954.

347 U.S. 483

MR. CHIEF JUSTICE WARREN delivered the opinion of the Court.

These cases come to us from the States of Kansas, South Carolina, Virginia, and Delaware. They are premised on different facts and different local conditions, but a common legal question justifies their consideration together in this consolidated opinion.[1]

---

\*Together with No. 2, *Briggs et al.* v. *Elliott et al.,* on appeal from the United States District Court for the Eastern District of South Carolina, argued December 9–10, 1952, reargued December 7–8, 1953; No. 4, *Davis et al.* v. *County School Board of Prince Edward County, Virginia, et al.,* on appeal from the United States District Court for the Eastern District of Virginia, argued December 10, 1952, reargued December 7–8, 1953; and No. 10, *Gebhart et al.* v. *Belton et al.,* on certiorari to the Supreme Court of Delaware, argued December 11, 1952, reargued December 9, 1953.

[1]In the Kansas case, *Brown* v. *Board of Education,* the plaintiffs are Negro children of elementary school age residing in Topeka. They brought this action in the United States District Court for the District of Kansas to enjoin enforcement of a Kansas statute which permits, but does not require, cities of more than 15,000 population to maintain separate school facilities for Negro and white students. Kan. Gen. Stat. § 72–1724 (1949). Pursuant to that authority, the Topeka Board of Education elected to establish segregated elementary schools. Other public schools in the community, however, are operated on a nonsegregated basis. The three-judge District Court, convened under 28 U.S.C. §§ 2281 and 2284, found that segregation in public education has a detrimental effect upon Negro children, but denied relief on the ground that the Negro and white schools were substantially equal with respect to buildings, transportation, curricula, and educational qualifications of teachers. 98 F. Supp. 797. The case is here on direct appeal under 28 U.S.C. § 1253.

In the South Carolina case, *Briggs* v. *Elliott,* the plaintiffs are Negro children of both elementary and high school age residing in Clarendon County. They brought this action in the United States District Court for the Eastern District of South Carolina to enjoin enforcement of provisions in the state constitution and statutory code which require the segregation of Negroes and whites in public schools. S.C. Const., Art. XI § 7; S.C. Code § 5377 (1942). The three-judge District Court, convened under 28 U.S.C. §§ 2281 and 2284, denied the requested relief. The court found that the Negro schools were inferior to the white schools and ordered the defendants to begin immediately to equalize the facilities.

In each of the cases, minors of the Negro race, through their legal representatives, seek the aid of the courts in obtaining admission to the public schools of their community on a nonsegregated basis. In each instance, they had been denied admission to schools attended by white children under laws requiring or permitting segregation according to race. This segregation was alleged to deprive the plaintiffs of the equal protection of the laws under the Fourteenth Amendment. In each of the cases other than the Delaware case, a three-judge federal district court denied relief to the plaintiffs on the so-called "separate but equal" doctrine announced by this Court in *Plessy* v. *Ferguson,* 163 U.S. 537. Under that doctrine, equality of treatment is accorded when the races are provided substantially equal facilities even though these facilities be separate. In the Delaware case, the Supreme court of Delaware adhered to that doctrine, but ordered that the plain-

---

But the court sustained the validity of the contested provisions and denied the plaintiffs admission to the white schools during the equalization program. 98 F. Supp. 529. This Court vacated the District Court's judgment and remanded the case for the purpose of obtaining the court's views on a report filed by the defendants concerning the progress made in the equalization program. 342 U.S. 350. On remand, the District Court found that substantial equality had been achieved except for buildings and that the defendants were proceeding to rectify this inequality as well. 103 F. Supp. 920. The case is again here on direct appeal under 28 U.S.C. § 1253.

In the Virginia case, *Davis* v. *County School Board,* the plaintiffs are Negro children of high school age residing in Prince Edward County. They brought this action in the United States District Court for the Eastern District of Virginia to enjoin enforcement of provisions in the state constitution and statutory code which require the segregation of Negroes and whites in public schools. Va. Const., § 140; Va. Code § 22–221 (1950). The three-judge District Court, convened under 28 U.S.C. §§ 2281 and 2284, denied the requested relief. The court found the Negro school inferior in physical plant, curricula, and transportation, and ordered the defendants forthwith to provide substantially equal curricula and transportation and to "proceed with all reasonable diligence and dispatch to remove" the inequality in physical plant. But, as in the South Carolina case, the court sustained the validity of the contested provisions and denied the plaintiffs admission to the white schools during the equalization program. 103 F.Supp. 337. The case is here on direct appeal under 28 U.S.C. § 1253.

In the Delaware case, *Gebhart* v. *Belton,* the plaintiffs are Negro children of both elementary and high school age residing in New Castle County. They brought this action in the Delaware Court of Chancery to enjoin enforcement of provisions in the state constitution and statutory code which require the segregation of Negroes and whites in public schools. Del. Const., Art. X, § 2; Del. Rev. Code § 2631 (1935). The Chancellor gave judgment for the plaintiffs and ordered their immediate admission to schools previously attended only by white children, on the ground that the Negro schools were inferior with respect to teacher training, pupil-teacher ratio, extracurricular activities, physical plant, and time and distance involved in travel. 87 A. 2d 862. The Chancellor also found that segregation itself results in an inferior education for Negro children (see note 10, *infra*), but did not rest his decision on that ground. *Id.,* at 865. The Chancellor's decree was affirmed by the Supreme Court of Delaware, which intimated, however, that the defendants might be able to obtain a modification of the decree after equalization of the Negro and white schools had been accomplished. 91 A. 2d 137, 152. The defendants, contending only that the Delaware courts had erred in ordering the immediate admission of the Negro plaintiffs to the white schools, applied to this Court for certiorari. The writ was granted, 344 U.S. 891. The plaintiffs, who were successful below, did not submit a cross-petition.

tiffs be admitted to the white schools because of their superiority to the Negro schools.

The plaintiffs contend that segregated public schools are not "equal" and cannot be made "equal," and that hence they are deprived of the equal protection of the laws. Because of the obvious importance of the question presented, the Court took jurisdiction.[2] Argument was heard in the 1952 Term, and reargument was heard this Term on certain questions propounded by the Court.[3]

Reargument was largely devoted to the circumstances surrounding the adoption of the Fourteenth Amendment in 1868. It covered exhaustively consideration of the Amendment in Congress, ratification by the states, then existing practices in racial segregation, and the views of proponents and opponents of the Amendment. This discussion and our own investigation convince us that, although these sources cast some light, it is not enough to resolve the problem with which we are faced. At best, they are inconclusive. The most avid proponents of the post-War Amendments undoubtedly intended them to remove all legal distinctions among "all persons born or naturalized in the United States." Their opponents, just as certainly, were antagonistic to both the letter and the spirit of the Amendments and wished them to have the most limited effect. What others in Congress and the state legislatures had in mind cannot be determined with any degree of certainty.

An additional reason for the inconclusive nature of the Amendment's history, with respect to segregated schools, is the status of public education at that time.[4] In the South, the movement toward free common schools, supported by general taxation, had not yet taken hold. Education of white children was largely in the hands of private groups. Education of Negroes was almost nonexistent, and practically all of the race were illiterate. In fact, any education of Negroes was forbidden by law in some states. Today, in contract, many Negroes have achieved outstanding success in the arts and sciences as well as in the business and profes-

---

[2]344 U.S. 1, 141, 891.

[3]345 U.S. 972. The Attorney General of the United States participated both Terms as *amicus curiae.*

[4]For a general study of the development of public education prior to the Amendment, see Butts and Cremin, A History of Education in American Culture (1953), Pts. I, II; Cubberley, Public Education in the United States (1934 ed.), cc. II–XII. School practices current at the time of the adoption of the Fourteenth Amendment are described in Butts and Cremin, *supra,* at 269–275; Cubberley, *supra,* at 288–339, 408–431; Knight, Public Education in the South (1922), cc. VIII, IX. See also H. Ex. Doc. No. 315, 41st Cong., 2d Sess. (1871). Although the demand for free public schools followed substantially the same pattern in both the North and the South, the development in the South did not begin to gain momentum until about 1850, some twenty years after that in the North. The reasons for the somewhat slower development in the South *(e. g.,* the rural character of the South and the different regional attitudes toward state assistance) are well explained in Cubberley, *supra,* at 408–423. In the country as a whole, but particularly in the South, the War virtually stopped all progress in public education. *Id.,* at 427–428. The low status of Negro education in all sections of the country, both before and immediately after the War, is described in Beale, A History of Freedom of Teaching in American Schools (1941), 112–132, 175–195. Compulsory school attendance laws were not generally adopted until after the ratification of the Fourteenth Amendment, and it was not until 1918 that such laws were in force in all the states. Cubberley, *supra,* at 563–565.

sional world. It is true that public school education at the time of the Amendment had advanced further in the North, but the effect of the Amendment on Northern States was generally ignored in the congressional debates. Even in the North, the conditions of public education did not approximate those existing today. The curriculum was usually rudimentary; ungraded schools were common in rural areas; the school term was but three months a year in many states; and compulsory school attendance was virtually unknown. As a consequence, it is not surprising that there should be so little in the history of the Fourteenth Amendment relating to its intended effect on public education.

In the first cases in this Court construing the Fourteenth Amendment, decided shortly after its adoption, the Court interpreted it as proscribing all state-imposed discriminations against the Negro race.[5] The doctrine of "separate but equal" did not make its appearance in this Court until 1896 in the case of *Plessy* v. *Ferguson, supra,* involving not education but transportation.[6] American courts have since labored with the doctrine for over half a century. In this Court, there have been six cases involving the "separate but equal" doctrine in the field of public education.[7] In *Cumming* v. *County Board of Education,* 175 U.S. 528, and *Gong Lum* v. *Rice,* 275 U.S. 78, the validity of the doctrine itself was not challenged.[8] In more recent cases, all on the graduate school level, inequality was found in that specific benefits enjoyed by white students were denied to Negro

[5]*Slaughter-House Cases,* 16 Wall. 36, 67–72 (1873); *Strauder* v. *West Virginia,* 100 U.S. 303, 307–308 (1880):
"It ordains that no State shall deprive any person of life, liberty, or property, without due process of law, or deny to any person within its jurisdiction the equal protection of the laws. What is that but declaring that the law in the States shall be the same for the black as for the white; that all persons, whether colored or white, shall stand equal before the laws of the States, and, in regard to the colored race, for whose protection the amendment was primarily designed, that no discrimination shall be made against them by the law because of their color? The words of the amendment, it is true, are prohibitory, but they contain a necessary implication of a positive immunity, or right, most valuable to the colored race,—the right to exemption from unfriendly legislation against them distinctively as colored,—exemption from legal discriminations, implying inferiority in civil society, lessening the security of their enjoyment of the rights which others enjoy, and discriminations which are steps towards reducing them to the condition of a subject race."
See also *Virginia* v. *Rives,* 100 U.S. 313 318 (1880); *Ex parte Virginia,* 100 U.S. 339, 344–345 (1880).

[6]The doctrine apparently originated in *Roberts* v. *City of Boston,* 59 Mass. 198, 206 (1850), upholding school segregation against attack as being violative of a state constitutional guarantee of equality. Segregation in Boston public schools was eliminated in 1855. Mass. Acts. 1855, c. 256. But elsewhere in the North segregation in public education has persisted in some communities until recent years. It is apparent that such segregation has long been a nationwide problem, not merely one of sectional concern.

[7]See also *Berea College* v. *Kentucky,* 211 U.S. 45 (1908).

[8]In the *Cumming* case, Negro taxpayers sought an injunction requiring the defendant school board to discontinue the operation of a high school for white children until the board resumed operation of a high school for Negro children. Similarly, in the *Gong Lum* case, the plaintiff, a child of Chinese descent, contended only that state authorities had misapplied the doctrine by classifying him with Negro children and requiring him to attend a Negro school.

students of the same educational qualifications. *Missouri ex rel. Gaines* v. *Canada,* 305 U.S. 337; *Sipuel* v. *Oklahoma,* 332 U.S. 631; *Sweatt* v. *Painter,* 339 U.S. 629; *McLaurin* v. *Oklahoma State Regents,* 339 U.S. 637. In none of these cases was it necessary to re-examine the doctrine to grant relief to the Negro plaintiff. And in *Sweatt* v. *Painter, supra,* the Court expressly reserved decision on the question whether *Plessy* v. *Ferguson* should be held inapplicable to public education.

In the instant cases, that question is directly presented. Here, unlike *Sweatt* v. *Painter,* there are findings below that the Negro and white schools involved have been equalized, or are being equalized, with respect to buildings, curricula, qualifications and salaries of teachers, and other "tangible" factors.[9] Our decision, therefore, cannot turn on merely a comparison of these tangible factors in the Negro and white schools involved in each of the cases. We must look instead to the effect of segregation itself on public education.

In approaching this problem, we cannot turn the clock back to 1868 when the Amendment was adopted, or even to 1896 when *Plessy* v. *Ferguson* was written. We must consider public education in the light of its full development and its present place in American life throughout the Nation. Only in this way can it be determined if segregation in public schools deprives these plaintiffs of the equal protection of the laws.

Today, education is perhaps the most important function of state and local governments. Compulsory school attendance laws and the great expenditures for education both demonstrate our recognition of the importance of education to our democratic society. It is required in the performance of our most basic public responsibilities, even service in the armed forces. It is the very foundation of good citizenship. Today it is a principal instrument in awakening the child to cultural values, in preparing him for later professional training, and in helping him to adjust normally to his environment. In these days, it is doubtful that any child may reasonably be expected to succeed in life if he is denied the opportunity of an education. Such an opportunity, where the state has undertaken to provide it, is a right which must be made available to all on equal terms.

We come then to the question presented: Does segregation of children in public schools solely on the basis of race, even though the physical facilities and other "tangible" factors may be equal, deprive the children of the minority group of equal educational opportunities? We believe that it does.

In *Sweatt* v. *Painter, supra,* in finding that a segregated law school for Negroes could not provide them equal educational opportunities, this Court relied in large part on "those qualities which are incapable of objective measurement but which make for greatness in a law school." In *McLaurin* v. *Oklahoma State Regents, supra,* the Court, in requiring that a Negro admitted to a white graduate

[9]In the Kansas case, the court below found substantial equality as to all such factors. 98 F. Supp. 797, 798. In the South Carolina case, the court below found that the defendants were proceeding "promptly and in good faith to comply with the court's decree." 103 F. Supp. 920, 921. In the Virginia case, the court below noted that the equalization program was already "afoot and progressing" (103 F. Supp. 337, 341); since then, we have been advised, in the Virginia Attorney General's brief on reargument, that the program has now been completed. In the Delaware case, the court below similarly noted that the state's equalization program was well under way. 91 A. 2d 137, 149.

school be treated like all other students, again resorted to intangible considerations: ". . . his ability to study, to engage in discussions and exchange views with other students, and, in general, to learn his profession." Such considerations apply with added force to children in grade and high schools. To separate them from others of similar age and qualifications solely because of their race generates a feeling of inferiority as to their status in the community that may affect their hearts and minds in a way unlikely ever to be undone. The effect of this separation on their educational opportunities was well stated by a finding in the Kansas case by a court which nevertheless felt compelled to rule against the Negro plaintiffs:

"Segregation of white and colored children in public schools has a detrimental effect upon the colored children. The impact is greater when it has the sanction of the law; for the policy of separating the races is usually interpreted as denoting the inferiority of the negro group. A sense of inferiority affects the motivation of a child to learn Segregation with the sanction of law, therefore, has a tendency to [retard] the educational and mental development of negro children and to deprive them of some of the benefits they would receive in a racial [ly] integrated school system." [10]

Whatever may have been the extent of psychological knowledge at the time of *Plessy* v. *Ferguson,* this finding is amply supported by modern authority. [11] Any language in *Plessy* v. *Ferguson* contrary to this finding is rejected.

We conclude that in the field of public education the doctrine of "separate but equal" has no place. Separate educational facilities are inherently unequal. Therefore, we hold that the plaintiffs and others similarly situated for whom the actions have been brought are, by reason of the segregation complained of, deprived of the equal protection of the laws guaranteed by the Fourteenth Amendment. This disposition makes unnecessary any discussion whether such segregation also violates the Due Process Clause of the Fourteenth Amendment. [12]

Because these are class actions, because of the wide applicability of this decision, and because of the great variety of local conditions, the formulation of decrees in these cases presents problems of considerable complexity. On reargument, the consideration of appropriate relief was necessarily subordinated to the primary question—the constitutionality of segregation in public education. We

[10]A similar finding was made in the Delaware case: "I conclude from the testimony that in our Delaware society, State-imposed segregation in education itself results in the Negro children, as a class, receiving educational opportunities which are substantially inferior to those available to white children otherwise similarly situated." 87 A. 2d 862, 865.

[11]K. B. Clark, Effect of Prejudice and Discrimination on Personality Development (Midcentury White House Conference on Children and Youth, 1950); Witmer and Kotinsky, Personality in the Making (1952), c. VI; Deutscher and Chein, The Psychological Effects of Enforced Segregation: A Survey of Social Science Opinion, 26 J. Psychol. 259 (1948); Chein, What are the Psychological Effects of Segregation Under Conditions of Equal Facilities?, 3 Int. J. Opinion and Attitude Res. 229 (1949); Brameld, Educational Costs, in Discrimination and National Welfare (MacIver, ed., 1949), 44–48; Frazier, The Negro in the United States (1949), 674–681. And see generally Mydral, An American Dilemma (1944).

[12]See *Bolling* v. *Sharpe, post,* p. 497, concerning the Due Process Clause of the Fifth Amendment.

have now announced that such segregation is a denial of the equal protection of the laws. In order that we may have the full assistance of the parties in formulating decrees, the cases will be restored to the docket, and the parties are requested to present further argument on Questions 4 and 5 previously propounded by the Court for the reargument this Term.[13] The Attorney General of the United States is again invited to participate. The Attorneys General of the states requiring or permitting segregation in public education will also be permitted to appear as *amici curiae* upon request to do so by September 15, 1954, and submission of briefs by October 1, 1954.[14]

*It is so ordered.*

[13]"4. Assuming it is decided that segregation in public schools violates the Fourteenth Amendment

"(a) would a decree necessarily follow providing that, within the limits set by normal geographic school districting, Negro children should forthwith be admitted to schools of their choice, or

"(b) may this Court, in the exercise of its equity powers, permit an effective gradual adjustment to be brought about from existing segregated systems to a system not based on color distinctions?

"5. On the assumption on which questions 4 (a) and (b) are based, and assuming further that this Court will exercise its equity powers to the end described in question 4 (b),

"(a) should this Court formulate detailed decrees in these cases;

"(b) if so, what specific issues should the decrees reach;

"(c) should this Court appoint a special master to hear evidence with a view to recommending specific terms for such decrees;

"(d) should this Court remand to the courts of first instance with directions to frame decrees in these cases, and if so what general directions should the decrees of this Court include and what procedures should the courts of first instance follow in arriving at the specific terms of more detailed decrees?"

[14]See Rule 42, Revised Rules of this Court (effective July 1, 1954).

## BOLLING ET AL. v. SHARPE ET AL.

*CERTIORARI TO THE UNITED STATES COURT OF APPEALS*
*FOR THE DISTRICT OF COLUMBIA CIRCUIT.*

No. 8. Argued December 10–11, 1952.—Reargued December 8–9,
1953.—Decided May 17, 1954.

347 U.S. 497

MR. CHIEF JUSTICE WARREN delivered the opinion of the Court.

This case challenges the validity of segregation in the public schools of the District of Columbia. The petitioners, minors of the Negro race, allege that such segregation deprives them of due process of law under the Fifth Amendment. They were refused admission to a public school attended by white children solely because of their race. They sought the aid of the District Court for the District of Columbia in obtaining admission. That court dismissed their complaint. The Court granted a writ of certiorari before judgment in the Court of Appeals because of the importance of the constitutional question presented. 344 U.S. 873.

We have this day held that the Equal Protection Clause of the Fourteenth Amendment prohibits the states from maintaining racially segregated public schools.[1] The legal problem in the District of Columbia is somewhat different, however. The Fifth Amendment, which is applicable in the District of Columbia, does not contain an equal protection clause as does the Fourteenth Amendment which applies only to the states. But the concepts of equal protection and due process, both stemming from our American ideal of fairness, are not mutually exclusive. The "equal protection of the laws" is a more explicit safeguard of prohibited unfairness than "due process of law," and, therefore, we do not imply that the two are always interchangeable phrases. But, as this Court has recognized, discrimination may be so unjustifiable as to be violative of due process.[2]

Classifications based solely upon race must be scrutinized with particular care, since they are contrary to our traditions and hence constitutionally suspect.[3] As long ago as 1896, this Court declared the principle "that the Constitution of the United States, in its present form, forbids, so far as civil and political rights are concerned, discrimination by the General Government, or by the States, against any citizen because of his race."[4] And in *Buchanan* v. *Warley,* 245 U. S. 60, the Court held that a statute which limited the right of a property owner to convey his property to a person of another race was, as an unreasonable discrimination, a denial of due process of law.

Although the Court has not assumed to define "liberty" with any great precision, that term is not confined to mere freedom from bodily restraint. Liberty under law extends to the full range of conduct which the individual is free to pur-

---

[1] *Brown* v. *Board of Education, ante,* p. 483.

[2] *Detroit Bank* v. *United States,* 317 U.S. 329; *Currin* v. *Wallace,* 306 U.S. 1, 13–14; *Steward Machine Co.* v. *Davis,* 301 U.S. 548, 585.

[3] *Korematsu* v. *United States,* 323 U.S. 214, 216; *Hirabayashi* v. *United States,* 320 U.S. 81, 100.

[4] *Gibson* v. *Mississippi,* 162 U.S. 565, 591. Cf. *Steele* v. *Louisville & Nashville R. Co.,* 323 U.S. 192, 198–199.

sue, and it cannot be restricted except for a proper governmental objective. Segregation in public education is not reasonably related to any proper governmental objective, and thus it imposes on Negro children of the District of Columbia a burden that constitutes an arbitrary deprivation of their liberty in violation of the Due Process Clause.

In view of our decision that the Constitution prohibits the states from maintaining racially segregated public schools, it would be unthinkable that the same Constitution would impose a lesser duty on the Federal Government.[5] We hold that racial segregation in the public schools of the District of Columbia is a denial of the due process of law guaranteed by the Fifth Amendment to the Constitution.

For the reasons set out in *Brown* v. *Board of Education,* this case will be restored to the docket for reargument on Questions 4 and 5 previously propounded by the Court. 345 U.S. 972.

*It is so ordered.*

[5] Cf. *Hurd* v. *Hodge,* 334 U.S. 24.

1955 ARGUMENT

IN THE SUPREME COURT OF THE UNITED STATES

OCTOBER TERM, 1954

OLIVER BROWN, MRS. RICHARD LAWTON, et al.

vs.

BOARD OF EDUCATION, TOPEKA, KANSAS, et al.

Case No. 1


FRANCIS B. GEBHART, et al.

vs.

ETHEL LOUISE BELTON, et al.

Case No. 5


SPOTTSWOOD THOMAS BOLLING, et al.

vs.

C. MELVIN SHARPE, et al.

Case No. 4


HARRY BRIGGS, JR., et al.

vs.

R. W. ELLIOTT, et al.

Case No. 2


DOROTHY E. DAVIS, et al.

vs.

COUNTY SCHOOL BOARD OF PRINCE EDWARD COUNTY, VIRGINIA, et al.

Case No. 3


Washington, D.C.

April 11, 1955

The above-entitled matter came on for oral argument at 12 noon.

PRESENT:

The Chief Justice, Earl Warren and Associate Justices Black, Reed, Frankfurter, Douglas, Burton, Clark, Minton
and Harlan.

APPEARANCES:

On behalf of the Board of Education of Topeka, Kansas:

HAROLD R. FATZER, Attorney General of Kansas.

On behalf of Oliver Brown, Et Al:

ROBERT L. CARTER.

On behalf of Francis B. Gebhart, Et Al:

JOSEPH DONALD CRAVEN, Attorney General of Delaware.

On behalf of Ethel Louise Belton, Et Al:

LOUIS L. REDDING.

On behalf of Spottswood Thomas Bolling Et Al:

GEORGE E. C. HAYES and JAMES M. NABRIT, JR.

On Behalf of C. Melvin Sharpe, Et Al:

MILTON D. KORMAN.

On Behalf of Harry Briggs, Et Al:

THURGOOD MARSHALL and SPOTTSWOOD W. ROBINSON, III;

On Behalf of R. W. Elliott, Et Al:

ROBERT McC. FIGG, JR., and S. E. ROGERS.

On behalf of Dorothy E. Davis, Et Al:

THURGOOD MARSHALL and SPOTTSWOOD W. ROBINSON, III.

On behalf of County School Board of Prince Edward County, Virginia, Et Al:

ARCHIBALD G. ROBERTSON, and LINDSAY ALMOND, JR., Attorney General of Virginia.

Amicus Curiae:

Richard W. Ervin, Florida.

Ralph E. Odum, Florida

I. Beverly Lake, North Carolina.

Tom Gentry, Arkansas.

Mac Q. Williamson, Oklahoma.

C. Ferdinand Sybert, Maryland.

John Ben Shepperd, Texas.

Brunell Naldrep, Texas

THE CHIEF JUSTICE: No. 1 on the Calendar, Alfred Brown, Mrs. Richard Lawton, et al, vs. Board of Eudcation of Topeka, Kansas, et al.

THE CLERK: Counsel are present, sir.

THE CHIEF JUSTICE: Attorney General Fatzer.

ARGUMENT ON BEHALF OF BOARD OF EDUCATION

by MR. FATZER

MR. FATZER: Chief Justice and Members of the Supreme Court: I am Harold R. Fatzer, the Attorney General of Kansas and with me today is Mr. Paul E. Wilson, the First Assistant Attorney General who has previously argued the

State's position when the question of the answer to Questions 1, 2 and 3 was argued heretofore.

Today, we appear not as an adversary. We appear here to be of assistance if we can to the Court in helping it see that proper decrees are imposed and made.

Now in answer directly to the questions, Your Honors, of Nos. 4 and 5 and the subsequent subsections, we want to say that traditionally in Kansas, segregation has not been a policy of that state, on a state level. We suspect that the Kansas case is probably the least complex of any that is before it. We wish to say that that has never been a matter of state policy. We believe that the decision of the Court has been received by the students, teachers, school administrators and by the parents of both colored and white with approval.

In answering the—assisting this Court, I shall be very brief in stating our position, what we believe should be done with respect to the case that is now before the Court, that is, the Topeka Board of Education.

Your Honors, we believe that 4(a) should be answered in the negative. We do not believe that the immediate and forthwith admission of the plaintiffs—although they may be in the school; I am not prepared to tell the Court that they are not, I suspect that they are—would, and as the Board of Education found, work a hardship, would impair administrative procedures, and so we would suggest to the Court that no decree be entered which would forthwith admit any student to the school of his choice. Rather, we believe that the Court should exercise its equitable jurisdiction at all times in these cases because of the public interest involved, notwithstanding the fact that the plaintiffs in the case would undoubtedly have some present and immediate right and personal right of admission to the schools.

We believe, Your Honors—and I want to make a brief report of a situation that has developed since the brief in the Kansas case was filed—we believe that this case should be reversed, that it should be remanded to the Federal District Court in Kansas. I should like to tell you and briefly review the efforts of the Topeka Board of Education to terminate segregation in the public schools in that city.

It was commenced on September 3, 1953. The policy announced by the School Board was to terminate maintenance of segregation in elementary schools as rapidly as was practicable. Five days following that date to wit, September 8, 1953, segregation was terminated in two schools in the city. It involved only approximately ten colored children, but they were living in the district. They were permitted to attend those schools.

JUSTICE BURTON: You referred to the termination of segregation in the elementary schools?

MR. FATZER: That is correct.

JUSTICE BURTON: Has it been terminated in the other schools?

MR. FATZER: There is none in grades one to six, Mr. Justice.

That was called the first step. The second step was made on January 20, 1954. And that was effective for the school term, current school term, 1954-1955.

At that time, and by order of the Board of Education, segregation was terminated in twelve school districts in the city and transportation was not provided to the Negro school children living in those twelve districts on the basis that the child could attend the school of that district but with the privilege, if he preferred, to attend the colored school which he had been attending. This affected approximately 113 children, plus the ten that had been previously affected from Step 2—123 Negro children were placed in the integrated school.

JUSTICE FRANKFURTER: What is the total of school population into which these 123 were merged, roughly?

MR. FATZER: I will have to refer—

JUSTICE FRANKFURTER: What magnitude? Was it 10,000, or 50,000?

MR. FATZER: No, nothing of that kind. I think perhaps the school population in Topeka is roughly 8200, Mr. Justice.

JUSTICE FRANKFURTER: So there was no problem of space and buildings, and none of those problems?

MR. FATZER: In one school there was. One school in which, in the so-called Polk School there was the space problem and I think three children were admitted to that school and others were not because of this space problem.

JUSTICE FRANKFURTER: And there was no redistricting of the districts you have?

MR. FATZER: Not at that time.

Now I spoke to Your Honors of a subsequent event that occurred subsequent to the filing of the state's brief here in response to the request of the Court, which occurred on February 23, 1955. We have with us today the minutes of the Topeka Board of Education adopted February 23, 1955, which we have filed in the Clerk's office as a supplement to the brief filed in this Court in response to Questions 4 and 5 propounded by the Court. We file it simply for informational purposes to show the good faith of the members of the Board of Education of Topeka in carrying out the previous announced policy of terminating segregation as rapidly as practicable.

Now this third step, Your Honors, is effective September, 1955. It provides, (1) that segregation has been terminated in all remaining buildings; (2) that the McKinley Elementary School, one of the colored schools, be closed and that it be placed on a standby basis for the coming year; (3) that colored schools, Buchanan School, Monroe and Washington Schools be assigned districts within the areas of the city, the same as any other school area in the city and that any child who is affected by the change in the school district—I will go ahead—any child who is affected by the change in school district lines as recommended on a map which we did not attach hereto, be given the option of finishing the elementary grades in the school in which he attended in 1954 and 1955. That is, he could attend the school in the district in which he resided or, if the new district overlaps now into a district that formerly existed before the redistricting, he can attend the school that he attended last year. In other words, it is equally available to both the white and the colored students.

JUSTICE FRANKFURTER: Have I missed a statement as to the basis or the reasons for which this redistricting was done?

MR. FATZER: The basis of it was done, of course, Your Honor, on the Court's decision of May, 1954, to comply with the order of this Court that segregation, per se, was unconstitutional. That is the basis of it.

JUSTICE FRANKFURTER: You mean there were exclusively Negro schools?

MR. FATZER: Yes.

JUSTICE FRANKFURTER: And those were withdrawn from use by the city?

MR. FATZER: One was, Your Honor.

JUSTICE FRANKFURTER: One was. And the others are now available to children, intermixed, is that it?

MR. FATZER: Yes.

JUSTICE FRANKFURTER: Was that districting a geographic districting?

MR. FATZER: Yes.

JUSTICE FRANFKURTER: Was there any indication in the minutes of the Board or in any document you filed as to the exact geographic nature of this districting?

MR. FATZER: Unfortunately, Your Honors, we did not have attached to this the map of the Board of Education which designated the particular districts of the city school system.

JUSTICE FRANKFURTER: Could you supplement that later?

MR. FATZER: Yes, we would be glad to.

JUSTICE REED: Could you also supplement that by showing the percentage of actual white children in the districts?

MR. FATZER: I think that is set forth here in the figures of the Superintendent of Public Instruction and approved by the Board.

This shows roughly, Your Honors, an estimation of—on the assumption of one-third of the children attending the strictly colored schools, Washington, Monroe and the Buchanan Schools, who would be given the choice to attend the schools which they attended last year, those three schools, or to go into the new district in which they might reside and attend the formerly all-white schools—one-third of the colored children will attend the school at which they attended last year or this present term.

Bear in mind this is effective in September of this coming term.

There is another provision in this resolution of the Topeka Board of Education and that is with respect to kindergarten children, that those children entering kindergarten in 1955–1956, September of this coming year, this coming September, those who are affected by the change in the school district boundaries as recommended, be given the option of attending the same school in 1955–1956 that they would have attended in 1954–1955 had they been opened up then.

It has been reported to the Attorney General's office that the purpose of this clause is that if a parent who had a child that would enter kindergarten this year formerly lived in a segregated district and as a result of the change of school district boundaries, a result of this policy, the parent can send his child to the school he would have attended last year or this current term if he had been old enough or he can always send him to the school in the district in which he resides.

It has been suggested to us that the purpose of that is to permit any parent to move from the area where he lives to some other area in the city.

JUSTICE REED: Have you indicated the number of each in each of these districts, the number of white and colored children?

MR. FATZER: Yes, if you have it, Your Honor—

JUSTICE REED: I have it.

MR. FATZER: On page 2 it shows approximately the number of students changing from the four colored schools to the non-segregated schools.

JUSTICE REED: Those I suppose are the integrated schools?

MR. FATZER: That is correct. I used the term "non-integrated schools" as of the date of this order.

JUSTICE REED: It does not show the schools—under paragraph 4, it does not show the number of white and colored in different grades?

MR. FATZER: Well, if Your Honors will go down to the last four schools listed in paragraph 4—Buchanan, Monroe, McKinley and Washington—you will note the estimated total of attendance this year is considerably lower than the actual attendance on this present school term. Whereas, the reverse is true of the other schools affected.

JUSTICE CLARK: What was the attendance this past session, this present system?

MR. FATZER: In the whole school system?

JUSTICE CLARK: No, the last three schools.

MR. FATZER: Buchanan, 110. Monroe, 181. No, I beg your pardon, Buchanan 136; Monroe, 256.

JUSTICE CLARK: That is these figures here, I see. I thought that was the next year.

MR. FATZER: No, this is the actual, 10–15–54, Mr. Justice Clark, turn to the right-hand side of the page.

JUSTICE CLARK: Yes, I see. Thank you.

JUSTICE REED: Are your opponents here? Are they going to argue?

MR. FATZER: Yes, they are.

JUSTICE HARLAN: Could I ask you a question?

MR. FATZER: Yes, sir.

JUSTICE HARLAN: Is the difference between those two columns, for example, the difference between 110 and 136 in the case of Buchanan, is that a result of your redistricting?

MR. FATZER: That is the estimated result of redistricting.

JUSTICE HARLAN: Without regard to the possible exercise of the option that you referred to?

MR. FATZER: Well, that is taken into consideration on this estimate on the basis that one-third of the children attending Washington, Monroe, Buchanan, will remain. Two-thirds of them will go to some other school.

JUSTICE REED: Are all the schools under four, are they colored, or only the last three?

MR. FATZER: The last four are, Buchanan, Monroe, McKinley, and Washington.

JUSTICE REED: That is my understanding, but I still do not understand how many colored pupils are estimated to be in grammar school next year.

MR. FATZER: Fifty-eight, your Honor, at the top of page 2.

JUSTICE REED: Fifty-eight. That is the estimate for next year?

MR. FATZER: Yes, sir. Now, I am not quite sure that that takes into consideration, and it probably does not, the 123 students that have been integrated on Steps 1 and 2. This is an estimate of Step 3 to complete the program.

We believe, Your Honors, that this Board has complied with the Court's decision in good faith. That it has done everything it could as expediently and as rapidly as possible. It has taken approximately a year and five months of this willing Board to meet its administrative program and problems, to provide for teacher assignments, student assignments. The administrative intent of compliance has been declared. And we believe, your Honors, that the rule of *Eccles* v. *Peoples Bank* in 333 U.S. 426 is applicable, that where the administrative intention is expressed but has not yet come to fruition, we have held that the controversy is not ripe for equitable intervention. We believe that the cause should be remanded but that this Board be permitted to carry out its orderly process of integration.

Now perhaps the Court might be interested in the other cities that are not affected by the decree in this case, governing solely the Topeka Board of Education. I shall briefly cover them.

In the first place, as I told the Court, this decision has received no adverse reaction from the people of our state. For instance, the City of Atchison, on the Missouri River, approximately 30,000 people, with about 10 per cent Negro population. On September 12, 1953 the Board of Education adopted a resolution terminating segregation in grades seven through twelve, and so as to complete the plan, segregation is to be terminated in grades one through six as soon as practicable.

In Lawrence, the seat of the University, approximately 24,000 population, with about 7 per cent of Negro population, they have maintained segregated schools since 1869. That city and that Board of Education has terminated segregation in its system.

In Leavenworth, a city of approximately 20,000, there is a population, Negro population, of about 10 per cent. The system was established, the segregated system was established in 1858 and has been maintained constantly since that time. They have adopted resolutions in that Board, in that city, and the first positive step was taken in the current year in which children of kindergarten and first-grade pupils were to be admitted to the schools nearest their residence and presumably in the ensuing school term it will be extended to grades two, three and perhaps higher.

I should like just briefly, Your Honors, to quote from a report from one of the school authorities in Leavenworth with respect to the time that, in his judgment, they require to complete their voluntary program, because I think, in the first place, this man is one of the leading public school educators in Kansas, he has started the movement in Leavenworth to comply with the Court's decision and I would like, just briefly, to read part of his report to our office:

> In my judgment, the solution will have to be carefully and slowly introduced. You and I and most Board members will readily agree to the righteousness of the complete integration from the standpoint of our established principles of decency, Christianity and democracy. However, there is a sufficient number of biased and prejudiced persons who will make life miserable for those in authority who attempt to move in that direction too rapidly. As a consequence, many of us will be accused of "dragging our feet" in the matter, not because of our personal feelings or inclinations, but because, in dealing with the public, its general approval and acceptance is indispensable. One cannot force it. He can only coax and nurture it along.

In Kansas City, Kansas, with a population of approximately 130,000 persons, about 20.5 per cent are members of the Negro population. I should point out that this city has a greater per cent of Negro population than some southern cities, such as Dallas, Louisville, St. Louis, Miami, Oklahoma City, and only slightly less than in Baltimore.

Up to the present school term, including the present school term—excuse [me], up to the present school term—the city has maintained seven elementary schools, one junior high school and one high school for its approximately 6,000 Negro students, while it had twenty-two schools which were attended by more than 23,000 white students.

Just briefly, the Board of Education of that city has adopted this resolution which provides in substance to begin integration in all public schools at the opening of school on September 13, 1954; second, to complete the integration as rapidly as class space can be provided; to accomplish the transition from segregation to integration in a natural and orderly manner designed to protect the interest of all the pupils and insure the support of the community, and they seek to avoid disruption of professional life of career teachers.

So that city, although no limit is set, they are proceeding in good faith and with dispatch to end segregation.

Parsons, a city of 15,000, located in the southern part of the state, has less than 10 per cent of Negro population, and they have announced their policy to end segregation, effective last term with respect to all schools except one school, due to its crowded condition and the fact that there was a lack of adequate facilities and it required new buildings, and when those are completed, there will be complete integration in that system.

In Coffeyville, a city on the state line, the southern state line, (approximately 60,000 to 70,000 people,) approximately 10 per cent colored population, they adopted resolutions terminating segregation at the end of the school year.

Only one city that we have not heard from, Fort Scott. We have reports that in that city the only protest against the proposed segregation was from Negro citizens. I am sure that we shall have no difficulty with that city. We, therefore, suggest to this Court that the case be reversed, that it be remanded to the district court and that the Board of Education be permitted and allowed, without the interference of any decree, to carry out the program in good faith, subject to any objections that any person might have with respect to its completeness or with respect to its application, and that, at that time, notice be given by the Court to counsel at which time those matters may be dealt with by the lower court.

JUSTICE FRANKFURTER: May I ask whether, in Kansas, you have a centralized authority over the local school boards or are they autonomous?

MR. FATZER: They are autonomous. They are elected by the people. They are financed by the people locally, except with respect to state aid, but it is not conditioned upon local action. It is conditioned upon daily, average daily attendance.

JUSTICE FRANKFURTER: And on the law enforcement side, does the Attorney General of Kansas, assuming that there is a statewide law or an order of this Court, is the authority of enforcement vested over localities in the Attorney General?

MR. FATZER: With respect to state laws, I think that is correct, sir. I am doubtful if we would have any duty to enforce the decrees of this Court.

JUSTICE FRANKFURTER: Who would? In a particular case you have Topeka. Suppose this Court enters a decree, assume we follow your suggestion of remanding the particularities to the appropriate district court of the United States and a decree is then entered, binding against the School Board of Topeka—I think it would be, would it not?

MR. FATZER: That is correct, the members of the Board.

JUSTICE FRANKFURTER: What would be the enforcing authority, the federal authority? Has the Attorney General of Kansas any responsibility in that regard?

MR. FATZER: In this case, when the three-judge court was convened, the statute was complied with, with respect to notice to the Governor and the Attorney General of the state.

It would be my judgment, Mr. Justice, that the great inherent power of the federal district court, that it can enforce its own decrees.

JUSTICE REED: Mr. Attorney General, do you have in Kansas at present a law which permits segregation?

MR. FATZER: We do not now, no, sir. We have considered it to be declared invalid by decision of this Court.

JUSTICE REED: That is you have interpreted the decision as invalidating your law?

MR. FATZER: Yes, sir, we have.

JUSTICE REED: Therefore, you feel no obligation to enforce that state law?

MR. FATZER: We feel any statute—

JUSTICE REED: You have no obligation to enforce that state law?

JUSTICE FRANKFURTER: What were the sanctions of that state law, Mr. Attorney General, in connection with Mr. Justice Reed's question—what was the nature of that law?

MR. FATZER: Purely permissive.

JUSTICE FRANKFURTER: Just authorizes local school boards to introduce it?

MR. FATZER: They could introduce it or reject it, which some of them did. One city in the state never even used it. Two cities in the state previously, which had segregation previously terminated on their own volition. It is a purely permissive. It was a purely permissive statute. We consider it without force and effect at this time.

JUSTICE FRANKFURTER: And you are in this litigation by virtue of the requirement of notice to the Governor and the Attorney General under the three-judge court statute?

MR. FATZER: That is correct, Your Honor. We felt that this system was apparently being maintained under authority of this Court, under authority of our Supreme Court, and other appellate courts. We felt that we owed a duty to uphold the decisions of our state courts with respect to this state statute and that is why we were here originally. And we are here now not as an adversary but to assist the

Court in any way we can in helping it arrive at a correct decree if any need be entered locally.

JUSTICE DOUGLAS: How many students are involved here in the Topeka case?

MR. FATZER: Eight thousand two hundred, I think Your Honor, was the figure.

JUSTICE DOUGLAS: I mean in this litigation.

MR. FATZER: The whole school system was involved.

JUSTICE DOUGLAS: In Topeka?

MR. FATZER: My recollection is that there were 836 Negroes, 7,418 white children for a total of 8,254 children altogether, 836 colored children 7,418 white children, or a total of 8,254.

JUSTICE DOUGLAS: These appellants in No. 1 you say, you do not know whether they have all been taken into the schools that they sought to enter?

MR. FATZER: I cannot tell you that, sir. I assume they have. I do not know. I am sure that counsel for the appellant can advise the Court on that. I do not know.

JUSTICE DOUGLAS: I suppose, if there were just an application by one Negro student to enter the school that was closest to his home which happened to be a white school, and he was admitted, that that case would become moot then?

MR. FATZER: I assume, sir, that there are more children involved, all the children of the city school system are involved, in my judgment.

JUSTICE CLARK: Under the plan in Topeka, there will be no segregation, enforced segregation after when?

MR. FATZER: Commencing September, 1955, sir.

JUSTICE CLARK: That is this next September?

MR. FATZER: That is this next school term.

JUSTICE CLARK: There will be no enforced segregation?

MR. FATZER: No enforced segregation.

JUSTICE CLARK: Now skipping over to the city of Kansas City, what is the schedule there? I understood you to say they did not have a definite schedule, is that correct?

MR. FATZER: Well, if I said that, I did not want to leave that impression, Mr. Justice Clark.

JUSTICE CLARK: I may have misunderstood you.

MR. FATZER: I shall read with some care here the resolution of this Board adopted August 2.

JUSTICE CLARK: Where is it? I can read that if you want to go ahead.

MR. FATZER: It is on page 20 of the Supplemental Brief of the State of Kansas as to Questions 4 and 5 propounded by the Court.

JUSTICE REED: Going back to page 2 of what you filed here on April 11 on the schools, I may be stupid about it, but in the fourth section, that refers only to Negroes.

MR. FATZER: That is Item No. 4, "The following is the estimate of the number of students in 1955–1956 that would be in the affected schools."

JUSTICE REED: Does that mean Negroes, too?

MR. FATZER: Yes.

JUSTICE REED: You don't know the percentage of Negro students in each school?

MR. FATZER: No, I am in error, Your Honor. That is total enrollment.

JUSTICE REED: I understood you had a total enrollment of some 8,000?

MR. FATZER: Yes, that is correct.

JUSTICE REED: Then there is only 2750 accounted for here.

MR. FATZER: We would be glad, Your Honor, to provide this breakdown with respect to these schools, with respect to whether they are white or colored in each grade.

JUSTICE REED: It would help me.

MR. FATZER: All right. In other words—

JUSTICE REED: You have redistricted and what I was interested in is to know whether the redistricting has resulted in essential—whether all the school population will be unsegregated, or whether you will have all of the schools in one section all colored population.

MR. FATZER: The colored schools are in the areas that are predominantly, through history, geographic residential colored areas.

JUSTICE REED: Very normal that there is a separation of population.

MR. FATZER: Now on the fringe, some of the colored students under this plan would go to the white schools, the white children that are in the new areas, new districts, could likewise complete their course. They can attend either school. It is a privilege that is given to either child.

JUSTICE REED: And we do not know how long that will continue, strictly speaking?

MR. FATZER: Well, from now on. I mean, segregation.

JUSTICE REED: The plan could result in not a segregated school, but an all-white school and an all-Negro school?

MR. FATZER: It is my understanding, sir, that that would not be the case. Now for the children, if you will note under No. 2(d), any child who is affected by the change in district lines as herein recommended, be given the option of finishing elementary grades. That would be, if he was in the first grade, he could finish the elementary grades one to six in the school which he attended this current year. Now that is equally available to both the colored and the white students.

JUSTICE REED: I understand that, but it is also equally available that all the Negroes could go to one school and all the whites to another.

MR. FATZER: I am not prepared to say on that, sir, but my understanding is that that would not be the case. We will be glad to furnish the Court maps showing this area and we would be glad to show a breakdown under No. 4, Mr. Justice Reed, of the per cent and the number of the different white and colored students.

JUSTICE FRANKFURTER: I would be grateful to you if you would add to that what is not fully clear in my mind and I do not want to take the Court's and your time—if you would be good enough to state why there had to be, in the judgment of the School Board, redistricting and the basis on which the redistricting was done.

Is my question clear?

MR. FATZER: Why redistricting—

JUSTICE FRANKFURTER: Why was it necessary, in order to carry out the desegregation, the abolition of segregation, why was it necessary to have new or changed school districts and what were the considerations which led to the kind of districts that they carried out?

MR. FATZER: It is my understanding, Mr. Justice, that the reasons they required the redistricting of the schools, as this proposal would establish, is that colored schools did not have a district previously, that is, in a general large way, that children living in this particular part of the city would attend this particular school.

JUSTICE FRANKFURTER: They just took them by bus to schools set aside for colored children?

MR. FATZER: That is right.

JUSTICE FRANKFURTER: I see.

MR. FATZER: They gathered them up. So that now they have definite proposed districts for each of these schools with definite geographic lines.

JUSTICE FRANKFURTER: And your maps will show the nature of the districts, the contours of the districts, will they not?

MR. FATZER: That is correct.

Thank you, Your Honors, very much.

THE CHIEF JUSTICE: Mr. Carter?

### ORAL ARGUMENT ON BEHALF OF BROWN, ET AL

#### by MR. ROBERT L. CARTER

MR. CARTER: We are in accord with Mr. Fatzer that the case should be reversed and remanded to the district court. We feel that the decree should be entered by this Court declaring the Kansas statute by which power the Topeka Board proceeded to organize and have segregated schools, that that statute be declared unconstitutional and void.

JUSTICE FRANKFURTER: I understood that the Attorney General had already expressed an opinion to that effect.

MR. CARTER: He had expressed an opinion.

JUSTICE FRANKFURTER: I am not saying what you said should not be done, but he has already announced that this Court's decision on May 17 of last year invalidated that statute. Is that a correct understanding?

MR. CARTER: Yes, sir. That is invalidated, that invalidated the statute but, as far as Topeka is concerned, any power to organize and segregate a school must emanate from a specific statute or else, under the state law, there is no power to maintain segregation. Therefore, the invalidation of this statute means there is no power at all in Kansas to maintain and operate segregated schools as the law has been interpreted by the state courts of Kansas.

JUSTICE REED: That was involved in the suit you brought here?

MR. CARTER: Yes, sir.

JUSTICE REED: What do you mean, you want a specific invalidation of this specific statute?

MR. CARTER: We think, Your Honors, that such a decree ought to be entered, declaring the statute unconstitutional because as of now the implications are that the statute is unconstitutional by the May 17 decision, but the May 17 decision has no specific declaration or judgment or decree. And in the reversal, we think this should be set forth in your reversal and remanding to the lower court.

JUSTICE REED: If we had said that in the opinion, then it would not be necessary in the decree, or would it?

MR. CARTER: I think it would in terms of the decree. It seems to me that is the thing that the lower court gets and acts upon rather than the opinion of the Court.

JUSTICE REED: If a decree is reversing the decision of the court below to allow all children, a complete integration—I do not just understand your point.

MR. CARTER: We think that the May 17 decision in effect means that the Kansas statute which was here in this case is void. What we are asking for is specifically a decree, reversing and specifically saying the statute is unconstitutional and has no force and effect.

JUSTICE FRANKFURTER: You would rather go to the decree, rather than the opinion?

MR. CARTER: Yes.

JUSTICE FRANKFURTER: Because the decree is the thing that counts.

MR. CARTER: Yes. Secondly, we would like a decree that would indicate that—an order to the Topeka Board to cease and desist at once from basing school attendance and admission on the basis of race so that as of September, 1955, no child in Topeka would be going to school on the basis of race or color. We would think that an instruction should be issued to the district court to hold jurisdiction and hold preceedings to satisfy itself that the school board of Topeka as of September, 1955, has a plan which satisfies these requirements in that the school system has been reorganized to the extent that there is no question of race or color involved in the school attendance in its rules.

We also think that the court should hold jurisdiction, the district court should hold jurisdiction to issue whatever other orders the Court desires.

We feel that everything that Mr. Fatzer has said argues for a forthwith decree in this case.

The plan which has been issued as the third step is not one that indicates that there are any reasons why desegregation should not be obtained as of September, 1955. The plan says that desegregation will obtain as of September, 1955. We take objection to the plan. We think there are a number of points in the plan which will mean there will be a modified form of segregation being maintained for many years as the plan now operates, but we do not think that this is the place for us to argue about the question of the plan.

We think that if this Court issues a decree as we have suggested to the lower court, the school board and the attorneys for the appellants can argue as to whether or not a specific plan which is being adopted by the Board conforms with the requirements of this Court's opinion and its decree, that segregation be ended as of September, 1955, which we think should be done.

JUSTICE FRANKFURTER: As of September. Can you tell specifically when the classes are formed in the Topeka schools? When is the makeup of the classes affected in this litigation? When, in September, the first of September, or—do you happen to know about that? The point of my question is as to the time when this must be determined if it is to affect the entering classes in September, when it is that the district court will have to hear these things?

MR. CARTER: I do not have that information. I know from one of the resolutions that school opened September 15, I think, this year. I do not know when they open in 1955.

JUSTICE FRANKFURTER: The Attorney General will be able to tell us then?

MR. CARTER: I would think that we would of course want to have a hearing before the district court at as early a date as possible so that this matter could be settled and there would be no question but that the Board in Topeka would be going to unsegregate schools on a plan which conforms to the court's decree in all its requirements as of September, 1955. With that we would be satisfied.

JUSTICE CLARK: Are the appellants segregated at this time?

MR. CARTER: Yes, sir. There are five who are in the junior high school who have moved out of this class because they are not in a non-segregated school. About six of them are attending Washington, Buchanan, and Monroe schools which are the segregated schools.

JUSTICE HARLAN: Is that the result of compulsion, or their own choice?

MR. CARTER: Well, Your Honor, as a result of expulsion, this plan, what is known as the third step—there were eighteen school districts in Topeka. The first six schools listed on page 2 of the order, the papers which the Attorney General gave you, those schools are the remaining six schools in which segregation still obtains, the all-white schools. The lower four schools are the all-Negro schools.

In all of the other districts, that is approximately twelve, Negro and white children are attending schools together, that is the Negro children are able to go to the schools that are nearest to their homes.

This third step purports to complete the integration of the system and to bring into the system the three Negro schools and make it part of the total school system. Now instead of eighteen schools, you will have twenty-one schools purportedly servicing every one. Our objection to this is the fact that in our opinion these three schools will remain segregated, all Negro children will be attending them for many years to come and we think that does not conform to your order.

JUSTICE DOUGLAS: Are those Buchanan, Monroe and Washington?

MR. CARTER: Yes, sir.

JUSTICE CLARK: Will that be on a voluntary basis, you think?

MR. CARTER: No, that will not be on a voluntary basis because the Negro children who now live in the district, as this thing is reorganized in the district serviced, for example, by Buchanan, as you will note, the children in this district have an option to go to a school outside of the district, but since the Negro children only had the option or the right before this thing was put into effect, to go to Buchanan, Monroe and Washington, they cannot exercise an option to go to any other school than the Negro school. That means this, that the white children will go out of the district and continue to go to the schools they are going to and the Negro children will be forced to continue in Buchanan, therefore you will have segregated schools.

I think that is as much segregation as before the May 17 order.

JUSTICE HARLAN: Do you attribute that result to the way the option system may work rather than the way the district is made up?

MR. CARTER: Yes, sir. I know nothing about the district. I cannot say whether the districting is done fairly. I do not know anything about the matter. But on the face of it, this is my objection to the plan as it is given to us by the Attorney General.

JUSTICE CLARK: I thought all the students would be given a choice as to whether they want to stay there or go to another school under section 3, page 1, the bottom of the page. It does not say all, but it says the estimated number of students who will transfer is indicated as one-third.

MR. CARTER: I know, Justice Clark, but if you will look on page 1, Item D on the third step, this is the option, that "Any child who is affected by change in the district lines as herein recommended, be given the option of finishing elementary grades in the school which he attended 1954–1955 and continue therein."

This is the option to be exercised and this is the option where the Negro child has no option and the white child in the district that is serviced by one of the former Negro schools, has an option to go out of the district and the Negro child has not.

THE CHIEF JUSTICE: Thank you, Mr. Carter.
Mr. Attorney General, can you tell us when the schools open in Topeka?

MR. FATZER: My understanding is, sir, that it commences on the second Monday in September and that the enrollment of students is generally completed during a three-day period just about, just before the second Monday in September.

THE CHIEF JUSTICE: The determining as to where a child shall go is not made until in September?

MR. FATZER: I think that is true. I assume that it will be worked out under this plan. If the lower court would approve it or if it were to be modified by that date, surely the schools authorities want to know how many children are going to be in some school and whether facilities are going to be adequate and whether or not, under the program and the plan as proposed or as may be modified, that what children are going, whether they are eligible under the plan to go to this school and whether existing facilities are available to take care of them.

THE CHIEF JUSTICE: I think generally what this Court would be interested in knowing would be in the event there is a remand to the district court, if it might be said when it gets there, that it was too late for next year.

MR. FATZER: No.

THE CHIEF JUSTICE: That it should have been there before some date, say, in July or August when those things are done.

MR. FATZER: I am sure that would not be the case, Your Honors. I can tell this Court that I am pretty certain.

JUSTICE REED: From what you say, I take it that you consider it proper to allow an option to a child to go to another school, that is within the limits of the Constitution?

MR. FATZER: Bearing in mind, sir, that our understanding at present—

JUSTICE REED: Before you answer that, may I make another statement. I understand that normally a child in Topeka goes to the school in the school district in which he resides?

MR. FATZER: Yes, sir.

JUSTICE REED: Now, there is a variation from that which allows him to go to another school if he has been going there before. That is the 2(e) section?

MR. FATZER: Yes. He can complete his elementary course in the other school, if he should be in another district.

JUSTICE REED: A child who goes to school for the first time, for the first year, in the first grade, may he choose a school to which he goes?

MR. FATZER: The first year only.

JUSTICE REED: And after having chosen the first year, then he continues there?

MR. FATZER: He must attend in the district in which he resides under Plan 2(e).

JUSTICE REED: If he attends in 1955–1956 you interpret that to mean only for 1955–1956, for that year?

MR. FATZER: That is the interpretation placed upon it by the attorney for the Board of Education to our office, yes, sir, that they only attend there one year.

If, in the area of the Monroe school, some child by geographic area would be within that boundary and within another district prior to this redistricting and could have attended last year if they had been old enough, they could attend the so-called white school for the one-year period on the basis that it would permit time for the parents to move if they so desired.

I am told that, very frankly, that is the purpose of the section.

JUSTICE BURTON: That applies to the particular year. In years to come there will not even be that option.

MR. FATZER: Just one year, the next school year, Mr. Justice.

THE CHIEF JUSTICE: Thank you.
No. 5, Francis B. Gebhart et al, Petitioners, vs. Ethel Louise Belton, et al.

THE CLERK: Counsel are present.

## ARGUMENT ON BEHALF OF GEBHART, ET AL

### by MR. JOSEPH DONALD CRAVEN

MR. CRAVEN: Mr. Chief Justice and Members of the Supreme Court, the brief for the State of Delaware was filed by my predecessor, Mr. Young. I find myself in agreement with that brief except for one modification which I will mention to the Court a little later, but we are before the Court asking for a firm answer of the Court of Chancery of the State of Delaware and the Supreme Court of the State of Delaware. That is based on two considerations. First, that the "separate but equal" doctrine under which these cases were brought here is, of course, no longer in effect in view of the Court's decision of May 17 and secondly, because these children have been integrated into the two school districts which were involved in those cases, that is, the Hockessin and Yorklyn school districts.

There have been no untoward events in connection with that integration and the state is asking for a firm answer.

JUSTICE FRANKFURTER: You mean each one of these parties is now in a school or has been in a school in which segregation in any aspect has terminated?

MR. CRAVEN: Yes.

JUSTICE FRANKFURTER: Are all these children now in school?

MR. CRAVEN: Some of them I think have been graduated, are through. This was back in 1952. But they are either all in—

JUSTICE FRANKFURTER: What schools are we talking about?

MR. CRAVEN: Yorklyn and Hockessin.

JUSTICE FRANKFURTER: What grade are they?

MR. CRAVEN: They are both elementary and high school.

JUSTICE FRANKFURTER: Some of these children were in high school and are now out of high school?

MR. CRAVEN: Yes, some of them are still in high school.

JUSTICE FRANKFURTER: Some of them are still in high school?

MR. CRAVEN: That is correct.

JUSTICE FRANKFURTER: You say as to no child is there any question as to any aspect of segregation affecting that child?

MR. CRAVEN: In those two cases, in the two cases before the Court.

JUSTICE FRANKFURTER: In your cases.

MR. CRAVEN: That is right.

JUSTICE DOUGLAS: In No. 5?

MR. CRAVEN: In No. 5.

JUSTICE DOUGLAS: So specifically, a decree as to some of these children is completely moot because the children are out of school?

MR. CRAVEN: Yes.

JUSTICE DOUGLAS: And as to some, the children are in a school as to which no order prohibiting something is real or practical or alive because the child is now enjoying what he should?

MR. CRAVEN: That is correct.

JUSTICE DOUGLAS: That is your understanding?

MR. CRAVEN: That is my understanding, however, I would like—

JUSTICE REED: What decree do you recommend?

MR. CRAVEN: A simple affirmance of the holding of the Supreme Court of Delaware and affirm the Court of Chancery decision.

JUSTICE FRANKFURTER: What did your court decree?

MR. CRAVEN: Our court decreed, Court of Chancery decreed that the children should be entitled to immediate admittance into nonsegregated schools on the theory that they had this present constitutional personal right and having found that the facilities were not equal in those two districts and that decision of our Court of Chancery was appealed to our State Supreme Court which affirmed and the state again appealed on the narrow question that the districts in question should have been given time in which to make the facilities equal.
Of course, that is no longer a matter for argument before this Court.

JUSTICE REED: The matter of constitutionality was not dealt with at all?

MR. CRAVEN: No, it was not. We did not come up here on the question as to whether segregation per se was unconstitutional.

JUSTICE FRANKFURTER: At the time the case was here, inasmuch as they were admitted by the decree of this Court, what was the thing that the parties asked that you resisted?

MR. CRAVEN: We took the appeal on the basis that our local court, our Court of Chancery should have afforded the defendants time in which to make the facilities equal and that by denying time, they erred.

JUSTICE FRANKFURTER: I suppose that they would say the case is still alive inasmuch as their rights rested on not being equal rather than on the prohibition upon the states, equal or not equal, to make segregation?

MR. CRAVEN: We do not take that position. We think that is not before the Court. We think that is moot. We recognize the binding effect of the Court's decision in the other cases in which the specific question of segregation was raised.

I say to that extent I, as the present Attorney General of the state, am in accord with my predecessor in asking that the cases be affirmed. And it would seem to me that that is all that there is before the Court as far as Delaware is concerned, in the nature of the cases that come here.

However, my predecessor did argue at some length—I will not argue at length but I feel in duty bound to have something to say about the situation in Delaware. I wish I were in the happy position of my friend Mr. Fatzer from Kansas, and to say that there is no problem as far as Delaware is concerned, but we are a border state and ever since the Civil War, it seems to me, the border states have had their particular problems. I should be happy to be able to tell this Court that all is well and will be well whatever the form of the mandate of this Court is. That I can not, either in justice to this Court, nor in justice to the people of Delaware, say, because we are a divided and a troubled people in the face of the mandate of the Court.

That is where I depart from my predecessor who asked that this Court out of the bounty of its wisdom, set an ultimate date beyond which segregation would no longer be permitted. With the greatest deference in the world to this Court, I do not think that it has such wisdom. I think it would be presumptuous of me to come here and ask this Court to name a date which I could not name as a native of Delaware, who has lived there all my life and I say that it seems to me in order to implement the mandate of the Court, it is going to be necessary to remand the cases in question, because we feel of course that we are going to be bound by the action of the Court as well as where those particular issues have been raised, that the cases should be remanded to the courts of first instance, with a direction that the suitable state authority, whether it be the State Board of Education or the local boards, submit plans under the direction of this Court, and that the local courts see that those plans are carried out. We have many problems in Delaware.

JUSTICE REED: You mean the specific precincts, school districts are involved?

MR. CRAVEN: Well, of course the Court has before it certain specific cases and I assume it will not reach out but will direct its mandate to those particular cases. We, in Delaware, as in all other states where segregation has had, we believe up to this time, constitutional sanction will naturally be bound by and will be interested in the form of that mandate because we assume—and I may say that those of us who are the Attorneys General of our respective states and are conscious of our duty as constitutional officers to respect and carry out the mandate of this Court—recognize and feel that we have great problems coming before us. I can conceive of a plethora of suits in the State of Delaware involving a great many of the various school districts in which the attorney general or his deputies will have to, as we do represent the State Board of Education, unless some orderly process or plan can be worked out to see the spirit as well as the letter of the Court's mandate is effectively implemented.

JUSTICE FRANKFURTER: Mr. Attorney General, may I interrupt you to ask whether, in Delaware, you have a centralized educational authority or is it decentralized as it is in Kansas?

MR. CRAVEN: I think it is perhaps a compromise of the two, Your Honor. We have a State Board of Education which has supervisory power of all the school districts of the state. Then we have special school districts which have a large amount of autonomy, and which raise their own taxes. Then we have what we call school districts that are entirely supported by the state, and which are more directly responsible to the State Board of Education.

JUSTICE FRANKFURTER: In relation to a problem like that what is the diffusion or division of authority in your state? I ask it in view of the litigation you had in your state.

MR. CRAVEN: We have had some litigation. And I think I might say in passing, that I think the litigation that we have had is indicative of intent and desire on the part of both the people and the courts of Delaware to comply with the decision of May 17 and with the implementation which I assume will be forthcoming.

We have had one decision by our Supreme Court which has declared the provisions of the Delaware Constitution and the statutory provisions thereunder providing for segregated education to be unconstitutional. That is a late case, 1955, and is the case of *Steiner* v. *Simmons,* found in 111 Atlantic 2d at 574, and I read from the Court's opinion. I have a mineographed opinion so I think the page reference would not be very helpful. However, it is on page 11 of this mimeographed opinion and reads:

> We think that the opinion in the segregation cases is a final one. Its necessary present effect is to nullify the provisions of the Delaware Constitution and statutes requiring separate schools for whites and Negroes.

And so far as Delaware is concerned, our constitutional provisions and our statutes have been declared unconstitutional, the ones requiring segregation, in conformance with the opinion of this Court.

I will not pass on to some other litigation which perhaps is at the Court's notice, some of which is still pending. I am not asking the sympathy of the Court, but the Attorney General of the state has these problems to face, and I sometimes feel that the making of the decision and the implementing of the decision is not a matter of mandate, it is a matter of the local officers, their attitudes and their ability to cope with local conditions. And so I strongly urge the Court that it not set an ultimate date, that it not attempt to decide in forty-eight states how the thousands of school districts are going to conform with its mandate, but that it trust the local judgments, and that under some general direction it refer these cases back to the local courts, assuming that the judges and the local officials and the Attorneys General will do their duty.

JUSTICE HARLAN: There is one thing I do not quite understand, Mr. Craven. I understood you to say first because of the Delaware situation, that all that was required was a straight affirmance of this Court, no mandate, nothing.

MR. CRAVEN: That is correct.

JUSTICE HARLAN: Therefore, what you have been saying more recently relates to your views as to what decrees should be issued in the case of other states?

MR. CRAVEN: In the other states, others similarly situated.

THE CHIEF JUSTICE: Mr. Redding?

### ORAL ARGUMENT ON BEHALF OF BELTON, ET AL

#### by MR. LOUIS REDDING

MR. REDDING: May it please the Court, there are two important circumstances I believe which distinguish the consolidated Delaware cases now before Your Honors from all the other school segregation cases. The Attorney General has alluded to both of those circumstances. He has pointed out that the respondents here, the Negro school children who are respondents here, were admitted to the schools previously ascribed by the state constitution exclusively for white children, by the decree of the Court of Chancery, which was affirmed by the Supreme Court of Delaware in August, 1952, and except in three instances where those children have graduated from high school, they have been or they are now just about completing their third successive year of attendance on a nonsegregated basis.

I should like to point out what is in the brief of the Attorney General to the effect that this attendance has been without incident and without social repercussion. The other circumstance to which Mr. Craven has alluded is the fact that the Delaware Supreme Court has had occasion to construe the effect of the decision in the school segregation cases on school segregation as it has been practiced in Delaware since May 17, 1954, and the Attorney General is, of course, correct in pointing out that the Supreme Court of Delaware has said in three places in its opinion that the decision of this Court on May 17 renders null the Delaware constitutional and statutory provisions providing for public school segregation. But the Supreme Court's opinion in this case to which Mr. Craven has alluded, *Steiner* v. *Simmons,* 111 Atlantic 2nd 574, does create a peculiar problem in Delaware. The respondents here, as we have already said, were immediately admitted by the Delaware courts to the schools previously for white, and they were admitted to those schools because both the Court of Chancery of Delaware and the Delaware Supreme Court interpreting this Court's opinions in the Gaines, the Sipuel and the Sweatt cases decided that this right to the equal protection of the laws in so far as that applied to public schools, was a present and personal act, and it was for that reason that it admitted Negro school children to the schools. However, in this opinion of the State Supreme Court, decided on February 8, this year, the Court seems to take another position. The Court says that, and I would like with the Court's indulgence, to read just a few lines of the opinion which Mr. Craven did not read, the Court says:

> The right to unsegregated education has been established. The plaintiffs in the segregation cases and the plaintiffs in the case now have that right. But as to the plaintiffs in the segregation case, the enforcement of that right has been deferred. The Supreme Court of the United States has not entered a decree directing immediate admittance.

And a little further down, the Court says: "Under such circumstances, can the right of the plaintiffs"—who were there respondents—"be considered a present and personal right?"

JUSTICE FRANKFURTER: Those are different children?

MR. REDDING: Yes, sir, so that now we have the situation that in Delaware the persons who are now respondents in this case have been recognized by the Court, the Supreme Court of Delaware, as having a present and personal right to equal opportunity to a nonsegregated education.

But children who have been segregated since that time do not have such a right. It is for that reason that I would like to advert, as Mr. Craven did, to the decrees which this Court will enter in other cases. We believe that those decrees should require forthwith desegregation. We are certain that if they do require immediate desegregation, the Delaware Supreme Court will regard the decrees as binding and will order immediate desegregation in the schools in Delaware, and thus relieve Delaware of this duality which now exists with respect to the constitutional rights of Negro school children.

JUSTICE FRANKFURTER: Mr. Redding, in this case do you join the Attorney General of Delaware in saying that mere affirmation is required?

MR. REDDING: I do, sir, but only because the Attorney General addressed his remarks to the form of the mandates in the other cases.

JUSTICE FRANKFURTER: I see. I quite appreciate your position. But one has to enter a decree in this case. Since this was not a class suit but appears to be a personal suit, you agree with the Attorney General?

MR. REDDING: Yes.

JUSTICE REED: By this recent decision in Delaware they refused to direct the immediate entry of other Negro school children?

MR. REDDING: Yes, sir. If Your Honor please, this is what happened. Ten Negro school children were admitted to the Milford High School in September of 1954. They were then ejected from the school. They obtained a preliminary injunction ordering their readmission, and the Milford Board of Education appealed to the State Supreme Court, and the opinion in *Steiner* v. *Simmons* eventuated from that appeal. The Court reversed and the children are not now in the Milford High School.

JUSTICE REED: They did not direct their integration?

MR. REDDING: They did not, sir.

JUSTICE DOUGLAS: Counsel, you answered Justice Frankfurter— (unintelligible).

MR. REDDING: If I did say that, I was, of course, mistaken. Of course, there was a cause of action.

JUSTICE FRANKFURTER: Did you sue on behalf of others?

MR. REDDING: Yes, sir.

JUSTICE DOUGLAS: The decree that I read that the Chancellor entered, the relief runs, not only to the instant plaintiff, but others.

MR. REDDING: Yes.

JUSTICE DOUGLAS: That is right.

THE CHIEF JUSTICE: Mr. Attorney General, did you have anything further?

MR. CRAVEN: No, nothing.

THE CHIEF JUSTICE: You agree it is a class suit?

MR. CRAVEN: Yes, I do.

JUSTICE DOUGLAS: That all members of the class have been or should be integrated?

MR. CRAVEN: If not, they can be within a reasonable length of time. We do not wish to change our position because it is a class suit.

JUSTICE REED: What was the order in the Steiner case?

MR. CRAVEN: The Court of Chancery which had ordered the children back was reversed. However, I think the Court ought to know the reason for that. The State Board of Education had put out directions to the various school boards, saying that they should submit plans to the State Board of Education for approval, plans for integration, and in the Milford case, they did not submit the plan. Our Supreme Court held that the Director of the State Board of Education had the force of law and because the Milford School Board had not submitted a plan for the approval of the State Board of Education, it had not complied with the law and the children had not attained status.

JUSTICE REED: And, therefore, it did not direct immediate integration?

MR. CRAVEN: Did not direct the immediate integration.

JUSTICE FRANKFURTER: Mr. Attorney General, as to *Gebhart,* these named children, the decree of your Court was immediate admission here which was done, is that right?

MR. CRAVEN: Yes.

JUSTICE FRANKFURTER: Now, as I understand it, the latest pronouncement of your court does not call for immediate admittance of the children who were before the Court in the Steiner case. Therefore, the decree in the Gebhart case for immediate admission of all children similarly situated, the very problem which you ask this Court to consider in a different light is presented in a troublesome light, is it not?

MR. CRAVEN: Well, in the first place, there are two different questions and two different courts. That may offer some explanation. At the time our Court of Chancery ordered the children back on the basis of the facilities not being equal, we still thought that was good constitutional law in Delaware and the children went back. Now the appeal was taken by the State to our Supreme Court and we were still arguing separate but equal.

JUSTICE FRANKFURTER: Yes, but the decree was immediate, was it not?

MR. CRAVEN: It was.

JUSTICE FRANKFURTER: Thank you.
(Whereupon, at 2:00 p.m., a recess was taken.)


AFTER RECESS


THE CHIEF JUSTICE: No. 4, Spottswood Thomas Bolling, et al, vs. C. Melvin Sharpe, et al.

THE CLERK: Counsel are present.

THE CHIEF JUSTICE: Mr. Hayes.

ARGUMENT ON BEHALF OF SPOTTSWOOD THOMAS BOLLING, ET AL

by MR. GEORGE E. C. HAYES

MR. HAYES: May it please the Court, this suit involves the District of Columbia, and as Your Honors well know, integration has been started in the District of Columbia. With respect to the two questions that are being asked of us, I shall address myself to Question 4 and Mr. Nabrit, with whom I am associated, will address himself to Question 5.

By way of specific answer to Question 4(a), we answer by saying, yes, the question being, would a decree necessarily follow, providing that within the limits set by normal geographical school districting Negro children should forthwith be admitted to the schools of their choice.

And we take the position that in all of these cases since the rights are personal and present, that the answer to that question should be yes. With respect to the District of Columbia, there are additional reasons why that answer should be yes.

First of all, there are presently, as far as we know, no factors which would justify any request for a decree that is not forthwith. The President of the United States by his own statement, has indicated that it is his desire that the District of Columbia should be a model, as far as the integrated school system is concerned. The Corporation Counsel of this District, as soon as the mandate came down, being called upon by the Board of Education, pronounced that in his opinion the decision of May 17 rendered unconstitutional the provisions of the DC Code that pretended to have our system a segregated one.

The Board of Education almost immediately after the decision came down came forth with a very forthright statement of policy, and because of the fact that I shall attempt to, in some measure, contrast a little further along as to what they said by way of policy and what has actually been undertaken by the Superintendent of Schools, I call the attention of the Court to the language of the Board of Education in its expression of policy. If Your Honors please, on pages 8 and 9 of the brief for the respondents on the formulation of the decree, they have set forth the expression of the Board of Education. I shall not read all of it to you but call your attention to the fact that in section 3 they provide:

> Attendance of pupils residing within school boundaries hereafter to be established, shall not be permitted at schools located beyond such boundaries except for the most necessitous reasons or for the public convenience, and in no event for reasons related to the racial character of the school within the boundaries in which the pupils reside.

They end their statement by saying:

> In support of the foregoing principles which are believed to be cardinal, the Board will not hesitate to use its full powers. It is pledged to a complete and wholehearted pursuance of these objectives. We affirm our intention to secure the rights of every child within his own capacity to the full, equal and impartial use of all school facilities and the right of all qualified teachers to teach where needed within the school system.
> And finally, we ask the aid, cooperation and good will of all citizens and the help of the Almighty in holding to our stated purposes.

We read that to Your Honors because we feel that is a very fine pronouncement of a policy. Pursuant to that, the Board of Education called upon the Superintendent of Schools to offer a plan, and in this regard, we addressed ourselves to what was done in the hope that the experience of the District of Columbia may be helpful to Your Honors in arriving at conclusions as far as all of the cases may be concerned. In that situation what was done was for the—will Your Honors indulge me just a second? After having gotten the pronouncement the Corning plan was asked to be put in operation. Mr. Corning, at that time, the Superintendent of Schools, indicated that he would find it impossible to give a zoning map prior to September. The Board of Education, however, called upon the Superintendent to have that map by the first of July, and in spite of the fact that there had been suggestions of administrative reasons that would make that impossible by the first of July, this zoning map was produced. We call attention to that because, as I have indicated to you, we think it will be helpful, that sometimes when the administrators in candor and in honesty think that something cannot be done, that is there be an affirmative action taken, that ways are found to meet that situation, and that was done in the instant case.

Mr. Corning did furnish the zoning maps. Now, I have heard the question asked as I have sat here this morning, as to the reason why the zoning maps were necessary. In our jurisdiction they would be necessary because, prior to the time of the decision of May 17, there were schools designated for Negroes and schools designated for whites, and persons within the respective areas would go to the designated schools because of that circumstance. And when this Court, by its decision of May 17, struck down the segregated setup, it became necessary to have zones having to do simply with the geographic situation, rather than being based on the question of race or color. And that was undertaken. That is what was done by the first of July. And then with those zones set up, Mr. Corning, as the Superintendent, presented to the Board a plan which, by various steps, would be carried forward until, according to the plan, in September of 1955, the school system was to be completely integrated.

I call Your Honors' attention to the fact at the outset that there would be no need for anything beyond a decree saying what the Board of Education has indicated, what the Superintendent has set forth as a plan is to be envisioned for our schools as of September, 1955. That, according to the plan, is to be a complete integration. If that were all, we would ask nothing other at the hands of this Court, than a decree which would set forth that there should no longer be an administering of the school system in the District of Columbia where the question of race or color was in any sense involved, as a part of any administrative action, as a part of any attendance as far as school children were concerned, as far as teachers were concerned.

And be it said to the credit of the Board of Education in this jurisdiction, they have gone forward in the doing of all of that. They have gone forward in the matter of integration both as to pupils, and as to teachers and as to administrative officers.

However, we have concern, because as far as some of the plan, it lends itself as we see it, to the possibility of error. Even though, as has been indicated, the provision is that students—if I have not indicated to Your Honors that this is fundamental in it, I should perhaps first say that. That the suggestion is that students under the new zoning will have the right to go to schools of their choice within this area.

In other words, if I be in a given area, school area, I have the preferential right to go to that school that is in that area. But it allows the option of remaining at school until graduation is had if the individual desires to do so.

In other words, as we conceive it, a geographic school district which in, and of itself, would lay the proper foundation for the integrated schools is superimposed on a right that may be exercised by a student, the result of which is, as we see it, that race is still made the issue, and the question of the segregation is carried forward just as before, because by the exercise of this option, a child may continue to stay in the school until the time of his graduation.

JUSTICE REED:  Is there more than one grade school in a school district?

MR. HAYES:  Yes, Your Honor.

JUSTICE REED:  They have several in a single district?

MR. HAYES:  Yes, Your Honor, or there will be a number of elementary schools within each school district.

There would probably be not as many junior high schools but I venture to say there are some in which the district takes over one junior high school. If I be incorrect as to that, as I say that may not be. But the districting has to do with the question of the elementary school area, the junior high school area, the high school area.

JUSTICE REED:  That is unusual in my thinking.
I was not aware that there was more than one elementary school in a district.

MR. HAYES:  I am certain, if Your Honor please, that that is correct.

JUSTICE REED: In that district any white child or Negro child can select his own school?

MR. HAYES: He goes to the school nearest to him in his own area.

JUSTICE REED: It is measured by feet or something?

MR. HAYES: I do not think there are instances very often where there would be a question—

JUSTICE REED: It would be easy enough if you have one school in a district. If you had only one school, everybody closer to that school than any other, he would go then to that school?

MR. HAYES: Yes, it is my understanding as I say, that a number of schools may be within a district.

JUSTICE REED: That was true before with segregation.

MR. HAYES: I beg your pardon.

JUSTICE REED: That was true when you had segregation, you had overlapping districts?

MR. HAYES: Yes, sir. Well, now, with the present school districting there will be schools still as I conceive it in so far as the elementary schools are concerned as Your Honor will see—in the junior high schools—and it may well be that that is not true then, but I am relatively certain and as I say, my friends can give you the statistics actually with respect to that, that there will be elementary schools, there may be other elementary schools in the same district but he goes to the one that is nearest to him.

JUSTICE REED: Is that in the statement?

MR. HAYES: Well, there is nothing in the statement, if Your Honor please, that breaks it down into whether one—

JUSTICE REED: Do you have a regulation?
How do you know that the child is to go to the nearest school in the district?

MR. HAYES: The only way I can say that to you, sir, is that that is a part of what I understand the Corning plan to be. The Corning plan would provide that the child shall go to the school nearest to him in his district.

JUSTICE BURTON: Mr. Hayes, you referred to the right of a child to stay in a given school until his graduation from that school. I take it that this is merely a temporary measure, is it not, that has to do with the status at the moment and it will work out over a period of two or three years? That is not to break up the continuity of the course?

MR. HAYES: It would presumably work out at the end of the graduation period through the intermediate grade from the time the child graduated from that to the junior high school, that would end his right to exercise his option.

JUSTICE BURTON: If so, the child last year, if he was in junior high school, he could complete his junior high school course without breaking into it and being forced to go somewhere else?

MR. HAYES: That is what I understand the plan to suggest and the plan purports to suggest that immediately you go into the new area, in others words, when you go from the intermediate to the junior, when you go from the junior to senior high school, you have the right to stay until graduation is over.

JUSTICE BURTON: You are talking about matters of continuity for the child in a given school?

MR. HAYES: That is what is urged as being the reason for the thing, I suggest, that it is the question of continuity within the graduation period of a child in a particular school.

JUSTICE MINTON: You do not contend that it is done for any purposes of discrimination?

MR. HAYES: No, the actual language, if Your Honor please, would not result in discrimination. We are concerned as to whether or not the administering of it might not be distorted, and not in any sense saying that the present administration has done any such distorting. I am in no position to say that and would not say that. But we are concerned that the language of a decree which we are asking would be of such character as would render impossible the use of that device as a means of discrimination.

JUSTICE BLACK: How would this be done?

MR. HAYES: By leaving this option—

JUSTICE BLACK: I mean how could the plan which you have just outlined that they are suggesting be used for discrimination?

MR. HAYES: Well, this type of thing could occur as we see it, that a child who had a right to go to a particular school by reason of the geographic area might not be allowed to go to that school because in that school there was a child who exercised the preferential right to stay there until graduation.

JUSTICE BLACK: I thought the plan provided that they were given a choice, some were given a choice and others had to go to specific schools.

MR. HAYES: If Your Honor pleases, what the option is that is allowed is that, if I am in school "A", I can remain in school "A" until graduation unless—

JUSTICE BLACK: You do not object to that, do you?

MR. HAYES: Well, when Your Honor says we do not object, we object to it simply because of the fact that we feel that the allowance of that is still the carrying forward of the old idea of the segregated setup, because the right to remain in that school was basically one of color.

In other words, the person went into that school because of this segregated setup.

JUSTICE BLACK: You mean you want a decree that will prevent an option being given to the children where there are two or three schools to go to, to permit them to go to that one school?

MR. HAYES: No, we do not think that the decree from this Court should do any forbidding. We think rather, that the decree from this Court should simply indicate that there should be nothing done where color was used as a criteria. Now we feel that this is a possibility and is a perpetuating of the old idea of color being the criterion.

JUSTICE BLACK: Is it your idea that because there is a possibility that there should be no option left to the children of either race to select their own schools?

MR. HAYES: No, we think rather, if the decree were to take the shape which I have suggested to Your Honor, that then in the event that there were showings, flagrant showings of a violation of this right of option, that then there would be the right to go to the courts without the establishing of a principle that we feel has already now been established.

JUSTICE BLACK: I have not quite made my question clear. Can that come from mere option of the child to choose one school rather than another?

MR. HAYES: Well, we feel—

JUSTICE BLACK: Would you object to that under any circumstance?
Do you believe the parents of the child or the child would be left free to select one of the schools? I ask you that because I know that has been the rule all over the country where they have two or three schools.

MR. HAYES: Well, if Your Honor please, as we conceive it, as I have said to Your Honor, in fairness so far as the District of Columbia is concerned, I do not find too much to give me concern. But I would be concerned since we have adjusted ourselves to other decrees, about a decree that left an option to the individual, himself, because, if that option were left, it seems to me that the very force of the decree might be obviated by that sort of a device.

JUSTICE BLACK: Would you go then far enough to say that this Court should provide that the law is compelled to deny option of children to go to one school rather than another?

MR. HAYES: No, I have said, Your Honor, there should not be any such denial. I do not think this Court should undertake to say that. I think, rather, that a decree of the character which we have in mind would not require that at all. It would not estop the question of options properly exercised, but may, as I say, give rise to the possibility of overcoming what might then become a flagrant violation.

JUSTICE BLACK: You mean that coercion instead of option, freedom of choice, you would want that prevented?

MR. HAYES: A number of things of that character might come in and might come in under the heading of "option." And that is the reason I believe that I should bring these things up.

JUSTICE REED: Let me pursue that point.

MR. HAYES: Yes, Mr. Justice.

JUSTICE REED: I am surprised to find there are two or more schools in a district in the District of Columbia, but let us assume that there are two schools. One of them used to be a Negro school and the other white. Now then you have an objection to allowing the students to choose which one they go to?

MR. HAYES: Mr. Korman has stated to me that what happened was only true in two instances where they were so close together that they could not draw two circles.

That may answer what was in Your Honor's mind and may correct what is in my mind except for these two exceptions.

JUSTICE REED: Let us take those two exceptions. Do you object to a choice of schools in that one area or two areas when there are two in the same district?

MR. HAYES: No, it is not that.

JUSTICE REED: The ultimate result would be one of them could be all-Negro, the other could be all-white?

MR. HAYES: Well, with a small overlapping to which Mr. Korman makes reference, in a city such as ours, I do not believe that that would come as a possibility. It might be but I do not think by any type of gerrymandering or anything else, there could be any such situation that would end up with there being simply a white as against a colored school. Now there may be areas from a geographic districting which might end up in what Your Honor says with respect to all-white and all-colored. That might be.

JUSTICE REED: Concerning Justice Black's questions, you have no objection constitutionally to the selection in the District by children?

MR. HAYES: Well, when Your Honor says it in that wise, I have a concern that I did not gather just what Justice Black's question was.

We do not think that this Court should say by its mandate that no one shall have the right to exercise an option. We do not think that that would be right.

JUSTICE REED: We do not say that. We say that they can exercise an option.

MR. HAYES: No. If Your Honor please, if Your Honors would confine the decree to the language and character which we think ought to be, then we feel that abuse of the option period would fall within the purview of such a decree. And, as Mr. Justice Black has indicated, at some time further along the line, somebody says, "Oh, I am going to exercise my option," if you could go in and say this wasn't an exercise of option, if it was coercion or anything else, that is what we would be concerned with. May I call Your Honor's attention to an example of something which has happened in our school system which gives us concern as to the actual putting into effect of the regulations as provided?

I just answered a question by saying that when you graduate from one level to another, that the person who goes into this new level, presumably then comes under this geographic condition. He does not have any right not to claim promotions or anything of that character. We had the situation develop that there were, according to what we are advised, a graduation in which there were 1,018 junior high graduates entering the high schools, according to new nonracial boundaries. Of the students promoted, 571 came from schools of the old Negro division and 525 came from formerly white schools.

One hundred twenty-two of the students from former all-Negro schools were promoted to six former all-white high schools. One Negro boy moved from an integrated former white junior high into vocational high which had retained its Negro enrollment.

No white students were promoted to former Negro schools. Now, we call attention to that sort of circumstance, that it would be a rather unusual thing with the zoning change as has been indicated, zoning now without regard to color, new zoning with overlapping districts where in one instance—there were certain Negro areas that—now the new zone which is unsegregated situation goes deep into that area, it seems to us a rather unusual circumstance that under those conditions 120-some Negroes would go, be graduated into a new area, to a white high school, and that there would be no whites, who, having been promoted, would go to a Negro school. It is the type of administering of that kind that gives us the concern.

JUSTICE FRANKFURTER: May I ask you to what issue more readily you are addressing yourself? Is it to the kind of decree this Court should fashion in directly greater detail than fashioned by the district court of which?

MR. HAYES: If Your Honor please, just what I have in mind is the type of decree that this Court should pass in remanding the case to the district court.

JUSTICE FRANKFURTER: Do you think this Court can go into particularities?

MR. HAYES: No, sir.

JUSTICE FRANKFURTER: As to what would or would not operate not as a fair opportunity for a fair choice but some kind of a "huggamugga," some kind of a manipulation whereby what is deemed to be a fair choice is not really a fair choice.

Do you think we could particularize that?

MR. HAYES: No, I do not think you can. If Your Honors please, we have attempted to draft what we think would cover the situation having to do with the question of the nonsegregated setup and that the defendants and agents and the like should be estopped from using race as a criteria.

JUSTICE FRANKFURTER: Have you in your brief set forth a proposal for the kind of decree that you would like this Court to issue?

MR. HAYES: No, Your Honor, we have not.

JUSTICE FRANKFURTER: Would that appeal to you or would it be agreeable to you?

MR. HAYES: Yes, Your Honor.

JUSTICE FRANKFURTER: Perhaps I might suggest to other counsel that they take their hand in drafting the kind of decree they want this Court to consider—not in generalities but in terms [of] the kind of decree that they propose as is so often the case in chancery, proposed by the states—specifically the kind of decree they want submitted for consideration by the Court, because generality of language easily evaporates in memory, let alone in speech.

MR. HAYES: Yes, Your Honor. I am appreciative of that. May I simply address myself and say in respect to 4(b), our answer to that is yes, that the Court does have executive power that is referred to in there and to say to Your Honors that, as I indicated to you, Mr. Nabrit is going to talk to the Court about Question 5 and a part of that is the type of decree and I think you will have the specific answer to what Your Honor is asking.

## ARGUMENT ON BEHALF OF SPOTTSWOOD BOLLING, ET AL

### by MR. JAMES M. NABRIT, JR.

MR. NABRIT: Mr. Chief Justice, if the Court please, I should like to add to what Mr. Hayes has said about the situation in the District of Columbia. There are 160-some odd schools in the District of Columbia and they were divided into two divisions, white and colored, prior to the decision May 17.

Essentially 17 of the schools that were formerly white, there are now only 11 elementary schools, no junior high schools and 1 senior high school and 3 vocational high schools which do not have Negroes in them.

In other words, Negroes have gone into all of the formerly white schools in the District except those indicated, a total of 16. In the case of those schools that were formerly all Negro schools, there are 15 elementary schools now with no whites, 9 junior high schools and 4 high schools. In the case of the teachers colleges they have two, Wilson, which was formerly all white now has thirty-six Negroes, and Miner, formerly all Negro, still has no white students.

Now we would be remiss in our obligations to the Court if we did not say and make it clear that the progress in integration in the District has been amazing since May 17, 1954.

We, also, feel that we would be remiss in our obligations if we did not point out to the Court some things which we think ought to be taken into account in deciding what disposition to make finally of this litigation which has now taken the greater part of five years, and also, if we did not suggest to the Court something which we think we have learned in the District of Columbia which might be of some aid in the resolution of the difficult problems inherent in Questions 4 and

5 in the cases before the Court. We feel that we may do that since so many representatives of the various states have been asked to give some aid to the Court, and two things we think may be helpful to the Court from our own experience in the District of Columbia. In the first place, implicit in many of the requests for delay and for a gradual effective desegregation process, inherent and implicit in these replies is that integration involves manifold administrative difficulties and that to do this short of a long delayed process may prove educationally unsound.

Now we concede that there is merit in both of those positions, but we have to give the Court our experience as an aid in the view which the Court gives to these representations.

Now the experience which we have had in the District I think ideally illustrates it. When the decision was handed down immediately thereafter, thinking of all of the things that may stand in the way, the Superintendent announced that we could not take any steps toward a desegregation until this Court had handed down its decree.

But that was the first flush of an expression without having had an opportunity for conference. After a conference and study with other officials, the Board of Education of the District in cooperation with the Superintendent and the officers of the District decided upon instituting this plan for integration.

At the time that this policy that you have had brought to our attention was adopted, the Superintendent presented a plan with certain graduated steps by which we would have gradual integration in the District.

And, in presenting his plan, he stated that the reasons for the delays involved in the various steps were administrative difficulties which stood in the way, and because of the rapid acceleration of this program, would be educationally unsound.

Now one of the things which was in that was a statement that in order to draw the educational boundaries for the new districting of an unsegregated system, the difficulties were so involved that it would be impossible to draw those boundaries until September, 1954, and that hence any steps towards effective integration other than a relieving of overcrowding would be impossible educationally.

The Board of Education did not agree with that. The Board voted that these boundaries be drawn by July 1, and that the program begin on September 1. The Superintendent proceeded to draw the boundaries by July 1, and to accelerate the program by September 1. Now the only reason I call that to the Court's attention is to say that the Court must be carefully observant of representations that long periods of time are needed for these integration steps, because we have found in the District that when a decision was made, the difficulties vanished, the administrative difficulties, educationally questionable results did not come as a consequence of the action taken. As a matter of fact, the Superintendent himself has accelerated the entire program in the District of Columbia so that today he will be hard pressed to tell the Court what he purports to do in the future. So that it would appear to us that of all the cases before the Court, that is the case in which the Court can take the decision of May 17, which reached such a high point in our democracy, and bring a fitting conclusion to this case by writing a decree that desegregation or integration shall be effective forthwith. Even the Corporation Counsel does not disagree with that. He does not agree to a consent decree, but that is beside the point.

He says that integration is progressing rapidly and will be completely finished by September 1. Therefore, he is in no position to object to a decree which says that that be done. Now it would appear to me that in these cases in order that there might not be the kind of confusion which seems to be inherent in the Delaware situation, ought not to be placed in the District of Columbia where this Court supervises all of our courts and where we have a school board that we can not elect and where the judges of the courts below supervised by this Court in their judicial functioning operate administratively to appoint the School Board over which this Court has no jurisdiction, and thus place us in a very uncertain position in the District. For example, the distinguished lower court judge who is now the Chairman of the Committee to select the school board members, announced last week that there were three persons who would come to the end of their term this year, and that he wanted names submitted for people to be on the Board.

In quoting him, I think it would be a good idea to have somebody from southwest Washington or southeast Washington, and we have got a number of lawyers on the Board now, too many lawyers. Now we have nothing to do with that as citizens of the District of Columbia, so that when we deal with the policies which have been adopted by the Board, they get tangled in this administrative setup with our traditional judicial function. So that in this case, if ever the Court should make it clear that integration in education in the District of Columbia must take place immediately—because if we go back down into the district courts with any type of uncertainty we run into that type of situation in our local courts, and that is not to question any philosophy, program, or integrity of any judge. It is simply to state a fact which is a part of our system.

Now, it would seem to me that this also could be of assistance to the Court in dealing with the question if, in a situation where the Court has as wide a supervisory power as in this, the Court directed the courts below here to enter a decree which is in effect, Mr. Justice Frankfurter, this judgment reversed and cause remanded to the district court for proceedings not inconsistent with this Court's opinion, and entry of a decree containing the following provisions:

(1) All provisions of District of Columbia Code or other legislative enactments, rules or regulations, requiring, directing or permitting defendants to administer public schools in the District of Columbia on the basis of race or color, or denying the admission of petitioners or other Negroes similarly situated to the schools of their choice within the limits set by normal geographic school districting on the basis of race or color are unconstitutional and of no force or effect:

(2) Defendants, their agents, employees, servants, and all other persons acting under their direction and supervision, are forthwith ordered to cease imposing distinctions based on race or color in the administration of the public schools of the District of Columbia; and are directed that each child eligible for public school attendance in the District of Columbia be admitted to the school of his choice not later than September, 1955, within the limits set by normal geographic school districting;

(3) The District Court is to retain jurisdiction to make whatever further orders it deems appropriate to carry out the foregoing;

(4) Defendants are to pay the costs of the proceedings.

Now we would suggest that as a fitting climax to the District case. And we would like to say that the decision of the Court in the District of Columbia case which bore out the hopes and expectations of the citizens of the District has carried the hopes of the Negro people of the United States to such a high point that it would be tragic indeed, in my opinion, if we should recede from that high point by not giving a decree and bringing to a decisive and final end the litigation in this case.

THE CHIEF JUSTICE: Mr. Nabrit, would you please make copies of that for the Court?

MR. NABRIT: I shall be happy to.

JUSTICE FRANKFURTER: May I ask you whether you have thought of considerations peculiarly relevant to the District of Columbia for what you call amazing progress that do or do not obtain in comparable states—by comparable, I mean the proportion of Negro to white population. You spoke with special emphasis of the progress of the District here. With your considerable thinking on this subject, have you any reasons why you think that is so in the District?

MR. NABRIT: Well, I should think so, Mr. Justice Frankfurter.

JUSTICE FRANKFURTER: So far as these things are relevant as to what a court in its discretion may or may not do.

MR. NABRIT: Precisely. I thing there are several considerations. I think one, the Court may well be advised that in the District of Columbia there are approximately 104,000 pupils of whom the majority of these are Negroes, so that numerically, I doubt if there is a place in the South where, from that standpoint, this would not be a very excellent guide to the large number of children that may be integrated in a shorter period of time even when the Negroes outnumber the whites. So I think that is a relevant consideration. I think, No. 2, the fact that there was a firm administrative executive hand in the District of Columbia in support of integration even prior to the decision of this Court must be conceded to be a very effective element.

JUSTICE FRANKFURTER: You mean the Superintendent?

MR. NABRIT: No, I mean the Superintendent, the Board of Education, I was speaking about, the Board, the District Commissioners and the law-enforcement officers, the general theory that where that exists you have a much better situation in which to do it.

But the primary thing that this seems to me to show its relevance to the whole question before the Court is that firm action and firm decisions, and certainly here where both dovetail always improves the desegregation or integration steps, so that in the District where we have all of these together, we have this extraordinary speed. But, even in the District we find that the very fact of firm decision in itself militated against ordinary objections.

Now, I think one further relevant consideration in the District of Columbia was the whole general community relationship. We would not be giving the Court all of the picture if we did not say that.

JUSTICE FRANKFURTER: You mean this in the nation's capital with all its concentrations and influences that that implies?

MR. NABRIT: Precisely and I think I should say that. And I also ought to say to the Court that in our opinion in thinking about this problem in the Deep South, where it would seem to me we have so many things that may appear to be different, that there has always been in our philosophy, in our system, the notion that our law is supreme and that we are a nation of laws rather than of individuals, and that although we may have had attitudes which differ—and in some instances violently—with the decisions or with laws, that we are, after all, governed by them, and two cases illustrate it to me. One is the case of the National Labor Relations Acts, the Wagner Act, the Taft-Hartley Act. The other is income tax, where the attitude of many people is just the same.

They do not want to pay minimum wages, they do not want to pay this, they do not want to have that; but the law is there; they keep the attitude but they obey the law.

The same thing with income tax. Everybody is worrying now for a few days that they are going to have to pay income tax. Very few people are running around happy over it. The attitude is not good but all of them pay it. And therefore, I say, it seems to me that in this area a firm decision calling for forthwith integration will be accepted and will be complied with by the South where I have lived all of my life and that thus, in spite of all their protestations and the attitude which many of them generally genuinely have, they will follow a decision of this Court just as other Americans follow the law.

JUSTICE REED: Mr. Nabrit, before you sit down I do not understand this language of your proposed decree, giving a choice. I have asked questions about it before. Are you familiar with the problems of choice that came up?

MR. NABRIT: Yes, I am and I would like to address myself for a moment if I may, to that. In the District of Columbia there is a system of administration and operation of the school which is known as the Districting Plan. Now there are different plans educationally in the United States that you are familiar with. In some places, there are no districts. You just go to whatever school you want to until that school is full, and then you find another one and go to that. Baltimore has a system something like that.

In other schools they have the boundary system, the districting, and you go to the school in your district except as—and all of them have this which relates to Mr. Justice Black's question—all of them have some ground upon which they will excuse you from going to a particular school. There are many grounds of hardships, where they will do that, in the sibling case and others. In the District of Columbia, however, we have this system based upon districting. That is the basis on which the school board says children shall be assigned, and they voted a policy that it would be done, and only the hardship or necessary situation of overriding necessity would permit any departure from that.

Now that was the policy.

JUSTICE REED: The Board policy?

MR. NABRIT: Yes. Now when the plan was proposed which the Board adopted, there was a difference between the policies and this plan, and it is that difference to which we call the Court's attention, that is, that in this plan which provided for this forthright imposition of the boundary or district system, there was set up inside the system, a system which provided that all of the pupils in all of the schools could stay right where they were until they graduated, unless—and you should know this because this even weakens the position still further, we want you to know that—unless your remaining there prevented a student who lived in that district from getting into it.

So that takes some more of the sting out of it. But we consider that bad because, looking at the Labor Relations cases and others, where this Court has said where you have a choice regarding a union or not, here is a company union, here is another union, that the choice is not a choice. You do not have freedom of choice. And where you come out of a segregated system where everybody in the system is segregated and you say to the Negro child, sure, you have a choice and to the white child, you have got a choice, I mean that is not choice. So that we simply point it out because it goes for five years and there is nothing that we have found that indicates that at the end of the fourth year the Board would adopt another plan with that in there.

JUSTICE REED: That is in it—

MR. NABRIT: I think it is on page 10 of our brief, Mr. Justice Reed. It is on page 10, No. 3 in the next to the bottom paragraph, "All pupils at present enrolled in a given school may remain until graduation provided the school is not overcrowded and provided the priority rights of pupils within the new boundaries of the school are not denied."

JUSTICE REED: There is another angle to that same choice. In your own decree, you provided a choice.

MR. NABRIT: Now in ours, we said, do not deny any child the right to go to the school of his choice on the grounds of race or color within the normal limits of your districting system.

In other words, you have this districting system here. Now, we say in that system, let children go to the schools of their choice within that system.

JUSTICE REED: Within that district.

MR. NABRIT: That is right.

And do not assign them on the basis of race or color, and we have no complaint. If you have some other basis, all boys, all girls, sixteen or fourteen, any other basis, we have no objection. But just do not put in race or color as a factor. And on that basis, we do not complain. But I do not think that it will be found to help the Court very much to try to look at a system where nothing existed by choice, and contrast it with the districting system in which there is this type of choice.

THE CHIEF JUSTICE: Thank you, Mr. Nabrit.
Mr. Korman.

ARGUMENT ON BEHALF OF SHARPE, ET AL

by MR. MILTON D. KORMAN

MR. KORMAN: Mr. Chief Justice, may it please the Court, I am in hopes that we could come here today without any controversy between the appellants and the respondents, and indeed, now that almost an hour has been spent by my adversary addressing the Court, I still see no reason for being here opposing each other. The only reason I can assign to it is that apparently my friends on the other side are determined that there must come from this Court or from the District Court some directive by which they can point in the future to the proposition that they have forced the District of Columbia to do certain things, and that is not the fact. These are the facts.

May 17, 1954, this Court declared, "We hold that racial segregation in the public schools of the District of Columbia is a denial of the due process of law guaranteed by the Fifth Amendment to the Constitution."

The next day, May 18, the members of the Board of Education and the Commissioners of the District of Columbia, met with the Corporation Counsel in private session at which time the Corporation Counsel of the District advised them that that language from this Court had effectively and forever struck down the validity of any laws on the books which provided for separate schools for whites and Negroes in the District of Columbia. And on the following day, May 19, the Board of Education met and appointed a committee to draft a set of principles. On May 22, three days later, that committee met and drafted a statement of policy.

May 25, three days after that, the Board of Education adopted that statement of policy and it appears in the Appendix to our brief. And in that same statement of policy they said that they thereafter proposed to so integrate the schools of the District of Columbia as quickly as it could be done.

On June 2, seven days later, or eight days later, the Superintendent of Schools, having worked on the matter for a year or more, presented to the Board of Education a complete plan for the desegregation of the schools of the District of Columbia. That plan is set forth in the Appendix to our brief.

Incidentally, that plan which was submitted by the Superintendent was approved by the Board of Education. On June 23, the Superintendent presented to the Board of Education a schedule of dates for putting into effect that plan, and the final date for anything to be done was September, 1955. Before schools opened on September 13, 1954, an attack was made upon that plan sponsored largely by the Federation of Citizens Association. The case was *Sabine and others* v. *Sharpe and others*.[1] It was heard by Judge Schweinhaut of the United States District Court. We presented to the District Court the proposition that the decision of this Court of May 17 had struck down all requirements for segregated schools and that the Board of Education was entirely within its rights in providing for the integration of schools to commence at the first opportunity, the opening of schools in the fall of that year. Judge Schweinhaut sustained the position we had taken and dismissed that suit, so that we have a determination by our District Court that

[1]Sabine v. Sharpe, 1 R.R.L.R. 305 (D.D.C. 1954).

our interpretation of this Court's decision was correct. The schools opened on September 13, 1954 as an integrated system, and it is completely integrated today and I do not know what my opponents point to in all these things that they have talked about here. What are the options that they talk about? Let us read them. They appear in the Appendix to our Brief, and this is the Superintendent's plan.

JUSTICE REED: What color brief?

MR. KORMAN: This is the one here. I suppose that would be called buff. And it is entitled, I think, somewhat differently than the other briefs of respondents, on formulation of the decree.

On page 13, the last paragraph, we find this from the statement of the Superintendent,

In order to provide stability, continuity and security in the educational experience of pupils during the transition period, it is agreed that it will be educationally sound to permit pupils at present enrolled in any school to continue in that school even though they are not living in the new boundaries.

If I may interject there, the plan proposes to set boundaries for each individual school in the District of Columbia, except in one or two instances where there were two schools so close together that two circles could not be drawn for them and one circle was drawn around the two buildings as the district for that school.

All others have a single area to be served by a single school.

Going on:

By this means immediate displacement of unnecessarily large numbers of pupils will be avoided. Progressively with the establishment of new boundaries, all children will attend the schools serving the areas in which they live.

The following procedures will be needed to carry out this plan:

1. Fixed zones are to be established for each elementary, junior high and senior high school to insure balanced use of school facilities.

2. All pupils new to the school system or to a particular school level will be assigned to the schools designated to serve the zones in which they live.

3. All pupils at present enrolled in a given school may remain until graduation provided the school is not overcrowded and provided the priority rights of pupils within the new boundaries of the school are not denied. If they prefer they may transfer to the school serving the zone in which they live. Elementary school pupils who change residence will be transferred to the school assigned to the area of the new residence.

4. Transfers from one school to another will be required when necessary to relieve overcrowded conditions.

And then on the following page, I skipped one paragraph, there is an example of what takes place:

These must attend School A—that is a school formerly in Division 1:

1. All children living within the new boundaries who formerly attended School A.

2. All children living within the new boundaries who are entering a school of that level for the first time.

3. All children who are newly residing in the area served by School A.

4. Children now attending School B but living within the boundaries of School A if School B becomes overcrowded.

Now, on that, who may attend School A—not who must but who may:

1. Children now enrolled in School A whether or not their residence is within the boundaries of School A may continue to attend until their graduation subject to the following conditions:

   a. If school A becomes overcrowded, pupils previously attending School A who live in the area now served by School B or any other school will be transferred to that school.

   b. If further relief from overcrowding is necessary after all children not living in the area served by School A have been transferred, it will then be necessary to provide additional relief by further changing the boundaries of School A.

Can anything be clearer?

Wherein, my friends, can you read race into that? How you do it is beyond me. Yet they say we must have a decree which enjoins us from putting race into this arrangement.

This plan, incidentally, has been mentioned by the Attorney General in his brief before this Court. May I read to you what he has to say of this plan in the District of Columbia. I read from a footnote in the brief of the United States on page 20 of their brief.

> In presenting his program for integration for the approval of the Board of Education, the Superintendent of Schools of the District laid emphasis on the consideration of the educational growth and welfare of the school child. Thus, in justification of the proposal that each presently enrolled pupil be granted a limited option to remain in the school he now attends even though he does not reside within its new attendance boundaries the Superintendent enumerated the ways in which this would provide stability, continuity and security in the educational experiences of pupils during the transition period. While we do not describe the District of Columbia program in detail here since this is undertaken in a brief for the respondents in No. 4, we think it reflects credit upon those responsible for its formulation and execution. In every significant respect the plan evidences painstaking care on the part of school officials to realize the expressed objective of a speedy transition calculated to make the best use of the total resources of the school system in plant and personnel to serve the best interests of all the pupils and to promote the general welfare of the community.

That is an evaluation which we did not write. The only ones, or largely the only ones in point of fact who are taking advantage of the option are children in the junior high schools and the high schools where they have elective subjects and where those children have mapped out a course of education for themselves, they have made selections, they have adopted certain courses and they want to continue and they have the right to remain in those schools until they have completed the particular level at which they are going to school. If a child is going to a particular junior high school and the boundary of that school leaves out his residence as it is finally fixed, and he wants to stay in there, he should have that right, whether he is white or colored.

This is not a question of race at all. It is a question of the continuity of education of that child, the security he has, the right to continue to go to school with the pupils that he has come to know, the right to continue with the teachers that he has selected to instruct him until he graduates from that particular level.

That is all that the plan provides for.

Actually, the plan has been stepped up and there remains at this time nothing to be done so far as integration of the schools of the District with the exception of putting into effect finally the boundaries of the senior high schools which have not all been fixed, and not all pupils have been required to go to the particular high school in which they reside, in the boundaries of which they reside.

Except for that one point, the schools of the District are completely integrated. Mr. Nabrit gave you the figures showing that only a comparatively few schools have no pupils of both races on their enrollments, and he points to the fact that only 122 or some number like that, out of a graduating group of some 500 went into schools formerly occupied by other races. He is mentioning the white students—let me see whether I made a note of that when he gave it. Out of 525 who came from Division 1 schools, that is the white schools, 122 went into Division 1 schools and one went into a Division 2—that is, a formerly colored vocational school, but no white children went into a formerly colored school.

Obviously, the reason is that whether we like it or not, when they change, they have been changing from white to colored and not the other way, so when neighborhoods change, there are no longer white children going into the neighborhoods where colored now live, but colored children are coming into the neighborhoods that were formerly occupied by white.

So, it is only logical that, when people graduate from one level of a school, we find that colored children may go to schools formerly occupied by white, but it is not likely that the other will occur, that the white children will go into schools formerly occupied by colored because the neighborhoods have been changing the other way.

That is the only answer to that. We cannot read race into that as something that the school system is putting on for these children. It is just not so.

JUSTICE REED: What is your explanation for several all-white schools?

MR. KORMAN: Just that in certain areas in the District, there are no Negro residents and in certain areas of high schools and we have two teachers colleges. Those are now open to pupils of both races.

JUSTICE REED: Take the elementary schools. They go up to the eighth grade?

MR. KORMAN: No, sir, it means up to the sixth grade. It used to be up to the eighth grade, when I went to school—I suppose when you did, too.

Then we even went from elementary to high school but in the interim they have introduced the junior high school which takes in the seventh, eighth and ninth grades, the last two grades of what we used to think of as elementary school, and what we used to call the first grade of high school.

JUSTICE REED: So there would be several first grade rooms in each school?

MR. KORMAN: Yes, sir, in the particular school where my children attend, there are some four first-grade classrooms. That is true of many schools.

JUSTICE REED: The total number is what in an elementary school building, is that several hundred?

MR. KORMAN: Yes, sir, it varies. In the particular school I know about it runs between 800 and 900 children. As I view this case, this proceeding is really moot. There is nothing here to enjoin. And if this Court found that this situation in the District presented a moot proposition, it would be entirely within not only its rights, but within the framework of decisions which it has laid down heretofore. I refer to the case—the opinion which was written by Mr. Justice Clark just two years ago next month—the *United States* v. *W. T. Grant*,[2] where it was held specifically where there is no reasonable expectation that the wrong will be repeated, the case is moot. Here is that situation.

I hope the Court may not think I am using undue levity when I say that if anyone should attempt to disintegrate the local schools, if we had, the local school board would promptly be disintegrated.

There is no chance whatever in this District of Columbia that we should have a return to the segregated schools. I say that this proposition is completely a moot one. This is not a case where the respondents have violated the law and by reason of a decree of a court, are required to do something.

I think that the Court must know that long before this case came on for hearing there was a pronouncement at the suggestion of the President of the United States by the governing authorities of the District of Columbia that segregation should be cast out in all of the various fields that the District had any supervision of, and they have been doing that and are practically complete in having eliminated any vestige of segregation, of discrimination in any of the areas of the District Government that the District has any supervision over and indeed, some of the members of the school board, I think perhaps it probably engendered some of the discussion they had when I rose to address the Court last time, had expressed themselves rather forcefully that they wanted to have integration in the schools but they were not able to because the law then forbade it.

But within two or three days, as I pointed out to the Court, we had this—when this Court said those laws were unconstitutional, they put into effect a system of complete integration of the schools. That system is in effect now because they wanted to do so not because they were compelled to do so.

I say to you, gentlemen of the Court, that there is no need for any decree in this case, requiring anyone to do anything. If the Court sees fit to remand to the lower court with the suggestion that the lower court enter a decree for a declaratory judgment, which is the first prayer of the complaint that was filed, that the laws which required segregation of schools are unconstitutional, I would have no objection. I see no necessity for it. That has been established. The matter is, in fact, moot.

I would like to see this Court declare it moot, because that is the situation.

Unless there are questions from the Court, I have nothing further.

[2]United States v. W. T. Grant, 345 U.S. 629 (1953). The Court declared that even after a violation of law has been proven the moving party must show his right to relief and that judicial discretion to grant or withhold relief is very broad.

THE CHIEF JUSTICE: Mr. Korman, in the event the Court does not determine to declare it moot, would you prepare the form of the decree that you think would be appropriate? Would you do that?

MR. KORMAN: I would be glad to do that, and unless I am directed to do otherwise, I would like to limit it to a direction that only a declaratory judgment be entered based on the decision of last May. That would be my preference.

THE CHIEF JUSTICE: Whatever you think might be reasonable.
If there are two or three alternatives, would you suggest them?

MR. KORMAN: Yes, sir.

JUSTICE CLARK: Mr. Korman, do you know of any protest with the Board, Superintendent Corning, by parents or children, students, as to their assignments to schools in the District under this new plan?

MR. KORMAN: I now know of none with the exception that there was a provision approved by the Board of Education that so-called hardship cases might be specially dealt with. Out of the 105,000 children approximately, there were 377 such so-called hardship cases. Many of them were accompanied by physician's certificates that it was needful that a child should go to some other school than the one he would normally be assigned to. In many of them the change was made as I understand it by the sibling rule.

That is, that a family had a child going to one school because he was transferred there, he was in the higher grade and another child would enter the school system during that year and they wanted the older child to take the younger one by the hand to that school. But only 377 so-called hardship cases out of 105,000 children. Other than that, there have been no protests and so far as I know, everyone is content here except my friends.

JUSTICE BLACK: Was there a hardship rule of that kind in effect before?

MR. KORMAN: I do not know of any. That was especially set up for this transition period. If we had the hardship transfers, they were only for this particular year and would have to be reviewed again and application made again next year.

JUSTICE BLACK: You mean there is a rule in the District, come what may, however much that it may be thought necessary for one person to go into another district, the District has a rigid rule that it is never done?

MR. KORMAN: That has been the rule in the past when we had a segregated system and I assume that will be the rule in the future with the integrated system.

I do not think it was for economical reasons. It was not called or thought valid in the Division 1 schools. There was a great deal of laxity in the Division 2 schools. I think it was largely because of instances where parents of children were working and wanted to take the children to certain schools on the way to work. I know it was not adhered to as strictly in the Division 2 schools, the colored schools, but it was in the white schools.

If you lived in a particular district served by that school, you had to go there. That was to prevent parents selecting certain schools for their children to go to. What the reason for selection was, I do not know.

JUSTICE BLACK: Can you offer any explanation for that?

MR. KORMAN: No. Some schools had more of a social cast or something of that sort. I do recall I was, in one instance in the office of the superintendent discussing some business and a rather poor individual called up and said he wanted his child to go to a particular school as they lived a half block over the line of the other area, and the Superintendent said, "That is the rule, we cannot break it, even for you."

JUSTICE FRANKFURTER: To what particular virtues do you attribute this progress that has taken place in the District?

MR. KORMAN: Well, I think, for one thing, it is entirely within the scope of the program of the President of the United States. I think for a second thing, it is entirely in the program of the thing.

JUSTICE FRANKFURTER: Does that mean responsiveness or respect for the great office or because in the District people are without any other political loyalties to worry about, they are appointees?

MR. KORMAN: No. I do not think so. Because, while there has been a great deal of criticism of our Board of Education, the Board of Education are not appointees of any political party.

JUSTICE FRANKFURTER: I understand that. The Commissioners are. The atmosphere is different than we find with elected officers.

MR. KORMAN: I do not think so.

JUSTICE FRANKFURTER: You don't?

MR. KORMAN: No.

JUSTICE FRANKFURTER: I thought there was a good deal of excitement about no voting in this District?

MR. KORMAN: There is, in some quarters.
But I think that possibly there is a general awareness that the time has come when some change must take place and some thought this would come sometime ago. Others thought it was a little too soon. The argument, it seems to me, was always just who should make the decision.

JUSTICE DOUGLAS: Of course, you had in the District—I do not think you have mentioned it in your brief—but you had in the district a pretty high standard and quality of teaching staff.

MR. KORMAN: Yes. We have always had a school system which largely, though in two halves, was perfectly equal side by side.

JUSTICE FRANKFURTER: Is that an established fact, that the standards of teaching in the District are higher than in some of the other states?

MR. KORMAN: I would not say that.

JUSTICE DOUGLAS: I was thinking of the standard of teaching in Negro schools before the desegregation.

MR. KORMAN: All of the courses of instruction in our teachers colleges, all of the books that they used, all of the criteria that were laid down for instruction on both sides of the dual school system were identical.

JUSTICE DOUGLAS: That was part of the case, they were separate, equal.

MR. KORMAN: Yes.

THE CHIEF JUSTICE: Thank you, Mr. Korman. Do you have anything further, Mr. Nabrit?

MR. NABRIT: No, thank you.

THE CHIEF JUSTICE: May I revert for a moment to No. 1, the Kansas case. I see General Fatzer is here and Mr. Carter is here. Gentlemen, would you, if you wish, present the form of decree that you think would be appropriate in your case? I believe it would be helpful to the Court if you did.

MR. FATZER: We shall be glad to.

THE CHIEF JUSTICE: Thank you. I do not know whether counsel in the Delaware case are here or not.

MR. KORMAN: I think they left.

THE CHIEF JUSTICE: Mr. Redding, if you would care to, I believe it would be helpful for you to propose the kind of decree you believe would be appropriate and we will have the Attorney General do the same.

No. 2 and No. 3, Harry Briggs, Jr., et al vs. R. W. Elliott, et al, Dorothy E. Davis, et al, vs. County School Board of Prince Edward County, et al.

Mr. Robinson.

### ARGUMENT OF HARRY BRIGGS, JR., ET AL

#### by MR. SPOTTSWOOD ROBINSON

MR. ROBINSON: May it please the court, as the Chief Justice has already indicated, the arguments in numbers 2 and 3 are being combined and it is principally for that reason that at the outset I request the indulgence of the Court to first outline the argument that will be presented in these two cases on Questions 4 and 5 and the part of the argument that Mr. Marshall will present.

And I think that perhaps this can be best done by starting with the specific answers to Questions 4 and 5 that we suggest to the Court.

As to Question 4, we submit that a decree should be entered which would require desegregation of the public schools involved as soon as the necessary administrative and mechanical procedures prerequisite to such desegregation can be accomplished.

We do not feel and therefore we submit that the equity powers of this Court should not be exercised so as to delay relief in these cases beyond the time that is essential for the taking of the administrative steps essential to desegregation.

In answer to No. 5, on the assumptions on which that question is predicated, we would submit in answer to part (a) thereof that this Court should not formulate detailed decrees in these cases which in our opinion makes it unnecessary for us to submit an answer to part (b) of that question.

In answer to part (c), as to whether or not this Court should appoint a special master to hear evidence with a view to recommending specific terms for such decrees, we would suggest an answer in the negative. And in answer to part (b), we submit that this Court should remand these cases to the courts of first instances with directions to frame decrees in these cases in accordance with the mandate of this Court; the decree entered by this Court, however, to contain certain provisions that Mr. Marshall will outline in his portion of the argument.

We think that beyond those considerations, the lower courts may, by the exercise of ordinary procedural devices reach such further provisions in the decrees as might be necessary.

I will undertake to present our argument on Question 4 and Mr. Marshall will undertake to present our argument on 5.

In the normal course of judicial procedure, the decision of this Court that was entered on May 17, declaring that racial segregation in public educational facilities afforded by a state is a violation of equal protection of the laws secured by the Fourteenth Amendment, would have been followed by decrees which would have forthwith enjoined the continuation of the practice that this Court at that time found to be unlawful.

As a matter of fact, in a somewhat analogous situation that this Court found itself presented with a *Sipuel* v. *Board of Regents,* where an effort was there made to secure a postponement of the rights that were involved, this Court not only refused to delay the relief sought but accelerated the granting of the relief by directing that its mandate issue forthwith.

If that course of procedure had been followed, if that course of procedure is now followed, it would mean a disposition in these cases which would require we think, two principal things, first, the initiation immediately of the administrative procedures and steps that are necessary in order to desegregate the public schools in question and secondly, the admission at the commencement of the school term of the appellants and others who are similarly situated.

JUSTICE BLACK: May I ask you who would that include, those similarly situated?

MR. ROBINSON: Mr. Justice Black. I would answer that question by suggesting that it would include all Negroes who are residents in the Virginia case of the County of Prince Edwards and in the South Carolina case of District No. 1.

JUSTICE BLACK: Mr. Robinson, it is relevant to point out in view of your remarks that in the Delaware case, in order to avoid loose talk about class suits, the decree merely related to the specifically named pupils and others seeking admission in that school.

MR. ROBINSON: In the Virginia case there are actually three schools involved.

JUSTICE BLACK: In the Delaware complaint—I do not know whether you have seen it—

MR. ROBINSON: I have not.

JUSTICE BLACK: The schools are mentioned by name. One is a high school and the other an elementary school—by name.

MR. ROBINSON: I do not know whether, in the Delaware case, the prayer for relief in the complaint was the admission of the named plaintiffs to a particular school.

JUSTICE FRANKFURTER: That was the complaint and all other similarly situated seeking admission as pupils in the Claymont High School and in the other case in the Hockessin School No. 29. The class suit was not class-at-large, but class defined with reference to that particular school.

MR. ROBINSON: In both the Virginia and South Carolina cases, however, the suits were brought as class actions under Rule 23 of the Federal Rules of Civil Procedure and in these cases there was a prayer for admission to a specific school as distinguished from a prayer for declaratory relief and also for an injunction which would prevent the use of race in the assignment of pupils to schools.

JUSTICE FRANKFURTER: Why restrict it to a county, why not to the whole state?

MR. ROBINSON: I answered Mr. Justice Black's question in the fashion I did, that in Virginia we have a situation in which our local school communities possess such a degree of autonomy that I do not believe that a decree that this Court would enter in the Prince Edward County case would be binding except of course as a matter of *stare decisis* in some other county for the simple reason that we do not have the school authorities who operate those other school units before the Court in this litigation.

JUSTICE FRANKFURTER: What is the relevant school population in the suit now?

MR. ROBINSON: At the time we filed the suit—Your Honors will understand in Prince Edward County the litigation embraced only the high schools—there were 451 Negro high school and 384 white high school students in the county overall according to the 1950 census.

JUSTICE FRANKFURTER: Your suit does not cover it?

MR. ROBINSON: No. I have the information if you want it.

JUSTICE FRANKFURTER: Well, when one talks about class suits it is important to determine the content of the class. In your case, the content of the class is what, 700, all told, 800—

MR. ROBINSON: Approximately 800, I should say.

JUSTICE BLACK: Why do you say it includes the entire county?

MR. ROBINSON: In Virginia, unlike the situation, Mr. Justice Black, in other states the entire county is one school unit. In other words, in school terminology, one school district or one school division, there are no subdivisions of a county geographically or otherwise for school purposes.

JUSTICE BLACK: You mean they can be sent to any school in any county?

MR. ROBINSON: In terms of this situation under a segregated system there would be no choice with respect to Negro students because there is only one Negro high school and with respect to white students there would be very little choice. While there were two white high schools, one was really a small high school department of essentially an elementary school accommodating something like seventy-five students and as the testimony in the record of the case indicates, was being maintained primarily for reasons of convenience of some of the people living in that neighborhood and, as a matter of fact, was a school that we understood at that time probably was slated for abolition at sometime in the near future.

JUSTICE BLACK: Did the petitioners ask that these students be sent to a particular school?

MR. ROBINSON: No. In our complaint we did not.

JUSTICE FRANKFURTER: Did the state or county give bus service to all the high school students in the county?

MR. ROBINSON: Yes, all those who required it, both white and Negro.

JUSTICE REED: (Unintelligible.)

MR. ROBINSON: Very definitely.

JUSTICE REED: That is not involved?

MR. ROBINSON: Yes, I think that it is.

JUSTICE REED: I do not recall the specific situation.

MR. ROBINSON: I cannot say that it has been. I will direct Your Honors to the fact that within the district court's decree which was an equalization decree, the court continued to provisions with respect to school bus transportation.

JUSTICE BLACK: If there is a decree such as you suggest with reference to all the people in the county, what statutory sanctions could be invoked for enforcement of a decree of that nature if it were violated?

Suppose we entered a decree requiring that all the colored children in the whole county must be admitted into the county schools of a certain type and suppose someone violated that, what sanction can be imposed under the statute?

MR. ROBINSON: I am still not sure that I am clear.

JUSTICE BLACK: How would you enforce the order?

MR. ROBINSON: Through the normal contempt procedures—

JUSTICE BLACK: Anything else?

MR. ROBINSON: —Very definitely involved.

JUSTICE BLACK: In other words, you would have to try contempt procedures for everybody in the county that violated the order?

MR. ROBINSON: I would say that would be available, yes.

JUSTICE BLACK: Any others?

MR. ROBINSON: I cannot recall that there is.

JUSTICE FRANKFURTER: You mean contempt in the district court in the federal court for violating the decree?

MR. ROBINSON: Yes, in whatever court it emanates.

JUSTICE FRANKFURTER: In this case. This is in the district court. Assuming such a decree as you would like to have were entered, then obedience to it would be by the contempt process for disobedience?

MR. ROBINSON: Yes.

JUSTICE REED: And contempt would be the process against the parties in this case?

MR. ROBINSON: In the Prince Edward County case, yes.

JUSTICE REED: The school board?

MR. ROBINSON: In this situation it would be the school board which is a corporation under Virginia law and the Division Superintendent of Schools.

We have a situation in which, back in 1948, there was an instance of a violation by school authorities of a federal court decree. It was the same court in which we took this appeal except that it was a single, rather than a three-judge district court. That is a case which was referred to in the first brief we filed for Virginia on the first appeal. The case is *Ashley* v. *the School Board of Gloucester County.*[3]

---

[3]Ashley v. School Board of Gloucester County, 82 F. Supp. 167 (E.D. Va. 1948). Negro school teachers brought and won an action against the school boards of three Virginia counties claiming their constitutional rights were violated by the payment of lower salaries to them than were paid to white teachers.

That was a situation in which the district court entered a decree, an equalization decree and after the expiration of a certain period of time contempt proceedings were initiated predicated upon the basis that the decree provisions had not been complied with. The district court found that the school authorities were in contempt. It imposed a fine upon the members of the Board and the Division Superintendent as well as I can recall. There were no subsequent contempt proceedings because shortly after that at least a measure of equalization was forthcoming in that county. That is the only instance to which I might direct your attention.

JUSTICE BLACK: With reference to the scope of your decree, the number of people involved, it would be important to state, would it not, as to what sanctions the law provided, or whether we would be entirely dependent upon contempt proceedings, and so forth, statutory or common law?

MR. ROBINSON: I would volunteer this, but readily confessing I would not be in a position to argue that point: whether or not now that the law has been made plain as to what the rights of these people are, a school official who declines to afford constitutional rights of this character at the time they are applied for does not violate one of the federal statutes having to do with activities under authority of the state law which are in deprivation of rights secured by the Constitution.

JUSTICE BLACK: I was thinking that there was a federal statute which made it criminal contempt—that general safeguard. I had an idea without looking at it, that there was some kind of a provision made for civil action for damages.

MR. ROBINSON: Well, yes, there is a section to which Your Honor refers, section 1983 of Title 42, it is the old section 43 of it.

JUSTICE BLACK: Civil Rights Act.

MR. ROBINSON: Yes. We had some amount of discussion about that the last time we were here.
In this situation we submit if there is any—if there is going to be any postponement of relief beyond the date we suggest the burden is on these defendants to state what they propose to do and establish, as a matter of fact, that the postponement of relief beyond the date we suggest—the burden is on these defendants, those which are inherent in the prompt vindication of the appellants' constitutional right.

JUSTICE FRANKFURTER: You suggested a terminal date but did not give a date in your sketch of proposed decree, but you also gave a consideration, namely, administrative requirements.

MR. ROBINSON: Yes, that is right.

JUSTICE FRANKFURTER: Since that is a criteria, that is a condition which you take into account, can this Court take judicial notice relevant to the enforcement of the decision we made last May, can this Court take into account that that would be satisfied, that requirement, that would be fulfilled by September, 1955, if not this Court, could the district court take notice or if it is not one of those things that either court can take into account, doesn't that require determination with evidence and testimony and so on?

MR. ROBINSON: I think that speaking as of this moment, it is a matter of which this Court could take judicial notice.

JUSTICE FRANKFURTER: This Court could take judicial notice of the conditions in Prince Edward County with regard to relevant administrative considerations in the disposition of plant, personnel, and so forth?

MR. ROBINSON: Not quite in that fashion, sir. This Court has before it the case in which argument was just completed, involving a much larger and a much more complicated school system than exists in Prince Edward County. The Court has had before it the school systems in two other states. Now absent any showing of judicially relevant considerations that would administratively delay the accomplishment of desegregation beyond September of 1955, we feel that this Court, on the basis of the experience had in those instances which we think has now been had by the Court and certainly is a matter of which the Court could take judicial notice, would fully justify this Court in fixing as the terminal date of the desegregation process September 1955.

JUSTICE FRANKFURTER: We have heard from both counsel that the District represented some very special considerations.

MR. ROBINSON: I think, Mr. Justice Frankfurter, that the considerations which are really important to the question which is now before the Court—and that is ways and means and particular time of accomplishing desegregation—are considerations which obtain in Prince Edward County as well as in the District of Columbia and in these other areas.

JUSTICE FRANKFURTER: Maybe so, but my attitude and mind do not necessarily lead to that conclusion.

MR. ROBINSON: I am sure our opponents will urge considerations to the contrary. Mr. Marshall proposes in his presentation to go fully into those. If Your Honors want me to—

JUSTICE FRANKFURTER: No, no, divide your time as you please.

JUSTICE REED: The only problem that we suggest that is the burden of your opponents is to show that here in Court.

MR. ROBINSON: I think so.

JUSTICE REED: Just tell us what they think about it.

MR. ROBINSON: No, I think they should come forward in this Court and demonstrate—

JUSTICE REED: Demonstrate how, by evidence?

MR. ROBINSON: Yes, by evidence. I suppose that is the only way we can formulate—

JUSTICE REED: Or their statement that it would be difficult as part of the school situation, because of the attitude of the people, because of lack of bus transportation?

MR. ROBINSON: I do not think that, sir.

JUSTICE REED: Because of lack of schools of adequate size.

MR. ROBINSON: If there were a fact that was brought to the attention of the Court, I should think that would be one way of doing it.

JUSTICE REED: Perhaps that would be better to take up in the district court.

MR. ROBINSON: We feel when it comes to the question of fixing the terminal date, that here we have a consideration that is so all-important in so far as the realization and satisfaction of constitutional rights may be concerned, it is a matter that occupies just that degree of importance that the thing is a matter which should be fixed by this Court, assuming that there is no lack of basis upon which this Court can proceed to that conclusion.

JUSTICE REED: How would you find that, according to the percentage of the minority race there may be in a particular county?

MR. ROBINSON: No, without undertaking how much time this particular activity would take or that would take, this Court would be justified in concluding that if a school system like the District desegregated in the space of time it did, that a school system far less complicated and far smaller in size than the District could desegregate in an equal space of time, absent any showing by our opponents that an additional period of time would be needed.

JUSTICE REED: Before you make that, that carries the connotation to me that every place in the country is just alike. There would be no difference in the time that would be required in the District; if they may do it that quickly, in a certain time, every other place should do it.

MR. ROBINSON: As I say, that is a consideration that Mr. Marshall is directing his argument to. We think the burden on our opponents is increased by reason of the fact that the rights that these appellants seek to postpone are rights which have been characterized in a number of cases by this Court as personal and present. We think that that consideration is a measure—a consideration of the appellees and makes it even more difficult.

Then there are two additional considerations that we submit here. In the first place, as this Court has pointed out, the continuance of racial situations in public education is a matter that causes irreparable harm and damage to the students. Every day that this illegal system of racial segregation continues, it would mean that we have not one child but a multitude of children who are really being seriously injured. Additionally, the rights asserted by the appellants in these cases are the rights of the children and if they are ever going to be satisfied they must be satisifed while they are still children, and the period for attendance in public schools is a short period.

We think they are important considerations that must be weighed in making any determination as to whether the burden upon our opponents of demonstrating a justification for the delay has been met.

I would like to look first at the precedents because we have some and they have some, that are specifically urged upon the Court as decisive of this question. I would like to call attention first to the Youngstown case,[4] a decision by this Court in which the Court even in the face of the gravest of public emergencies, declined to delay the satisfaction of the rights involved.

The case of course is familiar to the Court. Preliminary injunctions had been entered by the district court against the enforcement of a Presidential order involving a seizure of steel mills. The appeal was taken here and among the arguments to this Court was the argument that the public interest in the uninterrupted production of steel which was so closely and so necessarily connected with the production of sensitive and essential war materials was superior to the constitutional rights of the owners of the properties that had been seized to the immediate return of their properties, and out of the seven opinions that were filed by this Court, no one apparently saw any merit in that argument.

We submit that, if in a situation of that kind, equity could not appropriately exercise its broad discretion to withhold an immediate right of relief, then such a postponement would be completely inappropriate in these cases where no consideration that even touches the magnitude of the one there involved is present here.

I would like to make reference to *Ex parte Endo,* that I think is much more closely related to these cases than the cases upon which our opponents rest. That was the case in which the Government argued that disorder and hardship and community hostility and prejudice that was supposed to flow from the unsupervised release of a loyal American citizen of Japanese ancestry; in other words, the argument there was made that even though the detention of the party in that habeas corpus proceeding was illegal, that there was such a hostility, there was such a prejudice in some areas, that it was necessary for the detention to be continued at least temporarily in order that the relocation program of our Government could be successfully continued; but this Court, in a unanimous opinion, there being in addition two concurring opinions, held that notwithstanding this, the party must be given her unconditional release. The Court said that here the petitioner had one of these rights in that sensitive area of rights specifically guaranteed by the Constitution, and notwithstanding the weight in a time like that, that the Government's contention was bound to carry, nevertheless concluded that she must be immediately released.

JUSTICE REED: That follows the Hirabayashi case, which said that they could be and only after Miss Endo had demonstrated her loyalty.

MR. ROBINSON: But when her loyalty—when we got to that point—had been demonstrated to us, her right to constitutional freedom was clear.

---

[4]Youngstown Sheet and Tool Co. v. Sawyer, 343 U.S. 579 (1952). In the famous steel seizure case, the President ordered most of the steel mills of the country seized to avert a steel strike. The Court ordered the mills returned. John W. Davis argued the case for the steel companies.

JUSTICE REED: Yes.

MR. ROBINSON: I think the significance of the Endo holding is that once we get to that point, she could not be illegally detained. In other words, the postponement—there could be no postponement. There was no justification for postponing or delaying her constitutional right to freedom just like that of any other American.

JUSTICE REED: In the Hirabayashi case we did not have that.

MR. ROBINSON: In the Hirabayashi case we had a situation until there had been an opportunity to make a determination as to who was loyal and who was disloyal, we would not be in a position to know who had the right and who did not have it. I think that is the difficulty.

In answer to the Court's question, for in our efforts to get the thing answered, we have made a very extensive study of the cases and we have come up with no case, we have come across no case wherein this situation, this case, where it is found that there is a violation of a constitutional right, nevertheless, [this Court] has postponed relief or satisfaction of that right on the ground that, because of some local community hostility or prejudice or customs, delay in effectuating that right is justified.

As a matter of fact, we think that it would be strange in these cases for this Court to conclude that here we have a situation where for the first time it may now be decided that the enjoyment of such fundamental and basic human rights may be justifiably delayed. These are rights asserted in these two cases that are secured by the Fourteenth Amendment and as a matter of history, that Amendment was designed to protect these rights against the same type of local hostilities and prejudices and customs and all that our opponents rely on.

Not only do we have the Amendment itself but we have congressional legislation that was designed for the very purpose of affording protection to the enjoyment of rights of this kind when their infringement, predicated upon local customs, was forthcoming. We cannot find any situation anywhere in the cases nor do we think that the principle should be established here that rights of that character should be enforced at a pace that is geared down to the very customs and practices and usages that the Constitution and federal legislation were designed to protect against.

I would like to get into the cases which are relied upon by our opponents and I would like to have the opportunity to distinguish them. They rely upon a number of decisions of this Court and other courts as well in which there has been some measure of delay in the absence of rights but are cases that involve totally different considerations.

We find upon our examination of these cases that they fall principally into two groups: First, they make reference to the nuisance cases, the situations in which delay and enforcement of a right, usually a property right against conduct that is essentially commission of a tort, has been forthcoming. They also rely upon a number of decisions of this Court in antitrust litigation in which, because of some phase of the activity which was to follow this Court's decision, some measure of time was afforded.

THE CHIEF JUSTICE: We will recess now.

(At 4:30 p.m. the hearing was recessed.)

(Oral argument was resumed at 12:00 p.m., April 12, 1955.)

THE CHIEF JUSTICE: Harry Briggs, Jr., et al, vs. W. Elliott, and Dorothy E. Davis, et al, vs. County School Board of Prince Edward County, Virginia, et al, numbers 2 and 3 on the Calendar.

THE CLERK: Counsel are present.

THE CHIEF JUSTICE: Mr. Marshall.

### ARGUMENT ON BEHALF OF HARRY BRIGGS, ET AL AND DOROTHY E. DAVIS, ET AL

### by MR. THURGOOD MARSHALL

MR. MARSHALL: May it please the Court, as was pointed out in argument yesterday by Mr. Robinson, it is our opinion that in answering specifically the questions propounded by this Court that the Court should issue a forthwith decree, and I say on that when we use "forthwith decree" in our briefs and argument as explained in the brief for this case, we actually are urging, not tomorrow or as of whatever day the opinion comes down in this case, but we are urging as of the September school term being this year of the next school term, and as I use "forthwith" that was what we were urging.

I am just using it as a shorthand way of saying September, 1955.

JUSTICE FRANKFURTER: You do not want that word in the decree, then?

MR. MARSHALL: It came about this way, Mr. Justice Frankfurter: We took the position that in any decree issued that says "forthwith," that normal administrative details always come into consideration. So as far as we are concerned, if the decree says "September of 1955," that will be exactly what we want.

JUSTICE FRANKFURTER: I am sure you will agree in this kind of litigation, it is of the utmost importance to use language of fastidious accuracy.

MR. MARSHALL: Absolutely, we agree with you fully. That is why we would rather have it say September of 1955.

The other specific point is that we believe that the appellants in these cases, those of high school age from Prince Edward County and those of elementary and high school age of District 1 which includes Clarendon County, should be admitted as of September, 1955, and the entire class that they represent.

JUSTICE HARLAN: Mr. Marshall, on page 19 of your joint brief—

MR. MARSHALL: Yes, sir.

JUSTICE HARLAN: —as I read it, you suggest as an alternative date, September 1, 1956.

MR. MARSHALL: Yes, sir.

JUSTICE HARLAN: You indicate that that would be acceptable?

MR. MARSHALL: Yes, sir.

JUSTICE HARLAN: Have you receded from that view?

MR. MARSHALL: No, sir, I was going to limit the argument to two sections, and as I understand it, the two questions can be divided. We say that we are entitled to forthwith action as of September. We felt obliged by the wording of Question 5 to, at that stage of our argument, assume that this Court had then agreed that forthwith was not proper, and in answering that in good faith to the Court, we took the position that, if we cannot have forthwith, the least this Court should do would be to put a date certain and put certain other safeguards. And we most certainly do not recede from that position.

If I may just bring this particular issue down to the present point, I think we should also, at the outset of this argument, recognize that these present and personal rights we are talking about that were in the beginning of this case, they are still there and we are still talking about the same personal and present rights of the type that this Court enforced in the Sipuel case, the *Sweatt* v. *Painter* case, the *McLaurin* v. *Oklahoma State Regents* case, and other cases set out in our brief, and that even in the consideration of Questions 4 and 5, which you are now considering, we still are considering those questions in the light of this personal and present right. We want to continue to emphasize that point.

The question then resolves itself as to, it seems to us, whether or not this immediate relief is granted or the delayed action, and we believe that there is much to support our position that it should be—not only should be, but could be—forthwith. We believe that the three cases other than South Carolina and Virginia cases, the three cases that were argued yesterday, argued very well to the proposition that forthwith should be the term included—I mean, September, 1955, should be the term included in the decree. And I say that for each one of the cases. In the Kansas case, it is significant that the resolution they produced yesterday said specifically that segregation in so far as they were concerned, was going to be over as of September, 1955. So, certainly, a decree in these two cases would be unnecessary, as a precedent or anything else for Kansas. They do not need it. According to their story, they will be through with it by September of 1955.

In the Delaware case, despite the fact that the new Attorney General says that they need time, I believe that his statement which has no documentation, no support except his personal opinion, should be weighed with the long detailed argument which his predecessor made in the brief which is before this Court which says they do not need time. And what will happen in Delaware is that already 50 per cent of the children living in the State of Delaware have already been integrated so they do not need any time. And, as for the others, this Steiner case, this last case that was adverted to in argument of both sides in the Delaware case, stands on the books in Delaware. And they say that these rights which they recognize as being personal and present could not be enforced as of the time of the decision in that case but had to be delayed until this Court decides the broad question. Bear in mind that the original decision of the Delaware case said—on, of course, a basis to which I do not agree—the separate but equal basis, but they said that the relief had to be immediate. And if at some later date the schools were made equal, of course the Attorney General would come in for nonenforcement. But that judgment said "immediately."

The Steiner decision says depending on what this Court says, that it might be a delayed action. So, if, in the decisions in the Virginia and South Carolina cases, this Court should say that time can be recognized as a factor as to this relief, in fact the decision of the original Delaware case would be destroyed. It would destroy the present and personal, and I do not have the slightest idea what the status of the law in the State of Delaware would be.

In the District of Columbia case, it is wholly significant when we apply it to these cases we are now on, for, in the District of Columbia, they did it between May and September and I say, in all frankness, they must have been working on it before because it is a very complicated, involved school system in a city the size of Washington. But it is significant that they not only began on it in September, but they found that it was necessary to speed it up. And the other thing that we must bear in mind, it seems to me, in answer to all of the arguments to the contrary, running through them is this great number of Negroes involved, this terrific number makes the Fourteenth Amendment different. And, fortunately, in so far as this argument is concerned, the District of Columbia has the largest number of Negroes in its school system of any city in the country, not only the southern cities, but any other city. It is approximately 60–40.

And so that argument, it seems to me, is lost because on one hand, we have theory that numbers are bad, and that numbers are this, and we have unsupported opinions of Attorneys General, and so forth, that numbers are this, and we have right here in our face in the District of Columbia that if you take everything else aside, numbers could not possibly be important.

JUSTICE FRANKFURTER: The argument is lost only if all other factors are the same.

MR. MARSHALL: That portion of my argument would be, Mr. Justice Frankfurter, and I would like to get to the other factors.

The question was raised yesterday that a partial reason for this fine development in the District of Columbia was the good policy of the Administration, of the school system, good will, firm hand, and so forth. And I say that that does not, in any way, negate my argument, for this reason: It is admitted within all of the studies of desegregation—and considerable scientific studies have been made—that, yes, the situation needs a firm hand of government to say, "We are going to desegregate." And that is it.

But I take the position that it matters not whether that firm hand is executive, legislative or judicial, and in these cases we are urging that the district court, once properly instructed by this Court, will be the type of firm hand, and I support that by the citation some time back in this very case, not the Virginia case, the South Carolina case, where, during the trial of the case, the question was raised as to whether or not, assuming the district court would issue an injunction, somebody might not obey it, and the question was raised by the attorney for the defendants as to the question, and I think Judge Parker's statement was wholly significant, and it was a very short statement: "Any injunction issued by this court will be obeyed."

And I think that applies to any decree that this Court issues, plus the fact that, as late as March 14, this year, in a case involving recreation in Baltimore, Maryland, recreation facilities, not school facilities, state recreation facilities, the Fourth Circuit, with Judge Parker presiding, issued a per curium decision, in which they said, not only that the decision of this Court on May 17, declared unconstitutional the laws as to public schools, but declared all the other laws involved in segregation unconstitutional.[5] So, so far as I am concerned with the proper instructions and a decree in this Court, I have no hesitance in worrying about the firm hand of the judiciary in the Fourth Circuit carrying out the instructions of this Court. And, second, I have no doubt whatsoever that the people in South Carolina and North Carolina, once the law is made clear, will comply with whatever that court does.

JUSTICE REED: Mr. Marshall, your comments about the District of Columbia—

MR. MARSHALL: Yes, sir.

JUSTICE REED: In the District of Columbia, as I understand it, there is one board that has authority over the District of Columbia schools?

MR. MARSHALL: That is my understanding.

JUSTICE REED: Now do you know whether or not that is true in any of the other states?

MR. MARSHALL: I do not. It varies, Mr. Justice Reed, and they have been changing. But I can positively say this: I know of no state where the state board has complete control. As a matter of fact, every system that I know of, varies only from complete autonomy of the local board, to the state board having supervisory authority as to policy, which, incidentally, Mr. Justice Reed, they cannot enforce.

JUSTICE REED: Yes. That has given me concern. One can see the advantage that the District of Columbia has. It is part of what you are saying in regard to a strong hand of the Judiciary, because obviously, the Judiciary has no hand until other cases have been brought before it.

While, if the policies of the state are in the hands of the state authorities, the power to enforce by direction of the state would result in a situation as they had in New Jersey. As I understand it, they did desegregate there.

MR. MARSHALL: Yes, sir, they did.

JUSTICE REED: The policies of the central power.

MR. MARSHALL: Plus a commission that worked.

JUSTICE REED: Which had power.

[5]Lonesome v. Maxwell, 220 F. 2d 386 (4th Cir. 1955).

MR. MARSHALL: Which had power. I might say, Mr. Justice Reed, I think I would feel they would have to do two things. They both can be done by the court. In the first case, to equalize teachers' salaries in Maryland, an effort was made to bring in the state board and, frankly, the purpose was to get one suit instead of twenty-three or twenty-four. Judge Chestnut of the district court, said the evil would be, if there be an evil, it would be of the one who was actually administering the school system, paying out the money that it was complained was paid out unequally.

Then the case was filed against the county and the district court ruled they could not pay Negroes less salaries than they paid others.[6]

Two other cases were filed in the state court on the same basis whereupon the state legislature passed the necessary legislation to compel the equalization.

JUSTICE REED: If there was more time than between now and the first of September, 1955, say the first of September, 1956, the first of September, 1957, there would be opportunity for the enactment of state law that would put into a central body authority to carry forward desegregation.

MR. MARSHALL: On the contrary, Mr. Justice Reed, at least one state—I think it is North Carolina—but at least one state has further decentralized for the express purpose of requiring anybody that wants to enforce this decree, whatever it might be from this Court, to go from district to district.

So, I do not know whether that would help or not. And I might say, in addition to the Maryland situation about teachers, and we may say Maryland is at least a border state, but Louisiana did the exact same thing. The area is unimportant.

The question was asked yesterday—at least we have been unable to find a lawyer-like argument to support a case that would cover any of the states involved, the whole state. It might be some day somebody might think of one. So we now are on the assumption that we are required, if necessary, we would be required to litigate. But I just do not believe that people, even assuming that they are in this frame of mind, would necessarily continue—I do not believe these school boards, many of them I know are the finest people in the community and there is nobody more law-abiding, and once the law is made clear, I do not believe—the primary case,[7] Mr. Justice Reed, you wrote the opinion—it only involved one little election precinct in Harris County, Texas, which is part of Houston, one precinct. And, as a result of the decision which actually only applied to the two men, the two registrars, the primaries were open to Negroes in every single southern state within a year or less, except one or two counties of Georgia. As a result, we had to file a case which the Court knows about, *Chapman* against *King,* and in South Carolina, where we had to eventually file two cases, the

----

[6]Mills v. Board of Education of Anne Arundel County, 30 F. Supp. 245 (D. Md. 1939). Thurgood Marshall argued the case for the Negro teachers. The earlier case referred to is Mills v. Lowndes, 26 F. Supp. 792 (D. Md. 1938).

[7]Smith v. Allwright, 321 U.S. 649 (1944). The exclusion of Negroes from voting in a Democratic party primary election was declared invalid.

Elmore case and the Baskins case.[8] So the precedent established by this Court—and that would be the primary issue as to whether Negroes could vote in the Deep South—was, at the worse, one that raised terrific racial feeling and it worked out. In the Sweatt and McLaurin cases, involving the Law School of Texas, the Graduate School of Oklahoma, University of Oklahoma, as a result of this Court's decision, the universities, the graduate and professional schools, were open in twelve southern states, and the reports show, as a matter of fact, Professor Guy Johnson, we cite in our brief, made a study and the important thing is that there was only one untoward incident in the whole twelve states of integrating into professional schools. And I also would like to remind the Court that you will remember at that time the Attorneys General of the southern states, with the exception of Alabama, filed a brief amicus in this case in which they said everything that they are saying in this brief and despite all of their predictions, not a single prediction came true except that Mississippi, Georgia, South Carolina, Florida and Alabama have not admitted them yet, and we are convinced that within the next six months, for reasons that are not important to this Court, that Alabama will be open. So it will leave only four.

Finally, in the Henderson case, where not only the other side made all of these dire predictions of what would happen in these areas if Negroes rode with white people on the trains, and I remember only too well the brief filed by Congressman Hobbs and his argument to this Court.[9] There is no argument that can be made that was stronger and with more dire predictions, and we have had less trouble than we had before. So, it seems to me that in considering this, I, for one, and the lawyers representing the appellants in these cases, and the people they represent, there is nobody more conscious that this is a real difficult problem. We recognize it as such. But we believe that in considering the difficulty of the problem, you have to take, not only the fact that some Attorney General would be unhappy about supporting the decision in this case or that he would have problems.

I say, in all deference to the Attorneys General, they get paid for the handling of problems. It is not just the consideration of one side of this, but the large number of Negroes in the South who have, for years—since 1870—been suffering the denial of rights which this Court said on May 17, that they have been injured in a way that there is only one way to correct. And I think that it is our job to constantly urge to this Court that in taking all of this into consideration, it take that,

[8]Chapman v. King, 154 F. 2d 460 (5th Cir. 1946); an action against Georgia officials who refused to let a Negro citizen vote in a Democratic primary was upheld. Rice v. Elmore, 165 F. 2d 387 (4th Cir. 1947; the South Carolina democratic primary was ordered open to Negro citizens in an opinion by Judge J. Waties Waring (see n. 1, p. 180, *supra*). The decision was upheld on appeal. When South Carolina tried to convert the Democratic primary system into private clubs, Negro citizens successfully attacked the new procedures in Baskins v. Brown, 174 F. 2d 391 (4th Cir. 1949).

[9]Henderson v. United States, 339 U.S. 816 (1950). See n. 35, p. 66, *supra*. Congressman Sam Hobbs (1887–     ) of Alabama, a member of the House Judiciary Committee submitted an individual brief supporting the Southern Railway Company's segregation policy in its dining cars. He said that to desegregate the dining cars "would be the kiss of death and render operation of the railway impossible."

too, into consideration. And on these difficult problems, whenever our Government faces them, the history of our Government shows that it is the inherent faith in our democratic process that gets us through, the faith that the people in the South are no different from anybody else as to being law-abiding. And in that connection, you will find that in our brief, we set out in a footnote the several studies that have shown by people who take polls, not the takers, but the brains behind the taking—that it is almost impossible to predict from, one person's opinion, what he will actually do. You just cannot do that. You get his opinion. He would not like to go to school with the Negro, he would not like to have his children to go to school with the Negro, but that is not saying he won't, and that is not saying that he would prefer for his child to grow up and be an imbecile as to going with the Negroes. It does not say that. It says that in the context of an area where segregation has not only been considered lawful but it has been considered on a very high level, to ask somebody as to whether or not you want to destroy my present system, his answer would be no.

Automatically people do that. And I cannot see the basis for any statement that gradual, indeterminate delay of relief in this case will do anything. It is significant. I think it would be a better position if somebody came before this Court from Carolina and Virginia and said, if you give us five years or four years, we can work it out. They don't say that. And they are taking no step to say it. As a matter of fact, in the brief filed by the State of Virginia, their reply brief, the whole brief relies upon the initial statement that it is this commission that has been appointed, that is working on the May 17 decision. And it is very interesting what they are working on, which appears at page 3 of the appendix, the final paragraph of this official State Commission:

> That in view of the foregoing, I have been directed to report that the Commission, working with its counsel, will explore avenues towards formulation of a program within the framework of law designed to prevent enforced integration of the races in the public schools of Virginia.

That is what they are working on. And they are coming to this Court, asking to be given time to work on that, and I submit that when you consider the decision of May 17 and questions 4 and 5, it was obvious that the average state official involved would be obliged to first make it clear to the general public in his state that the state segregation statutes requiring segregation in public education by order of this Court, is unconstitutional. Kansas did that almost immediately. Delaware, at least did it before, as a matter of fact, before the decision in the case, I mean, the decision in the Steiner case.

The District of Columbia, Mr. Korman, the responsible officials said it right off. Neither of these states has made any statement that their laws on segregation are unconstitutional. To the contrary, they take the position that, despite this decision, they are still constitutional, and all they are asking for is one of two things. It is either a moratorium on the enforcement of the Fourteenth Amendment, or local option. And in this case, throughout the briefs of both sides, throughout the arguments on yesterday and possibly throughout the arguments today, will be the effect of these decrees not only in the individual areas involved, but for other areas. And, whereas, this Court has said—I would say as far back as at least the Gaines case, and I think farther back—that there is no local option on the Fourteenth Amendment in the question of rights, that just because there is a southern area involved or border area involved, that is no reason to delay it.

And now, once having done that, I find it very difficult to draw an exception as to enforcement so that—if this is referred to the district courts and I use that advisedly, I mean I know technically, but the effect would be to say to all the district courts of the states, the several states could decide in their own minds as to how much time was necessary—then the Negro in this country would be in a horrible shape. He, as a matter of fact, would be as bad, if not worse off than under the "separate but equal" doctrine for this reason. When they produce reasons for delay, they are up in the air, they are pretty hard to pin down.

And, as a lawyer, it is difficult to meet that type of presentation. In separate but equal, we could count the number of books, the number of bricks, the number of teachers and find out whether the school was physically equal or not. But now, enforcement of this will be left to the judgment of the district court with practically no safeguards, and that, most certainly, we submit, would not be in keeping with the principle of our Constitution at first, and as it is today. It is a national Constitution. There is no place for local option in our Constitution. And we would have, as far north as southern Illinois—whereas of today there are some segregated schools—that in Illinois, the district judge there, if he wanted to, could say, because unlimited time was given by the Supreme Court in South Carolina, and Virginia, "I can give undetermined time in Illinois."

And it would apply all over the country.

JUSTICE REED: You certainly would not say, I am sure you would not, that the problems of Delaware and Kansas are the same as they are in South Carolina, would you?

MR. MARSHALL: I would say—

JUSTICE REED: I grant you that they might be the same.

MR. MARSHALL: Yes, sir, they are different but it can be argued both ways.

Kansas is north of Missouri. The Attorney General of Kansas yesterday, on two occasions in commenting on—I have forgotten the name of the cities—excused them on the ground they were down near the Missouri line, a southern state. But the record will show that Missouri is further advanced on desegregation than any of the other states. So here we have Kansas saying they cannot do it, and Missouri saying, let us do it faster. So, it will not be a geographical difference there. And in Kansas, it has always been non-understandable to me that the state could have been running so long on the theory that you have integrated high schools but segregated elementary schools.

I mean, the fact that the mixed high schools have been existing all these years without trouble, that they could do the same in the elementary schools without any trouble. Take Delaware, Delaware is no better off than Maryland, and Baltimore desegregated. The rest of the state has not. The rest of the state has taken a "wait-and-see" attitude to see what this Court does. But Baltimore is south of Delaware. And so I say that in this it is, of course—I recognize that there are difficult situations, and even as they mention in the briefs for the states, they vary within a state. But area alone could not be important because, in two counties in Arkansas, Charleston and Fayetteville, Arkansas, there were a very small number of Negroes involved, something like ten or eleven in these places but they integrated in September without any problem. But the number point could not be significant because of the numbers that were integrated here. So I think that all of these arguments, when you add them up, they all end with this: that there has to be in this type of presentation to this Court, there has to be, it seems to me, something that will help. We have taken in our brief, and I think we have taken in argument, the position that we say that there is no question but that we are entitled to relief under 4(a). However, in good faith, we are going to assume that we are not entitled to it as the question is asked in 5, at which stage we go out and get all of the available scientific materials that we think will help the Court. We take the different plans that have been put into segregation for that and we, in good faith, answer the question because it is considered by this Court to be material and once it is considered by this Court, to be material, it is material to us.

On the other hand, Virginia and South Carolina are rearguing Question 3, which was decided on May 17. It is the exact same argument.

JUSTICE FRANKFURTER: Mr. Marshall, you referred to Arkansas a little bit ago.

MR. MARSHALL: Yes, sir.

JUSTICE FRANKFURTER: And earlier, you said something about which I have deep sympathy, that on the whole, people are the same, there are no great biological differences between white people in South Carolina and white folk in Arkansas.

MR. MARSHALL: Yes, sir.

JUSTICE FRANKFURTER: That is your position?

MR. MARSHALL: Yes.

JUSTICE FRANKFURTER: Why is it that Fayetteville desegregated and other parts of the State of Arkansas did not; because there is some individual reason?

MR. MARSHALL: The best I can get from reading the writeup of it, which is in the *Southern School News,* is the statement from the superintendent who emphasized the fact they made no preparation about it, they just put them in there, but then he said that the smallness of number was what encouraged them to do it.

JUSTICE FRANKFURTER: Well, isn't that very important, and is it not something—is it not the same thing that is involved in carrying them by bus?

MR. MARSHALL: Yes.

JUSTICE FRANKFURTER: That is a direct statement, is it not?

MR. MARSHALL: Yes.

JUSTICE FRANKFURTER: That is a great saving?

MR. MARSHALL: It is also a great saving—there would be a saving because to equalize the facilities in the southern states would take around four and a half billion dollars.

That would save money all over the South for them if they did that.

JUSTICE FRANKFURTER: Maybe they couldn't. If I am to take any stock in what the Chief Justice of Delaware said, he pointed out the complexities of the various school districts in that state.

MR. MARSHALL: Yes.

JUSTICE FRANKFURTER: I do not know whether it is so or not but I assume it would be so, if he said so.

MR. MARSHALL: But Mr. Justice Frankfurter, granting the complexity and assuming throughout each of these states there are terrific complexities, the only thing that this Court is dealing with, this Court is not dealing with the complexities, this Court is dealing with whether or not race can be used. That is the only thing that is before this Court.

JUSTICE FRANKFURTER: But the physical situation in the different districts may make the result not because of race, but because of those physical differences.

MR. MARSHALL: No, sir, physically, Mr. Justice Frankfurter, I submit it will have to be further attended to by the people who are working on it.

JUSTICE FRANKFURTER: Yes, sir.

MR. MARSHALL: But this Court cannot do it.

JUSTICE FRANKFURTER: I do not imagine this Court is going to work out the details of all the states of the Union.

MR. MARSHALL: I certainly would not want to be a party to thinking about it. But that is why, it seems to me, that the real basic issue as I said in the beginning, is that what we want from this Court is the striking down of race.

Now, whatever other plan they want to work out, the question is made about the educational level of children. That has been an administrative detail since we have had public schools.

They give tests to grade children so what do we think is the solution? Simple. Put the dumb colored children in with the dumb white children, and put the smart colored children with the smart white children—that is no problem.

JUSTICE FRANKFURTER: I hope you will not swallow whole that science can tell us that that is a great certainty any more than the polls can tell us these things.

MR. MARSHALL: The proof is that in my own profession some of the greatest lawyers—they had difficulty in getting out of law school—but they turned out to be the greatest lawyers in the country, I think there is no question about it. But the point is that all of these problems that they urge are problems which are peculiar in administrative detail and have no merit in either the constitutional issue involved, or the question of decree in this case, if for no other reason than you cannot sell it.

JUSTICE FRANKFURTER: In the northern states where there is not a problem of race at all, at least in some of them, there are problems of districting schools which are of the same nature as those that involve southern states, is that right?

MR. MARSHALL: Yes, sir.

JUSTICE FRANKFURTER: Not because of race, but because of the inherent problems.

MR. MARSHALL: And they should be solved in the north, without regard to race.

JUSTICE FRANKFURTER: But that may take an amount of time that is not definitively determined by the authority of this Court.

MR. MARSHALL: Then we get to our suggestion of the September of 1956 point. We say that we believe that, if we do not get immediate relief, then the least—

JUSTICE FRANKFURTER: Well, we should not use "immediately enforce." I thought that we agreed that we would not use words like "immediately" or "forthwith" except the declaration that this Court has made on May 17, 1954, that you cannot make distinction because of race.

MR. MARSHALL: Yes, sir. If we cannot get that, then we say that the least that would do us any good at all would be a decree which included four items: (1) That this Court make the clearest declaration that not only those statutes but others are in violation of the Fourteenth Amendment. We think it is necessary for that to be put in the decree. (2) That they start immediately to desegregate. (3) File reports; (4) That it must end at a day certain, and that, we take the position, is the minimum that we should expect if we cannot get the decree which will say that as of the next school term—

JUSTICE FRANKFURTER: What you are saying is that the decision of this Court on May 17, 1954, was not empty words, that was a declaration of unconstitutionality of everything that made a differential on the ground of race.
    What you want is a manifestation clear and unequivocal on that, that states, the counties, the cities and the schools, all are affected because we have specific cases and not the world at large?

MR. MARSHALL: Yes, sir.

JUSTICE FRANKFURTER: That, in good faith, this declaration should be carried into action?

MR. MARSHALL: That is what we would like to have, because we take the position that this Court could have ordered this done immediately after the May 17 decision, could it not?

JUSTICE FRANKFURTER: It could have. It might as well say some physical thing that can be done should be done in the next five minutes.

MR. MARSHALL: No, sir.

JUSTICE FRANKFURTER: There are certain unalterable facts of life that can not be changed even by this Court. I am not talking about the feelings of people, I am talking about districting the accommodations, the arrangement of personnel, and all the complexities that go with the administering of schools.

MR. MARSHALL: What I would say, Mr. Justice Frankfurter, is that it should be done as of the school term which is September, 1955. I am getting to using words again.

And now we take the position that the Court should do it. That is the fundamental place we are now. It is whether or not the Court should do it. And we take the position that having done this, having gone into answering the broad equity powers, there is no question about the gradual and effective—we say it can never be effective and that having answered those, we then say that we come back to the point that this Court at this time should enter that type of decree, that is the substance of our position.

JUSTICE HARLAN: I want to ask you this question: It may appear to be a little on the technical side, but I think it is bound up with the basic problem. Do you consider that the decree, whether it is entered by the district court or this Court, do you consider that its enforcement provisions can run in favor of any other than those who are named as plaintiffs in these particular suits?

MR. MARSHALL: It is my understanding, Mr. Justice Harlan, that in the federal class suit, that if the entire class is not actually receiving relief, the only way other members of the class can enforce it is to intervene.

JUSTICE FRANKFURTER: In other words, you recognize these so-called class suits as pure experience class suits and only those who become parties prior to the decree can actually take advantage of the enforcement provisions?

MR. MARSHALL: We had a situation like that in one of our teacher salary cases and rather than to try to do anything more, we merely had them file a regular intervention that was after judgment and appeal and it was back in the district court and it was granted and once the intervention was granted, the relief was extended to the whole class. But I would assume, sir, that any school board, including the two school boards before this Court, would grant relief to the local class. There is one case— the *Williams* v. *the Kansas City Park Commission*.[10] It

[10]205 F. 2d 47 (8th Cir. 1953). The Court of Appeals held that the city must allow Negroes to use all recreational facilities in the city parks.

is a court of appeals case. The district court said that declared suit was no class suit, that it was no good in regard to these personal rights but the court of appeals said that we overrule the decision, but we do not have to pass on the class action because we are sure the district court will protect the class. I say I am sure whatever decree is entered in this case, I have every faith that the local school board would give it to the whole class. I do not think they will restrict it to the individuals.

JUSTICE FRANKFURTER: We have to define the class. I understood your associate, Mr. Robinson, to say in the Virginia case we have before us, Prince Edward County and that is the only county.

MR. MARSHALL: Yes, sir, and only the high school students.

JUSTICE FRANKFURTER: So that is the only class before us?

MR. MARSHALL: Yes.

JUSTICE FRANKFURTER: In Delaware it was indicated that the class is the pupils seeking admittance to two named schools.
The word "class" cannot be used to cover a state or the nation?

MR. MARSHALL: I do not see how it can.

JUSTICE BLACK: May I ask you this about the South Carolina case. That is a school district. How many are involved or will be involved in that? How many schools.?

MR. MARSHALL: The number of students—I got through Mr. McC.Figg, the lawyer on the other side. The total number is 2,858. That is in School District 1.

JUSTICE BLACK: That is the only school, that is the only district involved?

MR. MARSHALL: That is the only district involved.

JUSTICE BLACK: How many schools?

MR. MARSHALL: Four schools, one combination on the same grounds of an elementary and high school for white students and three schools for Negroes.

JUSTICE BLACK: As I understand it, as far as South Carolina is concerned, this order would affect the pupils in that district and no others?

MR. MARSHALL: Absolutely. I do not see how the decree could—

JUSTICE BLACK: It would require new litigation to affect other students in South Carolina.

MR. MARSHALL: Unless in the two cases I mention in Maryland and Louisiana, there could be a possibility that the others would agree. For example, getting back to our university and graduate schools, Arkansas operated its graduate school while the Sipuel case was in this court before it was decided and there was a willingness to go along.

JUSTICE BLACK: They might do it voluntarily.

JUSTICE FRANKFURTER: As far as the court order was concerned, it would have to be as definite and specific as the statute on which a charge was being made against a person for an offense?

MR. MARSHALL: I think so. In addition to that, Mr. Justice Black, as I said before, maybe I could say it but I do not believe that anybody under the jurisdiction of the Fourth Circuit would disobey a judgment issued by that Court of Appeals and I think there would be considerable compliance. Maybe some would argue it back to the point where well, if you do not, we will sue. But we would have *stare decisis* in a circuit where *stare decisis* is quite important.

JUSTICE BLACK: But the courts would be left with an order which involves only 2,000 pupils, as to the enforcement, rather than one which would involve all the pupils in the state.

MR. MARSHALL: I would say that—Mr. Justice Black, I just do not believe it is that important. I think that the whole state is involved, for example, in Virginia, according to the Attorney General—it is practically unanimous about that.

JUSTICE BLACK: Do I understand that it is your position that we must consider this order with reference to South Carolina involving one district as though it affects the whole state?

MR. MARSHALL: No. I say that I gathered, maybe mistakenly, from the preliminary sentence at the end of the May 17 decision where the statement was made this was going to be set for further reargument that because these are class actions and the wide applicability—and I for one, and others, construed that, that although nobody but these two counties were involved, that consideration would be given our ideas as to the rest of it with the understanding that it did not apply. That is the only reason I bring this in. I would be perfectly willing. I do not think there is anything in my argument except the first part about how this would affect Topeka, Kansas as that would be changed either way.

JUSTICE FRANKFURTER: May I say this apropos of your last statement. Of course you could not have local operation with reference to the applicability of the Fourteenth Amendment.

MR. MARSHALL: Yes, sir.

JUSTICE FRANKFURTER: And say that race is not allowed to be, is an inadmissible differential as to Clarendon County, South Carolina, but admissible in some other county. Therefore, any general language in the opinion dealing with the substantive constitutional question is one thing.

MR. MARSHALL: I think so. I think there is no question about that. But I think we ought to also make it clear while we are talking about the effect of this decree or rather, this takes in the judgment of this Court, that we point out at the end of our reply brief a point that we have not wanted to point out but we felt obliged to, is that a decree in this case, a judgment in this case, which says that the enforcement of the Fourteenth Amendment as it applies to Negroes can be postponed at the judgment of any district court, in my mind presents a very difficult prospect for postponement of enforcement of other provisions of the Constitution that this Court has never even thought about. And I would assure [you] that I am convinced this Court would not do it, but I am most sure that they will be urged over and over again on the basis of the Briggs case that this newspaper, which the local state judge did not like, and said go out of business—that because of their terrific love for the judge and hatred for the newspaper, we had better let you stay out of business for six months.

To my mind that is just horrible to think of.

JUSTICE FRANKFURTER: I am going to suggest, Mr. Marshall, speaking for myself, the question is not what we should not like in a decree but what we should like.

MR. MARSHALL: That is the very question we have here and which the Court has copies of. These are two decrees. The first one is the decree that we think we are entitled to which would require admission by September of 1955 and the other is the alternative decree, assume that the Court would not enter that, requiring admission as of September of 1956.

On those decrees, I would like also to say to Chief Justice Warren and the Court, that with your permission—this is the joint suggestion of the lawyers in Topeka, Delaware, Virginia, and South Carolina and we could have made different ones for each one with the state and the defendants, but we would like, if the Court would indulge us, to leave this one because it is the joint agreement of all of the lawyers that this is the type we would recommend to the Court. We had it drafted before the argument and we expected to ask permission to submit it after argument because we were not too sure, so as of last night we—is it all right—we agreed, is it all right for that to apply to Topeka?

THE CHIEF JUSTICE: It is all right.

JUSTICE REED: Do these decrees take into consideration the making of the school districts?

MR. MARSHALL: Yes, sir. I might get to that. We take the position that—you will notice here that it says—the one that gives the time.

JUSTICE REED: Three.

MR. MARSHALL: Yes, sir.

3(a), the third page shows the district court—"that the transition to a school system not based on race and color distinctions involve such administrative factors,"—and we used that because the districting, the assigning of pupils, the assignment of buildings, the assigning of teachers, are all administrative details.

At least we think they are administrative details. Once that is shown to the district court satisfactorily, the district court would give them another year.

JUSTICE CLARK: How much time did the Fourth Circuit of South Carolina have when they were thinking of separate but equal?[11]

MR. MARSHALL: Six months.

JUSTICE CLARK: That was to build facilities, or what was the purpose of that?

MR. MARSHALL: The purpose was to provide for facilities and if I remember correctly, when they appeared in the court, they had made all of the preparations including the fact that they had let, not only appropriated the money, and so forth, they let the contract to build the new Negro schools and we took the position that merely for the purpose of the separate and equal point which we were willing to, for all intents and purposes—that would be all of that.

JUSTICE CLARK: Was there any question of facilities in this particular district?

MR. MARSHALL: There is no question about the facilities in Prince Edward. We agreed as of the first argument in this case, there was no question in Clarendon County and there is no question in Prince Edward County. So, the physical facilities are entirely out of the case so far as we can see.

JUSTICE FRANKFURTER: Mr. Marshall, in all the prior cases, the Gaines cases, and Sweatt cases, and all that class of cases—

MR. MARSHALL: Yes, sir.

JUSTICE FRANKFURTER: —in any of them was there any requirement of reorganization of the school system other than the mere admission of a few colored students?

MR. MARSHALL: It was nothing but the registration detail, they had nothing to do otherwise.

JUSTICE FRANKFURTER: There was no problem of what you call administration?

MR. MARSHALL: None that I conceive of. There would have been problems if they wanted to assign them to a different place, but they did not do it.

JUSTICE FRANKFURTER: It was only the question of admitting them?

MR. MARSHALL: The question of admitting them. We think in our brief, we have recognized this in these cases, that there will be problems, but we take the position that, if they can work out the details in the District of Columbia, in that highly involved system, they can work them out in Clarendon County with 2,800 children.

In conclusion, in so far as this particular, as our side is concerned, I am trying to leave some time for rebuttal—in summing up, while we still believe that

---

[11] See p. 545, *infra*, for lower court decision in Briggs v. Elliott.

we are entitled to this type of decree that would come under the answer to 4(a), and we are convinced that any other form of gradual adjustment would not meet the words of the question of this Court which is effective gradual adjustment. We say only at that stage that assuming that that is done, then we believe that the least we should expect is that protection be given to these cases. For example, the children in these cases and the class that they represent.

They are graduating every day. That is the one narrow issue involved in this case. When we go from the narrow issue of the individual named plaintiffs involved and get to the class, the class is limited to children of school age. Your school age is something you cannot control and any delay in that is costly. The Court has said that the segregation system could very well be harming these children personally. On the other hand, we have this effort to—these plans to protect people's rights against these theories, these predictions of what cannot be done. And even if this Court should take that position, we believe that a deadline date is the only thing that will prevent our arriving at the position in the Attorney General of Virginia's reply brief where on the last page he says the only thing that would do him any good is an interminable period of desegregation, and, as between that and what we think we are clearly entitled to, we say that the only thing that will protect us is a deadline because we hope that the Court will recognize that there is practically no way under the sun that a lawyer seeking relief under any other decree, could show that the delay was not one way or the other, and that in this effort to solve this very difficult problem, it seems to us that the answer should be that this is not a matter for local option. This is not a matter that shall be geared down to the local mores and customs of each community in the country, to the extent that, not the Constitution, but the mores and customs of some people in some community will determine what are and how they shall be enforced in so far as constitutional rights are concerned.

JUSTICE REED: Mr. Marshall, I gather from your argument that "gradual" has no place in your thinking as far as the decree is concerned?

MR. MARSHALL: I would say pretty well, yes. I would say gradual is involved in this case as of now because Virginia and South Carolina and the other states have had from May 17 until now, which is almost a year.

JUSTICE REED: I was thinking of a decree which would say that segregation, or desegregation would start through the first grade and run through the years.

MR. MARSHALL: Yes, the twelve years.

JUSTICE REED: Two grades at a time or whatever it might be that in places like South Carolina where I understand the percentage of the races is quite disproportionate—90 per cent Negroes against white?

MR. MARSHALL: Yes, the twelve years.

JUSTICE REED: There have been suggestions made—perhaps it was used, I think in New York.

MR. MARSHALL: It was Indiana that had a five-year plan. I forget how it was broken down. The interesting thing there is that most of them cleaned up right quick and some of them waited until the five years—the last day. You had that variation within the state. But I would say, sir, that on this—if I may extend your plan of two years or a year, the studies that I have had on it show that the original was a twelve-year plan, the first year coming in, next year and going up that way. It is our idea—

JUSTICE REED: I think that has been used in some of the schools here in the District?

MR. MARSHALL: Not that I know of.

JUSTICE REED: In the public schools?

MR. MARSHALL: Not that I know of.

But my answer to that is that there you not only destroy completely the rights of the individual pupils, you destroy the rights of the whole class.

Nobody in that class will ever get mixed education. That is our answer to that.

THE CHIEF JUSTICE: Mr. Rogers?

### ARGUMENT OF MR. R. W. ELLIOTT ET AL

#### by MR. S. E. ROGERS

MR. ROGERS: Mr. McC.Figg will make the principal argument, Mr. Chief Justice.

I would like to just have the indulgence of the Court for about five or ten minutes, since I come from the district involved.

I live in the district involved. I am associated daily with the problems that we have. I would like to have just an opportunity to point to some of those problems.

It seems to be recognized by our opponents that these are terrific problems. They are the greatest problems that have been presented to our people in this district, probably this century.

We are not in the position of Kansas where we have only a few Negroes who would be involved in the integration or the desegregation. We are not in the position of the District of Columbia, where our school authorities are not responsible to the people in the District. We are not in the position of the District where our school funds come from others than the people in the District. We are an agricultural community. We have no industries as you will note from the record. As our children are educated from generation to generation, some remain at home to farm and supervise the farming, some to work and labor on the farms, but most of them have to leave the district and find employment elsewhere. We are tied to the land. Therefore, we are not in the position as I noticed here in Washington yesterday, Mr. Korman stated that some of the districts where there was a complaint that there were no white children sent to this particular Negro school, that the problem could not be solved by just moving away from the district, because we can not—we are tied to the land and we cannot take the land with us.

So our school district, being an agricultural district, and being tied as we are to the land, we have to face our problems there, without moving away.

JUSTICE REED: What is your district, is it a county district?

MR. ROGERS: No, sir, it is only one-third. Our district is composed of the old plantation section of the country, fronting along a deep curve in the Santos River. It is for that reason that our Negro population is so large in that district and our white population so small. There has not been very much change in the texture of the population over the years. We differ from the school district adjoining us, another school district in the county. Yet, if you go to the next school district, No. 3, we start as 1, 2, 3, in No. 3 there probably you will find their problem is not as bad as ours. We do not have the concentration of population.

So, if we did—if this Court should order the immediate desegregation, the immediate integration of the schools of this district, we would be—it would not produce an integration that most people have in their minds of mixing the white and the colored in school. It would actually be the sending of the few white children that we have there to the Negro schools, because our ratio of population is approximately nine to one in students in the school population.

JUSTICE FRANKFURTER: Could I trouble you to state the schools that are involved in your district and the population of those schools, both in numbers and in division between white and Negroes? And, also the distances that they are apart.

MR. ROGERS: I think I can give you those, sir. The total enrollment in the district is 2,858 down about 200 students by the way, from the time of the commencement of this case. Of that, colored students are 2,559. The white students are 299. That drop has been entirely in the colored children.

The first school is the Somerton High and Elementary School which occupies one lot and two adjoining buildings. The elementary school has a total of 176 students, this is the white school. The high school has 123. The Scotch Branch School, which is in the town of Somerton, approximately a quarter of a mile away, has 700—that is the colored school has 738 in the elementary school and 408 in the Springhill—which is located about four miles to the south of the Somerton school—southeast—it is an elementary school, and has 650 Negroes, that is the Negro school. The St. Paul school, which is located about 4 miles to the south of the Somerton School, has 763 Negroes.

They are all Negro students. The Negro high school is run on the basis of four years, the nine-four plan, nine years in the elementary and four years in high school. The white school is run on the basis of six years in the elementary and six years in the high school.

Having that population to deal with, we, of course, have the administrative functions that our opponents have referred to.

JUSTICE FRANKFURTER: I take it that the colored schools would be taught by all colored teachers, and the white schools—

MR. ROGERS: They are now.

JUSTICE FRANKFURTER: That kind of condition?

MR. ROGERS: Yes, sir, there is no integration of the teaching.

JUSTICE FRANKFURTER: The size of the classes, are they the same in the respective schools?

MR. ROGERS: Generally they are, sir. You have—you get that largely from your classrooms. In the districts there are fifty-four colored classrooms and thirteen white classrooms.

They are divided out among the various schools, I can give you those proportions, if you want them.

JUSTICE FRANKFURTER: The proportions are a little bit in favor of the white classes?

MR. ROGERS: Yes. It is like the overhead of a business, you have a minimum to run a school that you have to have.

But in addition to those things we must remember that in the very statement that was filed by the appellants, called a social science statement in the original causes, attention was called to the fact that the question of desegregation involved problems that were as they [saw] them, in the frontiers of scientific knowledge. We realize that very much in this district because we have had a biracial society for more than two centuries. As this Court called attention to the fact that we could not turn the clock of progress back to 1895 or even 1868, using the basis that we are now doing—[we] are now exploring the frontiers of scientific knowledge—I do not believe that in a biracial society, that we can push the clock forward abruptly to 2015 or 2045. We can help.

Great progress has been made. We have equalized in this district. We have spent a great deal of money in that equalization. We are doing good work. The Negroes from that district are going out as lawyers, doctors, and teachers. The white children are doing the same. Whether we like it or not, there is a feeling in the district that the desegregation of the elementary and the high school does affect the social life of the community, and for that reason, we have to remark that to say that the decision is [un]popular in the area is the understatement of the year, but we would wish to work within the framework of the decision. But we do know that we are faced with problems that cannot be solved except with a change of attitude and those attitudes will have to be changed slowly, not quickly.

As a result, we are asking that the cases be sent back without instructions, but to be sent back to the lower court for action in conformity with the provisions of the decision.

JUSTICE FRANKFURTER: Would it not be fair to say that attitudes in this world are not changed abstractly, as it were, by reading something, that attitudes are partly the result of working, attitudes are partly the result of action?

MR. ROGERS: I think so.

JUSTICE FRANKFURTER: Would that be a fair statement?

MR. ROGERS: Yes, sir. I think so. Our sociologists have had a very difficult time in saying what attitude comes from or how it can be changed. But it does have to be in the society as it works.

JUSTICE FRANKFURTER: But you do not fold your hands and wait for an attitude to change by itself?

MR. ROGERS: No, sir. You cannot. That has not been done here. That is not being done in this district. We have made progress and greater progress will still be made. I am sure. But to simply say you have to change your attitude is not going to change it.

JUSTICE HARLAN: Mr. Rogers, what is the total adult population in the district between the races—whites and Negroes?

MR. ROGERS: I do not have the division of the adults. I can tell you it is about eight to one. It is not quite as much as in the school age. Our colored population is about eight to one. It is not quite the same.

THE CHIEF JUSTICE: Is your request for an open decree predicated upon the assumption that your school district will immediately undertake to conform to the opinion of this Court of last year and to the decree, or is it on the basis—

MR. ROGERS: Mr. Chief Justice, to say we will conform depends on the decree handed down. I am frank to tell you, right now in our district I do not think that we will send—the white people of the district will send their children to the Negro schools. It would be unfair to tell the Court that we are going to do that. I do not think it is. But I do think that something can be worked out. We hope so.

THE CHIEF JUSTICE: It is not a question of attitude, it is a question of conforming to the decree. Is there any basis upon which we can assume that there will be an immediate attempt to comply with the decree of this Court, whatever it may be?

MR. ROGERS: Mr. Chief Justice, I would say that we would present our problem, as I understand it, if the decree is sent out, that we would present our problem to the district court and we are in the Fourth Circuit. Our opposition has just told this Court how the Fourth Circuit has been—he has no fear of the Fourth Circuit. I feel we can expect the courts in the Fourth Circuit and the people of the district to work out something in accordance with your decree.

THE CHIEF JUSTICE: Don't you believe that the question as to whether the district will attempt to comply should be considered in any such decree?

MR. ROGERS: Not necessarily, sir. I think that should be left to the lower court.

THE CHIEF JUSTICE: And why?

MR. ROGERS: Your Honors, we have laid down here in this Court the principle that segregation is unconstitutional. The lower court we feel is the place that the machinery should be set in motion to conform to that.

THE CHIEF JUSTICE: But you are not willing to say here that there would be an honest attempt to conform to this decree, if we did leave it to the district court?

MR. ROGERS: No, I am not. Let us get the word "honest" out of there.

THE CHIEF JUSTICE: No, leave it in.

MR. ROGERS: No, because I would have to tell you that right now we would not conform—we would not send our white children to the Negro schools.

THE CHIEF JUSTICE: Thank you.

JUSTICE BURTON: Mr. Rogers, that might not mean that you would violate the decree—

MR. ROGERS: No, sir.

JUSTICE BURTON: —it would mean that you would send your children to some other school, some other than public school?

MR. ROGERS: Yes. We do not want to say that we would violate it. We are trying to work within it. We hope the Court will give us a decree that we can work within.

JUSTICE FRANKFURTER: May I ask one more question? Am I right—I am not asking a leading question—in thinking that you have said or implied, are you asking this Court to reconsider the declaration of unconstitutionality of last May?

MR. ROGERS: No. We are asking the opportunity to work the matter out at the local level.

JUSTICE FRANKFURTER: You are not inferentially or remotely coming before this Court and saying that decision was a mistake and what went on before should be continued?

MR. ROGERS: I am certainly not saying that in my argument, no, sir.

JUSTICE FRANKFURTER: All right.

THE CHIEF JUSTICE; Mr. McC.Figg, you may proceed.

### ARGUMENT ON BEHALF OF R. W. ELLIOTT, ET AL

#### by MR. ROBERT McC.FIGG

MR. McC.FIGG: All right, sir.

JUSTICE FRANKFURTER: I take it you and your associate will address yourselves to our minds in your argument. We are dealing with the secret recesses of the mind.

MR. McC.FIGG: No, I do not believe we have any mental reservations in what we are trying to say. I think Mr. Rogers and I both understand that we were not invited up here to reconsider the decision of May 17, 1954.

It seems to me that that decision might be said to be the declaration of the rights of the parties that were asked for when this declaratory action was brought. In many cases of declaratory judgment, the courts go no further. The Court may, however, proceed to grant such orders as may be warranted by the showing made in actions involving declaratory judgments as I understand the procedure, and it would seem that maybe the question which we are discussing here, is how much further the Court should go than the declaration of the rights of the parties. We are here answering in particular two specific questions with subdivisions. The fourth question we answered in our original brief, that we did not think that a decree should necessarily follow, providing that Negro children should forthwith be admitted to schools of their own choice within the limit of normal geographical school districting.

We did say that we think that this Court in the exercise of its equity powers, does have the power to permit an effective gradual adjustment to be brought about from existing systems to a system not based on color distinctions. In the argument yesterday it seemed to me to be suggested that the characterization of the rights of the appellants as personal and present, cast some doubt in the minds of our adversaries as to whether these equity powers were as broad in this case as they are traditionally held to be in the equitable jurisdiction of the United States courts. In the briefs which have been filed by the Attorney General of the United States in this matter, all three of them, it has been emphasized that the power of the Court in their opinion is not limited by the characterization of the rights as personal and present.

And reference is made in one of those briefs to Chief Justice Marshall's statement in *Cohens* against *Virginia*.[12] that general expressions in every opinion are to be taken in connection with the case in which those expressions are used, and that if they go beyond the case, they may be respected, but ought not to control the judgment in a subsequent suit when the very point is presented for decision.

And Attorney General McGranery, and Attorney General Brownell[13] in both briefs which have been filed by them in this case, have urged the view that the Court does not have its full equitable discretion to deal with this litigation. They say that a court of equity is not bound to direct any particular form of relief, that it has full power to fashion a remedy which will best serve the ends of justice in the particular circumstances. They say that Congress expressly empowered the Court to enter such appropriate judgment, decree or order or require such further proceedings to be had as may be just under the circumstances. And that the needs of the public and the effect of proposed decrees on the general welfare are always a relevant if not paramount concern to a court of justice, and that where public

[12]Cohens v. Virginia, 6 Wheat. 264 (1821). In one of John Marshall's famed Constitutional opinions, he upheld the right of the Supreme Court to review final decisions of the state courts in cases arising under the federal Constitution and laws.

[13]James P. McGranery (1895–     ); United States Attorney General, 1952–1953; Democratic Representative from Pennsylvania, 1937–1943; Assistant Attorney General, 1943–1946; United States District Judge, Pennsylvania, 1946–1952. Herbert A. Brownell, United States Attorney General, 1953–1957.

interests are involved, equitable powers assume an even broader and more flexible character than when only a private controversy is at stake.

That is a quotation from the decision of this Court in *Porter* v. *Warner* in 327 U.S. [395].

We think that the suggestion in the argument yesterday that there may be some limitation on the equity power of this Court to consider the circumstances or to authorize the consideration fully of the circumstances involved in the particular cases by the District Court is not sustained by the decisions of this Court and that nowhere does the history of the phrase "present and personal" sustain the thought that its use by the Court in the case where it has been used was intended to limit the equity powers of this Court where those rights were involved in litigation instituted as this was by plaintiffs in the equity jurisdiction court.

Now then, we have been handed a copy of the forms of decree suggested by the appellants, the one which they say is the least that they should have, and the other, if the Court does not follow Question 4(a). And the difference seems to be that in the one they say that the officials of this school district should be ordered to carry out this decision beginning September 1, 1955. The other is apparently quite similar, but it says that if the district officials will come before the federal court and make a showing of administrative difficulty, that the district may go as far as September 1, 1956. That seems to be the difference between the two decrees. Now it is our view of the case that, as Mr. Rogers has told you, we conceive that this case should be remanded in the usual course for proceedings in conformity with the declaration which the Court made on May 17, 1954, and that the school authorities may then, or the appellants may then, present the circumstances facing the authorities of this district in trying to carry out the duty imposed upon them by the laws of the state and provide an efficient public system of education in this district. What we think is that, certainly if the September, 1955, limitation as an outside time limit is put upon this district, it would mean the end of the public school system in the district.

That would not be the voluntary action of the trustees and I do not think Mr. Rogers meant to show that. He was trying to tell the Court, I think, that there are forces at play in this situation over which the trustees have no control. There is the question of whether you are going to have funds to run a school, there is the question of whether you are going to have the legislation to run the schools.

The Attorney General's brief in this case points out that in South Carolina heretofore the state aid to the district, which is in the form of a guaranteed minimum teachers' salary, has been computed and is distributed by the state statute on the basis of white teachers and the Negro teachers in the school district, and that statute is one of the changes which the Attorney General suggested would have to be made by legislation in our state in order to expect trustees to be able to run the schools and pay the teachers.

JUSTICE FRANKFURTER: Is it the amount of the appropriation, or the allocation?

MR. McC.FIGG: That is all an allocation. The amount is a lump sum amount for the whole state which of course is arrived at by an overall budget, and then the allocation is on—there are school funds from the state allocated on average daily attendance, and enrollment. That is a factor in that. Now the figures that

Mr. Rogers gave you about the district I understood were enrollment figures, and it should be said in reference to the teacher load about which inquiry was made, that the schools are largely built, the classrooms provided and the teachers provided on average daily attendance. Our records will show you that the white attendance has always been almost 100 per cent and that the attendance of the Negro pupils has been down as low as 80 per cent and the planning has been for the experience in attendance and not on enrollment.

If they built classrooms for the enrollment, there would be vacant classrooms. They build them for the attendance and employ teachers to teach the pupils who come. An explanation of that very low attendance as I understand it—I do not live in the district and I am associated with Mr. Rogers in personally presenting the case of this litigation, but as I understand it, the Negro parents are, in great measure, tenant farmers and they want their children on the farms and there is a constant struggle with them, especially at planting and harvest time, to have school attendance rather than the children helping their parents plant the seeds and gather the crops.

JUSTICE CLARK: What is your compulsory age?

MR. McC.FIGG: The compulsory age was seven through sixteen. Of course, our compulsory education laws, we, at that time, were principally an agricultural state, so we did not have as many teeth in this as it may have in some more industrial states because wherever a parent certifies that he needs his child for any reason, the law does not require the attendance.

The first two months of school, the first two months of the school year, it was developed in the district court, that about 50 per cent attendance among the Negro pupils as against almost 90 per cent for the white students, so that what concerns us about this and why we would rather have an opportunity for the officials of this district to lay their problems before the lower court where it could be done in full and by concrete showing which we, as counsel in the case, are not able to make before this Court—our friends on the other side call it unsupported when we make statements and I think that they are largely predictions rather than—we have no instructions from the trustees to tell this Court that they will or will not be able to continue to operate the schools.

But one of the great reasons is that the state action that is necessary in our state has got to be taken before any trustee knows exactly how he is going to be able to operate schools in the future.

And then the attitude of the people in voting on tax levies or even in electing school board members. This district is to a considerable extent autonomous and represents local government and it is not like the District of Columbia where the school board is appointed by members of the judiciary and the voters do not have any ability other than persuasion or letters to the newspapers to influence in any effective manner the members of the school board.

But in District 1 of Clarendon County, the democratic process of the ballot box has a great effect on the taxation to run the schools, and as was suggested here, when it is said that white children will not enter the schools which can be realistically called Negro schools, if there were a forcible requirement of entrance, if they were made to enter, they will have other ways of educating their children.

The white people are in a vast minority but they do happen to pay most of the taxes, and they have a considerable influence in the affairs of the district as would be known and is natural.

The school trustees just cannot tell what is going to be the showdown when the time comes.

JUSTICE REED: Is the tax provided by the state or by the district?

MR. McC.FIGG: The trustees?

JUSTICE REED: No, the tax.

MR. McC.FIGG: There is a state contribution toward teachers' salaries. There has been a state loan for capital construction as a result of which the school program was carried to fruition, but a considerable percentage of the funds that run this district are district imposed, and that would be by the people in the district and by the trustees in the district. They are real estate taxes, the local taxes are all real estate.

The taxes in the state are direct taxes.

JUSTICE REED: Does the State Board of Education have any directional power over the local Board of Education?

MR. McC.FIGG: The County Board of Education has supervisory power from the local board of trustees and then the state board has appellate jurisdiction. That is not controlling. I think it would have to come up as the case does in court. There would have to be some direction by the State Board of Education.

JUSTICE REED: Do you think the State Board has the power to direct?

MR. McC.FIGG: Yes.

JUSTICE REED: And say that certain persons should not be employed?

MR. McC.FIGG: I think they could reverse the local action in proper cases. I think they would have to find their power to do—to segregate—in the state law. I do not think they have any power—I do not say they could not—I have definitely never considered the question from that angle but their powers are granted by state statute and their power is to enforce the state school law. I do not think they would find anything in our state school laws—

JUSTICE REED: Take a state school law, for instance, which said you should have not more than fifty pupils to a teacher in the elementary grades, would the State Board have the power to enforce that?

MR. McC.FIGG: On a complaint. The complaint normally would be made to the trustees and they would pass on it. Then a complaining party, an aggrieved party—I think the statute uses the word, aggrieved, may go to the county board and then go to the State Board.

JUSTICE REED: As an administrative matter, is that it?

MR. McC.FIGG: Yes. Of course, I do not think they would deal with fifty pupil enrollment question. It would be how many people use the room as a practical matter.

THE CHIEF JUSTICE: Mr. McC.Figg, you made the distinction between the District of Columbia and your school district. Is there any inherent distinction between your school district and, let us say, Baltimore or St. Louis?

MR. McC.FIGG: I am not familiar with those. I think that probably—

THE CHIEF JUSTICE: I mean so far as the board of education is dependent upon the community?

MR. McC.FIGG: Well, I would assume not. They probably are run somewhat the same, those particular cities I have never had any information about.

One thing that has been mentioned in the briefs, the Attorney General's brief was mentioned and others, has been the matter of disparity of numbers as bearing upon this problem. Another thing, and it seems to me a very important thing that has been mentioned as proper to be taken into account by the Court, is the matter of community acceptance of the very idea that it be, or can be carried out. It is easy enough to say that that is of no moment, of no relevance, but if the failure to achieve community acceptance in a short time results in the destruction of public support for the idea of public education, that is a very serious matter and it is serious to both classes of pupils. It is serious to the Negroes in this district, nine times as serious as it is to the white pupils and maybe more because they may not be as well able to take care of themselves if an impasse occurs in the public education affairs of the district, and the people of the district, after all, have lived there for at least ninety years in what my associate called a biracial society.

That has been a long time to develop habits and relationships toward each other, and there has to be some opportunity as we see it, for community acceptance of this idea. We think that that is an important consideration in the employment of the discretion of the court of equity which, after ninety years, has established the unconstitutionality of their school system. It seems that it would be reasonable not to try to establish a six-month time limit or a twelve-month time limit or an eighteen-month time limit but to rely on the district courts in the states and particularly the court that this district is in, to receive representations from the citizens both white and Negro as to what the best interests of both classes of children in the district might require in the way of handling its school affairs.

THE CHIEF JUSTICE: I was thinking of what Mr. Rogers said his suggestion was, that perhaps these attitudes that he relies on could not be changed until 2015 or 2045. I wonder if the decision of May 17 last year would be of much value to these people if they waited until 2045 for that change in the attitude of these people.

MR. McC.FIGG: I do not hardly think that time element is going to be—I never have thought it was involved in the disappearance of the institution of segregation in the southern states. But the southern states have not been so far behind the time table of those who, in other sections of the country have had the same problem and ended it in their own time.

For instance, I think it was the Act of 1938 that abolished segregation in New York State, and counsel today referred to the fact that in southern Illinois there are still segregated schools, and we know the trouble that they were having in 1952 trying to put the white and Negro children in the same schools in southern Illinois for the first time in the history of the state. The Attorney General of Kansas, yesterday, in talking about plans, said a willing school board had started working in September, 1953, and it had not yet achieved the carrying out of its attack on a very simple problem in a state that has never had the usages and customs that this school district had, a state which has only been permissive in its segregation legislation and confined it to the first six grades and required mixed schools above that, and then, as counsel conceded here today, the District of Columbia obviously has been working on its plan for a good while before your decision of May 17, 1954, and as a result of that and with their comparatively streamlined educational setup, they say they can meet a September 1, 1955, deadline. Then I was interested in reading about the constitutional change in the New Jersey people, that prohibited separate schools in 1947, and by September, 1951, they were still worrying with the problem of getting rid of mixed schools in a district in New Jersey. There have been forty-three such districts in 1947 and all but three I think have been integrated, as they called it, by September, 1951.

Now, I do not know of any school district which has been mentioned here or that I have heard about, that has as much of every kind of factor in this serious problem that the other side admits is a problem of primary magnitude. This district has all of the adverse factors to contend with. The trustees have not one favorable circumstance. In New Jersey every board was in favor of accomplishing what the Constitution—the constitutional change of 1947 demanded. The majority of every board and the majority of the people apparently in the community, and yet there were three stragglers four years later.

Now how, in the face of that, can it be suggested by counsel that for some other purpose or for effect in southern Illinois or for effect in some other part of the United States that the children and the parents and the school authorities of this district should have imposed upon them a six-month or an eighteen-month outside deadline by this Court on no evidence, not a scintilla of evidence—because our record is utterly barren as far as any evidence properly bearing upon the exercise by this Court of equitable discretion usually to be exercised by the district court after this Court has declared it law.

We just do not think these people should be treated as an example or as a theoretical case, or as you may say, we just passed it as an act to be applied in all the states or in all school districts. Their problem is personal and present to the trustees.

It is not theoretical. It is very serious. It is as serious as any board or any school district in the whole United States will face. There is no doubt about that.

Therefore, we ask this Court to give us an opportunity to let our school officials, who are charged with providing efficient public education to the children, white and Negro in this district, an opportunity to go before the district court in the district in which they live, in a reasonable time, where they will have ample opportunity to offer their evidence, to have other people come in, to have the citizens, and then trust the district judge to carry out the constitutional provisions. Counsel, it seems to me, thought the school boards were going to disobey the

Constitution, the school authorites, everybody connected with the state, everybody involved in this thing except they seem to have a distrust of allowing a district judge in the district where this school is or the one in Virginia from performing the function which the statutes of this country envisaged that he would perform, to hear evidence on a serious question and then make a decision not on a record barren of the testimony, not on considerations pulled out of the air, but on real concrete evidence and facts and considerations. And I do not believe that in a problem of this kind that anybody is going to suffer any real lack of educational advantage by giving a proper opportunity to the people involved, the officials involved, to study and present and canvass their problems before the district court.

There are not enough, as we suggest in our brief—this is a case, we are talking to a court of equity, and when you weigh these things quantitatively, there will be no great denial in this district of the educational advantage of mixed schools because the white content of those schools, even if they were completely gone tomorrow, would be inconsiderable, in an educational aspect.

So that we respectfully suggest, if Your Honor please, that what concerns us is that counsel in this case is not avoiding or getting around or rearguing your decision, but it is whether that decision, unless the things that we are aware of and are concerned about are given a chance to be presented to the court in an orderly fashion without limitation upon the traditional equitable jurisdiction which we think the district judge is as capable of properly using as any court in the federal setup. We say this is a school district in which it may well prove impossible to have unsegregated schools in the reasonably foreseeable future.

THE CHIEF JUSTICE: And on what do you base that conclusion?

MR. McC.FIGG: Failure to allow opportunity and time for community acceptance of the idea, on the large numbers involved, on the long biracial society that has developed there, and there is other evidence in the community of course, we can look to see how much acceptance is going to have to be achieved. The churches are not biracial, the PTA is separate, everything else in the community is separate and the Attorney General's brief refers among other things, and I think it is an important reference in many school districts, to the fact that even in New Jersey and other places it was found necessary to institute programs in the community apart from the school to at least gain community acceptance of an idea of mixing the children in the schools, that there had to be some start in districts far removed from the South in making the adults willing to entertain the idea before it was possible to gain their consent, both by funds and by authority to their elected representatives to have unsegregated schools. And I base it on that. I just do not see the signs in the community at this writing of a situation you can confidentially say, "This will be no problem."

JUSTICE: FRANKFURTER: In view of the emphasis you have placed upon the unique factors in Clarendon County, I naturally inferred you do not think this a typical school district of South Carolina.

MR. McC.FIGG: I think it is typical of others in South Carolina.

JUSTICE FRANKFURTER: It may be, but something that is unique cannot be typical.

MR. McC.FIGG: Well, I did not say, I do not believe I used the word "unique."

JUSTICE FRANKFURTER: No, no, but you emphasized these special factors and I wondered whether I had the right to think that this may not be duplicated in every other district.

MR. McC.FIGG: No, I think that you may well find it in almost the same degree or perhaps in the same degree in 25 to 30 per cent of our school districts because of the way the population is situated. About a third of the state is agricultural, intensively agricultural and this district, this county, has not the greatest percentage of Negro population over white, Calhoun County is heavier and Buford County, I believe, is heavier and Berkeley County. There are others where there is going to be a difficult—

JUSTICE FRANKFURTER: The situation you describe is not uniform in the state?

MR. McC.FIGG: No, not in every district. There are districts that will have problems, some of the districts in states other than the South that have been solved in three or four years as in the State of New Jersey or in other places.
I think that about a third of our state is regarded as intensively agricultural and I believe this is typical of that kind of—

JUSTICE FRANKFURTER: We have this case?

MR. McC.FIGG: That is right, you have this case and it is different from any other cases you have here, I believe, certainly different from the Virginia case in the amount of people involved.

JUSTICE BURTON: Is that saying that there are 25 or 30 school districts that might be approximately like the first?

MR. McC.FIGG: No, we have 46. On school districts—there may be more than that. We have several hundred school districts.

JUSTICE BURTON: Twenty-five or 30 would be like this and about 75 would be unlike?

MR. McC.FIGG: Yes, that is, in degree, would be less of an expensive problem. I do not say that is going to be easy anywhere in South Carolina. The history of the way of life there, the biracial society that my associates spoke about, of course, has been maintained for nearly a century, since the war, and it is going to be difficult to be able to obtain community acceptance of that everywhere.
As counsel in this case what worries us is the fact it may be impossible to obtain that without some time to do it.

THE CHIEF JUSTICE: On the other hand, do you argue that we should wait until attitudes have changed until compliance with the opinion of the Court is had?

MR. McC.FIGG: No, I do not say that you should wait at all on that. You see, all we suggest is that the proper court to be considering this matter is not this Court, because it does not have the opportunity to consider the evidence and to consider the circumstances. If you lay down such a time as the other side has asked you to do, you are not considering this district, you are considering a general problem that is not involved in our particular litigation, and we approach this as a lawsuit.

THE CHIEF JUSTICE: It makes a considerable difference whether the school district is making a valid effort to comply with decisions of the Court or whether it is exercising every effort that it can put forth to prevent it from becoming a reality. I understood from Mr. Rogers that your school district there and your people, because of your attitude, would not permit white and colored children to go to school together, notwithstanding the opinion of this Court. Now when it comes to remanding this to the court below, do you not believe that it is essential for us to take into consideration, since it is a court of equity, whether there is an attempt to comply or an attempt at frustration?

MR. McC.FIGG: To speak frankly, I think, if the case were remanded in the usual course, for action in the local court upon such considerations as advanced, it would advance public acceptance, the action which this Court would take. I believe, if it was set down almost like a legislative act, that it would retard public acceptance. You asked me that?

THE CHIEF JUSTICE: Yes, and that is a very fair answer. Let me ask you, do you not think that it might be of some value to the court below to have some guidance as to the manner in which progress can be expected?

MR. McC.FIGG: My conception was the other way, if Your Honor please. My conception was that the district judge would sit as he does in many cases, in full possession of his equity powers and if it was thought that he misused them, one side or the other would complain. I think he would be better off if he may fully consider the situation. It would mean the public would feel better about it. I think definitely one of our major problems is public acceptance. I am talking about every part of the country when I say that that has been the problem.

We do not regard ourselves as too far behind the timetable because we have had the problem for many years. Ninety years ago a way of life had to be worked out, it was thought that would accommodate these two races in a certain area.

We think great progress has been made. Even in my time, I have seen the areas of the real relevance of race, the life, and many of our people think that the last frontier is the schools and that the school situation may be ahead of the time table in orderly progress. But there has been so much improvement.

We have great belief in the fact that the evolutionary process has done a very, very good job. It is still a matter that anything that forwards public acceptance of this undertaking and doing this job is going to speed the day.

I think if you ordered the trustees tomorrow to comply or else, that that would destroy the public school system of South Carolina.

THE CHIEF JUSTICE: We will recess at this time.
(At 2 p.m. a recess was taken until 2:30 p.m.)

AFTER RECESS

THE CHIEF JUSTICE: Mr. Robertson.

## ARGUMENT ON BEHALF OF COUNTY SCHOOL BOARD
### PRINCE EDWARD COUNTY OF VIRGINIA, ET AL

### by MR. A. G. ROBERTSON

MR. ROBERTSON: If the Court please, Virginia has no plan, no panacea for the complete solution of the segregation problem. We cannot foresee any definite future date when it can be completely solved.

What we are up against, of course, is that the government is determined upon the consent of the governed and many people in all parts of Virginia have expressed their unwillingness at this time to consent to the compulsory integration of the races in the public schools. In August, 1954, the Governor appointed a legislative commission and that has finally filed an interim report in January of this year which was to the same effect, the opposition to compulsory integration in the public schools at this time. And to the same effect the resolution of the Board of Supervisors of Prince Edward County which I represent, and of 54 other counties in the state comprising altogether 55 of the 90 counties in the state, indicating the opposition to compulsory integration.

What we are up against is that neither a court decree, for that matter, nor an executive order, can produce the result which is opposed by a united majority in the place where it must be enforced.

A solution is being sought, however, in good faith by the Governor's Legislative Commission. That Commission is composed of thirty-two members, comprising almost one-fourth of the General Assembly of Virginia. The Commission has sought and obtained advice of organizations and of people in all walks of life in general and is seeking, as I say, in good faith to find a legislative program within the decision of May 17, 1954.

The first question to be decided here, of course, is the power of this Court to permit gradual adjustment. We maintain the Court has the power and that the power should be exercised by the Court in this case. That has been intimated here before, if the Court lacked the power, it would seem that it would long since have reversed this case and remanded it with a direction for immediate desegregation. But if it had done that, it would have nullified the public school laws of Virginia, without any provisions for other laws in their place and would have practically destroyed the public school system of Virginia.

As a result, the existing laws having been wiped out, there would have been a vacuum without any other laws to justify the operation of the schools and it just could not have been operated without the sanction of laws.

This action, of course, is an equity proceeding where the appellants seek an injunction against segregation and in an equity proceeding this Court may, of course, withhold, delay or condition its remedy as the situation may require.

As the court said in the Virginia-West Virginia Debt case,[14] the state cannot

[14]Virginia v. West Virginia, 246 U.S. 565 (1918). The State of Virginia successfully sued West Virginia for $12 million due it under the original compact creating the latter state. When West Virginia refused to pay, Virginia brought the problem to the Supreme Court which reserved action to let Congress settle the matter.

be expected to move with the zealotry of a private individual. It is enough if it proceeds with all speed and to adjust Virginia to the decision of May 17,1954. The General Assembly of Virginia must consider and must enact new legislation and, of course, this Court must grant time, adequate for that.

The next session of the General Assembly of Virginia convenes in January, 1956. Though the rights are personal and present, the allowance of an immediate remedy in a court of equity is within the discretion of the Court in view of the circumstances of the particular case before the Court.

This Court has the power to permit adjustment to new conditions, which present many problems in Virginia and Prince Edward County.

That power is conceded by all the parties to this action and the Attorney General of the United States, we understand now. Virginia does not appear before this Court as a convicted culprit to be punished for wrongdoing. Segregation was declared legal in *Roberts* against *The City of Boston* in 1849 and in some cases the "separate and equal" doctrine was promulgated in *Plessy* against *Ferguson* in 1896. That doctrine was not repudiated until May 17, 1954.

At least—I say it with deference—it took this Court more than sixty years to change its mind and decide that segregation was illegal per se, and it would seem now that justice would require that Prince Edward County and the State of Virginia be afforded fair opportunity to adjust itself to this revolutionary decision.

Since *Plessy* v. *Ferguson,* Virginia has maintained a segregated public school system in good faith, and the separate but equal requirements of *Plessy* against *Ferguson* have been met in this case so we say we are not here as a convicted culprit subject to punishment.

Repudiation by this Court on May 17, 1954, of the "separate but equal" doctrine created the problem which confronts Virginia now and just points up the necessity that Virginia be afforded time and opportunity for the solution of that problem. We come now to the evidence in this case. The evidence of record in this case applies to the effects of segregation. There is not a scintilla of evidence in this case now regarding the effects of desegregation. Much has been said of the emotional and psychological effects of segregation upon Negro children. What we are confronted with now and concerned with now, are what the emotional and psychological effects will be upon the white children. In Charles City, within twenty-five miles of Richmond, the Negro school children outnumber the whites three to one. And whites constitute the minority group in Prince Edward County. Fifty-five per cent of the school children are Negroes.

In 17 of the 98 counties of Virginia, the Negro population exceeds the white.

What, also, the emotional and psychological effect of desegregation is upon the white citizens in Virginia, generally—they, in large part, pay the taxes and bear the cost of operating and maintaining the public school system.

Surely, evidence regarding the effects of transition to non-segregation is required for the formulation of an appropriate decree here.

Without a favorable community attitude, no satisfactory adjustment is possible.

I certainly have not heard anybody else mention it in this case but I lived through the prohibition era and that noble experiment keeps coming back to my mind in what the experiment ended in.

The greater the percentage of Negroes in the community, the more difficult the problem of desegregation.

The ratio of Negro groups, Negro pupils in the State of Virginia varies from zero, not one, in three counties, Highland, Craig and Buchanan Counties to more than 77 per cent in Charles City County.

Education now follows one single pattern in Virginia. But the plan for local variation must obviously be devised and time is needed for the preparation of such a plan. A single pattern to be applied under one general rule will no longer apply. A plan acceptable and which might be enforced in Highland County or Craig County or Buchanan County where there is not a single Negro student will not be accepted in Prince Edward County where 55 per cent are Negro or in Charles City County where almost 78 per cent are Negroes or in a majority of the other counties in the State of Virginia.

Some workable plan must be devised and that is one of the purposes of the legislative state commission. Without a plan that the public will accept and support, Virginia schools may have to be closed for the time necessary to devise such a plan. The reason I have said that the existing laws would be nullified is there will not be any new laws to take their place and there would be no authority for the operation of the schools.

Just as in South Carolina, the greater part of the money for the public schools must be provided by the localities and the remainder will come from the state.

About this matter of public acceptance, what if they refuse to supply the necessary funds?

JUSTICE REED:  How is that money raised in Virginia?

MR. ROBERTSON:  The Board of Supervisors raises it.

JUSTICE REED:  That is not the school board?

MR. ROBERTSON:  No, the Board of Supervisors levies the tax which includes the fund for the operation of the schools and then the Board of Supervisors allocates the funds to school districts.

JUSTICE REED:  So the Board of Supervisors is distinct from the School Board?

MR. ROBERTSON:  Yes.

JUSTICE REED:  They raise the money and appropriate it to the various schools?

MR. ROBERTSON:  Yes.

JUSTICE REED:  The school board has no control over what it gets?

MR. ROBERTSON:  Not until it gets it, not in raising it.

JUSTICE REED:  They cannot pass a resolution if they want so much money for the schools?

MR. ROBERTSON:  That is within the discretion of the Board of Supervisors whether they provide it or not.

JUSTICE REED: Is there any central state control over the school boards?

MR. ROBERTSON: The State Board of Education has general supervisory control but the real government is in the district school board.

JUSTICE REED: You probably heard me ask this question of South Carolina. As I understand, there was administrative appeal from the local board?

MR. ROBERTSON: The State Board of Education issues general rules and regulation, but if there is a question of whether or not the school board is violating the law, that will take the normal course in the courts.

JUSTICE REED: Promulgates whether it should be the law. Suppose the State Board issues a regulation that there should be three schools in the district and the local board did not have three, they thought two would be better?

MR. ROBERTSON: I speak, subject to correction by the Attorney General. My idea is that that would be appealed to the State Board of Education and then would be subject to redress in the courts by a court decree.

Application in good faith of the "separate but equal" doctrine and statewide enforcement since 1940 for compulsory school attendance were hard-won victories which produced magnificent results. I wish I had time to say what some of those results were. A few of them appear in a footnote on page 7 of our brief which shows how much illiterateness in the state has been reduced and is being reduced and as appears from the other briefs here we do not stand here as a convicted culprit. We are proud of our public schools and think we have gotten great results and we are trying to maintain it and preserve it and defend it for the benefit of all the children in the state the best way we know in good faith and with good will.

The next thing is the necessary support of public schools. That may create a situation whereby we will have nonenforcement of the compulsory attendance law. That would increase teen age idleness and delinquents and I think the Court will be interested in this.

In Danville, Virginia, since this case in Baltimore was decided, a bond issue for public swimming pools which everybody thought would be passed was defeated. In Prince Edward County last week the Board of Supervisors declined to levy the tax necessary to raise the funds for the school budget for 1955–1956 until they could find out and know what they were up against.

In Albemarle County which encircles Charlottesville, the University of Virginia's seven-year capital improvement fund, the present fund of which would have provided two fine Negro elementary schools and two equally good white schools, has been brought to a halt.

I am not speaking in defiance or in any ill will but I am trying to tell the Court as vividly as I can what we are up against in public acceptance and in searching for a solution here to meet this problem.

JUSTICE MINTON: If a deadline was fixed in the decree entered by this Court of 1956, what would be the attitude of your people?

MR. ROBERTSON: I think they would be greatly hampered. I have no authority to speak in that way for anyone but myself. My feeling is that as I will come to that in a moment in my argument, that if this case was remanded to the district court without instructions, other than to proceed in conformity with the opinion delivered here on May 17, 1954, as rapidly as can be done, without serious jeopardy or impairment of the public school system of Virginia, then the district court in its normal process with this case serving as a precedent for all the state, would bring about desegregation in the different localities in the state as rapidly as could reasonably be done and as the law could be enforced.

Does that answer your question?

Virginia employs some six thousand Negro teachers, more than employed in all the states where they do not have segregation and those Negro teachers must be treated fairly and justly in the solution of this problem.

The general level of educational capacity and attainment must be determined. Standard reading tests of 31,000 Virginia school children in eight grades for the school session 1950–1951 showed that the lowest 25 per cent of white students were further advanced than the highest 25 per cent of the Negro students.

The standard IQ test given to all high school students in Virginia for the session 1951–1952 showed the same thing.

I know that it may be said, well, that is your fault, you denied them opportunity, you denied them equality. It is the result of environment. We think that is irrelevant in this case. We are not aware of any unfairness or inequality and we are not responsible for that.

We say that the standards of health and morals must also be taken into account. Tuberculosis is almost twice as prevalent among the Negroes as it is among the whites. Negroes constitute 22 per cent of the population of Virginia but 78 per cent of all cases of syphilis and 83 per cent of all cases of gonorrhea occur among the Negroes.

One white child out of every fifty born in Virginia is illegitimate. One Negro child out of five is illegitimate.

Of course, the incidence of disease and illegitimacy is just a drop in the bucket compared to the promiscuity. We say that not as a moral issue, not as to where the fault lies, but that the fact is there and the white parents at this time will not appropriate the money to put their children among other children with that sort of a background.

That is just one of the factors of life with which we are confronted. There are some 130 different school districts in Virginia and each one of them presents a different problem in a different locality.

An integrated system of public schools would require more than a court decree. It would require an evolutionary change in the attitude of people in Virginia, both Negro and white.

An intelligent, orderly and effective transition must be accomplished under new legislation to be accomplished with good will and in good faith and all within the requirements of the decision of May 17, 1954.

We come now to the consideration of the decree. We say that this Court should not formulate a decree, a detailed decree and this Court should not appoint a special Master.

We think that this Court should remand the case to the court below and direct that court to take further evidence to determine a program for effective enforcement of the decision of May 17.

THE CHIEF JUSTICE: Mr. Robertson, would you prepare the form of decree that you suggest for the Court, please?

MR. ROBERTSON: Yes, sir.

JUSTICE HARLAN: Mr. Robertson, we wonder when this commission you refer to is due to report.

MR. ROBERTSON: I do not know the date—September, 1955. The record in this case contains no evidence as to the facts on which a detailed decree must be based and without such evidence a detailed decree would be based upon surmise and conjecture. Moreover, it is not the function of an appellate court to prepare detailed decrees and as has been said here, this Court has never previously formulated such decrees in the school cases.

I have to say this in fairness to the Court—this case may require months or years of trial courts' attention and this Court cannot give the case that kind of attention effectively.

This Court at this time does not know the issues that must be met and decided. This Court will not undertake to decide unknown issues.

If this Court enters a detailed decree now, the decree will be based upon issues developed in the briefs of counsel and through the assertion of facts made by the counsel.

It will be based upon general notions of propriety, not upon the testimony of witnesses. It will be entered upon undetermined issues, without a hearing upon the issues, without evidence and without cross-examination.

Reference to a Master is a practice of this Court only when the original jurisdiction of the Court is invoked. Where the original juisdiction of this Court is invoked, the Court receives evidence and makes findings of fact.

In this case the original jurisdiction of the Court has not been invoked and the Court cannot properly receive evidence or enter a decree not based on evidence.

That is beyond the function of the Court. In this case no overall rule can properly be applied. Countless different facts and circumstances are involved, the flexibility is absolutely necessary.

This Court is remote from the scene. On the other hand, the court below clearly has much greater familiarity with local conditions than this Court can ever acquire.

The court below in pretrial conference could confer with counsel, with school authorities and with others. It could consider administrative programs here and formulate an appropriate decree.

The court below should be free to supervise future action in Prince Edward County and enforce the decisions of this Court as speedily as may be done, consistent with the maintenance of the public school system in Prince Edward County.

The court below is fully equipped to follow the general directions of this Court. It is under the same oath as this Court to obey the law and thereby, it will proceed in good faith and with all reasonable speed.

We agree with the Attorney General of the United States that no decree should be entered now in this Court providing that Negro children shall forthwith be admitted to schools of their choice. We agree with him that this Court in exercise of its equity powers should permit an effective, gradual adjustment.

We agree with him that this Court should not formulate a detailed decree and that this Court should not appoint a special master to hear evidence and to recommend specific terms for a detailed decree.

We agree with him that this Court should remand the case to the court below for further proceedings in conformity with the opinion of May 17, 1954.

We differ with the Attorney General in that we believe that no specific direction should be given to the court below for all the reasons I have stated and that no definite time limit should be set. Any specific directions to the court below will crimp its efficiency.

There is no short or easy path to the solution of the segregation problem in Virginia. New phases of the same problem will continue to be present and the generations of litigation that Mr. Justice Jackson apprehended when these cases were decided here before cannot be forestalled by any action of this Court now.

It can be forestalled and the progress can be pushed along in the district court.

This Court—and I say "this"—this Court can tell Virginia what not to do, but what I apprehend and what I think presents a much more difficult problem, this Court cannot tell Virginia what kind of public schools to operate. And if public opinion refuses to go along, not in disobedience of the decree of the Court—we would not for one minute say that they would disobey the Court, defy the Court and continue segregated schools against the mandate of this court, but there are more difficult and subtle ways of doing it which we as counsel in this case do not know how to meet. They could refuse to vote the money, refuse to support necessary laws, and repeal usual public attendance laws.

You mar and impair the public school system of Virginia in a way that has taken a whole era to produce. You encourage a recurrence of the bitterness that was engendered by the old Reconstruction era.

What is worst of all, in our opinion, you impair the public school system of Virginia and the victims will be the children of both races, we think the Negro race worse than the white race, because the Negro race needs it more by virtue of these disadvantages under which they have labored. We are up against the proposition: What does the Negro profit if he procures an immediate detailed decree from this Court now and then impairs or mars or destroys the public school system in Prince Edward County?

THE CHIEF JUSTICE: Mr. Almond.

### ARGUMENT ON BEHALF OF THE ATTORNEY GENERAL OF VIRGINIA

#### by MR. LINDSAY ALMOND

MR. ALMOND: Mr. Chief Justice, may it please the Court. Several questions have been propounded from the bench to various of counsel relative to the statutory setup of the various cases with regard to the operation of the public school system. We have in Virginia a constitutional provision, section 133 of our state constitution which vests the control and direction of the school board in the various counties and cities of Virginia.

By statute pursuant to that constitutional provision, the supervision and control is gone into more detail. The State Board of Education has supervisory direction. The appropriations for the operation of the public schools in Virginia, 56 per cent comes from the localities.

The rest from the state. The state may condition its appropriation. The State Board of Education is vested with power to make rules and regulations requiring equalization relative to curricula, teachers' salaries and whatnot.

But the whole system in Virginia, if it please the Court, is one of local autonomy. The school boards of Virginia are appointed by a school trustee electoral board which board in turn is named by the circuit judges of the various circuits comprising the counties of Virginia.

The appropriations for public schools in Virginia at the local level work in this fashion:

The statute requires the local school board to present its budget to the board of supervisors as to its requirement for the coming session. That has to be done some time in advance. Then it is lodged within the legislative discretion of the board of supervisors which is the governing body of the county and the city council which is the governing board of our city, to appropriate such funds as it deems sufficient for the efficient operation and maintenance of the public school system.

I wanted to clear that up with reference to my own state. And then another question has been asked that I think it will be appropriate for me to answer here now. The question has been asked from the bench relative to the authority of the Attorney General respecting the enforcement of law in Virginia. No state officer has any right to undertake to enforce federal law. But as to the enforcement of state law in Virginia, the statute prohibits the Attorney General from entering into the institution or trial of criminal cases in the circuit and other courts of the county and state.

His jurisdiction attaches only upon a writ of error being granted by the Supreme Court of Appeals and then he must take over and represent the Commonwealth.

I trust that was not a digression but the Court had manifested its interest in those quesions.

Now if the Court please, knowing that I shall say, because I harbor no spirit of defiance—I do not agree as a lawyer and I must say it in all deference with the momentous decision of May 17. It is the law of the land.

I trust that we may be given an opportunity to work out a solution at the state and local level, acceptable to our people and consistent with the Constitution of our country.

That is all we ask in this case. As far as my constitutional obligations as an officer of my state and my status before the bar of this Court which I cherish, I shall advise and have advised the officers of my state to proceed with expedition in view of all the circumstances and problems facing Virginia to work out a solution to this grave problem.

Just a word, if you please, on the power of this Court to permit gradual adjustment. There seems not the shadow of a doubt that this Court may—it does not have to—in the exercise of its equity powers permit an effective gradual adjustment to be brought about from existing segregated systems to a system not based on color distinction.

As I shall try to develop in my argument, that does not mean enforced integration to us in Virginia.

Now on the power of the Court, there is almost unanimity of agreement on this point among counsel of both sides. This Court, itself, entered upon the threshold of the exercise of that power on May 17. Otherwise it would have entered an order reversing the decree of the court below with the mandate that the relief sought be granted. This Court has frequently in the application of its judgment, resorted to the flexibility of equitable rules and remedies and adopted them toward the circumstances of particular cases.

If there were argument or dispute on this point, the Congress has settled it by removing every vestige of room for debate by expressly empowering the Court in molding effective relief to enter such appropriate judgment, decree or orders or require such further proceedings to be had as may be just under the circumstances.

I close that point of my argument with a statement. My honest judgment is that clearly the Court possesses the power. Should it exercise that power in these cases? This, I think, has been removed from the realm of debate.

On May 17, this Court handed down a decision in principle. The Court refrained from formulating decrees necessary to implement its decision.

It recognized that these are not individual but class actions. It recognized the wide and sweeping applicability of its decision. And so the Court recognized that the decision involved the rights, the mode of life, the customs, the mores of 50 million people and 11 million school children.

It recognized and so stated the various local conditions with their varying problems, problems interstate, intrastate, community-wise, county-wise and village-wise. And it recognized that the formulation of decrees represented problems of considerable complexity and I venture to add, problems of overwhelming magnitude.

The Court then by its own conclusions without more action, would seem to have answered the question. And I maintain, if Your Honors please, that the consequences of the alternative answers the question.

The alternative to the exercise of the power to permit gradual adjustment would be to adopt the view asserted by the plaintiffs that their rights are personal and present and require immediate enforcement within the limitation stated by Mr. Marshall, forthwith enforcement, subjugative of the rights of millions, superior to the preservation of any semblance of public education in many parts of this country, provocative of unending chaos, engendering of racial bitterness, strife and possible circumstances more dire.

Forthwith enforcement, in terms of the definition of our adversaries would be preemptive of the right of a sovereign people to call upon their own elective representatives in their state legislatures to promulgate state policy and enact laws consistent with the Constitution for the maintenance and administration of their own public school system.

Our adversaries ask this Court—and I say without any spirit of bitterness, they ask this Court to arm them with the power to destroy, which this Court has said to be perhaps the most important function of state and local governments. Prince Edward County with a Negro population of 55 per cent of the total, one of the poorer counties of Virginia, has, at really tremendous cost, borne largely and in disproportionate measure by the white people, constructed and now operate a high school facility for Negroes not equal to, but far superior to its facilities for white children.

The white people there are not complaining. They seek an education for their children and for the Negro children. Now, after these things was the final mandate requiring admittance forthwith or without provision for a reasonable time for state and local government to proceed to an orderly solution within the framework of constitutional legislative and administrative process.

You will have placed in their hands, unbridled power to destroy the most important function of state and local government.

The high schools of Prince Edward County, not in defiance of the mandate of this Court, but under the imperative necessity of relentless circumstance over which they have no control, would cease to operate.

They would remain dormant until an orderly and lawful solution could be brought about.

I say, in all candor and frankness to this Court, that solution whatever it may be, will not in my judgment in the lifetime of those of us hale and hearty here, be enforced integration of the races in the public schools of that county.

Mr. Robertson has pointed out, it is nothing to boast about. I certainly do not assert it as a threat but as a fact. The governing body of the state, in response to the demand of the people who pay the taxes, have deferred action on the school levy.

Forthwith admittance would serve to perpetuate that action for some time to come.

Now, in view of the broad scope of the decision of May 17, its crushing impact upon a system of public education established and progressively maintained with the sanction of the Congress since 1868, with the sanction and approval of this Court since 1896, the sudden shock entailed by the uprooting and demolishing of a way of life enshrined and institutionalized in the hearts and minds of the overwhelming majority of millions of law-abiding citizens, their fierce and deepseated devotion to their customs and traditions composing as they do, the warp and woof of their mores of life and their devout and firm conviction as to the legal and moral soundness of their public school system which they have maintained for generations and into which they have poured their souls, their substance and their sacrifices, we, in Virginia and in the South, if it please the Court, steeped in the concept of the right of people to govern, to support or not support a system of public education as they may choose, we are facing the bleak prospect of serious impairment or possible destruction of our public school system—and I measure my words.

This Court, in all deference, should, therefore, afford a reasonable opportunity to work with as much expedition as possible, in good faith as state governmental machinery will permit, to evolve a solution acceptable to a majority of our people and consistent with the Constitution of our country.

We therefore respectfully submit that this case be remanded and that the Court of first instance be allowed discretion in the light of relevant circumstances and tradition.

Now, only one phase of this great problem has ever been considered by this or any other court. When this Court repudiated the "separate but equal" doctrine, it then proceeded to deal only with the affect of segregation upon the colored children; that type of segregation which they denoted as segregation with the sanction of law. They held that the plaintiffs, by reason of segregation complained of, were deprived of the equal protection of the law.

No consideration has ever been given, nor did the record in its present state so require, to the effect of integration on white children, to what it would do to their hearts and minds or to the effect of integration on the ability of a state to maintain a public school system or to how a state might shape its legislative policies to evolve a solution to the dilemma which confronts it.

These, in my judgment, are considerations of policy and legislation belonging to the states. As to such matters I say in all deference, this Court has no power to legislate or to delegate nonexistent authority to the court of first instance. I further say, with due deference, it has no power to give to a state or a local school board affirmative directions as to the operation of its school system.

There is no authority in law nor can we submit to any situation whereby any court takes charge of and supervises our public schools.

On the surface the problems confronting us do not stem from racial antipathies. Those who spout that propaganda are either abysmally ignorant of the facts of life or are as reckless with truth as Sherman was with fire in some parts of our country.

If permitted to delve into and cope with these problems on state and local legislative and administrative levels, we are hopeful—we are determined to salvage a rational and constructive system from the wreckage which the future otherwise tends to hold for us.

May I for a moment, touch upon this problem of uniformity of approach with the decree? Our problem cannot be solved if it please the Court, through uniformity of approach statewide at the state level.

Broad non-discriminatory discretion to be exercised without discrimination must be vested in local school boards to cope with varying conditions extant throughout the state.

No blanket forthwith decree entered by any court could possibly do aught but preclude an approach to a solution and not only turn the clock back educationwise, far beyond *Plessy* v. *Ferguson,* but wreak damage upon the hearts and minds of children, to quote the opinion of May 17, in a way unlikely to be ever undone and to the extent that such final adjudication would constitute precedents in law. The remaining southern states here, amicus curiae and others not before this Court in any role, could and would tell their people in fact, that they had not had their day in court to test the constitutionality of any solution which they might evolve in an honest effort to save their public school system from destruction.

This Court has said that public education is the most important function of state and local government. Virginia and her sister states of the South are in full accord with the soundness of that statement, for nearly a century we have proceeded under the sanction of law.

Suddenly we are told we are performing the most important function of state and local government in violation of law.

If education—and we agree—is the most important function of state and local government, then the state and local government have the right to cope with the problems thus created in the discharge of their functions and to be given a reasonable time to set in motion governmental processes designed to respond to the educational requirements of their own people.

It is difficult and dangerous. The percentage of Negro children, as Mr. Robertson has pointed out, range from zero in three counties to 77 per cent in one. One-fourth of Virginia's counties have 50 per cent or more of Negro population, one-half have 25 per cent or more. Over one-half of Virginia's twenty-nine cities have 25 per cent or more of Negro school population.

Six of our cities have less than 10 per cent. The ratio of population is of pressing significance in any approach to a solution of this problem. While it is not the final determinant, it is the most powerful single influence on racial attitudes which we must recognize.

A county with 10 per cent or less of Negro population will be found in many instances to have a district or area where the ratio will approximate 50 per cent. Now it is pointed out in the brief of opposing counsel that in May of 1954 Negroes were admitted to previously all white parochial schools in Virginia and this was accomplished without a bit of discontent. The fact remains that out of a total of 21,048 pupils, only 7 per cent of them were Negro and that the schools were not tax-supported. While the public schools of Virginia with a population approximately 800,000 of which 25 per cent are Negroes must depend upon local taxation for 56 per cent of their support.

Mr. Robertson went into the achievement standards. I am going to say this: In a typical class of thirty-six, according to these tests, accepted appropriate standard tests, in a typical class of thirty-six, half white and half Negro, the range of comprehension would extend all the way from six Negro pupils with a reading age of nine years and four months to a top group of six white pupils with a reading age of sixteen years and two months.

In dealing with the how of integration, which they tell us we must deal with, how would it be possible to proceed with an effective teaching program on any such basis if the teaching level is pitched for the level of the median Negro child?

Then the education of the white group must suffer. Regardless of why and as to any other reason, it is a fact that these great differences do exist. And these are not intangibles, they are measurable.

They are substantially the same variations as turn up year after year by race in the county and city schools.

These realities cannot be ignored. I am not going further into the matter of health, Mr. Robertson brought it out, but with the same drinking fountain, the same toilets, the same physical daily habits, and all, our problem is increased. The conclusion as a result of these conditions with reference to health is inescapable, that white parents will keep their children out of school. They will withdraw their support. I do not say that as a threat.

Now, with the attitude that has flourished, our friends sing their siren song entitled "The People of the South are Law-abiding People." In the next stanza they urge this Court with unwarranted and undue force, to press this crown of thorns upon our brow and hold the hemlock up to our lips. Yes, we are an orderly law-abiding people. We lead in giving law and order to the nation. We washed the Eighteenth Amendment out of the Constitution and flooded the Volstead Act to oblivion on the stream of our honest spirits because it affected the way of life of the American people.

We have that problem multiplied now. The people of Virginia devoutly committed to the cause of education, look to this Court as their trustee of the power and the bearer of the responsibility.

THE CHIEF JUSTICE: Mr. Marshall.

### REBUTTAL ARGUMENT ON BEHALF OF HARRY BRIGGS, ET AL

#### by MR. MARSHALL

MR. MARSHALL: May it please the Court, I had hoped as I saw the issues in this case, that by now I would be discussing the one point I think is still before the Court. That is, assuming that the Court decides to consider effective gradual adjustment, that by now somebody representing one of the two states would have been able to give the Court some idea as to when that could be done under any circumstance.

And to hear from the Lawyer Almond, not in his lifetime, some other place, it was so for hundreds of years, I say on that point, which as I understand is limited to the decision being effective, there is nothing before this Court that can show any justification for giving this interminable gradual adjustment. I am particularly shocked at arguments of the impotency of our Government to enforce its Constitution. I am shocked that anybody would put the right of the Negro child to participate in education, which this Court has said is the most important function, on a non-segregated basis. I am shocked that anybody classes that right to take a drink of whiskey involved in prohibition with the right of a Negro child to participate in education.

We are not talking about the same thing. There is nothing in anything that shows that there is any connection.

The point was made that in South Carolina they have had segregated schools for such a long time, and it would not be wise to get rid of them expeditiously. I remind this court that in two cases where certiorari was applied for here and denied, the two primary cases from South Carolina, *Elmore* and *Baskins,* Negroes have been denied the right to vote in South Carolina since, if I remember correctly, before the turn of the century, but yet when the district court issues a temporary injunction or preliminary—I have forgotten which, but before ultimate decision, Judge Waring, now retired, ruled that Negroes could not be excluded from the primary election in South Carolina in the very state he is talking about, they had to re-open their books which they did and register some sixty or eighty thousand Negroes within ten days of the decision.

They say, well, education has been here for a long time. And once again these general phrases of time and its significance at this step—I know I was correct in the beginning of trying to make clear the issues in this case.

Everybody on the other side takes the position that we are obliged to show that effectve gradual adjustment will not work.

As I read these questions they are obliged to show that it will work. It is said constantly that we have not shown anything. We have shown our right to immediate relief. And this is a court of equity. And although I, of course, recognize that the burden of proof never shifts in a case but the burden of going forward shifts back and forward, in this, a court of equity, it is unbelievable that at this late day and age the argument would be made that calls for consideration and that the person arguing it should be given advantage brought out by their own wrongdoing.

Both attorneys in the Virginia case say that all of these things they talk about, they admit frankly, are because of the denial of the rights to these people involved. They mention these educational tests. There again, we have use of figures that can be used any way. They use figures on a percentage basis. They leave out the fact that in each one of those percentages, there are Negro children that run the gamut in each one of those twenty-five figures, but they try to give the impression that all the Negro children are below all the white children when that is not true.

There are geniuses in both groups and there are lower ones in both groups, and it has no bearing. No right of an individual can be conditioned as to any average of other people in his racial group or any other group.

Now these health theories, and again we have figures that you can go any way you want. I did not check them because I think they are so completely immaterial unless the State of Virginia either has no public health service in its schools or they do not know how to use it.

It has always been interesting to me, if the Court please, from the Morgan case involving transportation, that, well, whenever Negroes are separated from other people because of race, they always make an exception as to the Negro servants.

In Virginia, it is interesting to me that the very people that argue for this side, that would object to sending their white children to school with Negroes, are eating food that has been prepared, served and almost put in their mouths by the mothers of those children, and they do it day in and day out, but they cannot have the child go to school. That is not the point involved in this case. The point is as to whether or not, at this late date, with emphasis, this government can any longer tolerate this extreme difference based upon race or color.

Not one man has stood before this Court yet representing the other side, and shown concretely what they have done in support of the May 17 decision. They have not even started to begin to think about desegregating.

Rather, their emphasis is based on the hope—without any foundation that I can imagine—that this Court will buy the idea of turning this over for a period of an indeterminate number of years. They say I do not have faith in the district courts.

That is untrue. My argument was that I was sure the district courts in these cases would do absolutely right and follow the ruling of the Court, but in this governmental protection of these rights and the governmental leadership in this so-called educational process, this changing-of-attitudes process can be brought about more effectively, and I submit anything else would be of no effect, than for this Court to issue the strongest type of a decree which will arm the district judge and the court of appeals judge with these necessary high level decrees so that they can operate from then on.

That is why we think that the instruction from this Court, we all agree—I do not know why there was so much argument about it—there should be this evidence given in the lower court.

That is in our proceedings. We say you can present it to the lower court, you can show all of these difficulties. We agree on that. The only thing we do not agree on is they want no time limit, and I do not believe that anybody in good faith could listen to these four arguments and not be certain that when they go to any court they are going to argue the same thing they are arguing here, which is never.

So I say, with a strong, forthright decree from this Court, all of the district courts in the country can solve this problem. To my mind—again I come back to it—despite the criticism that has been made of what I say, that we cannot continue to exist with this division in our country, whether it is on sectional lines or areawise.

This local option business, this question that there is always a two-fold score, that we cannot integrate Negroes because we have got so many in this country.

However, the reason we cannot integrate them is because we have to listen to what the people in that county want. Well, obviously, that is what they mean. They mean the 10 per cent of the white people. They mean specifically that the enforcement of our constitutional rights, recognized in this Court's decision on May 17, must be geared down to the point, as one of the lawyers said, you not only bring in people in the community, you bring in experts.

The district court would be a legislative body, and after listening to all the people in the community, there would be the decision as to when this could come about.

This is the opposite of orderly procedure. And we would have, for example, as was raised by Mr. Justice Reed, the number in Clarendon County, I do not think it is probable but you could have three different time limits in Clarendon County, one for each district. Obviously that is not what is intended. Obviously, I do not believe that our Constitution, that this Court,—and I most certainly do not believe that Questions 4 and 5 were either—intended to put the right of the children in these cases to be subjected to what the will of the majority of the people in that community want.

Finally, one thing that to my mind is completely without any semblance of legal authority is that, if you do not give me what I want, I will close up the public schools. It is quoted in the *Southern News* and in this very State of South Carolina in one of these hearings on these bills to abolish the public school system in South Carolina, they are already working on it, to be ready. And one leader who happened to be a white leader who is not in favor of integration, made the statement that "I do not know what the solution to this problem is, but as to foreclosing these schools, one thing I do know, we will not solve the problem by increasing ignorance." Now that is something I just do not believe, and proof is right in South Carolina, and immediately after this May 17 decision Governor Byrnes stopped the building of all schools under the equalization program.

A month or so later, he started the program again. So, sure, there will be noise here and there, but we have got to continue, if the Court please. I cannot over-emphasize that the problem is tough and we have faith in our government and not the belief that our government is not enforcing its Constitution in South Carolina and Virginia, just as it is any place else.

So far as I am concerned, the arguments that are made to the contrary, in addition to the arguments made in their briefs, they have shown only one point in so far as the legal argument is concerned.

That is, that they should have an opportunity to have time to make certain adjustments. We agree on that, and they should present them to the district court but we want a time limitation, a time limit. We believe we are entitled to our rights as of the next school term, and if we cannot get that type of decree in the judgment of this Court, then what is going to happen? They are making all the threats as to what will happen if they do not get the decree, putting that aside if this Court in its wisdom decides that you will not, in this case, issue a decree which will require admission of these students by September.

The only thing that will give us anything at the end of this lawsuit would be a decree which would do the four things I say. It is important to start that immediately, to report to the district court step by step, and to end it at a date certain. Otherwise, we will have in the State of Virginia and in the county involved, the State of South Carolina and throughout the country the continuation of what has been branded as an unlawful procedure, what has been branded by this Court as unconstitutional.

It is not the question of having my constitutional rights to day-by-day variations in county by county determined one way or the other according to the local option.

In my county they say my child will go to school, schools will be desegregated in five years. I move over into the next county, hoping that he will go in one year and they make it six years. I will be traveling all around the country trying to get my constitutional rights.

It makes no difference under this Constitution of the United States that your child is born in one state or one county or the other. You have the exact same rights in South Carolina and Virginia in so far as the Constitution is concerned as you have in New York or any place else.

Therefore, in so far as these cases are concerned, we believe that the first decree is the one we are entitled to, and if we are not entitled to that, in your judgment, at least, we get the second decree so that our plaintiffs in these cases and other Negroes will at least have some protection.

Without a decree, providing for a time limit, there will be no protection whatsoever for the decision of this Court rendered on May 17.

Thank you very much.

THE CHIEF JUSTICE: Referring to the South Carolina case, Mr. McC.Figg and Mr. Rogers, will you be good enough to furnish to the Court a decree as you would propose it for the state as the others have done? It would be helpful to the Court if you would.

We will now hear from the State of Florida, Friend of the Court.


## ARGUMENT ON BEHALF OF THE STATE OF FLORIDA, AS THE FRIEND OF THE COURT

### by MR. RICHARD ERVIN

MR. ERVIN: First I would like to express appreciation for the opportunity to be present and present the facts of our Amicus brief.

The decision of May 17 was momentous and it had a very serious impact potentially upon our Florida school system.

We believe the answer to this is that stated in Question 4(b), effective gradual adjustment.

We feel that the legal justification rests in equity jurisprudence considering the progressive state of society, the public interest, and that this Court should permit a situation where sociological and psychological factors can be considered as well as physical adjustments in each situation that comes before the courts for adjudication.

We feel that no constitutional rights are absolute but that all are exercised within the realm of the police power, the public welfare and regulations for the best interest of the people.

In overturning the present decision on the basis of advance and psychological knowledge, we feel that the Court in any implementation pattern that it sets in these cases, particularly in the South Carolina and Virginia cases, that it should give consideration to psychological and sociological factors in implementation.

The brief of the United States Attorney General says, "The impact of segregation upon children, the Court found, can so affect their entire life as to preclude their full enjoyment of their constitutional rights. In similar fashion, psychological and emotional factors are involved and must be met with understanding and good faith in alterations that must now take place in order to bring about compliance with the Court's decision."

We feel that he means that in the implementation of the Court's May 17 decision that consideration must be given to sociological and psychological factors. We think that in order to do that, that there must be essential preparation in the South, in the various school districts of the South to bring about some degree of public acceptance and diminution of sociological and psychological factors which militate against a nonsegregated school system.

The Attorney General's brief then says "General hostility is a relevant factor to be considered in determining the most effective method for ending segregation in a particular locality. School administrators have an obvious concern in obtaining public support and acceptance of the transition. Thoughtful preparation in advance will resolve the problem with as few disruptions as possible."

Harry Ashmore wrote the book, *The Negro and the Schools*. He based it on the Ford Foundation for advancement studies and he wrote, "It is axiomatic that separate schools can be merged only with great difficulty, if at all, where a great majority of the citizens who support them are actively opposed to the move. No public school is isolated from the community that supports it, and if the very composition of its classes is subject to deep-seated and sustained public disapproval, it is hardly likely to foster the spirit of united effort essential to learning."

As we understand it, the school system in the South, is close to the people and it is an important center of social life in many of our Southern communities. In arguments here, it has been suggested that the federal court could by decree, handle the situation without the cooperation of state and local officials; that public opinion of the community may be disregarded, provided positive leadership and action of responsible public officials is extended on behalf of the program of desegregation.

Such appears to be implicit in the sociological theory advanced by Mr. K. B.

Clark[15] and other scientists but whether this theory is correct or not, statewise and folkwise, in Florida, as between its public officials and people they are practically homogenous.

In other words, they view the problem of desegregation almost the same and they feel that Florida is not ready for a program of immediate segregation.

I want to read to you very briefly the findings of the survey made of leadership opinion in Dade County, Florida. Dade County is where Miami is located. This survey was made by the University of Miami social scientists of that University.

Dade County people are heterogeneous. They come from all parts of the nation and they have all types of racial people in that area. Here are some of the findings:

> Despite the fact that a majority of the white population of Dade County is opposed to the Court's decision as a matter of principle, they, nevertheless indicate that they will abide by the decision if integration is handled gradually with an adequate period of preparation. The present reluctance to assume positive leadership by public officials or any substantial number of leadership groups outside official circles indicates great difficulty if an attempt is made to move too quickly. A general belief exists that serious violence will occur if the decision is pushed by any minority group, white or colored.

With a majority of white population disagreeing with the Supreme Court decision principle, a state legislator was without question correct when he said what is needed is a change in the community. Such change obviously requires sufficient time.

We believe that it is wise in these cases where only the question is involved of race, that a decree remanding the case to the courts of first instance and in the general directions stating that the court will consider not only physical adjustments but sociological and psychological factors would be the right decree.

We feel on the other hand, that an abrupt decision, one that sets a time limit which could become the maximum limit, that it would seriously retard the efforts of all moderate, all liberal-minded people in the State of Florida, and would drive them probably in the opposition camp.

There will even be trouble in the legislature with regard to getting appropriations, state aid to the schools. There would be complete arousement of the people that it had to be done by a certain period of time with no advance preparation. You would not have the opportunity for university workshops where the problem is studied, where interracial committees, which are now in operation in Florida, are trying to solve the problem, continue their efforts. You would not have the churches, the civic groups, fraternal, the other people who are consciously trying to make this go forward there.

We feel that for the court, that is, the federal courts to assume the whole burden of enforcing the decision without taking into their confidence the school

[15]See "The Effects of Segregation and the Consequences of Desegregation: A Social Science Statement," Appendix to Appellants' Brief in Brown v. Board of Education, October Term, 1952, p. 17.

administrators and the people of the state, would be a great mistake and would have untoward results.

The idea that from the top, that is by federal contempt or by prosecution, under the federal Civil Rights statute, that the May 17 decision can be enforced, we think is an unsound one, we hope that the Court will not permit it.

We are making efforts in our state to work this out on a local basis. It is true some of the counties, some of the areas of the state are not making that effort. Others are. In Dade County alone there is a council, a Council of Human Relations. They are meeting next Sunday to talk about plans, well in advance of the Court's implementation decision. They are trying to devise means to prepare the people for acceptance. Any decree that would result in a specific, abrupt change would be completely devoid of cooperation of state officials, of state citizens, it seems to me.

I do not believe in the rule "Do it," that has been expressed here. The extremists are trying to take charge of this proposition. We want the Court acting as an executive council here at the very top to write in these cases where race is the sole question, that the lower courts can take into consideration the sociological and psychological factors involved in the integration, only for the transition period as well as the physical adjustment that is necessary, and then there will be the arguments all along the way, that is the federal district judge or perhaps the state court judge, where there is a dispute about administrative policy, to see whether or not the quotas of the school administrators in Florida and other areas of the South—whether they are trying to circumvent or whether they are really trying to adopt these programs of human engineering to bring about public acceptance.

I think that these ideas expressed here that what we want really is a delay, a moratorium or local option and that that is beside the point. We want an opportunity to show this Court that we can by local action, not by taking a vote but by people working with the school administrators, the PTA, interracial committees, talking this problem out, arrange some time of desegregation in the school districts. We want to show the Court that it can be done.

If it appears that this idea of gradual adjustment under the great power of the court of equity is not properly received by the people of the South, then the Court can abandon it. But at least they should give us the chance, just as you felt that you had to strike down racial segregation altogether in the schools because of the modern advance, the psychological knowledge, then you should take into consideration the psychological and sociological and allow us a period of grace to work on them.

We feel you have faith in your decision that ultimately it will be not only the rule but the accepted practice everywhere. But to ruin the good effect of this decision by abrupt decree is what we respectfully request that you guard against. The Prophet Isaiah said, "He that believeth will not make haste."

In this instance, this great problem before us, we would like to ask the Court that you write a broad decree remanding these cases under your equity power and your power to say that within the framework of reality these rights of the Negro children shall be exercised in such a way that they will not arouse our communities and they will not result in all kinds of trouble in the schools.

If you will allow us the opportunity to work under this decision, not against some deadline, we feel eventually we will bring about full integration.

As one county goes away from segregation, it will be an example to other counties. For that reason, we hope you will not feel that the rule "Do it and do it now," and federal compulsion is the only way. Give the people a chance through the democratic process to change the attitudes of the people in the community. If it does not work, you can change it in a later case and come back to a deadline time table.

Thank you.

THE CHIEF JUSTICE: We thank you for your cooperation and presentation.

Mr. Odum, will you want to say something by way of supplementation?

JUSTICE REED: Mr. Attorney General, could you be a bit more specific as to how time will have an opportunity to bring about acceptance of this?

Do you have in mind gradual integration by the first grade, second, and third grade, or starting at the top and have it the other way?

MR. ERVIN: Yes, all of that would be contemplated, but we do want the school administrator to try to work out the direction of the plan for his school system, sir.

Probably they can start in the first grade, that is a mixed group. Probably it should start at the high school level. But each school attendance area or district should make a showing of good faith to forward some type of plan. If that is done and there were no objection to it, if it were accepted by the Negro people involved, it could go on under that plan.

If it were not accepted and a case were brought then the question would be whether or not in good faith they were making any attempt at all.

I think the Chief Justice had that in mind this morning when he questioned some of the advocates of the gradual program.

We do contemplate any type of plan that would move toward the goal.

JUSTICE REED: As for instance, a choice between two schools in the same district?

MR. ERVIN: I do not know whether that could be done or not. That might be one solution if the interracial committees and the groups working with the school board decided that that was the way to start it, that might be all right. I have not examined that type, Your Honor, but that might be one of the ways.

THE CHIEF JUSTICE: Thank you, General.

THE CHIEF JUSTICE: Mr. Odum.

### ARGUMENT ON BEHALF OF THE STATE OF FLORIDA
### AS A FRIEND OF THE COURT

#### by MR. ODUM

MR. ODUM: Mr. Chief Justice, by way of supplementation of what I am going to say to you, I am aware that after argument of two days most of the subject matters have already been talked about. I do not want to take up the Court's time by way of repetition but I think it may be of interest to the Court to know some of our problems, specific problems in Florida that will have to be faced and overcome before we can comply with the Court's decision. Last May when this Court announced its decision in the Brown case, that news had a considerable impact in Florida. Everyone in Florida, of course, felt that he or she was directly, or would be directly, involved. There were a great many wild statements made and there was considerable discussion of the matter in the newspapers. We were confronted and found that we had two groups of people there.

We had extremists on both sides who were unable or unwilling to see any good in the other fellow's point of view, who were unwilling to reason or to be reasoned with. In between these two extreme groups we have a great many people, both white and Negro, who can give and take, and who are willing to work together and who are willing to try as good citizens to live within the law, at the same time recognizing the position that the other people have and their feelings and trying to work together. I think that position is best expressed as regards this decision by one of our outstanding Negro citizens in Florida. I would like to quote you what Dr. Mary McLeod Bethune had to say.

In a press statement this was announced. As you know, I am sure Mrs. Bethune has spent her life working for the welfare of Negro people. She is the founder and has developed the Bethune-Cookman College in Daytona Beach, Florida.

I do not believe that anyone can question her interest and her sincere devotion to the cause of the Negro people. She had this to say when she heard the news of the Court's decision:

> The High Tribunal has put a legal foundation under a belief many of us have long held and which is clearly and concisely stated in the most basic American ideal. 'All men are created equal.'
> In quietness and patience, people of culture receive this news, realizing the inevitable has at last come about. They also realize, however, that the absorption into our daily life of this new decision—the putting of it into practice—must represent an organic cultural assimilation which, like all social processes, will take time. But eventually, the wrongs and mistakes of history are righted and remedied and inhumanities are rectified . . . Let us enter into this integration calmly, with good judgment. Let us give and take, working out together the best possible means we can put into action so that there may be peace and understanding, and may I say, the spirit of brotherhood.
> There is much for the Negro to do as well as the white. We must use tact and wisdom. It will take conferences, thinking and planning and working side by side. More largely than is realized, we are good, loyal, American citizens. And whether we be north, east, south or west, we shall put forth every effort to meet the requirements of our new status.

JUSTICE REED: Where is that in the brief?

MR. ODUM: Page 43, Your Honor, this statement is included in our brief, our own brief, under the subheading "Reasons for Hope" because we do have reasons for hope in Florida.

All of these reasons for hope based on statements such as these whether they be from Negro leaders or white leaders, are always based on the assumption that there will be time, reasonable time to work out difficulties, because we do have difficulties, and it is foolish to try to ignore or brush aside these difficulties with the assumption that a little pressure from the top can overcome them, that they will crumble away. In the first place, that assumption, because of this, is false. We have to have leadership before any pressure can be exerted. And by that I mean leadership at the local level and the school board officials and the state officials who will be directly or indirectly concerned with trying to carry out the Court's decree and preserve our school system in good order, and the safety and health and welfare of our children and our people.

Our cabinet, our Florida cabinet, which is the governing body there, the Governor and the Attorney General and the Superintendent of Schools, the Commissioner of Agriculture and the State Treasurer and the Comptroller on the day after this decision was announced, tried to decide what was the best thing to do, so they took this decision, and I think this is in answer to the accusation that none of us in the South are doing anything about it, because they lost no time in doing something constructive about it. They said, "Let us find out what problems we have to face, what we have to overcome and what should be done."

The cabinet requested Attorney General Ervin to make a survey of leadership opinion, and that point is important. This was not a straw vote, a straw poll of people on the street as to what they thought. Everybody knew what they thought, practically all the white people were against the plan; practically all the colored people were for it. It would have been a waste of time to make such a survey as that. This survey was a survey of leadership opinion, because we assumed from a very hasty study of what the experience in other states was that without leadership willing and able to carry it out, it could not be carried out. So this survey was a leadership opinion in Florida.

With the help of an advisory committee, an interracial advisory committee consisting of some of the best people that we could find in the state, Negro and white leadership, educators, people who had some specialized knowledge that would help us in making this survey, and with the help of sociologists from the State Universities—we had, to mention a few of this committee, we had three of the outstanding Negro leaders, I feel, in Florida, Dr. Richard Moore who is President of the Bethune-Cookman College, Dr. George Gore, president of the State Negro College at Tallahassee, Florida and Dr. Gilbert Porter, head of the State Negro Teachers Association. They served and worked with this committee. Eight thousand-some-odd, I believe it was, questionnaires were carefully formulated under expert advice and sent out to such people as county school board members, trustees, supervisors, a sampling of teachers both Negro and white, of course, presidents of PTA associations both Negro and white, county judges, peace officers, and many other elected and appointed officials, and practically all officials that we thought would have some direct or indirect bearing or responsibility for carrying out an implementation of this decree. In addition to that, we sent trained interviewers into ten sample counties.

The counties were chosen at a number of spots in the state representing some urban, rural counties, some counties that had a high Negro population, and other counties a low Negro population, trying to get a cross section. In these interviews and in these questionnaires we tried to get at the root of what these leaders and their local community thought.

The results are in the brief. Time does not permit my going into these results but they have been obtained for the information of ourselves and the people of Florida who must try to work this problem out. Now this information presents the problems which they had time to overcome and solve. We do not know when. We maintain that many of these problems cannot be solved. We do feel this and we feel sure of this, that to set a definite date in Florida for compliance, an immediate overall compliance whether it is next year or the following year, would be to the best we can find out, totally impracticable.

There would be no sense to it, because Florida is a peculiar state. It extends for almost a thousand miles from Pensacola down to Miami and Key West, and in between this thousand miles you will find in the sixty-seven counties some really different situations. You will find counties which are populated largely by people who have migrated there from other states, white people who have different customs and traditions.

Then those in the Deep South counties further north. Even that generalization does not always hold true because some of the central and south central counties present some of our greatest problems.

We know of counties in Florida, in one end of the county, problems of integration would be very small because there is a low population of Negroes and most of the people there are people from the north who have no particular objection. At the other end of the county it is just the opposite situation, a heavy concentration of Negro rural workers whose cultural situation reveals a wide gap. Whether we like it or not, it is there and these gaps must be closed.

A decree telling that particular county "You must integrate all of your schools at one time" would make it almost impossible for that county school board to carry that out. We do not believe the Court, in a decision of this kind, has ever intended that our people, white and Negro, shall be made to suffer. We really believe that the Court in its equity power is willing to permit a course down the line.

The federal courts, the district courts, who are close to the situation and who can call before them the parties and examine into the real problems and decide these problems, that that discretion should be given.

We think in line with your questioning—that good faith always should be the answer. It should be the test. And if the district judges are adequate or capable of making a determination like that, they can decide whether or not a plan which is formulated by a local school board is a trumped up thing or whether it is offered in good faith.

Where the Board can come in and show—worrying about the burden of proof—I think it is on the Board of Instruction, but when the Board can come in and say, we have tried and here is what we have done, we have tried to work with the PTA, through parent groups, through teacher groups, we have done our best, but even so, we know that if we admit these children there will be disruption and our school is in confusion and our scholastic standards in that school will fall away; the school will be in danger.

In that case, we think the federal district court should be permitted to take those things into consideration after he is satisfied that there is good faith there, and say, we will listen to your proposal, what to do about it.

And then the school board gives a considered plan and says here is what we will do. If it is reasonable, we think that would justify the time.

How much time, the Court would have to decide at that time under those circumstances.

If it says six months or a year, that would be the time. Then at the end of that time the board would have the responsibility of showing that it had complied or why it had not complied.

The pressure would always be there. And yet, it would not be too much pressure, the kind of pressure that an overall immediate decree would bring which would take away the hope that we have of time for a reasonable adjustment, for reasonable compliance.

We think that the Court has the right to give us those things.

JUSTICE HARLAN: What you are really saying is that there should be a time limit but the time limit should be fixed by the district court?

MR. ODUM: Yes. We do not think that the time limit set for all states or all counties would be practical.

JUSTICE HARLAN: But you agree that a time limit at some level imposed by somebody is an essential part of this machinery?

MR. ODUM: Yes, that each case as it came up before the district court would have to have its own time limit set.

Thank you.

JUSTICE FRANKFURTER: Before you sit down, may I ask you apropos of the results of your survey, your Appendix A which I read with the greatest interest and even found enlightening, did the attorney general give that survey any kind of dissemination among the people in the state, the views set forth and the data?

MR. ODUM: Yes, sir, as I said, the purpose in making that survey was not only to give that information to you but to make it available to us, school leaders in Florida. We really printed 2,500 copies of this book.

JUSTICE FRANKFURTER: Was there any summary of it in the press?

MR. ODUM: Most of the daily newspapers in Florida carried it, one paper quoted it in full.

Two thousand five hundred copies were made available to various school officials in the state with the hope they would be used as a guide.

JUSTICE FRANKFURTER: You mean most of the papers printed your conclusion?

MR. ODUM: Yes, sir, not the whole story, but most of it.

THE CHIEF JUSTICE: Thank you, sir.

We will now hear from the State of North Carolina. Mr. Beverly Lake, Assistant Attorney General.

## ARGUMENT ON BEHALF OF THE STATE OF NORTH CAROLINA
## AS THE FRIEND OF THE COURT

### by MR. I. BEVERLY LAKE

MR. LAKE: May it please the Court, speaking on behalf of myself and the Attorney General of North Carolina, I would like to express my appreciation for the opportunity to participate in the argument of these cases, to which neither our state nor any of our citizens was a party.

In response to the invitation of the court, we are here as a friend of the Court. We have no reason to make North Carolina a party to these cases nor by anything that we may say or do here to commit her or her people to any course of conduct. No decree that is issued under your authority in these cases can reach directly any officer, agency or citizen of North Carolina. But whether or not the children of this state will or will not attend public school after this year and whether or not the people of North Carolina will or will not continue to live side by side in peace and friendliness will depend in a large measure on the decrees about to be issued.

To ignore those facts is simply to shut one's eyes to reality, and if ever there was need to come to grips with reality, that need is present in drafting of these cases.

So for that reason we have come in response to the invitation to direct the Court's attention to the public schools of our state and to the grave concern which the people of North Carolina have felt. They yield to no other Americans in their loyalty to the Constitution or in their respect for this cause. We are not here to re-argue the issue disposed of last May, but the proper discussion of the questions which we have been invited here to discuss requires that we start with the frank recognition of the indisputable fact that in North Carolina—contrary to the condition in Kansas—in North Carolina, there, the overwhelming majority of people regard that decision as a serious blow which they did not expect in view of the circumstances under which their schools are being operated. And the suggestion in the opinion that at this term that decision might be implemented by a decree requiring that Negro children be admitted forthwith to the schools of their choice has hung like a veritable sword of Damocles over the public schools of our state. It comes as a terrific blow and comments of the county, and city school superintendents which are quoted in the Appendix to our brief show that those people who know the North Carolina schools best believe that, if such a decree should fall from this Court upon the schools of our state, it would in all probability be a death blow, and if not, that it would put those schools in turmoil and confusion from which only the enemies of our country could derive satisfaction.

The people of North Carolina recognize that this issue is too great for hasty action. I speak on behalf of a state which is conscious of no wrongdoing in this matter. North Carolina is proud of her record in the field of Negro education. Today North Carolina is, in fact, educating more Negro children than any other state in the Union and she is educating them well. That is not the result of an eleventh hour attempt to avert the decision of last May. It is the result of a century of devotion to the cause of public education. It is the result of sacrifices of four generations made in reliance upon the interpretation placed on the Fourteenth Amendment by the Congress, by the courts of northern as well as southern states and by this Court. It is the result of a public school system in which both white and

Negro North Carolina children have a distinct pride because both white and Negro children have a share in its development. They participate in its benefits.

As I say, in equity, Maitland says we study the day before yesterday in order that yesterday may not paralyze today, and today may not paralyze tomorrow.

THE CHIEF JUSTICE: Very well. We will recess until tomorrow morning.

(At 4:30 p.m. the oral arguments were recessed to be resumed at 12 o'clock noon, Wednesday, April 13, 1955.)

(Oral argument was resumed at 12:00 p.m., April 13, 1955.)

THE CHIEF JUSTICE: Mr. Lake, you may proceed.

### ARGUMENT ON BEHALF OF THE STATE OF NORTH CAROLINA AS THE FRIEND OF THE COURT—Resumed

#### by MR. I. BEVERLY LAKE

MR. LAKE: May it please the Court, immediately after the decision of last May, the late Governor William B. Umstead appointed a special committee of nineteen distinguished men and women from all walks of life and all parts of North Carolina and directed them to study the problems which that decision placed before the people of North Carolina, and report back to him with their recommendation.

On that committee of nineteen was three Negroes. Two of those Negroes were and are presidents of great colleges owned and operated by the State of North Carolina for the education of young Negro men and women.

There are three other such colleges owned and operated by our State, and in those two alone there are today 4,000 students enrolled.

That committee made its report to the Governor after our brief was filed to this Court. It was a unanimous report. The committee said:

The mixing of the races forthwith in the public schools throughout the state cannot be accomplished and should not be attempted.

When the Legislature convened in January for its 1955 session, His Excellency, Governor Luther Hodges, transmitted that report to the Legislature with his unqualified endorsement and approval.

Last week the Legislature, without a dissenting vote, neither the House of Representatives nor the Senate, adopted a resolution approving that report, approving the brief which we have filed with this Court. Since that resolution is a statement, an authoritative statement of the position of North Carolina on this matter and was not available when our brief was filed, Mr. Chief Justice, I request permission to file a copy with the clerk for the Court's information.

THE CHIEF JUSTICE: You may have it.

JUSTICE FRANKFURTER: Will you file a copy for each member of the Court?

MR. LAKE: We will file as many copies as you like.

JUSTICE REED: Does that resolution embody the report you have made?

MR. LAKE: It does not, sir. There are some quotations but I have the report also and will be glad to file that, too.

There is nothing, we think, in the decision of last May which requires a decree that Negro children be admitted forthwith to the schools of their choice within the limit of their normal geographic school district. On the contrary, such a decree would go far beyond that decision and would, in our opinion, we respectfully submit, go beyond the authority of this or any other federal court.

This Court has now held that for a state to separate children in public schools solely on the basis of race reaches an unconstitutional result. So long as that decision remains unmodified, a state may no longer travel that road toward its goal of educated citizenry.

And under existing acts of Congress, it would certainly be within the authority of the federal court to enjoin a state official from attempting to travel that road again. But that is a far cry from a decree requiring that Negro children be admitted forthwith to the schools of their choice.

The federal Constitution does not confer upon the federal government, as a whole, authority to impose upon state officials affirmative duties in the administration of the state's schools, and it certainly does not give that power to the federal courts. Of course, Congress is authorized by the Fourteenth Amendment to enact legislation to enforce the rights guaranteed by that Amendment. But we submit that Congress has no authority to assign children to this or that building owned and operated by the state.

It must be remembered that in North Carolina this is not simply a matter of allowing Negro children to go where they wish. Such a decree would be tantamount to allowing a Negro child to push a white child out of his desk so that the Negro child may sit in it, for there are in none of our schools in North Carolina any substantial number of empty desks.

Therefore, if such a decree should be issued and next fall a substantial number of Negro children were to apply for admission to and be received in what is now a white school, it would necessarily follow that an equal number of white children could not attend that school even if they wanted to do so.

So a decree such as is contemplated by this Court's Question 4(a) would amount to taking the assignment of children to the public schools in North Carolina out of the hands of the school board and placing it in the hands of Negro children. And we respectfully submit that that would be as unconstitutional as it would be impractical.

JUSTICE FRANKFURTER: Is what you have just said just a way of saying that it takes time to make the necessary accommodations to carry out that which has been declared unconstitutional?

MR. LAKE: I think it will take a great deal of time, Mr. Justice Frankfurter.

JUSTICE FRANKFURTER: I am not asking how much. But does it mean any more than that adjustments must be made to prevent the continuance eventually of that which has been declared to be unconstitutional?

MR. LAKE: I think what I have said goes beyond that, but I think that that is also true. What I have said, sir, I think is more fundamental that that, because here I am speaking of the authority of the federal government to impose the duties upon the state officials, affirmative duties.

JUSTICE FRANKFURTER: What adjustment do you make in your analysis between what you have just said and what this Court has done in a number of cases requiring institutions to admit Negro students to law schools and medical schools? The University of North Carolina has admitted both, has it not?

MR. LAKE: The University of North Carolina has admitted Negroes to its law school and to its medical schools, yes, sir.

JUSTICE FRANKFURTER: Apart from a decree of this Court?

MR. LAKE: Apart from the decree of this Court. There was a decree of the circuit court requiring that to be done.

JUSTICE FRANKFURTER: Is such a decree beyond the authority of the Court?

MR. LAKE: I am not familiar with the exact terms of those decrees.

JUSTICE FRANKFURTER: *Sweatt* v. *Painter.*

MR. LAKE: I think, sir, in *Sweatt* v. *Painter,* if I am not mistaken, the Court ordered those Negroes admitted to the schools of the University of Texas because the state did not afford them an equal opportunity for a legal education in another institution.

JUSTICE FRANKFURTER: Whatever the reason, the direction of the Court, the affirmative direction, to admit a certain student in a certain institution, surely that isn't beyond the powers of a court, because of any doctrine of inherent limitation or separation of powers or what not.

MR. LAKE: Well, sir, it is our—

JUSTICE FRANKFURTER: I don't get the force of your argument that there is some suggestion that there is a limitation of the powers of the Court to direct an institution or anybody else to do something if there is a legal duty to do so.

MR. LAKE: No, sir, I agree with that, if there is a legal duty to do it. But our position, sir, is that the states are free to comply with the decision of this Court in several different ways, and the Question 4(a)—

JUSTICE FRANKFURTER: All the different ways, excluding one way, namely, making a distinction on the basis of color.

MR. LAKE: Oh, yes, sir, that would not be complying with the Court's decision. I say the state is free to select its course among the alternative routes which remain, and the Court in Question 4(a), as I understand it, does not state that choice. It says you must, if such a decree would be issued, it says you must allow the Negro child to go to the school of his choice.

JUSTICE FRANKFURTER: Where does 4 (a) say that?

MR. LAKE: Question 4 (a), sir.

JUSTICE FRANKFURTER: In the first place, these are questions, not answers.

MR. LAKE: Oh, yes, yes. I am speaking now to the question that the Court asked us to direct ourselves to. Question 4 (a) says:

> Would a decree necessarily follow providing that within the limits set by normal geographic school districting Negro children should forthwith be admitted to schools of their choice?

Now, as I understand it, counsel for the petitioners yesterday said that they would concede, that they would agree with the position which I now take, that this Court has never said that a state must operate a public school system.

It has never said that if a state does operate a public school system, it cannot separate children on the basis of age, sex, educational attainment, health or any other circumstance having a reasonable relation to education and the general welfare.

The Court has closed the road, as I understand it, of a public school system in which children are separated solely on the basis of race. And certainly this Court can issue a decree forbidding a state from attempting to travel that road again.

But within those alternatives which remain we submit, sir, that a state has the right to choose its alternative.

For example, in the matter of judicial procedure, when a state adopts a court procedure which leads to an unconstitutional result, this Court will throw out that result and require the state to adopt a different procedure. But this Court does not undertake to tell the state what other procedure it must adopt.

It said in *Honeyman* v. *Hanan,* 302 U.S. 375, that:

> The federal Constitution does not undertake to control the power of a state to determine by what process legal rights may be asserted.

And we submit that neither does the federal Constitution undertake to control the power of a state to prescribe by what process and by what criteria children are to be assigned to this or that public school of the state except the state may not use the criteria of race alone.

JUSTICE FRANKFURTER: You mean, for instance, if North Carolina would choose to abolish the public school system in her universities and high schools and follow on the suggestions of some people who think in those terms whereby all education is to be given through a central broadcasting system and every parent in the state is given a broadcasting set or TV set and all education is to be done from the central headquarters into the homes for the educating of the children; you think if the state wants to do that, it could do that. Is that what you mean?

MR. LAKE: I do think that the state would certainly be free to do two of those things. It could abolish the public school system.

JUSTICE FRANKFURTER: It could bring up its children in ignorance if it wanted to.

MR. LAKE: It could do that also. The state could abolish the public school system. It could set up such a TV system, but I do not think it could require the people to allow their children to listen to that alone.

I don't think that it could say that that shall be the only educational system available for the people in our state, no, sir. But with that qualification I think that a state might do so. I am not suggesting that North Carolina contemplates that method.

JUSTICE FRANKFURTER: You mean that it couldn't abolish private and parochial schools?

MR. LAKE: Oh, no; no, sir. Now, the decision of last May—

JUSTICE FRANKFURTER: You would agree under your argument, as you say, that while the Court can merely say this is bad, and day after day or term after term or whatever the period may be, did say this is bad, this is bad, and this is bad, every time it comes up it could do that, you say.

MR. LAKE: Oh, yes, sir.

JUSTICE FRANKFURTER: It couldn't finally say that there is such a pattern here that the only way to deal with this problem and to enforce these rights of constitutional sanctions is that when you have a school system which is for both white and colored people, you can't leave colored people out, the Court can't do that?

MR. LAKE: I would say, sir, that in the silence of Congress, the Court could say that you cannot exclude a child from that school solely on the basis or race, but if a state were to say, "We are going to send the girls to this school"—

JUSTICE FRANKFURTER: That is a very different proposition.

MR. LAKE: Yes, sir, but the Court's Question 4 (a), as I understand it, does not leave room for that. It says schools of their choice. Now, that is the only point to which I direct that remark.

Now, we do not have here for discussion the possibility of an action at law against a state official to deny these petitioners rights which this Court has now said that they have nor the imposition of criminal sanctions against such a state official. Those are possible methods of enforcing their rights.

If they do not apply and if they are deemed inadequate, Congress has authority under the Fourteenth Amendment to enact legislation which will provide an adequate remedy, so this Court's withholding from these petitioners the remedy which they now seek is not a nullification of their constitutional right. It is not a retreat from the decision of last May.

No counsel here has questioned the fact that this Court in the exercise of its equity powers which these petitioners have invoked has the authority to allow these defendants and others similarly situated ample time to find and put into operation an adequate and constitutional substitute for their present method of assigning children to the public schools or an adequate and constitutional substitute for their public school system as a whole.

In the New York-New Jersey case in 283 U.S. 336 this Court allowed the City of New York four years to make proper disposition of its garbage, and it is our position, we respectfully submit, that if the City of New York is entitled to four years to decide what to do with its garbage, the people of these counties in Virginia and South Carolina are entitled to a great deal of time in deciding what to do with our most cherished treasure.

In our brief, since no petitioner has questioned the fact that this flexibility of remedy which is characteristic of courts of equity is applicable here, we shall pass over any further authorities on that subject, because I think there is no debate about that, that this Court does have the power to grant ample time to make the adjustment in the exercise of its equity powers.

But I would like to call the Court's attention simply to this quotation from a letter of Lord Hardwick quoted in Pomeroy as to the reason why courts of equity may adjust their remedies to the circumstances of cases. Lord Hardwick said:

> No rule can be equally just in the application to a whole class of cases that are far from being the same in every circumstance.

So in the exercise of its equity powers this Court may certainly mold its decree to fit the conditions in the communities where those decrees are operating. But we respectfully submit that this Court cannot know and cannot determine those conditions so well as can the district courts which know those communities.

The records now before this Court do not concern themselves with the adequacy or inadequacy of this or that remedy. They were compiled at hearings where the issue was the constitutional right of these petitioners.

Here we are not concerned with that right. We are concerned only with the expediency or inexpediency, the adequacy or inadequacy of this or that remedy, where, whether and if that right is violated.

JUSTICE HARLAN: Could I ask you a question about your committee?

MR. LAKE: Yes, sir.

JUSTICE HARLAN: You said your committee had resolved that immediate desegregation is impracticable.

MR. LAKE: Yes, sir.

JUSTICE HARLAN: Is the committee now *functus officio* or is North Carolina going ahead to try to apply the Court's opinion? In other words, are you going to wait until a suit has been brought and North Carolina is under the impact of judicial process, or is it your contemplation that you will go ahead and try to work it out?

MR. LAKE: That committee has ceased to function, but this resolution which I am going to file with the Court provided for the creation of a permanent committee to continue the study of the problems directly and indirectly arising out of this decision.

Now, sir, as to the other aspect of your question, I cannot say what North

Carolina will do because we have had no pronouncement from the Legislature as to what will be done in the future.

I would like to call to the Court's attention this difficulty which all of the southern states now have before them. Under the Question 4(a) we have the possibility that there may come from this Court a decree—we do not think such a decree will be issued, but there may come from this Court such a decree—as to require forthwith admission of Negro children to the schools of their choice.

Now, under those circumstances, and if I may go back just a minute when that decision came out it was the expectation that we would be here last November for the argument. It was then postponed from day to day.

So for nearly a year the defendants and others similarly situated have been in the position that they did not know when a decree might come down requiring a certain action.

Now if I may by some analogy say this. A man who knows that there is a possibility that he may be executed in twenty-four hours is not in a good position to consider plans for remodeling his home. So I do not think that the facts that North Carolina has not come up with an answer to this problem should be regarded as an answer to our suggestions that we must have time.

We have not yet had that time. Now, I want to be completely frank, Mr. Justice Harlan. I do not know, of course, what the future will bring. But so far as I know now, I would say that the chance of North Carolina in the near future will mingle white and Negro children in her public schools throughout the state is exceedingly remote. That is the reason that I have the gravest fear that such a decree would result in the abolition of our public school system.

JUSTICE FRANKFURTER: May I ask you whether I am right in assuming that North Carolina, the school system of North Carolina is not centrally administered?

MR. LAKE: North Carolina, sir, has a State Board of Education, and of course that State Board of Education has general supervision of all the schools.

JUSTICE FRANKFURTER: Meaning by that there are legislatively laid down certain standards for educational administration?

MR. LAKE: Yes, sir, we have a general school law.

JUSTICE FRANKFURTER: But the financing, the appropriation, is that statewide?

MR. LAKE: The school system is a statewide school system in that respect. North Carolina operates its schools with state funds.

JUSTICE FRANKFURTER: Exclusively?

MR. LAKE: No. I believe the ratio is about 65 per cent state and 35 per cent local.

JUSTICE FRANKFURTER: That leads me to my next question.

MR. LAKE: Yes.

JUSTICE FRANKFURTER: Is there variety among the different counties, are there disparities and variations in the facilities, educational standards, et cetera, et cetera, et cetera?

MR. LAKE: Well, of course, sir, there are varieties in the size of the school buildings and so forth and so on. Our school buildings—if I may try to explain our system, it is this: Our school buildings are the county responsibility. The county owns all buildings and supplies the school buildings.

JUSTICE FRANKFURTER: Do they have to act according to the requirements of the State Board? In other words, the size of the schoolrooms, the number of pupils in a schoolroom, et cetera, et cetera, are important factors in the quality of education.

MR. LAKE: Yes, sir.

JUSTICE FRANKFURTER: Who determines that?

MR. LAKE: I believe sir, the County Board of Education. I am not positive of that, but I know of no power in the State Board to control it.

JUSTICE FRANKFURTER: So you may have varying conditions in the different counties?

MR. LAKE: We do.

JUSTICE FRANKFURTER: I notice the gamut of white and Negro children from the different counties runs from 1.5 to 62.57, from one point of a per cent to roughly 64 per cent.

MR. LAKE: Yes, sir.

JUSTICE FRANKFURTER: Is that reflected in differences of educational enjoyments, would you say? Does that mean that different accommodations would have to be made in different counties?

MR. LAKE: If I understand you, sir, yes, I think clearly that it would. We have a very complex system in North Carolina, sir. It grew up over this hundred years, you see.

Now, we began, of course, with local schools—local school districts. As the years have gone by, we have drawn certain powers from those local bodies to the state.

For example, certification of teachers is a matter of state authority. The selection of the curriculum, Justice Frankfurter, is entirely state.

Now, every child in North Carolina except insofar as local tax supplement to provide additional benefit for every child in their district, white and Negro alike, every child in North Carolina, regardless of race, residence, economic or social status, studies the same subjects, he goes to school the same number of days as the other children. That has been true for more than ten years. The length of the school term—

JUSTICE FRANKFURTER: Is school attendance equally enforced?

MR. LAKE: Yes, sir; yes, sir. There is no distinction in that respect. He goes to school the same number of days, he uses the same textbooks, and the state supplies the textbooks, so every child in North Carolina, white or Negro, has the books.

The Negro children, I may say, have certain advantages. Every teacher in North Carolina, having the same training, the same experience, teaching the same subjects, receives the same pay. Because of conditions outside the schools, that makes the teaching profession more attractive to Negroes than to white people.

Consequently there is a tendency—of course, there are exceptions—there is a tendency for the Negro teachers to remain in the profession longer than the white teachers.

The result is, since they get salary increments based upon experience, the average Negro teacher in North Carolina today receives more salary than the average white teacher, and that has been true for a whole school generation, for ten years.

The same circumstance, I believe, accounts for the fact that the average Negro teacher in North Carolina has had more years of college and university than the average white teacher.

And we have at this moment 288,000 Negro children sitting in the school-rooms of North Carolina. They are studying the same subjects, using the same textbooks, going to school the same number of days, to teachers better paid, more experienced, with more time in college and universities than our white children have.

Those Negro teachers should have a moment of our consideration here, I think. North Carolina employs more Negro teachers than any other state in the Union, and I am told more than all of the nonsegregated states combined. Hundreds of our Negro teachers have been trained in colleges and universities in the northern states. They have come to us because there was no room for them in the nonsegregated school system of the states where they were educated.

Now, we respectfully submit that those Negro teachers should be given consideration in this matter.

The comments of the county and city school superintendents quoted in the appendix to our brief shows that of 165 superintendents, only three believe that it would be possible to use Negro teachers in mixed schools in North Carolina. Now, if they are right, and as I said yesterday, those are the men who know more about this North Carolina public schools than any other people anywhere, if they are right, the jobs of 8,500 Negro teachers are hanging in the balance in North Carolina alone, awaiting the final decree of this Court.

We have called to the Court's attention in our brief certain major differences between North Carolina and other states in this respect, in this matter.

JUSTICE REED: Mr. Lake, before you proceed, are you familiar with the parochial school system in North Carolina?

MR. LAKE: I would say, sir, we have a very limited parochial school system in North Carolina, if I understand you. I assume you mean the Catholic school system.

JUSTICE REED: Yes, sir.

MR. LAKE: We have very few Catholics in North Carolina. There are some parochial schools. I am not familiar with it.

JUSTICE REED: Do you know whether they have integrated the classes in their schools?

MR. LAKE: I do not know, generally, but I am inclined to think they have. I know that there has been some such attempt—I won't say attempt—they have done so in the schools in and near Raleigh. Whether that is true all over the state I just don't know, but I suspect it has been true.

JUSTICE REED: Do you know how that was done?

MR. LAKE: By decree of the Bishop, as I understand, and again I am speaking—

JUSTICE REED: Did you discuss that question in your brief?

MR. LAKE: No, sir.
That, Mr. Justice Reed, is, in our opinion—I won't say in our opinion—it simply didn't occur to me before, because, as I say, the parochial schools in North Carolina are negligible in numbers.
Our state simply does not have many Catholic citizens in it. And so we do not have many parochial schools. Most of the Catholic children we have go, I believe, to the public schools, but there again, I am speaking only on the basis of belief.

JUSTICE REED: Do you have any other church schools?

MR. LAKE: Not many. The Baptist Church, and I believe it is true of the Methodists—I speak of the Baptists because I happen to know them—the Baptist Church formerly operated a number of academies in North Carolina. Some of these grew into what are now junior colleges. Other were abandoned when the state school system became much more effective.
Now, sir, if I may go on to those differences, because my time is running on. The problem created by this decisions is not the same in cities as in rural areas. In cities, North and South—and, Mr. Chief Justice, I don't know Baltimore and St. Louis, but I believe that would be true of Baltimore and St. Louis—in cities, North and South, the problem, by virtue of normal geographic school districting, obtains about the same proportion that it does in those states where a very small number of Negroes are mixed with a large white population. But normal geographic school districting is no help in the rural areas. North Carolina has the same differences when one part of the state is contrasted with another.
For example, Mitchell County in the western part of the state, with 49 Negroes and 15,000 white people, has a far different problem from that which confronts the people of Northampton County, in the eastern part of the state, where there are 71 Negro school children for every 29 white school children, or Anson County, where the population—in the central part of the state—is almost equally divided between white and Negro, where they are 50-50, approximately.

JUSTICE REED: Do you have a law in North Carolina that forbids whites and blacks to go to school together?

MR. LAKE: Yes, sir. That is in our state constitution. It is also in the statute.

I may say, sir, that that has been true since 1868. The law was enacted by the same legislature about the time of the Fourteenth Amendment.

JUSTICE REED: It covers only the grade schools?

MR. LAKE: It covers all schools.

JUSTICE REED: Your universities?

MR. LAKE: No, sir, I did not mean the universities. I had reference to high school and elementary. It covers all.

JUSTICE REED: It is worded to cover only the elementary schools?

MR. LAKE: All public schools, I believe, Justice Reed. The University of North Carolina is not mentioned in it. But, of course, until the Negro was admitted to the law school some four or five years ago, it was entirely possible.

JUSTICE REED: My interest is whether the law covered the state universities.

MR. LAKE: It does not, I am sure; I would have to look at the charter.

JUSTICE REED: You have no permissive authority to school boards in counties such as you speak of, where there is a small percentage of Negroes, to unify the school system?

MR. LAKE: Well, I hardly know how to answer that, sir, for this reason—

JUSTICE REED: I am asking because in my own state we have that permissive authority above high school.

MR. LAKE: Yes, sir.

Not specifically, but this is what we have had, and I offer this to refute the suggestion that the southern states are doing nothing and would do nothing, with additional time.

This legislature also passed a bill, and it is now the law, that each county or city administrative board is the sole authority in the assignment of children to the schools of that area. Now, because I drafted that bill, the legislature, when it was in session, asked me did that mean that a county, if it saw fit to do so, could admit Negro children to white schools. I told them that it certainly did mean that. The legislature passed that bill.

JUSTICE REED: So now you do have a law which would permit the integration of schools where the local board wanted it?

MR. LAKE: They also asked me this question, Mr. Justice Reed: "Does the decision of last May invalidate our constitutional provision?" And I told them that in my opinion the decision of last May did not technically invalidate our state constitution because North Carolina was not a party to those cases, but that in my opinion, as a lawyer, that precedent would make it obligatory upon a court to hold that those laws no longer had application.

I believe I have just about five more minutes.

THE CHIEF JUSTICE: You have a little more time than that. You have about ten minutes, I believe.

MR. LAKE: Thank you.

North Carolina differs from northern and border states in this important circumstance. In North Carolina we have no large metropolitan areas. We have no large sub-racial groups, such as is to be found, I believe, in all large metropolitan areas. Consequently, everybody in North Carolina, practically everybody in North Carolina, is either Anglo-Saxon or Negro. As a result of that, we have more consciousness of race in North Carolina than is to be found in some of the border and northern states.

That race consciousness is not race prejudice. It is not race hatred. It is not intolerance. It is a deeply ingrained awareness of a birthright held in trust for posterity.

There have been in every group, and are individuals, who, despising their birthright, have been faithless to that trust. So it has been and so it is in North Carolina.

But the majority of North Carolinians have been taught from infancy, and they understand, how it came about that Isreal became a great nation, while Edom faded into oblivion, and they agree with the great Disraeli, who said: "No man will treat with indifference the principle of race, for it is the key to history. The Negroes of North Carolina know the difference between race pride and race hatred. Every day there is in North Carolina a demonstration of the truth that two races, as fundamentally different as the Anglo-Saxon and the Negro can live side by side in freedom, security, peace, friendship, mutual helpfulness.

If our State Department will only use that demonstration of democracy in action in North Carolina, it will be a more effective answer to communism at home and abroad than would a decree of this Court which proclaims equality but destroys the public schools.

I do not know what decree should finally be entered in Prince Edward County, in Clarendon County, because I don't know the conditions in those counties. But I do know this:

I know that if a decree should be entered by this Court, or any other court, requiring the immediate intermixing of white and Negro children in the public schools of North Carolina, those schools will be in the gravest danger of abolition.

And the friendliness and peace which now characterizes the relation of white and Negro North Carolinians would be supplanted by racial tensions and bitterness and antipathies unparalleled in our state since those terrible days which called forth the original Ku Klux Klan.

If that statement be deemed an exaggeration, I invite the Court's attention again to the comments in our brief by county and city school superintendents, sheriffs and chiefs of police. A public school system does violence to the earnestly held conviction of that community, has always been and always will be a school system of inadequate equipment, shoddy instruction, and irregular attendance.

The people of North Carolina are convinced that a segregated school system is a just school system, and the only practical school system for their state.

That is not an opinion which originated on some tobacco road. That is an opinion which is justified by a century of experience, which has demonstrated the wisdom of this agreement reached a hundred years ago by the carpetbaggers, the scalawags, the Negroes, and the handful of Confederate veterans who comprised the legislature which adopted the Fourteenth Amendment in the name of North Carolina.

Mr. Chief Justice, the Attorney General of North Carolina is the attorney for all the people of our state. We have come here conscious of the sacred duty which we owe to the Negroes of North Carolina as well as to the white people. We have discharged that duty.

The people of North Carolina want to go on educating those 288,000 Negro children and their children's children, as well as the white people of the state, and we respectfully ask this Court not to make it impossible for them to do so.

THE CHIEF JUSTICE: Thank you, Mr. Lake. I know the Court will thank you for presenting your views.

Attorney General Thomas J. Gentry of Arkansas.

### ARGUMENT ON BEHALF OF THE STATE OF ARKANSAS, AS THE FRIEND OF THE COURT

#### by MR. THOMAS J. GENTRY

MR. GENTRY: Mr. Chief Justice.

THE CHIEF JUSTICE: Mr. Attorney General.

MR. GENTRY: May it please the Court, at the very outset of my oral argument, I should like to repeat for the purposes of emphasis what was said on page 3 of our written *amicus curiae* brief, filed in behalf of the State of Arkansas in these cases.

We there stated that nothing contained in our brief is intended to bring into question the directness of the May 17 ruling of this Court or its reasons for reaching that conclusion.

As we now view these cases, it is wholly immaterial whether the decision was right or wrong, advised or ill advised, or timely or untimely. It is now accepted as the law in Arkansas that in the field of public education the doctrine of separate but equal has no place, as was specifically held by this Court in its decision of May 17.

As a leader of this Court, I feel it is appropriate for me as the duly elected Attorney General of Arkansas to preface my argument with an explanatory statement as to the reasons for my presence before this Court today, and the reasons which prompted me to file a brief in these cases.

I am not here in obedience to any specific mandate or command from the General Assembly of Arkansas or from any branch of the Executive Department of my state. I am not here because of any political pressure, or pressure of any economic group or any propaganda of any kind.

But I am here because I honestly and sincerely conceive it to be my sworn duty to present to this Court the views of what I believe to be a majority of all of the people of Arkansas on the complex problem which affects substantially all the people of Arkansas in their daily walks of life.

Secondly, I am here because of what I have construed to be the sincere and earnest invitation, if not actual solicitation, of this Court extended to all the Attorneys General of the so-called segregated states.

Without intending any adverse criticism of the Attorneys General of several segregated states who have not seen fit to appear in these cases, yet it is my personal view that I would be derelict in my obligation as a member of the bar of this honorable Court to completely ignore what I choose to consider as an invitation from this Court, an invitation this Court was under no obligation or duty to extend and one which, as I believe, is very rarely extended.

May it please the Court, what is the up-to-date situation upon this matter in the State of Arkansas? In our written brief, on page 2, we set out fully the policy statement issued by the State Board of Education, which was issued on June the 14th, 1954, which was about a month after the decision of May 17 which was handed down by this Court.

It is not necessary to repeat that statement at this time. Suffice to say that up to the present time the statement of June 14, 1954 by our State Board has not been reversed or modified in any respect.

It is also pointed out on page 6 of our brief that two Arkansas school districts have already integrated the white and Negro children in the public schools, the integration being total as to one of these districts and only partial at the high school level in the other district.

We were advised by the State Board of Education just before we left Little Rock that there had been no other inauguration of any form of desegregation in this state by any of the school districts.

JUSTICE REED:  Did you have a law in Arkansas forbidding integration?

MR. GENTRY:  We have had such a state statute, Mr. Justice Reed, since 1868, prohibiting integration of the races from the first through the twelfth grades.

JUSTICE REED:  And was that repealed?

MR. GENTRY:  No, sir, that has not been repealed.

JUSTICE REED:  These school districts acted, then, under the belief that that was no longer a valid law?

MR. GENTRY:  They acted under the belief that by the doctrine of *stare decisis* that in the event that the action should have been taken against them for violation of the state law, that it would have been thrown out by our Supreme Court.

And, as a matter of fact, as the Attorney General of the state, I assume the prosecution in the Supreme Court, not in the lower courts, of all criminal cases, and frankly, Your Honor, I would have confessed error before our Supreme Court if there had been any conviction for violation of this statute.

JUSTICE REED: Does your office give advisory opinion to the school boards?

MR. GENTRY: Yes, sir; we do.

JUSTICE REED: You did not issue any opinion?

MR. GENTRY: No, sir. These two school boards did it on their own volition without consulting my office, without consulting the State Board, which, of couse, only has advisory authority, at any rate.

But as you will notice by the policy statement, that was somewhat against the policy even of the State Board which thought perhaps it would be best to wait and see.

There are some 422 separate autonomous school districts in the State of Arkansas, and the school board, the directors of the school, the school board in each district, is elected by the citizens of that district.

By the same token, these school directors on the school board, they propose what tax they think it will take to operate the schools for the succeeding year, and the millage based upon the property tax, of course, is placed upon the ballot, and the people in each school district vote upon whether or not they want that tax for the succeeding year.

There are actually 422 elections, different millages in each of the 422 districts. The taxes which are levied by the school districts are the principal source of revenue for the operation of the school districts, the 422 school districts in the State of Arkansas.

However, the legislature does appropriate supplemental funds to carry on the public school functions of the State of Arkansas, and these funds are distributed to the various and sundry school districts on the basis of enrollment in each district.

JUSTICE FRANKFURTER: Mr. Attorney General, may I trouble you, in view of your reference to the two districts in which integration has been successfully carried out, in view of your statement in your brief:

From a comparison of the factual situations of the Charleston and Fayetteville school districts with, for example, districts in St. Francis and Phillips Counties, it would certainly seem to follow as a matter of necessity that the process of integration must be applied as the circumstances in each district may require . . .

May I trouble you to sketch briefly the difference and make a comparison such as you indicated, which you know, and I do not.

MR. GENTRY: Yes, sir, I will be happy to.

The Fayetteville School District, Mr. Justice Frankfurter, is located in Washington County, Arkansas, and that happens to be where the State University is located. In that district there are approximately sixty-eight Negro students from the first to the twelfth grade. There was no Negro high school in that district.

Under the law as prevailed under the "separate but equal" doctrine, the eleven or twelve or ten, or whatever the number of Negro children who graduated into the high school level was, they were sent by trucks from Fayetteville to Fort Smith where there was a Negro high school, in order that they may obtain an education, some fifty or sixty miles, and arrangements were made to educate these people there.

Now when this decision was handed down, the eleven or twelve in the high school there, which was partially integrated in Washington County, they were placed right in with the five hundred or so high school students, the white high school students there in Fayetteville.

Now, the other district, the Charleston District is in Franklin County, Arkansas, which is one of the sparsely populated counties, and there were only a few Negro pupils there, and, of course, there was no particular problem. It was, as a matter of fact, less of a problem to integrate them than it was to keep them separated, and as a result in that situation they were immediately placed. That was the situation in those two instances.

I might say, Mr. Justice Frankfurter, that that has had a very quieting effect in Arkansas. It has been watched with a great deal of pleasure by a lot of people, and the outcome of it is being watched very closely by the other districts, but there have been no untoward incidences and it has worked very well so far.

Now, the other counties which you referred to, St. Francis and Williams—

JUSTICE FRANKFURTER: Phillips.

MR. GENTRY: St. Francis and Phillips. Phillips County is over in eastern Arkansas on the Mississippi River. St. Francis County is about halfway between Little Rock and Memphis on the St. Francis River.

Both of them are agricultural cotton communities and about the same situation exists in those two counties in all five districts, in each one of the two counties which, as I say, has been described by other attorneys who have argued before—

JUSTICE FRANKFURTER: You mean like Clarendon County?

MR. GENTRY: Yes, sir, maybe not the same percentage-wise, but the percentages, I believe, are in the appendix of the brief, Your Honor.

JUSTICE FRANKFURTER: But the crucial thing is the saturation, the large percentage of Negro population compared with the white. A lot of consequences follow from that, I understand.

MR. GENTRY: Yes, sir, but where they are located and the part of the county, and the rural counties getting the children to and from their homes to a school, bus transportation over roads in some of the rural counties in Arkansas presents a problem which certainly the school board directors of Washington, D.C., couldn't appreciate.

In our written brief which was dated November 15, we stated on page 3 that the General Assembly of Arkansas had not been in session since the rendition of the opinion of May 17.

We said in our brief on page 3 that:

> Without anticipating what action, if any, the General Assembly of Arkansas will take in its 1955 session—

And the 1955 session convened on January 10th of this year and adjourned sine die on March 10th of this year—

> it is probably safe to say at this time that some further words of advice and direction from this Court will go a long way toward charting the course of future action or inaction by the Arkansas General Assembly.

For reasons not material now, those solicited words of advice and direction from this Court were not forthcoming prior to the adjournment of the Legislature on March 10, 1955. So it may be said now that the Arkansas General Assembly is still anxiously awaiting the final words of this Court.

JUSTICE REED: When does it meet again?

MR. GENTRY: In 1957 in January. Every two years, Your Honor, on the odd number of years in January, I believe it is the second Monday after the first Tuesday.

It may be of passing interest, however, to mention that the House of Representatives passed a bill or an act to be entitled, "An Act to regulate the assignment and transfer of school children to and from the various schools within the separate school districts and for other purposes."

Now, the first section of this bill expressly provides, among other things:

Nor shall anything in this Act be construed as depriving any child of school age of the right to a free public school education as now provided by the Constitution and laws of the United States and the constitution and laws of the State of Arkansas.

Now, this bill provided that the effective date of this Act should be July 15, 1955. But the Senate amended this Act to make the effective date of the Act July 15, 1957. And the sponsors of the Act, in their wisdom, failed, after this amendment to the Act was adopted, to postpone the effective date of it, did not call the Act up for final passage in the Senate, realizing, I am sure that in view of the amendment, it would be advantageous to await further the final decision of this Court.

Thus the legislative history of the bill indicates very strongly that the Arkansas Senate still wants the advice of this Court before taking any definite action on the problem of integration of the races in the public schools.

And let me add parenthetically that I was not the draftsman of this bill, neither was I called upon officially or unofficially to rule upon its constitutionality. Thus is the situation in Arkansas upon this matter today.

JUSTICE CLARK: Mr. Gentry, I wonder would you tell me what county Little Rock is in?

MR. GENTRY: Pulaski County. That joins Bowie County in Texas.

There seems to me to be somewhat of a confusion in the arguments presented to this Court as to the rights of these appellants and the remedies these appellants seek.

Now, the appellants in their brief contended most earnestly that:

Where a substantial constitutional right would be impaired by delay, this Court has refused to postpone the injunctive relief even in the face of the gravest of public considerations suggested as justification therefor.

Appellants contend therefore that appellents' constitutional rights should be effectuated by decrees of this Court forthwith, forthwith ordering the abolition of segregation in the public schools. And as a starter for their contention, they cite the Youngstown case and the Endo case.

First in the Youngstown case, that was a case where the owner of a steel mill sought an injunction in the lower court, in the district court, where the injunction was sustained by the court of appeals, and this Court agreed with the lower court.

In the Youngstown case, this Court decided two points. First, that it was unnecessary to await the final order of the district court before passing on the validity of the executive order and, secondly, that the seizure order was not within the constitutional power of the President.

Now it is very significant in this case to note that the proceedings in the Youngstown case were instituted by the owner of the mills to preserve the status quo.

Therefore, by the very nature of this case, there was no need for this Court, acting under its apparent equity powers, to give any consideration to the necessity for a period of adjustment by reason of a change in the status quo. The injunction was granted.

On the other hand, let it be supposed that the presidential order had been authorized by Congress, and that this Court had held that the order was valid. Well, in that event there would have been brought about a complete change in the status quo, and this Court might very well, upon a sufficient showing by the owners, have exercised its equitable discretion and granted a reasonable time to make the adjustments brought about by the change in the possession.

So in the instant cases this Court, by its May 17 decision, has ordered a complete change in the status quo. This Court, by its May 17 decision, established the constitutional right of these appellants to attend integrated public schools. Therefore there is not now a question of right of these appellants before this Court.

This Court is not now concerned about rights. Its exclusive concern at this time is about equitable remedies.

Now, Mr. Pomeroy in his *Equity Jurisprudence,* points up this distinction.

The primary right of the complaining party—

the appellants in this case—

which has been broken may be purely legal, that is, the right which the law confers, while his remedial right and the remedy which he obtains may be entirle equitable, recognized and given by equity alone.

Mr. Pomeroy continues:

The distinguishing characteristics of legal remedies are their uniformity . . . their lack of an adaptation to circumstances and the technical rules which govern their use. There is in fact no limit to the variety and application. The court of equity has the power of devising its remedies and shaping it so as to fit the changing circumstances of every case and the complex relations of all the parties.

To the same effect are the decisions of this Court in *Hecht v. Bowles*[16] and

---

[16]Hecht Co. v. Bowles 321 U.S. 321 (1944). Although the Hecht Company was found to have violated the Emergency Price Control Act, the District Court refused to issue an injunction against it. The Supreme Court upheld the broad power of a lower court to mold a flexible decree in any case brought before it.

*International Salt Company* v. *United States,* which we cite on page 10 of our brief. The appellants in these cases have chosen to exercise equitable remedy.

Having appealed to equity jurisprudence, this Court may, if it sees proper to do so in the circumstances, devise the relief granted to fit the complex relationship of the parties. This Court clearly recognized in its May 17 opinion that the public interest is involved in these cases.

In the *Virginia Railroad* v. *Federation,* 300 U.S. [515, 552], the Court stated:

Courts of equity may, and frequently do, go much farther both to give and withhold relief in furtherance of the public interest than they are accustomed to go when only private interests are involved.

Remembering that this Court is now concerned about equitable remedies rather than constitutional right, we have asked this Court to bear in mind the language of Mr. Justice Holmes in *K.T. Railroad,* 194 U.S.[267,270][17] where he stated:

Great constitutional provisions must be administered with caution.

This Court has held in its May 17 decision that the complex problem which would be created by the granting of appellants' prayer for injunction would play no part in determining the rights of the appellants.

As stated by Mr. Justice Frankfurter, concurring in the Youngstown case:

'Balancing the equities' when considering whether an injunction should issue, is lawyers' jargon for choosing between conflicting public interests. When Congress itself has struck the balance, has defined the weight to be given the competing interests, a court of equity is not justified in ignoring that pronouncement under the guise of exercising equitable discretion. [343 U.S. at 609–610]

We interpret Mr. Justice Frankfurter's language, he is making the very point we insist distinguishes the holding of May 17 from the decision in the Youngstown case.

It is stated that the Court does not balance interest in determining whether the injunction should issue. Here the Court has already decided that the injunction shall issue.

The Court is now deciding how to administer the constitutional provision in the light of the Court's well recognized power to make nice adjustments and reconciliation between public interest and private need to use Mr. Justice Douglas's language in *Hecht* v. *Bowles.* At page 12 of their brief appellants say in reference to the Youngstown case:

If equity could not appropriately exercise its broad discretion to withhold the immediate grant of relief in the Youngstown case, such a postponement must certainly be inappropriate in these cases where no comparable overriding consideration can be suggested.

As I have pointed out, neither the Court in the Youngstown case nor in the concurring opinion engaged in any discussion as to the propriety of withholding

[17]Missouri, Kansas and Texas Ry. Co. v. May, 194 U.S. 267 (1904). The Court upheld a Texas law directed against railroad companies that allowed Johnson grass to mature and grow to seed upon its road.

immediate injunctive refief. The sole question there presented and decided was the right to the issuance of an injunction.

We submit, therefore, that the Youngstown case falls far short of what the appellants claim that it says.

Further, Mr. Justice Frankfurter in his concurring opinion in the Youngstown case stated:

> A court of equity ought not to issue an injunction even though the plaintiff otherwise makes out a case for it, if the plaintiff's right to an injunction is overborne by a commanding public interest against it. [343 U.S. at 596]

Also it is my contention that in the Endo case there is no support for appellants' contention. The Endo case arose under a petition for a writ of habeas corpus, and finally reached this Court where the writ was granted, and it was assumed by this Court that the original evacuation of all the Japanese from the Sacramento area was authorized as a matter of military authority based upon the existing war emergency.

But it was held that the detention of the petitioner, who was conceded to be a loyal citizen of the United States by the War Relocation Authority, a civilian agency, on the basis of race was in violation of the Fifth Amendment.

In that case there was no appeal to the equitable discretion of this Court in that proceeding because it was based upon a petition for a writ of habeas corpus. The Government there urged that this Court sustain the authority of the War Relocation Authority on the basis of the pending war emergency.

In other words, this Court was asking a balanced interest in deciding whether the petitioner was being unlawfully deprived of her right of liberty under the Constitution. This Court refused to permit the existing emergency to carry any weight when applied, as Mr. Justice Douglas said, to the sensitive area of rights specifically guaranteed by the Constitution.

The Court in passing on petitioner's rights under the Constitution decided that she had the right to her liberty. This Court in its May 17 decision balanced the interests and considered the national emergency in handing down its May 17 decision, and having done so, the Court finally and completely adjudicated the right of these appellants to attend integrated schools.

The question now before the Court in these cases was not and could not have been before the Court in the Endo case because the question of granting habeas corpus, as in the Endo case, was not based upon the equitable remedy of injunction. Here the exact reverse is true.

Now the appellants do contend in their brief that the antitrust cases and the nuisance cases relied upon by the appellees in their briefs are not in point because they did not involve the enforcement of constitutional rights.

We agree that these cases have no bearing upon the rights of appellants to an injunction.

Even if they did, they would be out of place in this hearing because the question of rights was decided by this Court in its decision of May 17.

On the other hand, all of those cases and many others of similar import are authority for our contention that this Court is not required to enter forthwith decrees in these cases as the appellants seem to contend.

May it please the Court, why is gradual integration necessary? We do not consider it necessary or even appropriate in this oral argument.

To repeat our several contentions as set forth in our brief, we are content simply to say that this Court should enter such decrees as will permit these cases and other similar cases which may hereafter arise to be determined on the basis of the particular facts then shown to exist, recognizing, of course, in all cases that the rights as distinguished from remedies have been adjudicated.

In determining the extent of the exercise of its discretion, this Court will recall that in discussing the First Amendment in *Cantwell* v. *Connecticut,* 310 U.S., it said:

> Thus the Amendment embraces two concepts, freedom to believe and freedom to act. The first is absolute but, in the nature of things, the second cannot be. Conduct remains subject to regulation for the protection of society.[18]

Chief Justice Marshall in *Von Hoffman* v. *City of Quincy,*[19] stated:

> Without impairing the obligation of the contract, the remedy may certainly be modified as the wisdom of the nation may direct.

And further Mr. Chief Justice Hughes, speaking in *Home Building & Loan Association* v. *Blaisdell,* 290 U.S. stated:

> But it does not follow that conditions may not arise in which a temporary restraint of enforcement may be consistent with the spirit and purpose of the constitutional provision and thus be found to be within the range of the reserved power of the State to protect the vital interests of the community. [290 U.S. at 439]

In *Interstate Consolidated Railway* v. *Massachusetts,*[20] speaking only for himself, Mr. Justice Holmes stated that it was his personal opinion that:

> constitutional rights like all others are matters of degree and that the great constitutional provisions for the protection of property are not to be pushed to a logical extreme, but must be taken to permit the infliction of some fractional and relatively small losses of compensation, for some at least of the purposes of wholesome legislation.

Further, Justice Holmes stated:

> If the Fourteenth Amendment is not to be a greater hamper upon the established practices of the States in common with other governments than I think was intended, they must be allowed a certain latitude in the minor adjustments of life, even though by their action the burdens of a part of the community are somewhat increased. The

[18]310 U.S. 296, 303–04 (1940). The Court struck down the conviction of three Jehovah's Witnesses who tried to sell religious literature from door to door in New Haven, Connecticut without securing a required permit.

[19]Van Hoffman v. City of Quincy, 4 Wall. 535 (1867). Justice Noah Swayne and not Chief Justice John Marshall (who died in 1835) wrote the opinion in this case. The quote comes from the decision of Marshall in Sturges v. Crowninshield, 4 Wheat, 122, 200 (1819) which is cited in the Van Hoffman opinion. The Court did not allow Quincy to repeal a law providing for certain taxes to be levied to meet interest payments on municipal bonds.

[20]Interstate Consolidated Railway v. Massachusetts, 207 U.S. 79, 86–87 (1907). A Massachusetts law requiring railways to transport children at half-fare was upheld.

traditions and habits of centuries were not intended to be overthrown when that amendment was passed.

Further, in *Block* v. *Hirsch*.[21]

A limit in time, to tide over a passing trouble, well may justify a law that could not be upheld as a permanent change.

So when this Court comes to decide the terms of the decrees in these cases, I respectfully urge this Court to remember Mr. Justice Holmes' admonition that traditions and habits of centuries were not intended to be overthrown when the Fourteenth Amendment was adopted, and that the decrees should be so framed as to tide over a passing trouble.

JUSTICE FRANKFURTER: What case is that from?

MR. GENTRY: *Block* v. *Hirsch,* 256 U. S. 135.

JUSTICE FRANKFURTER: Did that case turn on the kind of decree entered?

MR. GENTRY: No, sir.

JUSTICE FRANKFURTER: Not as I remember it. That was the constitutionality of the Rent Control Act.

MR. GENTRY: Yes, sir.

JUSTICE FRANKFURTER: But what you read doesn't refer to the decree, does it? Would you mind reading that again?

MR. GENTRY: "A limit in time to tide over a passing trouble may well justify a law that could not be upheld as a permanent change."

JUSTICE FRANKFURTER: You said something about a decree.

MR. GENTRY: I don't believe I did, sir, in the quotation.

JUSTICE FRANKFURTER: That was your comment?

MR. GENTRY: Yes, sir, that was.

In this litigation one side has said that what we need is an immediate and forthwith decree which will take effect in September, 1955, or not later than 1956. Then other statements have been made on the other side that this matter not be accomplished until 2045.

My guess in these cases is that the date would be somewhere in between, as is in most cases, the position taken by opposing sides and opposing lawyers.

I don't know the exact date. I don't think it is possible to determine an exact date. I think that any guess or any statement of an exact date would be purely a guess.

[21]Block v. Hirsch, 256 U.S. 135, 157 (1921). A Washington, D.C. emergency law permitting rent control and hold-overs by tenants was upheld.

But why guess upon a question which is as important as this, when it is not necessary.

Now, it seems to be logical we should charge the court of first instance with the responsibility of carrying out the mandate of this Court and placing the mandate of this Court into effect, and secondly, to give the court of first instance, along with the responsibility, the authority to do what is best under the circumstances in carrying out the mandate of this Court.

There are 422 separate instances in Arkansas. How many in other segregated states, I have no idea. But it would appear that by far the most logical thing to do would be to place the responsibility upon the court of first resort and give that court the authority to carry out the duties placed upon it by this responsibility, and not hamper him or the court, lower court, in any respect.

It must always be remembered that if there is any abuse of discretion, these people have their right of appeal to this Court, and certainly almost every week we have some allegations of abuse of discretion by courts below brought to this Court. It is not a new or a novel thing. But I do believe that the redress of the grievances of these people will be better, more promptly taken care of, by referring this matter back to the courts of first instance for solution.

Secondly, this Court might well leave some of the problems of integration to the Congress. After considerable reflection on the subject, since the filing of our written brief, I am still of the opinion that some of the problems of integration might well be worked out through appropriate legislation by Congress, pursuant to section 5 of the Fourteenth Amendment.

JUSTICE DOUGLAS: You refer to future litigation?

MR. GENTRY: Yes, sir, Your Honor.

What we who are not parties to this particular case have to look forward to, I, as the Attorney General of Arkansas, have to look forward to the possibility—not a probability, but a possibility—of 422 separate law suits in my state, a multitude of litigation. I think that the Congress might well assist in the problem which confronts the nation.

JUSTICE BLACK: May I ask you a question there?

The argument has been made heretofore largely on the basis that the Court is going to draw a decree which will decide when segregation should end in every state in the Union, draw up a broad legislative plan. What we have is litigation on the part of individuals, a very small number, perhaps a half dozen, that ask to be admitted into certain schools.

Does your argument suppose the decree would affect those individuals? Maybe it would have to. This is a lawsuit. Would your argument, which you are making, apply then?

In other words, if the decree of the Court is to treat this as a litigation between the parties, which will involve only the person named in the proceeding of today, would the argument you have made be applicable?

MR. GENTRY: I think it definitely would, Mr. Justice Black, because if that is the decision of this Court, I have no doubt but what there will probably be a case filed in practically every jurisdiction in the state where there is segregation, and although I am trying to talk about the broad aspect of this, if that be the law, insofar as these five or six or ten individuals are concerned, then under the doctrine of *stare decisis* it would be the law when the two thousand or three thousand or ten thousand came before this Court and asked for the same right and the same remedy.

JUSTICE BLACK: But assuming that is true, as you have assumed—properly, I suppose—that the Court has already passed on the basic question to that end, assuming that is true, we still have before us a lawsuit between individuals, certain individuals, perhaps a half a dozen which are admitted to certain schools.

If others wish to be admitted, it would require lawsuits, it is true. It is true there might be many. But would that not be the appropriate time to pass on whether, in that individual case, the number of individuals who apply could be admitted into the particular schools into which they sought entrance, and are the circumstances which this Court has declared on individual lawsuits not limited to circumstances of the individual case?

Is it your idea that the Court should attempt to draw some kind of a broad plan which would be in the nature of legislation to determine when and how, and so forth, the schools shall proceed all over the nation, or should the Court limit itself to the particular lawsuit before it?

MR. GENTRY: I think that the Court in these particular cases—far be it from me as a country boy from Arkansas to tell the Supreme Court—

JUSTICE BLACK: I am asking you. I appreciate the argument you have made.

MR. GENTRY: I believe that under the circumstances of taking the broad picture, that this argument would be feasible, it would be appropriate. Merely the ten or fifteen that are all we are talking about, they could be integrated, like the eleven were in Fort Smith.

JUSTICE BLACK: That is what I had in mind is connection with your Arkansas argument.

MR. GENTRY: If that is the problem, and that is all there is to it, then we have no problem.

JUSTICE FRANKFURTER: You yourself suggested in the exchange that you and I had that the situation in the Charleston school district is one thing, and the case in Clarendon is another.

MR. GENTRY: Yes, sir; that is true.

JUSTICE FRANKFURTER: In other words, *stare decisis* applies to the legal principle announced, but does *stare decisis* apply to the terms of a particular decree? They are very different things, aren't they?

MR. GENTRY: Yes, sir; they are very different things, but the ultimate result is what I am looking to. The ultimate effect of this opinion which is already the law in all of our country, that is what I am looking to ultimately.

JUSTICE FRANKFURTER: What you are saying is that if this Court enters a decree that requires implementation of the May 17 decision forthwith, you say you would, naturally, be troubled by the fact that you would have law suits all over the State of Arkansas asking for the same kind of a forthwith decree. Isn't that what you are troubled by?

MR. GENTRY: That is one of the problems which we must face. But the point that I am undertaking to make to the Court, that it would not be without precedent if this Court would supplement its opinion and call the attention of Congress to the particular problem that we have as a result of this decree or opinion of May 17, and that the solution to the situation could be helped by the Congress.

For example, in the case of *Board of Education* v. *Barnette*,[22] that was the flag salute case in which Mr. Justice Frankfurter, in a concurring opinion, stated that the opinion of the Court meant this, and in fact, as I read the opinion, told them how to require a salute of the flag within the meaning of the Court, and by the same means that the attention of the Congress may be called to some of the problems that we have here.

For example, as the Court stated in its opinion, the public school education is one of the most, or the most, important functions of the local and state governments. At the present time, in the opinion of this Court, the Supreme Court, on the part of the federal government, is now advising the local and state government how it must administer this function of the local and state governments.

Now, if the Fourteenth Amendment—and the Court has already said that the Fourteenth Amendment includes that, then it is also a federal problem as well as the state and local problem.

And by enactment of the Congress outlawing, for example, the deprivation of the constitutional rights under the Fourteenth Amendment by refusing to allow someone to go to an integrated school—[making it] punishable by a fine—I think it would have a deterring effect upon any violation, and it might be well that that is the solution rather than the decrees of this Court and the lower court in specific instances.

JUSTICE BLACK: May I ask you this question. I am asking your view. I want your view on whether it would apply only in a definite and specific instance.

MR. GENTRY: I don't believe that it could, Mr. Justice Black, because the decree would be there, and any violation of that decree would have to be enforced by contempt proceedings.

JUSTICE BLACK: With reference to the particular instance?

MR. GENTRY: With reference to the particular instance. There would have to be a decree in every instance where litigation was brought.

[22]West Virginia State Board of Education v. Barnette, 319 U.S. 624 (1943). A West Virginia law requiring all school children to salute the flag was held unconstitutional as violating the First Amendment rights of the children of Jehovah's Witnesses. Justice Frankfurter dissented, adhering to the earlier view of the Court in Minersville School District v. Gobitis, 310 U.S. 586 (1940).

JUSTICE BLACK: Do you suppose there might be many places in which no litigation would be necessary?

MR. GENTRY: That is correct.

JUSTICE BLACK: And they might not be faced with that litigation?

MR. GENTRY: But these cases, as I understand it, and the persons [who] may be ordered to do something by this decree are only litigants in the particular case.

JUSTICE DOUGLAS: If Congress did not act—you said there was a prospect of leaving some of this to Congress—I am not quite sure that I understand what you mean.

MR. GENTRY: Well, under the present circumstances, the responsibility of seeing that the constitutional rights of the appellants and all others similarly situated all over the segregated areas falls squarely within the Court because there is no law the Congress passed pursuant to section 5 of the Fourteenth Amendment which would protect the rights which this Court has given these appellants and others similarly situated in its decision of May 17.

Now, it has been held by the Court that there has been a violation of the Fourteenth Amendment, then the Congress can pass an act saying that the violation of the Fourteenth Amendment in this particular respect is unlawful, place what penalties it wishes, and if somebody wilfully violates the law, then you not only have the courts to assist in the enforcement of this but the criminal courts, the courts of equity, and the full power of the law enforcement of the United States Government, as well as the judiciary. That is the point that I was making.

JUSTICE HARLAN: Well, wouldn't you suppose that if the impact of the decree in these particular cases, which can affect only the individuals, is remitted to the district court, and then you have a flock of lawsuits by others who have not been enjoined, wouldn't it be within the discretion of the district court to stay those law suits, pending some proposal by the local school authorities to promulgate a plan to take care of the wider situation than that which affected the particular individual?

I thought that was inherent in your whole idea, that this should be remitted to the district court.

MR. GENTRY: I hope that that will be the case. But I am trying to submit alternative solutions, Mr. Justice Harlan.

May it please the Court, I am, of course, primarily interested in what is going to happen in Arkansas, and I am concerned about the attitude which will be taken by both the white and Negro people in some sections of Arkansas where many Negroes live.

There are many sections of Arkansas where integration in the schools will be worked out promptly and without the necessity of the supervision by any court, and regardless of what is contained in the final decree of this Court.

On the other hand, there are many sections of Arkansas where the Negro population is relatively heavy, and it is in these sections where there will have to be close supervision of some sort. It is in these sections, in my opinion, it will be extremely inadvisable for this Court to fix any definite deadline for the completion of integration.

During the transition period it will be my purpose, both officially and unofficially, to assist in every possible manner in bringing about complete transition without any unpleasant incidents.

JUSTICE REED: What do you mean when you say—the words you just used—time, definite time, for the completion of integration?

You said a few moments ago, before, that this judgment can only act on these few individuals, so if we admit, leaving the South Carolina cases for the moment, if these people were admitted immediately, would there be any particular difference?

MR. GENTRY: I fear that it might be an instruction to the lower court, and any further litigation which might come before the lower court, that it was the duty of the lower court to so order immediately. That is the fear.

JUSTICE REED: It depends on the circumstances, doesn't it?

MR. GENTRY: If the lower court was free and told by this Court that it was free to adjudicate the matter, depending upon his sound discretion, so long as the rights were protected and the circumstances considered.

JUSTICE REED: Well, that means to talk generally in an opinion, but to act specifically in a case.

MR. GENTRY: That is it, in effect.

JUSTICE REED: That is what you are suggesting?

MR. GENTRY: Yes, sir.

During the transition period which we have already started in Arkansas and, as a matter of fact, on last April 3, in an interview with the representative of the National Association for the Advancement of Colored People in the Arkansas *Gazette*, he stated that he had been in Arkansas since October measuring community reaction to the idea of racial integration in the public schools, and he stated that his experience, he had experienced no unpleasant incidents, and in this interview he is reported to have stated:

Arkansas represents perhaps the brightest among the Southern states, and it is expected to follow its previous pattern of pioneering.

Still quoting:

Arkansas represents a variable picture. There are extremes in terms of resistance and in favorable reaction. There are variations in how long it will take for integration.

I am in complete accord with the statements that Arkansas represents a variable picture, and I also agree with the statement of this educational specialist that there are variations in how long it will take for integration in the State of Arkansas.

And it is because of these facts that I am opposed to any decree of this Court which would fix a definite deadline for the completion of integration in these cases, because that might indicate to the other courts in Arkansas that immediate integration was the command of this Court.

JUSTICE HARLAN: If it were generally agreed among all you gentlemen representing the different states, as far as the administrative problems were concerned, as to these particular individuals, there wasn't any administrative problem, because there are only a half dozen or so, then this Court would never reach the question of time, would it? It would go back to the district court, and then it would be up to the district court, as an original matter, if other suits were filed, to grant time in relation to the handling of a large number of lawsuits that are going to pile up?

MR. GENTRY: Not only the handling of a large number of lawsuits, Your Honor, but the handling of these administrative matters which the appellants just choose to pass off with a brush. Some of the counties in Arkansas are going to have to have buildings built, and other things taken into consideration.

JUSTICE HARLAN: You misunderstood me.

In answer to Justice Black's question, you said there were no administrative problems, and in the nature of things I wouldn't suppose there would be in the case of only a half dozen individuals, or so.

MR. GENTRY: No, sir, not in the case of a half dozen individuals.

JUSTICE HARLAN: You could absorb those without administrative problems. Your administrative problems arise when there is a flood of applications, and they would result from new lawsuits being filed, and at that stage it would be the function of the district court to pass on the time elements.

MR. GENTRY: That is my contention, exactly.

I believe, if the Court please, with the questions, my argument as contained here is complete.

Thank you for the opportunity.

THE CHIEF JUSTICE: Thank you for the cooperation of your state and the presentation of your views.

MR. GENTRY: Thank you.

THE CHIEF JUSTICE: Attorney General Williamson of Oklahoma.

### ARGUMENT ON BEHALF OF THE STATE OF OKLAHOMA, AS THE FRIEND OF THE COURT

#### by MR. MAC Q. WILLIAMSON

MR. WILLIAMSON: Mr. Chief Justice, Your Honors, although Oklahoma is not a party contestant in any of the litigations currently being considered by the Court, I would like to say that Oklahoma is keenly interested in the principles heretofore enunciated by the Court of May 17, 1954, and we are further interested in the principles which will follow in due course this year.

We filed a very short brief herein upon invitation of the Court, for which invitation we are grateful. Our brief pointed out principally, Your Honors, the fact that Oklahoma has a unique, different system of raising funds for the support of our separate schools, and I may say at this point that Oklahoma, having been admitted into the Union in 1907 as the forty-sixth state of this Union, had in its constitution, imbedded in the constitution, the principle of compulsory segregation in the common public schools of Oklahoma. That has been the rule, the constitutional rule, in our state since 1907, and it is compulsory.

So when the occasion came for this Court to promulgate the opinion of May 17, 1954, that opinion posed at once a question involving the fiscal arrangement of our funds for public schools, and we met that question in due course, as I shall explain.

In our brief filed in November of 1954, I said to the Court that our State Legislative Council, which is an organization consisting of the entire current membership of both the Senate and the House of Representatives of the State Legislature, was giving careful and studious consideration to the impact of the May 17 decision upon fiscal arrangements of the State of Oklahoma, drafted, as they are, into the constitution, providing for funds to run separate schools. So upon the convening of the regular 1955 session of the Oklahoma Legislature, which did convene on January 10, 1955, and which is currently in session and about to wind up its duties, that Legislature, among other things, passed a resolution submitting to the people of Oklahoma at a statewide election the question of whether the people of Oklahoma wished to and would amend their own constitution, taking out of our constitution the segregation provisions for the raising of taxes on a basis of four mills to the dollar upon all the taxable property of the state, to be devoted to separate schools.

That question was submitted to the people of the state, and on April 5, 1955, that being the date called by the present Governor for the submission of the question, the statewide election was held.

I may say to the Court that the people of Oklahoma responded with more than 300,000 votes cast, perhaps nearly 350,000 and the question of removing the segregation feature as a constitutional feature and substituting therefore an amended constitutional section providing that the money so levied would go into what I may call a common jackpot for the distribution county-wide for the benefit of all children, based on an average daily attendance of the fiscal year preceding.

So this election, having been held, showed that the people of Oklahoma, by a majority of three to one, adopted and ratified that change, the spirit and significance of which was to take segregation out of the Oklahoma State Constitution.

So I point out that Oklahoma has already made substantial progress along the lines of putting our house in order, fiscally speaking, and I may say further that the fiscal question was the principal question which stood as an obstacle in the way of this plan for proposed gradual changeover.

JUSTICE REED: Is that section 9 of Article 10?

MR. WILLIAMSON: Yes, sir.

If Your Honor please, that will be found on page 8, and the following pages of our brief.

JUSTICE REED: As I understand it, the segregation clause was repealed from the constitution.

MR. WILLIAMSON: That is quite correct.

If Your Honor will notice the text—and we have it in our brief on page 9, rather close to the top there—you will see there is quite an extended provision there, and it writes segregation into section 9 of our Constitution. That section 9 of Article 10 of our Constitution is what we refer to as the fiscal section. It provides the fiscal framework for raising money, assessing taxes, and ad valorem taxes, statewide.

This fiscal problem being the big problem, our present section 9 as amended by this three to one vote of the people, provides, as I said, first, that the same four-mill levy on all taxable property, real and personal, which was heretofor levied for separate schools, is still to be levied against the property of the state, but when this four mills is collected by the various county treasurers, and there are seventy-seven of them—this millage is then distributed without regard to color, but based upon the average daily attendance of the school children of each county.

So there has been a transition of the four mills out of the segregation group.

Now, if Your Honors please, this amendment does another thing. It provides that whereas section 26 of Article 10 has provided a limit with regard to the issuing of bonds by school districts, that limit being 5 per cent of the net valuation, real and personal, of the school district, this constitutional amendment raises that limitation for the purpose of assisting impoverished and rural districts, it raises that limitation from 5 to 10 per cent, thereby allowing districts with modest or impoverished assessed valuations, the right, should they see fit, to go 5 per cent stronger for the purpose of erecting public improvements in the various school districts.

It will be understood, I am sure, that our method of financing contemplated county-wide assessment for separate schools, whereas the method of raising money for district or majority schools in Oklahoma has been a district basis, with geographical limitations, each district to itself.

So we have a rather incongruous situation in Oklahoma where the four mills for separate school purposes has been invested in buildings.

In the capital city, for instance, in Oklahoma City, which is the largest city of the state, some 350,000 people, that city has received the impact of most of the money collected throughout the length and breadth of Oklahoma County for public schools.

Farmers 45 miles southwest and southeast pay their two mills, but the money is gathered at the county treasurer's office, and then is administered as a separate school fund on a county unit basis and is administered by the Board of County Commissioners of the county, and in case there happens to be an independent school district, that is, the wider majority district, which needs the separate schools also in the district, they go to the County Commissioners and from the county treasurer they receive money which is allocated to the independent district for the purpose of separate schools.

So we have the county unit system on separate schools. In Oklahoma City alone, we have this sort of a situation. This separate school money, collected county-wide, doesn't belong to the Oklahoma City School District. That is the majority district. Yet we find erected in the Oklahoma City School District, out of this county-wide school fund, what is known as the Douglass High School, which is a high school for colored children.

That high school, as I have the figures, cost in excess of $2,100,000. That high school stands within the geographical limits of Oklahoma City, the majority school district, but that building doesn't belong to the taxpayers of the Oklahoma City majority school district. It belongs to the taxpayers in the county.

That is true in a greater or lesser degree. We have, for instance, in Oklahoma, 1,795 school districts. Out of those 1,795, we have 313 school districts which have within them separate schools. In each of those 313 instances the buildings and permanent improvements have been bought and paid for by people, many of them do not even live in the school districts which contain the situs of the building.

So we have the problem there of the permanent improvements in 313 school districts of that state which really do not belong to the people of the district where the buildings in each instance sit.

That is a problem which must be wrestled with. There are probably in the entire operation of 313 separate school districts 500 school buses. That is an item. They don't belong to the school district where that school is. They belong to the people of the county.

I point out to the Court there are property situations there with which our Legislature must concern itself, and which it will concern itself.

In addition to the fact that this amendment adopted by the people has not only taken away the separate school label on that four mills which was given generally to the schools, in addition to the fact that it has also given the impoverished school districts 5 per cent higher limitation on the right to vote bonds, since they raised the limit to 10 per cent of the taxable valuation, they have also set up and created by this new constitutional amendment a fund which is supplied from the various items of the state income, which are all provided by the statute.

This amendment creates the state public common school building equalization fund, and into that fund will flow moneys from various state sources.

That is the third benefit which the new constitutional amendment gives to the school situation.

That common school equalization fund will receive various public moneys from time to time, and the purpose and intent of that third item in this amendment to the constitution is to give to impoverished districts loans which will make up for their needs for buildings where they haven't got the money to pay for them.

In other words, we are trying to fix the fiscal pictures.

THE CHIEF JUSTICE: We will recess now.

(A recess was taken.)

AFTER RECESS

THE CHIEF JUSTICE: Attorney General Williamson, you may proceed.

### ARGUMENT ON BEHALF OF THE STATE OF OKLAHOMA
### AS THE FRIEND OF THE COURT

by MR. MAC Q. WILLIAMSON (Resumed)

MR. WILLIAMSON: Mr. Chief Justice, Your Honors, when the Court arose, I was speaking among other things about the features of the amendment which was adopted by the people. I think I finished my explanation of the third feature which is a state fund for assistance of impoverished districts.

There will be a burden thrown on some small rural districts in this state because of the fact that colored children are in some cases transported by the buses many miles and there may be the disposition of the rural school boards to cut out that charge and let these children go at home.

There will be a national shifting of the personnel of the minor population, school children population here and there and the basis on which that will be taken care of is by upping of five mills of the debt limit on bonds voted by the district. That is planned to take care of the need of some school districts for great public improvements, greater than they could pay for under the old system.

Now actually there is one district for instance in Oklahoma, that is in Carter County, that has 45 white children and 201 colored children and they bring those colored children from many parts of adjoining counties.

They have some four buses. There is a white district that is very limited in its area and limited in its taxability and there is going to be a shift of population there. Some of these children are transported many miles, will go to schools in their area.

We think the new amendment to section 9 of Article 10 of the constitution rather fully takes care of the physical problem that had been created by our there-tofore constitutional segregation levies.

Now, if I may say one thing at this juncture, section 9 of Article 10 of the Oklahoma constitution is the only amendment which was submitted to the people.

Reference to my brief will show that upon two other places there in the constitution, the term Negro and the reference to separate schools are found.

That will be found on page 7 in my brief.

At page 7 it is found right at the top, section 5, Article 1, makes provisions constitutionally for the establishment and maintenance of a system of public schools and the italicized language at the bottom provides constitutionally for the establishment and maintenance of separate schools.

Just under that section 3 of Article 13 provides again and in other places in the constitution that these separate schools shall be provided by legislature and impartially maintained and defines the terms of the children and then section 11 of Article 23 of the Oklahoma constitution defines the words wherever used in the constitution and statutes "colored" or "colored race."

I point out to the Court, lest there might be some confusion that none of these sections were amended but that only the section with the big obstacle, the fiscal section without which we could not run schools.

It was thought proper at that time not to load the special election ballot with four or five questions but to present to them the single sole question.

Will you be in favor of amending the constitution of Oklahoma to provide for the untying of the separate school levy and for the elimination of the separate school levy from the state constitution?

That question was put directly to the voters. No other questions. As I said to the Court a while ago it was approved by a vote of three to one.

The legislature now, as I said is in session. The legislature proposes to implement this newly adopted section 9 of Article 10.

It will implement it, no doubt, in the next two or three weeks.

Of course, the legislature could with better understanding implement that if we had the decision of this Court in the meantime.

But if we have that so well and good. If we do not have it—

JUSTICE BURTON: Mr. Attorney General, have you rendered any advice or opinion as to the status of these other three provisions?

MR. WILLIAMSON: No, sir. If Your Honor please, this matter has been pending continuously in litigation here. I will say to the Court that we have had a rule of long standing policy in the Office of the Attorney General of Oklahoma where I have had the honor personally to preside for several years, we have a rule in that office to the effect that we will not arrogate to ourselves the right to publish or prejudge a pending legal question and write an opinion of the Attorney General's Office when it is before some court.

We discuss informally with our state officers and with those who are entitled to inquire, we discuss legal questions but we do not formalize opinions on them.

JUSTICE BURTON: Are there any proposals pending in the Legislature for the amendment of these provisions?

MR. WILLIAMSON: Not at this time. The three I have just mentioned?

JUSTICE BURTON: Yes.

MR. WILLIAMSON: Not at this time.

JUSTICE REED: No provision for advisory opinions of the Attorney General?

MR. WILLIAMSON: No, there are not, Mr. Justice Reed. No provisions. However, we freely discuss the matters informally with anyone who cares to ask and is entitled to ask.

Now, that brings me to the last and final remarks I should like to make to the Court. In Question No. 4, as propounded by this Court some several months ago, providing as it did for (a) and (b), which have been alluded to by some, both lawyers and laymen, and without levity, as the $64 question. While the immediate impact of that question, as answered here in this litigation by this Court will not reach Oklahoma and many of the other so-called segregation-practicing states, yet we feel that it would be perhaps unfortunate and we feel that perhaps we should speak out against any proposed deadline now forthwith.

We feel that we should speak out because of the impact potentially which it may have on some of these segregation states in the future.

We feel that we should speak out at this time upon the question of an effective gradual adjustment, because we see in this historic occasion before this Court, we see balanced here the rights of young colored minors who wish to go to the school of their choice, and we see over as against that a tremendous public interest where men and women, the fathers of children, boys and girls, are disturbed and are vexed and are apprehensive and we see them having the tremendous public interest themselves in this situation.

And in view of that, we believe earnestly that there might be a situation, perhaps not in these cases pending now, but there might be a situation in the future sometime where something that the Court might say by way of laying down a deadline in these cases might be inferred to mean that there will be a deadline laid in all cases, a prejudgment if you please that it may amount to.

It might be twisted into that by somebody out yonder trying to interpret it.

It is our considered and earnest view that public officials as we are in Oklahoma trying to do our duty, trying to go along with a Governor who staked his personal and professional reputation with the people of our state on adopting this bill—and that is Answer 3—school officers, state officers, all over the segregating practicing states honestly and earnestly endeavoring to try to fit this thing together—we feel there might be a bit of potential stigma on any disposition to give a man a deadline or especially where the courts are open and active and vigorous and no suspicion is cast on the trial courts as to their ability to take care of situations.

It seems to us of Oklahoma that nothing even in the remotest instance constituting any driving or lashing some public official toward a deadline should ever appear until and unless it appears in the record such officials are negligent or malingering or not promptly attending to their duty.

Thank you.

THE CHIEF JUSTICE: Attorney General Williamson, we thank you and your state for this expression of your views.

MR. WILLIAMSON: Thank you, Mr. Chief Justice.

THE CHIEF JUSTICE: Attorney General Ferdinand Sybert of Maryland.


### ARGUMENT ON BEHALF OF THE STATE OF MARYLAND
### AS THE FRIEND OF THE COURT

#### by ATTORNEY GENERAL C. FERDINAND SYBERT

MR. SYBERT: With Your Honor's permission, on behalf of the State of Maryland I desire to express to the Court my thanks for this opportunity to appear and assist in the resolution of these momentous questions. I call the Court's attention to the effect that the *amicus curiae* brief filed herein on behalf of

Maryland was prepared and filed by my predecessor in office, Attorney General Edward Rollins, whom I succeeded last December.

I adopt and subscribe to that brief in its entirety. While Maryland was a slave state, they have always been considerate of its colored population. It is highly significant that at the beginning of the war between the states only one-half of the Negroes in Maryland were slaves and the rest were freedmen.

In its Constitution of 1867 Maryland provided for the free education of both the white and colored races.

While it is true that it did provide by statute for separate schools, this was the accepted pattern of the day. Our brief delineates and documents the progress that has been made in the education of our colored population in Maryland from 1867 to the present day.

That progress has really been remarkable. It is completely true that at the time the Court's opinion was handed down in these cases last year Maryland's educational facilities were already equal though separate.

Equal in physical fact and not in theory only. I cite this situation to indicate the bona fides of the state's goodwill toward all its citizens.

Maryland has of course for many years proceeded, like most of the nation, on the supposition that segregation in public education was not in violation of the provisions of the Fourteenth Amendment so long as the facilities provided for the races were substantially equal.

I do not intend to over-emphasize the difficulties occasioned by the impact of this honorable Court's opinion upon standard and established practices and traditions in Maryland.

But I feel it would be a disservice to the Court to say that no difficulties have been encountered or will arise.

To be at all helpful we must examine the situation factually and realistically. Shortly after the Court's opinion in these cases last year, several parent-teacher association groups in a Southern Maryland county adopted what they identified as the West River proclamation, a copy of which appears in the appendix to our brief at pages 62 and 63.

This manifesto in essence would prohibit any change in the existing educational pattern in Maryland, except by state law sanctioned by the people through referendum.

Another plan to circumvent this Court's decision was a petition circulated by a group known as the Maryland Petition Committee and signed, I have been informed, by approximately 36,000 citizens.

The petition called upon the Governor of the State to make provision for the establishment of a system of private schools for any groups which do not believe in integration, with freedom from school taxes for such citizens as might support those free schools.

The petition also affirmed the belief of its signers that the constitution grants them the right to withdraw their children from the public schools if denied the above-mentioned privileges; for the Court's information, the Maryland Petition Committee after a protracted difficulty in attempting to find a sponsor finally obtained the introduction late in the recent session of the Maryland Legislature of two bills designed to implement its petition.

When the legislature adjourned sine die last week the two bills died in the committee of the House in which they were introduced.

Maryland was one of the three states which refused to ratify the Fourteenth Amendment in the 1860s and which have not ratified it since.

A bill for such ratification was introduced in the recent session but died in committee.

Also the legislature made no changes in Maryland's segregation statutes although no bills were introduced toward that end.

The Office of the Attorney General of Maryland has received hundreds of letters since the opinion in these cases containing almost every conceivable suggestion as to methods of circumvention or implementation of the decision.

Many meetings of citizens have been held to the same ends.

I will now relate an incident which occurred in Frederick County, Maryland. Frederick is one of our northernmost counties, bordering on the Mason-Dixon line.

It is a highly conservative county and is one of the richest farming counties in the nation. Its colored population is not quite 7 per cent of the total. Last fall after the schools were opened, the county Board of Education gave orders for three colored children to be placed on a white school bus in order to be saved, those three children would be saved a mile and a half longer ride.

They would be left off at their own colored school. The next morning after this ban was put into effect irate parents descended upon the county board of education and persuaded it to reverse itself and put the colored children back on the colored bus.

Now if Your Honors please, let us inspect some other things which have been happening in Maryland, both before and after the May 17 opinion.

The University of Maryland has been operating its graduate schools on a nonsegregated basis for a number of years. Very soon after the opinion was handed down in these cases last year, its Board of Regents announced the ending of segregation in all undergraduate departments as well, of course, as graduate departments and Negroes were freely admitted last September.

The state has been spending approximately a quarter of a million dollars on out-of-state scholarships annually for Negroes who could not obtain in Maryland courses being taught at the University of Maryland but not theretofore available to them.

Due to the complete desegregation of the University, the granting of any further scholarships of this nature have now been eliminated.

The state for many years has operated Morgan College, Morgan State College as an institution of higher learning for Negroes with a regular and summer enrollment of about 2,300.

In recent years Morgan has admitted white students who desire to attend that institution. The number has been very small.

So much for the situation in Maryland with respect to higher education. In the City of Baltimore, which contains almost one-half of Maryland's population, the public school authorities began the process of desegregation in September 1954, with elementary and high school students attending the schools of their choice, regardless of race. Some early difficulties were encountered, such as picketing by some parents and absenteeism or, as sometimes termed, a strike of pupils.

Pupils marched in columns from one school to another, from two schools in the northern section of Baltimore. They formed columns and marched possibly two miles down to the central part of the city and marched on City Hall.

The police struggled to maintain order. That situation existed, began on a Thursday, continued on Friday, over the weekend. Colonel Ober, the Commissioner of Police of Baltimore issued a statement that picketing of the schools was a violation of the school's laws and could not be tolerated.

The school authorities in Baltimore City also made public announcement that absenteeism was of course a violation of the compulsory attendance laws and would not be tolerated.

As a result of those statements, the children came back to school on Monday and I am informed by the Superintendent of Schools of Baltimore City that no untoward incidents have taken place since.

I have been informed by a good many citizens that possible further trouble is feared this coming September. I might say that the process of integration in Baltimore has taken this shape: In Baltimore the students have been allowed to go to the school of their choice, except I might say there are 175 schools in the City of Baltimore—only 35 of those schools are districted because of crowded conditions.

Other than in those 35 schools—some of those are colored, some are white, any student is allowed to attend any school of his or her choice.

JUSTICE REED: How many schools do you have in Baltimore?

MR. SYBERT: One hundred seventy-five schools in Baltimore.

JUSTICE REED: He can go to any school he wants to?

MR. SYBERT: Any school except in 35 districted schools which are districted simply because of overcrowded conditions, some white and some colored.

I might add that any pupil in the district of a districted school may go to any other undistricted school but no person, no child from outside the district of a districted school might go to that school because it is already overcrowded.

About 2,400 or 2,500 Negro pupils availed themselves of the right to go from former colored schools in Baltimore City to theretofore white schools.

JUSTICE BURTON: Has that optional effect been in effect for a long time?

MR. SYBERT: Traditionally, right along. That optional situation has been in effect.

JUSTICE BURTON: It means in substance you can choose any school you want to provided that school is not already crowded?

MR. SYBERT: Yes, sir. 2,400 or 2,500 colored students last September entered in schools theretofore white and a handful of white students, I believe I was told three or four, availed themselves of the right to go to colored schools which happened to be nearer than the schools they previously attended.

In the twenty-three counties of Maryland outside of Baltimore City—

JUSTICE REED: I don't know if I fully understand that. The right to choice has existed for many years?

MR. SYBERT: The right to choice of white students as to white schools and colored students as to colored schools before September, 1954—

JUSTICE REED: Then the statute forbidding segregation was changed to allow them to go to any school?

MR. SYBERT. There wasn't any change in statute or ordinance. The school authorities in Baltimore City decided to desegregate and announced that policy in the summer and in September—

JUSTICE REED: It was carried out?

MR. SYBERT: —without regard to race from September on.

JUSTICE CLARK: How many colored students are there in Baltimore City?

MR. SYBERT: There are 57,000 colored students in Baltimore City and 87,000 white.

JUSTICE CLARK: And you say 2,500 chose to go to another school?

MR. SYBERT: Two thousand four hundred or 2,500, approximately 5 per cent. A total school population of 144,000 in Baltimore City.

There has been no integration or desegregation in the counties of Maryland up to the present time. In the twenty-three counties of Maryland the situation is extremely varied. Maryland has often been referred to as America in miniature.

We have the wooded mountainous western section, three or four counties, the rich grain area upland central district, the alluvial plains of southern Maryland and the eastern shore of Maryland bisected by the Chesapeake Bay with its seafood industry.

Baltimore City in approximately the center of the state, a great seaport.

I am bound to inform the Court that the existing ways of life and established patterns of thinking vary between the inhabitants of those dissimilar regions as much as does their habitat.

It is also true that great differences as to population of schools and school attendance by races exists among the counties.

I direct the Court's attention to Table B on page 38 of our brief, 38 of the appendix which reflects the number and percentage of white and Negro school population in the counties.

That shows there are actually no Negro children of school age in Garrett County. I might say the Negro population of Garrett County, the mountainous most westerly county is nine, but none of them are of school age.

In southern Maryland Calvert County has a colored school population of slightly over 50 per cent.

The other counties range in between. A few, 5, 6, 7 per cent and from there 16, 20, 30, 40 and so on, up to 50 per cent in Calvert County in southern Maryland.

Yet in every county except Garrett, of course, where the occasional colored child went to the white schools because there are seldom more than one or two colored children of school age, there being only one or two colored families that ordinarily live in that county; all the other counties have established and maintained since 1870 separate facilities.

In the last thirty years Maryland has undertaken a program of bringing the colored facilities equal with the white.

And for some years the facilities in the separated colored schools have actually physically and in all other respects been equal with those of the white schools.

Within a few days after this Court's opinion of May 17 the Maryland State Board of Education issued a statement appearing at Appendix page 17, pointing out that the problems involved in any program of integration would vary among the different school systems of the state but expressing confidence that they will be solved in fair, decent and legal manner and with good common sense.

The Board also stated that until the decree of this Court should be handed down any detailed plan of action for implementation would be premature, but it pointed out that the State Board and the local school authorities should not delay in analyzing the situation and making plans for implementing the decision of the Court.

Thereupon the Superintendents of all the school systems of the county, some twenty-three county school systems, appointed a committee to determine just what were the facts of the whole situation, the local situations, also to make recommendations as to policies to be adopted by the local systems and to suggest answers to the two questions propounded by this honorable Court.

The report of this committee of superintendents begins at page 1 of our appendix. It is exhaustive and illuminating. Its conclusions may fairly be said to represent the consensus of mature opinion of the counties of Maryland.

Its suggestions as to the answers to the questions here being discussed have been adopted by the Maryland Board of Education and by the Attorney General of Maryland.

The committee summarized its recommendations in part as follows—and this is found on page 16 of the appendix.

In summary the committee advocates a policy of gradual adjustment and remanding of responsibility for implementing the decree to the local school authorities.

Legal opinion would seem to indicate that the issues to be treated in moving from segregation to desegregation are not within the usual experience of the judiciary.

The state and local agencies which have been established to cope with such problems should be afforded the first opportunity to work out on a biracial basis the procedures for meeting the new principles of law as contained in the Court's decision of May 17.

Our adherence to this position is based on our desire to build at the local level in our respective counties a climate of goodwill between all parties concerned.

This climate is necessary to undergird the program of action which is necessary to carry out the program of the Court.

We recommend to the several counties formation of citizen's committees appointed by the local board and consisting of representatives of both races who will consult with the local educational authorities on the steps to be taken in each county, the program of desegregation and the setting up of safeguards for the protection of the rights of all children, and so on.

I respectfully commend to the Court's attention the whole report of the committee of superintendents which as I have just said represents the mature thinking of the school authorities on that and most of the other thoughtful citizens.

JUSTICE REED: Did they make any recommendations as to the steps to be taken?

MR. SYBERT: No, their report indicates that a process of education, getting together of the races through their parent-teachers' associations, by racial meetings, being first set up to discuss ways and means.

They have not gotten as far as discussing specific plans.

Therefore Maryland's position—

JUSTICE FRANKFURTER: Their theory is that the specific plan will derive out of an active and aggressive attitude of the state in carrying out this decree; is that a fair statement?

MR. SYBERT: I think so.

Maryland therefore specifically recommends to this Court that the questions propounded should be resolved in favor of an affirmative answer to Question 4(b) and an affirmative answer to Question 5(d), that is first that this Court may and should in the exercise of its equity powers so frame its decree as to effect an effective gradual adjustment be brought about from existing segregated systems in public education to systems not based on color distinction.

On that point that is the position taken in the brief of my predecessor. To my mind the same end would be attained if this Court, in considering these cases involving specific persons who have sued, would simply remand the cases to the lower courts for such further action in the light of the opinion in this case as should appear to be necessary.

Second, that the cases be remanded without specific direction as to methods of time or compliance which questions should be determined by the courts of first instance in the light of local conditions as they may be found to exist.

We respectfully submit that the ninety-day period suggested by the government within [which] the lower courts should order local authorities to present their plans for ending segregation as soon as feasible would make for makeshift and abortive planning.

The Baltimore *Evening Sun* gave its answer to this question in an editorial on November 26, 1954.

I quote:

From the evidence presented so far by the individual states, the plan is going to take time if done on a community by community basis. School authorities have expressed a need for full talks with all interested parties so that each community will know exactly what the plans are. If this attempt to get community understanding and cooperation is made, more than ninety days will be required for the planning stage.

THE CHIEF JUSTICE: Do you feel, General, that the district court is entitled to any guidance as a matter of help to them in supervising these cases?

MR. SYBERT: If Your Honors please, I really don't think that is necessary. I think the fact that this decision has been handed down in most instances is going to lead to the gradual and ultimate adoption of the principles there laid down.

In my state we are fortunate enough not to have any pending litigation with respect to schools.

The general consensus is that as this plan can be worked out, gradually, ultimately non-segregation will be achieved.

We feel that the ninety-day period—

JUSTICE FRANKFURTER: Do I infer from what you just said that you think no litigation will arise at all. There is no problem so far as Maryland is concerned about any action by a district court?

MR. SYBERT: That depends upon the degree of forbearance, the degree of intelligence with which both races approach this problem.

There is no question about it, we have a severe problem in some counties in Maryland.

If the members of the colored race find that honest, intelligent steps to work out a desegregated school system are being pursued, I think the great majority of them will bear the immediate filing of suits.

JUSTICE FRANKFURTER: None has been filed, I suppose?

MR. SYBERT: Not in recent years.

JUSTICE FRANKFURTER: I mean since last May, for instance?

MR. SYBERT: I did not understand.

JUSTICE FRANKFURTER: Since these litigations?

MR. SYBERT: None has been filed.

JUSTICE FRANKFURTER: On this school board were there members of the colored race, were there colored members on this school board?

MR. SYBERT: The State Board of Education has one colored member.

JUSTICE FRANKFURTER: The State Board?

MR. SYBERT: The Baltimore City Board of Education has one. Three or for counties in the State have colored members on the school board.

JUSTICE FRANKFURTER: I notice you point with pride, with justifiable pride, as I understand, to the number of colored teachers in Maryland schools compared with—I think it is always invidious to make comparisons with other places—

MR. SYBERT: Page 10.

JUSTICE FRANKFURTER: Are there any colored teachers in non-segregated colored schools?

MR. SYBERT: No, Your Honor.

JUSTICE FRANKFURTER: Do the colored teachers absorb the personnel requirement of teaching in the colored schools?

MR. SYBERT: Yes. Our qualifications have been exactly the same for years—

JUSTICE FRANKFURTER: No, I mean are there exclusively colored teachers in the colored schools?

MR. SYBERT: Exclusively colored teachers and in the white schools exclusively white teachers.

JUSTICE FRANKFURTER: Is that a requisite of law or practice?

MR. SYBERT: Our constitution provides for a free system of education; our statutes require segregated schools.

JUSTICE FRANKFURTER: Does it require segregation of teachers or has it just worked out that way?

MR. SYBERT: That has worked out that way. Our statute simply requires the setting up and maintenance of separate schools. The law does provide for colored normal schools and white normal schools.

JUSTICE REED: I understand that on the State Board of Education there is one member who is a Negro?

MR. SYBERT: One member of the State Board of Education, that is true, sir. As I said, not only that, but a colored member of the Baltimore City School Board of Education, we have had them in three or four counties. We have had colored policemen in Baltimore City for years; colored firemen for the last three or four years.

JUSTICE REED: Did that member participate in that report?

MR. SYBERT: There wasn't a colored member on the Committee of Superintendents because we don't have a colored superintendent in the state. We have twenty-four; one in Baltimore City and one in each of the twenty-three counties.

I might say that I am convinced that I am correct when I say that thoughtful leaders of both races in Maryland believe that we should make haste slowly. They feel that coercion and force can only lead to trouble in Maryland.

They believe that they themselves and local authorities can work the situation out now that the Court has enunciated the principle in a calm lawful manner and within a reasonable time.

Unless there are further questions that concludes my statement.

Thank you very much.

THE CHIEF JUSTICE: Thank you very much, General, for your cooperation.

Attorney General Shepperd of Texas.

### ARGUMENT ON BEHALF OF THE STATE OF TEXAS
### AS THE FRIEND OF THE COURT

#### by ATTORNEY GENERAL JOHN BEN SHEPPERD

MR. SHEPPERD: May it please the Court, the purpose of the State of Texas in appearing as an *amicus curiae* in these cases is to bring more fully to the attention of the Court the problems with which we will ultimately be faced as a result of the decision of last May 17. I shall discuss the background of the segregated system in Texas together with the factual information as to the varying degrees in which different areas of the state shall be affected.

My assistant, Mr. Waldrep will continue our discussion with observations relative to the questions propounded by the Court.

In order to determine the problems with which the Texas public school system is confronted, our office has made a sincere effort to obtain a correct cross-section of views of the people of our state.

Surveys were made of editors, legislators and others with a knowledge of the subject matter under consideration.

Public opinion was sampled and composite views of groups of Negro and white editors, civic leaders, school administrators, parents and many others were obtained.

We shall attempt to present the Texas picture as reflected from this research.

Expressive of the general attitude of our people is a statewide survey conducted by the Texas people on September 12 last. It was indicated in that poll that 71 per cent of our people are definitely opposed to the decision.

Seven per cent are in favor of putting the Court's ruling into effect immediately. Twenty-three per cent believe plans should be made to bring the races together in the schools within the next few years, and 65 per cent prefer continued segregation.

A later poll made public on April 6 of this year revealed that 45 per cent of the cross-section interviewed expressed determination to circumvent desegregation either by disobeying the law or by evading the law through legal channels.

Thirty-five per cent favored gradual mixing of the races and only 14 per cent wanted to obey the law to the letter.

The poll indicated that there would be less resistance to a plan of gradual integration.

JUSTICE FRANKFURTER: Am I right? Am I right in understanding that 35 were for gradual integration and 14 for immediate compliance?

MR. SHEPPERD: Yes, sir.

JUSTICE FRANKFURTER: That means about 50 per cent or 49 per cent close to 50 per cent—

MR. SHEPPERD: I think there were four different questions asked, Mr. Justice Frankfurter.

JUSTICE FRANKFURTER: On this last figure you gave I gathered from the figures in the State of Texas 50 per cent have indicated their readiness to carry out sooner or later the decision of this Court, is that right?

MR. SHEPPERD: Thirty-five per cent.

JUSTICE FRANKFURTER: Gradually and 14 per cent immediately?

MR. SHEPPERD: Thirty-five per cent answered the question as to whether or not there should be immediate integration as opposed to gradual mixing of the races.

JUSTICE FRANKFURTER: Thirty-five per cent said they would be for gradual?

MR. SHEPPERD: Yes.

JUSTICE FRANKFURTER: Fourteen for immediate?

MR. SHEPPERD: Yes.

JUSTICE FRANKFURTER: So half in your state—any validity that poll may have about which I am very skeptical—

MR. SHEPPERD: I might point out that this poll predicted the re-election of Mr. Truman in '48. That has been pretty accurate as far as the state—I would be ashamed if it were not more generally rated.

JUSTICE FRANKFURTER: That makes it scientific?

MR. SHEPPERD: The four questions propounded by the Court dealt with immediate integration and gradual integration and some of the same people answered all four questions.
Of the Texas Negroes interviewed only 32 per cent favored immediate desegregation. Thirty per cent approved gradual mixing of the races and 26 per cent wanted to continue separate school facilities for Negroes and whites.

THE CHIEF JUSTICE: What does that represent, General, these last figures you just gave us?

MR. SHEPPERD: It represents the Texas Negroes interviewed, Mr. Chief Justice.

THE CHIEF JUSTICE: Those figures are different from the first ones you gave us?

MR. SHEPPERD: Yes, sir.

It is in the same poll, but this is the Negroes that were interviewed in this poll.

THE CHIEF JUSTICE: I see. I did not understand that.

MR. SHEPPARD: Of this latter number about half or 12 per cent of the total number of Negroes polled were determined to prevent integration even if that meant disobeying the law. Sixty-seven per cent of the Negroes, 70 per cent of the Latin American whites and 85 per cent of other whites interviewed predicted trouble between white and Negro parents in the event of desegregation.

Three out of ten expected serious trouble. Seven out of ten predicted more than a little trouble and only 15 per cent of all races were optimistic enough to expect a minimum.

From its inception the Texas public school system has been operated and maintained on a segregated basis. That has existed for more than eighty years under the authority of section 7 of Article 7 of our Texas Constitution of 1876.

This provision requires that the state maintain separate schools for white and colored children with impartial provisions for both.

This constitutional authority was a direct and continuing result of the expressed will of the people of our state.

This doctrine of separate and equal schools was not the result of official or governmental prejudice or a desire to discriminate against either race nor caused by any hatred or feeling of superiority.

The truth is that the purpose of the system is to furnish equal opportunities, privileges and services for the children of the two races and at the same time to preserve the peace and harmony and public support of the public school system.

In certain localities it would have been impossible to maintain peace, order and harmony among the people and to have the taxpayers' support for the public school system if those people were forced to mingle together against the will of the majority.

This was a valid exercise of the police power of the state. The argument that the states have been violating the Constitution by maintaining separate and equal school systems is without foundation.

On the contrary they have been acting in accordance with numerous precedents of this and other courts.

With this background we now consider the geographical picture in Texas which points up the need for a decree which will preserve the administration of our educational system in local school boards.

According to the federal census of 1950, the State of Texas has a total population of 7,701,194, of which 977,458 or 12.7 per cent is colored.

Of the 1,786,918 persons of school age enumerated in our school scholastic census of last year, 13 per cent or a total of 230,546 are colored.

Texas has 254 counties, but one-half the colored school children of the state live in only 45 counties of the eastern section of the state. About 90 per cent of all the colored scholastics of Texas reside in the 88 counties comprising the eastern third of the state. The remaining 10 per cent of our colored school children are scattered throughout 125 central and western counties, thus the proportionate colored population of Texas counties vary sharply with five eastern counties having colored school children in the majority and 41 western counties having not a single colored school child.

Referring briefly to our Appendix No. 1, it will be seen that the colored population drops sharply as we move from the eastern boundary of our state to the western boundary.

In those counties designated in red, 50 per cent or more are colored. In those in blue 40 per cent or more. Those designated by the dashed mark, many along the Louisiana line and in the central eastern part of the state, 30 per cent or more are colored.

Those in green, 20 per cent or more. Those in pink, 10 per cent or more. Purple, 5 per cent or more.

The diagonal green, 1 per cent or more and those in white less than one-half of one per cent or no colored population at all.

Taking our next exhibit, which covers the scholastic population of Texas, you will notice depicted in brown in the eastern forty-five counties of our state 50 per cent of the Negro scholastic population.

In the next forty-three counties, an additional 40 per cent of our Negro scholastic population or a line drawn on the eastern third of our state roughly from Sherman, Texas to include Dallas and Fort Worth, Waco, Austin and San Antonio and back to the Gulf of Mexico to Jackson County or Edna, Texas, we find the total of 90 per cent of our Negro colored population.

The rest of the state comprising the vast area of western and southern Texas and the Panhandle of Texas has actually less Negro scholastics in that than does Harris County in which Houston is located and when we look at Harris County we find that actually only 17 per cent of the scholastics in that county are colored.

Thus it is obvious that the question of separate and integrated schools is as vast and as varied as Texas terrain and population and the varied situation that exists in these communities cannot be treated under a single blanket policy. They must be considered as they exist in local school districts.

This idea has been manifested in prior consideration of the subject matter made by our editors and our Texas Commissioner of Higher Education, Dr. [J. W.] Edgar who stated in June of last year:

> Texas has 2,000 problems as a result of the Supreme Court's decision. We have 2,000 school districts and they vary from totally white to totally Negro. The final decree of the Court ought to be to permit continued management of local districts by local boards. Schools must be run on a community basis. They cannot be run successfully from Washington or even from Austin. Experience in separating children on a language basis has proved to us that where the responsibility is put on the local community, they work honestly to resolve differences.
>
> Anything which schools do effectively must be done with public support. We don't care to tell others how to run their schools. But we certainly believe that our two thousand problems can be resolved best if the Supreme Court leaves control in local districts.

That is a quote from Dr. Edgar, the Commissioner of Education of Texas.

Of the 213 counties listing Negro scholastics 146 counties offer a complete Negro high school. Twenty-one counties offer some Negro high school but not 12 grades. Thirty-six counties offer only Negro elementary school and ten counties operate no schools for colored children. However, these counties have ten or fewer Negro scholastics and the Texas school laws requires that a district must have an average daily attendance of at least fifteen pupils authorized to maintain any type of school financed by state laws.

This law applies whether the pupils are white or colored. Negro scholastics in those counties not having a complete 12 grades are transported at state expense to other schools.

Texas provides public education for every colored pupil on an equal basis with the white people.

Texas in 1953–54 had 1953 active school districts; of these districts 292 offered a full twelve-grade school for both white and Negro.

One hundred twenty-five districts maintained a Negro school but did not have a white school. A total of 956 districts provide some colored schools. The districts that did not maintain a white or colored school were in areas that did not contain the requisite number of white or colored scholastics. So we see that the Texas educational system is predicated upon local self-governing school districts. They have full authority to administer the school system. The basic and historic concept of the public free schools is based upon the democratic and salutory privilege of local self-government.

The schools of Texas are operated, maintained and controlled by local school boards made up of men and women elected by their neighbors.

There are 911 of these school trustees in the state.

Each one, fellow citizens. Each one, familiar with their problems, temperament and economic conditions of his locality. Citizens may resolve their complaints or effect scholastic district policies quickly, face to face with the men and women who are responsible for them.

Justice for parent, child, teacher and administrator alike is of the greatest importance. Only a short distance across a town or down a farm to market road—it is local.

Expenses of these school districts are paid through local taxation voted by the taxpayer of the district and complemented by the legislature under an automatic system of finance called the minimum foundation program.

Capital expenditures are made through bond issues voted by the taxpayers of the district.

All personnel of the schools with the exception of the elected officials are employed by local officers and work under their supervision.

Considering the attitudes of the Texas citizens, the structure of the Texas school system, the variety of local situations, the urgency of saving and increasing facilities, and the necessity of maintaining peace and order, it is clear that any attempt to effect immediate or too sudden mixture of white and colored pupils, especially if made by an authority outside the individual school district, would be rash, imprudent and unrealistic.

Texas loves its Negro people and Texas will solve their problems in its own way. During the past decade in particular gigantic strides have been made in human understanding, in raising the standards of education and in elevating the level of education among our citizens. We are proud of our school system and we make no apologies for it.

We have worked exhaustively to make it a good one. We are proud of the nine thousand men and women who serve on our school boards without pay.

We are proud of the management and the fact that they have been able to raise the standards of our schools. We see no reason to subject our economy, our traditions, our state of social harmony or our children to the shock of forced or too rapid integration before the public conscience is prepared to accept it.

We see no reason to pluck local affairs out of local hands.

The question is more basic than laws and systems. This touches the deepest roots of human emotion. It touches mothers and fathers and children in an area of deep sensitivity.

It comes dangerously close to interference in the sacred inviolable relationship between parent and child and the right of parents to bring up their children in their own customs and beliefs.

Texas does not come here today to argue the cause of other states because its situation is unique.

It argues only that in Texas a man-made cataclysm must be made slowly and with wisdom. Our argument may be summed up in eight words, the simplicity of which I believe this honorable Court will appreciate.

It is our problem, let us solve it. Even as I talk here this afternoon my fellow Texans are working with diligence and prayer and with consciousness before God to bring enlightenment, with understanding and well being to all our people.

Were they alive the framers of our Constitution would not ask more.

THE CHIEF JUSTICE: General, have any steps been taken at all to bring about desegregation?

MR. SHEPPERD: No, sir, they have not. The only state action, Mr. Chief Justice, that was taken is an action by the State Board of Education shortly after the May 17 decree stating that in their opinion it did not apply at this time to Texas and during the present school year that we are in now that segregation would continue to be practiced. Our legislature has been in session since January 7 and they have taken no action and there are no bills pending before them.

THE CHIEF JUSTICE: You say you anticipated difficulties in some parts of your state but I notice over in the West and in the North and even down in the South, that there are a great many counties that have from two-tenths of one percent up to one percent, would you anticipate any real difficulty in integrating those schools.

MR. SHEPPERD: I don't believe that there would be any serious trouble in integrating those schools. It would depend upon the method in which it is presented to them.

Texans are kind of like Californians, they are a rugged breed of individualists and without any disrespect at all to the Court intended, I think if this thing is approached on a partnership basis rather than being told what to do that we are all going to get along better and I believe that is what the Court had in mind when they propounded these questions.

As Mr. Justice Black pointed out in his question earlier, in the cases before you the questions propounded in all probability would not be necessary.

THE CHIEF JUSTICE: The only point I make is this. You anticipated there would be some difficulties in some parts of the state. What probability do you believe there would be of having integration very quickly let us say, in these places where there are less than 1 per cent or 1 per cent, 2 per cent, 3 per cent, something like that, what is your prognosis there?

MR. SHEPPERD: I think that there are some of those particular counties in some of those particular districts that would like integration. It would be more economically feasible for them to integrate.

THE CHIEF JUSTICE: That is the only reason. I say that is the only reason they would do it?

MR. SHEPPERD: That is the only reason I have heard advanced. As far as difficulties are concerned, I would hesitate to speak for my brethren from west Texas because they too get a little rugged in spots.

We might find in many of those counties just as much feeling as we would in east Texas counties.

THE CHIEF JUSTICE: Thank you.

MR. SHEPPERD: Thank you, sir.

THE CHIEF JUSTICE: Mr. Waldrep.

## ARGUMENT ON BEHALF OF THE STATE OF TEXAS
### AS THE FRIEND OF THE COURT

### by MR. BRUNELL WALDREP

MR. WALDREP: Mr. Chief Justice Warren, may it please the Court. With every new change in our school system, we have many problems. The Texas public school system is no exception to this rule.

Inasmuch as these are class actions before this honorable Court and because of the great variety of local conditions which exist, this Court has stated that the decrees in these cases will present problems of considerable complexity.

Therefore the cases with regard to this were restored to the docket and all of those states now requiring segregation in public education have been permitted to appear and present argument with reference to questions four and five.

While we are not before this Court as a party litigant, Texas does appreciate this opportunity of presenting argument relative to these complexities referred to by the Court as they relate to the State of Texas and particularly to our public school system.

The educational system in Texas stems from a constitutional mandate to the effect that it shall be the duty of the legislature to establish and make provision for the support and maintenance of an efficient system of public free schools.

In keeping with this educational policy there was also a constitutional mandate in section 7 of Article 7 of the constitution of our state to the effect that the races should be separated in the public schools.

This condition has existed for more than approximately sixty years and in the remarks of General Shepperd it was shown that these problems that are peculiar to Texas appear primarily in the northern quadrant of the state of Texas.

For that reason we feel that no single equitable general decree could be formulated for the entire state of Texas because the establishment of an integrated system is not a problem which would apply equally to west or south Texas where there is only a small percentage of the population and to northeast Texas where the concentration of the Negro population is the heaviest.

In keeping with the pronouncement of this Court that education is perhaps the most important function of our state government Texas has worked diligently to improve its school facilities.

Not many years ago we established what is known as a Minimum Foundation School Program which provided that all possible control and responsibility be left to the school administrators and local school boards to meet the needs of the children in the various school districts within our state.

This program guaranteed to every school age child within the borders of our state regardless of his or her race, creed or color, economic status or his place of residence at least a minimum of a full nine months schooling each year.

This program has been in effect for five years and as a result the average daily attendance of school-aged children has risen from 77.3 per cent in 1900–1949 to 80.5 per cent during 1953–1954.

Seventy-nine point thirty-one per cent of the Negro school-age children were in average daily attendance in 1953–1954.

Now this program which is in operation in our state provides a system of financing which guarantees to the local school district that state funds will be available to pay the cost of a minimum school program when local funds are in sufficient amount. If a school program in the state superior to the minimum requirements is desired by any articular district, it may be paid for by the taxes voted and levied and collected from the taxpayers within that particular district.

Most of our minimum program in Texas reveals from the polls taken and the results of that program that the teachers and the school administrators salaries have risen from twenty-ninth in the nation to sixteenth.

Ninety-seven point one per cent of our teachers within our state now have college degrees. And there are approximately 8,500 Negro teachers and school administrators in Texas.

By reason of this emphasis which the state has placed upon the Minimum Foundation School Program, we respectfully submit that any decree of this Court should permit an effective gradual adjustment toward integration.

And unquestionably the integration of a particular program within a district should be left to the local school districts.

Inasmuch as our educational program is predicated upon local self-governing districts and the schools are operated and maintained and controlled by local school boards, these school boards are elected by the people within the particular district and the operational and maintenance costs are provided by taxation of the district and supplemented by the Minimum Foundation Program.

All of these capital expenditures which are being spent and more than half of the operational and maintenance costs are provided by local taxation of themselves directly after election by the voters of that particular school district.

Our citizens within the state have taxed themselves heavily with reference to this emphasis on an efficient school system within the borders of our state.

Subsequent to the decision of this honorable Court on May 17 of last year, the State Board of Education of our state adopted a resolution to the effect that the decision of the Court not being final, that the Board was obligated to adhere to and comply with the present state laws and the policies providing for segregation within the public school system until such time as they may be changed by constituted authority.

It was also stated by this Board that if the Texas laws were changed, each local district should have sufficient time to work out its own individual problems.

The school system within the borders of our state at this time is presently overcrowded and any immediate integration of course would create many problems and particularly additional facilities would be needed in many of our districts.

JUSTICE REED: Why is that necessary?

MR. WALDREP: The buildings within the districts.

JUSTICE REED: Additional facilities? There would be no more children.

MR. WALDREP: In some instances, Your Honor, where the daily average attendance is not sufficient to warrant a Negro school, these Negroes are required to go to the adjoining districts. Under our compulsory attendance law if they are required to return to the district that they are residents with our school buildings presently overcrowded, there are no facilities available for them until such time as additional wings or buildings are constructed.

JUSTICE REED: Why would they have to? Why wouldn't they go to the school they have been going to?

MR. WALDREP: In some instances they would provide a method of voluntary transfer, I am sure. But in the meantime that would take—

JUSTICE REED: I don't grasp the problem of space. Undoubtedly your schools are crowded, most schools are.

MR. WALDREP: That is right, sir.

JUSTICE REED: But there would be the same number of children. There would be the same number of schools.

MR. WALDREP: There would be the same—

JUSTICE REED: There would be the same number of seats.

MR. WALDREP: There would be the same number of schools and the same number of seats but there would be a shifting of the children, a shifting of the population by reason of the compulsory attendance laws.

JUSTICE REED: Couldn't they go just where they are going now?

MR. WALDREP: They could arrange it in those counties, particularly in west Texas where they are now being transported by bus to the adjoining district.

JUSTICE REED: A sufficient number could still be transported?

MR. WALDREP: Yes, sir.

JUSTICE REED: I still don't grasp why there would be a need for additional facilities.

MR. WALDREP: In some areas in the particular county of Red River for example, there are Negro students transported by bus from three communities to the high school at the county seat.

These particular children would be required to come back to the district of their residence and attend that high school within that area which is not equipped under our compulsory attendance law. Unless that was changed, we could make an additional provision under our compulsory attendance laws, I am sure, as pointed out by Your Honor.

JUSTICE REED: There would be no lack of facilities.

MR. WALDREP: There would be in many instances.

JUSTICE REED: But none on account of race?

MR. WALDREP: None on account of race. Within the geographic limits. If the districts were changed, it would create a problem I am sure.

For that reason with reference to the existing boundary lines and a utilization of the present housing facilities, it is our belief that no equitable general decree would be entered.

But it would appear that a particular decree, specific in nature would have to be entered which would be based upon the fact and conditions existing then in a particular locality.

No single formula can be applied to all of these localities as an effective and orderly transition will depend upon special conditions and problems that exist in a particular area. And in Texas there is a wide variance of the local conditions and a practical approach in one community may not be a practical approach in another community. So it is apparent that there can be no general statewide pattern of integration in our public schools.

We say that the school authorities in the local districts are best acquainted with conditions and are more familar with local conditions and can best evaluate the existing problem.

THE CHIEF JUSTICE: Doesn't that assume that they all want to conform?

MR. WALDREP: No, sir. That decision, Mr. Chief Justice, would be left primarily to the governing body of the local school district.

THE CHIEF JUSTICE: And you feel that even though there is just one colored child in a school district, as there are in some of your districts that I see here—

MR. WALDREP: Yes, sir.

THE CHIEF JUSTICE: —and there is no administrative problem, no financial problem, no physical factors to take into consideration; you believe that that should be left to the school board without any interference, even though there is an intention, a desire, not to conform to the law?

MR. WALDREP: It would be left to the—

THE CHIEF JUSTICE: Is that what you are asking, I mean?

MR. WALDREP: We are asking that it be left to the administrative discretion within the local governing districts of Texas, yes, sir.

THE CHIEF JUSTICE: Regardless of whether there are any physical problems or financial or administrative problems?

MR. WALDREP: Presumably those particular counties would integrate where there is no physical or practical problem at that particular time based upon the particular problems presented to them. That would be my construction, sir.

THE CHIEF JUSTICE: You would assume, then, that in places where there are no physical factors, financial problems or adminstrative problems, that they should and they would integrate?

MR. WALDREP: In all probability they would, sir, in compliance.

THE CHIEF JUSTICE: That is what I wanted to ask.

MR. WALDREP: Yes, sir.

JUSTICE BURTON: You are not advocating local option?

MR. WALDREP: No, sir; other than the administrative discretion within the local governing school district, as set up by statute in Texas.

JUSTICE FRANKFURTER: You are urging recognition of local differentiation?

MR. WALDREP: Yes, sir.
Well, in a sense, that conditions in one particular district would be different than conditions in another district within the State of Texas, yes, sir.

A gradual transition to an integrated public school system is not a denial of a constitutional right enunciated by the Court. So we feel in passing specifically to Question No. 4 propounded by the Court that the geographical school districting in Texas is such that there should be a gradual adjustment from a segregated system to an integrated one, and that this Court should not formulate a detailed decree, but the decree should remand the cases to the courts of first instance with directions to frame decrees in these cases in this manner, adjusting the equities between the parties without unduly hindering the public school system.

Texas urges that consideration—

JUSTICE REED: Which cases are you referring to, Nos. 2 and 3, South Carolina and Virginia?

MR. WALDREP: Yes, sir.

Texas urges that consideration be given to these traditions and usages that have grown up through the years as a result of separate but equal facilities, which includes a vast amount of capital expenditures and provision or facilities for the school children of Texas. A period of orderly transition will more certainly insure that the decree will meet with favor.

Texas enjoys harmonious relationships and has made excellent progress in economic, educational and social advancement. We have striven to create an atmosphere in which people can think clearly and act intelligently.

We want to respect community attitudes, preserve our public school system and solve the many social and legal, as well as economic, phases of this particular problem.

Fifty per cent of our Negro scholastics are located in forty-five of our northern counties, and 90 per cent of the total Negro scholastics are located in the eighty-eight counties comprising the northern quadrant of the state. This area is predominantly an agricultural area, and in cities and towns residential certification prevails, and there are separate schools in these areas for white and Negro school children.

The Negro school building, of course, is located in the Negro section of town, and the white school building within the white section of the town.

Each district should be permitted to adjust its own problems as the conditions exist.

By reason of these particular varying degrees within the State of Texas and with the background considered, in keeping with the segregated school system and the urgent necessity of utilizing all of our school facilities, both Negro and white, and the attitudes manifested by the people of our state, and the necessity for maintaining a harmonious relationship, it is clearly indicated that there should be a local self-governing administration of this particular problem and a gradual transition period which would better insure an orderly compliance with the decision of the Court.

Thank you.

THE CHIEF JUSTICE: Thank you, General Shepperd and Mr. Waldrep, for your views.

Mr. Sobeloff.

## ARGUMENT ON BEHALF OF THE GOVERNMENT OF THE
## UNITED STATES, AS THE FRIEND OF THE COURT

### by SIMON E. SOBELOFF

MR. SOBELOFF: May it please the Court, arising to address the Court toward the end of the third day of argument in this case devoted to a consideration of the Fourteenth Amendment, and occasionally the Fifth, almost, it seems to me, that the Court might invoke for its own protection the Eighth Amendment, which guarantees it against cruel and unusual punishment.

I am going to try not to be repetitious and yet reframe arguments that have been made here, restate them in a context that seems to us coherent from the Government's point of view.

I am not so presumptious as to claim that we have complete objectivity, but I am more than ordinarily conscious in this case that I am privileged to speak for the United States, and our approach to these problems is perhaps a little different than that of the plaintiffs or the defendants, or even of some of the States or other governmental authorities that might appear as plaintiffs or as defendants in future cases.

Of course, there are certain areas of agreement, obviously. There is some true concurrence. Some of the concurrence that has been voiced is more apparent than real; that is, it is verbal. I am not challenging the good faith or the sincerity of these declarations, but as often happens, different people say the same thing, but mean different things by it.

Everybody here has urged that this Court should not itself frame detailed decrees, but should remand the cases to the district courts. But the objectives of the different opponents of that idea are not always the same. Some would ask this Court, have asked this Court to remand the cases with specific and rigid directions to the district courts to specify a fixed date for desegregation by 1955 in September or at the latest a year later.

Others have gone to the other extreme, and they have urged a remand, but they have specifically asked that this Court shall fix no date, and more than that, it shall give no criteria in its decree to the lower courts for the guidance of those courts, leaving open, as is plain, the possibility that nothing would eventuate except delay.

The government rejects both extremes. Our brief, which sets forth our views at length and more in detail than it will be possible for me to present them, or even necessary to present them orally, our brief offers the counsel of moderation, but with a degree of firmness.

This, as everybody recognizes, is not a debate on the validity of the Court's decision. This is not a reargument. Segregation has been declared unconstitutional. While it continues, as has been said, constitutional rights are being denied, and in some cases the delay is irretrievable.

On the other hand, that doesn't mean that institutions and practices that have persisted for generations may be erased with a single stroke of the pen. No practical person will overlook that situation.

Difficulties undeniably exist in some places. In other places, as has been stated here at this table, the difficulties are practically nonexistent or are very slight. Obviously, the Court ought not to treat all these decisions as a lot. There has to be some discretion. Of course, it should be recognized that these cases are not like the Gaines case, or the Sipuel case, where a simple order to admit would suffice.

Affected here are seventeen states, and millions of pupils and school plants costing enormous sums, and school buildings that are not interchangeable, that are not readily augmented. That doesn't mean that the problem arises everywhere, but where it does arise, it can be severe. There are teaching and administrative organizations that have to be adjusted, and such organizations are not readily altered and intergrated. There are physical problems. There are financial problems. There are administrative problems. There are indeed emotional problems.

But this Court at this stage, on this record, lacks the materials for judgment either as to what ought to be done or as to the order or the time schedule within which it ought to be attempted in particular cases.

There are certain places where, for instance Delaware, both parties agree there should be a simple affirmance. That case practically disposes of itself.

Kansas says, "We are going to be integrated in September."

The Court can simply refer the matter back to the district court from which the case emanates, with the simple direction to pass an order in accordance with the decree. If the Court finds that there has been substantial integration by September, 1955, there is no difficulty about it. It may decide that the case calls for a simple order. It may decide that the case calls for no specific direction or injunction.

These cases present no difficulty. Even in the District of Columbia substantially they say they will have integrated by September. Oh, there is indeed some question, and it may be a serious question, as to the propriety of certain options.

I wish—and I must say this in all frankness—that there had been a more generous recognition and credit given to the District authorities for the readiness with which they proceeded to respect this Court's decision and indeed, as has been brought out here, they had planned even in advance of the Court's decision, in anticipation of it, and had laid plans for integration, which plans have been put into effect, and even though there is a legitimate basis for disagreement as to those as to some provisions, as in this option plan, I think on the whole they are entitled to considerable credit for the readiness with which they acted.

That doesn't mean that this Court should either approve or disapprove the option provision. The Court has not been informed in detail about that provision and how it is operating. An option provision that is perfectly all right in the District of Columbia might work in an entirely different way in another place, or it may be all wrong in the District of Columbia and might work better in other places.

This Court, I am sure, would be better advised and would be acting more consistent with its usual practice to say that as to a matter of that sort, where the record has not been made, the facts have not been developed, it will not pass on that. The problem may solve itself, as the more momentous problems in connection with desegregation in the District of Columbia seem to have been solved.

If it arises and is presented in orderly fashion, it can be dealt with.

Of course, it is obvious from what has been said here that there is such a great variety of conditions as between the states and within states and within counties and even within a particular school district, that no single formula can be devised by the ingenuity of man that will fit aptly all cases, and this Court could not, in any event, take unto itself the burden of acting as a super school board. It must necessarily repose some measure of discretion elsewhere, and I think, by common consent, by common agreement of the parties, and the others who have addressed this Court, the district courts are the appropriate agency.

Now, giving a measure of discretion to the courts, however, does not mean that they ought to be given no guide, no instruction, no criteria. This Court ought not to give a district judge a blank check and say, "Fill it out any way you want." It ought to tell him to consider all the facts, everthing that has been mentioned here. Some of these things are very weighty. But the court ought to be told, the district court ought to be told by this Court that that measure of discretion is not to be used for the purpose of frustration. He is not to permit delay to be had for the mere sake of delay. Where difficulties exist, the equity court, of course, has the right to fashion its remedy according to the needs and time where it is needed and to the extent that it is needed; but only to that extent, should be allowed.

The district courts ought to have it made plain that in the view of this Court a time shall be allowed, but not for the purpose of paralyzing action or of emasculating the Court's decision of last May.

JUSTICE HARLAN: Mr. Sobeloff, do you think these decrees, whatever they are, can affect anyone other than the litigants who are actually before the court?

MR. SOBELOFF: I would say that these decrees, like all decrees, affect only the parties, or if they are class actions, the people who are identifiable as belonging to the class.

JUSTICE HARLAN: That is the "if," though.

MR. SOBELOFF: But regardless of that, I am sure this Court will not overlook the immense importance of its declarations in a particular case as a guide to a general treatment of problems in other cases.

I don't mean to suggest that if this Court were to say that a certain time element should be allowed, if you decide that you ought to put in a time element, that you allowed in this particular case, that district judges generally ought to adopt that same schedule under entirely different conditions, but I do think it is important for this Court to indicate its approach and the approach of the district judges on the matter, and in most instances where the Court makes that clear, the tendency is to reduce litigation.

It has been pointed out here that in these college cases and the professional school cases, the Sipuel case was decided, and other states having similar problems didn't go through a process of litigation. They foresaw the inevitable result of a future case that made a future case unnecessary.

I don't mean to say that our position will fold up automatically. I don't mean to say that there will be no further litigation. But I think that what you do here will largely influence the temper, the spirit in which district courts will operate, will be guided by the way you fashion the decree here.

JUSTICE REED: Take the South Carolina case. What do you envisage would be the result of the judgment in that case?

MR. SOBELOFF: The judgment here?

JUSTICE REED: Either here or if it is sent back to the district court.

MR. SOBELOFF: I think in the South Carolina case—let's see. You have the Clarendon County case. You have about 2,500 Negro children and about 300 white children in that case.

JUSTICE REED: No. You have about seven or eight Negro children, and they represent as a class all of the Negro children, numbering about 2,500.

MR. SOBELOFF: Yes. I would say that ought to be referred to the district court there.

JUSTICE REED: What is his problem? To admit ten children whose names are on this list?

MR. SOBELOFF: I understand that these are class cases.

JUSTICE REED: So the problem would be the 2,500.

MR. SOBELOFF: Yes.

My own thought is that it would not serve any useful purpose to unduly narrow the scope of the case. I know you don't want to adjudicate questions that are not necessary to be adjudicated, but nothing is going to be gained by admitting ten and disregarding the situation of the others. I don't think that would be satisfactory, either to the plaintiffs or to the defendants. I think in that instance you have to look to the whole situation. I think you have to tell the district judge that he must consider that, but that doesn't mean that the district judge ought to be told nothing as to how to proceed.

JUSTICE REED: No.

MR. SOBELOFF: And our brief—and I will come to it presently—

JUSTICE REED: My question is directed to whether he is dealing with ten people or 2,500 people.

MR. SOBELOFF: I think he is dealing with 2,500 people there. If you were simply going to order the admission of ten people, I suppose that that would be of some value as a declaration of this Court, but you would be adjudicating an unreal situation. You know that you are not really dealing with ten people, you know you are dealing with 2,500 people, and I think what you ought to do is treat that as that kind of a case, and tell the judge below to treat it as that kind of a case, but that doesn't mean the judge ought to be left without any support, without any guidance. His hands ought to be strengthened.

He ought to be in a position, when the contesting litigants appear before him and make their contentions, he ought to be able to say, by reason of the Court's decree, this is what the Constitution directs me to do. I can allow time if you show me the need for the time, and if you show me a plan why the time is necessary and how you are going to employ the time, not merely give time and time indefinitely.

I think it would be an unfortunate thing for both sides if the thing were handled in that way.

JUSTICE BURTON: Following Justice Reed's question, you would frame your opinion in the light of the 2,500, and you would frame your decree in the light of the ten.

MR. SOBELOFF: I would say so. I don't know technically whether that is a class suit or not. I understand from the way the thing is written that it is a class suit, the way the briefs are treated. The Court's questions are predicated on the assumption that these are class suits. The Court says in so many words, in

addressing the parties and addressing the Attorney General of the United States
and the Attorneys General of the states, this Court says, since these are class
actions, and the impact will fall on a great many, we want further argument on
these questions.

So this Court has heretofore regarded these cases as class cases.

JUSTICE HARLAN: You would agree, would you not, whether they are
or not, goes to the very heart of the character of the decree we will enter, because if
only five or six plaintiffs are involved, what is the reason for delay?

MR. SOBELOFF: If only five or six persons were in that situation, let's
assume, even though they are not class suits, let's assume that five people came to
the court to sue for themselves and did not say they were suing for a class, I think
that the court, to be practical about it, would have to look at those five, not as
though they were the only ones on the scene, it would have to look at those five in
the context of the whole population where they are, white and colored.

The first thing that this Court should make clear is that any state constitutional provision or statute which conflicts with the opinion of the Court, with the
decision of the Court of last May, is void. There has been some confusion about
that. The Attorney General of Maryland has told you that in Maryland there is
this division in Baltimore City, because although the statutes are the same, they
went ahead and desegregated. In the counties, because of some things that were
said officially and unofficially, there has been some doubt about it.

Some of the counties who want to desegregate, school officials who want to
desegregate, were led to believe that they couldn't desegregate until there was a
final decree by this Court.

Although Maryland was not directly a party, they thought these laws did not
fall in Maryland from the mere rendition of the decision in May, but there would
have to be a decree. I don't think there is much doubt about it. Some of the attorneys here have said frankly that they think any conflicting statutes or constitutional provisions have fallen, but this Court ought to declare that, so there will be
no room for doubt or hesitation, so that those who want to obey the law will know
what that is.

JUSTICE REED: Even though the particular statute has not been involved
in this particular case?

MR. SOBELOFF: If this Court has said that under the Constitution there
can no longer be separate but equal; and the local law says, commands, separate
but equal, I think it is plain that that local law has to give.

JUSTICE REED: Yes, even though it is not raised here.

MR. SOBELOFF: You don't direct your decree to those who haven't
appeared in the court, but the impact of that will be felt if this Court says so, in
this decree.

I think as a matter of clarification that ought to be in the decree.

JUSTICE FRANKFURTER: The Delaware Supreme Court made a dis-
tinction. It said that the provisions in the Constitution and all the laws carrying

out the Delaware Constitution allowing or commanding segregation are null and void, but unless there is a decree entered, there is no compulsion in the translation of that nullification.

MR. SOBELOFF: This Court can very readily in the next few weeks set at rest any doubts about it. I don't think there could be any doubts in lawyers' minds as to what will happen, but I think it ought not to be left to further speculation.

JUSTICE FRANKFURTER: That is what the Delaware Supreme Court said, and it seems incontestable to me.

MR. SOBELOFF: But others have expressed different views.

JUSTICE FRANKFURTER: The decree, you say, should formalize what this Court said on May 17.

MR. SOBELOFF: Exactly. It ought not to be left to be gathered from the comments of the Court in the opinion. It ought to be in the decree itself.

The Court ought to also make clear that the remand is for the purpose of effectuating its decision, not for the purpose of frustration. I think it would be greatly of help to the judges in the performance of their duties if they knew that the Court wants or directs them to resume jurisdiction of the cases for the purpose of effecting the decision as soon as feasible, not limiting them specifically as to a date, but allowing them to fix dates with that in mind, not merely to wait until attitudes change in some remote generation, but consider the matter, hear the parties and, after debate, discussion and consideration, decide it with a view to effectuating the Court's decision as speedily as feasible.

JUSTICE BLACK: What does "feasible" mean?

MR. SOBELOFF: "Feasible" means like any other question of fact, a determination after considering all relevant facts.

If you find that the judge is not given enough time, or if he finds he has not given enough time, he can give further time. If either side feels he has abused his discretion, either side can, on appeal, have a review. The merit of that is that this Court does not undertake to pass on situations with which it is not intimately familiar.

The district court judge can familiarize himself with it. He is directed to familiarize himself with it, and to order the effectuation of the Court's decision as speedily as feasible, bearing in mind these facts, these circumstances, that will be brought out in the hearing before it.

JUSTICE BLACK: Does that include circumstances with reference to the feasibility to do this, or would it also include attitudes of the people?

MR. SOBELOFF: Attitudes ought to be considered, but attitudes are not to control. Attitudes ought to be considered, because there are certain things that cannot be done within a certain time, but that doesn't mean that whether or not a constitutional right shall be vindicated by a court shall depend upon a public opinion poll; these inquiries are interesting, but courts do not adjudicate constitutional questions on that basis.

JUSTICE BLACK: Does that not indicate the difficulty of "as soon as feasible"?

MR. SOBELOFF: I don't say the words "as soon as feasible" are self-interpreting. They cannot be. If it could be, then the government's recommendation to you would be to put in that date, and interpret it. It is because we recognize that the matter cannot be interpreted and translated into a precise date by this Court that you ask the district judge in the first instance to translate that; but you say to the district judge: "Give them all the time that is reasonably necessary to effectuate the Court's decision, to put into effect that decision, to give it, as this Court said, effective gradual adjustment."

The word "effective" is there, as well as the word "gradual."

JUSTICE MINTON: Would you put a deadline in at all?

MR. SOBELOFF: I don't think I would put a deadline in the more complicated situation. I think you could, if you saw fit, in the District of Columbia, if you decided it was necessary to have any time, you could perhaps put in a deadline. Even there I would prefer that the district court do it in the light of all the circumstances. I think that is the more orderly way. I think it is, on the whole, a more satisfactory way.

But in a complicated situation, I don't think this Court should put in a deadline. Our brief recommends: Don't put in a deadline.

JUSTICE BURTON: That is, you do not recommend any deadline for the completion, but you do mean the immediate start forthwith, to begin to make it effective.

MR. SOBELOFF: I think, Your Honor, that this Court ought to say to every district judge: Call for a plan within ninety days. Somebody here has said that ninety days is too short a time. I think a plan can be formulated in ninety days, especially after eleven months have already gone by since the decision. But I would say that if the plan cannot be formulated within ninety days, then [if] the district judge, as a judge in equity, is applied to for further time, he ought to be permitted to give further time; but the burden ought to be on him who wants the delay to show that he needs it, that he is engaged in a good-faith effort to solve this problem, not that he is waiting for the day after tomorrow, the day after the expiration of the period; but that he is moving, and then when the plan is presented, there should be hearings and all these relevant considerations are to be addressed to the court, and they ought to deal with it as the facts would indicate; and he should require a bona fide beginning.

I think he ought to be required to require a bona fide beginning, whatever he thinks can be done, not to put off everything until some future date, but let the first step be taken as speedily as it can be done without disruption.

That will be interpreted. Fortunately, it will be interpreted by people who live in these communities and understand them. But they ought not to be given an open-end time. He ought to be permitted to channel these efforts, not to impose his will, not to decide it abstractly without hearing, but to let the school officials formulate the plan and produce it, not some time in the remote future, but reasonably promptly.

If more time is needed, he can give it to them.

JUSTICE REED: While the local school board is before the district judge.

MR. SOBELOFF: Yes.

JUSTICE REED: But the state Attorney General and the State Board of Education have something to do with it, and perhaps furnish money or perhaps the statutes provide for the building of new schools, yet none of those parties are before the court.

MR. SOBELOFF: That is a difficulty. It may be that in a particular case, additional parties may be required, either at the suggestion of the plaintiffs, or the court may do that.

That illustrates how these complexities that cannot be foreseen here will arise and can be dealt with intelligently in the light of the situation. But the point is that they be dealt with in an orderly fashion.

Local sentiment, local conditions are not being overridden, but neither is action paralyzed because of an assertion of a local feeling.

Now, the experience in the District of Columbia since May 17 is not going to be exactly paralleled in other places; it can't be. The government recognizes, of course, that because of the President's particular relation to the local government here, his influence would be exerted and was exerted in a way that perhaps he wouldn't wish and couldn't properly attempt to exert it in other situations.

The very character of this community, drawn as it is from various parts of the country, engaged in government work, things that have happened here earlier in recent years, other litigation with which this Court is familiar, all those things have an impact to differentiate the District of Columbia situation from others, and yet the District of Columbia does teach a lesson.

It shows that despite these differences that very often problems that are said to be utterly insoluble, when approached with understanding and sympathy, reasonable good will, not rigidity, yet with a degree of firmness, can be dealt with, and sometimes the difficulties that are foreseen at the beginning do not materialize.

The authorities here in the District did not believe that they could effectuate as much as they did in the time they did.

In another situation, the estimate may prove to be insufficient. More time may be granted.

This Court ought not to make it impossible for the local judge to do that in a proper case.

The reluctance of the plaintiffs in this case to tolerate any delay at all is perfectly understandable, although I don't agree with them on this, although we recommend against setting a fixed date in this Court's decree, and we understand their skepticism about allowing any delay.

But I think that their fear stems from the fact that if the Court sends it back, sends the cases back without any directions, and without a time limit, the thing will be so gradual that there will be nothing affected, and the Court would really be frustrating its own decision of last May.

That is their fear.

The Court can minimize the danger which they apprehend, in a reasonable way, if these provisions—which I will defer until morning—that we have set forth in our proposal, are incorporated in a decree of the Court.

You can have that measure of flexibility which the defendants rightfully ask for and at the same time give the plaintiffs assurance against abuse.

Of course, there will be resistance in some places, and the progress will not be equal. No important change in social policy has been achieved without some resistance, but you must not assume—and I am sure the Court will not assume—that all men in the South are resisting the Constitution, any more than it would be safe to assume that everybody in the North gives enthusiastic support to every provision of the Constitution, but this Court should not, and I am sure will not, underrate the immense influence of its authority on men of good will and intelligence and patriotism in all sections of the country, and I am sure that is a factor that will not be lost sight of and will greatly come to the aid of an ultimate solution.

With the Court's permission, I will resume in the morning.

JUSTICE BLACK: Would you mind tomorrow addressing yourself a little more to the question of class suits, having in mind *Hansberry* v. *Lee,*[23] and other cases, as to who can be covered by a class suit?

MR. SOBELOFF: I will do that.

JUSTICE REED: Also the case of Ben Hur.[24]

MR. SOBELOFF: I am not familiar with that. I will get that.

THE CHIEF JUSTICE: We will now adjourn.

(Whereupon, at 4:30 p.m., the Court recessed, to reconvene at 12:00 noon, Thursday, April 14, 1955.)

(Oral argument was resumed at 12:00 p.m., April 14, 1955).

THE CHIEF JUSTICE: Mr. Solicitor General, will you proceed, please?

ARGUMENT ON BEHALF OF THE UNITED STATES GOVERNMENT (Resumed)

by SIMON E. SOBELOFF

MR. SOBELOFF: If it please the Court, my attention has been called to the answer I gave to a question by Mr. Justice Minton.

Mr. Justice Minton asked me, "Would you put a deadline in at all?" and I replied, "I don't think I would put a deadline in the more complicated situations."

That answer is not clear. What I wanted to say is that I would not have the Supreme Court put in any deadline. I thought that the whole tenor of my argu-

[23]Hansberry v. Lee, 311 U.S. 32 (1940). An attempt to hold a specified number of property owners to a restrictive covenant through a claim that they were bound by the outcome of a class action was rejected by the Court. The property owners were not parties to the so-called class suit and could not be affected by the judgment.

[24]Supreme Tribe of Ben Hur v. Cauble, 255 U.S. 356 (1921). All the members of a fraternal organization which brought a class action on their behalf were held bound by the outcome of the suit.

ment yesterday was that there should be no open orders by the district courts, that they should have deadlines but with freedom in proper cases on a proper showing of facts requiring further time to grant further time.

JUSTICE REED: You mean you would start with a deadline?

MR. SOBELOFF: I would start with a deadline first as to the requirement—we suggest ninety days for a plan to be submitted.

JUSTICE FRANKFURTER: Are you now speaking of the decree to be entered by this Court—

MR. SOBELOFF: No, sir.

JUSTICE FRANKFURTER: —or by the district court?

MR. SOBELOFF: What I said in answer to Mr. Justice Minton applies to the decree of this Court. I would not attempt the deadline in the decree of this Court.

JUSTICE FRANKFURTER: So I understand. But I am wondering, considering the reasons that make that undesirable for this Court to fix a deadline, the reasons that compel remission to the district court to formulate a more detailed decree, whether we should be here considering what deadline the district court should have. Are we not anticipating the very consideration that would urge a deadline?

MR. SOBELOFF: I don't think you ought to tie the hands of the district judge, but I think it would be useful to the district judge if you were able to say to the parties, I am required to ask you, to require you, to produce a plan within ninety days.

See what you can do in the ninety days. If anybody comes before me and shows that there has been a good-faith attempt to produce the plan but [that it] cannot be done within the time limit, I will entertain an application for further time.

There is the merit of requiring motion. That is also the saving grace of not tying people to a time limit that may prove in actuality unworkable.

JUSTICE FRANKFURTER: There are various ways of suggesting motion without being explicit about it.

MR. SOBELOFF: If the Court can devise any way that would suggest motion and require motion and encourage motion and without, however, restricting unduly that discretion which is necessary in the administration of this business, that is the thing that the Government would like to see.

JUSTICE FRANKFURTER: The point of my remark is that the wisdom which directs you to suggest this Court should not go into certain definitiveness or peculiarities is the wisdom that, for me at least, carries beyond guessing what actualities and definitiveness the district court should go into.

MR. SOBELOFF: On the other hand the district judges might appreciate some indication of a tentative limit with the knowledge that on a showing to them of the necessity for more time they can grant more time.

I think it is arguable and may work differently in different situations but in general I think two things are to be avoided: one, a fixed and inflexible limitation; on the other, no limitation at all.

I think that while this Court does not fix the time, the district courts ought to be required to fix some time in the knowledge that they can, on a proper showing, grant more time, but the thing ought not to be left hanging in the air indefinitely.

THE CHIEF JUSTICE: Mr. Solicitor General, this may be an appropriate time for me to ask if you would be willing to prepare a proposal for a decree as the other parties have. It would be helpful to the Court if you would do that.

MR. SOBELOFF: We will be very glad to do whatever the Court thinks would be helpful. I want to call attention to the fact that on pages 27 and forward from that point in that brief, we have with particularity set forth provisions which we think appropriate for the decree.

All that would be required would be the formulation of the words: it is hereby decreed and the provisions themselves are set forth.

THE CHIEF JUSTICE: Thank you.

JUSTICE FRANKFURTER: Plus such further thoughts as you may have had since November 24, 1954.

MR. SOBELOFF: Yes, sir.

JUSTICE HARLAN: For example, your item 1, Mr. Sobeloff, on page 27 is a fixed deadline of ninety days. I take it you are now suggesting flexibility there?

MR. SOBELOFF: Yes. Elsewhere we do speak of giving the court discretion to give further time but if that leaves in doubt the right of the judge to do that, that doubt ought to be resolved now, and there are two other matters that will not detain me very long that I should like to mention before I come to the question that the Chief Justice asked as we were—and others—as we were about to adjourn.

First, with regard to the time limit for the execution of a plan not for the formulation of the plan—my attention has been called to the fact that in the Government's brief in last year, that is in 1953, it was suggested that one year should be allowed, whereas in the present brief we do not make that recommendation.

The inconsistency is more apparent than real because even in the 1953 brief, where one year was suggested, it was stated that it should be one year plus such other time as on a proper showing may be found necessary.

The important thing, whatever the Court does is to make it clear to the lower courts and to the parties that there must be a bona fide advance toward the goal of desegregation. That doesn't mean that people ought to be ridden over roughshod; it doesn't mean that conditions ought to be ignored.

Adjustments have to be made and allowance should be made for the time.

Time ought to be allowed for those adjustments. But it does not mean that the matter ought to be left hanging in the air. And it is between these two extremes that we think that the Court should go and because of the familiarity of the lower courts with their particular conditions we think that the time limits can best be set there.

If, however, this Court thinks it would be wiser to suggest one year, with the opportunity on proper application for an extension, we have no objection to that.

Now, another detail that has not been mentioned in any of the discussions but is proposed in our brief that in a very hypothetical way we say that the Court may wish to appoint a special master to review such reports, that is the reports which will periodically be required of the lower courts to this Court, and to make appropriate recommendations through to this Court and to the lower courts.

Now, we are not recommending that a master be appointed to take testimony.

We are not recommending that he function as a director over the local school authorities.

We have in mind that the volume of these reports may be such that this Court could not effectively deal with them and this Court might find it desirable to have someone who will receive these reports, digest them, present the essence of them to this Court for consideration and from time to time perhaps consult with the lower courts and impart to the judges the reactions of this Court and the suggestions and recommendations, because these things can perhaps be handled better by that informal method than by a series of decrees.

JUSTICE REED: Do I correctly understand then that this Court is to retain these present cases here?

MR. SOBELOFF: Yes, sir.

JUSTICE REED: And what is then to be sent to the district court?

MR. SOBELOFF: It sends the cases back to the district court for the further proceedings for the framing of decree.

JUSTICE REED: Then the cases can be in two courts at the same time?

MR. SOBELOFF: The Court can send that back and yet retain jurisdiction for future purposes if conditions arise that make it, in the discretion of this Court, necessary to intervene, to give direction, you could still do it.

I see no inconsistency between that and these further proceedings in the formulation of decrees.

JUSTICE CLARK: Did we do that in the *Terry* v. *Adams*[25] case? That is the election case down in Texas a few terms ago.

MR. SOBELOFF: I don't know. I am not familiar with the situation there. I think it would be a very wholesome thing for this Court to do, so anybody who has the occasion to see a more specific direction from this Court could do it and it would not involve the delay of starting all over again.

[25]Terry v. Adams, see n. 45, p. 87, *supra*.

Now, with regard to the question—I may add in respect to this master that our view is that he should not be expected or perhaps not even be permitted to volunteer suggestions and certainly give orders to the parties though he perhaps should be permitted if called on to advise.

There may be certain plans that are under consideration which an educational unit, school board, might be in doubt about.

They may want to know what is being done in other jurisdictions. This master would be in a position to give them valuable information.

In that spirit rather than the imposition of a command from him, he might be able to render valuable service.

Now on the question of the class action, of course, the concern of the United States in this case is not primarily with a few individuals.

The importance that attaches to these cases is because we all realize that we are dealing here, not with named plaintiffs alone and not even with individuals who, by any interpretation of the rule, might be regarded as members of the class in the particular case.

We are dealing here with great populations, both white and Negro. It is an important principle. So it is not the fate of a handful that is involved here. The question is what is the procedure to be followed in resolving a much larger problem.

Now it seems to us that this massive litigation which has taken a number of years already would be ineffectual if the effect were limited to a few.

We think that the Court could at least embrace within its decree more than the named plantiffs but members of the classes in those communities who are in the same situation as the named plaintiffs and of course the effect under the doctrine those cases would have upon other future cases is obvious.

From the standpoint of the plaintiff, it would seem to me that the admission of a few might disappoint what they are really after. From the standpoint of the defendants too, I don't think that they would consider that this case was as vital as they do consider it if they thought it would only affect a few.

But if this Court should not take the view which I am about to elaborate as to the class nature of these actions, if you should decide that these are not class suits and that your relief has to be limited to the few, then neither side can have that both ways. On the one hand the plaintiffs can't expect that the decree will run in favor of people who are not before the Court.

On the other hand, the defendants, if they insist that the decree can only affect a few, can't say that the rights of those few shall not be fully adjudicated because there may be others that will be affected.

On the other hand, if you take the view that this case, for instance the case in South Carolina, involves only eleven high school students and not a greater number and it seems to me to be consistent, you can't say these people ought to have their rights postponed, because there may be others.

Either you take into account the others and ask the district court to consider the whole group or if you take the opposite view and say we are only going to consider the eleven who are named plaintiffs then you have to give them, it seems to me, the rights which the decision of May 17 entitles them to have.

JUSTICE BLACK: If that should be done, would there be any possible necessity of the machinery which you suggested, which would be pretty large, of having masters and reports from all over the country?

MR. SOBELOFF: If you should take that view and terminate the suits in that way, I don't think you would have to do any more. But there might be the danger of a volume of litigation that could perhaps, if you take the other view, be averted.

JUSTICE BLACK: What view is that?

MR. SOBELOFF: If you take the class action you don't have to have new suits. These other people can have their rights determined in these very proceedings.

JUSTICE BLACK: Beyond the Clarendon District?

MR. SOBELOFF: Obviously, no. Under no view of the class action rule can people in other districts be affected, either entitled to relief or bound by the proceedings in these cases.

JUSTICE BLACK: Then, even then litigation would continue, would it not, in other parts of the country?

MR. SOBELOFF: It might. Although as I say, that the prestige of this Court is such that people will be disposed to abide by the law and not invent spurious reasons for delay.

JUSTICE BLACK: Do you think they would be any less inclined to abide by that if there was a direct immediate order that these individuals should be admitted in these schools and nothing more?

MR. SOBELOFF: I don't think I know that they would be less disposed to obey, but you would be settling a much narrower question.

Perhaps from one point of view, that is desirable. But I think both sides want to have the situation settled in the light of these administrative problems, which they say and which we all recognize will happen if a great number will apply.

So far as these few are concerned, the problem may be resolved without great administrative difficulty. But what happens tomorrow?

The problem may come up in a milder form. I don't know. My guess is not any better than any other man's about that.

All I am suggesting to the Court is that if you should take the view contrary to what I suggested yesterday that these are class actions, and that other people in Clarendon County besides the named plaintiffs are to be entitled to the relief under the decree.

If you take the view that only the eleven are before the Court then it would not be consistent to say that these eleven should not have their constitutional rights because administrative problems may arise in the future with respect to plaintiffs who have not yet declared themselves and have not yet intervened.

JUSTICE HARLAN: On the other hand, there would be no reason for delay as far as these plaintiffs are concerned, in that view?

MR. SOBELOFF: Not in that view. If you take that view in the nature of these actions.

JUSTICE DOUGLAS: The question of the eleven might not raise administrative problems.

MR. SOBELOFF: That is right. At what point it is simple and raises no administrative difficulty, nobody can say abstractly. You would have to examine the record and satisfy yourself whether or not you can pass a fair judgment on this record.

JUSTICE CLARK: What happens to the other 2,500?

MR. SOBELOFF: That is just it. If it is a class action, then the 2,500 are all considered as part of the class.

JUSTICE CLARK: I mean, assuming it is not. You say there are only eleven. Originally it was thirty-one but now there are eleven to consider.

MR. SOBELOFF: If you consider the rights of the eleven in this individual action, the rights of the eleven are adjudicated. They get their relief. The others may or may not intervene in this case according to the rule I will discuss presently or they will have to start new actions.

Generally that has been held. This Court has never passed on this question but the lower court decisions generally held that there can be intervention at any time before judgment. There is one case that goes even further and says that a person who is covered, who is included in the class although not named as a plaintiff can come in and claim his relief, even after judgment.

There would be cases in which such a person came in and demanded a citation for contempt against the plaintiff for not complying with the Court's injunction although he had not theretofore declared himself and intervened as a plaintiff.

JUSTICE CLARK: Do you have a brief on this problem?

MR. SOBELOFF: We will be very glad to submit a brief to the Court.

JUSTICE HARLAN: The Fourth Circuit has even gone further. They have held you can have a class action without intervening at all.

MR. SOBELOFF: In what case is that?

JUSTICE HARLAN: I forget the name of it. It was in a suit to enjoin the enforcement of an alleged unconstitutional tax and the court in its opinion held that the decree could run for the benefit of all the class irrespective of joining.

JUSTICE FRANKFURTER: Mr. Solicitor General, there are other problems involved in this other than the mere question of who are the technical parties to the litigation.

Whoever writes the decree must write it in the context of what will actually happen and what could happen.

It is hard for me to believe that if this Court ordered eleven children to go to a school in a county in which there are 2,800 children—that is the figure—in the same situation, that somehow or other, the others will not manifest the desire for the decree, and therefore merely writing a decree for the eleven may amount to nothing except the ink that is written on a piece of paper—

MR. SOBELOFF: In answer to the question yesterday I think I indicated in answer to Mr. Justice Harlan that I think you have to remember that hovering over these few are a great many others who will be affected, but I don't know what conclusion the Court will come to.

If you come to that conclusion of course it is obvious that this is a class action, then you have to consider the effect on the whole area.

JUSTICE FRANKFURTER: My suggestion is I don't have to get into the fog of class action and spurious class action to consider the consequence of rights for eleven what might be called fungible subjects in relation to the 2,800.

MR. SOBELOFF: On the other hand, there is this to be said. You have here not a case where [a decision] in favor of these necessarily displaces other people. What the plaintiffs here are asking is not to be admitted to white schools. Technically what they are asking for is to go, to be permitted to attend schools that are nonsegregated.

That does not mean that all 2,500 will be in white schools. They are to go to schools in which they are admitted regardless of color.

The problem may not involve a complete redistribution of all. This Court might consider it wiser to defer dealing with the rest.

JUSTICE FRANKFURTER: But it may involve—and I do not see easily how it can avoid involving—considering the educational system of that county and the administrative problems.

MR. SOBELOFF: I am inclined to sympathize with that view. I point out if you take the other view it does not necessarily follow that you have to consider the whole picture. You may say sufficient unto this case is the litigation that is actually before us.

We are going to decide it with respect to the named plaintiffs and we are going to see what happens.

You may take that view. I am not urging that it is the better view. But I say that there is something to be said for the consistency if you limit it to the eleven of giving them their rights as they would appear if there were only eleven.

If, on the other hand, you want to consider it in determining the relief for the eleven whether there are others, the whole scene, then you have to include the whole group.

JUSTICE FRANKFURTER: It is not a question of wanting, exercising, a preference for this or that. I may speak for myself, the first requisite of a decree of equity is that it be effective and not be merely a piece of paper.

MR. SOBELOFF: I had intended to discuss this Rule 23 (a) [of the Federal Rules of Civil Procedure]. I see my time is up and I will be very glad to submit a memorandum.

THE CHIEF JUSTICE: Would you do that, please?

MR. SOBELOFF: Yes, sir.

23(a) which deals with representation is not too long and I think it would be well to have it before the Court by reading it.

> If persons constituting a class are so numerous as to make it impracticable to bring them all before the court, such of them, one or more, as will fairly insure the adequate representation of all may, on behalf of all, sue or be sued when the character of the right sought to be enforced for or against the class is . . .

And then there are three sub-paragraphs, 1, 2, and 3. If the right to be enforced is:

> (1) joint, or common, or secondary in the sense that the owner of a primary right refuses to enforce that right and a member of the class thereby becomes entitled to enforce it.

I think the classic example of that is a stockholder's suit where the officers and directors of the corporation refuse to vindicate the right of the stockholder which he holds derivatively as a stockholder. Under certain conditions he may come in and stand in the place of the corporation of which he is a stockholder. I think that is the typical case under one.

> (2) Where the rights sought to be enforced are several, and the object of the action is the adjudication of claims which do or may affect specific property involved in the action.

> For instance where there is a suit over a common fund or a creditor's action.
> And the third, which I think would cover this case:

> Where the rights sought to be enforced are several and there is a common question of law or fact affecting the several rights and a common relief is sought.

This Court could very well say that in the case that we have been talking about, the South Carolina case, these eleven are representatives of the larger group.

They profess to come in on behalf of others and that these others have with them a common question of law and fact, affecting the several rights and a common relief is being sought.

Here there is no attempt to recover separate damages. It isn't even a case where there is a common disaster and a number of people in an accident have sought relief.

There the Court could adjudicate at one time the question of liability and then have the measure of damages which would make the difference in different cases, determined separately.

Here what they are asking for is a declaration of the law. And an injunction. Now there is no practical impediment imposed here to adjustment that will apply to the whole class. The class at large has been adequately represented, fairly represented.

The unnamed plaintiffs as well as those who are separately, specifically named.

There have been a number of cases. The Court called my attention yesterday to two. I don't think that they are cases that fall within this group 3. The Hansberry case is a case involving a racial covenant on land. It is a case that arose, of course, before *Shelley* and *Kraemer*. The plaintiffs were not litigants in the first case, but they come in a later case and they say we are entitled to the benefits of the adjudication of this case in which we were not named parties. It was a class action and we are in the same boat.

The answer of this Court through Mr. Justice Stone was that the people who sold the land to the plaintiffs in the second case, they had rights which would be affected by the decree and they were not parties in the first suit, so therefore it was not really a class action.

That the sellers of the land whose rights would be determined here were not parties to the so-called class action in the first case and therefore their rights ought not to be determined.

So it was not only the plaintiffs having their rights adjudicated but their grantor. For that reason, the case was not considered a proper class action.

That is readily distinguishable from this situation. The other case that was mentioned, the Ben Hur case.

JUSTICE REED: There would be a good many defendants that are not present here.

MR. SOBELOFF: I don't know whether that could be said here or not. It may be because of the division of authority in the school districts.

JUSTICE REED: Yes. Also because this class suit [was] for the benefit of all the children in South Carolina.

MR. SOBELOFF: Is it for the whole of South Carolina?

JUSTICE REED: That is my understanding.

MR. SOBELOFF: It is just for those in the school districts. I will check on this.

JUSTICE REED: The defendants are in only the school districts.

MR. SOBELOFF: They could not possibly hope for the children in another district to be admitted in the schools of this district. It must be limited to this district.

JUSTICE CLARK: They allege South Carolina.

MR. SOBELOFF: I think in the classical joke, they cover too much territory. I think obviously they can't maintain an action against the school authorities in one district to admit all the children of South Carolina.

JUSTICE REED: I was just thinking of some possible defendants that were not before the Court.

MR. SOBELOFF: Of course a more serious problem would be where the authority or jurisdiction is fractionated, whether you have in a particular case all defendants before the court that ought to be there.

JUSTICE FRANKFURTER: You certainly haven't gotten the defendants in the other counties before the Court—

MR. SOBELOFF: Absolutely. That is not even debatable.

JUSTICE FRANKFURTER: —If you enter a decree in this litigation unless they want to come in.

MR. SOBELOFF: I don't see that it would avail anybody to get a decree. I don't think the plaintiffs would seriously insist on it.

But it does seem to me that this question never having been decided by the Court, that there is room for holding under this subsection (c) of 23 of Rule 23(c), that this is a class action and you could treat it that way and declare the rights of all these children—

JUSTICE REED: Even though they have not personally come in.

MR. SOBELOFF: Even though they have not personally come in.

JUSTICE CLARK: Could they come in?

MR. SOBELOFF: Even though they have not personally come in, you could say, "We will not include those who will come in and wish to come in but we will make provision in the district court to give them an opportunity to come in."

JUSTICE REED: Would you set a time on that?

MR. SOBELOFF: I think there ought to be a reasonable time like any order of the court that allows people to intervene. It is customary to have a reasonable time, thirty days, sixty days.

JUSTICE REED: Before judgment or after judgment?

MR. SOBELOFF: Generally the rule as stated applies before judgment. But as I indicated before, there is one case where even after judgment a party was allowed to intervene only for the purpose of seeking enforcement by the way of contempt against a violator against the injunction.

So the matter is entirely open in this Court. There are decisions both ways in lower courts and we will prepare a memorandum so the Court will have the cases before it.

THE CHIEF JUSTICE: Mr. Solicitor General, we thank you for your cooperation and for your helpfulness in these very important cases.

Mr. Marshall, you may close the argument.

### REBUTTAL ARGUMENT ON BEHALF OF HARRY BRIGGS ET AL

#### by MR. THURGOOD MARSHALL

MR. MARSHALL: May it please the Court, at this stage of the case I would like permission of the Court to break what I have to say into two points.

One, there are some things that I think should be commented upon as to the several state attorneys general and as in our brief we found there are certain general points that run through all of them.

I would like to reserve this time and take the specific ones first and then get to the general ones.

The Attorney General of the State of Florida, for example, had a pretty long argument on the point of leaving this to the local community and what would be done, pointing out the several areas where it had been done and I think at that stage it should be significant that in the State of Florida, right now, some five years after the decision in the Sweatt and McLaurin cases we still have a case tied up in the Florida courts that has been up here twice, back in the Florida courts and is still there seeking only to break down the exclusion of Negroes from the law school of the University of Florida.[26]

That has taken them five years and they have not gotten around to that yet. I think it is quite pertinent to consider how long it would take, without a forthright decree of this Court to get around to the elementary and high schools.

This same is true for North Carolina. Even after the Sweatt case it was necessary not only to go to the District Court in Durham for a judgment seeking admission of Negroes to the law school of North Carolina. It was not only defended by the Attorney General's office. We had to appeal to the Court of Appeals for the Fourth Circuit, which reversed the District Court and ordered the Negro admitted.[27]

The State then petitioned this Court for certiorari. So in North Carolina it took quite a bit of time to get around to the Sweatt and McLaurin decision.

It is significant that Arkansas, while waiting to see what happened in this Court, I think their good faith can be shown in two points, where, one, they adjourned the present session of the legislature and they won't be back until 1957, I assume to get around to then begin a discussion of the May 17 decision.

Oklahoma, it is significant that whereas most of these states complain about the terrific legislative problem involved in changing statutes to finance their schools as a result of whatever decree might come down from this Court, that Oklahoma in a few months not only passed necessary legislation but amended their constitution to do it and I think that pretty well takes care of the argument about the state being unable through its legislative machinery to make its necessary adjustments.

JUSTICE FRANKFURTER: Doesn't that indicate variations in state conditions?

MR. MARSHALL: It involves variations, Mr. Justice Frankfurter, but I think they are immaterial.

---

[26]Virgil Hawkins first sought admission to the University of Florida Law School in 1949. Litigation concerning his case is reported at Hawkins v. Board of Control, 47 So. 2d 608 (1950), 53 So. 2d 116 (1951), cert. den., 342 U.S. 971 (1951), 60 So. 2d 162 (1952), remanded, 347 U.S. 971 (1954), rehearing, 83 So. 2d 20 (1955), judgment vacated and plaintiff ordered promptly admitted to law school, 350 U.S. 415 (1956). On remand however, the Florida Supreme Court refused to order prompt admission, 93 So. 2d 354 (1957), cert. den., 355 U.S. 839 (1957). The plaintiff then brought an action in a federal district court, 162 F. Supp. 851 (N.D. Fla. 1958) which declined to order him admitted. That decision was reversed by the Fifth Circuit, 253 F. 2d 752 (1958).

[27]McKissick v. Carmichael, 187 F. 2d 949 (4th Cir. 1951).

JUSTICE FRANKFURTER: Maybe they are immaterial, but if they are necessary then since I cannot, with every respect to Oklahoma, attribute very special biological virtues to the inhabitants of that state, can only draw a conclusion that there must be some other factor.

MR. MARSHALL: I think you are right, Mr. Justice Frankfurter, and I think, at that stage, I should remind the Court that in the State of South Carolina, folks [after] *Smith* against *Allwright,* the primary case was in sight, had no trouble in calling a special session of the legislature to repeal all of their primary laws to circumvent the decision of this Court, and I would assume that all of the states could equally get a meeting of the legislature to comply with this Court.

And as for the argument of the State of Maryland, my native state, I think I should say in the beginning that the comment made by Attorney General Sybert that all of the thoughtful Negro and white people in the State of Maryland are for this long, prolonged, gradual business, I am afraid that as a Marylander I am in the thoughtless group, because there is no question in my mind about that.

And it is significant that the Attorney General of Maryland in asking for time, for unlimited time, based it on the fact that they were making such terrific progress on race relations to the point that this year, last year in 1954 they abolished the scholarship provision to send Negroes out of the state which was declared unconstitutional by this Court in 1938, and by the Court of Appeals of Maryland in 1936.[28]

So that it took them sixteen years to catch up with the law of their own Court of Appeals and the law of this Court and use that as the basis for saying that because of their good faith we should work the problem out.

As to the State of Texas, we pointed out in our reply brief something that I think is very significant.

That Texas poll, the exact same agency that took a poll in the Sweatt case, and they found in the Sweatt case an even larger number of people that were bitterly opposed to Negroes being admitted to the University of Texas.

And yet when we know that Negroes were admitted to the University of Texas, they are going there now, and our brief also points out that Negroes are attending parochial schools throughout Texas on a nonsegregated basis, and that many, more than half of the junior colleges in Texas, the municipal junior colleges, have been desegregated since this case has been pending.

The points I am only trying to make there is this: leaving out what I consider to be important points, and throughout all of this, it is very significant that the State of Texas had great difficulty through its representative here admitting that in these counties within this area with this very small number of Negroes, that they could not take some courage from what happened in Arkansas in those two counties.

I can see no reason that makes Texas so different from Arkansas. And finally as to the specifics, as I understand the position of the United States Government

---

[28]Missouri ex rel. Gaines v. Canada, 305 U.S. 337 (1938). University of Maryland v. Murray, 169 Md. 478 (1936). The University of Maryland was ordered to admit a qualified Negro to its law school. The case was argued before the Maryland Supreme Court by Thurgood Marshall.

on this one point of time, the original position was one year, then you could come in and ask for more time, and in the brief they filed just last November they take the position that they would not like to see a time limit fixed because what would be a minimum time limit might actually become a maximum time limit, that the school board might tend not to start work until the end of the year.

Well, so far as the appellants in these cases are concerned, if we could get the time limit on the year we would be willing to take our chances that it would not be done until the end of that year, we would be perfectly satisfied.

So there I think the Government's position gets back to its original position of one year.

The only thing we don't agree on is the question of extension of time.

As to what runs through all of these arguments of the states, if I remember correctly, practically every Attorney General who appeared before this Court and those representing the Attorney General either began or some time in the argument said there was no race prejudice involved, there was no racial hatred involved, there was no bitterness involved.

And then I think you can take the balance of each argument made by the State Attorneys General and find out whether or not that is true.

Most if not all of them said that it was all right, there were very few Negroes involved like in Arkansas, that it is possible they could be integrated, that there might not be friction.

And then they said "However, where there are a large number of Negroes involved and only a small number of white people involved, that is the most horrible situation."

So on the one hand they say that where the majority, the big majority are white, a very small minority is Negro, you can do it, that is the most feasible, the nicest problem.

And the other is the reverse; well, the only way to understand that is that in one category you have a small number of white students, and the only difference between the two is Negro and white, and if that is not race I don't know what race is.

And that is the argument that is made throughout these cases.

I think that we should keep coming back to this point. That we look at this case as a regular legal proceeding. And then we look at that in the broader perspective. The decision on May 17 [showed the] forthright straightforward position of the law of this country as pronounced by its highest Court. Since that time, partially because of the leaving open of these two questions, but throughout areas of this country, stimulated by statements of state officers, attorneys general, governors, et cetera, the whole country has been told in the South that this decision means nothing as of now.

It will mean nothing until the time limit is set. So when you conceive of it in that framework, this time limit point becomes a part of the effectiveness, forthrightness if you please, of the May 17 decision.

That is why yesterday and the day before this Court was told over and over again that these states were not moving at all until they found a time limit.

So to my mind whereas in an ordinary case the question of details of decree are more or less minor matters—or there are exceptions to it that do not reach the level of high constitutional principle, but in these cases they do reach an equal level with the forthrightness of the May 17 decision.

And when we take that position, at least we urge upon the Court, there is considerable difficulty in getting to the other problems.

One side, for example, said—of course, no court I am certain would agree, as was suggested by one of the Atttorneys General, that in deciding as to the time for enforcement of a constitutional right the Court would hit a middle ground between two positions.

We are not in this Court bargaining on a negligence case or something like that.

It is significant—I might be wrong. I know it has happened in cases involving statutes, even federal statues, even antitrust, for example, statutes.

But I don't believe any argument has ever been made to this Court to postpone the enforcement of a constitutional right. The argument is never made until Negroes are involved.

And then for some reason this population of our country is constantly asked, "Well, for the sake of the group that has denied you these rights all of this time," as the Attorney General of North Carolina said, to protect their greatest and most cherished heritage, that the Negroes should give up their rights.

If by any stretch of the imagination any other minority group had been involved in this case, we would never have been here.

I just cannot understand at this late date why we constantly are faced with that. But we are faced with it and we have to meet it as best we can.

The next point I want to make on the general side is what I made before, and that is the need for uniform application of our Constitution and all of its provisions throughout the country so that freedom of the press won't mean one thing in one state and another thing in another state, so that all of these rights in the Constitution—it has never been said on any other right that I know of that special exceptions should be made as to one state or the other.

And as of this stage of these arguments, there is the real possibility that in Clarendon County, South Carolina, for example, we could have three different rules in the same county because there are three school districts there, and the same of course would be true on and on.

To my mind that is not the way that our Constitution is to be applied. Local option I still say is what is urged.

And it is not local option even statewide, because each Attorney General said it is going to be different from one area of the state to the other, and Texas went so far as to bring in maps to show that it would operate from one area to the other in a different fashion.

I am sure that the State of Texas does not even administer their own constitution in varying areas of various sections of the country.

But they want the federal Constitution [to be administered that way]. And the most significant comment made over and over again was that the difference between acceptance and rejection of a constitutional position depended on whether it was pronounced from within or without a state.

I think maybe that is the best answer I know to any claim that this is not local option.

While I am on that point I would like to come back to the class action point which I was asked and which has come up again. It is true that in both of these cases the class was made for all of the Negroes in the category of school age within the state.

We expected at any time that that would be limited. The idea was to make the class as broad as possible and when it got limited, we would not be down to nobody.

Obviously I agree with the position that has been made here this morning by several of the Justices. Obviously we can get relief from nobody who is not in court, and there is no intention on our part to bring in any defendants from any other counties when we get to the district court.

We would not think of doing such a thing. It applies only to the Negroes in School District Number One in Clarendon County who are of school age, resident, et cetera, in School District Number One. In the present posture of this case it does not, could not even include the entire county.

The largest group it could cover would be those in School District Number One. The largest group it could possibly cover in Prince Edward County would be the Negroes of high school age in Prince Edward County and it could apply to no one else.

JUSTICE FRANKFURTER: In numbers, how many would that be?

MR. MARSHALL: In Clarendon County I think it is 2,800 and in Prince Edward it is 800.

JUSTICE FRANKFURTER: With reference to the high school age, 800 would be involved?

MR. MARSHALL: Yes, sir, a total of 800. I understand it is 863 white and colored, 400-and-some Negroes.

JUSTICE FRANKFURTER: The question is intermixing these students, allowing them free access, not allowing any students to be barred merely because of color?

MR. MARSHALL: Yes, sir, it would only apply to that number, 400.

JUSTICE FRANKFURTER: And numerically would that cover 400 or absorb 400?

MR. MARSHALL: It would be 450–some.

JUSTICE FRANKFURTER: That is 400 are now excluded merely because of color?

MR. MARSHALL: That is right, and the only thing we want is to say that you can't exclude that many which is all of the Negroes involved.

JUSTICE CLARK: How many are named in this case in Virginia?

MR. MARSHALL: I can tell you in Virginia it was forty-five, in the Clarendon County case that number is much smaller.

And I may say, Mr. Justice Clark, that after the questions yesterday I made every effort to get some of our people in Clarendon County on the phone to find out how many were actually in as of today, and I could not get ahold of anybody.

JUSTICE CLARK: How many in Prince Edward are named in the case?

MR. MARSHALL: There are 119 named, 119 named plaintiffs.

JUSTICE CLARK: The courts named them in that county?

MR. MARSHALL: Yes, sir.

On that particular point, if the Court please, I think we ought to emphasize the fact that this is an action under the three-judge statute aimed at having declared unconstitutional a state statute of statewide application, and the constitutional provision obviously, and that the class action is merely a procedural device that instead of naming five or six thousand people or what have you, instead of putting all of them down, it is just merely procedural.

But that the effect of a statute being declared unconstitutional by this Court does at least have statewide significance as witness the fact that the statute requires you to notify the state attorney general that you are about to attack his statute.

And so that so far as the basic issue in this case is concerned, it is to have the statute declared unconstitutional.

Once the constitutional provision in the statutes are declared unconstitutional, then we come up against the problem as to whether or not a state officer is going to operate under a statute that is unconstitutional.

Insofar as the district involved in this case is concerned, we, the Negroes not named, we are certain as our research will show that they can intervene any time before judgment and merely show that they are within the class involved.

Once they do that, they can take the same position that a named plaintiff would have.

THE CHIEF JUSTICE: Mr. Marshall, are your authorities on that subject in your brief?

MR. MARSHAL: No, sir.

THE CHIEF JUSTICE: Would you furnish them to us?

MR. MARSHALL: We will be very glad to, sir, but I say in all frankness that they are pretty much the same as the Solicitor—there is really very little dispute on it.

It has not been decided by this Court, but the thing I want to say is aside from these cases, that it is the most difficult problem if every Negro in the South has to go to court to get the rights that everybody else has been enjoying all these years.

I grant that it is not before the Court. But we thought the class action was this procedural device so that when it comes down to the district court, I mean when the judgement comes out of the district court, that whoever is administering that policy will recognize the law and not just admit McLaurin into the University of Oklahoma or Sweatt into the University of Texas but let all Negroes who are qualified in.

JUSTICE FRANKFURTER: If it would not interfere with the course of the argument you ultimately have in mind, would you care to sketch what you see to be the sequence of steps of events if there were a decree in terms, say, that not one of these four hundred–odd, whatever the number may be in the school districts, including the ones in Clarendon County, not one of these children should be excluded from any high school in that district for reason of color.

Suppose that were the decree, what do you see or contemplate as the consequence of that decree?

MR. MARSHALL: If that decree were filed with nothing more then I would be almost certain that the school board through its lawyers would come into the district court either before—this is a possibility that I have to put two on.

If they don't admit them and we file a suggestion of contempt with the district court—

JUSTICE FRANKFURTER: Before you get to contempt there must be some action which would be the basis of contempt. What do you think it would involve as the consequence?

MR. MARSHALL: They refuse.

JUSTICE FRANKFURTER: That is that the hundred, or four hundred students would knock at the door of the white schools.

MR. MARSHALL: Oh, oh, that, no, sir, not necessarily because there is not room for them.

JUSTICE FRANKFURTER: I should like to have you spell out with particularity just what would happen in that school district.

MR. MARSHALL: Well, I would say, sir, that the school board would sit down and take this position with its staff, administrative staff, superintendents, supervisors, et cetera. They would say, "The present policy of admission based on race, that is now gone. Now we have to find some other one." The first thing would be to use the maps that they already have, show the population, the school population, then I would assume they would draw district lines without the idea of race but district lines circled around the schools like they did in the District of Columbia.

That would be problem number one.

Problem number two would then be, "What are we going to do about reassigning teachers?"

Now that there is no restricting about white and Negro it might be that we will shift teachers here or shift teachers there.

Third would be the problem of bus transportation. We have two buses going down the same road, one taking Negroes, one taking whites.

So we might still do it that way or we might do it another way.

JUSTICE FRANKFURTER: Throughout all this period, I wouldn't know how long that would be, there would be no actual change in the actual intake of students, is that right?

MR. MARSHALL: I would say so, yes, sir.

JUSTICE FRANKFURTER: All right.

MR. MARSHALL: I would say so. That was the point I was going to get to.

And assuming that they are doing that and the time is going on, they might come into the district court and ask for further relief, which would be to say, "We are working in good conscience on this. We just can't do it within a reasonable time." Or we would go into court and say they are not proceeding in good faith. Either way the district court would at that stage decide as to whether or not they were proceeding in good faith, at which stage the district court would have the exact same leeway that has been argued for all along.

JUSTICE FRANKFURTER: Now as to primary schools, that is if that is what they are called.

MR. MARSHALL: Yes, sir.

JUSTICE FRANKFURTER: The problem would be a little different because the number makes a difference.

MR. MARSHALL: Well, it would be different because of numbers. The figure shift would be the shifting of the children.

JUSTICE FRANKFURTER: I am assuming that under the responsibilities of the law officers in various states, there would be a conscious desire to meet the order of this Court. I am assuming that this process which you outlined would proceed, wouldn't that be a process in each one of these school districts?

MR. MARSHALL: That would be and I think that that is the type of problem.

The only thing is we are now on this do-it-right-away point.

JUSTICE FRANKFURTER: Your analysis shows that do-it-right-away merely means show that you are doing it right away, beginning to do it right away.

MR. MARSHALL: I take the position, Mr. Justice Frankfurter, this has been in the back of our minds since Question 4 (a) and the others all along, as to whether or not we will be required to answer this in the context which we have been answering this, or whether it was not the question of contempt, that it would never come up except on contempt.

JUSTICE FRANKFURTER: That is the way it would come up.

MR. MARSHALL: The way you put it.

JUSTICE FRANKFURTER: The school authorities would say we have not got the room or we have not got the teachers or the teachers have resigned or a thousand and one reasons or twenty thousand reasons that develop from a problem of that sort; you couldn't possibly proceed in contempt, could you?

MR. MARSHALL: I doubt that we would even move for contempt.

JUSTICE FRANKFURTER: Except there might be different difficulties of interpretation as to the reasons for delay.

MR. MARSHALL: And for example we would not recognize as reason for delay the waiting for these attitudes to catch up with us. We would not recognize that.

JUSTICE FRANKFURTER: Well an attitude might depend on the non-availability of teachers. That might be an attitude.

MR. MARSHALL: There would always be availability of competent capable Negro teachers, always.
There is no shortage. And I think it is very significant in New York—

JUSTICE FRANKFURTER: I am not sure why you say that with such confidence. In different localities established as you well know, better than I—

MR. MARSHALL: Yes, sir.

JUSTICE FRANKFURTER: Why do you make such a statement?

MR. MARSHALL: Well, there are so many that are in areas that don't want to leave because of home ties or what have you and because they are so well trained there are school boards that won't hire them because they don't want them, and those are very available, I mean well qualified teachers, sir.
North Carolina, they take a most interesting position: They say the Negro teachers have more experience, more college training.

JUSTICE FRANKFURTER: You have heard that the bar of this Court with considerable pride stated those standards of Negro teachers.

MR. MARSHALL: Yes, sir, and it was followed by the fact that they would deprive the white children of the benefit of superior teachers and fire the Negro teachers.

JUSTICE FRANKFURTER: I merely suggested in the areas of education that I know something about a plethora of well equipped teachers is not there.

MR. MARSHALL: Well, it is on the broad general figures, Mr. Justice Frankfurter, but on the Negro side we are producing them and in all frankness as the Attorney General of North Carolina, Mr. Lake, said in the South that is about one of the few places they can get work.
And you have masters, M.A.'s, that are unemployed.
The other point that I would like to come back to is to continue this class point as I see it affects these cases.
The named plaintiffs, I think there is no question they are entitled to relief. And on some of the questions it seems to me that if the named plaintiffs in such a small number are admitted, I would not have the real physical difficulties if you only admitted, if the school board only admitted those named plaintiffs.
However, it seems to me we have to be realistic, and most certainly by the time the case, before the case gets to judgment, many if not all of the other

Negroes will have intervened when they find that they are not protected and the only way they can get protected is to intervene.

I would imagine with considerable reliance that they would intervene.

The only thing it seems to me is this, that it is going to be difficult to consider this in the narrow named plaintiff category without the understanding that the whole class will eventually be in it.

That brings me to the next point, which is that I hope the Court will bear in mind the need for this time limit, which I come back to, because in normal judicial proceedings in these and other cases, there will be so much time lost anyhow.

We have to go before the local school board, we have to exhaust our remedies before we can go into court, there is no question about that.

Then we get into court and then unless we have this time limit, we most certainly will have this terrific long extended argument and testimony as to all of these reasons for delay, which I or any lawyer would be powerless to stop.

It would depend of course on the district judge.

But as of this time, the only valid reasons that have been set up have been the reasons set up relating to the physical adjustments and not a single appellant, appellee and not a single Attorney General has said one thing to this Court in regard to physical difficulties which could not be met within a year.

I come back to our original position as to why we picked a year.

We picked a year because we talked with administrators, school officials and we just could not find anything longer than a year. I submit that the American Tobacco Trust case, which we have on about the next to the last page of our brief, which involved a dissolution of this trust, this Court said that because of the involved situation and everything, a time limit had to be set, and this Court set a six months' time limit and told the district court that you can give them an extension of sixty days if they show valid reasons.

However, if you are convinced they can do it in less than six months, see that they do it in less than six months. Now there is at least one case in which this Court did do it on the basis of whatever material was before them, and the material you have before this Court at this time shows that we certainly have a right, if nothing else was shown, we would have a right to this immediate action, the time to take care of these administrative details, and that you have nothing else to go on.

The other side has not produced anything except attitudes, opinion polls, et cetera.

On the basis of that, it seems to me we get back to the normal procedure which would be the type of judgment from this Court that would require them to be admitted at, let us say, the next school term, and the contempt side, as I mentioned before.

Or what I consider to be the more realistic approach, which would be to let the other states involved know and the other areas know that it will not do you any good. If there were no time limit fixed the school officials in the other states that will follow whatever this Court will say, if they knew that they had a chance, just a chance of getting interminable delay from the district court after the lawsuit was filed, then I would imagine that they would not begin action until after the lawsuit was filed.

However, if they knew that if a lawsuit was filed they would have to either desegregate immediately or would get no more than a year, they would start working.

So it seems to me that if I am correct in that, then this time limit gets so involved with this constitutional right that so far as not the plaintiffs in these cases are concerned but insofar as precedent, effect and so forth in the country is concerned, that now this time limit is involved with the constitutional right and that the statement on time should be just as forthright as the statement was made on the constitutional position taken in the May 17 decision. And so we submit to the Court that on behalf of the appellants and petitioners—we have been appreciative of all of this time that has been given.

The last thing that I could possibly say is what I said in the beginning. That in considering problems as tough as these, and they are tough, that what I said before is apropos now. It is the faith in our democratic processes that gets us over these, and that is why in these cases we believe that this Court, in the time provision, it must be forthright and say that it shall not under any circumstances take longer than a year.

And once having done that, the whole country knows that this May 17 decision means that the protection of the rights here involved of any person in the category, any Negro, will get prompt action in the court.

Once that is done, then we leave the local communities to work their way out of it, but to work their way out of it within the framework of a clear and precise statement that not only are these rights constitutionally protected, but that you cannot delay enforcement of it.

Thank you very much.

THE CHIEF JUSTICE: Attorney General Almond, do you have any rebuttal to the argument of the amici?

## REBUTTAL ARGUMENT ON BEHALF OF
## PRINCE EDWARD COUNTY, VA.

### by MR. ALMOND, ATTORNEY GENERAL

MR. ALMOND: Mr. Chief Justice, I thank you for that. We feel in Virginia that we have said all we could say in support of our contention before the Court.

I do not know that we could add anything further unless there were some questions which the Court wished to propound to us.

Otherwise I thank you.

THE CHIEF JUSTICE: Thank you very much.

Is counsel for South Carolina here?

The same opportunity would be tendered to them, of course, if they were here.

(At 1:15 p.m. the oral arguments were concluded.)

. . .

FINAL DECISION ON RELIEF

# BROWN ET AL. V. BOARD OF EDUCATION OF TOPEKA ET AL.

*Appeal from the United States District Court for the District of Kansas**

Reargued on the question of relief April 11–14, 1955—Opinion
and judgments announced May 31, 1955

349 U. S. 294

MR. CHIEF JUSTICE WARREN delivered the opinion of the Court.

These cases were decided on May 17, 1954. The opinions of that date,[1] declaring the fundamental principle that racial discrimination in public education is unconstitutional, are incorporated herein by reference. All provisions of federal, state, or local law requiring or permitting such discrimination must yield to this principle. There remains for consideration the manner in which relief is to be accorded.

Because these cases arose under different local conditions and their disposition will involve a variety of local problems, we requested further argument on the question of relief.[2] In view of the nationwide importance of the decision, we invited the Attorney General of the United States and the Attorneys General of all states requiring or permitting racial discrimination in public education to present

---

*Together with No. 2, *Briggs et al.* v. *Elliott et al.,* on appeal from the United States District Court for the Eastern District of South Carolina; No. 3 *Davis et al.* v. *County School Board of Prince Edward County, Virginia, et al.,* on appeal from the United States District Court for the Eastern District of Virginia; No. 4, *Bolling et al.* v. *Sharpe et al.,* on certiorari to the United States Court of Appeals for the District of Columbia Circuit; and No. 5, *Gebhart et al.* v. *Belton et al.,* on certiorari to the Supreme Court of Delaware.

[1]347 U.S. 483; 347 U.S. 497.

[2]Further argument was requested on the following questions, 347 U.S. 483, 495–496, n. 13, previously propounded by the Court:

"4. Assuming it is decided that segregation in public schools violates the Fourteenth Amendment

"*(a)* would a decree necessarily follow providing that, within the limits set by normal geographic school districting, Negro children should forthwith be admitted to schools of their choice, or

"*(b)* may this Court, in the exercise of its equity powers, permit an effective gradual adjustment to be brought about from existing segregated systems to a system not based on color distinctions?

"5. On the assumption on which questions 4 *(a)* and *(b)* are based, and assuming further that this Court will exercise its equity powers to the end described in question 4 *(b),*

"*(a)* should this Court formulate detailed decrees in these cases;

"*(b)* if so, what specific issues should the decrees reach;

"*(c)* should this Court appoint a special master to hear evidence with a view to recommending specific terms for such decrees;

"*(d)* should this Court remand to the courts of first instance with directions to frame decrees in these cases, and if so what general directions should the decrees of this Court include and what procedures should the courts of first instance follow in arriving at the specific terms of more detailed decrees?"

their views on that question. The parties, the United States, and the States of Florida, North Carolina, Arkansas, Oklahoma, Maryland, and Texas filed briefs and participated in the oral argument.

These presentations were informative and helpful to the Court in its consideration of the complexities arising from the transition to a system of public education freed of racial discrimination. The presentations also demonstrated that substantial steps to eliminate racial discrimination in public schools have already been taken, not only in some of the communities in which these cases arose, but in some of the states appearing as *amici curiae,* and in other states as well. Substantial progress has been made in the District of Columbia and in the communities in Kansas and Delaware involved in this litigation. The defendants in the cases coming to us from South Carolina and Virginia are awaiting the decision of this Court concerning relief.

Full implementation of these constitutional principles may require solution of varied local school problems. School authorities have the primary responsibility for elucidating, assessing, and solving these problems; courts will have to consider whether the action of school authorities constitutes good faith implementation of the governing constitutional principles. Because of their proximity to local conditions and the possible need for further hearings, the courts which originally heard these cases can best perform this judicial appraisal. Accordingly, we believe it appropriate to remand the cases to those courts.[3]

In fashioning and effectuating the decrees, the courts will be guided by equitable principles. Traditionally, shaping its remedies[4] and by a facility for adjusting and reconciling public and private needs.[5] These cases call for the exercise of these traditional attributes of equity power. At stake is the personal interest of the plaintiffs in admission to public schools as soon as practicable on a nondiscriminatory basis. To effectuate this interest may call for elimination of a variety of obstacles in making the transition to school systems operated in accordance with the constitutional principles set forth in our May 17, 1954, decision. Courts of equity may properly take into account the public interest in the elimination of such obstacles in a systematic and effective manner. But it should go without saying that the vitality of these constitutional principles cannot be allowed to yield simply because of disagreement with them.

While giving weight to these public and private considerations, the courts will require that the defendants make a prompt and reasonable start toward full compliance with our May 17, 1954, ruling. Once such a start has been made, the courts may find that additional time is necessary to carry out the ruling in an effective manner. The burden rests upon the defendants to establish that such time is necessary in the public interest and is consistent with good faith compliance at the earliest practicable date. To that end, the courts may consider problems related to administration, arising from the physical condition of the school plant, the school

[3]The cases coming to us from Kansas, South Carolina, and Virginia were originally heard by three-judge District Courts convened under 28 U.S.C. §§ 2281 and 2284. These cases will accordingly be remanded to those three-judge courts. See *Briggs* v. *Elliott,* 342 U.S. 350.

[4]See *Alexander* v. *Hillman,* 296 U.S. 222, 239.

[5]See *Hecht Co.* v. *Bowles,* 321 U.S. 321, 329–330.

transportation system, personnel, revision of school districts and attendance areas into compact units to achieve a system of determining admission to the public schools on a nonracial basis, and revision of local laws and regulations which may be necessary in solving the foregoing problems. They will also consider the adequacy of any plans the defendants may propose to meet these problems and to effectuate a transition to a racially nondiscriminatory school system. During this period of transition, the courts will retain jurisdiction of these cases.

The judgments below, except that in the Delaware case, are accordingly reversed and the cases are remanded to the District Courts to take such proceedings and enter such orders and decrees consistent with this opinion as are necessary and proper to admit to public schools on a racially nondiscriminatory basis with all deliberate speed the parties to these cases. The judgment in the Delaware case—ordering the immediate admission of the plaintiffs to schools previously attended only by white children—is affirmed on the basis of the principles stated in our May 17, 1954, opinion, but the case is remanded to the Supreme Court of Delaware for such further proceedings as that Court may deem necessary in light of this opinion.

*It is so ordered.*

# APPENDIX


District Court Decision in Brown v. Board of Education

Intermediate Supreme Court Order in Brown v. Board of Education

First District Court Decision in Briggs v. Elliott

Intermediate Supreme Court Order in Briggs v. Elliott

Second District Court Decision in Briggs v. Elliott

District Court Decision in Davis v. County School Board

Chancellor's Decision in Belton v. Gebhart

Decision of Supreme Court of Delaware in Gebhart v. Belton

Intermediate Supreme Court Order in All Cases

APPENDIX

District Court Decision in Brown v. Board of Education

BROWN ET AL. v. BOARD OF EDUCATION

OF TOPEKA, SHAWNEE COUNTY,

KANSAS et al.

Civ. No. T–316.

98 F. Supp. 797

United States District Court,
D. Kansas.

Aug. 3, 1951.

Before HUXMAN, Circuit Judge, MELLOTT, Chief Judge, and HILL, District Judge.

HUXMAN, Circuit Judge.

Chapter 72–1724 of the General Statutes of Kansas, 1949, relating to public schools in cities of the first class, so far as material, authorizes such cities to organize and maintain separate schools for the education of white and colored children in the grades below the high school grades. Pursuant to this authority, the City of Topeka, Kansas, a city of the first class, has established and maintains a segregated system of schools for the first six grades. It has established and maintains in the Topeka School District eighteen schools for white students and four schools for colored students.

The adult plaintiffs instituted this action for themselves, their minor children plaintiffs, and all other persons similarly situated for an interlocutory injunction, a permanent injunction, restraining the enforcement, operation and execution of the state statute and the segregation instituted thereunder by the school authorities of the City of Topeka and for a declaratory judgment declaring unconstitutional the state statute and the segregation set up thereunder by the school authorities of the City of Topeka.

As against the school district of Topeka they contend that the opportunities provided for the infant plaintiffs in the separate all Negro schools are inferior to those provided white children in the all white schools; that the respects in which these opportunities are inferior include the physical facilities, curricula, teaching resources, student personnel services as well as all other services. As against both the state and the school district, they contend that apart from all other factors segregation in itself constitutes an inferiority in educational opportunities offered to Negroes and that all of this is in violation of due process guaranteed them by the Fourteenth Amendment to the United States Constitution. In their answer both the state and the school district defend the constitutionality of the state law and in addition the school district defends the segregation in its schools instituted thereunder.

We have found as a fact that the physical facilities, the curricula, courses of study, qualification of and quality of teachers, as well as other educational facilities in the two sets of schools are comparable. It is obvious that absolute equality of physical facilities is impossible of attainment in buildings that are erected at different times. So also absolute equality of subjects taught is impossible of maintenance when teachers are permitted to select books of their own choosing to use in teaching in addition to the prescribed courses of study. It is without dispute that the prescribed courses of study are identical in all of the Topeka schools and that there is no discrimination in this respect. It is also clear in the record that the educational qualifications of the teachers in the colored schools are equal to those in the white schools and that in all other respects the educational facilities and services are comparable. It is obvious from the fact that there are only four colored schools as against eighteen white schools in the Topeka School District, that colored children in many instances are required to travel much greater distances than they would be required to travel could they attend a white school, and are required to travel much greater distances than white children are required to travel. The evidence, however, establishes that the school district transports colored children to and from school free of charge. No such service is furnished to white children. We conclude that in the maintenance and operation of the schools there is no willful, intentional or substantial discrimination in the matters referred to above between the colored and white schools. In fact, while plaintiffs' attorneys have not abandoned this contention, they did not give it great emphasis in their presentation before the court. They relied primarily upon the contention that segregation in and of itself without more violates their rights guaranteed by the Fourteenth Amendment.

This contention poses a question not free from difficulty. As a subordinate court in the federal judicial system, we seek the answer to this constitutional question in the decisions of the Supreme

Court when it has spoken on the subject and do not substitute our own views for the declared law by the Supreme Court. The difficult question as always is to analyze the decisions and seek to ascertain the trend as revealed by the later decisions.

There are a great number of cases, both federal and state, that have dealt with the many phases of segregation. Since the question involves a construction and interpretation of the federal Constitution and the pronouncements of the Supreme Court, we will consider only those cases by the Supreme Court with respect to segregation in the schools. In the early case of Plessy v. Ferguson, 163 U.S. 537, 16 S.Ct. 1138, 1140, 41 L.Ed. 256, the Supreme Court said: "The object of the amendment was undoubtedly to enforce the absolute equality of the two races before the law, but, in the nature of things, it could not have been intended to abolish distinctions based upon color, or to enforce social, as distinguished from political equality, or a commingling of the two races upon terms unsatisfactory to either. Laws permitting, and even requiring, their separation, in places where they are liable to be brought into contact, do not necessarily imply the inferiority of either race to the other, and have been generally, if not universally, recognized as within the competency of the state legislatures in the exercise of their police power. The most common instance of this is connected with the establishment of separate schools for white and colored children, which has been held to be a valid exercise of the legislative power even by courts of states where the political rights of the colored race have been longest and most earnestly enforced."

It is true as contended by plaintiffs that the Plessy case involved transportation and that the above quoted statement relating to schools was not essential to the decision of the question before the court and was therefore somewhat in the nature of dicta. But that the statement is considered more than dicta is evidenced by the treatment accorded it by those seeking to strike down segregation as well as by statements in subsequent decisions of the Supreme Court. On numerous occasions the Supreme Court has been asked to overrule the Plessy case. This the Supreme Court has refused to do, on the sole ground that a decision of the question was not necessary to a disposal of the controversy presented. In the late case of Sweatt v. Painter, 339 U.S. 629, 70 S.Ct. 848, 851, 94 L.Ed. 1114, the Supreme Court again refused to review the Plessy case. The Court said: "Nor need we reach petitioner's contention that Plessy v. Ferguson should be reexamined in the light of contemporary knowledge respecting the purposes of the Fourteenth Amendment and the effects of racial segregation."

Gong Lum v. Rice, 275 U.S. 78, 48 S.Ct. 91, 93, 72 L.Ed. 172, was a grade school segregation case. It involved the segregation law of Mississippi. Gong Lum was a Chinese child and, because of color, was required to attend the separate schools provided for colored children. The opinion of the court assumes that the educational facilities in the colored schools were adequate and equal to those of the white schools. Thus the court said: "The question here is whether a Chinese citizen of the United States is denied equal protection of the laws when he is classed among the colored races and furnished facilities for education equal to that offered to all, whether white, brown, yellow, or black." In addition to numerous state decisions on the subject, the Supreme Court in support of its conclusions cited Plessy v. Ferguson, supra. The Court also pointed out that the question was the same no matter what the color of the class that was required to attend separate schools. Thus the Court said: "Most of the cases cited arose, it is true, over the establishment of separate schools as between white pupils and black pupils; but we cannot think that the question is any different, or that any different result can be reached, assuming the cases above cited to be rightly decided, where the issue is as between white pupils and the pupils of the yellow races." The court held that the question of segregation was within the discretion of the state in regulating its public schools and did not conflict with the Fourteenth Amendment.

It is vigorously argued and not without some basis therefore that the later decisions of the Supreme Court in McLaurin v. Oklahoma, 339 U.S. 637, 70 S.Ct. 851, 94 L.Ed. 1149, and Sweatt v. Painter, 339 U.S. 629, 70 S.Ct. 848, 94 L.Ed. 1114, show a trend away from the Plessy and Lum cases. McLaurin v. Oklahoma arose under the segregation laws of Oklahoma. McLaurin, a colored student, applied for admission to the University of Oklahoma in order to pursue studies leading to a doctorate degree in education. He was denied admission solely because he was a Negro. After litigation in the courts, which need not be reviewed herein, the legislature amended the statute permitting the admission of colored students to institutions of higher learning attended by white students, but providing that such instruction should be given on a segregated basis; that the instruction be given in separate class rooms or at separate times. In compliance with this statute McLaurin was admitted to the university but was required to sit at a separate desk in the ante room adjoining the class room; to sit at a designated desk on the mezzanine floor of the library and to sit at a designated table and eat at a different time from the other students in the school cafeteria. These restrictions were held to violate his rights under the federal Constitution. The Supreme Court held that such treatment handicapped the student in his pursuit of effective graduate instruction.[1]

[1]The court said: "Our society grows increasingly complex, and our need for trained leaders increases correspondingly. Appellant's case represents, perhaps, the epitome of that need, for he is

In Sweatt v. Painter, 339 U.S. 629, 70 S.Ct. 848, 850, 94 L.Ed. 1114, petioner, a colored student, filed an application for admission to the University of Texas Law School. His application was rejected solely on the ground that he was a Negro. In its opinion the Supreme Court stressed educational benefits from commingling with white students. The court concluded by stating: "we cannot conclude that the education offered petitioner [in a separate school] is substantially equal to that which he would receive if admitted to the University of Texas Law School." If segregation within a school as in the McLaurin case is a denial of due process, it is difficult to see why segregation in separate schools would not result in the same denial. Or if the denial of the right to commingle with the majority group in higher institutions of learning as in the Sweatt case and gain the educational advantages resulting therefrom, is lack of due process, it is difficult to see why such denial would not result in the same lack of due process if practiced in the lower grades.

It must however be remembered that in both of these cases the Supreme Court made it clear that it was confining itself to answering the one specific question, namely: "To what extent does the Equal Protection Clause * * * limit the power of a state to distinguish between students of different races in professional and graduate education in a state university?", and that the Supreme Court refused to review the Plessy case because that question was not essential to a decision of the controversy in the case.

We are accordingly of the view that the Plessy and Lum cases, supra, have not been overruled and that they still presently are authority for the maintenance of a segregated school system in the lower grades.

The prayer for relief will be denied and judgment will be entered for defendants for costs.


FINDINGS OF FACT AND CONCLUSIONS OF LAW—Entered
August 3, 1951

FINDINGS OF FACT

I

This is a class action in which plaintiffs seek a decree, declaring Section 72-1724 of the General Statutes of Kansas 1949 to be unconstitutional, insofar as it empowers the Board of Education of the City of Topeka "to organize and maintain separate schools for the education of white and colored children" and an injunction restraining the enforcement, operation and execution of that portion of the statute and of the segregation instituted thereunder by the School Board.

II

This suit arises under the Constitution of the United States and involves more than $3,000 exclusive of interest and costs. It is also a civil action to redress an alleged deprivation, under color of State law, of a right, privilege or immunity secured by the Constitution of the United States providing for an equal rights of citizens and to have the court declare the rights and other legal relations of the interested parties. The Court has jurisdiction of the subject matter and of the parties to the action.

III

Pursuant to statutory authority contained in Section 72-1724 of the General Statutes of Kansas 1949, the City of Topeka, Kansas, a city of the first class, has established and maintains a segregated system of schools for the first six grades. It has established and maintains in the Topeka School District, eighteen schools for white children and four for colored children, the latter being located in neigh-

---

attempting to obtain an advanced degree in education, to become by definition, a leader and trainer of others. Those who will come under his guidance and influence must be directly affected by the education he receives. Their own education and development will necessarily suffer to the extent that his training is unequal to that of his classmates. State-imposed restrictions which produce such inequalities cannot be sustained.

"It may be argued that appellant will be in no better position when these restrictions are removed, for he may still be set apart by his fellow students. This we think irrelevant. There is a vast difference—a Constitutional difference—between restrictions imposed by the state which prohibit the intellectual commingling of students, and the refusal of individuals to commingle where the state presents no such bar. * * * having been admitted to a state-supported graduate school, (he), must receive the same treatment at the hands of the state as students of other races." [339 U.S. 637, 70 S.Ct. 853.]

borhoods where the population is predominantly colored. The City of Topeka is one school district. The colored children may attend any one of the four schools established for them, the choice being made either by the children or by their parents.

## IV

There is no material difference in the physical facilities in the colored schools and in the white schools and such facilities in the colored schools are not inferior in any material respects to those in the white schools.

## V

The educational qualifications of the teachers and the quality of instruction in the colored schools are not inferior to and are comparable to those of the white schools.

## VI

The courses of study prescribed by the State law are taught in both the colored schools and in the white schools. The prescribed courses of study are identical in both classes of schools.

## VII

Transportation to and from school is furnished colored children in the segregated schools without cost to the children or to their parents. No such transportation is furnished to the white children in the segregated schools.

## VIII

Segregation of white and colored children in public schools has a detrimental effect upon the colored children. The impact is greater when it has the sanction of the law; for the policy of separating the races is usually interpreted as denoting the inferiority of the negro group. A sense of inferiority affects the motivation of a child to learn. Segregation with the sanction of law, therefore, has a tendency to restrain the educational and mental development of negro children and to deprive them of some of the benefits they would receive in a racial integrated school system.

## IX

The court finds as facts the stipulated facts and those agreed upon by counsel at the pre-trial and during the course of the trial.

### CONCLUSIONS OF LAW

## I

This court has jurisdiction of the subject matter and of the parties to the action.[1]

## II

We conclude that no discrimination is practiced against plaintiffs in the colored schools set apart for them because of the nature of the physical characteristics of the buildings, the equipment, the curricula, quality of instructors and instruction or school services furnished and that they are denied no constitutional rights or privileges by reason of any of these matters.

---

[1] Title 28 U.S.C. § 1331; idem § 1343; idem Ch. 151. Title 8 U.S.C. Ch. 3. Title 28 U.S.C. Ch. 155.

## III

Plessy v. Ferguson, 163 U.S. 537, and Gong Lum v. Rice, 275 U.S. 78 upholds the constitutionality of a legally segregated school system in the lower grades and no denial of due process results from the maintenance of such a segregated system of schools absent discrimination in the maintenance of the segregated schools. We conclude that the above cited cases have not been overruled by the later cases of McLaurin v. Oklahoma, 339 U.S. 637, and Sweatt v. Painter, 339 U.S. 629.

## IV

The only question in the case under the record is whether legal segregation in and of itself without more constitutes denial of due process. We are of the view that under the above decisions of the Supreme Court the answer must be in the negative. We accordingly conclude that plaintiffs have suffered no denial of due process by virtue of the manner in which the segregated school system of Topeka, Kansas, is being operated. The relief sought is therefore denied. Judgment will be entered for defendants for costs.

  Walter A. Huxman, Circuit Judge, Arthur J. Mellott, Chief District Judge, Delmas C. Hill, District Judge.

Intermediate Supreme Court Order in Brown v. Board of Education

BROWN ET AL. v. BOARD OF EDUCATION
OF TOPEKA ET AL.

344 U.S. 141

APPEAL FROM THE UNITED STATES DISTRICT COURT FOR THE
DISTRICT OF KANSAS.

No. 8. November 24, 1952.

PER CURIAM.

This action was instituted by the appellants attacking a Kansas statute which authorized segregation in the schools of that State. It was urged that the State of Kansas was without power to enact such legislation, claimed by appellants to be in contravention of the Fourteenth Amendment.

In the District Court, the State, by its Governor and Attorney General, intervened and defended the constitutionality of the statute. The court upheld its validity.

In this Court, the appellants continue their constitutional attack. No appearance has been entered here by the State of Kansas, the Board of Education of Topeka, and the other appellees; nor have they presented any brief in support of the statute's validity. The Court has been advised by counsel for the Board of Education that it does not propose to appear in oral argument or present a brief.

Because of the national importance of the issue presented and because of its importance to the State of Kansas, we request that the State present its views at oral argument. If the State does not desire to appear, we request the Attorney General to advise whether the State's default shall be construed as a concession of invalidity.

First District Court Decision in Briggs v. Elliott

**BRIGGS et al. v. ELLIOTT et al.**

Civ. A. No. 2657.

98 F. Supp. 529

United States District Court

E. D. South Carolina, Charleston Division.

Heard May 28, 1951.

Decided June 23, 1951.

Before PARKER, Circuit Judge, and WARING and TIMMERMAN, District Judges.

PARKER, Circuit Judge.

This is a suit for a declaratory judgment and injunctive relief in which it is alleged that the schools and educational facilities provided for Negro children in School District No. 22 in Clarendon County, South Carolina, are inferior to those provided for white children in that district and that this amounts to a denial of the equal protection of the laws guaranteed them by the Fourteenth Amendment to the Federal Constitution, and further that the segregation of Negro and white children in the public schools, required by Article 11, section 7 of the Constitution of South Carolina and section 5377 of the Code of Laws of that state,[1] is of itself violative of the equal protection clause of the Fourteenth Amendment. Plaintiffs are Negro children of school age who are entitled to attend the public schools in District No. 22 in Clarendon County, their parents and guardians. Defendants are the school officials who, as officers of the state, have control of the schools in the district. A court of three judges has been convened pursuant to the provisions of 28 U.S.C. §§ 2281 and 2284, the evidence offered by the parties has been heard and the case has been submitted upon the briefs and arguments of counsel.

At the beginning of the hearing the defendants admitted upon the record that "the educational facilities, equipment, curricula and opportunities afforded in School District No. 22 for colored pupils are not substantially equal to those afforded for white pupils." The evidence offered in the case fully sustains this admission. The defendants contend, however, that the district is one of the rural school districts which has not kept pace with urban districts in providing educational facilities for the children of either race, and that the inequalities have resulted from limited resources and from the disposition of the school officials to spend the limited funds available "for the most immediate demands rather than in the light of the overall picture." They state that under the leadership of Governor Byrnes the Legislature of South Carolina has made provision for a bond issue of $75,000,000 with a three per cent sales tax to support it for the purpose of equalizing educational opportunities and facilities throughout the state and of meeting the problem of providing equal educational opportunities for Negro children where this had not been done. They have offered evidence to show that this educational program is going forward and that under it the educational facilities in the district will be greatly improved for both races and that Negro children will be afforded educational facilities and opportunities in all respects equal to those afforded white children.

There can be no question but that where separate schools are maintained for Negroes and whites, the educational facilities and opportunities afforded by them must be equal. The state may not deny to any person within its jurisdiction the equal protection of the laws, says the Fourteenth Amendment; and this means that, when the state undertakes public education, it may not discriminate against any individual on account of race but must offer equal opportunity to all. As said by Chief Justice Hughes in Missouri ex rel. Gaines v. Canada, 305 U.S. 337, 349, 59 S.Ct. 232, 236, 83 L.Ed. 208. "The admissibility of laws separating the races in the enjoyment of privileges afforded by the State rests wholly upon the equality of the privileges which the laws give to the separated groups within the State." See also Sweatt v. Painter, 339 U.S. 629, 70 S.Ct. 848, 94 L.Ed. 1114; Corbin v. County School Board of Pulaski County, 4 Cir., 177 F.2d 924; Carter v. School Board of Arlington County, Va., 4 Cir., 182 F.2d 531; McKissick v. Carmichael, 4 Cir., 187 F.2d 949. We think it clear, therefore, that plaintiffs are entitled to a declaration to the effect that the school facilities now afforded Negro children in Dis-

[1]Article 11, section 7 of the Constitution of South Carolina is as follows: "Separate schools shall be provided for children of the white and colored races, and no child of either race shall ever be permitted to attend a school provided for children of the other race."

Section 5377 of the Code of Laws of South Carolina of 1942 is as follows: "It shall be unlawful for pupils of one race to attend the schools provided by boards of trustees for persons of another race."

trict No. 22 are not equal to the facilities afforded white children in the district and to a mandatory injunction requiring that equal facilities be afforded them. How this shall be done is a matter for the school authorities and not for the court, so long as it is done in good faith and equality of facilities is afforded; but it must be done promptly and the court in addition to issuing an injunction to that effect will retain the cause upon its docket for further orders and will require that defendants file within six months a report showing the action that has been taken by them to carry out the order.

Plaintiffs ask that, in addition to granting them relief on account of the inferiority of the educational facilities furnished them, we hold that segregation of the races in the public schools, as required by the Constitution and statutes of South Carolina, is of itself a denial of the equal protection of the laws guaranteed by the Fourteenth Amendment, and that we enjoin the enforcement of the constitutional provision and statute requiring it and by our injunction require defendants to submit Negroes to schools to which white students are admitted within the district. We think, however, that segregation of the races in the public schools, so long as equality of rights is preserved, is a matter of legislative policy for the several states, with which the federal courts are powerless to interfere.

One of the great virtues of our constitutional system is that, while the federal government protects the fundamental rights of the individual, it leaves to the several states the solution of local problems. In a country with a great expanse of territory with peoples of widely differing customs and ideas, local self government in local matters is essential to the peace and happiness of the people in the several communities as well as to the strength and unity of the country as a whole. It is universally held, therefore, that each state shall determine for itself, subject to the observance of the fundamental rights and liberties guaranteed by the federal Constitution, how it shall exercise the police power, i.e. the power to legislate with respect to the safety, morals, health and general welfare. And in no field is this right of the several states more clearly recognized than in that of public education. As was well said by Mr. Justice Harlan, speaking for a unanimous court in Cumming v. County Board of Education, 175 U.S. 528, 545, 20 S.Ct. 197, 201, 44 L.Ed. 262, "while all admit that the benefits and burdens of public taxation must be shared by citizens without discrimination against any class on account of their race, the education of the poeple in schools maintained by state taxation is a matter belonging to the respective states, and any interference on the part of Federal authority with the management of such schools cannot be justified except in the case of a clear and unmistakable disregard of rights secured by the supreme law of the land."

It is equally well settled that there is no denial of the equal protection of the laws in segregating children in the schools for purposes of education, if the children of the different races are given equal facilities and opportunities. The leading case on the subject in the Supreme Court is Plessy v. Ferguson, 163 U.S. 537, 16 S.Ct. 1138, 1140, 41 L.Ed. 256, which involved segregation in railroad trains, but in which the segregation there involved was referred to as being governed by the same principle as segregation in the schools. In that case the Court said: "The object of the amendment was undoubtedly to enforce the absolute equality of the two races before the law, but, in the nature of things, it could not have been intended to abolish distinctions based upon color, or to enforce social, as distinguished from political, equality, or a commingling of the two races upon terms unsatisfactory to either. Laws permitting, and even requiring, their separation, in places where they are liable to be brought into contact, do not necessarily imply the inferiority of either race to the other, and have been generally, if not universally, recognized as within the competency of the state legislatures in the exercise of their police power. The most common instance of this is connected with the establishment of separate schools for white and colored children, which has been held to be a valid exercise of the legislative power even by courts of states where the political rights of the colored race have been longest and most earnestly enforced."

Later in the opinion the Court said: "So far, then, as a conflict with the fourteenth amendment is concerned, the case reduces itself to the question whether the statute of Louisiana is a reasonable regulation, and with respect to this there must necessarily be a large discretion on the part of the legislature. *In determining the question of reasonableness, it is at liberty to act with reference to the established usages, customs, and traditions of the people, and with a view to the promotion of their comfort, and the preservation of the public peace and good order."* (Italics supplied.)

Directly in point and absolutely controlling upon us so long as it stands unreversed by the Supreme Court is Gong Lum v. Rice, 275 U.S. 78, 48 S.Ct. 91, 93, 72 L.Ed. 172, in which the complaint was that a child of Chinese parentage was excluded from a school maintained for white children under a segregation law and was permitted to enter only a school maintained for colored children. Although attempt is made to distinguish this case, it cannot be distinguished. The question as to the validity of segregation in the public schools on the ground of race was squarely raised, the Fourteenth Amendment was relied upon as forbidding segregation and the issue was squarely met by the Court. What was said by Chief Justice Taft speaking for a unanimous court, is determinative of the question before us. Said he:

"The case then reduces itself to the question whether a state can be said to afford to a child of Chinese ancestry, born in this country and a citizen of the United States, the equal protection of the laws, by giving her the opportunity for a common school education in a school which receives only colored children of the brown, yellow or black races.

"The right and power of the state to regulate the method of providing for the education of its youth at public expense is clear. * * *

"The question here is whether a Chinese citizen of the United States is denied equal protection of the laws when he is classed among the colored races and furnished facilities for education equal to that offered to all, whether white, brown, yellow, or black. Were this a new question, it would call for very full argument and consideration; but we think that it is the same question which has been many times decided to be within the constitutional power of the state Legislature to settle, without intervention of the federal courts under the federal Constitution. Roberts v. City of Boston, 5 Cush. (Mass.) 198, 206, 208, 209; State ex rel. Garnes v. McCann, 21 Ohio St. 198, 210; People ex rel. King v. Gallagher, 93 N.Y. 438; People ex rel. Cisco v. School Board, 161 N.Y. 598, 56 N.E. 81, 48 L.R.A. 113; Ward v. Flood, 48 Cal. 36; Wysinger v. Crookshank, 82 Cal. 588, 590, 23 P. 54; Reynolds v. Board of Education, 66 Kan. 672, 72 P. 274; McMillan v. School Committee, 107 N.C. 609, 12 S.E. 330, 10 L.R.A. 823; Cory v. Carter, 48 Ind. 327; Lehew v. Brummell, 103 Mo. 546, 15 S.W. 765, 11 L.R.A. 828; Dameron v. Bayless, 14 Ariz. 180, 126 P. 273; State ex rel. Stoutmeyer v. Duffy, 7 Nev. 342, 348, 355; Bertonneau v. Board, 3 Woods 177, 3 Fed.Cas. 294, [Case] No. 1,361; United States v. Buntin (C.C.), 10 F. 730, 735; Wong Him v. Callahan (C.C.), 119 F. 381.

"In Plessy v. Ferguson, 163 U.S. 537, 544, 545, 16 S.Ct. 1138, 1140, 41 L.Ed. 256, in upholding the validity under the Fourteenth Amendment of a statute of Louisiana requiring the separation of the white and colored races in railway coaches, *a more difficult question than this,* this court, speaking of permitted race separation, said:

" 'The most common instance of this is connected with the establishment of separate schools for white and colored children, which has been held to be a valid exercise of the legislative power even by courts of states where the political rights of the colored race have been longest and most earnestly enforced.'

*      *      *      *      *      *

"Most of the cases cited arose, it is true, over the establishment of separate schools as between white pupils and black pupils; but we cannot think that the question is any different, or that any different result can be reached, assuming the cases above cited to be rightly decided, where the issue is as between white pupils and the pupils of the yellow races. *The decision is within the discretion of the state in regulating its public schools, and does not conflict with the Fourteenth Amendment."* (Italics supplied.)

Only a little over a year ago, the question was before the Court of Appeals of the District of Columbia in Carr v. Corning, 86 U.S.App.D.C. 173, 182 F.2d 14, 16, a case involving the validity of segregation within the District, and the whole matter was exhaustively explored in the light of history and the pertinent decisions in an able opinion by Judge Prettyman, who said:

"It is urged that the separation of the races is itself, apart from equality or inequality of treatment, forbidden by the Constitution. The question thus posed is whether the Constitution lifted this problem out of the hands of all legislatures and settled it. We do not think it did. Since the beginning of human history, no circumstance has given rise to more difficult and delicate problems than has the coexistence of different races in the same area. Centuries of bitter experience in all parts of the world have proved that the problem is insoluble by force of any sort. The same history shows that it is soluble by the patient processes of community experience. Such problems lie naturally in the field of legislation, a method susceptible of experimentation, of development, of adjustment to the current necessities in a variety of community circumstance. We do not believe that the makers of the first ten Amendments in 1789 or of the Fourteenth Amendment in 1866 meant to foreclose legislative treatment of the problem in this country.

"This is not to decry efforts to reach that state of common existence which is the obvious highest good in our concept of civilization. It is merely to say that the social and economic interrelationship of two races living together is a legislative problem, as yet not solved, and is not a problem solved fully, finally and unequivocally by a fiat enacted many years ago. We must remember that on this particular point we are interpreting a constitution and not enacting a statute.

"We are not unmindful of the debates which occurred in Congress relative to the Civil Rights Act of April 9, 1866, the Fourteenth Amendment, and the Civil Rights Act of March 1, 1875. But the actions of Congress, the discussion in the Civil Rights cases, and the fact that in 1862, 1864, 1866 and 1874 Congress, as we shall point out in a moment, enacted legislation which specifically provided for separation of the races in the schools of the District of Columbia, conclusively support our view of the Amendment and its effect.

"The Supreme Court has consistently held that if there be an 'equality of the privileges which the laws give to the separated groups,' the races may be separated. That is to say that constitutional invalidity does not arise from the mere fact of separation but may arise from an inequality of treatment. Other courts have long held to the same effect."

It should be borne in mind that in the above cases the courts have not been dealing with hypothetical situations or mere theory, but with situations which have actually developed in the relationship of the races throughout the country. Segregation of the races in the public schools has not been confined to South Carolina or even to the South but prevails in many other states where Negroes are present in large numbers. Even when not required by law, it is customary in many places. Congress has provided for it by federal statute in the District of Columbia; and seventeen of the states have statutes or constitutional provisions requiring it. They are Alabama, Arkansas, Delaware, Florida, Georgia, Kentucky, Louisiana, Maryland, Mississippi, Missouri, North Carolina, Oklahoma, South Carolina, Tennessee, Texas, Virginia, and West Virginia.[2] And the validity of legislatively requiring segregation in the schools has been upheld wherever the question has been raised. See Wong Him v. Callahan, C.C., 119 F. 381; United States v. Buntin, C.C., 10 F. 730; Bertonneau v. Board of Directors, 3 Fed. Cas. 294, No. 1,361; Dameron v. Bayless, 14 Ariz. 180, 126 P. 273; Maddox v. Neal, 45 Ark. 121, 55 Am. Rep. 540; Ward v. Flood, 48 Cal. 36, 17 Am.Rep. 405; Cory v. Carter, 48 Ind. 327, 17 Am.Rep. 738; Graham v. Board of Education, 153 Kan. 840, 114 P.2d 313; Richardson v. Board of Education, 72 Kan. 629, 84 P. 538; Reynolds v. Board of Education, 66 Kan. 672, 72 P. 274; Chrisman v. Mayor of City of Brookhaven, 70 Miss. 477, 12 So. 458; Lehew v. Brummell, 103 Mo. 546, 15 S.W. 765, 11 L.R.A. 828, 23 Am.St.Rep. 895; State ex rel. Stoutmeyer v. Duffy, 7 Nev. 342, 8 Am.Rep. 713; People ex rel. Cisco v. School Board, 161 N.Y. 598, 56 N.E. 81, 48 L.R.A. 113; People v. Gallagher, 93 N.Y. 438, 45 Am.Rep. 232; McMillan v. School Committee, 107 N.C. 609, 12 S.E. 330, 10 L.R.A. 823; State ex rel. Garnes v. McCann, 21 Ohio St. 198; Board of Education v. Board of Com'rs, 14 Okl. 322, 78 P. 455; Martin v. Board of Education, 42 W.Va. 514, 26 S.E. 348.[3] No cases have been cited to us holding that such legislation is violative of the Fourteenth Amendment. We know of none, and diligent search of the authorities has failed to reveal any.

Plaintiffs rely upon expressions contained in opinions relating to professional education such as Sweatt v. Painter, 339 U.S. 629, 70 S.Ct. 848, 94 L.Ed.1114, McLaurin v. Oklahoma State Regents, 339 U.S. 637, 70 S.Ct. 851, 94 L.Ed. 1149, and McKissick v. Carmichael, 4 Cir., 187 F.2d 949, where equality of opportunity was not afforded. Sweatt v. Painter, however, instead of helping them, emphasizes that the separate but equal doctrine of Plessy v. Ferguson, has not been overruled, since the Supreme Court, although urged to overrule it, expressly refused to do so and based its decision on the ground that the educational facilities offered Negro law students in that case were not equal to those offered white students. The decision in McKissick v. Carmichael, was based upon the same ground. The case of McLaurin v. Oklahoma State Regents, involved humiliating and embarrassing treatment of a Negro graduate student to which no one should have been required to submit. Nothing of the sort is involved here.

The problem of segregation as applied to graduate and professional education is essentially different from that involved in segregation in education at the lower levels. In the graduate and professional schools the problem is one of affording equal educational facilities to persons sui juris and of mature personality. Because of the great expense of such education and the importance of the professional contacts established while carrying on the educational process, it is difficult for the state to maintain segregated schools for Negroes in this field which will afford them opportunities for education and professional advancement equal to those afforded by the graduate and professional schools maintained for white persons. What the courts have said, and all they have said in the cases upon which plaintiffs rely is that, notwithstanding these difficulties, the opportunity afforded the Negro student must be equal to that afforded the white student and that the schools established for furnishing this instruction to white persons must be opened to Negroes if this is necessary to give them the equal opportunity which the Constitution requires.

The problem of segregation at the common school level is a very different one. At this level, as good education can be afforded in Negro schools as in white schools and the thought of establishing professional contacts does not enter into the picture. Moreover, education at this level is not a matter of voluntary choice on the part of the student but of compulsion by the state. The student is taken from the control of the family during school hours by compulsion of law and placed in control of the school, where he must associate with his fellow students. The law thus provides that the school shall supplement the work of the parent in the training of the child and in doing so it is entering a delicate field and one fraught with tensions and difficulties. In formulating educational policy at the common school level, therefore, the law must take account, not merely of the matter of affording instruction to the student, but also of the wishes of the parent as to the upbringing of the child and his associates in the formative period of childhood and adolescence. If public education is to have the support of the people

[2]Statistical Summary of Education, 1947–48, "Biennial Survey of Education in the United States, 1946–48", ch. 1, pp. 8, 40 (Federal Security Agency, Office of Education).
[3]See also Roberts v. City of Boston, 5 Cush., Mass., 198, decided prior to the Fourteenth Amendment.

through their legislatures, it must not go contrary to what they deem for the best interests of their children.

There is testimony to the effect that mixed schools will give better education and a better understanding of the community in which the child is to live than segregated schools. There is testimony, on the other hand, that mixed schools will result in racial friction and tension and that the only practical way of conducting public education in South Carolina is with segregated schools. The questions thus presented are not questions of constitutional right but of legislative policy, which must be formulated, not in vacuo or with doctrinaire disregard of existing conditions, but in realistic approach to the situations to which it is to be applied. In some states, the legislatures may well decide that segregation in public schools should be abolished, in others that it should be maintained—all depending upon the relationships existing between the races and the tensions likely to be produced by an attempt to educate the children of the two races together in the same schools. The federal courts would be going far outside their constitutional function were they to attempt to prescribe educational policies for the states in such matters, however desirable such policies might be in the opinion of some sociologists or educators. For the federal courts to do so would result, not only in interference with local affairs by an agency of the federal government, but also in the substitution of the judicial for the legislative process in what is essentially a legislative matter.

The public schools are facilities provided and paid for by the states. The state's regulation of the facilities which it furnishes is not to be interfered with unless constitutional rights are clearly infringed. There is nothing in the Constitution that requires that the state grant to all members of the public a common right to use every facility that it affords. Grants in aid of education or for the support of the indigent may properly be made upon an individual basis if no discrimination is practiced; and, if the family, which is the racial unit, may be considered in these, it may be considered also in providing public schools. The equal protection of the laws does not mean that the child must be treated as the property of the state and the wishes of his family as to his upbringing be disregarded. The classification of children for the purpose of education in separate schools has a basis grounded in reason and experience; and, if equal facilities are afforded, it cannot be condemned as discriminatory for, as said by Mr. Justice Reed in New York Rapid Transit Corp. v. City of New York, 303 U.S. 573, 578, 58 S.Ct. 721, 724, 82 L.Ed. 1024: "It has long been the law under the Fourteenth Amendment that 'a distinction in legislation is not arbitrary, if any state of facts reasonably can be conceived that would sustain it.' "[4]

We are cited to cases having relation to zoning ordinances, restrictive covenants in deeds and segregation in public conveyances. It is clear, however, that nothing said in these cases would justify our disregarding the great volume of authority relating directly to education in the public schools, which involves not transient contacts, but associations which affect the interests of the home and the wishes of the people with regard to the upbringing of their children. As Chief Justice Taft pointed out in Gong Lum v. Rice, supra [275 U.S. 78, 48 S.Ct. 93], "a more difficult" question is presented by segregation in public conveyances than by segregation in the schools.

We conclude, therefore, that if equal facilities are offered, segregation of the races in the public schools as prescribed by the Constitution and laws of South Carolina is not of itself violative of the Fourteenth Amendment. We think that this conclusion is supported by overwhelming authority which we are not at liberty to disregard on the basis of theories advanced by a few educators and sociologists. Even if we felt at liberty to disregard other authorities, we may not ignore the unreversed decisions of the Supreme Court of the United States which are squarely in point and conclusive of the question before us. As said by the Court of Appeals of the Fourth Circuit in Boyer v. Garrett, 183 F.2d 582, a case involving segregation in a public playground, in which equality of treatment was admitted and segregation was attacked as being per se violative of the Fourteenth Amendment: "The contention of plaintiffs is that, notwithstanding this equality of treatment, the rule providing for segregation is violative of the provisions of the federal Constitution. The District Court dismissed the complaint on the authority of Plessy v. Ferguson, 163 U.S. 537, 16 S.Ct. 1138, 41 L.Ed. 256; and the principal argument made on appeal is that the authority of Plessy v. Ferguson has been so weakened by subsequent decisions that we should no longer consider it as binding. We do not think, however, that we are at liberty

[4]See also, Rast v. Van Deman & Lewis Co., 240 U.S. 342, 357, 36 S.Ct. 370, 60 L.Ed. 679; Borden's Farm Products Co. v. Baldwin, 293 U.S. 194, 209, 55 S.Ct. 187, 79 L.Ed. 281; Metropolitan Casualty Ins. Co. v. Brownell, 294 U.S. 580, 584, 55 S.Ct. 538, 79 L.Ed. 1070; State Board of Tax Com'rs v. Jackson, 283 U.S. 527, 537, 51 S.Ct. 540, 75 L.Ed. 1248; Lindsley v. Natural Carbonic Gas Co., 220 U.S. 61, 78, 31 S.Ct. 337, 55 L.Ed. 369; Alabama State Federation of Labor v. McAdory, 325 U.S. 450, 465, 65 S.Ct. 1384, 89 L.Ed. 1725; Asbury Hospital v. Cass County, N.D., 326 U.S. 207, 215, 66 S.Ct. 61, 90 L.Ed. 6; Carmichael v. Southern Coal & Coke Co., 301 U.S. 495, 509, 57 S.Ct. 868, 81 L.Ed. 1245; South Carolina Power Co. v. South Carolina Tax Com'n, 4 Cir., 52 F.2d 515, 518; United States v. Carolene Products Co., 304 U.S. 144, 152, 58 S.Ct. 778, 82 L.Ed. 1234; Bowles v. American Brewery, 4 Cir., 146 F.2d 842, 847; White Packing Co. v. Robertson, 4 Cir., 89 F.2d 775, 779.

thus to disregard a decision of the Supreme Court which that court has not seen fit to overrule and which it expressly refrained from reexamining, although urged to do so, in the very recent case of Sweatt v. Painter [339 U.S. 629], 70 S.Ct. 848 [94 L.Ed. 1114]. It is for the Supreme Court, not us, to overrule its decisions or to hold them outmoded."

To this we may add that, when seventeen states and the Congress of the United States have for more than three-quarters of a century required segregation of the races in the public schools, and when this has received the approval of the leading appellate courts of the country including the unanimous approval of the Supreme Court of the United States at a time when that court included Chief Justice Taft and Justices Stone, Holmes and Brandeis, it is a late day to say that such segregation is violative of fundamental constitutional rights. It is hardly reasonable to suppose that legislative bodies over so wide a territory, including the Congress of the United States, and great judges of high courts have knowingly defied the Constitution for so long a period or that they have acted in ignorance of the meaning of its provisions. The constitutional principle is the same now that it has been throughout this period; and if conditions have changed so that segregation is no longer wise, this is a matter for the legislatures and not for the courts. The members of the judiciary have no more right to read their ideas of sociology into the Constitution than their ideas of economics.

It is argued that, because the school facilities furnished Negroes in District No. 22 are inferior to those furnished white persons, we should enjoin segregation rather than direct the equalizing of conditions. In as much as we think that the law requiring segregation is valid, however, and that the inequality suffered by plaintiffs results, not from the law, but from the way it has been administered, we think that our injunction should be directed to removing the inequalities resulting from administration within the framework of the law rather than to nullifying the law itself. As a court of equity, we should exercise our power to assure to plaintiffs the equality of treatment to which they are entitled with due regard to the legislative policy of the state. In directing that the school facilities afforded Negroes within the district be equalized promptly with those afforded white persons, we are giving plaintiffs all the relief that they can reasonably ask and the relief that is ordinarily granted in cases of this sort. See Carter v. County School Board of Arlington County, Virginia, 4 Cir., 182 F.2d 531. The court should not use its power to abolish segregation in a state where it is required by law if the equality demanded by the Constitution can be attained otherwise. This much is demanded by the spirit of comity which must prevail in the relationship between the agencies of the federal government and the states if our constitutional system is to endure.

Decree will be entered finding that the constitutional and statutory provisions requiring segregation in the public schools are not of themselves violative of the Fourteenth Amendment, but that defendants have denied to plaintiffs rights guaranteed by that amendment in failing to furnish for Negroes in School District 22 educational facilities and opportunities equal to those furnished white persons, and injunction will issue directing defendants promptly to furnish Negroes within the district educational facilities and opportunities equal to those furnished white persons and to report to the court within six months as to the action that has been taken by them to effectuate the court's decree.

Injunction to abolish segregation denied.

Injunction to equalize educational facilities granted.

WARING, District Judge (dissenting).

This case has been brought for the express and declared purpose of determining the right of the State of South Carolina, in its public schools, to practice segregation according to race.

The plaintiffs are all residents of Clarendon County, South Carolina which is situated within the Eastern District of South Carolina and within the jurisdiction of this court. The plaintiffs consist of minors and adults there being forty-six minors who are qualified to attend and are attending the public schools in School District 22 of Clarendon County; and twenty adults who are taxpayers and are either guardians or parents of the minor plaintiffs. The defendants are members of the Board of Trustees of School District 22 and other officials of the educational system of Clarendon County including the superintendent of education. They are the parties in charge of the various schools which are situated within the aforesaid school district and which are affected by the matters set forth in this cause.

The plaintiffs allege that they are discriminated against by the defendants under color of the Constitution and laws of the State of South Carolina whereby they are denied equal educational facilities and opportunities and that this denial is based upon difference in race. And they show that the school system of this particular school district and county (following the general pattern that it is admitted obtains in the State of South Carolina) sets up two classes of schools; one for people said to belong to the white race and the other for people of other races but primarily for those said to belong to the Negro race or of mixed races and either wholly, partially, or faintly alleged to be of African or Negro descent. These plaintiffs bring this action for the enforcement of the rights to which they claim they are entitled and on behalf of many others who are in like plight and condition and the suit is denominated a class suit for the purpose of abrogation of what is claimed to be the enforcement of unfair and discriminatory laws by the defendants. Plaintiffs claim that they are entitled to bring this case and that this court has jurisdiction under the Fourteenth Amendment of the Constitution of the United States and of a number of statutes of the United States, commonly referred to as civil rights statutes.[1] The plaintiffs demand relief under the above referred to sections of the laws of the United States by way of a declaratory judgment and permanent injunction.

It is alleged that the defendants are acting under the authority granted them by the Constitution and laws of the State of South Carolina and that all of these are in contravention of the Constitution and laws of the United States. The particular portions of the laws of South Carolina are as follows:

Article XI, Section 5 is as follows: "Free public schools.—The General Assembly shall provide for a liberal system of free public schools for all children between the ages of six and twenty-one years * * *."

Article XI, Section 7 is as follows: "Separate schools shall be provided for children of the white and colored races, and no child of either race shall ever be permitted to attend a school provided for children of the other race."

Section 5377 of the Code of Laws of South Carolina is as follows: "It shall be unlawful for pupils of one race to attend the schools provided by boards of trustees for persons of another race."

It is further shown that the defendants are acting under the authority of the Constitution and laws of the State of South Carolina providing for the creation of various school districts,[2] and they have strictly separated and segregated the school facilities, both elementary and high school, according to race. There are, in said school district, three schools which are used exclusively by Negroes: to wit, Rambay Elementary School, Liberty Hill Elementary School, and Scotts Branch Union (a combination of elementary and high school). There are in the same school district, two schools maintained for whites, namely, Summerton Elementary School and Summerton High School. The last named serves some of the other school districts in Clarendon County as well as No. 22.

It appears that the plaintiffs filed a petition with the defendants requesting that the defendants cease discrimination against the Negro children of public school age; and the situation complained of not having been remedied or changed, the plaintiffs now ask this court to require the defendants to grant them their rights guaranteed under the Fourteenth Amendment of the Constitution of the United States and they appeal to the equitable power of this court for declaratory and injunctive relief alleging that they are suffering irreparable injuries and that they have no plain adequate or complete remedy to redress the wrongs and illegal acts complained of other than this suit. And they further point out that large numbers of people and persons are and will be affected by the decision of this court in adjudicating and clarifying the rights of Negroes to obtain education in the public school system of the State of South Carolina without discrimination and denial of equal facilities on account of their race.

The defendants appear and by way of answer deny the allegations of the complaint as to discrimination and inequality and allege that not only are they acting within the laws of the State in enforcing segregation but that all facilities afforded the pupils of different races are adequate and equal and that there is no inequality or discrimination practiced against these plaintiffs or any others by reason of race or color. And they allege that the facilities and opportunities furnished to the colored children are substantially the same as those provided for the white children. And they further base their defense upon the statement that the Constitutional and statutory provisions under attack in this case, that is to say, the provisions requiring separate schools because of race, are a reasonable exercise of the State's police power and that all of the same are valid under the powers possessed by the State of South Carolina and the Constitution of the United States and they deny that the same can be held to be unconstitutional by this Court.

The issues being so drawn and calling for a judgment by the United States Court which would require the issuance of an injunction against State and County officials, it became apparent that it would be necessary that the case be heard in accordance with the statute applicable to cases of this type requiring the calling of a three-judge court.[3] Such a court convened and the case was set for a hearing on May 28, 1951.

The case came on for a trial upon the issues as presented in the complaint and answer. But upon the call of the case, defendants' counsel announced that they wished to make a statement on behalf of the defendants making certain admissions and praying that the Court make a finding as to inequalities in respect to buildings, equipment, facilities, curricula and other aspects of the schools provided for children in School District 22 in Clarendon County and giving the public authorities time to formulate plans for ending such inequalities. In this statement defendants claim that they never had intended to discriminate against any of the pupils and although they had filed an answer to the complaint, some five months ago, denying inequalities they now admit that they had found some; but rely upon the fact that subsequent to the institution of this suit, James F. Byrnes, the Governor of South Carolina, had

[1]Fourteenth Amendment of the Constitution of the United States, Section 1; Title 8 U.S.C.A. §§ 41, 43; Title 28, U.S.C.A. § 1343.

[2]Constitution of South Carolina, Article XI, Section 5; Code of Laws, 5301, 5316, 5328, 5404 and 5405; Code of Laws of South Carolina, Sections 5303, 5306, 5343, 5409.

[3]Title 28, U.S.C.A. §§ 2281–2284.

stated in his inaugural address that the State must take steps to provide money for improving educational facilities and that thereafter, the Legislature had adopted certain legislation. They stated that they hoped that in time they would obtain money as a result of the foregoing and improve the school situation.

This statement was allowed to be filed and considered as an amendment to the answer.

By this maneuver, the defendants have endeavored to induce this Court to avoid the primary purpose of the suit. And if the Court should follow this suggestion and fail to meet the issues raised by merely considering this case in the light of another "separate but equal" case, the entire purpose and reason for the institution of the case and the convening of a three-judge court would be voided. The 66 plaintiffs in this cause have brought this suit at what must have cost much in effort and financial expenditures. They are here represented by 6 attorneys, all, save one, practicing lawyers from without the State of South Carolina and coming here from a considerable distance. The plaintiffs have brought a large number of witnesses exclusive of themselves. As a matter of fact, they called and examined 11 witnesses. They said that they had a number more coming who did not arrive in time owing to the shortening of the proceedings and they also stated that they had on hand and had contemplated calling a large number of other witnesses but this became unnecessary by reason of the foregoing admissions by defendants. It certainly appears that large expenses must have been caused by the institution of this case and great efforts expended in gathering data, making a study of the issues involved, interviewing and bringing numerous witnesses, some of whom are foremost scientists in America. And in addition to all of this, these 66 plaintiffs have not merely expended their time and money in order to test this important Constitutional question, but they have shown unexampled courage in bringing and presenting this cause at their own expense in the face of the long established and age-old pattern of the way of life which the State of South Carolina has adopted and practiced and lived in since and as a result of the institution of human slavery.

If a case of this magnitude can be turned aside and a court refused to hear these basic issues by the mere device of admission that some buildings, blackboards, lighting fixtures and toilet facilities are unequal but that they may be remedied by the spending of a few dollars, then, indeed people in the plight in which these plaintiffs are, have no adequate remedy or forum in which to air their wrongs. If this method of judicial evasion be adopted, these very infant plaintiffs now pupils in Clarendon County will probably be bringing suits for their children and grandchildren decades or rather generations hence in an effort to get for their descendants what are today denied to them. If they are entitled to any rights as American citizens, they are entitled to have these rights now and not in the future. And no excuse can be made to deny them these rights which are theirs under the Constitution and laws of America by the use of the false doctrine and patter called "separate but equal" and it is the duty of the Court to meet these issues simply and factually and without fear, sophistry and evasion. If this be the measure of justice to be meted out to them, then, indeed, hundreds, nay thousands, of cases will have to be brought and in each case thousands of dollars will have to be spent for the employment of legal talent and scientific testimony and then the cases will be turned aside, postponed or eliminated by devices such as this.

We should be unwilling to straddle or avoid this issue and if the suggestion made by these defendants is to be adopted as the type of justice to be meted out by this Court, then I want no part of it.

And so we must and do face, without evasion or equivocation, the question as to whether segregation in education in our schools is legal or whether it cannot exist under our American system as particularly enunciated in the Fourteenth Amendment to the Constitution of the United States.

Before the American Civil War, the institution of human slavery had been adopted and was approved in this country. Slavery was nothing new in the world. From the dawn of history we see aggressors enslaving weak and less fortunate neighbors. Back through the days of early civilization man practiced slavery. We read of it in Biblical days; we read of it in the Greek City States and in the great Roman Empire. Throughout medieval Europe, forms of slavery existed and it was widely practiced in Asia Minor and the Eastern countries and perhaps reached its worst form in Nazi Germany. Class and caste have, unfortunately, existed through the ages. But, in time, mankind, through evolution and progress, through ethical and religious concepts, through the study of the teachings of the great philosophers and the great religious teachers, including especially the founder of Christianity—mankind began to revolt against the enslavement of body, mind and soul of one human being by another. And so there came about a great awakening. The British who had indulged in the slave trade, awakened to the fact that it was immoral and against the right thinking ideology of the Christian world. And in this country, also, came about a moral awakening. Unfortunately, this had not been sufficiently advanced at the time of the adoption of the American Constitution for the institution of slavery to be prohibited. But there was a struggle and the better thinking leaders in our Constitutional Convention endeavored to prohibit slavery but unfortunately compromised the issue on the insistent demands of those who were engaged in the slave trade and the purchase and use of slaves. And so as time went on, slavery was perpetuated and eventually became a part of the life and culture of certain of the States of this Union although the rest of the world looked on with shame and abhorrence.

As was so well said, this country could not continue to exist one-half slave and one-half free and long years of war were entered into before the nation was willing to eradicate this system which was, itself, a denial of the brave and fine statements of the Declaration of Independence and a denial of freedom as envisioned and advocated by our Founders.

The United States then adopted the 13th, 14th and 15th Amendments and it cannot be denied that the basic reason for all of these Amendments to the Constitution was to wipe out completely the institution of slavery and to declare that all citizens in this country should be considered as free, equal and entitled to all of the provisions of citizenship.

The Fourteenth Amendment to the Constitution of the United States is as follows: "Section 1. All persons born or naturalized in the United States, and subject to the jurisdiction thereof, are citizens of the United States and of the State wherein they reside. No State shall make or enforce any law which shall abridge the privileges or immunities of citizens of the United States; nor shall any State deprive any person of life, liberty, or property, without due process of law; nor deny to any person within its jurisdiction the equal protection of the laws."

It seems to me that it is unnecessary to pore through voluminous arguments and opinions to ascertain what the foregoing means. And while it is true that we have had hundreds, perhaps thousands, of legal opinions outlining and defining the various effects and overtones on our laws and life brought about by the adoption of this Amendment, one of ordinary ability and understanding of the English language will have no trouble in knowing that when this Amendment was adopted, it was intended to do away with discrimination between our citizens.

The Amendment refers to *all* persons. There is nothing in there that attempts to separate, segregate or discriminate against any persons because of their being of European, Asian or African ancestry. And the plain intendment is that all of these persons are citizens. And then it is provided that no State shall make or enforce any law which shall abridge the privileges of citizens nor shall any state deny "to *any person* within its jurisdiction the equal protection of the laws."

The Amendment was first proposed in 1866 just about a year after the end of the American Civil War and the surrender of the Confederate States government. Within two years, the Amendment was adopted and became part of the Constitution of the United States. It cannot be gainsaid that the Amendment was proposed and adopted wholly and entirely as a result of the great conflict between freedom and slavery. This will be amply substantiated by an examination and appreciation of the proposal and discussion and Congressional debates (see Flack on Adoption of the 14th Amendment) and so it is undeniably true that the three great Amendments were adopted to eliminate not only slavery, itself, but all idea of discrimination and difference between American citizens.

Let us now come to consider whether the Constitution and Laws of the State of South Carolina which we have heretofore quoted are in conflict with the true meaning and intendment of this Fourteenth Amendment. The whole discussion of race and ancestry has been intermingled with sophistry and prejudice. What possible definition can be found for the so-called white race, Negro race or other races? Who is to decide and what is the test? For years, there was much talk of blood and taint of blood. Science tells us that there are but four kinds of blood: A, B, AB and O and these are found in Europeans, Asiatics, Africans, Americans and others. And so we need not further consider the irresponsible baseless references to preservation of "Caucasian blood". So then, what test are we going to use in opening our school doors and labeling them "white" and "Negro"? The law of South Carolina considers a person of one-eighth African ancestry to be a Negro. Why this proportion? Is it based upon any reason; anthropological, historical or ethical? And how are the trustees to know who are "whites" and who are "Negroes"? If it is dangerous and evil for a white child to be associated with another child, one of whose great-grandparents was of African descent, is it not equally dangerous for one with a one-sixteenth percentage? And if the State has decided that there is danger in contact between the whites and Negroes, isn't it requisite and proper that the State furnish a series of schools one for each of these percentages? If the idea is perfect racial equality in educational systems, why should children of pure African descent be brought in contact with children of one-half, one-fourth, or one-eighth such ancestry? To ask these questions is sufficient answer to them. The whole thing is unreasonable, unscientific and based upon unadulterated prejudice. We see the results of all of this warped thinking in the poor underprivileged and frightened attitude of so many of the Negroes in the southern states; and in the sadistic insistence of the "white supremacists" in declaring that their will must be imposed irrespective of rights of other citizens. This claim of "white supremacy," while fantastic and without foundation, is really believed by them for we have had repeated declarations from leading politicians and governors of this state and other states declaring that "white supremacy" will be endangered by the abolition of segregation. There are present threats, including those of the present Governor of this state, going to the extent of saying that all public education may be abandoned if the courts should grant true equality in educational facilities.

Although some 73 years have passed since the adoption of the Fourteenth Amendment and although it is clearly apparent that its chief purpose, (perhaps we may say its only real purpose) was to remove from Negroes the stigma and status of slavery and to confer upon them full rights as citizens, nevertheless, there has been a long and arduous course of litigation through the years. With some setbacks here and there, the courts have generally and progressively recognized the true meaning of the Fourteenth Amendment and have, from time to time, stricken down the attempts made by state governments (almost entirely those of the former Confederate states) to restrict the Amendment and to keep Negroes in a different classification so far as their rights and privileges as citizens are concerned. A number of cases have reached the Supreme Court of the United States wherein it became necessary for that tribunal to insist that Negroes be treated as citizens in the performance of jury duty. See Strauder v. West Virginia,[4] where the Court says 100 U.S. at page 307, 25 L.Ed. 664; "* * * What is this but declaring that the law in the States shall be the same for the black as for the white; that all persons, whether colored or white, shall stand equal before the laws of the States, and, in regard to the colored race, for whose protection the amendment was primarily designed, that no discrimination shall be made against them by law because of their color? The words of the amendment, it is true, are prohibitory, but they contain a necessary implication of a positive immunity, or right, most valuable to the colored race,—the right to exemption from unfriendly legislation against them distinctively as colored—exemption from legal discriminations, implying inferiority in civil society, lessening the security of their enjoyment of the rights which others enjoy, and discriminations which are steps towards reducing them to the condition of a subject race."

Many subsequent cases have followed and confirmed the right of Negroes to be treated as equals in all jury and grand jury service in the states.

The Supreme Court has stricken down from time to time statutes providing for imprisonment for violation of contracts. These are known as peonage cases and were in regard to statutes primarily aimed at keeping the Negro "in his place."[5]

In the field of transportation the court has now, in effect declared that common carriers engaged in interstate travel must not and cannot segregate and discriminate against passengers by reason of their race or color.[6]

Frequent and repeated instances of prejudice in criminal cases because of the brutal treatment of defendants because of their color have been passed upon in a large number of cases.[7]

Discrimination by segregation of housing facilities and attempts to control the same by covenants have also been outlawed.[8]

In the field of labor employment and particularly the relation of labor unions to the racial problem discrimination has again been forbidden.[9]

Perhaps the most serious battle for equality of rights has been in the field of exercise of suffrage. For years, certain of the southern states have attempted to prevent the Negro from taking part in elections by various devices. It is unnecessary to enumerate the long list of cases, but from time to time courts have stricken down all of these various devices classed as the "grandfather clause," educational tests and white private clubs.[10]

The foregoing are but a few brief references to some of the major landmarks in the fight by Negroes for equality. We now come to the more specific question, namely, the field of education. The question of the right of the state to practice segregation by race in certain educational facilities has only recently been tested in the courts. The cases of Missouri ex rel. Gaines v. Canada, 305 U.S. 337, 59 S.Ct. 232, 83 L.Ed. 208 and Sipuel v. Board of Regents, 332 U.S. 631, 68 S.Ct. 299, 92 L.Ed. 247, decided that Negroes were entitled to the same type of legal education that whites were given. It was further decided that the equal facilities must be furnished without delay or as was said in the Sipuel case, the state must provide for equality of education for Negroes "as soon as it does for applicants of any other group." But still we have not reached the exact question that is posed in the instant case.

We now come to the cases that, in my opinion, definitely and conclusively establish the doctrine that separation and segregation according to race is a violation of the Fourteenth Amendment. I, of

[4]100 U.S. 303, 25 L.Ed. 664.

[5]Peonage: Bailey v. Alabama, 219 U.S. 219, 31 S.Ct. 145, 55 L.Ed. 191; U.S. v. Reynolds, 235 U.S. 133, 35 S.Ct. 86, 59 L.Ed. 162.

[6]Transportation: Mitchell v. U.S., 313 U.S. 80, 61 S.Ct. 873, 85 L.Ed. 1201; Morgan v. Virginia, 328 U.S. 373, 66 S.Ct. 1050, 90 L.Ed. 1317; Henderson v. U.S., 339 U.S. 816, 70 S.Ct. 843, 94 L.Ed. 1302; Chance v. Lambeth, 4 Cir., 186 F.2d 879, certiorari denied Atlantic Coast Line R. Co. v. Chance, 341 U.S. 941, 71 S.Ct. 1001, May 28, 1951.

[7]Criminals: Brown v. Mississippi, 297 U.S. 278, 56 S.Ct. 461, 80 L.Ed. 682; Chambers v. Florida, 309 U.S. 227, 60 S.Ct. 472, 84 L.Ed. 716; Shepherd v. Florida, 341 U.S. 50, 71 S.Ct. 549.

[8]Housing: Buchanan v. Warley, 245 U.S. 60, 38 S.Ct. 16, 62 L.Ed. 149; Shelley v. Kraemer, 334 U.S. 1, 68 S.Ct. 836, 92 L.Ed. 1161.

[9]Labor: Steele v. Louisville & N. R. R. Co., 323 U.S. 192, 65 S.Ct. 226, 89 L.Ed. 173; Tunstall v. Brotherhood of Locomotive Firemen, 323 U.S. 210, 65 S.Ct. 235, 89 L.Ed. 187.

[10]Suffrage: Guinn v. U.S., 238 U.S. 347, 35 S.Ct. 926, 59 L.Ed. 1340; Nixon v. Herndon, 273 U.S. 536, 47 S.Ct. 446, 71 L.Ed. 759; Lane v. Wilson, 307 U.S. 268, 59 S.Ct. 872, 83 L.Ed. 1281; Smith v. Allwright, 321 U.S. 649, 64 S.Ct. 757, 88 L.Ed. 987; Elmore v. Rice, D.C., 72 F.Supp. 516; 4 Cir., 165 F.2d 387 certiorari denied, 333 U.S. 875, 68 S.Ct. 905, 92 L.Ed. 1151; Brown v. Baskin, D.C., 78 F.Supp. 933; Brown v. Baskin, D.C. 80 F.Supp. 1017; 4 Cir., 174 F.2d 391.

course, refer to the cases of Sweatt v. Painter, 339 U.S. 629, 70 S.Ct. 848, 94 L.Ed. 1114, and McLaurin v. Oklahoma State Regents, 339 U.S. 637, 70 S.Ct. 851, 94 L.Ed. 1149. These cases have been followed in a number of lower court decisions so that there is no longer any question as to the rights of Negroes to enjoy all the rights and facilities afforded by the law schools of the States of Virginia, Louisiana, Delaware, North Carolina and Kentucky. So there is no longer any basis for a state to claim the power to separate according to race in graduate schools, universities and colleges.

The real rock on which the defendants base their case is a decision of the Supreme Court of the United States in the case of Plessy v. Ferguson, 163 U.S. 537, 16 S.Ct. 1138, 41 L.Ed. 256. This case arose in Louisiana and was heard on appeal in 1895. The case related to the power of the State of Louisiana to require separate railroad cars for white and colored passengers and the Court sustained the State's action. Much discussion has followed this case and the reasoning and decision has been severely criticized for many years. And the famous dissenting opinion by Mr. Justice Harlan has been quoted throughout the years as a true declaration of the meaning of the Fourteenth Amendment and of the spirit of the American Constitution and the American way of life. It has also been frequently pointed out that when that decision was made, practically all the persons of the colored or Negro race had either been born slaves or were the children of slaves and that as yet due to their circumstances and surroundings and the condition in which they had been kept by their former masters, they were hardly looked upon as equals or as American citizens. The reasoning of the prevailing opinion in the Plessy case stems almost completely from a decision by Chief Justice Shaw of Massachusetts,[11] which decision was made many years before the Civil War and when, of course, the Fourteenth Amendment had not even been dreamed of.

But these arguments are beside the point in the present case. And we are not called upon to argue or discuss the validity of the Plessy case.

Let it be remembered that the Plessy case decided that separate railroad accommodations might be required by a state in intra-state transportation. How similar attempts relating to inter-state transportation have fared have been shown in the foregoing discussion and notes.[12] It has been said and repeated here in argument that the Supreme Court has refused to review the Plessy case in the Sweatt, McLaurin and other cases and this has been pointed to as proof that the Supreme Court retains and approves the validity of Plessy. It is astonishing that such an argument should be presented or used in this or any other court. The Supreme Court in Sweatt and McLaurin was not considering railroad accommodations. It was considering education just as we are considering it here and the Supreme Court distinctly and unequivocally held that the attempt to separate the races in education was violative of the Fourteenth Amendment of the Constitution. Of course, the Supreme Court did not consider overruling Plessy. It was not considering railroad matters, had no arguments in regard to it, had no business or concern with railroad accommodations and should not even have been asked to refer to that case since it had no application or business in the consideration of an educational problem before the court. It seems to me that we have already spent too much time and wasted efforts in attempting to show any similarity between traveling in a railroad coach in the confines of a state and furnishing education to the future citizens of this country.

The instant case which relates to lower school education is based upon exactly the same reasoning followed in the Sweatt and McLaurin decisions. In the Sweatt case, it was clearly recognized that a law school for Negro students had been established and that the Texas courts had found that the privileges, advantages and opportunities offered were substantially equivalent to those offered to white students at the University of Texas. Apparently, the Negro school was adequately housed, staffed and offered full and complete legal education, but the Supreme Court clearly recognized that education does not alone consist of fine buildings, class room furniture and appliances but that included in education must be all the intangibles that come into play in preparing one for meeting life. As was so well said by the Court: "* * * Few students and no one who has practiced law would choose to study in an academic vacuum, removed from the interplay of ideas and the exchange of views with which the law is concerned." [339 U.S. 629, 70 S.Ct. 850.] And the Court quotes with approval from its opinion in Shelley v. Kramer, supra: "* * * Equal protection of the laws is not achieved through indiscriminate imposition of inequalities." The Court further points out that this right to a proper and equal education is a personal one and that an individual is entitled to the equal protection of the laws. And in closing, the Court, referring to certain cases cited, says: "In accordance with these cases, petitioner may claim his full constitutional right: legal education equivalent to that offered by the State to students of other races. Such education is not available to him in a separate law school as offered by the State."

In the companion case of McLaurin v. Oklahoma State Regents, McLaurin was a student who was allowed to attend the same classes, hear the same lectures, stand the same examinations and eat in the same cafeteria; but he sat in a marked off place and had a separate table assigned to him in the

[11]Roberts v. City of Boston, 5 Cush., Mass., 198.
[12]See cases cited in Note 6.

library and another one in the cafeteria. It was said with truth that these facilities were just as good as those afforded to white students. But the Supreme Court says that even though this be so:

"These restrictions were obviously imposed in order to comply, as nearly as could be, with the statutory requirements of Oklahoma. But they signify that the State, in administering the facilities it affords for professional and graduate study, sets McLaurin apart from the other students. The result is that appellant is handicapped in his pursuit of effective graduate instruction. Such restrictions impair and inhibit his ability to study, to engage in discussions and exchange views with other students, and, in general, to learn his profession.

"Our society grows increasingly complex, and our need for trained leaders increases correspondingly. Appellant's case represents, perhaps, the epitome of that need, for he is attempting to obtain an advanced degree in education, to become, by definition, a leader and trainer of others. Those who will come under his guidance and influence must be directly affected by the education he recieves. Their own education and development will necessarily suffer to the extent that his training is unequal to that of his classmates. State-imposed restrictions which produce such inequalities cannot be sustained." [339 U.S. 637, 70 S.Ct. 853.]

The recent case of McKissick v. Charmichael, 4 Cir., 187 F.2d 949, 953, wherein the question of admission to the law school of the University of North Carolina was decided follows and amplifies the reasoning of the Sweatt and McLaurin cases. In the McKissick case, officials of the State of North Carolina took the position that they had adopted a fixed and continued purpose to establish and build up separate schools for equality in education and pointed with pride to the large advances that they had made. They showed many actual physical accomplishments and the establishment of a school which they claimed was an equal in many respects and superior in some respects to the school maintained for white students. The Court of Appeals for the 4th Circuit in this case, speaking through Judge Soper, meets this issue without fear or evasion and says: "These circumstances are worthy of consideration by any one who is responsible for the solution of a difficult racial problem; but they do not meet the complainants' case or overcome the deficiencies which it discloses. Indeed the defense seeks in part to avoid the charge of inequality by the paternal suggestion that it would be beneficial to the colored race in North Carolina as a whole, and to the individual plaintiffs in particular, if they would cooperate in promoting the policy adopted by the State rather than seek the best legal education which the State provides. The duty of the federal courts, however, is clear. We must give first place to the rights of the individual citizen, and when and where he seeks only equality of treatment before the law, his suit must prevail. It is for him to decide in which direction his advantage lies."

In the instant case, the plaintiffs produced a large number of witnesses. It is significant that the defendants brought but two. These last two were not trained educators. One was an official of the Clarendon schools who said that the school system needed improvement and that the school officials were hopeful and expectant of obtaining money from State funds to improve all facilities. The other witness, significantly named Crow, has been recently employed by a commission just established which, it is proposed, will supervise educational facilities in the State and will handle monies if, as and when the same are received sometime in the future. Mr. Crow did not testify as an expert on education although he stated flatly that he believed in separation of the races and that he heard a number of other people say so, including some Negroes, but he was unable to mention any of their names. Mr. Crow explained what was likely and liable to happen under the 1951 State Educational Act to which frequent reference was made in argument on behalf of the defense.

It appears that the Governor of this state called upon the legislature to take action in regard to the dearth of educational facilities in South Carolina pointing out the low depth to which the state had sunk. As a result, an act of the legislature was adopted (this is a part of the General Appropriations Act adopted at the recent session of the legislature and referred to as the 1951 School Act). This Act provides for the appointment of a commission which is to generally supervise educational facilities and imposes sales taxes in order to raise money for educational purposes and authorizes the issuance of bonds not to exceed the sum of $75,000,000, for the purpose of making grants to various counties and school districts to defray the cost of capital improvement in schools. The Commission is granted wide power to accept applications for and approve such grants as loans. It is given wide power as to what schools and school districts are to receive monies and it is also provided that from the taxes there are to be allocated funds to the various schools based upon the enrollment of pupils. Nowhere is it specifically provided that there shall be equality of treatment as between whites and Negroes in the school system. It is openly and frankly admitted by all parties that the present facilities are hopelessly disproportional and no one knows how much money would be required to bring the colored school system up to a parity with the white school system. The estimates as to the cost merely of equalization of physical facilities run anywhere from forty to eighty million dollars. Thus, the position of the defendants is that the rights applied for by the plaintiffs are to be denied now because the State of South Carolina intends (as evidenced by a general appropriations bill enacted by the legislature and a speech made by its Governor) to issue bonds, impose taxes, raise money and to do something about the inadequate schools in the future. There is no guarantee or assurance as to when the money will be available. As yet, no bonds have been printed or sold. No money is in the treasury. No plans have been drawn for school buildings or order issued for materials. No allocation has been made to the Clarendon school district or any other school districts and not even application blanks have, as yet, been printed. But according to Mr. Crow, the Clarendon authorities have requested him to send them blanks for this purpose if, as and when they come into being. Can we seriously consider this a bona-fide attempt to provide equal facilities for our school children?

On the other hand, the plaintiffs brought many witnesses, some of them of national reputation in various educational fields. It is unnecessary for me to review or analyze their testimony. But they who had made studies of education and its effect upon children, starting with the lowest grades and studying them up through and into high school, unequivocally testified that aside from inequality in housing appliances and equipment, the mere fact of segregation, itself, had a deleterious and warping effect upon the minds of children. These witnesses testified as to their study and researches and their actual tests with children of varying ages and they showed that the humiliation and disgrace of being set aside and segregated as unfit to associate with others of different color had an evil and ineradicable effect upon the mental processes of our young which would remain with them and deform their view on life until and throughout their maturity. This applies to white as well as Negro children. These witnesses testified from actual study and tests in various parts of the country, including tests in the actual Clarendon School district under consideration. They showed beyond a doubt that the evils of segregation and color prejudice come from early training. And from their testimony as well as from common experience and knowledge and from our own reasoning, we must unavoidably come to the conclusion that racial prejudice is something that is acquired and that that acquiring is in early childhood. When do we get our first ideas of religion, nationality and the other basic ideologies? The vast number of individuals follow religious and political groups because of their childhood training. And it is difficult and nearly impossible to change and eradicate these early prejudices, however strong may be the appeal to reason. There is absolutely no reasonable explanation for racial prejudice. It is all caused by unreasoning emotional reactions and these are gained in early childhood. Let the little child's mind be poisoned by prejudice of this kind and it is practically impossible to ever remove these impressions however many years he may have of teaching by philosophers, religious leaders or patriotic citizens. If segregation is wrong then the place to stop it is in the first grade and not in graduate colleges.

From their testimony, it was clearly apparent, as it should be to any thoughtful person, irrespective of having such expert testimony, that segregation in education can never produce equality and that it is an evil that must be eradicated. This case presents the matter clearly for adjudication and I am of the opinion that all of the legal guideposts, expert testimony, common sense and reason point unerringly to the conclusion that the system of segregation in education adopted and practiced in the State of South Carolina must go and must go now.

*Segregation is per se inequality.*

As heretofore shown, the courts of this land have stricken down discrimination in higher education and have declared unequivocally that segregation is not equality. But these decisions have pruned away only the noxious fruits. Here in this case, we are asked to strike its very root. Or rather, to change the metaphor, we are asked to strike at the cause of infection and not merely at the symptoms of disease. And if the courts of this land are to render justice under the laws without fear of favor, justice for all men and all kinds of men, the time to do it is now and the place is in the elementary schools where our future citizens learn their first lesson to respect the dignity of the individual in a democracy.

To me the situation is clear and important, particularly at this time when our national leaders are called upon to show to the world that our democracy means what it says and that it is a true democracy and there is no under-cover suppression of the rights of any of our citizens because of the pigmentation of their skins. And I had hoped that this Court would take this view of the situation and make a clear cut declaration that the State of South Carolina should follow the intendment and meaning of the Constitution of the United States and that it shall not abridge the privileges accorded to or deny equal protection of its laws to any of its citizens. But since the majority of this Court feel otherwise, and since I cannot concur with them or join in the proposed decree, this opinion is filed as a dissent.

Intermediate Supreme Court Order in Briggs v. Elliott

BRIGGS ET AL. v. ELLIOTT ET AL.

342 U.S. 350

APPEAL FROM THE UNITED STATES DISTRICT COURT FOR THE
EASTERN DISTRICT OF SOUTH CAROLINA.

No. 273. Decided January 28, 1952.

PER CURIAM.

Appellant Negro school children brought this action in the Federal District Court to enjoin appellee school officials from making any distinctions based upon race or color in providing educational facilities for School District No. 22, Clarendon County, South Carolina. As the basis for their complaint, appellants alleged that equal facilities are not provided for Negro pupils and that those constitutional and statutory provisions of South Carolina requiring separate schools "for children of the white and colored races"* are invalid under the Fourteenth Amendment. At the trial before a court of three judges, appellees conceded that the school facilities provided for Negro students "are not substantially equal to those afforded in the District for white pupils."

The District Court held, one judge dissenting, that the challenged constitutional and statutory provisions were not of themselves violative of the Fourteenth Amendment. The court below also found that the educational facilities afforded by appellees for Negro pupils are not equal to those provided for white children. The District Court did not issue an injunction abolishing racial distinctions as prayed by appellants, but did order appellees to proceed at once to furnish educational facilities for Negroes equal to those furnished white pupils. In its decree, entered June 21, 1951, the District Court ordered that appellees report to that court within six months as to action taken by them to carry out the court's order. 98 F.Supp. 529.

Dissatisfied with the relief granted by the District Court, appellants brought a timely appeal directly to this Court under 28 U.S.C. (Supp. IX) § 1253. After the appeal was docketed but before its consideration by this Court, appellees filed in the court below their report as ordered.

The District Court has not given its views on this report, having entered an order stating that it will withhold further action thereon while the cause is pending in this Court on appeal. Prior to our consideration of the questions raised on this appeal, we should have the benefit of the views of the District Court upon the additional facts brought to the attention of that court in the report which it ordered. The District Court should also be afforded the opportunity to take whatever action it may deem appropriate in light of that report. In order that this may be done, we vacate the judgment of the District Court and remand the case to that court for further proceedings. Another judgment, entered at the conclusion of those proceedings, may provide the basis for any further appeals to this Court.

*It is so ordered.*

MR. JUSTICE BLACK and MR. JUSTICE DOUGLAS dissent to vacation of the judgment of the District Court on the grounds stated. They believe that the additional facts contained in the report to the District Court are wholly irrelevant to the constitutional questions presented by the appeal to this Court, and that we should note jurisdiction and set the case down for argument.

*S.C. Const., Art. XI, § 7; S.C.Code, 1942, § 5377.

Second District Court Decision in Briggs v. Elliott

BRIGGS et al. v. ELLIOTT et al.

Civ. No. 2657.

United States District Court

E. D. South Carolina, Charleston Division.

March 13, 1952.

Before PARKER and DOBIE Circuit Judges, and TIMMERMAN, District Judge.

PARKER, Circuit Judge.

On June 23, 1951, this court entered its decree in this cause finding that the provisions of the Constitution and statutes of South Carolina requiring segregation of the races in the public schools are not of themselves violative of the Fourteenth Amendment of the federal Constitution, but that defendants had denied to plaintiffs rights guaranteed by that amendment in failing to furnish for Negroes in School District 22 educational facilities and opportunities equal to those furnished white persons. That decree denied the application for an injunction abolishing segregation in the schools but directed defendants promptly to furnish Negroes within the district educational facilities and opportunities equal to those furnished white persons and to report to the court within six months as to the action that had been taken to effectuate the court's decree. See Briggs v. Elliott, D.C., 98 F.Supp. 529. Plaintiffs appealed from so much of the decree as denied an injunction that would abolish segregation and this appeal was pending in the Supreme Court of the United States when the defendants, on December 21, 1951, filed with this court the report required by its decree, which report was forwarded to the Supreme Court. The Supreme Court thereupon remanded the case that we might give consideration to the report and vacated our decree in order that we might take whatever action we might deem appropriate in the light of the facts brought to our attention upon its consideration. Briggs v. Elliott, 342 U.S. 350, 72 S.Ct. 327. When the case was called for hearing on March 3, 1952, defendants filed a supplementary report showing what additional steps had been taken since the report of December 21, 1951, to comply with the requirements of the court's decree and equalize the educational facilities and opportunities of Negroes with those of white persons within the district.

The reports of December 21 and March 3 filed by defendants, which are admitted by plaintiffs to be true and correct and which are so found by the court, show beyond question that defendants have proceeded promptly and in good faith to comply with the court's decree.[1] As a part of a state-wide educational program to equalize and improve educational facilities and opportunities throughout the State of South Carolina, a program of school consolidation has been carried through for Clarendon County, District No. 22 has been consolidated with other districts so as to abolish inferior schools, public moneys have been appropriated to build modern school buildings, within the consolidated district, and contracts have been let which will insure the completion of the buildings before the next school year. The curricula of the Negro schools within the district has already been made equal to the curricula of the white schools and building projects for Negro schools within the consolidated district have been approved which will involve the expenditure of $516,960 and will unquestionably make the school facilities afforded Negroes within the district equal to those afforded white persons. The new district high school for Negroes is already 40% completed, and under the provisions of the construction

[1]The facts disclosed by the ordered and supplemental report are these: In order to qualify for state aid the old school district 22 has been combined with six other districts to become district 1, whose officials have requested and have by order been admitted as parties to this action. Teachers' salaries in the district have been equalized by local supplement, bus transportation has been instituted (none was furnished previously for either race), and $21,522.81 has been spent for furniture and equipment in Negro schools. Enabling legislation has been secured in the state legislature which permits the issuance of bonds of the school district up to 30% of the assessed valuation. (The enabling legislation was made possible by an Amendment to the Constitution of South Carolina passed in 1951. Const. art. 10, § 5, as amended, see 47 St. at Large, p. 14. The maximum had theretofore been 8%). Compliance with the requirements of the newly formed State Education Finance Commission has resulted in funds being made available to District 1 and a plan of school house construction based on a survey of education needs has been prepared, approved and adopted. Plans have been approved for the building of two Negro elementary schools at St. Paul and Spring Hill and advertisements for bids have been circulated in the press. The contract for remodeling the Scotts Branch Elementary School and for construction of the new Scotts Branch High School has already been let, construction has been commenced, and will, according to the record, be completed in time for the next school year.

contract will be ready for occupancy sometime in August of this year. That the State of South Carolina is earnestly and in good faith endeavoring to equalize educational opportunities for Negroes with those afforded white persons appears from the fact that, since the inauguration of the state-wide educational program, the projects approved and under way to date involve $5,515,619.15 for Negro school construction as against $1,992,018.00 for white school construction. The good faith of defendants in carrying out the decree of this court is attested by the fact that, when in October delay of construction of the Negro high school within the consolidated district was threatened on account of inability to obtain release of necessary materials, defendants made application to the Governor of the State and with his aid secured release of the materials so that construction could go forward.

There can be no doubt that as a result of the program in which defendants are engaged the educational facilities and opportunities afforded Negroes within the district will, by the beginning of the next school year in September 1952, be made equal to those afforded white persons. Plaintiffs contend that because they are not now equal we should enter a decree abolishing segregation and opening all the schools of the district at once to white persons and Negroes. A sufficient answer is that the defendants have complied with the decree of this court to equalize conditions as rapidly as was humanly possible, that conditions will be equalized by the beginning of the next school year and that no good would be accomplished for anyone by an order disrupting the organization of the schools so near the end of the scholastic year. As heretofore stated, the curricula of the white and Negro schools have already been equalized. By the beginning of the next scholastic year, physical conditions will be equalized also. This is accomplishing equalization as rapidly as any reasonable person could ask. We dealt with the question in our former opinion where we said, 98 F.Supp. at 537:

> "It is argued that, because the school facilities furnished Negroes in District No 22 are inferior to those furnished white persons, we should enjoin segregation rather than direct the equalizing of conditions. In as much as we think that the law requiring segregation is valid, however, and that the inequality suffered by plaintiffs results, not from the law, but from the way it has been administered, we think that our injunction should be directed to removing the inequalities resulting from administration within the framework of the law rather than to nullifying the law itself. As a court of equity, we should exercise our power to assure to plaintiffs the equality of treatment to which they are entitled with due regard to the legislative policy of the state. In directing that the school facilities afforded Negroes within the district be equalized promptly with those afforded white persons, we are giving plaintiffs all the relief that they can reasonably ask and the relief that is ordinarily granted in cases of this sort. See Carter v. County School Board of Arlington County, Virginia, 4 Cir., 182 F.2d 531. The court should not use its power to abolish segregation in a state where it is required by law if the equality demanded by the Constitution can be attained otherwise. This much is demanded by the spirit of comity which must prevail in the relationship between the agencies of the federal government and the states if our constitutional system is to endure."

For the reasons set forth in our former opinion, we think that plaintiffs are not entitled to a decree enjoining segregation in the schools but that they are entitled to a decree directing defendants promptly to furnish to Negroes within the consolidated district educational facilities and opportunities equal to those furnished white persons. The officers and trustees of the consolidated district will be made parties to this suit and will be bound by the decree entered herein.

Injunction abolishing segregation denied.

Injunction directing the equalization of educational facilities and opportunities granted.

DOBIE, Circuit Judge, and TIMMERMAN, District Judge, concur.

District Court Decision in Davis v. County School Board

## DAVIS et al. v. COUNTY SCHOOL BOARD
## OF PRINCE EDWARD COUNTY,
### VA., et al.

Civ. A. No. 1333.

103 F.Supp. 337

United States District Court
E. D. Virginia, at Richmond.

Heard Feb. 25–29, 1952.

Decided March 7, 1952.

Before DOBIE, Circuit Judge, and HUTCHESON, and BRYAN, District Judges.

BRYAN, District Judge.

Prince Edward is a county of 15,000 people in the southern part of Virginia. Slightly more than one-half of its inhabitants are Negroes. They compose 59% of the county school population. At the high school plane the average pupil attendance is 386 colored, 346 white. For themselves and their classmates, a large number of these Negro students, their parents, or guardians now demand that their county school board and school superintendent refrain from further observance of the mandate of section 140 of the Constitution of Virginia and its statutory counterpart,[1] the former reading: "White and colored children shall not be taught in the same school." Defendants' adherence to this command, it is averred, creates a positive discrimination against the colored child solely because of his race or color, constituting both a deprivation of his privileges and immunities as a citizen of the United States and a denial to him of the equal protection of the laws. The prohibition is denounced as a breach of the Civil Rights Act[2] and as inimical to section 1 of the 14th Amendment of the federal constitution.

Demandants pray a declaration of the invalidity, and an injunction against the enforcement, of the separation provisions. In the alternative, they ask a decree noting and correcting certain specified inequalities between the white and colored schools. That the schools are maintained with public tax moneys, that the defendants are public officials, and that they separate the children according to race in obedience to the State law are concessa. The Commonwealth of Virginia intervenes to defend.

Plaintiffs urge upon us that Virginia's separation of the Negro youth from his white contemporary stigmatizes the former as an unwanted, that the impress is alike on the minds of the colored and the white, the parents as well as the children, and indeed of the public generally, and that the stamp is deeper and the more indelible because imposed by law. Its necessary and natural effect, they say, is to prejudice the colored child in the sight of his community, to implant unjustly in him a sense of inferiority as a human being to other human beings, and to seed his mind with hopeless frustration. They argue that in spirit and in truth the colored youth is, by the segregation law, barred from association with the white child, not the white from the colored, that actually it is ostracism for the Negro child, and that the exclusion deprives him of the equal opportunity with the Caucasian of receiving an education unmarked, an immunity and privilege protected by the statutes and constitution of the United States.

Eminent educators, anthropologists, psychologists and psychiatrists appeared for the plaintiffs, unanimously expressed dispraise of segregation in schools, and unequivocally testified the opinion that such separation distorted the child's natural attitude, throttled his mental development, especially the adolescent, and immeasurably abridged his educational opportunities. For the defendants, equally distinguished and qualified educationists and leaders in the other fields emphatically vouched the view that, given equivalent physical facilities, offerings, and instruction, the Negro would receive in a separate school the same educational opportunity as he would obtain in the classroom and on the campus of a mixed school. Each witness offered cogent and appealing grounds for his conclusion.

On this fact issue the Court cannot say that the plaintiffs' evidence overbalances the defendants'. But on the same presentation by the plaintiffs as just recited, Federal courts[3] have rejected the proposi-

---

[1]Constitution of 1902; Sec. 22–221, Code of Virginia 1950, q. v., post, p. 339.

[2]8 U.S.C.A. §41.

[3]Briggs v. Elliott, D.C., 98 F.Supp. 529 and Carr v. Corning, 86 U.S.App. D.C. 173, 182 F.2d 14, citing Plessy v. Ferguson, 163 U.S. 537, 16 S.Ct. 1138, 41 L.Ed. 256, Gong Lum v. Rice, 275 U.S. 78, 48 S.Ct. 91, 72 L.Ed. 172, and Cumming v. County Board of Education, 175 U.S. 528, 20 S.Ct. 197, 44 L.Ed. 262.

tion, in respect to elementary and junior high schools, that the required separation of the races is in law offensive to the National statutes and constitution. They have refused to decree that segregation be abolished incontinently. We accept these decisions as apt and able precedent. Indeed we might ground our conclusion on their opinions alone. But the facts proved in our case, almost without division and perhaps peculiar here, so potently demonstrate why nullification of the cited sections of the statutes and constitution of Virginia is not warranted, that they should speak our conclusion.

Regulations by the State of the education of persons within its marches is the exercise of its police power—"the power to legislate with respect to the safety, morals, health and general welfare."[4] The only discipline of this power by the 14th Amendment and the Civil Rights Act of Congress is the requirement that the regulation be reasonable and uniform. We will measure the instant facts by that yardwand.

It indisputably appears from the evidence that the spearation provision rests neither upon prejudice, nor caprice, nor upon any other measureless foundation. Rather the proof is that it declares one of the ways of life in Virginia. Separation of white and colored "children" in the public schools of Virginia has for generations been a part of the mores of her people. To have separate schools has been their use and wont.

The school laws chronicle separation as an unbroken usage in Virginia for more than eighty years. The General Assembly of Virginia in its session of 1869–70, in providing for public free schools, stipulated "that white and colored persons shall not be taught in the same school, but in separate schools, under the same general regulations as to management, usefulness and efficiency."[5] It was repeated at the session 1871–2,[6] and carried into the Code of 1873.[7] As is well known, all this legislation occurred in the period of readjustment following the Civil War when the interests of the Negro in Virginia were scrupulously guarded. The same statute was reenacted by the Legislature of 1877[8] and again in 1878[9], still within the Reconstruction years of Virginia. In almost the same words separation in the schools was carried into the Acts of Assembly of 1881–2[10], and similarly embodied in the Code of 1887[11], in the Code of 1919[12], and now it is placed in the Code of 1950, in a single section, 22–221, in the same words: "White and colored persons shall not be taught in the same school, but shall be taught in separate schools, under the same general regulations as to management, usefulness and efficiency." The importance of the school separation clause to the people of the State is signalized by the fact that it is the only racial segregation direction contained in the constitution of Virginia.

Maintenance of the separated systems in Virginia has not been social despotism, the testimony points out, and suggests that whatever its demerits in theory, in practice it has begotten greater opportunities for the Negro. Virginia alone employs as many Negro teachers in her public schools, according to undenied testimony, as are employed in all of the thirty-one non-segregating States. Likewise it was shown that in 29 of the even hundred counties in Virginia, the schools and facilities for the colored are equal to the white schools, in 17 more they are now superior, and upon completion of work authorized or in progress, another 5 will be superior. Of the twenty-seven cities, 5 have Negro schools and facilities equal to the white and 8 more have better Negro schools than white.

So ingrained and wrought in the texture of their life is the principle of separate schools, that the president of the University of Virginia expressed to the Court his judgment that its involuntary elimination would severely lessen the interest of the people of the State in the public schools, lessen the financial support, and so injure both races. His testimony, corroborated by others, was especially impressive because of his candid and knowledgeable discussion of the problem. A scholar and a former Governor and legislator of the State, we believe him delicately sensible of the customs, the mind, and the temper of both races in Virginia. With the whites comprising more than three quarters of the entire population of the Commonwealth, the point he makes is a weighty practical factor to be considered in determining whether a reasonable basis has been shown to exist for the continuation of the school segregation.

In this milieu we cannot say that Virginia's separation of white and colored children in the public schools is without substance in fact or reason. We have found no hurt or harm to either race. This ends our inquiry. It is not for us to adjudge the policy as right or wrong—that, the Commonwealth of Virginia "shall determine for itself."[13]

[4]Briggs v. Elliott, supra, D.C., 98 F.Supp. 529, 532.
[5]Acts of 1869–70, c. 259, p. 402.
[6]Acts of 1871–2, c. 370, p. 461.
[7]Title 23, c. 78, sec. 58.
[8]Acts of General Assembly 1876–7, c. 38, p. 28.
[9]Acts of General Assembly 1877–8, c. 14, p. 10.
[10]C. 40, pp. 36, 37.
[11]Sec. 1492.
[12]Sec. 719.
[13]Judge Parker in Briggs v. Elliott, supra, D.C., 98 F.Supp. 529, 532.

On the second phase of this case, the inequality in the Negro schools when compared with the white, the defendants confess that the buildings and facilities furnished for Negro high school education are below those of the white school. We think the discrepancy extends further. We find inequality also in the curricula of the schools and in the provision for transportation of the students.

Undoubtedly frankness required admission by the defendants of their dereliction in furnishing an adequate school plant and facilities for the Negro. His high school is the Robert R. Moton. It is composed of one permanent brick building and three temporary, one-story, frame buildings. No gymnasiums are provided, no shower or dressing rooms to accompany physical education or athletics, no cafeteria, no teachers' rest room and no infirmary, to give some of the items absent in Moton but present in the white high school. Moton's science facilities and equipment are lacking and inadequate. No industrial art shop is provided, and in many other ways the structures and facilities do not meet the level of the white school.

In offerings we find physics, world history, Latin, advanced typing and stenography, wood, metal and machine shop work, and drawing, not offered at Moton, but given in the white schools. While the school authorities tender their willingness to give any course in the Negro school now obtainable in the white school, all courses in the latter should be made more readily available to the students of Moton.

In supplying school buses the Negro students have not been accorded their share of the newer vehicles. This practice must cease. In the allocation of new conveyances, as replacements or additional equipment, there must be no preference in favor of the white students.

On the issue of actual inequality our decree will declare its existence in respect to buildings, facilities, curricula and buses. We will restrain immediately its continuance in respect to the curricula and conveyances. We will order the defendant to pursue with diligence and dispatch their present program, now afoot and progressing, to replace the Moton buildings and facilities with a new building and new equipment, or otherwise remove the inequality in them.

The frame structures at Moton were erected in 1948 and 1949 as temporary expedients, upon the advice and authority of the State Board of Education. Through the activities of the school board and the division superintendent, defendants here, $840,000.00 has been obtained, the land acquired, and plans completed, for a new high school and necessary facilities for the Negroes. Both local and State authorities are moving with speed to complete the new program. An injunction could accomplish no more.

A decree will be entered in accordance with this opinion.

## Chancellor's Decision in Belton v Gebhart

### BELTON et al. v. GEBHART et al.

### BULAH et al. v. GEBHART et al.

Civ. A. Nos. 258, 265.

87 A. 2d 862

Court of Chancery of Delaware.

New Castle.

April 1, 1952.

SEITZ, Chancellor.

The question for decision in both cases here presented is whether the State of Delaware, through its agencies, has violated the plaintiffs' rights under the Equal Protection Clause of the Fourteenth Amendment to the United States Constitution.

Two actions were filed. They were consolidated for trial purposes and are here being decided. Although the plaintiffs sued by guardians ad litem, shall embrace only the minors when referring to "plaintiffs."

In the first action the plaintiffs are eight minors who sue on behalf of themselves and others similarly situated. Plaintiffs are Negroes and residents of the Claymont Special School District in New Castle County, Delaware. They have been refused admission to the Claymont High School, a public school maintained by the State of Delaware for white children only. They applied for and were expressly refused the right to attend the Claymont High School solely because of their color and ancestry. However, plaintiffs are permitted to attend Howard High School and Carver Vocational School, both operated under a single administration, by the Wilmington Special School District. Howard High School and Carver Vocational, for Negro children are located in the city of Wilmington approximately nine miles from the residences of these plaintiffs.

Incidentally, the Wilmington School District is not under the jurisdiction of the State Board of Education, and its members and agencies are not parties. The "arrangement" between the State Board and the Wilmington Board is completely informal. Consequently the State Board could not compel the Wilmington Board to take any action, nor could this Court compel the Wilmington Board to act since it is not a party.

Plaintiffs, including the guardians, belong to a class which, when its members own real property, are subjected to tax levied on such property to meet obligations on bonded indebtedness incurred in connection with the construction of the Claymont High School.

Plaintiffs contend that the State of Delaware, through its designated agencies and agents, has violated plaintiffs' rights under the Equal Protection Clause of the Fourteenth Amendment in that: (1) State-imposed segregation in education is itself in violation of the Fourteenth Amendment, and (2) the facilities and educational opportunities offered to the plaintiffs, and those similarly situated, are inferior to those available to white students similarly situated.

Defendants deny that segregation in education, in and of itself, violates the Fourteenth Amendment, and they deny that there is any substantial disparity between the facilities and educational opportunities offered the plaintiffs and white children similarly situated.

The second action was brought by a seven year old child residing near Hockessin, Delaware. Plaintiff is a Negro. She was refused admission to Hockessin School No. 29, a free public elementary school maintained for white children by the State of Delaware, solely because of her color and ancestry. Plaintiff is permitted to attend Hockessin School No. 107, an elementary school maintained for Negro children in the same general geographic area as the Hockessin School No. 29.

Plaintiff and defendants in the second action, make the same charges and defenses as are contained in the first case.

It is not disputed that under Article X, Section 2 of the Delaware Constitution, and under 1935 Code, Paragraph 2631 the State has directed that there be separate free school systems for Negroes and whites. The questions here presented follow:

(1) Are the Constitutional provision and the statute, in so far as they provide for segregation, in and of themselves in violation of the Fourteenth Amendment to the United States Constitution?

(2) Assuming a negative answer to question (1), are the separate facilities and educational opportunities offered plaintiffs equal to those furnished white children similarly situated?

## Segregation Per Se

As stated, plaintiff's first contention, and this applies to both cases, is that the evidence demonstrates that the refusal to permit plaintiffs and members of their class to attend schools for white children similarly situated, results in their receiving educational opportunities markedly inferior to those offered white children. This consequence flows, say plaintiffs, solely from the fact that they are Negroes. Simply stated, plaintiffs contend that the evidence shows that legally enforced segregation in education, in and of itself, prevents the Negro from receiving educational opportunities which are "equal" to those offered whites.

Plaintiffs produced many expert witnesses in the fields of education, sociology, psychology, psychiatry and anthropology. Their qualifications were fully established. No witnesses in opposition were produced. One of America's foremost psychiatrists testified that State-imposed school segregation produces in Negro children an unsolvable conflict which seriously interferes with the mental health of such children.[1] He conceded that the form, or combination of forms of hardship, vary in different cases and he further conceded that the results are not caused by school segregation alone. However, he pointed out that State enforced segregation is important, because it is "clear cut" and gives legal sanction to the differences, and is of continuous duration. He also pointed out other factors which viewed against the social background of the Delaware community, necessarily have the effect of causing the Negro child to feel that he is inferior because, in an indirect fashion, the State has said so. The other experts sustained the general proposition as to the harmful over-all effect of legally enforced segregation in education upon Negro children generally. It is no answer to this finding to point to numerous Negroes who apparently have not been so harmed. It leads to lack of interest, extensive absenteeism, mental disturbances, etc. Indeed, the harm may often show up in ways not connected with their "formal" educational progress. The fact is that such practice creates a mental health problem in many Negro children with a resulting impediment to their educational progress.

Defendants say that the evidence shows that the State may not be "ready" for non-segregated education, and that a social problem cannot be solved with legal force. Assuming the validity of the contention without for a minute conceding the sweeping factual assumption, nevertheless, the contention does not answer the fact that the Negro's mental health and therefore, his educational opportunities are adversely affected by State-imposed segregation in education. The application of Constitutional principles is often distasteful to some citizens, but that is one reason for Constitutional guarantees. The principles override transitory passions.

I conclude from the testimony that in our Delaware society, State-imposed segregation in education itself results in the Negro children, as a class, receiving educational opportunities which are substantially inferior to those available to white children otherwise similarly situated.

But my factual conclusion does not dispose of the first question presented. I say this because it is necessary to consider the decisions of the United States Supreme Court construing the Fourteenth Amendment as they apply to this general problem. Specifically, I must decide whether such a finding of fact as I have here made, is a proper basis for holding that such separate facilities can not be equal. In other words, can the "separate but equal" doctrine be legally applied in the fields of elementary and secondary education?

Plaintiffs say that the situation here presented has never been passed upon by the United States Supreme Court, or the Supreme Court of Delaware, and so is an open question. I agree with the plaintiffs that the Supreme Court has not, so far as I can find, passed upon a case containing a specific finding as to the effect on the Negro, educationally, of State-imposed segregation in education. The question, however, which judicial integrity requires me to answer is this: Has the U.S. Supreme Court by fair or necessary implication decided that State-imposed segregated education on the grammar and high school levels, in and of itself, does not violate the Fourteenth Amendment?

The United States Supreme Court first announced what has come to be known as the "separate but equal" doctrine in Plessy v. Ferguson, 163 U.S. 537, 16 S.Ct. 1138, 1144, 41 L.Ed. 256. It is, of course, true that that case involved a railway car situation. However, the defendants rely most strongly on Gong Lum v. Rice, 275 U.S. 78, 48 S.Ct. 91, 72 L.Ed. 172, decided by the U.S. Supreme Court in 1927. In that case a Chinese citizen was required to attend an elementary school for Negroes in Mississippi, even though he claimed that he was entitled to admission to the school for whites. The court accepted the conclusion that he was "colored" and stated that the facilities available for Negroes, and therefore available to the Chinese plaintiff, were equal to those offered to the whites. Thus, the question was whether the State was required, under those circumstances, to admit him to the school for white children. The Supreme Court held that the State was not so required, citing many cases for the proposition that such a practice was within the Constitutional power of the State, without interference because of the United States Constitution. It is true that there was no proof in that case concerning the

---

[1]At least two of the experts examined some Delaware children and while not at all conclusive, their findings gave some support to the conclusions reached.

effect of such State-imposed segregation on Negroes. But it seems to me that the very use of the "separate but equal" doctrine in an elementary school case, has implicit therein a recognition that in such a case there can be separate but equal educational opportunities in a Constitutional sense. Of course, this could not be true were my finding of fact given Constitutional recognition, but if it were, the principle itself would be destroyed. In other words, by implication, the Supreme Court of the United States has said a spearate but equal test can be applied, at least below the college level. This Court does not believe such an implication is justified under the evidence. Nevertheless, I do not believe a lower court can reject a principle of United States Constitutional law which has been adopted by fair implication by the highest court of the land. I believe the "separate but equal" doctrine in education should be rejected, but I also believe its rejection must come from that Court.

My legal conclusion is not inconsistent with my finding of the fact on this point, because by applying the "separate but equal" test, the Supreme Court has said in effect that inequality arising from segregation itself is not that type of inequality which violates the United States Constitution. While not set forth in so many words, it seems to me that many other lower courts have followed this same reasoning in reaching a similar conclusion. See, e. g., Briggs v. Elliott, D.C., 98 F.Supp. 529, appeal pending; cf. Davis v. County School Board of Prince Edward County, D.C.E.D.Va., 1952, 103 F.Supp. 337. Plaintiffs point to a decisional trend from which they would have this Court conclude that the "separate but equal" doctrine as applied to education should be rejected. Certainly such a trend is "in the wind" but, as stated, it is for the Supreme Court to say so in view of its older, and as yet, unrepudiated decisions. See Parker v. University of Delaware, Del. Ch., 75 A.2d 225.

I, therefore, conclude that while State-imposed segregation in lower education provides Negroes with inferior educational opportunities, such inferiority has not yet been recognized by the United States Supreme Court as violating the Fourteenth Amendment. On the contrary, it has been by implication excluded as a Constitutional factor. It is for that Court to re-examine its doctrine in the light of my finding of fact. It follows that relief cannot be granted plaintiffs under their first contention.

## Separate But Equal

We turn now to a consideration of the second question, to-wit, are the separate facilities and educational opportunities offered these plaintiffs, and those similarly situated, equal to those furnished white children similarly situated?

The issues on this point can best be resolved by first setting forth the facts as I find them, based on the testimony and exhibits, plus the inspection which I made of all the structures involved. I first consider the High School case.

## Claymont High Versus Howard High and Carver Vocational

One of the eight Negro plaintiffs in the so-called Claymont versus Howard-Carver case, is Ethel Louise Belton. She lives in Claymont. Each morning about quarter or ten of 8:00 she leaves her home north of Claymont to travel to Howard High School in Wilmington. She walks a distance to the Philadelphia Pike where she takes a public bus to Wilmington. The entire trip one way consumes about fifty minutes.

She takes, inter alia, a business course requiring two hours, two days a week. For this course she must leave the Howard High building at the end of the regular school hours, and travel to the so-called Carver Vocational building (under Howard administration), a distance of nine and one half city blocks. This course is not given in the Howard building itself. This trip consumes about fifteen minutes one way. A similar course is given at Claymont. She is also engaged in the study of the piano after school.

If she were white she could attend Claymont High School which is about a mile and a half from her home. If she walked to Claymont High School she would have for other use, an extra half hour each afternoon spent in travel. If she took the bus to the Claymont school she would have still more time.

Plaintiffs produced an expert witness who testified that bus travel increased fatigue and irritability, thereby impairing the learning process. Also it was pointed out that this infant plaintiff's travel time consumes about 25% of a most valuable block of the child's time, that which permits self-initiated activities, roughly, the hours from three to five in the afternoon.

I turn now to a comparison of the Claymont plant versus the Howard-Carver plant.

The Claymont building and the Howard building are both fairly good, with neither suffering by a comparison, except that for its purpose, Claymont has an admitted advantage over Howard with respect to the gymnasium. The same general equality, however, is not true of the Carver building which is a part of the Howard administration. It is an old building without an auditorium, gymnasium or regular cafeteria. The makeshift cafeteria is in a dingy basement and has neither seats nor tables. Carver has but one lavatory which has an unsanitary cement floor. It goes without saying that students traveling from Howard to Carver are not protected from the weather.

Claymont is located on a fourteen acre site, containing ample room for playground and equipment, as well as for sports of most any character. Aesthetically speaking it is very attractive. The Howard structure is located on a three and one half acre site with inadequate playing space, even considering the use of the public park with its restrictions. The Howard building is flanked by industrial buildings and poor housing. The area surrounding the Carver site is even more congested. There is no land in front, or play space in the rear.

An analysis of the teaching staffs at Claymont and Howard reveals that at Claymont 59.00% have master's degrees, while at Howard 37.73% have master's degrees. At Claymont 41% have bachelor's degrees , while approximately 52% have such degrees at Howard. There are none at Claymont without degrees while Howard has 9.4% of its faculty without degrees. It appears that of those of the Howard faculty without degrees one teaches a vocational subject, another wood working, and a third physical education.

In so far as the sizes of the classes at the two high schools are concerned, the comparative figures are as follows:

|  | Claymont | Howard |
|---|---|---|
| English | 25.56 | 32.26 |
| Foreign Languages | 25.75 | 31.10 |
| Home Economics | 16.2 | 24.71 |
| Industrial Arts | 17.14 | 23.9 |
| Mathematics | 30.60 | 33.25 |
| Natural Sciences | 34.87 | 32.26 |
| Physical Education | 24.28 | 43.67 |
| Social Studies | 33.88 | 32.05 |

The "average" teacher at Howard carries a teaching load of 178 pupils per week, while at Claymont the figure is 149 pupils per week. In so far as Physical Education classes are concerned there is a tremendous disparity in favor of Claymont.

Turning to the academic subjects, plaintiffs contend that courses in Public Speaking, Spanish, Mathematics Review, Trigonometry, and Economics And Sociology are not offered at Howard but are offered at Claymont.

Defendants point out that in general practice, each school offers only one foreign language. For a period of time Claymont offered Spanish as its modern foreign language but it is now shifting back to French. The fact that for one year Claymont has both French and Spanish (second year) is caused only by the shift from Spanish to French.

Defendants say that the subject matter of the course called Economics And Sociology is offered at Howard as "Problems in Democracy."

Defendants contend that the course offered at Claymont entitled "Mathematics Review" is only for those too lazy or too dull to continue the study of mathematics, and is a sort of "open air course."

Defendants argue that, contrary to plaintiff's contention, trigonometry is offered at Howard, and that, in fact, one student is now being taught trigonometry. Defendants say the course will be offered at Howard if there is any demand for it.

It is true that no public speaking course is offered at Howard. However, it appears that debating is available at Howard and Howard does offer related English in some vocational courses.

Although Claymont and Howard have trained librarians Carver does not. In fact, Carver's librarian has a degree from an unaccredited school.

Claymont has many more extra curricular activities than does Howard. Thus, Claymont has a school newspaper, an Art Club, Drivers Club, Mathematics Club, Square Dance Club, Leaders Corps and an organization to tickle the imagination called "Tumbling Girls." Howard has only a Story Hour, a Science Club, and a French Club.

I now consider whether the facilities of the two institutions are separate but equal, within the requirements of the Fourteenth Amendment to the United States Constitution. Are the separate facilities and educational opportunities offered these Negro plaintiffs, and those similarly situated, "equal" in the Constitutional sense, to those available at Claymont High to white children, similarly situated? The answer to this question is often much more difficult than appears, because many of the factors to be compared are just not susceptible of mathematical evaluation, e. g., aesthetic considerations. Moreover, and of real importance, the United States Supreme Court has not decided what should be done if a Negro school being compared with a white school is inferior in some respects and superior in others. It is easy, as some courts do, to talk about the necessity for finding substantial equality. But, under this approach, how is one to deal with a situation where, as here, the mental and physical health services at the Negro school are superior to those offered at the white school, while the teacher load at the Negro school is not only substantially heavier than that at the white school, but often exceeds the State announced educationally desirable maximum teacher-pupil ratio. The answer, it seems to me is this: Where the facilities or educational opportunities available to the Negro are, as to any substantial factor, inferior to those available to white children similarly situated, the Constitutional principle of "separate but equal" is violated, even though the State may point to other factors as to which the Negro school is superior. I reach this conclusion because I do not believe a court can say that the substantial factor as to which the Negro school is inferior will not adversely affect the educational progress of at least some of those concerned. Moreover, evaluating unlike factors is unrealistic. If this be a harsh test, then I answer that a State which divides its citizens should pay the price.

Thus, I ask. Are the facilities and educational opportunities at Howard-Carver inferior to those offered at Claymont as to any substantial factor? The answer to this question requires an analysis of the facts as I have found them.

From the points of view of location and landscaping and overall aesthetic considerations, Claymont is vastly superior to Howard-Carver. But defendants' counsel say that the differences are almost inevitable in any comparison of urban and suburban schools. Granting that this may be so, it only goes to demonstrate the dreary fact that segregated education, as here provided, means that white children in the Claymont school district may have the benefits which flow from living in the suburbs, but Negro children similarly situated may not. In other words, according to defendants, white parents may move into the Claymont suburbs in order to give their children the benefits which flow from attending a suburban school, but Negro parents may not. The cold, hard fact is that the State in this situation discriminates against Negro children. The court fully realizes that there are many white children who do not have the advantages which are provided at the Claymont School, but the point is that they are not white children whose position is otherwise similar to that of these plaintiffs. As the Supreme Court has said, there is a vast difference—a Constitutional difference.

Plaintiffs next point to the fact that part of the curriculum is offered at Howard and part at Carver; that these schools are some distance apart and that the facilities at Carver are markedly inferior to those available at Claymont for similar courses. I find as a fact from the record and from my visit, and defendants tacitly concede, that the facilities at Carver, with due regard for its vocational emphasis, are woefully inferior to those available at Claymont. A further repetition of the comparative facts is better forgotten.

The teacher training at Claymont is substantially superior to that at Howard-Carver, as the comparative figures demonstrate.

The teacher load at Howard-Carver is substantially greater than that at Claymont. Many more of the classes at Howard-Carver exceed the twenty-five to one student-teacher ratio, than at Claymont. Moreover, the twenty-five to one ratio has been fixed by the State educational authorities as a desirable maximum.

I conclude that with respect to teacher training, pupil-teacher ratio, extra curricular activities, physical plants and aesthetic considerations, the Howard-Carver School is inferior to Claymont under the "separate but equal" test. These factors are all a part of the educational process, as the experts stated.

One other factor of importance remains to be considered. At least one of the plaintiffs travels, by foot and by public bus, over nine miles each way to attend Howard, whereas, she could reach Claymont by traveling somewhat over one mile. Thus, a substantial portion of the plaintiff's time is taken traveling to and from school. Indeed, it is much more time than is taken by white children similarly situated.

I recognize that some authorities have refused to recognize the travel factor as justifying a holding of inequality,[2] however, I do not believe that those cases involved the burden time-wise and distance-wise which is here involved. I find that, under the facts here presented, the requirement that plaintiffs travel such a distance while whites similarly situated are subjected to no such burden, results in inferior educational opportunities for these plaintiffs because of time and fatigue factors.

I have enumerated the several respects in which I have found the facilities and educational opportunities at Howard-Carver to be inferior to those offered at Claymont. Viewing such factors, both independently and cumulatively, I conclude that the separate facilities and opportunities offered these plaintiffs, and those similarly situated, are not equal to those offered white children in the Claymont District, and that, in consequence, the State by refusing these plaintiffs admission to Claymont solely because of their color, is violating the plaintiff's rights protected by the Equal Protection Clause of the Fourteenth Amendment.

However, the defendants' counsel say that the evidence demonstrates that the Wilmington Board of Education plans to abandon Carver, and transfer its courses to the Howard building. It also intends to make Howard a senior high school, and remove the crowded condition of that school by creating a junior high school for Negroes at what is now the Bancroft School for whites. A new high school for Negroes at Middletown is supposed to help. The evidence shows that some of the building program is under way, while other parts of it are merely in the planning stage.

---

[2]See Brown v. Board of Education, D.C., 98 F.Supp. 797, appeal pending. Dameron v. Bayless, 14 Ariz. 180, 126 P. 273; People v. Gallagher, 93 N.Y. 438. Defendants also cite Gong Lum v. Rice, 275 U.S. 78, 48 S.Ct. 91, 72 L.Ed. 172, for this proposition, but I believe the language of the opinion negates any such a sweeping generalization.

Under these circumstances, defendants urge that even though the Court should find inequalities, it should do no more than direct the defendants to equalize facilities and opportunities, and give them time to comply with such an order. Passing over the fact that the Wilmington Board is not before this court, there are three reasons why I cannot agree with this approach. (1) I do not see how the plans mentioned will remove all the objections to the present arrangement. (2) Moreover, and of great importance, I do not see how the Court could implement such an injunction against the State. (3) Just what is the effect of such a finding of a violation of the Constitution, as has here been made. It is true that in such a situation some courts have merely directed the appropriate State officials to equalize facilities. I do not believe that such is the relief warranted by a finding that the United States Constitution has been violated. It seems to me that when a plaintiff shows to the satisfaction of a court that there is an existing and continuing violation of the "separate but equal" doctrine, he is entitled to have made available to him the State facilities which have been shown to be superior. To do otherwise is to say to such a plaintiff: "Yes, your Constitutional rights are being invaded, but be patient, we will see whether in time they are still being violated." If, as the Supreme Court has said, this right is personal,[3] such a plaintiff is entitled to relief immediately, in the only way it is available, namely, by admission to the school with the superior facilities. To postpone such relief is to deny relief, in whole or in part, and to say that the protective provisions of the Constitution offer no immediate protection.

I conclude that the State's future plans do not operate to prevent the granting of relief to these plaintiffs by way of an injunction, preventing the authorities from excluding these plaintiffs, and others similarly situated, from admission to Claymont High School on account of their color. If it be a matter of discretion, I reach the same conclusion. If, at some future time, defendants feel that they can demonstrate that all the Constitutional inequalities have been removed, then it would be for them to take the initiative.

### School No. 29 (White) Versus School
### No. 107 (Negro)

Let us now compare School No. 29 (for white children), and School No. 107 (for Negroes).

No. 29 is a four classroom building constructed in 1932 at a cost of $55,000.00, with a present value of about $77,000.00. No. 107 is a one room building converted by a sliding partition into two rooms. It was constructed in 1922 at a cost of $21,000.00 and has a present value of $13,000.00. This obvious appreciation in the value of the white school, versus the depreciation in the value of the Negro school reflects, aside from their age, differences in maintenance, upkeep and improvements. Until recently the white school was unlawfully favored in the receipt of State funds. The first six grades are taught at each school. However, at No. 107 each teacher has three grades while at No. 29 each teacher has only two grades. This is significant apart from the over-all number of children taught.

No. 29 has a very attractive auditorium, as well as a basketball court, a partial basement which provides storage space and more adequate space for heating and hot water. No. 107 has none of these. The auditorium serves a valuable purpose as the happenings on the occasion of my visit demonstrated.

No. 29 has several of the accepted forms of drinking fountains. No. 107 does not. No. 29 has modern spacious sanitary toilet facilities, while No. 107 has one commode in a very small room which adjoins the space where the children's lunches, the janitorial materials and the school drinking water bottles are kept. No. 29 has a well equipped nurse's office, while No. 107 has only a first aid packet. The fire protection facilities at No. 29 are more numerous than those at No. 107. No. 29 is also superior in other items too numerous to mention.

No. 29 is so beautifully situated that the view immediately catches the eye. The landscaping is also outstanding. No. 107 is unlandscaped, and apparently always has been. Its location just cannot compare with the location of No. 29. An over-all evaluation of the locations and the facilities of the two schools reflect such an obvious superiority in favor of No. 29 as to be depressing. Many of the items were given to No. 29 by the P.T.A. or the public. These, say the Attorney General, should be excluded from this comparison. It is conceded that the items mentioned belong to the school and are therefore State property. My answer is that we are comparing State facilities. We cannot conjecture what the State might or might not have furnished in the absence of such items.

On the Strayer-Englehart Score Card, used by educators to evaluate the physical condition of a school plant, No. 29 far surpassed No. 107.

The teacher preparation at No. 29 is superior to that at No. 107. Also, the County Supervisor rated every teacher at No. 29 higher than either teacher at No. 107.

The experts in the field of education testified that the various factors mentioned are all of importance in evaluating educational opportunities. The courts have so recognized.

The substantial factors above mentioned, whether viewed separately or cumulatively, lead me to conclude that the facilities and educational opportunities offered at No. 29 are substantially superior to those offered at No. 107.

[3]See Sweatt v. Painter, 339 U.S. 629, 70 S.Ct. 848, 94 L.Ed. 1114.

Another factor connected with these two schools demands separate attention, because it is a consequence of segregation so outlandish that the Attorney General, with commendable candor, has in effect refused to defend it. I refer to the fact that School bus transportation is provided those attending No. 29 who, except for color, are in the same situation as this infant plaintiff. Yet neither school bus transportation, nor its equivalent is provided this plaintiff even to attend No. 107. In fact, the State Board of Education refused to authorize the transportation of this then seven year old plaintiff to the Negro school, even though the bus for white children went right past her home, and even though the two schools are no more than a mile apart. Moreover, there is no public transportation available from or near plaintiff's home to or near the Negro school. The State Board ruled that because of the State Constitutional provision for separate schools, a Negro child may not ride in a bus serving a white school. If we assume that this is so, then this practice in and of itself, is another reason why the facilities offered this plaintiff at No. 107 are inferior to those provided at No. 29. To suggest, under the facts here presented, that there are not enough Negroes to warrant the cost of a school bus for them is only another way of saying that they are not entitled to equal services because they are Negroes. Such an excuse will not do here.

I conclude that the facilities and educational opportunities at No. 107 are substantially inferior in a Constitutional sense, to those at No. 29. For the reasons stated in connection with Claymont I do not believe the relief should merely be an order to make equal.

An injunction will issue preventing the defendants and their agents from refusing these plaintiffs, and those similarly situated, admission to School No. 29 because of their color.

Orders on notice.

Decision of Supreme Court of Delaware in Gebhart v Belton

GEBHART et al. v. BELTON et al.

GEBHART et al. v. BULAH et al.

BELTON et al. v. GEBHART et al.

BULAH et al. v. GEBHART et al.

Nos. 15–18.

91 A.2d 137

Supreme Court of Delaware.

Aug. 28, 1952.

SOUTHERLAND, Chief Justice, WOLCOTT, Justice, and CAREY, Judge, sitting.

SOUTHERLAND, Chief Justice.

Two cases, alike in respect of basic principles of law, but differing in respect of the facts, were filed in the court below by certain citizens of Negro blood, seeking the admittance of the plaintiffs[1] to public schools maintained for white pupils only. The first case, brought against the members of the State Board of Education and certain other school officials, concerns the claim of the plaintiffs, Ethel Louise Belton and others, residents in the Claymont Special School District in New Castle County and all of high school age, to be admitted to the high school maintained in that district for white pupils. The second case, brought against the members of the State Board of Education and certain other school officials, concerns the claim of the plaintiff, Shirley Barbara Bulah, a resident of Hockessin, New Castle County, to be admitted to School No. 29, an elementary school at Hockessin maintained for white pupils.

The relief sought in each case is a declaratory judgment that the provisions of the Delaware Constitution and laws requiring segregation in the public schools are in contravention of the equal protection clause of the Fourteenth Amendment to the federal Constitution, and also an injunction restraining the defendants from denying the plaintiffs admittance to the schools maintained for white pupils.

The cases were consolidated and tried before the Chancellor, who rendered a judgment denying the prayers of the complaints for a declaratory judgment but enjoining the defendants from refusing the plaintiffs admittance to the schools for whites. 87 A.2d 862.

It appears from the pleadings and testimony that the following issues were made below and determined by the Chancellor and are here for review:

I. Do the provisions of the Fourteenth Amendment forbidding a state to deny to any citizen the equal protection of the laws forbid segregation of pupils in the public schools on the basis of color?

II. If state-imposed segregation is not in itself unlawful, are the educational facilities afforded by the State to the plaintiffs substantially equal to those afforded white pupils similarly situated?

Upon the authority of applicable decisions of the Supreme Court of the United States the Chancellor resolved the first question in the negative. Upon a review of the evidence pertaining to the second question he held, first, as to the plaintiffs Ethel Louise Belton and others, that the educational facilities afforded them, i.e., those of the Howard High School in the City of Wilmington, maintained for Negro pupils, are substantially inferior to those of the Claymont High School; and second, as to the plaintiff Shirley Barbara Bulah, that the educational facilities afforded her, i.e., elementary school No. 107 at Hockessin, maintained for Negro pupils, are substantially inferior to those of School No. 29.

We take up these questions in the above order.

I. *Segregation per se.*

Article X of the Constitution of the State of Delaware provides in part as follows:

"Section 1. The General Assembly shall provide for the establishment and maintenance of a general and efficient system of free public schools, and may require by law that every child, not physically or mentally disabled, shall attend the public school, unless educated by other means.

[1]"Plaintiffs" in this opinion refers to the infant plaintiffs.

"Section 2. In addition to the income of the investments of the Public School Fund, the General Assembly shall make provision for the annual payment of not less than one hundred thousand dollars for the benefit of the free public schools which, with the income of the investments of the Public School Fund, shall be equitably apportioned among the school districts of the State as the General Assembly shall provide; and the money so apportioned shall be used exclusively for the payment of teachers' salaries and for furnishing free text books; provided however, that in such apportionment, no distinction shall be made on account of race or color, and separate schools for white and colored children shall be maintained. All other expenses connected with the maintenance of free public schools, and all expenses connected with the erection or repair of free public school buildings shall be defrayed in such manner as shall be provided by law."

Paragraph 2631, Revised Code of Delaware 1935 provides as follows:

"Sec. 9. Shall Maintain Uniform School System; Separate Schools for White Children, Colored Children, and Moors; Elementary Schools:—The State Board of Education is authorized, empowered, directed and required to maintain a uniform, equal and effective system of public schools throughout the State, and shall cause the provisions of this Chapter, the by-laws or rules and regulations and the policies of the State Board of Education to be carried into effect. The schools provided shall be of two kinds; those for white children and those for colored children. The schools for white children shall be free for all white children between the ages of six and twenty-one years, inclusive; and the schools for colored children shall be free to all colored children between the ages of six and twenty-one years, inclusive. The schools for white children shall be numbered and the schools for colored children shall be numbered as numbered prior to the year 1919. The State Board of Education shall establish schools for children of people called Moors or Indians, and if any Moor or Indian school is in existence or shall be hereafter established, the State Board of Education shall pay the salary of any teacher or teachers thereof, provided that the school is open for school sessions during the minimum number of days required by law for school attendance and provided further that such school shall be free to all children of the people called Moors, or the people called Indians, between the ages of six and twenty-one years. No white or colored child shall be permitted to attend such a school without the permission of the State Board of Education. The public schools of the State shall include elementary schools which shall be of such number of grades at the State Board of Education shall decide after consultation with the Trustees of the District in which the school is situated."

Do these provisions, in so far as they require segregation in public schools based on race or color, offend against the provisions of the Fourteenth Amendment to the Constitution of the United States, forbidding any state to deny to any citizen the equal protection of the laws?

The leading case in the Supreme Court of the United States approving the right of a state to establish separate school systems for whites and Negroes is Plessy v. Ferguson, 163 U.S. 537, 16 S.Ct. 1138, 41 L.Ed. 256. That case involved directly only segregation required by Louisiana law in railway passenger coaches. Mr. Justice Brown, however, supported his conclusion that the statute before the court was constitutional by pointing to state statutes establishing separate schools as affording a "common instance" of the validity of segregation laws, and observed that such statutes for separate schools had "been held to be a valid exercise of the legislative power even by courts of states where the political rights of the colored race have been longest and most earnestly enforced." 16 S.Ct. 1140. Even if this holding could be deemed dictum, the subsequent case of Gong Lum v. Rice, 275 U.S. 78, 48 S.Ct. 91, 93, 72 L.Ed. 172, admits of no such distinction. In that case a citizen of Chinese ancestry was denied admission to a state school maintained for white pupils because she was of the "yellow race" and was deemed to be "colored." Stating the question presented to be whether a Chinese citizen is denied equal protection of the laws when he is classed among the colored races and furnished facilities for education equal to that offered to all, Chief Justice Taft said:

"Were this a new question, it would call for very full argument and consideration; but we think that it is the same question which has been many times decided to be within the constitutional power of the state Legislature to settle, without intervention of the federal courts under the federal Constitution."

After citing numerous state decisions upholding segregation in the public schools, the Chief Justice quoted with approval the language of Mr. Justice Brown in Plessy v. Ferguson, supra, dealing with that subject, and concluded:

"Most of the cases cited arose, it is true, over the establishment of separate schools as between white pupils and black pupils; but we cannot think that the question is any different, or that any different result can be reached, assuming the cases above cited to be rightly decided, where the issue is as between white pupils of the yellow races. The decision is within the discretion of the state in regulating its public schools, and does not conflict with the Fourteenth Amendment."

These cases, we think, are decisive of the question. Moreover, in the recent decisions of Sweatt v. Painter, 339 U.S. 629, 70 S.Ct. 848, 94 L.Ed. 1114, and McLaurin v. Oklahoma State Regents, 339 U.S. 637, 70 S.Ct. 851, 94 L.Ed. 1149, the Supreme Court of the United States has refused to overrule Plessy v. Ferguson, though expressly urged to do so.[2] It is nevertheless argued that the cases of Plessy v. Ferguson and Gong Lum v. Rice, supra, are without force today and that we should assume that they will be overruled. We can make no such assumption. "It is for the Supreme Court, not us, to overrule its decisions or to hold them outmoded." Boyer v. Garrett, 4 Cir., 183 F.2d 582, per curiam. It is our duty to uphold the Constitution of our State, and not to abrogate its provisions except in so far—and only in so far—as required to do so by a ruling of the Supreme Court of the United States that they infringe upon rights protected by the federal Constitution. We must hold that segregation in the state's public schools is not illegal *per se*.

Our conclusion is supported by the following decisions of the federal courts, all rendered within the past three years: Corbin v. County School Board, 4 Cir., 177 F.2d 924; Carr v. Corning, 86 U.S.App.D.C. 173, 182 F.2d 14; Boyer v. Garrett, 4 Cir., 183 F.2d 582; Briggs v. Elliott, D.C., 98 F.Supp. 529; Brown v. Board of Education of Topeka, D.C., 98 F. Supp. 797; and Davis v. County School Board, D.C., 103 F.Supp. 337. A recent holding of the Supreme Court of Missouri is to the same effect. State ex rel. Toliver v. Board of Education, 360 Mo. 671, 230 S.W.2d 724.

A detailed review of these cases is unnecessary, since we are cited to no case holding to the contrary. They establish the principle that the constitutional guarantee of equal protection of the laws does not prevent the establishment by the state of separate schools for whites and Negroes, provided that the facilities afforded by the state to the one class are substantially equal to those afforded to the other (often referred to as the "separate-but-equal" doctrine). The question of segregation in the schools, under these authorities, is one of policy, and it is for the people of our state, through their duly chosen representatives, to determine what that policy shall be. When so determined, it must be given effect by our courts, subject always to the rule enjoined both by the Constitution of the United States and our own statute, that substantially equal treatment must be accorded. State ex rel. Toliver v. Board of Education, supra.

The refusal of the Chancellor to enter the declaratory judgment prayed for was therefore, in our opinion, correct.

But it is said that the uncontradicted evidence adduced by the plaintiffs shows that state-imposed segregation in the public schools and equality of educational opportunity are inherently incompatible, and that the Chancellor so held. The Chancellor indeed found on the evidence that segregation itself results in the Negro's receiving inferior educational opportunities, and expressed the opinion that the "separate-but-equal" doctrine should be rejected. He nevertheless recognized that his finding was immaterial to the legal conclusion drawn from the authorities above cited. We agree that it is immaterial, and hence see no occasion to review it. The Supreme Court of the United States has said that the states may establish separate schools if the facilities furnished are substantially equal for all. To say the facilities can never be equal is simply to render the Court's holdings meaningless—in effect, to say that that Court's construction of the Constitution is wrong. If so, it is for that Court to say so and not for us.

On the issue of segregation *per se,* we affirm the Chancellor's legal conclusion that it does not contravene the Fourteenth Amendment.

II. *Substantial equality or inequality of educational facilities.*

We turn to the second branch of the controversy. It is subdivided into two parts, the first concerning the claim that the facilities of Howard High School are substantially inferior to those of Claymont High School, and the second concerning the claim that the facilities of School No. 107 are substantially inferior to those of School No. 29.

Preliminarily it is to be observed that the facts in both cases, though developed largely from oral testimony, are almost wholly undisputed. The areas of disagreement concern the inferences of equality or inequality of facilities to be drawn from undisputed facts; hence, the rule requiring affirmance of the Chancellor's findings upon disputed issues of fact, if there be supporting evidence, has little application to this case. The holding in the case of Blish v. Thompson Automatic Arms Corporation, 30 Del.Ch. 538, 584, 64 A.2d 581, 604, cited to us by plaintiffs, and our recent holding in Pierce v. Wahl, Del., 86 A.2d 757, concern findings upon sharply disputed issues of fact. We think it our duty to review the evidence and draw our own conclusions.

Before proceeding to an analysis of the evidence touching the comparison of the educational facilities of one school with another, we inquire whether there are any principles or standards evolved by the

[2]See Education, Segregation and the Supreme Court, 99 Pa.L.Rev. 949.

courts to determine what constitutes "substantial equality." As the Chancellor indicated, it is not difficult to state the rule but it is quite difficult to apply it. Identity or absolute equality in all respects is, as observed by Judge Dobie, "impractical and somewhat Utopian." Corbin v. County School Board, supra [177 F. 2d 928]. Yet substantial equality in the essential and the more important aspects of educational opportunity there must be if segregation is to be upheld. There is thus imposed upon the courts the difficult and delicate task of drawing the line between the unimportant and incidental differences inevitably occurring in any comparison of two schools, whether for whites or Negroes, and a substantial disparity placing the plaintiff at a material disadvantage because of his race or color. We must avoid the tendency, natural enough in these circumstances, to magnify minor variations, and at the same time we must be vigilant to strike down unhesitatingly any instance of discriminatory treatment.

From the recent cases which have dealt with the question of "substantial equality" we extract the following general principles:

The right to equal opportunity is a personal one. State of Missouri ex rel. Gaines v. Canada, 305 U.S. 337, 59 S.Ct. 232, 83 L.Ed. 208. Rights under the equal protection clause are "personal and present". The state must provide education for the applicant "and provide it as soon as it does for applicants of any other group." Sipuel v. Board of Regents of University, 332 U.S. 631, 68 S.Ct. 299, 92 L.Ed. 247; quoted and reaffirmed in Sweatt v. Painter, supra.

Since the right to equal opportunity is a personal one, it cannot be denied because of limited demand, nor depend on the number of applicants. State of Missouri ex rel. Gaines v. Canada, supra.

The opportunities afforded, as between white and Negro schools, need not necessarily exist in the same place or school district; the state may choose the place. Gong Lum v. Rice, supra; Winborne v. Taylor, 4 Cir., 195 F.2d 649; Trustees Pleasant Grove Independent School District v. Bagsby, Tex.Civ. App., 237 S.W.2d 780; Pearson v. Murray, 169 Md. 478, 182 A.590, 103 A.L.R. 706.

Differences in travel, as between white and Negro pupils, do not necessarily show substantial inequality, particularly if the state furnishes transportation. Winborne v. Taylor, supra. But travel, coupled with inadequate transportation, may become sufficiently burdensome to constitute a substantial inequality. Corbin v. County School Board, supra.

The cases also disclose that in determining whether substantial equality or inequality exists, the usual approach is to determine whether, upon a comparison of the two schools concerned, the facilities of one are, upon over-all examination, so manifestly inferior to those of the other that the plaintiff necessarily suffers injury. See, for example, Parker v. University of Delaware, Del. Ch., 75 A.2d 225; Corbin v. County School Board, supra. Even in the absence of general inferiority, however, if it appears that the plaintiff, by reason of his race or color, is denied some one course of high school instruction indispensable to his education and available to others, substantial inequality exists as to him. State ex rel. Brewton v. Board of Education. 381 Mo. 86, 233 S.W.2d 697. And conversely, if the facilities are otherwise substantially equal, plaintiff is not injured because some courses offered in the white school are not offered in the Negro school if it appears that he is receiving substantially equal instruction in all the courses he desires to take. Brown v. Ramsey, 8 Cir., 185 F.2d 225.

A further question must be asked: What if some of the facilities at school A are superior to similar facilities at school B, and other facilities at school B are superior to similar ones at school A? Which school is to be deemed the better? As will hereafter appear, the question is pertinent to one of the cases before us. We agree with the Chancellor that the comparison cannot be made by attempting to offset an advantage of one kind against a disadvantage of another kind. "Equivalency cannot be determined by weighing the respective advantages furnished to the two groups." Carter v. School Board of Arlington County, 4 Cir., 182 F.2d 531, 535. The Chancellor met this difficulty, however, by holding, as a matter of law, that if the facilities or educational opportunities available to the Negro are, as to any substantial factor, inferior to those available to white children similarly situated, the constitutional principle of "separate but equal" is violated. This conclusion, he held, followed from the consideration that a court could say that such a substantial factor would not adversely affect the educational progress "of at least some of those concerned." 87 A.2d 868. But this is in effect to say that even if the plaintiff be not injured by the inequality, there are probably others who are now or who may hereafter be injured by it; and hence substantial inequality must be found in any such case. Upon the basis of the legal principles we have stated, particularly the principle that the right to the equal protection of the laws is a personal and present one, we think the rule announced by the Chancellor too sweeping and must disapprove it in so far as it purports to lay down a rule of universal application. We think that in a case where substantial inequality exists only in a few of the many factors entering into the comparison, the inquiry must be, Is the plaintiff injured by those inequalities? If he is not, he may not have relief. Cf. McCabe v. Atchison, T. & S.F.R. Co., 235 U.S. 151, 35 S.Ct. 69, 71, 59 L.Ed. 169, involving a class suit to enjoin the enforcement of an Oklahoma statute requiring segregation in railway passenger coaches. The bill was dismissed by the trial court, and its decision was affirmed by the Supreme Court of the United States, Justice Hughes saying: "The complainant cannot succeed because someone else may be hurt." But if such substantial inequalities do injure the plaintiff, then he is entitled to relief. These conclusions follow, we think, from the principles we have above derived from the applicable decisions.

With these general observations in mind, we turn to a review of the evidence.

*First. Howard High School and Claymont High School.*

Ethel Louise Belton, as well as the other plaintiffs in this case, pupils of high school age, made application to enter the Claymont High School and were refused admittance as pupils solely on account of race or color. The plaintiff, Ethel Louise Belton, was at the time of trial fifteen years of age, and was attending Howard High School in the tenth grade, the lowest grade of the senior high school. She and all the other plaintiffs are residents of the Claymont Special School District in New Castle County, in which a public school with grades 1 to 12 (both elementary and secondary grades) is maintained for white pupils by the school authorities of the State and of the special school district. Howard High School is a public school with grades 7 to 12 (junior and senior high schools only), maintained for Negro pupils by the Board of Education of the City of Wilmington, with some supervision by the State Board of Education and substantial financial support from the State. It is the only public school in New Castle County offering a complete high school course to Negroes. The Claymont School is distant from plaintiff Belton's home about a mile and a half; the Howard School in Wilmington, about nine miles. The State provides no transportation from Claymont to Wilmington.

Under the administration of Howard High School is the Carver building in which certain vocational courses are given. Plaintiff Belton takes certain academic courses at the Howard building. On two days of the week, at about three o'clock in the afternoon, she leaves that building and walks to the Carver building, a distance of about nine city blocks, to take courses in shorthand and typewriting, which are given between the hours of three-thirty and five-thirty.

No other plaintiff testified, and the record fails to show whether any of them takes or expects to take any of the vocational courses given in the Carver building, nor, if so, whether he is or would be required to take it after three o'clock in the afternoon.

Plaintiffs assert that the educational facilities and opportunities afforded them at Howard High School are substantially inferior in many respects to those offered at the Claymont School to white pupils similarly situated.

The following is a summary of the evidence relating to the facilities of the two schools:

(1) *Public Funds.*

No contention is made of any inequality of financial treatment. It affirmatively appears that Howard receives the same treatment as the other Wilmington high schools and (so far as comparison can be made) the same treatment as Claymont.

(2) *Buildings.*

The Howard building proper and the Claymont building are admittedly equal, except that the Howard gymnasium is insufficient for physical education, and some instruction must be given in the Walnut Y.M.C.A. gymnasium, distant three and one-half blocks from Howard. The Carver building is a very old one and markedly inferior. We approve the Chancellor's finding, not seriously challenged by the defendants, that the physical plant at Howard-Carver is substantially inferior to that at Claymont.

(3) *Sites.*

Claymont, in a suburban community, is on a site of fourteen acres; the Howard building proper, in an urban community, on a site of three and one-half acres. The Carver building is on a plot with about forty feet of land on either side of the building and no land in front or play space in the rear. There is testimony, not denied, that the space at Carver is inadequate as a playgound for pupils in that building.

As between Claymont and Howard proper, the Claymont playing space is larger and includes regulation atheletic fields, but Howard has the use, exclusive when required, of Kirkwood Park, a public park of ten and one-half acres adjacent to the site of the Howard building, which has, however, no regulation playing fields. As for organized athletics, Howard, like the Wilmington High School, has the use of the athletic fields of the P. S. duPont High School and the George Gray School, each at least half a mile distant from the Howard building.

So far as concerns physical education there is no testimony in the record that the playground space available to Howard-Carver is inadequate for that purpose. The inadequacy of Howard-Carver in respect of physical education appears to be attributable to the insufficiency of the gymnasium, above noted.

In respect of esthetic considerations, the Claymont site is admitted to be superior.

The defendants argue that, disregarding Carver, the difference in sites as between Claymont and Howard lies in esthetic considerations only and that this difference is not in itself a substantial inequality. We are inclined to agree that if these two schools were substantially equal in all other respects such a difference would hardly justify a finding of substantial inequality; but in this case esthetic considerations do not stand alone. All other considerations apart, the playground space of Carver is concededly inadequate. The Chancellor also found that the playing space available to Howard proper as well as at Carver is inadequate; but this finding appears to rest solely on the lack of regulation fields in Kirkwood Park, and we do not think that the evidence justifies a finding that any of the plaintiffs has suffered injury from this lack. However, for the purpose of the trial and decision of the case below Howard-Carver was treated as a unit, and on this basis the finding of substantial inequality in respect of the sites is justified.

In this connection we add an observation in connection with the Chancellor's comments with respect to the relative advantages and disadvantages of urban and suburban schools. In our opinion substantial inequality between two schools does not result from the mere fact that one is in the suburbs and another in the city. The question is always whether there are differences between the schools of such a nature as to make them substantially unequal. Indeed the policy of consolidation of schools, apparently proceeding at an increasing rate, necessarily requires more and more pupils to attend a school situated in a community of a different type from that in which they live. It may reasonably be inferred that in the opinion of authorities on education school attendance in one's own community is not an important attribute of educational opportunity.

(4) *Accreditation.*

Both schools are approved by the Association of Colleges and Secondary Schools of the Middle States and Maryland.

(5) *Curriculum.*

Plaintiffs adduced testiiony from an expert witness, who made a survey of both schools, to the effect that the Claymont curriculum in respect of college preparatory work was superior to that of Howard, seven courses, it was stated, being offered at Claymont that are not offered at Howard. It was established that one of these courses is no longer offered at Claymont, that four others (or their equivalents) are in fact offered at Howard, and that the other two are of minor importance. It is admitted that seven vocational courses are offered at Howard that are not offered at Claymont. There is no evidence that any of the plaintiffs is denied any course of instruction that he seeks. The Chancellor made no finding of inequality in respect of the curriculum, and we think he was right. The evidence shows that they are substantially equal.

(6) *Faculty and Instruction.*

Claymont has 404 high school pupils with 20 teachers, a pupil-teacher ratio of 20.1. Howard has 1274 pupils with 53 teachers, a ratio of 24. Of the teachers at Claymont, 59% hold master's degrees, and 36% bachelor's degrees. Of the teachers at Howard, 38% hold master's degrees and 49% bachelor's degrees. One teacher at Claymont holds no degree and five teachers at Howard (three of them vocational) hold no degree. The average annual salary at Howard is higher than that at Claymont by $169. We find no evidence in the record of the length of experience of the teachers of either school. The methods of instruction are modern in both schools.

A comparison of the size of the classes in eight different subjects shows that at Howard classes in five of these subjects were larger, though not substantially larger,[3] than at Claymont, and in two subjects the Howard classes are slightly smaller. In one subject, Physical Education, the disparity is substantial, the average class at Claymont being 24.88 and at Howard 43.67, with some classes so large (one with an enrollment of 88) as probably to prevent satisfactory instruction.

Viewing the situation as a whole, we think that plaintiffs have clearly shown substantial inequality in one respect, that of instruction in Physical Education, which (we infer from the record) is a required course at Howard for all pupils except for those excused for cause. It is evidently related to the inadequacy of the Howard gymnasium, already noted. We cannot agree with the Chancellor, however, that the other differences (pupil-teacher ratio, formal teacher training, and average size of classes) represent substantial inequality. They seem to us to be such differences as might be found between any two high schools, whether for whites or Negroes. As against the differences in the formal training of teachers, it is to be noted that the testimony from both sides indicates that it is still not unusual for vocational teachers to lack academic degrees, and that the larger number of such teachers at Howard appears fairly attributable to the emphasis in Howard on vocational training. It further appears that the general policies of the Wilmington Board of Education, which include a policy to avoid as far as possible the employment of teachers without academic degrees, have been as nearly accomplished in Howard as in any other public school in Wilmington. As for the average size of the classes, it appears that the Chancellor's finding of substantial inequality was based in great part upon the fact that several classes at Howard exceeded twenty-five in number, and upon his conclusion that a pupil-teacher ratio of twenty-five to one "has been fixed by the State educational authorities as a desirable maximum." This conclusion does not appear to be supported by the record. It is clear to us, from the testimony of the Director of Research of the State Board of Education and of the Assistant State Superintendent in charge of secondary schools, that the ratio derives directly from the legislative policy establishing the method of allotting state funds for the employment of teachers, and bears no necessary relation to the

---

[3]The average differences, expressed arithmetically, range from 2.65 to 8.51.

size of any particular class.[4] Moreover, since principals and specialists are included in the determination of the ratio for the allotment of funds, the actual ratio of pupils to teachers usually exceeds the ratio for fund allotments. A tendency to smaller classes is said to be desirable, but we do not find any formal fixation by the State authorities of a desirable maximum size. In short, we do not think the evidence on these matters discloses anything more than such variations as are inevitable concomitants of the administration of any school system.

(7) *Equipment and Instructional Materials*
These are conceded to be equal.

(8) *Libraries.*
These are conceded to be equal. As is to be expected, the Howard Library is the larger.

(9) *Physical and Mental Health and Nursing Services.*
The Howard health services are admittedly superior and the Chancellor so found. An attempt was made to show that the nursing services at Claymont were superior, but this contention appears to be abandoned.

(10) *Extra-curricular Activities.*
It was testified that Claymont has seven extra-curricular activities (clubs of various kinds) and Howard only three. In addition to these clubs, however, individual students at Howard, selected by their classmates, participate in the Wilmington program of radio activities. The inclusion of the "Drivers Club" as one of the seven is a manifest error since Howard, like all high schools in the state, has a drivers' class.[5] It is a fair conclusion from the evidence that the organization of student clubs depends in large part upon individual interest. Differences in number and kind of extra-curricular activities thus reflect differences in interests and tastes and not inadequacy of facilities. We think these differences too insubstantial to support a finding of inequality.

(11) *Travel.*
As above stated, plaintiff Ethel Louise Belton is required to travel to Wilmington every morning on a public bus, and then, on two afternoons of the week, to walk nine blocks to the Carver building, which she leaves at five-thirty o'clock. She is within walking distance of the Claymont School, and it appears that the courses she takes at Carver are given at Claymont during the regular school day and before three o'clock in the afternoon. Moreover, high school pupils at Claymont who live farther than two miles from the school are furnished transportation in the school buses provided by the State school authorities. No transportation is furnished to the plaintiff. These facts, we think, constitute clear evidence of substantial inequality and unlawful discrimination on account of race or color. We approve the Chancellor's ultimate finding on this point. We should add, however, that we do not agree that the question of travel, as a factor in determining substantial equality, is to be resolved on the basis of comparative distance alone. There are other pertinent aspects of the question. The present trend toward consolidation of the public schools, mentioned above, inevitably entails many miles of travel for many pupils, white as well as Negro, particularly for those in high schools. Thus this consequence does not flow from discrimination an account of race or color but from the general state policy with respect to the consolidation and location of schools—a policy with which the courts have nothing to do. The recent decision of the Fourth Circuit Court of Appeals in Winborne v. Taylor, supra. supports this view. That case involved a consolidation of three Negro high schools in the towns of Plymouth, Roper and Creswell into one improved school at Roper to be equal in all respects (in fact superior) to the schools for whites. This consolidation required the Negro pupils at Plymouth to travel eight miles, and those at Creswell sixteen. The sole question before the court was whether the travel distance was so unreasonably burdensome as to justify a finding of substantial inequality. The court below found such travel to be a normal and usual incident of the school system and not unreasonably burdensome. The Court of Appeals affirmed [195 F.2d 651], observing that "[t]he drawing of fine lines and minute differences, in the face of manifest substantial equality, is a burden neither the law requires nor reason suggests." To the same effect is Brown v. Board of Education of Topeka, D.C., 98 F.Supp. 797.[6] As we

---

[4] The Act of June 30, 1949, 47 Laws of Del.Ch. 364, provides that no state funds (as distinct from funds raised locally) shall be appropriated for teachers' salaries to any school district in excess of one teacher for each unit. A unit is, in grades one to six, twenty-five pupils or major fraction thereof, and, in grades seven to twelve, twenty pupils or major fraction thereof. In the case of a twelve-grade school, the teachers may be divided between the elementary and secondary schools in any way desired. It is clear that reasonable variations in the size of classes are to be expected in all schools, both white and Negro.
[5] See 1951 Report of the State Superintendent of Public Instruction, p. 119.
[6] On appeal to the Supreme Court of the United States, probable jurisdiction noted, 72 S.Ct. 1070.

have above stated, educational facilities need not be furnished in the same place or in the same school district. See the authorities cited supra.

We are accordingly unwilling to assent to the plaintiffs' argument that the travel distance here involved is in itself a substantial inequality. All the facts must be considered. But in the circumstances of this case, i. e., the extra travel to Carver and the failure of the State to supply transportation, such a finding must be made.

We have reviewed in detail the facts bearing upon the comparative educational facilities afforded by the two schools. We have found that the physical plant of Howard-Carver, including the sites, is substantially unequal to that of Claymont; that the classes in physical education at Howard are so large as probably to jeopardize satisfactory education; and that the plaintiff Belton is subjected to unequal and discriminatory treatment in respect of travel.

We think that these findings compel the conclusion that the plaintiff Belton is not afforded educational facilities substantially equal to those afforded white pupils at Claymont, and has suffered injury therefrom. In respect of the differences in facilities for and instruction in physical education, and in respect of transportation from Claymont to Wilmington, the other plaintiffs have also been injured. These inequalities are not incidental or unimportant differences, and it is our clear duty to say that they constitute unlawful discrimination on account of race or color. We so find, and the plaintiffs' suit must prevail.

*Relief.* There remains the question of the relief to be given. Both in the court below and here defendants press the argument that even if the finding of inequality was correct, the form of the decree, in effect directing the school authorities to admit plaintiffs to the Claymont School, was erroneous. The judgment, it is said, should have taken the form of a judgment directing the defendants to equalize the facilities and affording them a reasonable time within which to do so. In support of this contention, the Attorney General cites the cases of Briggs v. Elliott, supra, and Davis v. County School Board, supra, both of which are decisions of three-judge courts in federal districts in South Carolina and Virginia, respectively.

In the Briggs case, the court declared the facilities of the Negro schools unequal and directed the defendants to equalize the facilities promptly and to submit within six months a report showing the action taken. Plaintiffs appealed and the Supreme court vacated the judgment and remanded the case to the District Court to permit it to consider the report and to take whatever action thereon it might deem appropriate. 342 U.S. 350, 72 S.Ct. 327, 328. Upon the filing of the report, the District Court found that the action taken by defendants would result in the equalization of facilities by the opening of the next school year and again entered a judgment directing equalization of facilities. D.C., 103 F.Supp. 920. Plaintiffs have again appealed to the Supreme Court of the United States and probable jurisdiction has been noted. 72 S.Ct. 1078.

In the Davis case, the court enjoined the continuance of certain inequalities that it found to exist, and as to others directed the school authorities to pursue with diligence their program to replace the inadequate facilities with new ones or otherwise remove the inequalities.

Urging that, if inequality be found in this case, an order directing the defendants to equalize facilities will afford the plaintiffs adequate relief, the Attorney General shows that there is now under way in the City of Wilmington a far-reaching program for the betterment of facilities in the Negro schools. As to the Howard-Carver buildings, plans have been approved for the transfer of the junior high school pupils at Howard to another junior high school, for the enlargement of the Howard building, with additional equipment, and for the closing of Carver and the transfer of its pupils to Howard. It is said that all these changes are expected to be completed by September, 1953, and that they will completely equalize the Howard facilities. It is also shown that plans are under way to build a modern high school for Negroes at Middletown, New Castle County. Hence the defendants say that a decree to equalize the facilities will afford plaintiffs adequate relief.

There are two preliminary difficulties with the defendants' position. First, the Board of Education of the City of Wilmington, which has direct supervision of the Wilmington schools, is not a party to the cause; second, it is difficult to see how a court of equity could effectively supervise and direct the expenditure of state funds in a matter committed to the sound administrative discretion of the school authorities. But we prefer to rest our decision upon another ground. With reference to the decisions in the Briggs and Davis cases, which we have carefully examined and considered, we cannot reconcile the denial of prompt relief with the pronouncements of the Supreme Court of the United States. If, as we have seen the right to equal protection of the laws as a "personal and present" one, how can these plaintiffs be denied such relief as is now available? The commendable effort of the State to remedy the situation serves to emphasize the importance of the present inequalities. To require the plaintiffs to wait another year under present conditions would be in effect partially to deny them that to which we have held they are entitled. It is possible that a case might occur in which completion of equalization of facilities might be so imminent as to justify a different result, but we do not pass on that question because it is not presented. We think that the injunction of the court below, in effect commanding the defendants to admit the plaintiffs to the Claymont school, was rightly awarded.

*Second. Hockessin School No. 29 and Hockessin School No. 107.*

We take up the second case, involving the claim of the plaintiff Shirley Barbara Bulah to be admitted to Hockessin School No. 29.

The plaintiff, a Negro child eight years of age, is a resident of the village of Hockessin, New Castle County. At or near Hockessin the State Board of Education maintains two elementary schools with grades one to six, School No. 29 for white children and School No. 107 for Negro children. School No. 29 is a four room school with four teachers and 111 pupils. School No. 107 is a two-room school with two teachers and 44 pupils. The school districts have separate boards of trustees, but are, we understand, largely overlapping in area though the boundaries are not identical. Plaintiff lives at a distance of two miles from School No. 107. No transportation is furnished by the State for pupils in School 107. The State provides a school bus for pupils in School 29, which passes by plaintiff's house. In September, 1950, application was made on plaintiff's behalf for transportation to School 107 in the school bus serving School No. 29, and the request was refused. The present suit raises the general question of inequality of educational facilities furnished at School 107.

The following is a review of the pertinent evidence relating to a comparison of the two schools:

(1) *Public Funds.*

It is admitted that until recently School No. 29 was favored in the allocation of public funds. For the year 1949–1950 it was given $178.13 per pupil; No. 107 only $137.22 per pupil. This inequality has since been remedied and School No. 107 now receives equal or greater support, but the prior inequality is of importance, as will be seen.

(2) *Buildings and Sites.*

Both buildings are of brick, that of No. 29 on a site of five acres and that of 107 on a site of two acres. School No. 29 was built in 1932 at a cost of $55,438; No. 107, in 1921 at a cost of $21,382. No. 107 was until 1949 an oversized one-room school. In that year, its enrollment having reached 46, it was converted into a two-room school by installing a temporary movable partition through the middle of the room. According to the insurance records in the office of Business Administration of the State Board of Education, the present value of the building and equipment of No. 29 is $77,107; that of No. 107, $13,100. There was testimony on behalf of plaintiff that the appreciation of one and the depreciation of the other must reflect differences in maintenance upkeep and improvements. The inference is certainly not unreasonable. Some corroboration of this testimony is to be found in the record. Discrimination in the appropriation of public funds has already been noted. A comparative survey in 1951 of the equipment of the two schools shows the exterior painting and the floors to be in good condition in No. 29, but in poor condition in No. 107. The toilet facilities at No. 29 are substantially superior to those at No. 107. The fire hazard at No. 107 appears to be greater. No. 29 has an auditorium and a basement; No. 107, neither. These differences just mentioned may be attributable to the fact that one building is a four-room school and the other a two-room school; but , as hereafter pointed out, the State makes no point of this fact. Plaintiff further contended that the custodial service at No. 107 was inadequate.

Now it is to be noted that, although the plaintiff's evidence on the matter of the physical deficiencies in the building of School 107 rests in part on inference, and is lacking in many details, the defendants made no real effort to meet it. The State produced the school official who made the survey referred to, but he gave no evidence contradicting the testimony of plaintiff's witness either as to the past and present valuations of the schools plants or as to the inference of disparity in maintenance, upkeep and improvements. There is testimony that the State in recent years has spent or allotted funds for School 107, in excess of those budgeted for "delayed repairs." This fact would indicate an attempt to improve the condition of the building of No. 107, but the State proffered no testimony that such expenditures had been made or had substantially equalized the condition of the physical plants of the two schools, or would equalize them in the near future. Knowledge of the facts must certainly be attributed to the defendants, and this failure to adduce them, or to show that disparities in the physical plant would be promptly remedied, is significant.

Plaintiff's expert witness testified that he had made a comparison of the physical plants and equipment of the two schools by using the "Strayer-Englehart" score card.[7] Of a maximum possible rating of 644 points, School 29 was given 594 points; School 107, 281 points. No doubt this evaluation

---

[7]"This score card is used by a person, a qualified person, making a survey of the school in checking and giving certain weights to the items that are listed on the score card. Those items in general cover site, building—when I say 'building' I am referring to classrooms, general service rooms, internal structure, service systems, fire protection system, cleaning systems, electric service systems, water supply systems, toilet system, movable equipment, classroom illumination and placement. When I refer to site, I am speaking of location, topography, and provisions for use." (Testimony of Dr. Paul E. Lawrence.)

included some items of relatively minor importance, but the over-all disparity is great. Again, the defendants failed to challenge this testimony in any effective way. The card does not appear to have been put in evidence nor was the weight accorded the various items upon its developed by cross-examination or otherwise. An attempt was made to prove that the Strayer-Englehart card is obsolete, but it was shown without contradiction that it was used recently in a survey of the District of Columbia schools made under Congressional authority. At all events, it embodied a comparison of the two schools by an experienced educator, and no such comparison was offered by the State.

As for the sites, that of No. 29 is conceded to be superior, but the defendants say that this superiority consists largely in the landscaping which is attributable, it is said, to the voluntary efforts of the parent-teachers association of School 29. The record on this point is not wholly clear. Defendants' list of items given by the P.T.A. refers to "large shrubbery and trees." Plaintiff urges that that State owns and maintains them, and that the source of its title is legally immaterial. We think it unnecessary to resolve this question. Taking the physical plants as a whole, No. 29 appears to be substantially superior and defendants failed to meet in any satisfactory way the plaintiff's case on this point. True, the defendants' witness who made the comparative survey above mentioned testified that the facilities of School 107 "are certainly equal to and better than the majority of two-teacher schools [in the State], both white and colored." This testimony was not controverted, but it does not reach the point. The case was tried by both sides upon the theory that School No. 29, a four-room school, was to be compared with the School No. 107, a two-room school. Whether this theory is legally correct, or whether the comparison should have been between two schools of comparable size, or upon some other basis, we may not consider. The question is not before us. It was suggested by the Chancellor in a colloquy with counsel, but it was not followed up by the defendants. They accepted the plaintiff's tendered basis of comparison, and it cannot be changed here. Indeed the defendants do not suggest that it should be changed.

One other circumstance should be noted. The Chancellor himself inspected the two school buildings, and evidently based his finding of substantial inequality partly upon his own observation. To his conclusion from his own inspection we must give due weight.

We find that the physical plant of No. 29 is substantially superior to that of No. 107.

### (3) *Equipment.*

There appears no substantial inequality in physical and instructional equipment, including the libraries, with the exception of medical supplies and equipment, which appear to be superior at No. 29. Some attempt was made to show inequality of instructional materials but the Chancellor made no finding of inequality on this point, and we think none is justified.

### (4) *Teachers.*

The testimony shows that teachers at School No. 29 posses a superiority in formal training and are rated somewhat higher than the teachers at School No. 107. If these facts stood alone we should have difficulty in concluding that they represent anything more than accidental differences. However, they are to be viewed in the light of the admitted discrimination against School 107 in respect of the allotment of State funds. As above stated funds appropriated for the years prior to the year 1951–1952 were unequally allotted, to the detriment of School 107, and this inequality extended to teachers' salaries.[8] This was a direct violation of our constitutional and statutory provisions, above quoted, requiring that in the apportionment of funds for the support of the public schools no distinction shall be made on account of race or color. Beginning with the fiscal year of 1951–1952 this inequality has been remedied. The plaintiff's testimony, however, related to conditions at School No. 107 in October, 1951, and thus tended to show that the effect of the prior wrongful apportionment of funds still persisted. The burden was clearly upon the defendants to show the extent to which the remedial legislation had improved conditions or would improve them in the near future. This the defendants failed to do. It is natural to suppose that with the equality of funds any substantial disparities will shortly be eliminated, but we must take the record as it was made below, and it affords some support for plaintiff's general contention of substantial inequality. In view of our other findings in the case it is unnecessary to evaluate the weight to be given to this factor.

### (5) *Transportation.*

The facts with respect to this point have been stated. It admits of no doubt that the refusal of the defendants to furnish transportation to plaintiff, while furnishing it to pupils at School No. 29, constitutes substantial inequality of treatment because of race or color. The fact that there are insufficient Negro pupils to meet the requirements of defendants' rules for the establishment of a separate bus is legally irrelevant. State of Missouri ex rel. Gaines v. Canada, supra; Brown v. Ramsey, supra.

[8]In addition to the evidence in the record for the year 1949–1950, we note similar disparities for teachers' salaries in the appropriation acts of 1947, Vol. 46 Laws of Del.Ch. 67, and 1945, Vol. 45 Laws of Del. Ch. 23.

The above review of the evidence leads us to the conclusion that plaintiff has established, by a preponderance of the evidence, her contention that the facilities of School No. 107 are, to the extent set forth, substantially unequal to those at School No. 29, and that she has suffered injury.

We have already discussed, in the Howard-Claymont case, the matter of relief. It accordingly follows that the Chancellor's order in respect of the admittance of the plaintiff Bulah to School No. 29 must be affirmed.

In affirming the Chancellor's order we have not overlooked the fact that the defendants may at some future date apply for a modification of the order if, in their judgment, the inequalities as between the Howard and Claymont schools or as between School No. 29 and School No. 107 have then been removed. As to Howard, the defendants, as above stated, assert that when the Howard-Carver changes are completed, equality will exist. The Chancellor apparently thought the contrary. We do not concur in his conclusion, since we think that that question, if it arises, is one which will have to be decided in the light of the facts then existing and applicable principles of law. The Chancellor properly reserved jurisdiction of the cause to grant such further and additional relief as might appear appropriate in the future, and we construe this reservation to be a general reservation to any party to the cause to make an application to modify the order in any respect if and when changed conditions are believed to warrant such action.

We also note, with respect to both of the cases, that each cause is a so-called "spurious class suit" brought for the benefit of plaintiffs "and others similarly situated." We express no opinion whether, as to those "similarly situated" other than the plaintiffs, the judgment is *res judicata* or whether it has force only under the rule of *stare decisis*. Cf. 3 Moore's Federal Practice, § 23.11 (3). That question is not before us.

In conclusion, we add one further observation applicable to both cases, that is, that there are some points of comparison of the schools developed in the evidence and discussed on the briefs that, for the sake of brevity, have not been specifically mentioned. For the benefit of counsel, we may say that we have not overlooked them, but have regarded them either as of minor importance or as cumulative only.

The judgment of the Court of Chancery is affirmed.

Intermediate Supreme Court Order in All Cases

## BROWN ET AL. v. BOARD OF EDUCATION OF
## TOPEKA EL AL.

344 U.S. 1

NO. 8 APPEAL FROM THE UNITED STATES DISTRICT COURT
FOR THE DISTRICT OF KANSAS.*

October 8, 1952.

PER CURIAM.

In two appeals now pending, No. 8, *Brown et al.* v. *Board of Education of Topeka et al.,* and No. 101, *Briggs et al.* v. *Elliott et al.,* the appellants challenge, respectively, the constitutionality of a statute of Kansas, and a statute and the Constitution of South Carolina, which provide for segregation in the schools of these states. Appellants allege that segregation is, *per se,* a violation of the Fourteenth Amendment. Argument in these cases has heretofore been set for the week of October 13, 1952.

In No. 191, *Davis et al.* v. *County School Board of Prince Edward County et al.,* the appellants have filed a statement of jurisdiction raising the same issue in respect to a statute and the Constitution of Virginia. Appellees in the *Davis* case have called attention to the similarity between it and the *Briggs* and *Brown* cases; by motion they have asked the Court to take necessary action to have all three cases argued together.

This Court takes judicial notice of a fourth case, which is pending in the United States Court of Appeals for the District of Columbia Circuit, *Bolling et al.* v. *Sharpe et al.,* No. 11,018 on that court's docket. In that case, the appellants challenge the appellees' refusal to admit certain Negro appellants to a segregated white school in the District of Columbia; they allege that appellees have taken such action pursuant to certain Acts of Congress; they allege that such action is a violation of the Fifth Amendment of the Constitution.

The Court is of the opinion that the nature of the issue posed in those appeals now before the Court involving the Fourteenth Amendment, and also the effect of any decision which it may render in those cases, are such that it would be well to consider, simultaneously, the constitutional issue posed in the case of *Bolling et al.* v. *Sharpe et al.*

To the end that arguments may be heard together in all four of these cases, the Court will continue the *Brown* and *Briggs* cases on its docket. Probable jurisdiction is noted in *Davis et al* v. *County School Board of Prince Edward County et al.* Arguments will be heard in these three cases at the first argument session in December.

The Court will entertain a petition for certiorari in the case of *Bolling et al.* v. *Sharpe et al.,* 28 U.S.C. §§ 1254 (1), 2101 (e), which if presented and granted will afford opportunity for argument of the case immediately following the arguments in the three appeals now pending.

*It is so ordered.*

MR. JUSTICE DOUGLAS dissents from postponing argument and decision in the three cases presently here for *Bolling et al.* v. *Sharpe et al.,* in the United States Court of Appeals for the District of Columbia Circuit.

*Together with No. 101, *Briggs et al.* v. *Elliott et al., Members of Board of Trustees of School District #22,* on appeal from the United States District Court for the Eastern District of South Carolina; and No. 191, *Davis et al.* v. *County School Board of Prince Edward County et al.,* on appeal from the United States District Court for the Eastern District of Virginia.

INDEX

# INDEX